China in the Global Economy

Governance in China

ORGANISATION FOR ECONOMIC CO-OPERATION AND DEVELOPMENT

ORGANISATION FOR ECONOMIC CO-OPERATION AND DEVELOPMENT

The OECD is a unique forum where the governments of 30 democracies work together to address the economic, social and environmental challenges of globalisation. The OECD is also at the forefront of efforts to understand and to help governments respond to new developments and concerns, such as corporate governance, the information economy and the challenges of an ageing population. The Organisation provides a setting where governments can compare policy experiences, seek answers to common problems, identify good practice and work to co-ordinate domestic and international policies.

The OECD member countries are: Australia, Austria, Belgium, Canada, the Czech Republic, Denmark, Finland, France, Germany, Greece, Hungary, Iceland, Ireland, Italy, Japan, Korea, Luxembourg, Mexico, the Netherlands, New Zealand, Norway, Poland, Portugal, the Slovak Republic, Spain, Sweden, Switzerland, Turkey, the United Kingdom and the United States. The Commission of the European Communities takes part in the work of the OECD.

OECD Publishing disseminates widely the results of the Organisation's statistics gathering and research on economic, social and environmental issues, as well as the conventions, guidelines and standards agreed by its members.

This work is published on the responsibility of the Secretary-General of the OECD. The opinions expressed and arguments employed herein do not necessarily reflect the official views of the Organisation or of the governments of its member countries.

Publié en français sous le titre :
La gouvernance en Chine

© OECD 2005

No reproduction, copy, transmission or translation of this publication may be made without written permission. Applications should be sent to OECD Publishing: *rights@oecd.org* or by fax (33 1) 45 24 13 91. Permission to photocopy a portion of this work should be addressed to the Centre français d'exploitation du droit de copie, 20, rue des Grands-Augustins, 75006 Paris, France (*contact@cfcopies.com*).

Foreword

The OECD and the People's Republic of China have been engaged in a comprehensive programme of co-operation since 1995. In 2002, soon after China became a member of the WTO, the OECD published a landmark report, China in the World Economy: Domestic Policy Challenges which reviewed the policies needed to reap the benefits of China's further integration in the world economy.

Improving governance mechanisms and practices is now widely seen as a critical requirement to ensure continuing progress by China on its rapid development path. Redefining the role of the state, modernising public management, adjusting relations between levels of government and consolidating the institutional framework for market forces are key if China is to take the transition and development processes one step further. Improving governance will also be crucial to address the problems that threaten the sustainability of China's growth path, such as growing inequalities and environmental deterioration.

These considerations led China and the OECD to make governance the focus and the "unifying theme" of their programme of co-operation for 2003 and 2004. The launch of the China Governance Project led to two years of intense policy dialogue on governance issues and their impact on public action in several sectors. The project aimed to analyze current practices in China and share with Chinese policy-makers the experiences of OECD member countries on how to improve governance in order to help ensure sustained growth and social cohesion.

This report, covering the results of the China Governance Project, includes contributions from all relevant OECD Directorates and was jointly co-ordinated by the Directorate for Public Governance and Territorial Development and the Centre for Co-operation with Non-Members. The report provides a unique set of insights on governance practices in China and their recent evolution. It identifies a number of key challenges and discusses ways of addressing these in order to enhance the capacity of Chinese authorities to achieve their policy goals and ensure sustainable development.

Donald J. Johnston
Secretary-General of the OECD

About the Study

This study has been undertaken in the framework of the OECD-China programme of dialogue and co-operation. It draws on the understanding gained from several years of dialogue with a number of Chinese ministries and institutions. However, the report remains an independent study of the OECD Secretariat and is published under the Secretary-General's responsibility.

Acknowledgements. *This study has been produced by an OECD-wide team, which has been led by Irène Hors and overseen by Frédéric Langer for the Center for Co-operation with Non-Members and by Jón R. Blöndal for the Public Governance and Territorial Development Directorate.*

OECD Contributors: Janos Bertok, Jón R. Blöndal, Louis Bouchez, Kenneth Davies, Gretta Fenner, Lennart Goranson, Irène Hors, Kazutomi Kurihara, Andrzej Kwiecinski, Peter Ladegaard, Edwin Lau, Mathilde Mesnard, Krzysztof Michalak, Margit Molnar, Bernard Phillips, Elsa Pilichowski, Joachim Pohl, Anders Reutersward, Paul Schreyer, John Thompson, Ian Whitman and Gang Zhang. Sean Dougherty and Charles Pigott made useful comments on several chapters and the synthesis.

Outside Contributors: Jun Bi, John P. Burns, Xinyu Chen, Shiji Gao, Brad Gilmour, Nina Hachigian, Carsten Holz, Sylvie Mouranche, Jack Linchuan Qiu, Hiroko Uchimura, Terry Winslow and Christine Wong.

Research support for the synthesis and editorial support: Isabelle Gras. Technical assistance: Jennifer Gardner.

Experts from OECD member countries and China contributed important comments on the study in a seminar under the auspices of the Public Governance Committee on 3 February 2005 in Paris. Experts from China, who took part in their personal capacity in this seminar, were: Mr. Yanfeng Ge, Development Research Centre; Mr. Haiyan Li, National Development and Reform Commission; Mr. Zhaoxi Li, Development Research Centre; Ms. Wei Lu, Development Research Centre; and Ms. Hongri Ni, Development Research Centre.

Table of Contents

Synthesis 7

Part I
Public Sector Management

Chapter 1. Civil Service Reform in China....................................... 49
Chapter 2. The Reform of Public Service Units: Challenges and Perspectives 75
Chapter 3. Fighting Corruption in China.. 101
Chapter 4. E-government in China.. 133
Chapter 5. Institutional Arrangements for the Production of Statistics 169

Part II
Public Finance

Chapter 6. Governance in Taxation in China 199
Chapter 7. Public Sector Budgeting Issues in China 223
Chapter 8. China's Public Expenditure Policies 247

Part III
Institutional Framework for Market Forces

Chapter 9. Regulatory Management and Reform in China 275
Chapter 10. Reforming State Asset Management and Improving Corporate Governance: The Two Challenges of Chinese Enterprise Reform 301
Chapter 11. Labour Protection: Challenges Facing Labour Offices and Social Insurance 323
Chapter 12. Competition Law and Policy in China.............................. 349
Chapter 13. Governance of Banks in China...................................... 369
Chapter 14. Intellectual Property Rights in China: Governance Challenges and Prospects 403
Chapter 15. The Governance Challenges of Foreign Investment Policy in China 433
Chapter 16. Institutional Framework for Effective Agricultural Policy: Current Issues and Future Challenges 465

Part IV
Ensuring Sustainable Development

Chapter 17. **Environment and Governance in China** 487

Chapter 18. **Higher Education – Finance and Quality** 535

Postface by the Business and Industry Advisory Committee (BIAC) to the OECD 557

Postface by the Trade Union Advisory Committee (TUAC) to the OECD 563

Glossary 569

ISBN 92-64-00842-X
Governance in China
© OECD 2005

Synthesis

Table of Contents

1. Introduction: the China Governance Project and the Chinese context 11
   1.1. The China Governance Project 11
   1.2. China's governance in transition 12
   1.3. Governance matters to ensure China's sustainable development 17
2. Evolution of the role of the state and subsequent organisational challenges 19
   2.1. Public spending: narrowing scope and changing priorities 19
   2.2. New institutions to frame the state's participation in economic sectors are needed 20
   2.3. The reform of public service units is a pressing issue 21
   2.4. Half-way organisational changes create huge challenges of co-ordination 23
3. Modernising governing tools to improve the efficiency and the effectiveness of public action 24
   3.1. From control to regulatory governance 24
   3.2. Public management 28
4. Adjusting the relations among levels of government 30
   4.1. Fragmentation of authority and localism 31
   4.2. A dysfunctional intergovernmental fiscal system 33
5. Consolidating the institutional framework for market forces 34
   5.1. Labour protection and market integration 34
   5.2. Creating conditions for competition 36
   5.3. Corporate governance 37
6. Conclusions 39

Notes 41
Bibliography 42
Annex 0.A1. OECD Member Countries and Good Governance 43
Annex 0.A2. The Chinese Political System 44

List of boxes

0.1. Theoretical framing of China's transition: from the Four Modernisations to the Harmonious Society 13
0.2. Territorial divisions 16
0.3. The *tiaokuai guanxi* 32

List of tables

0.1. The five major administrative reforms of the transition period 15

Synthesis[1]

1. Introduction: the China Governance Project and the Chinese context

Governance is recognised as critical to economic development and the achievement of a society's objectives. OECD member countries target a development path built on three pillars: good governance, economic growth and social cohesion. Good governance[2] is thus seen as a crucial element to address challenges and fault lines facing a nation and to ensure sustainable development.

China is now undergoing a crucial transformation in its system of governance, adapting institutions and the functioning of the state to an increasingly market-oriented economy. This transformation is also being spurred by key strains that have emerged related to fiscal and financial imbalances, rising inequalities and environmental deterioration.

In 2003, the OECD initiated a project to share with China the expertise of its member countries on governance issues. The China Governance Project was also the opportunity to better understand the challenges faced by China and to organise policy dialogues on these issues. This project was undertaken in the framework of the programme of co-operation between the OECD and China, initiated in 1996. It thus benefited from a relationship of mutual trust established between the OECD Secretariat and Chinese ministries and bodies in many areas.

The first section of this introduction describes the China Governance Project. The second section gives an overview of changes that have affected the Chinese system of governance since the beginning of the reforms in the late 1970s. The third section points out the challenges ahead and outlines the overall structure of the synthesis.

1.1. *The China Governance Project*

The project took both a whole-of-government and a sectoral approach. In the whole-of-government approach, the project took stock of the progress made and examined remaining problems in budget processing and public expenditure, the tax system, the civil service, the fight against corruption, regulatory management and organisational structures of government entities.

The sectoral approach looked at how governance issues affect policy-making, its efficiency and effectiveness in different sectors. Again, the idea was to review progress made and to identify and analyse remaining weaknesses. The project covered 10 policy sectors: labour policies, the banking sector, competition, intellectual property rights, foreign investment, statistics, corporate governance, agriculture, environment protection and higher education.

This project took the dialogue beyond the general statement that "governance matters", by showing how, in practice, governance indeed affects public action in the different policy sectors covered. The following issues contribute to weaken public action:

organisational weaknesses (*e.g.* institutions inherited from the planned regime co-existing with "new" institutions that have been added one after the other), fiscal issues (*e.g.* mismatch between responsibilities and resources), managerial issues (*e.g.* low quality bureaucracy in poorer areas), central-local relations issues (*e.g.* decentralisation not accompanied by appropriate reorganisation of state structures), inadequate accountability structures and inadequate participation mechanisms in policy-making.

This study is the final report of the China Governance Project, organised in four parts: two whole-of-government parts, public sector management and public finance, and two policy sector parts: the institutional framework for market forces and sustainable development. The synthesis gives an overview of the analysis and conclusions of the 18 chapters of this report.

Several important dimensions of the system of governance are not covered in this report (*i.e.* organisation of elections, constitutional law, etc.), either because they do not pertain to the mandate of the OECD or because OECD-China co-operation has not yet been developed in these areas. The ambition of the report is not to provide a systematic analysis of China's governance system, but rather, through several entry points, to grasp some of the highlights and difficulties of the ongoing process of state reform.

In addition to descriptions and analysis, the chapters provide some key messages drawing on the experience of OECD member countries. It is hoped that they will provide landmarks for policy-makers and serve as a basis for further policy dialogue with China.

1.2. *China's governance in transition*

Since 1978, China has undertaken comprehensive reforms, which progressively transformed the former planned economy into what has been designated by Chinese leaders as a "socialist market economy". Framed in successive themes (*cf.* Box 0.1), the reform process was primarily driven by the desire to transform the economic system, but it also reconfigured the Chinese state and the system of governance. The following paragraphs sketch the transition process and provide landmarks on the evolution of the Chinese system of governance since the beginning of the reforms.[3]

Before the reforms, economic activities were tightly controlled, the state's control affecting not only the types of products produced, but also the quantities, pricing and distribution. The provision of raw materials, the distribution of funds, the staffing of technical personnel, agricultural production, the allocation of grain, textiles, and even paper, were controlled by the state.

China's economic transition has brought significant changes in all dimensions of the economy. Recognising that the system in place discouraged productivity, Chinese leaders authorised the development of a productive capacity outside of the state sector, first in rural, then in urban areas, by establishing collective enterprises, then private enterprises. This implied a progressive liberalisation of prices and an evolution of the monetary regime. The development of the private sector also called for an evolution of the financial system, away from being a passive channel of allocation of financial resources toward an important mechanism of the market economy. The progressive opening of the Chinese economy to foreign trade and investment, culminating in China's accession to the World Trade Organisation in 2001, is another important structural dimension of the transition process.

> **Box 0.1. Theoretical framing of China's transition:
> from the Four Modernisations to the Harmonious Society**
>
> The theoretical framework underpinning the transition process started with the concept of the *Four Modernisations (sige xiandaihua)*, announced by Zhou Enlai in the mid-1960s and revived by Deng Xiaoping to launch the economic reforms in 1978. It envisaged the development and rise of the Chinese economy until the middle of the 21st century by modernizing agriculture, industry, national defence and science and technology.
>
> In the mid-1980s, Deng Xiaoping elaborated a development strategy of "three steps" quantifying political and economic objectives. The first step or objective was to double the level of real GDP during the 1980s and thus solve the problem of inadequate clothing and food (*wenbao wenti*). The second step was to build a *Xiaokang (well-off) Society* by the year 2000 by quadrupling the 1980 real GDP level. The third step was to raise the per capita GDP within the following 30-50 years to the level of an intermediate developed country. The concept of *xiaokang* society is particularly interesting since it was reused (and redefined) by Jiang Zemin to describe "Chinese-style" modernization and notion of prosperity.
>
> The concept of *Three Represents (sange daibiao)* proposed by Jiang Zemin in 2000 mainly served to re-orient and re-position the Communist Party of China, but it also officially legitimised private entrepreneurship for the first time.
>
> Two concepts put forward by the fourth generation leadership (Hu Jintao/Wen Jiabao) in 2004, the *Scientific Development Concept (kexue fazhan guan)* and the *Harmonious Society (hexie shehui)* concept, take on a more comprehensive approach towards development. They complement the discourse about the Chinese modernization path with a social dimension and stress the need to reconcile conflicts between rural and urban areas and between different social groups to promote social stability. The Scientific Development Concept moreover accords high importance to the needs of individuals and to a co-ordinated and sustainable development. The *hexie shehui* concept is further linked to the notions of social welfare and more equal income distribution and to the rule of law. As for the role of the government, the concept envisages a closer relation between government and people.

Although obviously incomplete, these reforms have been impressive. Over the past two decades, they have allowed China to develop at an average growth rate of 9%. Today, the transition to a market-driven economy is well advanced, as in 2003 private businesses created 59% of GDP (OECD, 2005).

The evolution in the economic sphere called for changes in the system of governance. Before the reforms, Chinese society was organised in four types of organisations: industrial units (*qiye danwei*), agricultural units (*nongye danwei*), service units (*shiye danwei*) and administrative units (*xingzheng danwei*). The governance system was quite simple. The power structure was highly centralised as local governments, enterprises, institutions and social organisations had no autonomy and were *de facto* branches of the government in Beijing. These organisations executed the plan under the guidance of the State Planning Commission (now named National Development and Reform Commission, NDRC), and the central government controlled the distribution of human and financial resources. Macro-economic regulation was carried out through the planning system and orders from the government. The allocation of resources was fixed through the plan and controlled by the planning commission.

The departments for sectoral economic management directly controlled the productive units within the sectors they managed. The result was an extensive and bloated bureaucratic structure with bodies generally charged with the responsibility to oversee the production or control of one commodity rather than manage an entire sector of the economy. Overstaffing, functional overlapping and low efficiency were pervasive and debilitating problems. A disproportionate share of public resources was expended on the considerable number of public employees. Consequently the state had no discretionary resources to finance economic and social development programmes.

The transition process has implied a profound reshuffling of the map of power. The role of the state has been changing not only in its relation to the economy but also as a public service provider: private sector entities are becoming increasingly important actors and sub-national governments have seen their role increase. In a schematic way, the transition entailed two centrifugal movements: from a centralised system to a more decentralised system, and from a system in which administrative, productive and social service functions are folded into one same (or closely linked) organisation to a setting in which different functions are undertaken by different organisations.

The reform process has been bringing a progressive separation of state-owned enterprises (SOEs) from the administration and the transfer of responsibility for welfare services from enterprises to local governments. The monetisation of the economy led to the hardening of budget constraints, for SOEs as well as for the administration. Successively, in 1982-1985, 1988, 1993, 1998 and 2003 (see Table 0.1), the Chinese Government conducted five administrative reforms. Each had a different priority, but all contributed to four broad objectives: i) to modify the role of the government; ii) to transform the government's organisational structure; iii) to address the problem of over-staffing; and iv) to increase the efficiency of public action.

In 2002, the public sector employed 69.2 million people: 35.4 in the public administration and 33.8 in SOEs. Only 50 000 worked in core ministries and state bodies, while eight million worked in sub-national governments. The number of public employees has declined in recent years, but mostly as a result of the contraction of the SOE sector. Over the past decade, employment in public administrations and in public service units (PSUs or *shiye danwei*) remained relatively steady. These PSUs, 1.3 million organisations, are in charge of the delivery of services "for the purpose of social public benefit", most of them in the sectors of health, education, science and technology, and culture. Structures are inherited from the planned regime and are yet to be reformed; the stakes are high as PSUs attached to the national level employ 1.9 million staff, while PSUs attached to the sub-national levels employ 23 million.[4]

The decentralisation process occurred in an incremental and uncoordinated fashion. Beginning in the 1980s, local governments started assuming increasing responsibilities for economic development (see Box 0.2 for an overview of the territorial divisions in China). They intervened in the determination of prices, the establishment of new enterprises and the investment of locally accumulated funds. Public spending also was increasingly decentralised, local government becoming responsible for education, health and housing. As local governments kept an increasing share of locally collected taxes, this created the unexpected consequence of "localism", in which local authorities sought to protect their industries, as these were important sources of fiscal revenues.

At the Fourteenth National Party Congress of the Communist Party of China (CPC) in October 1992, Chinese leaders acknowledged the need for recentralisation, in order to correct the excesses of the decentralisation of the 1980s. However, local governments at

Table 0.1. **The five major administrative reforms of the transition period**

	Event/document	Objectives/measures
1982/83	12th CPC Party Congress (September 1982) and 5th Session of 5th NPC (December 1982).	*Re-organisation and downsizing;* central level: State Council's organs cut from 100 to 61, staff from 51 000 to 30 000; local levels: staff and organs cut. *Decentralization* of powers. Strengthening comprehensive departments, reducing economic management departments.
1988	1st Session of the 7th NPC (March).	*Re-organisation and downsizing;* central level: State Council's organs reduced from 67 to 60, staff from 50 000 to 44 000. *Transformation of government functions:* separating government bodies from profit-making enterprises, restructuring economic management departments, separating Party and state.
1993	CPC "Directions for Implementing the Restructuring of the Party and Government Units". State Council: "Provisional Rules and Regulations on Civil Servants".	Overall objective: Government restructuring for a socialist market economy. *Re-organisation and downsizing;* central level: State Council's organs cut from 86 to 59, staff reduced by 20%; local levels: 20-30% of staff cut. *Transformation of government functions:* focus on economic government function, separating government bodies from profit-making enterprises, strengthened macro-control and supervision. Establishment of a *civil service system* within three years; reclassification of public sector employees; recruitment, retirement and promotion processes formally established; age limits introduced and rejuvenation of civil service accelerated.
1998	1st Session of the 9th NPC.	Most decisive and thorough *re-organisation and downsizing* of the bureaucracy; central level: ministries/commissions downsized from 40 to 29; more than 200 bureau-level units cut; proposal to downsize 50% of personnel; local level: major cuts. *Functional adjustment* of the government to meet the demands of a socialist-market economy, focus on separating government bodies from running profit-making enterprises (by abolishing operational bureaucratic control). Increasing central control and macro-management capacity. Promoting the rule of law.
2003	16th CPC Party Congress (November 2002) 1st session of the 10th NPC (March 2003).	*Re-organisation:* 28 ministries/commissions; restructuring of administrative competencies; set-up of the State-owned Assets Supervision and Administration Commission (SASAC); the State Development and Planning Commission renamed the National Development and Reform Commission (NDRC); the State Economic and Trade Commission merged with Ministry of Foreign Trade and Economic Cooperation to become Ministry of Commerce (MOFCOM), comprising competencies for domestic and foreign trade management set-up of the China Banking Regulatory Commission (CBRC).

the county and township levels are still saddled with unusually heavy expenditure responsibilities, including for areas such as education and health. This has led to a large gap between available financial resources and expenditure responsibilities.

The devices through which power is exercised are also being progressively modified: from governing through economic planning and administrative orders to governing through budget, tax and regulatory tools. In parallel with administrative reforms, China has undertaken important fiscal reforms. The revenue mechanisms of the planned economy became progressively ill-suited to the changing economic regime. This led to a progressive decline of public revenues relative to GDP, down to a low 11% in the early 1990s. The Chinese central government had significantly devolved tax collection powers to local governments in view of increasing revenue mobilisation. The result was that by 1993, the central share of revenues had fallen to just 22% of the total. Fiscal reform therefore became a priority reform issue. The 1994 tax reform overhauled the tax system, adapting it to an

> **Box 0.2. Territorial divisions**
>
> China has four sub-national levels of state administration and a fifth level which is essentially local. At the end of 2003, the numbers of units were as follows:*
>
> - *Province* level: 31 units comprising 22 provinces, five autonomous regions and four big city municipalities. The provinces dominate in population terms, having on average over 45.3 million inhabitants per province.
> - *Prefecture* level: 333 units. Most provinces are entirely subdivided into prefecture-level cities, whose governments thus administer large areas of mostly rural character, divided into counties, as well as city districts. But 51 prefectures have a different structure.
> - *County* level: 2 861 units comprising 1 642 counties, 374 county-level cities and 845 districts in higher-level cities. These units, too, include both rural and urban areas.
> - *Township* level: About 44 000 units including 18 100 mostly rural townships, 20 200 towns and 5 750 street communities in cities.
> - *Grassroots* level: 680 000 villages with village committees; urban neighbourhood communities (number not known).
>
> * *China Statistical Yearbook 2004*, Table 1.1.

increasingly market-driven economy and allowed to increase both the share of revenues in GDP and the central share of total revenues. It was only then, in the late 1990s, that attention turned to improving the efficiency of public expenditures. Since 1999, broad reforms in budgeting are being progressively introduced, covering budget preparation, budget classification, treasury management, government procurement and information systems. However, while both the 1994 tax reform and the budget reforms bore fruits, the efforts to build a modern tax and budget system are far from complete. The notion of using the budget process as a strategic governance tool is still underdeveloped in China.

Complementary to these changes in the fiscal system, steps to progressively shift the mode of governance from governing by executive orders toward the rule of law have been taken. Before the beginning of the reforms, orders issued by the CPC and different parts of the government were the main basis for administering state affairs. After the Cultural Revolution, however, China aimed to develop a legal system to restrain abuses of official authority and revolutionary excesses. First in 1982, and again in 1999, the Constitution was revised to emphasise the concept of rule of law by which state organisations are all subject to the law. This turn is widely recognized as a change of significant symbolic importance.

The drive to establish a functioning legal system has brought about the promulgation of 300 laws and regulations, most of them in the economic area. Legislation designed to modernize and professionalize the nation's lawyers, judges, and prisons was enacted. China's entry into the WTO in 2001 also led to the adoption of many new economic laws and the amendment of others. The adoption of laws such as the Administrative Litigation Law (1989), the State Compensation Law (1994) and the Administrative Licensing Law (2003) are important landmarks.

The political regime *de facto* still is a one-party system. Nevertheless within these limits, there has been some evolution towards more checks and balances on the executive. There have been some moves to bring the ruling Party under the rule of law, such as the constitutional amendment in 1999 (United Nations, 2005), with further moves evident from the policy directions set out in the Fourth Plenum of the Sixteenth CPC Party Congress. In recent years, the National People's Congress has also increasingly asserted its power, through the drafting of laws, but also regarding the design and monitoring of the budget. Another important advancement has been the growing prominence of the State Audit Administration, whose annual reports criticise the Ministry of Finance and other government bodies at the central and local level.

1.3. Governance matters to ensure China's sustainable development

The "growing out of the plan" approach (Naughton, 1995) in economic transition and the gradual reduction of government control have worked wonders in the productive sectors by releasing pent-up energies and resources and improving allocative efficiency. As reflected in the above description, Chinese leaders have been aware of the need to adapt state institutions to an increasingly market-based economy.

Governance improvements appear crucial to support economic growth. The transformation of the system of governance is also necessary to address a Web of fault lines that may otherwise undermine China's development path.

Three sources of pressure on public finances coexist, which reinforce one another: the restructuring of the state-owned sector, the risk of insolvency of banks and the rising demand for social welfare. The state sector has withdrawn significantly from many parts of the economy in terms of numbers of SOEs and employees. Important progress has also been made in the restructuring of the state-owned sector: overall productivity has improved, although it is still less than in the private sector (OECD, 2005). But a significant core of distressed state-held companies with financial problems (7% of firms, 11% of workers, 23% of assets and 22% of outstanding debt) remains at all administrative levels. These include companies with negative equity, negative value added, or sub-zero rates of return on assets. Increasing competition resulting from the rising prevalence of market prices in both upstream and downstream markets combined with the growth of the non-state sector means that less efficient state enterprises face increasing financial difficulties. Growing budgetary pressures on local governments (*cf. infra*) have meant that loss-makers increasingly cannot be subsidized.

At the same time, restructuring or withdrawing from loss-making public enterprises reveals their insolvency. Indeed, while analysis of debt associated with distressed firms shows that the burdens have declined over time, a substantial number of firms hold debt that is, or is likely to become, non-performing. And, in spite of progress being made, much remains to be done before the banking sector, and in particular the state-owned commercial banks and rural credit co-operatives, can be said to be financially healthy.

Restructuring of the state sector also implies laying off workers. Employment in state-controlled industrial companies fell by almost 40% from 1998 to 2003, as close to 30 million workers by official estimation were laid off. This is a major source of social tensions, partially eased by the introduction of an urban minimum living standard for laid-off urban employees in 1997, which represents increasing costs for local government. More broadly, a government-based social insurance system comprising pension, health, unemployment, injury and maternity was established in 1997. Prior to this date, benefits were provided by the companies to employees. The costs of this shift of responsibility for the provision of social services from productive units to local governments also took place in former communist countries such as Poland and the corresponding costs were widely underestimated.

In addition, an increasing number of protests and demonstrations of various forms reflect growing social discontent. There are multiple causes, including unemployment, growing individual, regional and rural/urban economic inequalities, increasing demand for services from an ageing population and corruption or abuse of power. Another source of social protest are the important environmental deteriorations brought by rapid economic development, which have created large numbers of ecological migrants. To give examples, acid rain is falling on one-third of the Chinese territory, one-third of the urban population is breathing polluted air, and less than 20% of the trash in cities is treated and processed in an environmentally sustainable manner.

These interlinked problems create a particularly difficult situation for reform. Many actors (loss-making SOEs, banks with negative capital that survive only through regulatory forbearance, governments, employees) have a short-term interest in the *status quo*. But the *status quo* is unsustainable. Reform is all the more important as the weak financial environment is limiting the potential development of the private sector – and thus the creation of jobs. Also, public resources that could be used to finance social services are absorbed to subsidise non-performing loans.

The recently adopted Scientific Development Concept (*kexue fazhan guan*) and the Harmonious Society (*hexie shehui*) concept take on a more comprehensive approach towards development (*cf.* Box 0.1). They complement the discourse about the Chinese modernization path with a social dimension and stress the need to reconcile conflicts between rural and urban areas and between different social groups to promote social stability. The evolution of the political discourse shows a raising awareness regarding the importance of governance among Chinese leaders.[5]

Four broad areas appear to require further reform efforts:

1. Pursue the redefinition of the **role of the state**, and address the consequent organisational challenges this evolution raises. This question precedes that of the sustainability of public expenditures and of efficiency of public action.

2. Modernise the **governing tools** (regulatory framework, budgeting, civil service) and adapt these to a market-driven economy. This is necessary to improve the efficiency and effectiveness with which public resources are used. Strengthening the rule of law and regulatory stability will provide citizens and businesses with greater confidence concerning state institutions. This is also crucial to strengthen the state capacity and non-state mechanisms to arbitrate between conflicting interests, and between short-term and long-term objectives.

3. Adjust the **relations between levels of government**. This vertical dimension of the system of governance is crucial in many respects: to handle the remaining difficulties of the transition process, but also to provide better public services for citizens and enterprises. This comprises both fiscal and administrative aspects.

4. Consolidate the **institutional framework for market forces**. This is a necessary condition to strengthen the role of the private sector both as an engine of economic growth and as a provider of basic services.

The following four parts of this synthesis gather results of the China Governance Project on these four topics. A final part summarises the conclusions.

2. Evolution of the role of the state and subsequent organisational challenges

The transition process has implied an evolution of the role of the state, reflected in changes in the structure of public expenditures as well as in the organisational architecture of the public administration. The state has taken on a new role in relation to production and service units, from which the state is not retrieving totally. This evolution required the setting up of new institutions (to regulate SOEs and the financial sector) and new modes of functioning, both in regulation and service delivery. Drawing on several chapters, this part reflects the progress made on these issues.

2.1. Public spending: narrowing scope and changing priorities

Chapter 8 analyses the evolution of the structure of on-budget public expenditure since 1997. It concludes that the structure of public expenditure appears out of line with China's development needs and goals in three respects. Public spending on education is too low, not reaching the target of 4% of GDP fixed by the government. Spending on science and technology is also relatively low. Building a national system of innovation is crucial at this stage of development, to support technological upgrading. Finally, public spending on health is too low. The entry of private capital in the health sector alone is unlikely to meet the increasing needs for healthcare services. These expenditure gaps affect both economic growth and social cohesion.

At the same time, there is growing pressure for spending on social welfare (health but also pensions and unemployment/social relief). The pressure on public spending has been partially alleviated by increased revenues, thanks to economic growth and to the reform of the tax system, and to improved collection and compliance. However, as in most developing countries, informality and low productivity make it difficult to collect income tax and social insurance contributions outside the developed parts of the urban economy, comprising barely one-fifth of all employed persons (*cf.* Chapter 11). While this can put pressure on the authorities to rely on other revenue sources, such as consumption taxes, recent decisions to abolish various rural taxes and fees suggest that the government may see little room for additional taxation of any form in rural areas in the near future.

Although many recent reform efforts have been designed to improve the targeting and so increase the efficiency of public spending, there is still a need to consider fundamental questions about the role of the state. This is relevant at two levels: at a macro-, strategic level, *i.e.* setting priorities, in a perspective of macroeconomic regulation of growth and income distribution; and within each category of expenditure, assessing which activities or parts of activities should be left to the private sector, should be financed partially by users, etc.

The share of public spending allocated to investment is well above the OECD average; only Korea presents a higher share. Part of the investment spending has been motivated and justified by the government's policy of promoting development in Western regions (the so-called *xibu kaifa* policy). Investment has also been undertaken by provincial leaders in order to maintain the growth rate locally. These investment decisions have contributed to the overheating of the Chinese economy observed at the beginning of 2004.

Spending is also still high on public sector administration. Successive attempts to reduce the number of public sector employees have not been very effective. It is indeed not easy to cut the public labour force, since in the poorer areas, public sector employment functions as a social safety net.

2.2. New institutions to frame the state's participation in economic sectors are needed

The Chinese state will remain active, if not dominant, in a number of sectors. Important steps have been taken to change the governance framework of this participation, with in particular the creation of several regulatory bodies. But further efforts are needed to improve this new mode of state participation in economic sectors. Efforts to fine-tune the functioning and role of these new regulatory bodies should also be accompanied by measures to improve the internal governance regime of regulated entities (*cf.* Chapter 10 and Section 3) and by measures fostering competition and market scrutiny.

As competition in the economy is increasing, loss-making SOEs are creating unaffordable financial liabilities and inadequate services are affecting economic development overall; thus, improving the management of state-owned assets has become a top priority area for the current government. Chapter 10 recalls the different phases of the reform of SOEs and analyses in particular the impact of the creation of the State-owned Assets Supervision and Administration Commission (SASAC) in 2003. The fundamental objective behind the creation of SASAC has been to "fulfil the functional responsibilities of capital investors", implying a clear separation of ownership from management, a focus on investment returns and the use of legal means and mechanisms for shareholder intervention. But Chapter 10 shows why the reform effort does not yet allow for fully effective management of state-owned assets. The transition to a more efficient system of control would imply a number of supplementary measures, including: *i)* the creation and enhancement of the role of boards in SOEs, and the improvement of recruitment and performance evaluation procedures for their senior management; and *ii)* strictly separating the government's exercise of its ownership in SOEs from its regulatory and other functions and eliminating interference in SOE management.

Another important evolution has been that of the governance framework of financial institutions. In order to avoid destabilising systemic crises, to reduce the size of the future bail-out of failed institutions and to enable the financial system to allocate resources to the real economy, significant changes are necessary. In the banking sector, it has become clear that injecting funds into the banks will not help repair their balance sheets if the basic framework under which they operate is not reformed. As described in Chapter 13, the China Banking Regulatory Commission (CBRC) was created in 2003 to assume the responsibility of banking supervision from the People's Bank of China, in order to separate supervisory functions from that of monetary policy. Other financial regulatory commissions created earlier, the China Securities Regulatory Commission (CSRC, 1992) and the China Insurance Regulatory Commission (CIRC, 1998), have been given enhanced powers and have been steadily upgrading their capabilities.

At different rates from one sector to the other, institutional reforms have also taken place in the public utilities sector. The State Electricity Regulatory Commission (SERC) was set up recently to promote the development of a regional electricity market. As for other network industries (*cf.* Chapter 9), their reform has accelerated since the late 1990s, in response to rapidly increasing demand and to fulfil WTO commitments. Yet in the sectors of gas, rail and to a lesser extent telecommunication, reforms have still not significantly modified the institutional framework in place.

Although important steps have been taken in the right direction (*cf.* Chapters 9, 10 and 13), remaining problems call for sustained and co-ordinated reform efforts. To take one example, despite the creation of the CBRC and substantial official efforts to improve credit quality, the 2003 credit boom suggests that borrowing and lending decisions are still not fully made on the basis of strict commercial criteria. The chapters highlight several issues concerning the relations between state regulatory bodies, government authorities and the regulated entities.

A primary issue is to ensure that regulatory bodies are "distant enough", that is sufficiently independent, from the entities they regulate. Regulatory authorities necessarily need to have regular information and communication with the businesses subject to their authority if they are to effectively perform their functions. Yet too close a relation can result in the regulated using the regulator ("regulatory capture") to establish monopoly positions or otherwise inhibit competition.

A second issue is to maintain the right distance between government authorities and regulatory bodies. This is particularly relevant in the case of the oversight of SOEs, as there is a need to clearly separate the objectives and strategy assigned to companies by the state, as a majority shareholder, from its regulatory and other functions and from the management of these companies. As described in Chapter 10, the creation of SASAC has clearly contributed to shift the objective of supervision from direct intervention in enterprise management to capital oversight. However, SASAC continues to be responsible for the nomination, assessment and dismissal of not only the CEO but also of senior executives in those state-owned assets that have not yet been incorporated. Therefore it is likely that state interference in those companies' operations will continue to take place. If, where existing, boards in SOEs may not be in a position to take on these functions immediately, the procedures through which top management will be recruited and assessed should at least be transparent and based on criteria of relevant business competencies.

A third issue is to clarify and consolidate the accountability relationship between the government authorities and the regulatory actors. If the process of "controlling the controllers" is transparent, it helps avoid undue interference. The accountability of the regulatory bodies, rather than just their reporting lines, needs to be clearly defined.

Finally, it is also important to clearly identify the division of responsibilities between the different regulatory bodies. Clarifying the division of responsibilities between the SASAC and the CSRC, and their link with upstream authorities, are of particular importance to allow for adjudication, as for instance, at the time of initial public share offering on capital markets, these may have diverging interests. A transparent division of responsibilities between the CSRC, the stock exchanges and other self-regulating organisations is also crucial as it is a precondition for improving the efficiency and effectiveness of administrative enforcement.

2.3. The reform of public service units is a pressing issue

Under the pre-reform regime, public service units (PSUs) were all owned and managed by the government, receiving funds from the budget to finance all their operations. Their activities were conducted according to the state plan, insulated from any competition mechanism. In order to respond as much as possible to a growing demand with insufficient public funding, past reform measures have led to a substantial modification of the institutional status of PSUs, increasing their flexibility and autonomy in terms of financing, accounting, staffing and management practices. To find alternative sources of financing, a PSU would then either commercialise some of the services delivered or develop in parallel commercial activities with no direct link with the initial purpose of the PSU. Also, to make up for the insufficiency of services delivered, private companies have been authorised to develop in some of the sectors of activity of the PSUs.

After a series of piecemeal reforms, often implemented sector by sector, the Chinese Government is currently embarking on an important reform of PSUs. The stakes of such a reform are considerable, as the 1.3 million PSUs employ 25.5 million people. The problem is multi-dimensional: financial, organisational, managerial and regulatory.

The chapter on higher education gives a good illustration of the increasingly complex situation that has developed around PSUs, describing the evolution of the financing and of the organisational forms in this sector. In the past two decades, higher education institutions (HEIs) and the higher education sector in general underwent a radical transformation. HEIs used to be affiliated with ministries at the central level, but 85% of them were subsequently decentralised to provincial or sub-provincial level. HEIs were encouraged to find alternative sources of financing as the central and the local budgets could not finance the expansion of the sector that was needed. As a result, there are four sources of financing today: central budget (even for HEIs affiliated to sub-national governments), sub-national budgets, students' tuitions and fees and private sector contracts. Only 50% of the total budget of HEIs is covered by public funds.

This increased flexibility and opening of the higher education sector has allowed a rapid increase in both the volume of higher education and its quality. The number of students has increased by a multiple of 15 within 10 years, and private capital has allowed the modernisation and renovation of HEIs. On the other hand, relying heavily on private sources for financing tends to increase social and territorial disparities, in particular as long as the loan schemes that have been introduced do not function very well. Higher education becomes accessible only to those who can afford it. In addition, it is not uncommon that professors combine working in public HEI with teaching in private HEIs or prefer to spend time working on lucrative contracts (with the private sector but also with international or foreign agencies), to the detriment of basic teaching assignments or support to students. Third, the management of resources coming from private sources is not always transparent or done to serve the public interest. As a result, quality is uneven and difficult to monitor. Finally, the development of other sources of financing has not always been accompanied by efforts to increase the efficiency and performance of the HEIs.

The reform of PSUs today is driven by three issues: i) the need to clarify what should be the role of the state in the different sectors of operation of PSUs; ii) the need to improve the performance of PSUs; and iii) the need to clarify the management and accountability of PSUs to ensure they serve the public and not themselves.

Chapters 2, 17 and 18 discuss possible reform approaches. The question of what should be the best organisational form for PSUs, and thus of the role of the state, should not only be guided by fiscal considerations and related issues of equity (who should pay for what), and considerations of efficiency (including the necessity to introduce some degree of flexibility in formulating public actions in order to take local factors into account). Decisions on the organisational form should also take into account the broader organisational and management context in which public action will take place. The increase in autonomy and flexibility that PSUs have known does not mean that the government and line ministries should play no role at all – but rather calls for an evolution of that role. In the context of the PSU reform, it is important that measures be taken to strengthen the accountability relationship between those PSUs that will keep their independent agency-like type of status and the government body to which they are affiliated. If the operating context does not allow for the formal arrangements to be put in place efficiently, it might be wiser to promote integration into line ministries.

2.4. Half-way organisational changes create huge challenges of co-ordination

A multitude of successive sector-specific and administration-wide reforms have contributed to modifications of the organisational structure of the Chinese administration. However, many chapters in this report refer to organisational and co-ordination problems, which are linked to the co-existence of structures inherited from the past with new institutions. Five types of issues were detected in the policy areas covered by this report: i) lack of co-ordination between closely related organisations, leading to efficiency losses (e.g. budget, intellectual property rights); ii) lack of co-ordination between organisations with overlapping mandates, affecting the coherence of public action (e.g. water, statistics or agriculture); iii) hierarchical structure between organisations not corresponding to their mandates (e.g. FDI policy); iv) fragmentation of decision-making responsibilities (e.g. public expenditure); v) co-existence of institutions with conflicting working rationale/mandates (planned-economy *versus* market-based; e.g. agricultural policies).

An example illustrating the fragmentation of decision-making responsibilities in a complex institutional framework is the management of public expenditure. Even if the role of the economic and social development plans has changed, the NDRC continues to be the body co-ordinating their design and implementation. Decisions related to capital expenditures continue to be the responsibility of NDRC, while the budget, managed by the Ministry of Finance, covers only recurrent expenditures. Capital spending decisions are not required to be co-ordinated with fiscal authorities, even when these decisions will create large recurrent costs downstream. Similarly, staffing decisions, which have major spending implications, are made by the State Commission Office for Public Sector Reform (SCOPSR) and its local branches, with little consultation with fiscal authorities.

This fragmentation of decision-making responsibilities not only creates co-ordination difficulties but also affects the "readability" of public policy. Integrating all decisions related to public expenditure would allow better control and would better ensure fiscal sustainability. Moreover, it is not clear who will be the final guarantor of fiscal balance in China. Currently, this outcome will inevitably depend more on the balance of power between the different institutions than on policy choices.

An example of co-existing institutions with conflicting working rationale/mandates is detailed in the chapter on the institutional framework of agricultural policies. Despite important strides made in the 2003 reform, a complex Web of 14 ministries and commissions are still directly involved in governing agriculture and its upstream and downstream sectors. The introduction of measures towards the liberalisation of production, pricing and marketing has led to the creation of new institutions or to the redefinition of the mandate of old ones. At the same time, the production and trading of commodities considered of strategic importance, such as staple foods, have continued to be managed through state-linked enterprises. Institutions still carrying characteristics of the planned economy co-exist with institutions charged with the implementation of policy measures based on market principles.

In such a complex and highly fragmented institutional framework, with conflicting mandates, it is difficult to create incentives for co-operation and co-ordination among state actors (*cf.* in Chapter 16 the example of the grain sector). Therefore, further efforts are needed to streamline the organisational structure for the design and implementation of agricultural policies. But this organisational reform should be guided by redefining the role of the state in agricultural policy. The focus of public action should increasingly be on services that will increase the competitiveness of farms and rural enterprises and that will facilitate the restructuring process. Accession to WTO and the resulting opening to foreign competition make the need for restructuring and the improvement of efficiency even more pressing.

3. Modernising governing tools to improve the efficiency and the effectiveness of public action

Drawing again on several chapters of this study, this part gathers the results related to the need to modernise the governing tools (regulatory framework and public management) and adapt these to a market-driven economy. As mentioned previously, this is necessary to improve the efficiency and effectiveness with which public resources are used.

3.1. From control to *regulatory governance*

China has taken a series of steps to improve the regulatory capacity of the government, the regulatory framework and to strengthen the rule of law (*cf.* Chapter 9). For instance, the 2000 Legislation Law has clarified the role of the National People's Congress (NPC) and of the State Council in the law-making process, thus increasing its transparency and coherency. In many respects, as for example concerning intellectual property rights or individual employment contracts, China has adopted regulations that are well in line with international standards, but their enforcement has become a major challenge (*cf.* Chapters 14 and 11). In other areas there are still many traces of the previous planning system, resulting often in an overly complex and incoherent regulatory framework (see for instance Chapters 5 and 16, and Section 2.4). Several chapters point to the lack of secondary-level regulations or to their poor quality. Regulatory coherence is a significant problem. The National People's Congress and the State Council normally play a supervising role, but the large volume of sub-national legislation makes this task difficult to achieve.

Strengthening the rule of law and the regulatory framework will provide citizens and businesses with greater confidence concerning state institutions' evolution of the devices through which power is exercised. This is also crucial to strengthen the state capacity and non-state mechanisms to arbitrate between conflicting interests, and between short-term and long-term objectives. The following paragraphs summarise findings related to two aspects of the ongoing transition from control to regulatory governance: *i*) the reform of the administrative approval system and more generally, the evolution of the relationship between the state and non-state actors; and *ii*) the problem of application and enforcement of regulations.

3.1.1. *Reform of the administrative approval system*

Until recently, state control on economic activities through administrative approvals had continued to be an important characteristic of the Chinese economy. This was a legacy from the planned system, in which state controls penetrated virtually all sectors of economic life – from access to raw materials to price setting to distribution and sales. In its transition to a "socialist market economy", China is taking important steps in order to reduce restrictions on enterprises' ability to enter and exit the market, or otherwise respond efficiently to consumer demand, in particular with the reform of the administrative approval process.

In recent years, the reform of administrative approvals has become a high priority of the Chinese Government, as reflected by the creation of the Leading Group for Administrative and Examination Approval System Reform in 2001. Important reform measures have been taken recently (*cf.* Chapter 9), with the adoption of the Plan for Administrative Approval System Reform and of the 2003 Administrative Licensing Law (which covers a significant subset of the items subject to administrative approval, those primarily relating to business activities). The related Administrative Approval Reviews have led to the elimination of 1 795 approval requirements at the central level, out of a total of more than 4 000. The Licensing Law narrows the scope of activities for which a licence is required, and even in cases where a licence is required, it encourages self-regulation. This law should make the licensing process less burdensome, more open and less subject to delay. Some regulatory barriers to market entry will continue to exist, but will need to have a stronger connection to the several concepts of public interest specified in the Law. As noted in Chapter 9, it is too early to assess the impact of this law, but the significant efforts made to guide public bodies and civil servants for its implementation indicate a high level of political will.

In parallel, in July 2004, the State Council issued the Decision Concerning the Reform of the Investment System to streamline the investment approval process (*cf.* Chapter 15). This Decision simplifies the process through a single application report, and mandates a greater delegation of approval powers to local authorities. The revised Catalogue for Guidance of Foreign Investment adopted in February 2002 also represents a major step forward in foreign direct investment regime liberalisation. In view of the experience of OECD member countries, the Chinese Government, if it wishes to attract more and better foreign investment, may consider replacing the catalogue, which lists prohibited, restricted and encouraged categories, with a single list of sectors barred to foreign participation.

In the labour market, an important step was taken in 2003 with the elimination of administrative controls on the recruitment of migrant workers. As discussed in Chapter 11, this has not led to equal treatment of urban and rural workers in all respects, but it means that employers are free to hire the workers they want, and job seekers are free to compete for jobs anywhere in the country.

In relation to theses issues, two important messages emerge from the different chapters of this report.

First, in spite of the overall liberalisation trend, many activities continue to be subject to a large amount of government control. This is the case for instance with grain production, pricing, marketing and distribution and also with the land tenure system (*cf.* Chapter 16). The Chinese state should aim to further reduce its intervention, shifting the emphasis from planning activities to enabling activities, providing services and infrastructure. This is valid at the national level but also at the local level, since the experience of OECD member countries shows that policies to improve the business environment are key to local development. In the context of agriculture, allowing farmers, rural citizens and agro-rural enterprises to make their own decisions is likely to increase the efficiency of the allocation of resources. More generally, Chinese leaders should let investors determine which investment will be profitable and which will not, and bear associated risks. In addition, to the benefit of the Chinese people, this evolution could also allow to shift the state focus further toward regulation with respect to the protection of public health and safety, away from restrictions on competition.

As stressed in Chapter 16, such evolution of the government's role implies a profound shift in mentalities and in the relations between state and non-state actors: from a top-down hierarchical approach, implementation through direct control and objectives formulated as outputs and capital targets, to one that is service- and needs-oriented, responsive and accountable, servicing the needs of citizens and economic actors, setting up appropriate incentive systems and creating circumstances that allow winners to emerge. It also implies a change in competencies for mid-level managers, who have to learn to operate in a very different environment. This dimension of the transition should not be overlooked by Chinese leaders, and in this regard, opportunities for exchange with foreign officials and experts could be helpful.

Second, efforts made to streamline the regulatory framework of private businesses should be pushed further. Indeed, the operating environment for businesses continues to be quite complex, creating opportunities for extortion and bribery. In some cases, successive piecemeal reforms have added to the complexity of the regulatory framework. As noted above, recent efforts will certainly contribute to the improvement of the regulatory environment. As described in Chapter 6, China has also simplified the administrative regulations in the area of taxation, introducing one-stop shops and simplifying procedures for permits and licenses and by putting time limits on decision-making. Although commendable, there is still a long way to go. The costs born by enterprises linked to the complex administrative environment affect the profitability of domestic and foreign investments in China. Again the experience of OECD member countries with reducing administrative and regulatory burdens on enterprises could be pertinent for China.

3.1.2. Enforcement

The main challenge concerning the regulatory framework is that of application and enforcement of regulations; as described throughout the report, the application of laws and regulations is not always systematic, sometimes biased by corrupt arrangements or reflecting the local balance of interests.

The solution to problems of enforcement will probably not lie in occasional enforcement campaigns as are regularly organised in different fields, including anti-corruption, intellectual property rights or environment protection. These campaigns remind economic actors of the existence of the laws and correct a few misdeeds, but in the end they have little effect on behaviour patterns.

Part of the solution lies in strengthening the inspection bodies and the administrative and judicial enforcement bodies. Under the regime prior to the economic reforms, officials were under the close scrutiny of their supervisors. Organisations had cumbersome book-keeping procedures, but there were few agencies or effective procedures to control the overall functioning of public entities. Today, China needs to strengthen formal systems of financial and performance audit. Chapter 9 mentions the problem of inspectors being dependent on the local level, leading to poor enforcement (further discussed in Section 4).

As for judicial enforcement, trained judges are short in supply, in particular in less developed areas (see Chapter 10). Some chapters (for instance Chapter 15) point to other inadequacies of the court system, such as judicial ignorance of the law, corruption within the judicial system, pressures on judges from local government and CPC officials and inability of courts to enforce their own decisions. Chapter 17 on environment explains that courts tend to decide on the cases by relying on Party policy, the views of the local government and a court's individual sense of justice and fairness in contractual dealings. Factors such as *guanxi* (social connections) between Environmental Protection Bureau (EPB) staff and enterprise managers, interventions by local officials, and an enterprise's profitability often lead to outcomes that are far from those specified in environmental regulations. Chapter 14 points to the difficulty of launching a criminal lawsuit and to the fact that civil and administrative sanctions are not strong enough to dissuade infringers.

But the focus should not only be on strengthening the bodies involved in enforcement. Section 4 exposes the impact of the dysfunctional managerial and fiscal relations across levels of government on the enforcement problem. More fundamentally, regulatory governance implies a paradigm shift in which application and enforcement of regulations are based primarily on voluntary compliance. The deterrent effect of possible sanctions is only one element that contributes to create attitudes of compliance. Other elements relate to the quality of regulations, the regulatory-making process, public participation in this process, public participation in the application and enforcement of regulations, and thus the overall context of access to information. Indeed, the problem of regulatory enforcement is not just a technical problem. It rather reflects limited acceptance of new rules of the game and consequent tensions between interests of various groups. In other terms, the "regulatory enforcement problem" also reflects underlying dynamics of social change. Solving it will necessarily imply increasing public participation.

The nature of the political regime necessarily places constraints on possible progress in the areas of public participation and access to information. Special interest groups such as business, workers or farmers are generally prevented from forming associations outside the control of political leaders. There is still a lack of involvement of constituencies and stakeholders in policy-making and implementation. Chapter 15 for instance shows that while the Chinese Government has in recent years started to involve foreign companies in consultations leading to the promulgation of legislation related to foreign-investment, this process appears to be inconsistent and incomplete. Similarly, Chapter 14 explains that Chinese enterprises and other institutions have complained that relevant intellectual property authorities did not extensively solicit opinions and comments when compiling laws, regulations and policies. This insufficient consultation has led in some cases to inadequate protection standards.

In some areas, Chinese leaders have understood that pressure from public opinion usefully complements enforcement efforts. For instance, Chapter 17 shows that the SEPA has become interested in public disclosure because China's pollution problem remains severe, despite long-lasting attempts to control it with traditional regulatory instruments. Various tools and mechanisms are being used to inform and consult citizens, and to involve their participation: public hearings, advisory committees, document reviews, informational meetings, forums and Environmental Impact Assessments (official process of analysis of the anticipated effects of planned projects or activities on regional and local areas).

Another case in point is the labour law's provisions about working time and other working conditions (Chapter 11). Such rules are generally difficult to enforce when labour supplies are abundant, a situation that gives most job-seekers a weak bargaining position. Nevertheless, recent developments have suggested that a growing awareness of the importance of working conditions can make many job-seekers more demanding, and so put market pressure on employers to improve these conditions.

Although the media continue to be controlled by the state and there is limited freedom of expression and of association, positive steps can nevertheless be observed related to access to information, in part linked to the WTO accession process which requires increased transparency in public affairs. Several chapters note that information on rules, regulations and projects and their implementation by officials has become much more accessible in recent years. This trend has sometimes been reflected in the legal framework, as the obligation to provide information to citizens has been integrated in several sectoral laws. The Administrative Procedures Act mandates increased transparency in a wide variety of public policy areas. Progress is uneven at the local level. For instance, its seems that many local authorities are reluctant to provide copies of their local rules or regulations regarding intellectual property rights (IPR) as well as any local enforcement decisions. The Chinese Government argues that the provision of requested information is in itself a huge task, given the quantity of legislation.

3.2. Public management

The following paragraphs review the main results of the study on the two principal pillars of public management: the budget and the civil service. The potential benefits of the introduction of e-government and the need to simplify and rationalise administrative procedures are then discussed. In spite of progress made on all these fronts, corruption continues to be a major problem in China, symptomatic of the weaknesses of the public management environment. The analysis of these different elements of public management in China shows that progress varies from one region to another, in particular in improving the quality of the civil service. It also shows the interdependences of the different reform efforts, between budget and civil service, in particular in a perspective of managing performance; between e-government and administrative reforms. All these reforms, complementary to a repressive anti-corruption policy, are fundamental to curb the widespread problem of corruption.

3.2.1. The budget

Chapter 7 describes the reforms introduced since 1999 in budget management, from budget preparation with the introduction of departmental budgets to budget implementation. China appears to be, step-by-step, putting in place the infrastructure necessary for building a modern system of budget management. However, the budget management system remains marred by several weaknesses, impeding it from becoming a fully effective tool for policy management and implementation.

On-budget public expenditure represents only 20.3% of GDP in 2004. This is the part of the funds that can be discussed and allocated in a place where pros and cons are discussed and evaluated, above and beyond direct or local interests. Extra-budgetary revenues and expenditures (fees and levies collected by branches of government and spent off budget, tax expenditures, payment arrears, etc.) remain large, estimated to represent 10% of GDP in 1998. There are on-going efforts to move extra-budget activities onto the budget.

As mentioned before, the Ministry of Finance still does not have comprehensive oversight authority on spending. Co-ordination between central and local governments is improving but remains weak, and revenue forecasting also remains weak. In part due to the fiscal gaps described previously, improvement of budgeting at sub-national levels is limited. And finally, compliance with existing laws and regulations needs strengthening.

In the reform process, the government has focused mainly on tackling the technical issues, and has shied away from reforms that more directly involve political challenges. In particular, there has been little public discussion of the need for a major realignment of the intergovernmental fiscal system in spite of the many changes underway since 2000, as a result of reforms in the rural sector. Other important and needed steps include the refocusing of budget priorities and limiting policy initiatives which are not disciplined by the budget process in order to improve orderly prioritization. Finally, the recent audit reports of the State Audit Administration highlight the many difficulties government faces in enforcement of fiscal discipline and in holding spending units accountable for results. Strengthening accountability mechanisms and enforcing aggregate fiscal discipline constitute the critical next challenges for reforms in the next phase.

3.2.2. The civil service

The Chinese Government has undertaken extensive reforms to its civil service system over the past 10 years. Chapter 1 discusses these reforms and analyses remaining challenges.

In this field as in others, a first problem is to ensure that the rules – in relation to recruitment, reward, promotion, etc. – are applied. For instance, not all recruitments go through the established mechanisms. This gap between rules and practice is particularly important in less developed regions, where the public sector plays a role of employer of last resort.

Another important challenge for the Chinese civil service is its high geographical heterogeneity. In the centre and in the richer coastal areas, civil service is relatively performance-oriented, selects "the best and brightest" through competitive mechanisms, links rewards to performance, and controls indiscipline and corruption. In the less developed hinterland, civil service operates as an employer of last resort and presents relatively high levels of indiscipline and corruption. Improving the systems in these poorer areas depends on improving levels of economic development, which in turn is most likely with a competent and committed bureaucracy. Intervening to break out of the vicious circle linking underdevelopment and inefficient bureaucracy is an important task for the foreseeable future. Chapter 1 discusses possible measures, such as transfers of experienced officials to poor areas or flexible pay scales.

3.2.3. Administrative simplification and e-government

Several chapters note the complexity of procedures and regulations and thus stress the potential benefits of further administrative simplification. For instance, the current organisational structure of the tax administration based both on "type of tax" and "function" could be flattened and streamlined through centralizing and merging replicated and overlapping functions. Also, a simplification of regulations could lead to a substantial reduction of compliance cost for taxpayers and of administrative cost for tax authorities.

Such administrative simplification reforms are necessary to increase effectiveness in the adoption of information and communication technologies (ICT). Chapter 6 notes the importance of developing a unified information and technology system to integrate the varied functions of tax collection and administration. More broadly, Chapter 4 depicts the promotion of e-government adopted by the Chinese leadership. It shows that e-government initiatives are moving from simply encouraging the adoption of ICT to promoting substantive reform in the public sector.

But the success of e-government programmes is contingent upon progress in other fronts: administrative reforms that seek to standardise operational procedures and clarify responsibilities, strengthening of the rule of law for instance. These issues in turn involve broader transformations to which the e-government strategy can act as an additional catalyst. The stakes are high, both in terms of allocation of the ICT resources and in terms of the opportunity cost of not focusing on e-government as a major element of the reform agenda.

3.2.4. Curbing corruption

Corruption has become one of the most important problems in China today. The fight against corruption has become a priority on the political agenda: former President Jiang Zemin defined "anti-corruption mechanisms" as a "major political task for the Party" in his report to the Sixteenth Congress of the CPC in November 2002; President Hu Jintao has made anti-corruption a top priority of his government. Corruption indeed indirectly undermines the Party's legitimacy and thus affects the country's political and social stability. Corruption also affects economic development. Among other effects, as pointed out in Chapter 15, it deters foreign direct investment because it imposes a cost on the foreign-invested enterprise for which there is no corresponding benefit. It may also affect the implementation of public policies, such as the protection of intellectual property rights, banking regulations or environmental regulations.

The reasons for the magnitude of the challenge are manifold. Chapter 3 analyses the problem of corruption in China in perspective with four aspects of the transition process: the monetisation and the redefinition of the public sphere, the transition of control mechanisms, the emergence of non-state actors and the new regulatory role of the state.

China has undertaken a number of measures to develop its legal and institutional framework to more effectively detect and sanction corruption. Reforms have primarily focused on the penal regime as well as on the complementing disciplinary sanction system applicable for officials and Party members. Chapter 3 suggests that the effectiveness of repression efforts on corruption would benefit from equal attention attached to the prosecution of all actors involved in corruption schemes, i.e. not only bribe recipients but also bribe payers, legal persons and those involved in the laundering of proceeds of corruption. The deterring effect of the sanction system is weakened by significant gaps in enforcement, as reflected in the low conviction rates and a growing number of citizens absconding with ill-gotten assets. The harsh penalties, including death penalty, which characterise the penal provisions on corruption do not compensate for these gaps.

Until recently, much less effort had been made to examine the sources of corruption and to develop preventative measures. More attention should be paid to reviewing risk areas prone to corruption, eliminating opportunities for corruption and creating conditions conducive to ethical behaviour. More generally, in a context of widespread corruption, efforts to improve the efficiency and effectiveness of public action through the modernisation of the governing tools as described previously (reform of the administrative approval system, regulatory enforcement, management of fiscal and human resources, administrative simplification and introduction of e-government) contribute most effectively to curb corruption.

4. Adjusting the relations among levels of government

If according to its Constitution China is a unitary state, China's system of governance *de facto* features a mixture of non-federal and federal aspects derived from the central planning era and from successive decentralisation and recentralisation reforms. A major landmark in the evolution of relations across levels of government is the 1994 tax reform. Before then, the major problem was the lack of fiscal control of the central government over the local levels. After 1994, redefining the functional responsibilities of the different levels of government and organising fiscal transfers across levels of government became priorities. However, the lack of central government control over local levels persists through problems of enforcement and localism. The evolution of the broader economic and governance regime suggests that resolving these problems will mean improving the management of the relations between the central level and the local level.

Problems linked to the "vertical dimension" of the governance system are mentioned in almost all chapters of the report. The consequences of these problems are multiple: tensions between national and sub-national policies; inadequacy of the public services delivered at the local level; extensive inequalities in public services provided across provinces and between urban and rural areas; and imposition of illegal taxes, corruption and other forms of mismanagement of public funds.

This part of the synthesis focuses on two major aspects of these problems: i) the fragmentation of authority and the resulting problems of enforcement and localism, i.e. local officials seeking primarily to develop the local economy and to maintain local employment, using illegal means or measures that counter policies set at the national level; and ii) the dysfunctional intergovernmental fiscal system.

4.1. Fragmentation of authority and localism

The Chinese administrative system is far from a pyramidal pattern, in which decisions taken at the top are implemented smoothly at lower levels. It is also far from a federal model with a clear division of labour between levels of government. Instead, the complex multiplicity of hierarchical lines leads to unclear responsibilities and accountability relationships, creating situations in which it is not always easy to foresee which authority has priority over others. Box 0.3 describes the complex pattern of vertical organisation of executive power. Chapter 16 details the example of land ownership rights. As these are not clearly defined and as authority over these rights is diluted across various levels of government, there is considerable scope for arbitrary decisions to be taken by local leaders. This can lead to conflicting situations when, for instance, local leaders at the township, village or *xiaozu*[6] level, assuming the role of *de facto* landowners, decide to lease land to external investors without consensus from local farmers and without proper compensation for lost access to land.

Because of this general fragmentation of authority in the system, resolving a matter below the centre often requires building a consensus among an array of relevant officials. This need to construct a consensus generally predisposes officials to negotiate with other relevant officials from an early point. This reinforces the functional importance of relationships or *guanxi*, leading in some instances to clientelism and corruption.

Another consequence is that this complex institutional setting provides an opportunity for the Communist Party to play a strong horizontal role. The Party does not solely play a vertical linking role between top leaders at the centre and the local level. As local government heads (governors or mayors) and local people's congresses are not powerful enough to achieve local horizontal co-ordination, local Party committees play the role of leading and co-ordinating the work of the various state institutions at each level. But the linkages created through Party structures, between enterprises, local government officials and judicial entities, make application and enforcement systems even more vulnerable to interference from special interests.

> **Box 0.3. The *tiaokuai guanxi****
>
> Each ministry or bureau has entities at the different territorial levels, at least down to the county level. Administrative departments, government and Party organs at different levels are linked following a complex pattern of vertical relationships (*tiao*) and horizontal relationships (*kuai*). The term *tiaokuai guanxi*, litterally the relationships between the vertical and horizontal lines, refers to the complex issue of which authority has priority over others.
>
> To present this pattern, we take here the example of the Zhongshan county statistical bureau. This hypothetical statistical bureau under the Zhongshan county government would be subordinate both to the Zhongshan county government and the statistical bureau under the Guangdong provincial government. But these relationships of subordination are of different nature. The Zhongshan county government will exercise administrative leadership (*xingzheng lingdao*) on the statistical bureau: this involves funding, appointment of staff including senior positions and supervisory functions. The Guangdong provincial statistical bureau will exercise business leadership (*yewu zhidao*) over the county bureau.
>
> At the same time, the Zhongshan county government must answer to both the Zhongshan county Communist Party committee and the Guangdong provincial government. In addition, the organisation department of the Zhongshan county Communist committee will strongly affect the career opportunities of the leaders of the Zhongshan county statistical bureau, who must also obey Party discipline as members of the Party committee of the statistical department.
>
> * This box is based on Lieberthal (1995).

A related important problem mentioned in many chapters of this report is that of localism. For instance, Chapter 5 describes that local statistical offices are closer to local governments than to the National Bureau of Statistics (NBS); this facilitates interference to modify statistics to convey a more favourable image of local conditions. Incentives for local authorities to counter national policies are sometimes encouraged by the existence of substantial spill-overs of their benefits or costs. The chapter on IPR explains that loose enforcement of IPR protection may occur when local leaders judge that the local, short-term benefits of a strict IPR enforcement exceed the costs. Problems of enforcement at the local level are further aggravated by the fact that local administrative entities in charge of enforcement are often dependent on the respective local government through their budget and career management of staff. The judicial entities are similarly not independent.

The weak governability of the state apparatus, resulting from fragmentation of authority and localism, is all the more problematic in an increasingly market-driven system. The planning system tended to limit the "world of the possible" and thus the scope of power of officials. Economic planning resolved *ex ante* the possible contradictions between different objectives. In such a context, the multiplicity of overlapping hierarchical links was not so problematic and could even well serve to control a huge body of civil servants. The introduction of market mechanisms in the economy together with decentralisation has loosened the centralised top-down links between top leaders and the mass of officials, as they are obliged to turn increasingly to servicing citizens and private businesses. In addition, a market-driven economy hardens budget constraints and thus imposes the obligation for efficiency on the state.

Reform efforts have been undertaken in various fields to reinforce vertical lines of authority. Tax is one of the fields in which such reforms have been taken the furthest (*cf.* Chapter 6). In the area of statistics (*cf.* Chapter 5), when appointing the head and deputy-heads of the provincial statistical bureau, suggestions by the NBS need to be taken into consideration. This amounts to a *de facto* veto right for the NBS. The same pattern is repeated at the municipal and county level; the suggestions of the next higher level statistical bureau have to be sought before appointing the head and deputy-heads. More recently, the implementation instructions to the Statistics Law go a step further in that they stipulate higher level statistical bureau approval for appointments of all "mid-ranking" and higher statistical "special" and "technical" regular staff, although this may in practice not amount to much more than an advisory role.

Improving co-ordination between the central and local levels will also require progress on other fronts: the improvement of capacities of sub-national governments to properly handle new responsibilities, the development of external control mechanisms at the local level, reform of the incentive mechanisms for local leaders, and an increased participation of local leaders in debates of national policies.

In some cases, differences between the national and the local levels could reflect the difficulty to sustain the policy set at the national level and be an indication of the need of its revision. For instance, state intervention, through local officials, in the current system of allocation of land rights in rural areas is meant to ensure an egalitarian distribution of land rights. But strong interests related to expanding cities create situations conducive to corruption, leading to an allocation process guided *de facto* by power and money. A progressive shift to a rural land rights market would allow the rationalisation of farms and achievement of the benefits of larger scale farming. Through an appropriate regulatory framework, it would also allow implementing appropriate compensation schemes.

4.2. A *dysfunctional intergovernmental fiscal system*

As mentioned previously, there is a significant mismatch between revenues and expenditure assignments. Local governments at the county and township levels are still saddled with unusually heavy expenditure responsibilities, including in areas such as education and health. For instance, cities at the third and fourth tier account for all expenditures for social security: pensions, unemployment insurance, and other income support and welfare schemes. Counties and townships (fourth and fifth tier) are together responsible for providing basic education and public health for the rural populace – these two tiers accounting for 70% of budgetary expenditures on education, and 55-60% of expenditures on health. In addition, 90% of distressed state firms are located at sub-national levels, along with three-quarters of employment. Potential liquidation of the most problematic firms raises significant employment concerns.

As described in the chapters on budgeting and public expenditures, these heavy responsibilities are supported neither by an appropriate set of revenue assignments nor an effective system of transfers to ensure they could meet minimum service provision standards. Fiscal revenue-raising is quite decentralised, but it is less so than expenditure, in particular since the 1994 tax reform which significantly increased the central government's overall share of total revenue. Transfers from the central to the provincial governments to bridge the resulting gap have risen substantially. However, they fall short of covering the gap between expenditure responsibilities and tax revenue resources. Moreover, many earmarked transfers arrive late in the year and in unpredictable amounts.

Another aspect of this problem is the overly centralised character of the policy-making process. Policies made by central government usually have financing implications for local governments, but local governments are not always consulted before rollout. For example, most local officials reportedly learned of a salary increase for civil servants from TV broadcasts even though the costs were mostly borne at the local level. But improvements in consultation with local governments have clearly been evident in recent years. For example, the recent reforms in rural fees and agricultural taxes have been worked out with local governments.

The dysfunctional intergovernmental fiscal structure has important negative consequences. It contributes to local disparities and to problems of enforcement.

Provision of services to the local populace is vulnerable to variations in local fiscal health, and inequality has been rising among provinces, but more severely even below the provincial level. The decentralisation process has aggravated inequality in social welfare, in particular between rural and urban areas. According to the Ministry of Health,[7] rural Chinese enjoy only 20% of the country's medical resources though the vast rural areas are home to 900 million of the 1.3 billion population. The shortage of revenues at the lower tiers and especially in poor regions constitutes a bottleneck to national policy implementation in the sectors of social security, basic education and health, in which, as explained previously, China should be spending more.

A major consequence has been the growth of illegal taxes and fees. According to some estimates, these illegal fees could well equal official budgets at lower sub-national levels, in counties and townships. However, the exact situation seems to vary from one county to another.

The shortage of funds biases the enforcement of policies. For instance, in the environmental field, many Environmental Protection Bureaus (EPBs) are heavily dependent on collecting pollution levies to cover their operating costs. It is then in the interest of EPBs to allow enterprises to continue polluting and so paying their pollution levy, rather than to comply with discharge standards and stop paying. The shortage of funds also contributes to corruption and rent-seeking behaviour. When pay arrears are serious or operating funds insufficient, the temptation is great to use official power to extort bribes from citizens or companies. Some observers describe an effective "IPR protection industry", as bribes are often given to activate the participation of the different actors in the investigation of cases of infringement. At the same time, the same officials may receive bribes from infringing companies to turn a blind eye on their activities.

5. Consolidating the institutional framework for market forces

Market-driven economies require no fewer institutions then planned economies. The "invisible hand" of the market does not operate in an institutional vacuum. This part examines the progress made in China in building the necessary institutional framework for market forces. It first looks at the labour market and labour protection institutions and their impact on inequalities. It then examines the efforts made to build a level playing field with sound rules of competition. Finally, it looks at the progress made in the development of a corporate governance framework.

5.1. Labour protection and market integration

China's economic reforms have established a new relationship between enterprises, workers and the state, placing the public administration at arm's-length from most economic decisions in the market. This has shifted the responsibility of government toward promoting the functioning of efficient labour markets and replacing the "iron rice bowl" of the planning era with a social safety net and provisions for old-age security to cover all segments of the market. Chapter 11 focuses on three aspects of this relationship, for which the 1994 Labour Law makes the government responsible: employment services, labour inspectorate and social insurance. Issues concerning the integration of rural with urban labour markets are further discussed in Chapter 16.

Specialised labour office networks have been developed in urban areas, but much less so in rural areas. By international standards, the offices appear relatively well equipped for dealing with the urban formal economy – their main field of operation until now – but further rapid expansion will be required in order to cover additional labour market segments. As a general rule, labour bureaus need to respond to the needs of the local economy, but at the same time, it will be essential to consolidate their independence and to ensure their neutrality between the two sides of the labour market. The labour inspectorate supports the enforcement of labour policies in a complementary manner, not least of all by responding to individual complaints. This appears particularly important in a context where other possible channels for workers' complaints, such as trade unions, are not independent of political powers or enterprise management. Foreign actors and non-governmental organisations can play a complementary role in putting pressure on some enterprises, but they cannot replace an effective labour inspectorate.

Even though the household registration (hukou) system has been partly liberalised and restrictions on recruitment of migrants abolished, the limited coverage of social insurance and other forms of labour protection contributes to a continued labour market segmentation that distorts the competitive climate and the income distribution, and ultimately the conditions for economic development. Implementing labour law and social insurance is generally difficult in the less productive rural and informal segments of the labour market. But real incomes are rising in most parts of the economy, and the present scale of rural-urban migration and economic interdependence makes it urgent to reduce institutional inequity as far as possible.

The governance of social insurance involves many decentralised decisions about contribution rates and benefit levels. In contrast to most OECD member countries, which standardise these decisions at the national level, China's size, diversity and situation as a developing economy require flexibility. The central government encourages provincial governments to harmonise the system and to centralise the pooling of social insurance funds in each province. But contribution rates are often reduced for certain groups, especially rural migrants and workers in small private firms, who may also be offered a choice between alternative insurance packages. While such differentiation is justified, it may not be sufficient to overcome the disadvantages faced by rural migrants unless the accumulated entitlements are portable. The social insurance system as a whole needs to be revised with a view to actual mobility patterns in the labour market. The pension programme, in particular, is unsuitable for migrants because it requires 10 contribution years in the same locality. This limit should be abolished, and the administration should be equipped to take account of all contributions made by an individual during his or her lifetime, regardless of where they were paid. A more centralised administration might facilitate this, but with good co-ordination it should also be possible in a decentralised system.

5.2. Creating conditions for competition

Competition is the basic driving force of market-economies and is recognized as key to economic efficiency. The report examines three main components of the competition framework: tax policy, competition policy and intellectual property rights.

A country's tax system provides a level playing field to participants in its market in order for the market to work in the most efficient way, while raising necessary revenue for the government. As shown in Chapter 6, 10 years after the 1994 tax reform, a number of issues have emerged, which call for a new round of reforms. These reforms will embrace, in particular, transforming the production-type value-added tax to a consumption-type value-added tax, fine-tuning the excise tax, unifying the now separate corporate income tax codes (one for domestic enterprises and the other for foreign invested), reforming the individual income tax, restructuring local taxes and streamlining agricultural taxes.

In contrast to many transition and developing countries, China has not adopted a general competition law yet. Chapter 12 recommends the enactment of a general competition law, several drafts of which have been submitted though to the State Council for consideration. This indeed would provide a clear regulatory basis for combating localism and other "monopolistic" conduct by enterprises and local governments. As mentioned previously, such practices are indeed obstructing economic integration and thus affect development.

More generally, based on the experience of OECD member countries, it would be beneficial for China to progressively adopt a "national competition policy", referring to a systematic approach to government regulation by which laws and regulations should not contain restrictions on competition and consumer choice that are not necessary to achieve their goals. The idea is for the central government, ministries, agencies and local governments to progressively include competition policy principles in their policy-making and regulatory activity.

Competition is undermined by the selective foreign investment regime, which involves project screening in accordance with a catalogue divided into prohibited, restricted, permitted and encouraged foreign investments, as explained in Chapter 15. In addition to implementing an industrial policy within the framework of five-year economic planning which enables the government to protect what it perceives as infant industries, this screening procedure also allows it to protect certain SOEs – deemed "strategic" or "core" – that dominate specific economic sectors. This policy may not be producing the desired result. On the contrary, it is those sectors that were fully open to competition from both imports and from foreign-invested enterprises since early in the reform period that have tended to produce strong domestic companies.

In the past two decades, China has adopted a set of intellectual property rights (IPR) laws and regulations that are today basically in conformity with international practice and standards. The main subsisting problem with the overall regulatory framework is the lack of transparency at the local level. There has been a clear shift in approach to this issue, as the protection of intellectual rights is now understood as not only important for foreign investment and technology transfer, but also to promote Chinese innovation, and thereby to ensure China's future competitiveness. Chapter 14 describes in detail the relatively comprehensive IPR administration and judicial frameworks that have also gradually taken shape.

As described and analysed in Chapter 14, enforcement is problematic as IPR infringement remains a widespread problem. A report published by the State Council Development Research Centre estimates that the value of counterfeited goods in market circulation in 2001 was between 19 and 24 billion USD – an amount comparable to the GDP of Tunisia. Underlying causes of the problems, also present in other sectors as already discussed in Sections 3 and 4, seem to be mainly of two types: the complexity of the administrative enforcement channel and weaknesses in its organisational and financial structure. In particular, local administrative entities in charge of enforcement are dependent on the local government through the arrangements for their budget and career management of the staff. The vertical line of authority comes after the horizontal links to local governments, which are not always in the practice of strictly adhering to the policy of IPR protection announced at the national level. At the same time, several factors contribute to weaken the judicial channel of enforcement: weak sanctions, high thresholds to launch a criminal suit, and lack of capacity and independence of the judiciary. In light of the experience of OECD member countries, enforcement campaigns alone do not seem to be a sufficient answer to the problem of IPR infringement. It seems necessary to develop a multidimensional strategy, which would include a reorganisation of the administrative enforcement channel, as well as an increased participation of non-governmental actors in policy-making and implementation.

5.3. Corporate governance

A fundamental role of the government in supporting the market economy is to provide means for the effective governance of business entities. This involves legal and regulatory provisions for the organisation of various types of businesses, including rules for the relations among owners of incorporated businesses and their agents. It also requires market mechanisms to discipline enterprises and to contest ownership and control.

Traditionally these arrangements in China have been designed largely for state-owned entities and collective enterprises, and foreign-invested companies, with different sets of rules for each type. However authorities have long recognised the need to transform these arrangements into ones suitable for a market economy and have made much progress in recent years toward codifying the status of private companies and toward placing all businesses regardless of their type of ownership on a comparable legal and regulatory basis. The comprehensive change in the company law now being drafted is expected to largely complete this process.

As discussed in Chapter 10, China has to a certain extent brought its corporate governance codes for listed companies into line with international practices. However there remain some important gaps. As noted earlier, many state-owned assets have not yet been incorporated and so lack boards and other essential governance structures. Both Chapters 10 and 13 indicate that the board of supervisors of Chinese corporations tends to focus on enforcement of government regulations rather than the corporation's (long-term) goals.

Chinese authorities have long recognised the critical importance of stock markets in underpinning the effective corporate governance of listed companies. Until fairly recently, though, the stock markets were used more to support SOEs than to foster the development of private business or to bolster corporate governance. The effectiveness of the market in supporting governance has been further impeded by the fact that only a minority portion of listed SOE shares can be traded, participation by institutional investors is relatively low, disclosure by listed companies is limited while sanctions for inadequate disclosure are weak, and limited protections for minority shareholders leave consequent scope for abuse by controlling (typically state) shareholders.

The CSRC has been making vigorous efforts to address many of these weaknesses and is putting into place a new regulatory framework for listed companies aimed at protecting the interests of investors based on the principles of "transparency, fairness, and justice". Strong efforts have been made to improve the quality and accuracy of information provided to the public by listed companies. The introduction of Qualified Foreign Institutional Investors (QFII) is expected to help to dilute the dominance of state shareholders in listed companies. The recent decision, announced in April 2005, to allow state shares to be sold or transferred to outside investors (although outside of the stock exchanges) is also an important positive step.

Nevertheless, much remains to be done, particularly, as Chapter 10 emphasises, in terms of proper implementation and enforcement of existing laws and regulations. As elsewhere, formal enforcement of corporate governance provisions in China depends on a mix of administrative, civil and criminal mechanisms. However the effectiveness of enforcement mechanisms has been somewhat compromised by the predominance of state ownership of listed company shares, the state's control of key enforcement bodies such as the CSRC and stock exchanges, and by the weaknesses in the effectiveness of the judiciary discussed earlier. More generally, effective enforcement starts with the need for both national and local authorities to commit to the rule of law and strengthen regulatory and judicial capacities. Procedural barriers to private enforcement or enforcement through self-regulatory bodies should also be reduced.

As discussed in Chapter 13, corporate governance of banks presents special challenges owing to their fiduciary responsibilities and the "public good" functions that banks perform in supplying the means of payment and allocating resources to the real economy. Banks in China have been moving away from their passive role in allocating credit according to state directives under the planned economy. But in most cases they still have ownership structures and governance regimes that are not yet adequate to allow them to serve as purely commercial entities. This is particularly important in the case of the four large state-owned commercial banks (SOCBs) which account for the predominant share of bank assets. Strong efforts are being made to improve corporate governance of these banks by converting them into commercial companies with modern governance structures. This happens with a view to their future listing on the stock exchanges and ownership diversification. Bank regulators along with the prospect of stronger competition have spurred significant improvements in banks internal systems for assessing credit and managing risks. These efforts as well as government financial aid to restore the banks' capital adequacy represent very important positive steps. At the same time, continued state majority ownership of the SOCBs with dispersed minority stakes as well as the possibility that they will be perceived as ultimately backed by the government ("too big to fail") will seriously weaken monitoring by the market of bank performance and partially insulate them from the effects of market competition. For these reasons, it is unclear how far the reforms that are being undertaken will go toward making the SOCBs operate as market-based institutions.

6. Conclusions

China's rapid change since the beginning of the transition process is not only visible in the flourishing private sector enterprises and the radical renewal of its urban landscapes: it can also be seen in the transformation of its institutions. Over the past 25 years Chinese leaders have taken measures to adapt the role of government and public administration to an increasingly market-driven economy. The administrative, productive and social service functions previously folded into a structure of closely linked organisations have been dispatched to different public and private organisations. SOEs have been separated from the public administration and new regulatory bodies have been set up. Chinese leaders have laid bases for modern tax, budget and civil service systems. China has also taken steps toward a system based on the rule of law, and has embarked on an ambitious regulatory reform programme.

Progress in governance was achieved in a relatively short period of time and has contributed in a crucial manner to sustain China's high growth rate. Such achievements are all the more commendable since the size of China renders reforms difficult by requiring longer chains of command and by multiplying the sources of potential problems.

In his Report on the Work of Government to the 10th National People's Congress (National People's Congress, 2005), Prime Minister Wen Jiabao stressed three objectives for the government's 2005 work plan: continuing to ensure steady and rapid economic development; pressing ahead with economic restructuring and opening up; and developing social undertakings and building a harmonious society. In the last part of this Report, the Prime Minister highlights a fourth objective, that of improving "the government's capacity and style of work". This study fully confirms the importance of reform efforts aiming at reforming government institutions. But it goes further in two respects.

First, it shifts the focus from government to governance. This implies thinking about government, its role and mode of functioning in relation to non-government actors. For instance, the discussion on the problem of regulation enforcement led to stress the importance of public participation in policy-making and in the implementation process. It also implies paying particular attention to the relations between ministries and non-core public bodies such as regulatory bodies and public service units, and to relations across levels of government.

Second, this study has shown the interdependence of the different objectives set in the 2005 Government Report. Indeed, organisational problems, fiscal imbalances, managerial weaknesses, loose accountability structures and inadequate participation mechanisms affect the efficiency and effectiveness of public action in all policy sectors. Improving governance is a necessary pre-condition for the design and implementation of the policies that will be necessary to sustain economic growth and to address existing sources of tensions (fiscal pressure, social tensions linked to inequalities, corruption and environmental deterioration, etc.).

The analysis conducted in the framework of the China Governance Project identified four overall directions along which China should sustain reform efforts to improve its system of governance.

The fundamental issue, underpinning many of the challenges facing China today, is the redefinition of the role of state. This question precedes that of the sustainability of public expenditures and of efficiency of public action. It is the context for reforms affecting organisational structures, public service units and the civil service. Much has been achieved but, overall, the state needs to do much less directly and to focus its efforts on areas where markets cannot accomplish national objectives. The main recommended lines of action include: *i)* increasing public expenditure in education, health and science and technology; *ii)* consolidating the institutional framework of the newly created SASAC and of other regulatory bodies; *iii)* redefining the role of the state in the delivery of services provided by public service units, increasing the performance of PSUs and consolidating their accountability relationships with government authorities; and *iv)* rationalising the administrative organisational structure and improving co-ordination.

The on-going modernisation of governing tools needs to be sustained. This is crucial if the system of governance is to be further adapted to a market-driven economy and to improve the efficiency and effectiveness with which public resources are used. The experience of OECD member countries has shown that the systemic links between these tools requires a co-ordinated approach. The main recommended lines of action include: *i)* further shifting from control to regulatory governance, simplifying the administrative approval system and better ensuring the application and enforcement of regulations; *ii)* consolidating budgeting process in view of using it as a strategic governance tool; *iii)* improving the quality of the civil service; *iv)* pursuing efforts of administrative simplification, using new technologies to improve overall public management; and *v)* sustaining anti-corruption efforts, complementing policies based on investigation and sanction with a preventive approach. Part of the solution to the problem of policy enforcement noted in several chapters lies in strengthening the associated administrative and judicial enforcement bodies, and adjusting relations between levels of government. But the focus should not stop there. Regulatory governance implies a paradigm shift in which application and enforcement of regulations are based primarily on voluntary compliance. The deterrent effect of possible sanctions is only one element which contributes to create attitudes of voluntary compliance. Other elements are the quality of the regulation and of the regulatory process, sound public management processes, streamlined administrative procedures, adequate resources and overall access to information and public participation.

Adjusting the relations between levels of government is equally important. Devising means to ensure that local governments act in accordance with national objectives, and with resources corresponding to their responsibilities, is a major governance challenge. The main recommended lines of action include: *i)* improving co-ordination between the central and local levels; and *ii)* bolstering this with a new framework of fiscal relationships across levels of government.

Finally, further steps should be taken to consolidate the institutional framework for market forces. High growth will be necessary to meet social development objectives. Fixing the institutional framework for market forces is necessary to facilitate technological upgrading and further market integration. The main recommended lines of action include: *i)* supporting the enforcement of labour policies; *ii)* revising the social insurance system with a view of actual mobility patterns in the labour market; *iii)* further reforming the tax system to provide a level playing field to all actors; *iv)* adopting a competition law; *v)* strengthening the enforcement of intellectual property rights; and *vi)* improving corporate governance structures of listed companies, SOEs and banks. A sound competition policy approach would facilitate progress on many of these fronts.

Governance reforms, in China as everywhere else, happen incrementally, when favourable political circumstances coincide with technical capacity. On all the identified governance weaknesses, China will need to ensure that it has the technical know-how to proceed as and when the circumstances allow. Although the overall Chinese context remains very different from that of OECD member countries, much can be learned from these countries' reform experience. For instance, OECD member countries have also experienced the need to adjust for too much devolution to the local level or to arm's-length agencies, and have looked for means to consolidate accountability while increasing flexibility and performance. Through extended exchanges with OECD practitioners and experts, China could draw lessons on various technical aspects of the system of governance as well as on implementation strategies. A comparative and critical review of the experiences of different OECD member countries allows for understanding the conditions necessary for a governance reform to produce the wished results. Therefore, if this study has identified the governance challenges facing China, it is also a summary of the areas in which China would benefit from increased exchanges with OECD member countries.

Notes

1. The synthesis was written by Irène Hors, Public Sector Management and Performance Division, Directorate for Public Governance and Territorial Development, OECD, with the help of Charles Pigott, Consultant, and research assistance by Isabelle Gras, Consultant. It draws on all the chapters of this study and benefited from comments from authors of the different chapters.
2. See Annex 0.A1.
3. See Annex 0.A2 for an overview of the Chinese political system.
4. The Armed Forces employed 2.5 million people in 2002.
5. The domestic fault lines such as looming social instability as well as examples of weak governance capability of ruling parties abroad and inner-Party problems in fact also made the Communist Party of China (CPC) put its own governance capability on the agenda for the first time. In September 2004, the Fourth Plenary Session of the Sixteenth Central Committee of the CPC adopted a 36-page Decision on the Enhancement of the Party's Governance Capability. The document defines the Party's governance capability as its ability "to put forth correct theories, guidelines, principles, policies and tactics, lead in the formulation and enforcement of the Constitution and laws, adopt a scientific system and mode of leadership, mobilize and organize the people to manage state and social affairs, economic and cultural undertakings according to law, effectively run the Party, the state and the military, and build a modernized socialist country". According to the Decision, the CPC aims at improving the effectiveness of its governance by strengthening leader's capabilities; co-ordinating interests of different social groups; introducing institutional mechanisms to ensure leaders take into account the interests of the people, including private investors; changing decision-making mechanisms from top-down to bottom-up and by governing according to law.
6. Groups of 30-40 households (remnants of production teams of the collective era), often *de facto* collective owners of land.
7. "Public Health System Needs Overhaul", *China Daily*, 2 April 2005.

Bibliography

Lieberthal, Kenneth (1995), *Governing China: from Revolution through Reform*, WW Norton and Company.

Naughton, Barry (1995), *Growing Out of the Plan: Chinese Economic Reform, 1978-1993*, Cambridge University Press.

National People's Congress (2005), "Report on the Work of the Government", Third Session, 10th National People's Congress and Chinese People's Political Consultative Conference, 5 March.

OECD (2002), *China in the World Economy: the Domestic Policy Challenges*, OECD, Paris (also published in 2003 as *Shijie Jingji zhong de Zhongguo* by Qinghua University Press, Beijing).

OECD (2005), *OECD Economic Surveys: China*, OECD, Paris.

United Nations (2005), "About China: The Rule of Law", *www.unchina.org/about_china/html/rule.shtml*, accessed in June 2005.

ANNEX 0.A1

OECD Member Countries and Good Governance

OECD member countries target a development path built on three pillars: good public and corporate governance, social cohesion and economic growth. Good public and corporate governance are thus seen as crucial elements to address challenges and fault lines facing a nation and to ensure sustainable development. **Public governance** has been defined as "the formal and informal arrangements that determine how public decisions are made and how public actions are carried out, from the perspective of maintaining a country's constitutional' values as problems, actors and times change" (*cf.* mandate of the Public Governance Committee). **Corporate governance** involves "a set of relationships between a company's management, its board, its shareholders and other stakeholders. Corporate governance also provides the structure through which the objectives of the company are set, and the means of attaining those objectives and monitoring performance are determined" (*cf.* preamble of the OECD Principles of Corporate Governance).

The OECD Public Management Committee has adopted a set of principles that explain the key components of good public governance:

- **Rule of Law.** All actions and decisions should be applied equally and only based on the application of law.
- **Accountability.** All government actions, decisions and decision-making processes need to open to scrutiny by parliament, civil society and the public – and in some cases supra-national bodies.
- **Transparency.** Government needs to be able and willing, through the provision of information and explanation to show the extent to which its actions and decisions are consistent with clearly defined and agreed-to objectives based on sound analysis.
- **Efficiency and effectiveness.** Governments need to produce high quality cost-effective public outputs to citizens, and monitor and evaluate their performance.
- **Responsiveness.** Government needs the capacity and flexibility to respond rapidly to changes, consult widely and be willing to re-examine critically the role of government.
- **Forward-vision.** Government is able to anticipate future problems and issues based on current data and trends and develop policies that take into account future costs and anticipated changes (*e.g.* demographic, economic, environmental, etc.).

These principles take for granted the basic values shared by all OECD member countries, *i.e.* an open market economy and democratic pluralism.

ANNEX 0.A2

The Chinese Political System

The current Chinese political system was established in 1945. It is characterised by the pre-eminence of the Communist Party of China (CPC), which governs all central and local level state organs.

With about 67 million members, the CPC is the largest political party in the world. The broad lines of its formal organisation are set in the CPC Constitution. The Party exercises political, ideological and organisational leadership and has organisations at the five territorial divisions. In contrast to the former Soviet Union and most other soviet-type political systems, the CPC bureaucracy does not duplicate state administrations. The Central Committee of the Party, which contains the leading figures of the Party, state and army, has direct control of only a few departments, such as the Organisation Department which oversees the recruitment and career of the highest officials in the Party.

The National People's Congress (NPC) is China's Parliament. According to the Constitution, the National People's Congress is the "highest organ of state power". In reality, however, it has in practice less power then the State Council and several Party organs. The NPC and its permanent Standing Committee exercise the power of legislation, decision, supervision, election, appointment and dismissal.

The court system consists of the Supreme People's Court, local people's courts and special people's courts such as the military court. The state prosecution system consists of the Supreme People's Procuratorate, local people's procuratorates and special people's procuratorates such as the military procuratorate.

The President is the head of the state. He promulgates laws, appoints the Premier, Vice-Premiers, state councillors, ministers of various ministries and state commissions and the auditor general, according to decisions of the NPC and its Standing Committee.

State administration is governed by the State Council, the chief administrative body of the People's Republic of China which supervises ministries, commissions and bureaus. It is chaired by the Premier and contains the heads of each governmental department. There are about 50 members in the Council. The actual executive is the Standing Committee of the State Council, composed, at present, of the Premier and four Vice-Premiers, five state counsellors and a secretary-general. This restricted cabinet meets twice a week and takes all important governmental decisions. The state administrative system is composed of ministries and commissions. Each ministry supervises one sector. Commissions set policies on matters which require horizontal co-ordination of various substantive areas and generally outrank ministries.

Groupings of Party, government and/or military bureaucracies which are functionally related are called *xitongs*. These are headed by corresponding "leading groups" (*lingdao xiaozu*). These leading groups create bridges between leaders at the apex of the political system and thus contribute to the coherence and co-ordination of policy decisions. The strengthening and formalization of the role of different leading groups has been critical in the development of more coherent policies and in expediting decision-making.

The pre-eminence of the Party over the executive takes different forms. At the different territorial levels, access to positions of power in the government is very much determined by the positioning of individuals within the Party. At the central level, the Party Central Committee and its related bodies are where important decisions are taken. The Party controls the number of established posts in all Party or government administrative organs, public service units and working units. All important non-Party organisations at the district level and above host Party groups.

PART I

Public Sector Management

PART I

Chapter 1

Civil Service Reform in China

Table of Contents

Summary 53

Civil Service Reform in China 55

  1. Introduction 55

  2. Background 56

  3. Issues 60

      3.1. Recruiting and selecting the "best and brightest" 60

      3.2. Building a culture of performance 64

      3.3. Motivating public employees 66

      3.4. Level of institutionalization 69

  4. Conclusion and recommendations 69

Notes 71

Bibliography 71

Annex 1.A1 74

List of boxes

    1.1. Selection of bureau chiefs in the Ministry of Personnel, 2004 62

List of tables

    1.1. Number and distribution of civil servants by administrative level, 1998 60
    1.2. Number of vacancies and applicants for centrally managed civil service positions, 1994-2004 61
    1.3. Main components of civil service pay: pay scale for post wage and grade wage (2004) 67
1.A1.1. Estimated number of public sector employees 74

List of figures

    1.1. Total staff and workers in state-owned units, 1993-2002 56
    1.2. Total staff and workers employed by government agencies, parties and social organisations, 1993-2002 57
    1.3. China's central civil service management system 58
    1.4. Chinese civil service positions and grade structure 59
    1.5. Leading cadres in China with university education, 1981-98 62

Summary

The Chinese Government has undertaken extensive reforms to its civil service system over the past 10 years. These have encompassed recruitment and selection, training, appraisal, rewards and punishments, compensation, discipline and other areas. This chapter reviews each of these elements.

The chapter argues that the capacity of the civil service has improved during the past 10 years. But the capacity improvements may be explained by reasons other than civil service reform, such as by improvements in China's system of education. The rapid expansion of higher education since 1980 has produced a large population that is eligible for civil service employment.

China's civil service system is far from being homogeneous. To simplify, it may perhaps be viewed as two systems: one that is relatively performance-oriented, selects "the best and brightest" through competitive mechanisms, links rewards to performance, and condemns indiscipline and corruption; and another one that *de facto* operates as an employer of last resort, selects based on many different criteria some of which may be irrelevant to the job, ties rewards to positions, and is characterised by relatively high levels of indiscipline and corruption. (There are undoubtedly many gradations in between.)

Considerable evidence indicates that the performance-oriented systems operate primarily at the centre and in the richer coastal areas, while the traditional systems operate in the poorer, less developed hinterland. Improving the systems in these poorer areas depends in no small part on improving levels of economic development. Development is most likely with a highly competent and committed bureaucracy. Intervening to break out of the symbiotic relationship between poverty and inept bureaucratic leadership is an important task for the foreseeable future.

The following policy recommendations follow from this review:

1. To enhance legitimacy and accountability and to attract the best possible candidates to work for the government, civil service personnel policies and practices should be as transparent as possible. In addition to the material now provided on the Internet, for example, the Ministry of Personnel should maintain a publicly available database on the civil service, regularly publishing information on the size, distribution, gender composition, age distribution, and educational background of the civil service. Publishing this information will improve confidence in the civil service, especially in that the service is being fairly and impartially managed.

2. The practice of permitting entry to the civil service outside the established mechanisms should be reduced and eliminated. To strengthen the civil service's meritocracy, all candidates for entry-level positions including de-mobilized soldiers should be required to take and pass the civil service entry examination.

3. To reduce corruption, authorities should ensure that the rotation system for officials is implemented as widely as possible and that leading officials, their offices and their families are audited on a regular basis.

4. Transfers to poor areas should focus on improving human resources in those areas through training and transfers of experienced officials from more developed areas.

5. Salaries for civil servants should be maintained at a competitive level, determined locally. To ensure this, pay level surveys should be carried out regularly and their results should be published. Pay awards should be based in part on the surveys.

Civil Service Reform in China[1]

1. Introduction

Since 1980, China's leaders have sought to increase the capacity and legitimacy of the state in part through civil service reform. Attempts to improve governance in China by increasing accountability, predictability, transparency, participation, and efficiency and effectiveness (see Asian Development Bank, 1995) have been accompanied by civil service reforms to make the bureaucracy more meritocratic. Given the central role played by the civil service in China's political system, attempts to improve governance have appropriately focused on reform of the bureaucracy. "Good" governance requires a strong civil service that is accountable to the political executive, operates within the law, is open and transparent, and encourages the participation of the community. An efficient and effective civil service is also critical for high capacity and legitimate government, which "good governance" also seeks to achieve.

High capacity government is usually associated with bureaucracies that are competent, committed and coherent, and where bureaucrats have relatively high prestige and integrity (Weiss, 1998). Human resource management policies and practices for building capacity emphasize performance, flexibility, selection based on "fit" and the appropriate utilization of talent (Hilderbrand and Grindle, 1997). Accordingly, an effective public personnel system in a developing country[2] may be said to be characterized by the following: i) a legal and regulatory regime that ensures not only the rule of law but in which the rules and regulations give appropriate flexibilities to managers; ii) a relatively high degree of institutionalization to ensure predictability; iii) a selection system that is able to attract "the best and brightest" in the country and to utilize talent appropriately; iv) a performance management system that is able to motivate, reward and retain talented people and that effectively manages under-performers; and v) a discipline system that is both just and effective at maintaining a coherent and corruption-free service.

Since 1993, the Chinese Government has taken significant steps to reform the country's civil service system, which is still evolving. Bureaucracies with the most potential to contribute to high capacity government are not surprisingly found at the centre and in more developed parts of the country. Service in the public sector carries with it considerable prestige in China. Central ministries are staffed by many highly competent and committed employees and conform in many respects to the performance paradigm articulated above. Outside the centre the quality of the public service varies considerably, however. More developed parts of the country are able to support a more efficient and effective public service. In less developed parts of the country, where the civil service is viewed as an employer of last resort, the quality and capacity of the civil service is considerably lower.

In the sections that follow, the size and scope of the civil service will be examined and the political, economic and social context of civil service reform in China as well as the reforms themselves will be discussed. This is followed by a discussion of critical issues in the management of the civil service including selection, performance management, motivation, and discipline and corruption.

2. Background

In 2002, the public sector employed an estimated 70 million people, about half of whom worked in government in one capacity or another (see Annex 1.A1). Another 33 million worked in state-owned enterprises. The total number of public employees has declined in recent years mostly as a result of the contraction of the state-owned enterprise sector (see Figure 1.1). Employment in government and Public Service Units (PSUs, in sectors such as education, public health, research, etc.) has been relatively steady over the past decade. The press reported in March 2004 that PSUs employed between 28 and 29 million people at the end of 2003 in contrast to the 25 million reported by the National Bureau of Statistics for the end of 2002.[3]

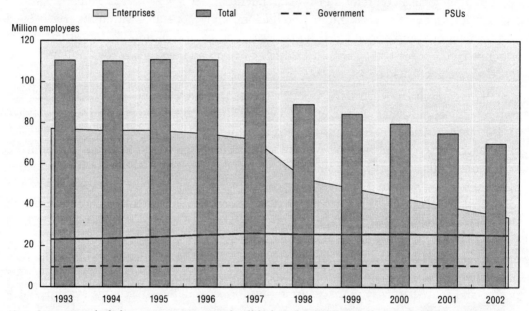

Figure 1.1. **Total staff and workers in state-owned units, 1993-2002**

Note: Government includes core government and political parties. Public Service Units (PSUs) include hospitals, schools, research institutes.
Source: National Bureau of Statistics, China Statistical Yearbook (various years), Beijing, China Statistics Press.

Of those employed in government departments and bodies in 2004, only 4.98 million[4] were formally classified as "civil servants" according to China's civil service regulations (Ministry of Personnel, 1993) (see Figure 1.2). This chapter focuses primarily on the management of this group. The regulations identify civil servants as the managers, administrators and professionals who work for government bodies (i.e. white collar employees who since 1993 have required a university degree to enter the service). This definition is both more inclusive and less inclusive than definitions of the civil service commonly used overseas. Unlike the practice in many Western countries, the civil service in China includes the most senior politicians such as the Premier, Vice Premier, state councillors, ministers and provincial governors, vice ministers and vice governors, etc. – the leadership positions (Ministry of Personnel, 1996, Article 9). White collar government employees at both central and local levels, including towns and townships, are also civil servants (Organisation Department, Ministry of Personnel, 1998).

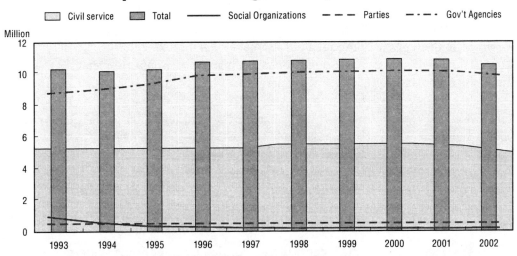

Figure 1.2. **Total staff and workers employed by government agencies, parties and social organisations, 1993-2002**

Source: National Bureau of Statistics, *China Statistical Yearbook* (various years), Beijing, China Statistics Press.

The scope of the Chinese civil service, however, is less inclusive than the scope of civil services in many Western countries. The Chinese civil service definition excludes: i) all manual workers employed by the government; and ii) the employees of all "public service units" (officially translated as "institutions" or *shiye danwei*). "Public service units" (schools, universities, hospitals, research institutes, radio and TV stations, cultural organisations, publishers, etc.) have their own personnel management arrangements and are funded through a variety of mechanisms. Some are mostly dependent on the state for funding (such as most schools, universities and hospitals) while others have been turned into economic enterprises and are expected to pay their own way. In 2004, most public service units were publicly funded. In 2002, public service unit employees numbered about 25 million (see Annex 0.A1) and worked in some 1.3 million units.

From 1993 to 1997, the Communist Party of China (CPC) extended the "civil service system" of personnel management (that is, competitive hiring, civil service-type performance evaluation, salaries and benefits pegged to civil service pay and benefits, etc.) to many other public organisations including the CPC itself and organisations on the Central Committee-controlled *nomenklatura*, such as mass organisations, the legislature, the Chinese People's Political Consultative Conference and the democratic parties.[5] Interviews with mainland judges indicate that the judiciary and the procuratorate are also managed according to the civil service system.[6] If this larger group is included, then in 2002 about 10.56 million people were managed according to civil service personnel arrangements (see Figure 1.2) (National Bureau of Statistics, 2003).

These data indicate the stability of the non-state owned enterprise portion of public employees. In spite of numerous downsizing campaigns (supervised in the 1990s by the State Commission for Public Sector Reform [SCOPSR, *zhongyang jigou bianzhi weiyuanhui*]), the number of government employees, including civil servants, has apparently changed little over the past decade (see Burns, 2003a).

The Communist Party plays an extensive role in the management of personnel, including the civil service, in all public organisations. Indeed, the first principle of personnel management in China is that "the Party manages cadres (*ganbu*)", of whom civil servants are a part.[7] One member of the seven-member Standing Committee of the Politburo (see Figure 1.3), the highest organ of political power in China, has responsibility for overseeing "organisation and personnel work", including management of the civil service. The CPC Central Committee has entrusted policy making for the civil service to its Organisation Department. The State Council's Ministry of Personnel implements the policy under the Organisation Department's supervision. The two bodies, one Party and the other one government, are tightly linked. A Vice Minister of the Ministry of Personnel is concurrently a Deputy Head of the Organisation Department, and personnel of the two bodies may be seconded to the other body for special projects as needed. By all accounts, Party and government bodies in charge of the civil service work seamlessly together. With one authority structure, they form a single system. Anti-corruption work is handled by the Party's Central Inspection Discipline Commission, the government's Ministry of Supervision and the People's Procuratorate (see Figure 1.2).

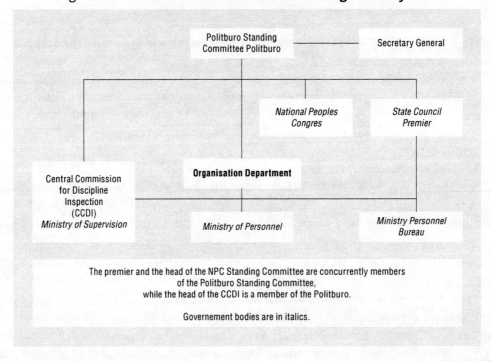

Figure 1.3. **China's central civil service management system**

All civil servants recruited into positions in the Ministry of Personnel are Party members, and civil servants recruited into personnel departments of all government bodies, even the most specialized and technical, must be Party members. The Party exercises control over public personnel appointments and dismissals of civil servants to leading positions (including the lowest level leadership positions such as deputy section head) through the *nomenklatura* system that gives the CPC final authority to approve these personnel movements (see Burns, 1989 and 1994). These arrangements make "civil service neutrality" in relationship to political parties an alien concept – arguably, this kind of civil service neutrality is irrelevant in one-party monopoly political systems.

The civil service is organised into 12 positions ranging from Premier at the top to clerical staff at the bottom and 15 grades that are determined by "level of responsibility and degree of difficulty of the task and the civil servant's capability, political integrity, practical success, work performance and work record"[8] (see Figure 1.4). "Political" positions that in developed capitalist democracies are usually not part of the civil service are considered to be civil service jobs in China. These include the Premier, Vice Premiers, state councillors at the centre, and governors and vice governors of provinces as well as mayors and vice mayors of provincial level municipalities, such as Beijing, Tianjian, Shanghai and Chongqing. In China civil service grades are divided into leadership and non-leadership positions (all positions in Figure 1.4 are leadership positions except for those of section member and Clerical Staff) (Ministry of Personnel, 1993, Article 9).

Figure 1.4. **Chinese civil service positions and grade structure**

Positions	Grades														
	1	2	3	4	5	6	7	8	9	10	11	12	13	14	15
Premier	√														
Vice Premier, state councillor		√	√												
Minister, governor			√	√											
Vice minister, vice governor				√	√										
Bureau chief					√	√	√								
Deputy bureau chief						√	√	√							
Division chief							√	√	√	√					
Deputy division chief								√	√	√	√				
Section chief, responsible section member									√	√	√	√			
Deputy section chief, Deputy responsible section member									√	√	√	√	√		
Section member									√	√	√	√	√	√	
Clerical staff										√	√	√	√	√	√

Source: Ministry of Personnel, *Provisional Regulations on Civil Servants* (in English), Beijing, Ministry of Personnel, mimeo, 1993, Article 10.

Most civil servants work in local government in one of China's 2 800 or so counties. Based on information published in 1998 (see Table 1.1), only about 10% of civil servants work at the central level.[9] Another 11% work at provincial level, 21% at prefectural level, 41% at county level, and 17% at town or township level. Less than 1 000 civil servants are ranked at minister/provincial governor level, while most civil servants who work in China's counties hold the rank of section chief or deputy chief (35.7%) or section member (46.8%). Bureau-level officials, employed in the central government and at provincial level, make up less than half a per cent of the total, while about 5.5% of civil servants are division chiefs (employed in central ministries and in provincial government) or county heads (Xi, 2002).

Table 1.1. **Number and distribution of civil servants by administrative level, 1998**

Administrative level	Number of civil servants	Percentage
Central-level	495 022	9.28
Provincial-level	592 589	11.11
Prefectural-level	1 133 977	21.26
County-level	2 186 263	40.98
Township-level	926 471	17.37
Total	**5 334 322**	**100.00**

Source: Xi Liu, Chinese Civil Service System (Zhongguo gongyuyuan zhidu), Beijing, Qinghua daxue chubanshe, 2002, p. 29.

Civil service reform in China dates from 1993 and grew out of post-Cultural Revolution elite-level dissatisfaction with the management of the leadership system. As early as 1980, paramount leader Deng Xiaoping put reform of the leadership system on the Party's agenda. Deng and his allies perceived that the "cadre system" (see Barnett, 1967), which was borrowed from the Soviet Union in the 1950s and under which the Party managed all cadres according to uniform rules and regulations, had outlived its usefulness. As the economy developed and liberalized, the positions of managers, administrators and professionals became more specialized. Accordingly, the CPC designed a management system for cadres working in government (civil servants) that took into account the non-market nature of much of government work, on the one hand, and the existence of newly emerging labour and wage markets, on the other. The CPC has also sought to reform personnel management of public service units to make them more market friendly. The reforms sought to improve the efficiency and effectiveness of the civil service, to boost its quality and integrity, and to improve its performance.

The 1993 reforms included policies designed to improve the capacity of the civil service and make it more competitive. In essence, first, all newly recruited civil servants were to be selected based on open competition, usually through an examination process and limited to the most part to university graduates. Second, civil servants were to be provided with a career structure and stable employment. Third, personnel management systems were to be performance oriented. Fourth, civil service compensation was expected to be competitive with rates paid in the market. Fifth, civil servants were expected to be of high integrity.

3. Issues

High capacity civil service systems are characterized by open and competitive selection processes, mechanisms that appropriately utilize talent, ensuring that all employees are appropriately trained, setting and communicating performance standards, evaluating performance and feeding back the results of the evaluation to employees, and linking performance to rewards. The extent to which the Chinese civil service approaches this model will be reviewed in the following sections devoted to staffing, performance management, motivation and institutionalization.

3.1. Recruiting and selecting the "best and brightest"

High capacity civil service systems are staffed by appropriately qualified people selected through open and competitive means. A mix of generalists and specialists is usually the norm and talent is effectively utilized. The Chinese Government has been largely successful at attracting "the best and the brightest" to the civil service system especially at the centre. The quality of the civil service at local levels varies tremendously, however.

Although its prestige has declined since the heyday in the 1970s, serving in the civil service in China is still highly prestigious and jobs in the civil service are highly sought after. Entry into the civil service especially at the centre is keen and increasingly competitive. From 1994 to 2004, the number of applicants for each post has grown from about 10 to nearly 18 (see Table 1.2). Scattered data for the mid-1990s indicate that civil service jobs were more attractive in poorer provinces such as Liaoning and Jilin and in the western region and less attractive in richer areas such as Shanghai (Zhu, 1997). A popular career strategy for university graduates is to join government for a time upon graduation to "learn the bureaucratic ropes" before leaving to go into more lucrative careers, including the private sector.

Table 1.2. **Number of vacancies and applicants for centrally managed civil service positions, 1994-2004**

	Number of applicants (A)	Number of vacancies (B)	Ratio of A to B
1994	4 306	440	9.8
1995	6 726	490	13.7
1996	7 160	737	9.7
1997	8 850	n.a.	n.a.
2001	32 904	4 500	7.2
2002	62 268	4 800	13.0
2003	87 772	5 400	16.3
2004	140 184	8 000	17.5

Note: The number of vacancies and applicants grew as more and more posts were covered by the civil service system. Centrally-managed posts include posts in the central government and posts managed by central institutions (e.g. Customs, People's Bank of China, etc.).
Source: Interviews, Ministry of Personnel, 22 July 1996, 12 August 1999, and 19 March 2004.

To boost recruitment, the government has taken several measures including: i) raising civil service salaries (see below); ii) waiving the requirement that applicants for the civil service must have two years of work experience before they are selected; iii) increasing publicity especially in universities; and iv) relying more on the Internet and information technology in recruitment. The civil service in China, especially in the richer coastal areas, attracts – like more traditional civil services overseas – those who can accept lower base salaries than they could earn in the private sector and who are interested in relatively competitive benefits and a stable career.

Civil service selection methods especially at the centre are often very rigorous and may include problem-based exercises to assess potential that are often found in assessment centres[10] (see Box 1.1).

Civil service reforms and reform of higher education have increased civil service capacities especially at the centre and at provincial level. Thus, by 2003, nearly 70% of civil servants had university or community college degrees (Interview, Ministry of Personnel, 19 March 2004). Because a university degree has been a requirement for entry since 1993, the educational profile of the civil service is rising. By 1998, from 80 to 90% of the top civil servants at ministry, bureau, and division level were university or community college graduates (see Figure 1.5). This represents a substantial improvement in the capacity of the Chinese civil service.

Box 1.1. **Selection of bureau chiefs in the Ministry of Personnel, 2004**

Since 1999, the Ministry of Personnel has selected candidates for bureau chief and deputy chief positions using something like assessment centres. In 2004, for example, to fill four vacancies, the ministry first advertised the vacancies internally. About 100 people applied, of whom 60 were found to be qualified. The 60 were required to take examinations including an English-language examination. Based on the results of the examination and reviewing their performance appraisal results, 31 were identified for further consideration.

The 31 candidates were bussed to a township within Beijing Municipality and taken through an exhibit that detailed the development of the township by a local leader. They were then taken to an examination hall in the township and given an examination paper that required them to write answers to two questions analysing the development of the township. The paper was designed to test their analytical power and writing skills.

The 12 candidates who passed this stage were then invited to an interview board that included the Minister and several Vice Ministers. They were given a set of documents related to a particular problem (resembling an "in-basket" exercise) and given 30 minutes to prepare to answer questions on how they would handle the problems raised in the documents. Eight candidates passed this stage of the exercise. Based on their overall performance and the ministry's evaluation of their potential, the Minister and Vice Ministers chose four to fill the vacancies.

Source: Personal communication with a participant, Beijing, March 2004.

Figure 1.5. **Leading cadres in China with university education, 1981-98**

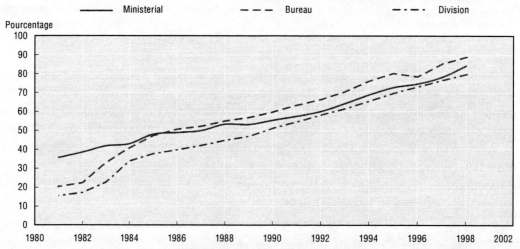

Source: Organisation Department (*Zhonggong zhongyang zuzhi bu*), Collection of Statistical Information on Party and Government Leading Cadres 1954-1998 (*Dangzheng lingdao ganbu tongji ziliao huibian 1954-1998*), Beijing, Dangjian duwu chubanshe, 1999.

Personnel reforms dating from the early 1980s have also lowered the age of China's civil servants. From 1982, when the CPC officially adopted a mandatory retirement policy (men retire at age 60 and women at age 55), China has increasingly selected younger people for leadership positions (Manion, 1993; Lee, 1991). From 1981 to 1989, the average age of officials of ministerial or bureau rank fell from 63.6 years to 56.9 years. In 1980, more than 80% of provincial or ministerial level officials were 60 years of age or older, whereas by 1998, the proportion over the age of 60 had dropped to about 54%. At the same time, at bureau level the number of officials over the age of 60 fell from 37% to 11%, while at county level those over the age of 60 are only about 1% of the total (Organisation Department, 1999). By the mid-1990s, more than half of the civil service as a whole was under the age of 40 (China Organisation, 1998).

The legitimacy of the political system depends in part on the extent to which the civil service is representative of the people. This is especially true in China's ethnic minority areas. China's civil service is both more and less representative of the population as a whole. Recognizing the multi-ethnic character of the country, civil service regulations require that authorities in ethnic minority regions give preference to ethnic minorities in hiring (Ministry of Personnel, 1993, Article 13). As a result, ethnic minorities hold about 8% of civil service posts compared to their approximately 6% of the total population (China Personnel Yearbook Editorial Office, 1989). In other respects, however, the civil service is unrepresentative of the general population. First, as we would expect, it is much better educated than the population as a whole. Second, women hold only about 20% of civil service posts overall (Interview, Ministry of Personnel, 19 March 2004), and less than 10% of leading positions at provincial or county level [7% at provincial level and 9% at county level (Organisation Department, 1999)]. If PSUs such as for health and education are included, the number of women increases, however. At the end of 2002, 58% and 45.5% of employees in public health and education respectively were women (National Bureau of Statistics, 2003).

Finally, Party members, who make up less than 5% of the total population, are over-represented in the civil service, where they hold about 80% of civil service posts (China Organisation, 1998). Although the regulations do not require civil servants to be Party members, in practice the Party requires that many posts be held by Party members.[11] These posts tend to be in politically sensitive departments (e.g. the State Council General Office, the Commissions and Ministries of Education, Science and Technology, National Defence, Ethnic Affairs, Public Security, Population and Family Planning, the China Securities Regulatory Commission and the State-owned Assets Supervision and Administration Commission) or in sensitive bureaus of ministries (the general office, policy and regulation, planning, personnel, education, social security and public security). Although the practice of reserving posts for Party membership is not new, publishing the list of such posts is new and indicates an increasing transparency. Generally the CPC Organisation Department determines which categories of posts should be held by Party members for recruiting departments and bodies to implement. With a few exceptions (e.g. the Cultural Revolution, the 4 June 1989 period, etc.), the policy has been successfully carried out.

Significant gaps characterize the implementation of civil service staffing reforms. For a variety of reasons, civil service positions, particularly at the local level, continue to be filled through non-competitive rather opaque processes. First, government policy and practice has been to move relatively large numbers of demobilized soldiers into the civil service after they have served their tour of duty. In Beijing's Haidian District, for example, in 2001 and 2002 each government body was expected to take several demobilized soldiers. Although some bodies refused (and apparently could refuse), the district government as a whole was assigned a quota of demobilized soldiers and expected to fill it. Neither examinations nor other competitive selection systems were used to place demobilized soldiers in civil service positions. Second, at the most local levels, particularly at township level, civil service posts continue to be filled by moving cadres from local economic enterprises, again without going through the centrally laid-down competitive processes (Interview, Ministry of Personnel, 19 March 2004).

Finally, relatively large numbers of official positions, again mostly at local levels (township and/or county), seem to have been filled through corruption. The sale and purchase of official positions has become a serious problem. In the late 1990s, for example, officials sold scores of government jobs in Wenzhou City (Zhejiang), Pizhou County (Jiangsu), Beihai City (Guangxi), Huaibei City (Anhui), Tieling City (Liaoning), Guanfeng County (Jiangxi) and in Heilongjiang Province.[12] Even very senior officials, such as former National People's Congress Vice Chairman Cheng Kaijie, executed for corruption in 2000, have been convicted of selling government posts (*Wenhui bao* [Hong Kong], 1 August 2000). These cases undoubtedly represent only the tip of the iceberg. The practice has apparently become so serious at the local level that it threatens to undermine the legitimacy of the civil service.[13] As a result of these and other loopholes, in 2002 alone some 38% of new civil service hires entered through non-competitive means (Interview, Ministry of Personnel, 19 March 2004).

In addition to the loopholes discussed above, the government's restructuring policy, which from 1998 to 2002 sought to downsize government bodies, clashed with the goal of improving the quality of the civil service through new hires (Burns, 2003a). In 1998, 1999 and 2000, to meet their downsizing targets many bodies could hire no new staff at all, thus undermining one of the objectives of the reform.

It can be concluded, then, that open, competitive hiring characterizes the civil service at the centre and probably in the richer coastal areas. Even in these areas, however, local government must provide employment for non-competitively selected demobilized soldiers. In less developed parts of the country, where government serves as an employer of last resort, the problems are much more severe.

3.2. Building a culture of performance

Building a culture of performance involves setting and communicating performance standards, ensuring that civil servants have appropriate knowledge, skills and abilities, evaluating performance and feeding back to employees the results of the evaluation, and linking performance to rewards (Hilderbrand and Grindle, 1997). Although formal systems have been established in China to achieve these objectives, the gap between objectives and what is happening on the ground remains relatively large, especially at local levels. The gap may be explained by a lack of resources in poorer communities and the widespread expectation in these communities that the bureaucracy will act as an employer of last resort.

Large numbers of civil servants have been trained every year (about 2.3 million people per year or 17 million from 1993 to 2003) and the number of civil servants trained per year has increased from about 26% in 1996 to 62.3% in 2002. But training opportunities are unevenly distributed. Budgets for training, even including opportunities for training overseas, are relatively generous at the central level and in richer coastal cities. In poorer counties and townships where government cannot even pay the salaries of local officials, training may appear to be a non-essential luxury.

An integral part of the cadre training programme is a system to rotate cadres that has sought to enhance their capacity and improve the capacity of local government, on the one hand, and to reduce opportunities for corruption, on the other. In particular, rotation has applied to leading officials and those who have worked in personnel, finance, materials management, licensing, and approval of funding and investment projects that were supposed to be moved every five years (Ministry of Personnel, 1996, Article 2). Large numbers of officials have apparently participated in the scheme. Thus, from 1996 to 1999, more than 400 000 officials nationwide were rotated to new positions (Chou, 2003). This policy put officials from rich coastal provinces in positions in poorer inland areas, in an effort to improve the capacity of local government there. The audits that precede an official rotation have sometimes also uncovered cases of corruption (Chou, 2003).

Officials have developed elaborate criteria for the evaluation of civil service performance that, especially at local levels, focused heavily on economic performance. According to national guidelines issued in 1991, local government leaders were to be evaluated according to 18 criteria, only three of which were not economic-related (population growth, forested area and nine-year compulsory education completion rate). The rest included GNP, gross value of industrial output, gross value of agricultural output, national income per capita, taxes and profits remitted, retail sales, etc. (Whiting, 2001). Although officials actually broadened the criteria adopted in the early 1990s to include more non-economic measures (*e.g.* public order and Party building), in practice, performance criteria were tightly linked to the economy. Dissatisfaction with the over-emphasis on economic measures and a focus on meeting the needs of higher authorities has prompted calls for reform. Experiments in Qingdao city, for example, have incorporated new measures which focus on public service, environmental impacts and market supervision – criteria that were not used previously (SCMP, 4 August 2004). Officials anticipate that more service-oriented criteria will be incorporated into civil service performance evaluations in the future.

Within government departments and bodies, performance appraisals focus mostly on merit-related criteria which seek to evaluate behaviour on the job. These criteria also evaluate "moral integrity", however, which includes the extent to which the civil servant implemented CPC policy during the reporting period (Ministry of Personnel, 1993, Article 20).

China's performance management policy seeks to link performance with rewards and stipulates the payment of bonuses to those who have performed well (Ministry of Personnel, 1993, Article 26). According to official policy, a bonus of one month's salary should be paid to those civil servants who are rated outstanding in annual appraisals. Outstanding awards are limited to 15% of the total, sometimes rising to 16 or 18% (Interview, Ministry of Personnel, 19 March 2004). Salary increments are also supposed to be based on performance. In poorer counties where personnel costs can amount to 70% or more of total expenditure (World Bank, 2002) paying bonuses and increments is undoubtedly a real hardship.

Because of a political preoccupation with stability, the government has foregone the use of management tools such as fixed-term contracts. After they serve a short period of probation, civil servants are employed on what amounts to permanent terms of service. As a result, removing poor or under-performers becomes relatively difficult. Because the consequences are so severe, few civil servants receive unfavourable performance ratings (only 0.1% of all civil servants are rated "unsatisfactory"). Officially, two consecutive "unsatisfactory" ratings should lead to dismissal.

Civil service regulations also stress that government officials should "be fair and honest and work selflessly in the public interest" (Ministry of Personnel, 1993, Article 6) which implies impartiality. An effective market economy requires that regulators implement rules and regulations even-handedly. In practice, however, the protection of local interests is a serious problem, especially in law enforcement. Authorities have accused the judiciary and procuratorate of colluding with local officials to undermine attempts to institutionalize the rule of law.

More serious than "localism" is corruption within the civil service which continues to be a significant problem, as reflected in China's relatively poor showing in Transparency International's Corruption Perception Index. Corruption has undermined civil service discipline (see Manion, 2004). Given the low probability of being prosecuted [from 1993-98, fewer than half of the corruption cases being investigated led to criminal charges being filed and, most strikingly, only 6.6% of these led to sentences (Hu, 2001; Hu in: SCMP, 24 March 2001)], engaging in corrupt practices appears to have been a relatively low-risk activity.

Corruption characterizes economies in development because they tend to have weak legal and regulatory systems and may not be able to pay adequate civil service salaries. Additional factors are at work in China, however. The design of China's anti-corruption institutional framework puts authority for anti-corruption work in the hands of the Party (the Central Commission for Discipline Inspection and its network of local commissions) and not in the hands of an independent body that would have authority over the CPC and that could call the CPC to account. This lack of an independent anti-corruption body makes the fight against corruption more difficult. Cases have shown that situations in which Party officials protect their corrupt subordinates with relative ease do occur.

The Party plays a direct role in the management of civil service performance. First, as we have seen, personnel officials in government departments and bodies are all Party members. Second, officials of CPC organisation departments participate directly in and approve personnel movements of all those holding leadership positions, no matter how lowly (for example, section chief and deputy chief). The CPC's *nomenklatura* system legitimizes this participation (see Burns, 1989 and 1994). In the 1990s, the Party has been a force for change and reform, especially within the central government. The care with which civil servants are selected for leading positions in the Ministry of Personnel (see Box 1.1 above) is evidence of this. In poorer parts of the country, however, where local Party committees may be captured by particularistic interests (triads, clans, chambers of commerce, or other interests) the CPC's stranglehold on civil service personnel administration may have undermined progress toward meritocratic outcomes.

3.3. Motivating public employees

Public employees like other workers are motivated by the expectation that if they perform well they will receive commensurate rewards that they value. High capacity organisations link performance to rewards. Like civil servants in other systems, public employees in China are motivated by the expectation of receiving both intrinsic and extrinsic rewards.

China's civil servants are paid according to a single uniform pay scale (see Table 1.3). A civil servant's total wage has four different components: basic wage, post wage, grade wage and seniority wage – which are then added together. The "post wage" refers to the current post that a person has. It is subdivided into 14 increments which are most often the result of how many years a person has been in the post. The "grade wage" reflects the individual

Table 1.3. **Main components of civil service pay: pay scale for post wage and grade wage (2004)**

Unit: RMB/month

Position	Post wage														Grade wage	
	1	2	3	4	5	6	7	8	9	10	11	12	13	14	Grade	Wage standard
President, Vice President, Premier	1 150	1 270	1 390	1 510	1 530	1 750									1	1 165
Vice Premier, State Councillor	940	1 045	1 150	1 255	1 360	1 465	1 570								2	1 030
Minister, Governor	780	870	950	1 050	1 140	1 230	1 320	1 410							3	903
Vice Minister, Vice Governor	645	725	805	885	965	1 045	1 125	1 205	1 285						4	790
Bureau Chief	520	590	660	730	800	870	940	1 010	1 080	1 150					5	686
Deputy Bureau Chief	425	485	545	605	565	725	785	845	905	965					6	586
Division Chief, County Magistrate	345	395	445	495	545	595	645	695	745	795	845				7	490
Deputy Division Chief, Deputy County Magistrate	280	320	360	400	440	480	520	560	600	640	680				8	408
Section shief	225	255	285	315	345	375	405	435	465	525	555				9	340
Deputy Section Chief	188	210	232	254	276	298	320	342	364	386	408	430			10	281
															11	231
Section member	157	173	189	205	221	237	253	269	285	301	317	333	349	365	12	190
															13	158
Clerical staff	130	143	156	169	182	195	208	221	234	247	260	273	286	299	14	133
															15	115

Source: Wenhui bao (Hong Kong), 3 December 2003. To come into force in July 2004.

capacity. Although obviously closely linked, it is separate from the post: one could theoretically have a lower grade than one's post would indicate. The combination of these two wages produces the greatest part of a civil servant's salary. The "basic wage" is the same for all government employees, from posts of "general office personnel" to the president: RMB 230 per month. The "seniority wage" represents very small amounts, as it is equal to the number of years of service in RMB: RMB 7 per month for a civil servant who has been working seven years. It is a means to count the years of service, which influences the attribution of other benefits to the civil servants.

Because average wages in the richest parts of the country are at least double the average wages in the poorest areas (National Bureau of Statistics, 2003), civil servants receive cash allowances to help defray cost-of-living differentials. The government has also laid down separate salary scales for major occupation groups employed by PSUs which are also topped up to reflect local conditions.

In addition to a basic salary, the government has provided public employees with goods (such as housing), services, cash subsidies and allowances (Burns, 2003b). Until 2003 virtually all civil servants were provided with housing at greatly subsidized prices. From the mid-1990s, the stock of civil service housing has been sold off gradually to civil servants at much below market prices. Since 2003, as part of the reforms, government departments have replaced the provision of departmental quarters with cash payments. Newly hired civil servants in Beijing complain, however, that the payments have not kept up with rising property prices.

Basic salaries are relatively low in China. However, this statement has to be put into perspective in two respects. First, basic salaries have not always been low in China compared to average national wages (see Burns, 2003b). In the 1950s, for example, officials in China pitched their own basic salaries at about 23 times the national average urban wage. Although the gap between the highest and lowest civil service salaries (vertical compression) has narrowed, officials have made up the difference to a large extent with generous benefits in kind (*e.g.* housing, official cars, travel, etc.), the provision of which has been mostly invisible. Official policy now calls for monetizing these benefits for junior and middle-level civil servants.

Second, the fact that the relatively high rate of corruption serves to compensate for relatively low base salaries has contributed, in some instances, to the tolerance of this phenomenon. Real incomes for most civil servants are probably much higher than the published low base salaries. Families may also benefit by having a family member in the civil service. Although the state has established rules of "avoidance" to reduce potential conflicts of interest, the evidence is clear that family members have benefited from access to the bureaucracy (Li, 2001).

Although in comparative terms China's base public salaries appear to be rather low, they pose a considerable burden for poorer parts of the country where personnel costs can be from 70 to 80% of total expenditure. The burden on local governments has been exasperated by salary increases for all civil servants, which the central government has mandated each year from 1998 to 2004. Transfers from the Ministry of Finance to cover the increases have apparently not been used to cover these costs. Poorer local governments have reacted by levying additional fees and charges on the local population and by deferring salary payments. The levying of such "illegal" fees and charges has been a contentious issue in rural China that has threatened the stability of many local communities.

This discussion has focused mostly on the material rewards of public office, which, after leading other sectors, such as public service units and enterprises in the 1950s, 1960s and 1970s, fell behind salaries paid by state-owned enterprises in the 1980s and 1990s, and behind the private sector. The gap is the greatest in the rich coastal parts of the country. Since 1998, the central government has raised civil service salaries each year. As we have seen, entry-level civil service positions remain competitive indicating that the policies to raise pay levels may have had an impact.

3.4. Level of institutionalization

An effective public personnel system is based on the rule of law that defines the rights and obligations of both employers and employees. Such a system provides predictability which is necessary for managing expectations. Systems that value the rule of law facilitate reforms becoming institutionalized.

Since 1980, the Chinese political system as a whole has become increasingly institutionalized. The 1980s, for example, saw a proliferation of Party and state institutions, regularization of institutional process, and emphasis on institutional discipline that has continued into the 1990s (Miller, 1999). Institutional restraints on China's leaders have increased during the past few years (Li, 2001). The CPC's management of the leadership succession in 2002-03 is evidence of a new higher level of institutionalization especially at the top. Such an environment is conducive for further institutionalization of China's civil service reforms.

To be successfully implemented, China's civil service reforms must become a norm and a matter of routine. Some of the reforms, such as the fixed tenure system which imposed retirement ages, have become institutionalized. Public employees around the country now accept that they will retire at 55 or 60 as laid down in personnel regulations (Manion, 1993). Other reforms have failed to live up to their promise. The existence of numerous loopholes in the competitive selection process has undermined the reforms. Widespread corruption and indiscipline have also reduced the capacity of local governments in many parts of the country. These practices have allowed sectional interests to capture local governments in some parts of the country, empowering kinship groups, chambers of commerce, or even criminal gangs.

The government recognizes that building norms and routines is a long-term process. Institutionalization of civil service reform goes hand in hand with the development of a system of rule of law.

4. Conclusion and recommendations

Ultimately, have China's civil service reforms had an impact on either improving the capacity of the civil service or on the performance of government bodies? One would expect that because the reforms were so extensive, touching recruitment and selection, training, appraisal, rewards and punishments, compensation, discipline and other areas, they should have improved civil service capacity. Although capacity has improved during the past 10 years, these capacity improvements may be explained by reasons other than civil service reform, such as by improvements in China's system of education (Walder, 2003). The rapid expansion of higher education since 1980 has produced a large population that is eligible for civil service employment.

The factors that influence the performance of government bodies are many and complex and may include resources, institutions and management mechanisms as well as political environments. According to research carried out in China, factors other than civil service reform are the most important for explaining agency performance. A study of municipal environmental protection and education bureaus in Beijing, Ningbo and Changchun, researchers found that agency leaders and their clients identified political leadership and financial support as more important than civil service reform for explaining improved agency performance. The research confirmed that civil service reform was perceived to play some role, however (Burns and Wang, 2003).

China's civil service system is far from being homogeneous. To simplify, it may perhaps be viewed as two systems – one that is relatively performance-oriented, selects "the best and brightest" through competitive mechanisms, links rewards to performance and does not tolerate indiscipline and corruption – and a second one that *de facto* operates as an employer of last resort, selects based on many different criteria some of which may be irrelevant to the job, ties rewards to positions, and is characterised by relatively high levels of indiscipline and corruption. (There are undoubtedly many gradations in between.) In China considerable evidence indicates that the performance-oriented systems operate primarily at the centre and in the richer coastal areas, while the traditional systems operate in the poorer, less developed hinterland. Improving the systems in these poorer areas depends in no small part on improving levels of economic development. Development is most likely with a highly competent and committed bureaucracy. Intervening to break out of the symbiotic relationship between poverty and inept bureaucratic leadership is an important task for the foreseeable future.

The following policy recommendations follow from this review:

1. To enhance legitimacy and accountability and to attract the best possible candidates to work for the government civil service, personnel policies and practices should be as transparent as possible. In addition to the material now provided on the Internet, for example, the Ministry of Personnel should maintain a publicly available database on the civil service, publishing regular information on the size, distribution, gender composition, age distribution and educational background of the civil service. Publishing this information will improve confidence in the civil service, especially that the service is being fairly and impartially managed.

2. The practice of permitting entry to the civil service outside the established mechanisms should be reduced and eliminated. To strengthen the civil service's meritocracy, all candidates for entry-level positions including demobilized soldiers should be required to take and pass the civil service entry examination.

3. To reduce corruption, authorities should ensure that the rotation system for officials is implemented as widely as possible and that leading officials, their offices, and their families are audited on a regular basis.

4. Transfers to poor areas should focus on improving human resources in those areas through training and transfers of experienced officials from more developed areas.

5. Salaries for civil servants should be maintained at a competitive level, determined locally. To ensure this, pay level surveys should be carried out regularly and their results published. Pay awards should be based in part on the surveys.

Notes

1. This chapter was written by John P. Burns, Department of Politics and Public Administration, University of Hong Kong, with the guidance of Jón R. Blöndal, Budgeting and Public Expenditures Division, Public Governance and Territorial Development Directorate, OECD.

2. Relatively developed countries with highly institutionalized public personnel systems may improve public sector performance through decentralization, de-regulation and giving management more flexibility to hire and fire. These "new public management"-type policies are less appropriate for developing countries that have weakly developed regulatory states. That is, in order to de-regulate, you first have to regulate.

3. See *People's Daily*, 24 March 2004 and *China Daily*, 24 March 2004 at www.english.peopledaily.com.cn/200403/24/print20040324_138315.html (retrieved on 8 April 2004) and www.chinadaily.com.cn/english/doc/2004-03/24/content_317402.htm (retrieved on 8 April 2004).

4. Figure for year end 2002. Interview, Ministry of Personnel, 19 March 2004.

5. The system was extended to the CPC in 1993, the Youth League, the Women's Federation, the Song Qingling Foundation, the National People's Congress (NPC) Standing Committee bureaucracy, the Chinese People's Political Consultative Conference (CPPCC) National Committee bureaucracy, the All-China Federation of Trade Unions, the Science and Technology Association and the Returned-Overseas Chinese Federation in 1994; the Association of Taiwan Compatriots, the Huangpu Military Academy Alumni Association, the eight democratic parties and the All China Federation of Industry and Commerce in 1995; the All-China Federation of Literature and Art Circles, the All-China Writers' Association, the All-China Journalists' Association, the All-China Staff and Workers Political Thought Work Research Association, the PSUs of all local Party committees, the All-China Legal Studies Association, the All-China Association for Friendship with People's Overseas, the All-China Foreign Affairs Studies Association, the All-China International Trade Promotion Association, and the All-China Red Cross in 1996; and the All-China Disabled People's Federation in 1997 [see Ministry of Personnel (ed.) *Renshi gongzuo wenjian xuanbian* (Selection of Personnel Work Documents) (various volumes) (Beijing: Renshi chubanshe, various years)].

6. Interviews with Supreme People's Court Judges, Hong Kong, May 2001.

7. Cadres are the managers, administrators and professionals found in all sectors of the economy including enterprises, in administrative agencies including government and in public service units.

8. Ministry of Personnel, *Provisional Regulations on Civil Servants*, Article 11.

9. More recent information is not available. An official of the Ministry of Personnel stated in an interview on 19 March 2004 that the relative distribution of civil servants had not changed since 1998.

10. Assessment centres are not places, but a method or process designed to assess skills or potential in a comprehensive and rigorous way. Typically, they involve the assessment of groups of participants by a team of trained observers. Candidates take part in a series of specially designed exercises or activities, including situational exercises that resemble the job being assessed for. See Margaret Dale and Paul Iles (1996), *Assessing Management Skills: a Guide to Competencies and Evaluation Techniques*, London, Kogan Page.

11. In 2004, the Ministry of Personnel published a list of civil service vacancies on the Internet, and indicated which ones required Party membership.

12. *People's Daily (Renmin ribao)*, 24 March 1998 in FBIS-CHI-98-097, 7 April 1998; *China Daily* in *South China Morning Post*, 22 September 1998; *New China News Agency (Xinhua)*, 29 October 1998 in FBIS-CHI-98-310, 6 November 1998; *Sing Tao Daily (Sing Tao Jih Pao)* (Hong Kong), 13 May 1998 in FBIS-CHI-98-133, 13 May 1998; *Ming Pao* (Hong Kong), 28 October 1998 in FBIS-CHI-98-301, 28 October 1998; and *Outlook (Liaowang)*, 10 March 1997 in FBIS-CHI-97-071, 10 March 1997.

13. On 7 May 1998 the central Organisation Department set up a 24-hour hotline to receive information on corrupt personnel practices. From then until November 1998 nearly 1 000 informants called them. See *New China News Agency (Xinhua)*, 29 October 1998 in FBIS-CHI-98-310, 6 November 1998.

Bibliography

Asian Development Bank (1995), *Governance: Sound Development Management*, Asian Development Bank, Manila.

Barnett, A. Doak (1967), *Cadres, Bureaucracy and Political Power in Communist China*, Columbia University Press, New York.

Burns, John P. (1989), *The Chinese Communist Party's Nomenklatura System Armonk*, M.E. Sharpe, New York.

Burns, John P. (1994), "Strengthening Central CCP Control of Leadership Selection: the 1990 Nomenklatura", *The China Quarterly*, No. 138, June, pp. 458-491.

Burns, John P. (2003a), "Downsizing the Chinese State: Retrenching the Government in the 1990s", *The China Quarterly*, No. 175, September, pp. 775-802.

Burns, John P. (2003b), "Rewarding Comrades at the Top in China", in Christopher Hood and B. Guy Peters with Grace O.M. Lee (eds.), *Reward for High Public Office: Asian and Pacific Rim States*, Routledge, London, pp. 49-69.

Burns, John P. and Wang Xiaoqi (2003), "The Impact of Civil Service Reform on Bureau Performance in China: Evidence from Beijing, Ningbo, and Changchun Environmental Protection and Education Bureaus", unpublished paper prepared for the Seventh International Research Symposium on Public Management, Hong Kong, 2-4 October.

China Organisation (Zhongguo jigou) (1998), July.

China Personnel Yearbook Editorial Office (1991), *China Personnel Yearbook, 1988-1989* (Zhongguo renshi nianjian 1988-1989), Beijing, Zhongguo renshi chubanshe.

Chou Kwok Ping (2003), "Conflict and Ambiguity in the Implementation of Civil Service Reform in China, 1993-2000", unpublished Ph.D. dissertation, the University of Hong Kong.

Hilderbrand, Mary E. and Merilee S. Grindle (1997), "Building Sustainable Capacity in the Public Sector: What Can be Done?", in Merilee S. Grindle (ed.), *Getting Good Government: Capacity Building in the Public Sectors of Developing Countries*, Harvard University Press, Boston.

Hood, Christopher and B. Guy Peters with Grace O.M. Lee (eds.) (2003), *Reward for High Public Office: Asian and Pacific Rim States*, Routledge, London.

Hu Angang (2001), *Zhongguo: tiaozhan fubai (China: Fighting Against Corruption)*, Hangzhou: Zhejiang renmin chubanshe.

Lee, Hong Yung (1991), *From Revolutionary Cadres to Party Technocrats in Socialist China*, University of California Press, Berkeley.

Li Cheng (2001), China's Leaders: the New Generation Lanham: Rowman and Littlefield.

Lieberthal, Kenneth (2004), Governing China: From Revolution through Reform, 2nd ed., New York: Norton.

Manion, Melanie (1993), *Retirement of Revolutionaries in China: Public Policies, Social Norms, and Private Interests*, Princeton, Princeton University Press.

Manion, Melanie (2004), *Corruption by Design: Building Clean Government in Mainland China and Hong Kong*, Cambridge, Mass., Harvard University Press.

Miller, H. Lyman (1999), "Institutions in Chinese Politics: Trends and Prospects", in *China's Future: Implications for Us Interests*, Web version www.fax.org/irp/nic/ china_future.html (accessed 11 November 2003).

Ministry of Personnel (1993), Provisional Regulations on Civil Servants, Beijing, mimeo.

Ministry of Personnel (1996), Provisional Regulations on Civil Service Position Exchange in China Personnel News, 31 August.

National Bureau of Statistics, *China Statistical Yearbook* (various years), Beijing, China Statistics Press.

Organisation Department, Ministry of Personnel (1998), "Guanyu zuohao xiangzhen jiguan shishi guojia gongwuyuan zhidu he canzhao guanli gongzuo de yijian" (Opinion on Doing Well the Implementation of the Civil Service System in Towns and Townships and Related Management Work), Zutongzi (1997), No. 48, in Ministry of Personnel (ed.) Renshi gongzuo wenjian xuanbian (Selection of Personnel Work Documents), Vol. 20, Beijing, China Personnel Press, pp. 135-138.

Organisation Department (Zhonggong zhongyang zuzhi bu) (1999), *Collection of Statistical Information on Party and Government Leading Cadres 1954-1998* (Dangzheng lingdao ganbu tongji ziliao huibian 1954-1998), Beijing, Dangjian duwu chubanshe.

Walder, Andrew (2003), "The Party Elite and China's Trajectory of Change", unpublished paper prepared for the International Conference on the Chinese Communist Party in a New Era: Renewal and Reform, National University of Singapore, East Asian Institute, 9-10 December.

Weiss, Linda (1998), *The Myth of the Powerless State*, Ithaca, N.Y., Cornell University Press.

Whiting, Susan H. (2001), *Power and Wealth in Rural China: the Political Economy of Institutional Change*, Cambridge, Cambridge University Press.

World Bank (2002), *China: National Development and Sub-National Finance: a Review of Provincial Expenditures*, Washington, D.C., World Bank.

Xi Liu (2002), *China's Civil Service System* (in Chinese), Beijing, Qinghua University Press.

Zhu Qingfang (ed.) (1997), *The Musts for Applying for the State Civil Service Recruitment Examinations* (Guojia gongwuyuan luyong kaoshi baokao xuzhi), Beijing, Zhongguo renshi chubanshe.

ANNEX 1.A1

Table 1.A1.1. **Estimated number of public sector employees**

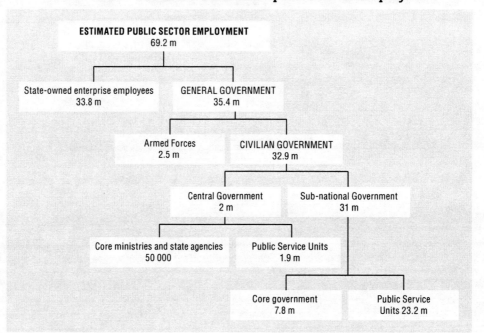

Note: These figures represent a conservative estimate based on published data from the National Bureau of Statistics of China. Only "staff and workers" employed in state-owned (not collectively-owned or "other"-owned) units are included. By the end of 2002, the total number of "staff and workers" employed by all state-owned units was 69.2 million. A further 10.7 million were employed in "urban collectively-owned" units and an additional 25.6 million were employed in "units of other types of ownership" which included co-operatives, joint ownership, limited companies, shareholding companies, etc.). "Staff and workers" exclude employees of township enterprises, private enterprises and teachers employed in *minban* schools (local publicly-supported schools). Many of these units could also probably be counted as "public". The central-local distribution of public employment based on the distribution in 2000 was estimated.

Source: National Bureau of Statistics of China (2003), *China Statistical Yearbook, 2003*, Beijing, China Statistics Press, p. 132.

PART I

Chapter 2

The Reform of Public Service Units: Challenges and Perspectives

Table of Contents

Summary 79

The Reform of Public Service Units: Challenges and Perspectives 81

   1. Introduction 81
   2. PSUs: A default organisational category under reform 81
      2.1. The evolution of PSUs 82
      2.2. The PSU problem today 82
      2.3. Current reform efforts 84
      2.4. Looking ahead 85
   3. The experience of OECD member countries 85
      3.1. A diversity of experiences 85
      3.2. General lessons learnt from OECD member countries 91
      3.3. Delivery by semi-autonomous government bodies 93
      3.4. Delivery by private firms and non-government organisations 94
   4. Key future reform challenges for China 94
      4.1. Clarifying the problems and challenges at stake 94
      4.2. Balancing coherence and diversity 95
      4.3. Applying appropriate reform levers 95
      4.4. Considering wider issues of governmental capacity 96
   5. Conclusions 96

Notes 99

Bibliography 100

List of boxes

2.1. OECD governments' role in sectors equivalent to PSUs
    (ownership and funding) 87

List of tables

2.1. Organisational classification of government bodies 89

List of figures

2.1. Organisational forms across OECD member countries 89

Summary

China's large and diverse sector of "public service units" (PSUs – *shiye danwei*) is a galaxy of public service providers operating alongside core government and separate from other state-owned or state-sponsored organisations such as state-owned enterprises (SOEs), state-owned financial institutions and state-sponsored "social organisations". Following on from the reform of SOEs and core government, the reform of PSUs represents the third major step of reforms that aim at transforming the organisational structure of the public sector into one that assists the socialist market economy.

Today, there are 1.3 million PSUs, employing more than 25 million people, comprising more than half of the best educated people in China and approximately one-third of staff working in the public sector. Education (schools, universities) and health (primary care centres, hospitals) account for more than 60% of PSU total employment.

PSUs have been undergoing reform to improve their efficiency for almost 20 years. Before the reform process started, the management of the sector had developed to fit the requirements of a planned economy with a highly centralized policy and resource allocation apparatus. Reform was carried out in a piecemeal fashion in the 1980s, focusing on granting additional autonomy to managers and employees of PSUs while encouraging PSUs to find non-budget subsidy revenues and increase labour market competition. However, the overall cost of PSUs has grown rapidly since the reforms. In addition, despite the growth in non-budget revenue, efficiency does not seem to have improved and some observers consider that non-budget revenue has constituted private rents for PSUs.

The additional autonomy granted to PSUs has not been matched with stronger reporting requirements on results or outputs, and without clear frameworks of accountability for the use of resources. In addition, the management modes and funding mechanisms of PSUs have evolved in a heterogeneous manner without much overall consideration of the sector, or of which management and funding mechanisms or governance structure should apply to which function.

Present reforms aim more at classifying, commercializing what can be commercialized, and restructuring the rest. In fact, as part of the transition from a central planning economy to a market economy, the reform of PSUs will be at the core of re-defining the size and role of government in the economy, as well as defining its modes of operating and funding mechanisms.

The experience of OECD member countries shows that these functions might potentially be assigned across the full range of organisational possibilities. The decisions on what should be public or "private" services need to take account of national and sectoral priorities, risks, private sector capacity and the quality of the wider institutions governing both public and private institutions. Sectors such as infrastructure, education, health and research require specific careful consideration. In some areas, while the ultimate desirable form may be clear, there will be serious transitional problems, including the private sector's capacity to take over, and for reporting ministries to steer, regulate and control.

For the delivery of public services, the Chinese Government will have to chose between the three different roles of government, depending on its priorities and on the sectors:

1. The government can be the regulator of service provision and delivery by the private sector. Apart from general market supervision by anti-trust authorities, this particularly involves sectors where forms of natural monopoly or undesirable forms of market power tend to emerge: telecommunications, banking, insurance, electricity, railways, etc. The issue of the quality of regulation becomes crucial to the delivery of services. In designing an overall reform strategy, considerable attention has to be paid to regulating entry, prices, quality and the availability of subsidies. The design of the institutions that carry out regulation is crucial in order for regulation to be predictable and transparent.

2. The government can be the contractor of services to private entities, especially for certain commercial goods with a clear public service function under certain conditions. When contracting out or establishing public-private partnerships, governments are strongly encouraged to invest in their contract management capacity, not to underestimate the sectoral capacity they need to monitor the performance of delivery by the privately owned entity, and to continuously put pressure on private providers. Governments need to ensure that they continue to have the operational knowledge to make good policies and choose – and alter – service delivery in a dispersed and networked environment.

3. Government organisations can remain directly responsible for the delivery of services. In this case, the government may define an overall framework for the delivery of services and define what services can be provided at arm's-length and what general relationships should be built for ensuring the good governance of the overall system. It is crucial that when establishing organisations at arm's-length from government, the whole governance framework should be considered, especially the capacity for central government entities to steer, control and conduct a dialogue with the management of these bodies especially on performance issues and the general capacity of the leadership of these organisations to manage the newly created organisations. Formally, this means that particular attention should be paid to the supervision, and ultimately to the ministerial right to intervene, as well as to financial and people management and on the means to maintain accountability to parent ministries.

It is clear that whatever the organisational form chosen for the provision of public services, governments have to retain an important policy making and enforcement capacity, as well as important co-ordination mechanisms.

PSU reform will not exempt the Chinese Government from a reform of the budgeting and tax system. Giving PSUs' additional autonomy in terms of raising revenues without improving the overall tax system is not sustainable. The reform of PSUs could be an opportunity to contribute to the reform of the budgeting system.

The Reform of Public Service Units: Challenges and Perspectives[1]

1. Introduction

China's large and diverse sector of "public service units" (PSUs – *shiye danwei*) is a galaxy of public service providers alongside core government and separate from other state-owned or state-sponsored organisations such as state-owned enterprises (SOEs), state-owned financial institutions and state-sponsored "social organisations". Following on from the reform of SOEs (see Chapter 10) and core government, the reform of PSUs represents the third major step of reforms that aim at transforming the organisational structure of the public sector into one that assists the socialist market economy.

PSUs are one of the four categories of legal persons defined in China's General Rules for Civil Law.[2] In the Interim Regulations on the Management of Public Sector Units (PSUs) registration adopted in 1998, it is stipulated that "a public institution is an organisation with the provision of social services in nature, established by the governmental agencies or other organisations with state-owned assets, working for the public good in activities such as education, science and technology, culture and health".[3]

Today,[4] there are 1.3 million PSUs, employing more than 25 million people (National Bureau of Statistics, 2002), comprising more than half of the best educated people in China and approximately one-third of staff working in the public sector.[5] Education (schools, universities) and health (primary care centres, hospitals) account for more than 60% of PSU total employment. PSUs, however, are characterized by their diversity in terms of services provided, governance structure, financing arrangements and relationship with government.

PSUs have been undergoing reform for almost 20 years to improve their efficiency. Reform started in a piecemeal fashion in the 1980s, focusing on granting additional autonomy to managers and employees of PSUs while encouraging them to find non-budget subsidy revenues and increase labour market competition. Present reforms aim more at classifying, commercializing what can be commercialized, and restructuring the rest. In fact, as part of the transition from a centrally planned economy to a market economy, the reform of PSUs will be at the core of re-defining the size and role of government in the economy, as well as defining its modes of operating and funding mechanisms.

This chapter provides an overview of the evolution of PSUs in the last two decades and the challenges at stake. It invokes the experience of OECD member countries to the extent that it may be useful, and suggests what main lines of reform could be taken by the Chinese authorities to transform PSUs into modern institutions appropriate to an opening economy.

2. PSUs: A default organisational category under reform

PSUs have been inherited from the formerly centrally planned economy. They have formal control rules that differ from those of core government organisations, and strong ties to the Communist Party of China (CPC) and the state in terms of ownership and control. They form a default organisational category that has developed over the years and has been under piecemeal reform for two decades. The government is now trying to take a whole-of-government perspective and is changing the PSU organisational structure to match its new role in a modern market economy.

2.1. The evolution of PSUs

While some PSUs date back to the early days of the CPC and the People's Liberation Army or the nationalist government, most were created under the planned economy under a rather simple regime, to provide a certain quantity and quality of goods and services as defined by the planned economy. The main difference between PSUs and state-owned enterprises (SOEs) was functional, in that PSUs provided mostly social and intangible services while SOEs provided mostly tangible and economic activities. SOEs were expected to be funded mainly through their own revenues whereas PSUs were mainly funded through direct transfers from government.

The management of the sector developed to fit the requirements of a planned economy and had a highly centralized policy and resource allocation apparatus. PSUs did not raise their own revenues and many did not have an independent accounting system. They were under strict hierarchical rules from reporting entities, either local or national. Their staff came under civil service personnel establishment (*bianzhi* system) control, and their activities were conducted strictly according to the state plan.

Reform started in the mid-1980s with successive sectoral reform policies in the fields of science and technology, education, culture and the arts, sports, and health. Until the mid-1990s, reforms were aimed at increasing the capacity of PSUs to raise their own revenues by limiting direct government funding to cover only basic salaries and by giving tax incentives to PSU earnings. PSUs were given an independent accounting system and in some cases a certain amount of management autonomy. Some staff have been put on contracts, giving their employers more capacity to lay off staff.

Some staff were encouraged to sell their services "in the market" (to public or private organisations), negotiating sharing arrangements for the revenues generated. The PSU sector was also encouraged to open up to non-PSU and non-state sector entities, allowing joint work with companies and mergers and co-operative agreements among PSUs across the boundaries of ministries and provinces, etc. At the same time, privately owned entities have also been encouraged to participate in sectors previously monopolised by PSUs. This resulted in the emergence of a number of private schools and hospitals.

There is little doubt that this strategy has been relatively successful in raising extra-budgetary revenues for some PSUs. However, it has not been sufficient to increase the efficiency of PSUs, as most PSUs do not operate in contestable markets and their reporting mechanisms do not provide good performance control for measurable and contestable goods. Successful reform would have required an overall reflection on the role of the state and its organisational forms in government activities, and the establishment of strong governance mechanisms in parallel with increased market incentives.

2.2. The PSU problem today

It would seem that today PSUs are benefiting both from their former status in the planned economy, where they received automatic budget appropriations, and from the market economy, which allows them to raise their own revenues and get involved in more commercial businesses. However, a common problem of public management reforms driven by market incentives arises, i.e. a situation where the accountability mechanisms provided in the formerly planned market economy have been weakened while market incentives are not yet functioning properly. Considering the size of the PSU sector, Chinese authorities had to change their reform strategy in the sector urgently.

2.2.1. The budget question[6]

The cost of PSUs has grown rapidly since the reforms. Data from the Ministry of Finance show that the total revenue of PSUs now accounts for RMB 1.38 trillion, or roughly two-thirds of total government spending.

Extra-budgetary revenue has also increased and continues to grow rapidly, while budget support has also risen significantly. Today, approximately 20% of PSUs are self-financed, and overall, initial data show that non-budgetary financial allocations currently represent approximately half of the total revenue of PSUs.

Pensions are an important liability for the future of PSUs. The vast majority of PSU employees receive pensions on a pay-as-you-go basis. These pensions are funded from current revenues and are escalating at a worrying rate. This is a very important factor that will have limiting consequences on PSU reforms in the coming years.

2.2.2. The performance question

Despite the growth in non-budget revenue, efficiency does not seem to have improved. Not only has there been a significant increase in the total number of employees, but the overall budget support per employee has also risen. Some data point to a continued significant increase of this ratio over the last few years, including very recently.

Many observers consider that non-budget revenue has constituted private rents for PSUs that have been used in ways that are not always in accordance with the general interest or with government policy.

The additional autonomy granted to PSUs has allowed them more budgetary freedom, without clear accountability for results or outputs. At the national level, since 1996 the budget has been allocated in two parts: basic funding is negotiated between the Ministry of Finance and the reporting ministry – often based on staffing numbers, and the second part is allocated for specific projects which are supposed to produce tangible outputs. This process, exacerbated by weaknesses in performance reporting and lack of oversight of extra-budget resources, has probably created a natural tendency for PSUs to increase their staff expenditure and other lavish expenses.

Some more anecdotal evidence, such as the difficulty of finding awardees for performance awards among PSUs, points to the possible serious underperformance of many PSUs.

2.2.3. The question of the role of the state and its organisational forms

Despite its common classification, the so-called "PSU sector" continues to cover a large variety of functions, management modes and organisational forms. Some PSUs have commercial functions that could be taken over by the private sector in a market economy (for example, they include some milk producers, entertainment book publishers and civil engineering organisations). Other organisations have functions whose take-over by the market is more debatable (hospitals, universities, etc.) or which raise questions about the capacity of government to regulate potential private monopolies. Finally, PSUs also include more traditional public services that are mainly carried out by government organisations in OECD member countries, such as basic education.

Because of these differences in functions, the management modes of PSUs have evolved in a heterogeneous manner without much overall consideration of the sector, or of which management and funding mechanisms or governance structure should apply to which function. Most importantly, they differ widely in their funding mechanisms (some having extensively developed external sources of funding), and in their operation through state planning.

2.3. Current reform efforts

Policy guidance on PSU reform, nationally and across sectors, is underdeveloped. The Tenth Five-year plan, adopted by the National People's Congress in March 2001, required an acceleration in the reform of those social services that are "suitable to be run as industries", as well as the separation of PSUs from government and enterprises, and of for-profit organisations from non-profit organisations. However, there is no clear definition of what constitutes an enterprise and what it means to be "non-profit".

The recent Decision on Some Issues Concerning Perfecting the Socialist Market Economic Systems, adopted by the Sixteenth Central Committee of the Communist Party of China (CPC) in October 2003, which is designed to provide overall guidelines for economic reform during the coming 10 years, includes the requirement to "implement PSU reform continuously". But it specifies nothing beyond the reform of personnel and the compensation system.

In practice, reform is being carried out at two different levels: at some sectoral levels, in particular in the science and technology sector; in some local governments (for example, the Zhejiang provincial government and the Nanjing municipal government). In addition, overall managerial reforms are being carried out by the Ministry of Finance and the Ministry of Personnel.

At the sectoral and local levels, current reforms attempt to:

1. classify PSUs (typically divided into categories such as administrative and law enforcement units, public benefit units and business-related units);
2. transform PSUs that are considered to be performing commercial activities into public enterprises or fully private companies; and
3. restructure the remaining PSUs (those considered to be public-benefit related) in terms of financing and personnel, and reduce their staff expenditure and staff numbers.

In some cases, non-profit organisations (NPOs) have been adopted as the preferred institutional form for reforming public-benefit PSUs. Further studies at national level have also encouraged transforming many PSUs into NPOs. The status of NPOs, however, remains unclear. While the functions would require management not to pursue an overall profit-making objective, the state would remain the owner of these NPOs, and would give them preferential tax treatment. This category should not be confused with non-governmental organisations (NGOs) that exist in OECD member countries. It would seem that a more similar organisational form in OECD countries would be government-created foundations. However, government-created foundations in OECD countries have a much more limited role in terms of service delivery compared to what is being proposed by the Chinese Government for its PSUs.

The question of changing the incentives of these PSUs is just starting to be addressed, mainly by the Ministries of Finance and Personnel. The Ministry of Finance is starting to think about how to best monitor the performance of PSUs. Personnel reform was launched in 2001 and aims at transforming guaranteed lifelong employment into fixed-term contracts, and at giving more flexibility in compensation, hiring and firing. While the general lines of the reform are known, it is not likely to be implemented for another few years. In addition, government officials point to the need to decrease employment in PSUs, and this has in fact been required for NPOs in the science and technology sectors since the 2000 reform. Actual staff cuts seem limited, however, which is understandable in view of the social consequences involved and the difficulties with pension liabilities.

2.4. Looking ahead

The problems of the PSU sector today differ according to the type of PSU involved.

While some – but not all – with functions of a clearly commercial nature are being privatized, others are being transformed into SOEs, often as a preliminary step towards privatization. The transformation of PSUs into private firms or SOEs needs to be completed. The first important challenge for the Chinese authorities is to define what can be run by the private sector and what should remain the function of government. This choice will depend on the public or private good nature of the functions concerned, on the capacity of the private sector to take over the functions carried out by PSUs, and, in some cases, on the regulatory capacity of government.

The role of government should remain minimal for newly created companies when they provide commercial goods or services in a purely private goods market that has an existing capacity. In other sectors, however, there will be a need to provide for good public regulation in order to maintain or create competition, as well as quality and cost standards when the market has a monopolistic tendency (network industries) and/or when the nature of the goods and services provided qualify clearly as public services (*e.g.* in the health and education sectors).

It is likely that many PSUs will remain non-company government organisations. The questions that remain for the Chinese authorities are how to best adapt the organisational forms of the different PSUs involved, and how to balance the need for management autonomy with accountability mechanisms for the use of resources. Although some of these entities might be able to raise some revenue, it is likely that many will remain mainly supported by state and local budgets for the purpose of social and cross-regional equity, organisational accountability and government coherence.

3. The experience of OECD member countries

3.1. A *diversity of experiences*

The most striking feature of the organisations in OECD member countries involved in sectors equivalent to those of PSUs is the diversity of the scope of state intervention and organisational structures.

3.1.1. Diversity in the scope of government intervention in ownership and funding of public services

If we look at the ownership of service delivery organisations in OECD member countries and at their funding mechanisms in the three most important PSU sectors – education, health and research – governments remain the most important player in the first two, and are of secondary importance to the business sector in the research area (see Box 2.1).

When comparing the organisation of the sectors involved in Chinese PSU reform with their equivalent in OECD member countries (see Figure 2.1), it is clear that, depending on the functions and the country's administrative culture, their functions could be allocated to many types of organisations, either government-owned or not.

After determining what should remain in the public service (and either suppressing or privatizing organisations providing services that do not qualify as public services), governments have a choice between owning public service delivery organisations or using private firms for the delivery of services.

3.1.2. The delivery of public services by government-owned entities[7]

In terms of the organisational form of public service delivery, a similar range of types for government-owned entities across OECD member countries can be observed:

- ministries – traditionally vertically integrated, which undertake essential government functions – diplomacy, finance, etc.;
- public law bodies – more arm's-length or indirectly controlled by government undertaking a range of defined service delivery functions;
- commercial government enterprises – state-owned enterprises or virtual SOEs operating in commercial markets under private law with a profit objective and full or partial government ownership, *e.g.* airlines, government electricity companies;
- other private law bodies – a range of organisations (trusts, foundations, etc.) established under private law but not with a for-profit objective, undertaking a non-commercial function.

Traditionally, in most OECD member country governments, core government is defined as the ministries and departments of the executive, under the direct hierarchical control of a minister and/or prime minister in parliamentary systems, or of the head of state in presidential systems. These direct accountability lines provide a simple and stable governance model in which policy making and the delivery of services fall under the responsibility of a government clearly accountable to parliament and ultimately to the people. The same set of financial and management laws and reporting mechanisms generally applies to all of these bodies.

All countries, however, have always had some degree of managerial autonomy for government bodies that are separate from traditionally structured ministries or departments but remain core government entities. Many such bodies are long-standing and have been created for a variety of reasons, both political and managerial. These bodies are removed from the direct and constant control of politicians, have different hierarchical structures from traditionally functioning ministries, and in some cases, have management autonomy or independence from political influence.

Box 2.1. **OECD governments' role in sectors equivalent to PSUs (ownership and funding)**

a) The education sector[1]

Today, OECD member countries spend 5.9% of their collective gross domestic product (GDP) on their educational institutions and 13% of total public expenditure on education.

Schools, universities and other educational institutions are still mainly publicly funded, with over 88% of all funds for educational institutions coming directly from public sources – and 93% for primary, secondary and post-secondary non-tertiary levels of education. There are however, significant levels of private funding in some countries, most notably Australia (15%), Germany (20%), Korea (19%) and Mexico (14%).

On average, across OECD member countries at the primary/secondary level, only 12% of the public funds designated for education institutions are spent on institutions that are privately managed (71% in the Netherlands and 50% in Belgium).

Tertiary institutions tend to mobilize a much higher proportion of their funds from private sources than primary, secondary and post-secondary non-tertiary institutions. The private share ranges from less than 3% in Denmark, Finland and Greece to 77% in Korea, but includes private payments that are subsidized from public sources.

b) The health sector[2]

Total expenditure on health varies between 14.6% of GDP in the United States and 5.6% in the Slovak Republic, with 23 OECD member countries out of 30 spending between 7% and 10% of their GDP on health. With the exception of the Netherlands and Poland, public expenditure on health varies between 5% and 8% of GDP.

The degree to which the delivery and financing of health care systems are publicly controlled or administered varies widely from one country to another. The OECD (OECD, 2004a) classifies them under one of the three approaches described below, but it is important to recognize that more than one of these approaches exists in most countries – even if one form is dominant.[3]

Broadly speaking, there are three main structural types of insurance/financing and delivery systems:

1. The public-integrated model combines budget financing of health care provision with hospital providers that are part of the government sector. These systems, which merge the insurance and provision functions, are organised and operated like any government department. Staff are generally paid on salary (although, in some cases, doctors can also have private patients) and they are most often public sector employees. Ambulatory doctors and other health care professionals can be either public employees or private contractors to the health care authority, with a range of remuneration packages. Broadly speaking, these systems exist in the Nordic countries, Australia (public hospitals), Italy, Greece, Portugal and, before the reforms of the early 1990s, the United Kingdom. New Zealand introduced a purchaser-provider split in the 1990s similar to developments in the United Kingdom, but it has since moved closer to an integrated model following reforms in 2000.

2. In the public-contract model, public payers contract with private health care providers. The payers can be either a state agency or social security funds. Single payer arrangements have a stronger position in relation to providers (as in the public integrated model) and tend to have lower administrative costs than multiple payer systems. In many public-contract systems private hospitals and clinics are run on a non-profit basis. Independent private

> Box 2.1. **OECD governments' role in sectors equivalent to PSUs (ownership and funding)** *(cont.)*
>
> contractors generally supply ambulatory care. In the past, payment of providers has been often on an *ex post* basis for services provided, although contract arrangements have been evolving.
>
> Canada, most of the remaining Continental European countries, Japan, and now, the United Kingdom, and, to some extent, New Zealand, belong to the public contract category.
>
> 3. A private insurance/provider model uses private insurance combined with private (often for profit) providers. Insurance can be mandatory (Switzerland) or voluntary (United States). Payment methods have traditionally been activity based.
>
> **c) Research[4]**
>
> In 2001, OECD member countries allocated about 2.3% of overall GDP to research and development (R&D). The business sector is the major source of financing of domestic R&D and accounted for more than 63% of funding in OECD member countries in 2001 (73% in Japan, 68% in the United States and 56% in the European Union).
>
> The business sector also performs most R&D. In 2001, R&D performed by the business sector reached close to 70% of total R&D in OECD member countries.
>
> The higher education sector performs about 17% of total domestic R&D in the OECD area. This percentage has increased steadily over the past decade in the European Union and the United States and has increased significantly in Japan.
>
> Business funding for public research is small. However, for the receiving institutions, the inflow from business in some cases already represents a considerable part of their income (more than 10% in Belgium, Canada, Finland, France, Germany, Iceland, Ireland, Korea, the Netherlands, Norway, Poland, Slovak Republic, the United Kingdom). An analysis of funding flows into the public sector has shown that financial support for public sector research from business has increased in many countries, in particular in the big "spender" countries.
>
> 1. See OECD, 2003a.
> 2. See OECD, 2003b; OECD, 2004a.
> 3. For example, in the United States, the hospital system for veterans belongs to a public integrated model, and Medicare and Medicaid are a form of public contract model, with the remainder a private insurance/provider model. Other countries are equally complex. France has a social insurance system that finances most of health care, but the public hospital system is part of the government sector and as such it is closer to a public-integrated model. This sits alongside public contract arrangements with private clinics or hospitals (some of which are non-profit).
> 4. See OECD, 2003c; OECD, 2003d.

In the past two decades, OECD member countries have significantly increased the number and scope of activity of these bodies at arm's-length from central ministries. In some cases, bodies have been newly created with new governance structures, while in other cases long-standing bodies have been given significantly more management autonomy.

In general, the rationale has been the need for organisations to put more focus on performance. Arm's-length bodies have been a favoured form of implementing performance management as they have the potential to function better than core ministries under clear performance contracts with their parent ministries; they benefit from a relaxation of their input controls but have a clear accountability line to the minister, and in most cases, remain institutionally part of their parent ministries.

Figure 2.1. **Organisational forms across OECD member countries**

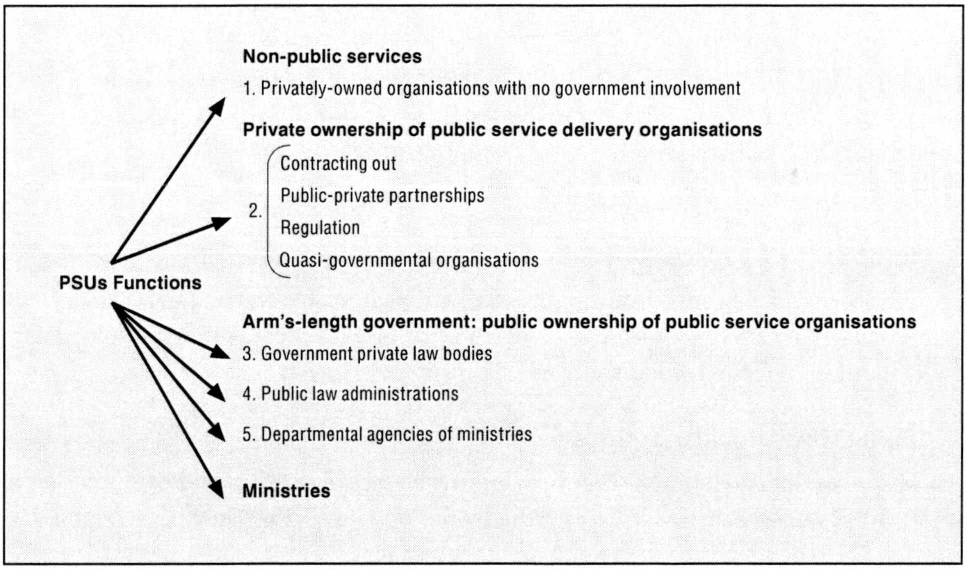

```
                         Non-public services
                         1. Privately-owned organisations with no government involvement

                         Private ownership of public service delivery organisations
                            ⎧ Contracting out
                         2. ⎨ Public-private partnerships
                            ⎨ Regulation
                            ⎩ Quasi-governmental organisations
PSUs Functions
                         Arm's-length government: public ownership of public service organisations
                         3. Government private law bodies
                         4. Public law administrations
                         5. Departmental agencies of ministries
                         Ministries
```

There is no universally accepted classification of arm's-length bodies. They differ widely in terms of organisation, legal status, and degree of management autonomy or political independence (see Table 2.1). But basically governments have used three main methods to distance these bodies from core ministries:

- a different governance structure and hierarchy from a traditional ministry;
- a different control environment, in other words partial or complete exemption from management, financial and personnel rules that usually apply to traditional ministries;
- a degree of management autonomy (including a separate financial administration).

Table 2.1. **Organisational classification of government bodies**

			Legal separation from the state	Rules applying to the entity	Status of staff	Funding
Traditional ministries			Indivisible from the state	General rules applying to ministries/public law	Civil servants	Tax funded
Arm's-length government		*Departmental agencies*	Tax funded (possibility of small fees)	General rules applying to ministries. Relaxation of some input controls	Civil servants	Largely tax funded
	Indirectly controlled bodies	*Public law administrations*	Partially or fully legally separate from the state	General rules applying to government entities/public law. Relaxation of some input and process control rules	Partly public servants	Some fees, some sales, some tax
		Government enterprises: 1. Commercial government enterprises (government companies)	Legally separate entities from the state	Private law bodies	Private law employments (sometimes some specific status)	Sales revenue funded/ subsidies
		2. Non-commercial other private law body (quasi corporations)	Id.	Id.		

These arm's-length bodies in central government now account for between 50% and 75% (or even more in very few cases) of public expenditure and public employment in some OECD member countries. This new institutional environment has created new challenges for governments to maintain central direction and control.

Some of the functions carried out by PSUs are in fact carried out in some OECD member countries by arm's-length bodies (many would be in the categories of public law administrations) such as hospitals, universities and research centres.

3.1.3. *The delivery of public services by private sector organisations*

In addition to the use of government organisations, the governments of OECD member countries have experimented with the greater use of private organisations to play a larger role in delivering publicly-funded services.

3.1.3.1. Public-private partnerships[8]

Public-private partnerships (PPPs) usually involve the financing and/or operation and management of public infrastructure projects by the private sector. They have mainly taken place in the fields of transport infrastructure and, to a lesser extent, for energy projects and in the health and education sectors. The use of PPPs remains limited: in the United Kingdom, the country which has made the most use of PPPs, about one-tenth of its total capital investments in public services in 2003-04 were through PPPs, and this has been relatively consistent over time. PPPs have had mixed results, with the gains in operational efficiency sometimes being undermined by the difficulty of contract management, the transaction costs involved in preparing and negotiating the project, and the difficulty of maintaining the balance of risk transfers between government and the private sector. In addition, from a public finance point of view, PPPs can only be justified if the transfer of risks and the efficiency gains outweigh the higher cost of capital of private sector financing.

3.1.3.2. Outsourcing[8]

Outsourcing is the practice whereby governments contract with private sector providers for the provision of services to government ministries and agencies, or directly to citizens on behalf of the government. Partial data show a significant increase of outsourcing in member countries in the last 15 years. The first activities that have been contracted out include "blue collar" support services such as cleaning, security and canteen services, maintenance and printing services, which are not considered as critical to the mission of the agency. The second group of activities that have been outsourced are high-value professional service, including "back office" activities (information technology, banking and financial services). This is where the greatest growth has occurred in recent years, but country variations are more pronounced. Outsourcing of mainline functions remains limited but has made important in-roads in some countries (employment placement services, child welfare services, long-term care institutions, R&D).

While experience in OECD member countries shows that when successful, contracting out can increase efficiency significantly, it also raises significant questions about the contracting capacity of the contractor (most importantly in terms of measuring the performance of the service provided).

3.1.3.3. Regulation

When governments decide that a public service with monopolistic tendencies, such as in the network industries (electricity distribution, telecommunications, water distribution, etc.), can be carried out by privately owned companies (whether as sole competitors or including publicly owned competitors), regulation is required to maintain competition and different standards of public services. Regulation has to do with business entry, prices, quality of goods and services, protection of the environment, work safety and health issues.

With the marketization and privatization of former state-owned enterprises and the establishment of competition in formerly monopoly-based industries with network characteristics such as energy and telecoms, independent regulators have mushroomed in OECD member countries. Although widely used, these new institutions often raise political challenges and involve significant design issues related to their independence, accountability, performance, and the quality of their regulatory activities.

3.1.3.4. Quasi-government

In all OECD jurisdictions, there is a range of bodies that are usually private law bodies with a governance board with some government appointees. They are partially financed on government grants and have no government controls on staff or others. It is in this category, for instance, that some of the government-created foundations can be found.

Governments run significant governance risks with these bodies. The line between public and private sectors is blurred. Government might remain legally responsible for the actions of bodies that it does not own (which is why they are outside the financial reporting entity) but is deemed to control. This risk suggests the need to use extreme caution in establishing quasi-government instrumentalities.

3.2. General lessons learnt from OECD member countries

Experience from OECD member countries and transitional economies suggests that considerable care is required in choosing an appropriate organisational form, both in terms of choice of function and in terms of capacities. Once the form has been chosen, many other conditions have to be fulfilled for the new organisational form to produce the expected positive effects. Experience in OECD member countries and transitional economies shows that when these conditions are not fulfilled, organisational reform can be counterproductive and result in losses that can have long-term effects not only on the capacity to deliver services but also on trust, and may even exacerbate corruption.

3.2.1. *Identify the public interest and divest from activities where there is no clear public interest*[9]

Across all OECD member countries there has been a widespread trend for governments to pull back from the delivery of commercial services – initially by placing commercial activities with commercial government organisations (state-owned enterprises) and subsequently through privatizations. OECD member country governments have redefined some of the basic rules for government involvement in an activity. Over the last two decades, privatization proceeds in OECD member countries have been in excess of three-quarters of a trillion dollars, with a slowing down since 2000.

In general, two types of assets have been privatized: i) assets in the commercial and competitive sectors which could be owned and provided for by the private market without government involvement (banking, manufacturing); *ii)* assets in the commercial sectors that have remained public services or monopolistic sectors, but provided by the private market – either in highly regulated sectors or through contracting arrangements (network industries). Exceptions that are justified by historical, sociological or political reasons exist in all countries, however.

There is little doubt that in China there are some PSUs whose functions should require little or no government involvement because they provide goods and services in the commercial and fully competitive sector. In this context, the Chinese authorities are continuing to privatize or close down these entities.

The privatization process requires several important preconditions for successful implementation and to avoid increasing corruption; these concern financial sector reform, having hard budget constraints and organising competition and wide-ranging divestment.

3.2.2. The right organisational forms for the delivery of activities where there is a public interest

Once the areas where the government should retain capacity have been identified, a choice of organisational form for the delivery of public services has to be made. The guiding principles for this choice are:

1. **Form follows function:** The chosen organisational form depends on the functions performed (policy making/service delivery, commercial/non-commercial, focused and measurable services/unfocused and non-measurable services are probably the most important splits). In general, two principles apply: *i)* commercial services tend to be outsourced and delivered by privately owned organisations (or, as a transition, by government companies); *ii)* arm's-length organisations should be used only for functions that aim at providing one or very few interrelated specialized services, that are focused and measurable, so that the use of resources remains highly controlled and performance measured.

2. **Maintain government capacity:** Whether the organisational form chosen means delivery by government or non-government actors or arm's-length delivery, the national or local government entities which are ultimately responsible for service delivery need to retain capacity in the sector in order to control performance and the use of government resources. Governments need to invest in their capacity to manage contractual relationships (this includes negotiating, drafting, controlling and directing contracts) and monitor the performance of organisations. This is recognized as a major challenge in OECD member countries.

3. **Avoid organisational zoo:** Organisational forms should be thought through within a coherent framework with a rather limited number of organisational forms. There should be specific sectoral and cross-regional coherence, to keep policies coherent and allow for accountability and control.

4. **Restructuring adds costs:** The benefits of organisational reform should be weighed against the disruption costs generated, the costs in terms of additional staff insecurity and the potential loss of institutional memory.

5. **The default organisational category is the classic vertically integrated ministry:** When in doubt about whether the preconditions for specific organisational changes have been fulfilled, governments are advised to choose what has proved to be the safest organisational form for public service delivery in the long run, *i.e.* the classic hierarchical ministry.

The following section develops the specific requirements for the various organisational forms.

3.3. Delivery by semi-autonomous government bodies[10]

The risks of semi-autonomous government are well known to OECD member countries and transition economies. They lie mainly in a weak accountability structure that could result in inefficiency, capture, lack of government and policy coherence and possibly patronage and corruption. The conditions for successful arm's-length government depend on the functions carried out, the general governance framework, the accountability mechanisms and the capacity of reporting entities to manage organisations by contract. These would include, in particular:

- A sound legal and institutional framework that limits the number of types of arm's-length bodies gives them a clear legal basis and justifies any exceptions to the stated rules. This legal and institutional framework should take into account the following:
  - grouping organisations into classes, establishing strict principles for the creation and removal of new entities;
  - assigning specific governance responsibilities;
  - providing a generic law for organisations;
  - establishing policy agreements with the different bodies;
  - establishing principles of public finance for these bodies;
  - specifying rules under which staff function;
  - specifying the external reporting and auditing procedures as well as the planning and control cycle;
  - assigning individual responsibilities;
  - establishing sound procedures to account for the use of public resources, the results achieved and good governance standards and for accounting to and consulting with stakeholders;
  - establishing standards of behaviour;
  - establishing control and audit procedures and principles.
- A well-thought-through structure for individual institutions is also important, including a gradual move to arm's-length systems. Not all bodies will be ready at the same time to function at arm's-length from government, not least because governments need to make sure they have enough managers available to work at arm's-length in a performance-based environment, and reporting entities need to be able to function well in a contract-based environment.
- Organisation of the necessary constant interface between arm's-length organisations and central (not necessarily parent) ministries.
- Accountability of and reporting by delegated managers, and the need for a strong oversight of bodies, including by Parliament.
- Sufficient time to move to arm's-length status. It takes months, and often years, to transform part of a traditional ministry hierarchy into an arm's-length body that functions well, and for the supervisory ministry to be able to steer it well. The process of getting things right cannot be entirely driven from the top but depends on co-operation and learning from both parties.

3.4. Delivery by private firms[11] and non-government organisations

Privately owned firms can only deliver public services that have easily identifiable and measurable products of a commercial nature.

The main risks in the delivery of public services by private firms lie in the danger of creating a private monopoly that is too costly to the public and does not provide services of the quality standards required by government.

When contracting out or establishing public-private partnerships, governments are strongly encouraged to invest in their contract management capacity, not to underestimate the sectoral capacity they need to monitor the performance of delivery by the privately owned entity, and to continuously put pressure on private providers. Governments need to ensure that they continue to have the operational knowledge to make good policies and choose – and alter – service delivery in a dispersed and networked environment. Specific conditions, applying to public-private partnerships and contracting out respectively, cannot be developed fully in this paper.

When the services are provided by privately-owned organisations that fall under government regulation for a public service, the issue of the quality of regulation becomes crucial to the delivery of services. In designing an overall reform strategy, considerable attention has to be paid to regulating entry, prices, quality and the availability of subsidies. The design of the institutions that carry out regulation is crucial in order for regulation to be predictable and transparent.

Some countries with a long civic tradition see private non-profit organisations delivering publicly funded services, particularly in health and education. These are country-specific exemptions to a general rule.

Public-service delivery by non-government organisations or private firms is not dominant in OECD member countries. In addition to the conditions described above for private firms, governments need to ensure that the NGOs, associations or foundations that provide services have a good governance structure in order to prevent capture by specific interests. It is also crucial that there be a clear distinction between the role of government and the role of the organisation chosen to deliver a specific service.

4. Key future reform challenges for China

The Chinese Government considers that PSUs have three main problems: they are too costly, underperforming and too heterogeneous. On the basis of the experience of OECD member countries, it is suggested that the Chinese Government could take the following approaches to address these problems:

4.1. Clarifying the problems and challenges at stake

The problems at stake in the reform of PSUs are various in nature and should be considered separately, although they should be coherent among themselves. In fact, behind the reform of organisational structures, the Chinese authorities are trying to implement four kinds of reform, for which different types of issues arise:

1. Redefining the boundaries of state intervention (what is a public service?) will require a reflection on the mission of the state, existing capacity in private market, and on ways to create and reinforce this capacity.

2. Determining what public service delivery organisations the government should own (public or private?): the decision as to whether public or private organisations should deliver public services will not automatically improve service delivery, decrease costs or help raise new revenues for public services. The success of contracting out to the private sector or regulating requires significant new capacity for central government. In its absence, the private delivery of public services might bring the opposite results than those expected.

3. Diversifying the source of revenue for public services (fees to the public): This touches upon a different set of issues that have to do with the costs of public services, the capacity of citizens to take over some of the direct funding of public services and equity.

4. Increasing the incentives for good performance of public PSUs: establishing a performance-based organisation requires establishing some performance-based financial and human resources management. It is how resource allocations are made and how accountability mechanisms for good performance are established that improve incentives for good performance. Organisational form can only embody this new priority and new management system but does not create incentives *per se*. A robust institutional framework is key to ensuring performance but in itself is not sufficient to guarantee it.

4.2. Balancing coherence and diversity

Considering the diversity of PSUs in terms of sectors, organisational forms, reporting structures and the different levels of reporting (national, provincial, municipal), it seems crucial that an overall governance framework for service delivery be thought through and general guidelines produced on how to analyse PSU reform. This framework would give some coherence to a reform that touches upon vital issues such as the role of the state in education and health and its modes of service delivery.

Coherence within sectors and across levels of government is crucial for organisational clarity, policy coherence, accountability and equity. As such, it is very important that a robust institutional framework is put in place and equal standards of service delivery be established for organisations across the country.

This framework should, however, allow for wide flexibility of choice of organisational forms according to sector.

4.3. Applying appropriate reform levers

Choosing different organisational forms for PSUs will not necessarily solve the issues of their funding and the lack of performance incentives for those organisations.

At present, PSUs are allowed to keep unspent revenue in their budget, one of their main incentives for good performance. However, in a weak performance monitoring environment, it is unlikely that this incentive helps organisations perform better. The core problem of PSUs is not the lack of autonomy, but their lack of incentive to perform.

Reflecting on the lack of incentives will require reviewing the following levers:

1. the central capacity to control performance and contract PSUs on performance;
2. human resources management, and in particular of senior management ; and
3. the management of financial resources and in particular budget allocation mechanisms.

Finding additional resources for funding PSUs will inevitably require a reform of the tax system in China which would help China raise more revenue. Indeed, it seems that it would be unwise to promote a model of general public service delivery – especially in the health and education sectors – where each organisation would generate a significant part of its own revenue from fees and other revenue drawn from citizens or firms. In addition to widening disparities in the provision of public services across regions and socio-economic backgrounds of citizens, such a policy would make the implementation of government-wide policies much more difficult.

4.4. Considering wider issues of governmental capacity

Today's problems in the field of PSUs reflect larger problems of government capacity in China.

Granting additional autonomy to PSUs will require stronger capacity in the centre (either at national or local government levels) to design government-wide policies, to govern more autonomous government entities by contract on performance, and to control performance and the use of resources. It will also require additional capacity in terms of leadership of these more autonomous entities.

5. Conclusions

The experience of OECD member countries leads us to caution against any assumption that PSUs are a "sector" with common characteristics – potentially, these functions might be assigned across the full range of organisational possibilities.

While there is some commonality across OECD member countries in terms of what is "public" and what is "private", the respective margins cannot be determined outside the particular country context. Decisions by the Chinese Government need to take account of national and sectoral priorities, risks, private sector capacity and the quality of the wider institutions governing both public and private institutions.

The experience of many OECD member countries shows that reforming government organisational forms first requires a better definition of the respective responsibilities of the public and private sectors in the provision and delivery of services. Some sectors are easier to classify than others: the banking, industry, and agriculture sectors are clearly areas in which government ownership of the delivery organisations should remain limited. On the other hand, services that are sovereignty functions of the state (*e.g.* diplomacy) or services that imply making administrative decisions (*e.g.* tax collection) are clearly functions of the state that require governments to retain overall responsibility for the provision and delivery of services.

Sectors such as infrastructure, education, health and research require more careful consideration and often result in a more mixed picture. In all countries, the government retains an important role, in both the overall regulation of sectors and in many cases in the direct provision of services – whether they are delivered by government-owned organisations or private entities contracted out by government entities. The delivery of public services by private sector organisations requires significant increased capacity for regulating the sectors, and existing capacity for the private sector to take over.

In some areas, while the ultimate desirable form may be clear, there will be serious transitional problems, including the private sector's capacity to take over, and for reporting ministries to steer, regulate and control.

For the provision of public services, governments have to retain an important policy making and enforcement capacity, as well as important co-ordination mechanisms. It is clear from the experience of OECD member countries that as much attention should be given to strengthening parent ministries' capacity to regulate or control and steer, as to the design of new organisations for the delivery of goods and services.

Diversity of organisational form in the public sector – especially in an immature market framework – can pose serious risks to the collective interest. The management of this risk can be facilitated by some umbrella legislation defining the authority and control of different kinds of organisations.

Once the responsibilities of the public and private sectors in the provision of public goods and services have been clarified, it is clear that there can be only a limited number of organisational structures and governance relationships for the provision and delivery of services for which the government remains responsible.

The government can have three different functions:

1. The government can be the regulator of service provision and delivery by the private sector. Apart from general market supervision by anti-trust authorities, this particularly involves sectors where forms of natural monopoly or undesirable forms of market power tend to emerge: telecommunications, the banking sector, the insurance sector, electricity, railways, etc.
2. The government can be the contractor of services to private entities, especially for certain commercial goods with a clear public service function under certain conditions.
3. Government organisations can remain directly responsible for the delivery of services. In this case, the government may define an overall framework for the delivery of services and define what services can be provided at arm's-length and what general relationships should be built for ensuring the good governance of the overall system. The fewer the categories, and the more uniform the rules applying to them, the more intelligible the public governance system is to politicians, civil servants and citizens alike. Having too many forms of government organisations and too many organisations increases the risk that they will not work together on important common objectives, or that complex problems of public policy "fall between the cracks" of organisations' responsibilities.

While the relative "autonomy" of some government entities may be desirable, changes in organisational form should aim at preserving good governance and accountability in the use of resources.

Establishing entities at arm's-length from reporting entities respond to two "good governance" reasons: to improve the performance of the public sector by bringing decision-making closer to the point of delivery, and to make public decision-making more credible by separating it from direct political intervention.

Arm's-length government, however, cannot solve the problems of a generally ill-functioning government. Experience from transition economies gives mixed messages about establishing new organisations to avoid general problems of governance in the public sector, as even autonomous bodies need to be strongly co-ordinated and overseen by parent ministries.[12] In addition, it is impossible to create a lasting performance culture in an environment where government under-performing prevails.

It is therefore crucial to consider the whole governance framework when establishing organisations at arm's-length from government. Essential are the capacity for central government entities to steer, control and conduct a dialogue with the management of these bodies especially on performance issues, and the general capacity of the leadership of these organisations to manage the newly created organisations. Formally, this means that particular attention should be paid to the supervision, and ultimately the ministerial right to intervene, including through the following devices:

- the general arrangements for a planning agreement, regular updates between the parent ministry and the agency, covering mission, specific performance targets and budgets, and covering reporting arrangements;
- powers for the minister or other political authority to give policy or operational directives transparently (by public notice or tabling in the legislature);
- emergency powers – for the political executive to intervene and dismiss the governing board or the chief executive if and when there is a failure of management.

This organisational change also requires a thorough reflection on financial and personnel management, as well as on the means to maintain accountability to parent ministries, by stressing:

1. The rules that apply to the appointment and dismissal of top management and governing boards (when they exist).
2. The detailed definition of relaxed controls on arm's-length bodies.
3. The emphasis on results management. In OECD member countries, it has taken years for organisations to learn how to specify results and how to supplement attenuated management through reports with other forms of surveillance. It is indeed difficult to define measures which properly represent desired results, are comprehensive in their coverage and reasonably few in number.
4. The individual accountability of managers for the performance of the organisation – and, related to this – how to create a general culture of performance (through mechanisms of staff accountability for results).
5. Getting the parenting right: the framework law establishing the arm's-length body needs to define a clear formal line of accountability from the agency to the political executive. A parent ministry should be clearly responsible for transmitting policy requirements and monitoring implementation. But even with the right formal framework, the problem is to get the supervision right. This requires the parent ministry to have the necessary competence to administer a performance management system which requires capabilities akin to the operational management skills of the body itself.
6. Safeguarding the accountability of resources: Financial and management autonomy incur considerable risks: if arm's-length bodies are able to raise their own resources, they can reduce the ability of government to control its overall spending and impact on the economy, and they can disguise inefficiencies by extracting more revenues from their clients. When they are permitted to do their own borrowing or enter into leases, they may create contingent liabilities for government. Managerial autonomy and freedom from the general rules regarding the hiring and remuneration of staff can attract skilled staff away from core government and also increase opportunities for corruption and patronage.

Increasing managerial flexibility over budgets and staff does not mean abrogating central control: it means substituting a form of governance based on detailed external rules and individual transaction-based approvals with one based on strong external budget disciplines, monitoring, reporting and audit; and assurance through good systems of internal controls and internal audit. No government should delegate without being satisfied that it has both the internal and external framework for effective steering and control in place.

When the conditions for the successful autonomy of organisations are not met, government authorities should not hesitate to draw some organisations back into the traditional vertical ministerial hierarchy. Some PSUs could then become bureaus or field units within integrated departments. While this might still be feasible in China right now, OECD member countries have usually found it very difficult to draw an autonomous body back into traditional ministerial hierarchies. This is another reason for using caution in developing semi-autonomous government bodies for service delivery.

PSU reform will not exempt the Chinese Government from a reform of the budgeting and tax system. Giving PSUs additional autonomy in terms of raising revenues without improving the overall tax system is not sustainable. Fees and revenues raised from the public will be hidden taxes which will significantly increase social and regional inequities. In addition, an improved budget allocation system should help better decide on resource allocation to match policy priorities. The reform of PSUs could be an opportunity to contribute to the reform of the budgeting system.

Notes

1. This chapter was written by Elsa Pilichowski, Public Sector Management and Performance Division, Public Governance and Territorial Development Directorate, OECD. Part of the research was carried out through a joint activity with the World Bank leading to the organisation of a joint conference with the World Bank and the National Development and Reform Commission in Beijing on 23-24 March 2004, entitled "International Experience with Public Service Reform and China's PSU Reform". In addition, some of the information and data included in this chapter draws on draft papers by the World Bank. Since the writing of this paper, the World Bank report has been finalised and is entitled *China: Deepening Public Service Unit Reform to Improve Service Delivery*, Poverty Reduction and Economic Management Unit, East Asia and Pacific Region, The World Bank, 12 June 2005. Their collaboration is gratefully acknowledged.

2. The other three basic forms of legal persons are: enterprises (*qiye*), government organs (*jiguan*), and social organisations (*shetuan*). "Reform of China's Public Institutions: Retrospect and prospects", by project team on "Reform of China's Public Institutions and Development of China's Non-profit Organisations", National Centre for Science and Technology for Development, address on International Symposium on Reform of China's Public Institutions and Development of China's Non-profit Organisations, October 2003, Beijing.

3. *Id*.

4. Data are for end 2001.

5. Data from the Ministry of Personnel.

6. Most data were provided by Ministry of Finance.

7. See Gill, 2002; OECD, 2002a; OECD, 2004b.

8. See OECD, 2004c.

9. See Joumard, Kongsrud, Nam and Price, 2004; OECD, 2003e; OECD, 2002b.

10. See Laking, 2002.

11. See OECD, 2004c.

12. The following part of the conclusions largely draws from a paper written by Rob Laking for the OECD and the World Bank reviewing the experience of "agencification" in transition and developing economies, and entitled "Agencies: their Benefits and Risks", to be published in *OECD Journal on Budgeting*, Vol. 4, No. 4.

Bibliography

Gill, Derek (2002), "Signposting the Zoo – From Agencification to a More Principled Choice of Government Organisational Forms", *OECD Journal on Budgeting*, Vol. 2, No. 1.

Joumard I., P.M. Kongsrud, Y.S. Nam and R. Price (2004), "Enhancing the Effectiveness of Public Spending: Experience in OECD Countries", *OECD Economics Department Working Paper*, No. 380, OECD, Paris.

Laking, Rob (2002), "Distributed Public Governance: Principles for Control and Accountability of Agencies, Authorities and other Government Bodies", in *Distributed Public Governance*, OECD, Paris.

Laking, Rob (2005), "Agencies: their Benefits and Risks", *OECD Journal on Budgeting*, Vol. 4, No. 4, OECD, Paris.

National Bureau of Statistics (2002), *China Statistical Yearbook, 2002*, China Statistics Press.

OECD (2002a), *Distributed Public Governance*, OECD, Paris.

OECD (2002b), *Recent Privatising Trends in OECD Countries*, OECD, Paris.

OECD (2003a), *Education at a Glance*, OECD, Paris.

OECD (2003b), "Health Care Systems: Lessons from the Reform Experience", *OECD Health Working Papers*, No. 9, OECD, Paris.

OECD (2003c), *OECD Science, Technology and Industry Scoreboard*, OECD, Paris.

OECD (2003d), *Governance of Public Research*, OECD, Paris.

OECD (2003e), *Privatising State-owned Enterprises*, OECD, Paris.

OECD (2004a), *OECD Health Data 2004*, OECD, Paris.

OECD (2004b), "Public Sector Modernisation", *OECD Policy Brief*, OECD, Paris.

OECD (2004c), "Public Sector Modernisation: The Use of Market-type Mechanisms in the Provision of Government Services", GOV/PGC(2004)19.

World Bank (2005), *China: Deepening Public Service Unit Reform to Improve Service Delivery*, Poverty Reduction and Economic Management Unit, East Asia and Pacific Region, The World Bank, 12 June 2005.

PART I

Chapter 3

Fighting Corruption in China

Table of Contents

Summary 105

Fighting Corruption in China 107

  1. The problem of corruption 107
      1.1. Monetisation and redefinition of the public sphere 108
      1.2. Transition of the control mechanisms 108
      1.3. Emergence of non-state actors. 109
      1.4. New role for the state as an economic and social regulator 110
  2. Sanctioning corruption in the People's Republic of China 110
      2.1. Criminal law 111
      2.2. Enforcement of Party and public service discipline 115
      2.3. China's enforcement priorities and future challenges 117
  3. Preventing corruption and promoting integrity in the public service 119
      3.1. Prevention: an emerging issue 119
      3.2. Creating supportive conditions for integrity 120
      3.3. Supporting prevention: an emerging role for oversight bodies 124
  4. Conclusion 127

Notes 128

Bibliography 130

List of boxes

3.1. How big is the problem of corruption in China? 107
3.2. Building an ethics infrastructure 120
3.3. Managing Conflict of Interest in the Public Service:
     OECD Guidelines and Toolkit 123

Summary

Corruption has been openly recognised as an emerging challenge to China's economic and social reform. In 2002, then President Jiang Zemin defined "anti-corruption mechanisms" as a "major political task for the Party". Incumbent President Hu Jintao has declared the fight against corruption a priority on the political agenda of his government, as corruption threatens both the economic development and the political and social stability of the People's Republic of China (PRC). This chapter tracks the development of corruption, analyses the causes for its perceived or real expansion, as well as reforms and policies that the Chinese authorities have adopted in response.

The reasons for the growing corruption challenges faced by the Government of China are manifold: large financial transactions undertaken in the course of the restructuring process may lead, in the absence of functioning control mechanisms, to the siphoning off of assets; the shift from traditional control to systems of accountability does not pass without frictions; and the utility of material wealth has increased, given the availability of consumer goods and the perception of wealth as a symbol of success. China has undertaken a number of important efforts in developing its legal and institutional frameworks to more effectively curb corruption. While these efforts were initially focused on bolstering China's sanction system, more recently efforts have shifted towards strengthening preventive measures.

Reforms aimed at further deterring corruption have primarily focused on the penal regime as well as on the complementing disciplinary sanction system applicable for officials and Party members. The modifications of the penal law have redefined a number of offences, introduced some new offences such as illicit enrichment, increased the penalties, and established the criminal liability of legal persons. It is further expected that corruption will be added to the list of predicate offences for money laundering in the near future.

Gaps in enforcement, reflected in low conviction rates and a growing number of citizens absconding with ill-gotten assets, continue to hamper the deterring effect of the sanction system. The harsh penalties, including death penalty, which characterize the penal provisions on corruption do not compensate this gap, and the uneven treatment of active and passive bribery – the latter being handled considerably stricter – detracts from the success of the current anti-corruption strategy. In the aim to enhance enforcement of the penal law with regard to corruption, the Chinese Government has established a number of specialized law enforcement bodies and increasingly engages in international cooperation. Future improvements appear to require foremost strengthening of the judiciary namely in terms of skills. The effectiveness of sanctions as a means to deter corruption would further benefit from equal attention attached to the prosecution of all actors involved in corruption schemes, including bribe payers, legal persons, and those involved in the laundering of proceeds of corruption. The PRC's recent joining as full member of the ADB/OECD Anti-Corruption Initiative for Asia-Pacific and its consequent commitment to implement the Anti-Corruption Action Plan for Asia-Pacific in matters related to both prevention and prosecution of corruption is expected to foster and fertilise the reform process through experience-sharing and policy dialogue and, as such, to bolster China's domestic anti-corruption framework.

Criminalizing, detecting and prosecuting corruption has been the primary focus of China's anti-corruption policy and much less effort has been made to examine the sources of corruption and to develop preventative measures. More gradually, and particularly over the last five years, more attention has been paid to reviewing risk areas prone to corruption, and creating conducive conditions and improving management arrangements that encourage ethical behaviour and make corruption harder to commit and easier to detect.

Prevention can nowadays be considered as an equal priority. Prevention measures have been included in a wide range of contemporary policy initiatives, in particular promoting professionalism in human resources management, reforming financial management and closing loopholes, particularly in risk areas such as public procurement and contract management, as well as simplifying procedures on administrative licensing. Corruption prevention has also become a key function of China's supreme oversight bodies, particularly the Ministry of Supervision, the Supreme People's Procuratorate and the China National Audit Office.

Fighting Corruption in China[1]

1. The problem of corruption

If often commented, the corruption phenomenon is difficult to circumvent. Data are approximate and rare: corrupt acts are by their very nature hidden, and are not easily turned into statistics (*cf.* Box 3.1). But, opinions converge on the fact that corruption has increased in the era of post-Mao economic reforms in terms of the incidence, the number of people and the layers of authority involved and the financial scale of abuse. It affects departments in charge of the domestic economy and foreign economic relations, but also the judicial, health, educational and military spheres. As articles from the press reveal, there is both grand corruption (which involves senior officials, major decisions or contracts, and the exchange of large sums of money) and petty corruption (low-level officials, the provision of routine services and goods, and small sums of money).

> Box 3.1. **How big is the problem of corruption in China?**
>
> A statistical analysis of cases of corruption involving officials at the provincial level and above investigated between 1978 and 2002 shows an increase of the corruption level at the end of the 1980s and the beginning of the 1990s, especially in the coastal areas (Guo, 2003).
>
> "According to a report made by Zhang Siqing, China's chief procurator, from 1993 to 1997, the procuratorate organs of the country investigated 387 352 cases of corruption, involving 54 805 cadres (among them 16 117 were Party and government officials, 17 214 judicial officials and 8 144 public security personnel, 13 330 economic management officials)" (Zhang, 1998).
>
> There seems to have been a sharp increase in particular towards the end of the 1980s. The International Country Risk Guide (ICRG) corruption index shows an increase in the level of corruption between 1988 and 1990, with no improvement afterwards between 1990 and 1999.
>
> Attempts to assess the economic cost of corruption have produced impressive orders of magnitude. Different definitions of corruption and different methodologies lead to quite different results. According to Minxin Pei (Pei, 2002), in aggregate, estimates of the magnitude of corruption range from 3-5% of GDP. Kick-backs from government purchases and construction projects account for a large share (about 1.5% of GDP).

We propose to look at the problem of corruption in perspective of four dimensions of the transition process in China: the monetisation and the redefinition of the public sphere, the transition of control mechanisms, the emergence of non-state actors and the new regulatory role of the state.

1.1. Monetisation and redefinition of the public sphere

Before the reforms, the development of corruption on a large scale was limited by the fact that money was not a real means of exchange: between firms, it was more like an accounting device, and for end users it could not always allow access to desired goods. In market economies, as money is hard to trace – in particular to the extent that China has remained a cash economy – readily transferable and easily changed into the goods desired, it is an ideal medium of exchange in corrupt transactions. Under the planned economy regime, money was strictly controlled. It was difficult, for instance, for a firm to stock cash. Companies had suppliers and buyers imposed on them. And as for consumers, goods were in scarce supply and the distribution of large goods such as housing was controlled by the state. Therefore, money might not buy what one wanted. Material goods, such as meat, cartons of cigarettes, fountain pens or rare Chinese medicine like tiger bones, were common payments for favours. Very often corrupt deals were barter deals. But whereas the functioning of the economy and its related complex division of labour was sustained by planning, no such device existed of course for corrupt deals. Thus, it was difficult to find the double coincidence of interests necessary to complete a corrupt transaction. Agents who held high-level positions had access to larger networks and were therefore in a position to complete longer strings of barter deals.

An important dimension of the transition process has been the separation of enterprises from the administration. The existence of special links between government departments and affiliated enterprises were normal under the planned economy regime. After almost 25 years of reform, a lot of progress has been made in this regard. The administration interferes much less in many competitive sectors and a lot of power has been transferred to macro-management departments such as the Ministry of Finance and the National Development and Reform Commission. The creation of the State-owned Assets Supervision Administration Commission (SASAC) in 2003 has been an important step toward clarifying the relationship between the government and state-owned enterprises.[2] Yet, formal or informal links between state-owned enterprises and administrative departments remain, especially for the network industries and at the sub-national level (Guo and Angang, 2004), as profits are an important source of revenue. The pursue of sector or local interests may lead to forms of state capture or corruption.

Finally, after decades of planned economy, the development of a market economy gave many people the wrong impression that there is a market for everything, including public power. With this impression in mind, officials trade their powers for private gains, and business people pay officials. They deem the corrupt deal between them as a fair trade.

1.2. Transition of the control mechanisms

Actors take advantage of corruption opportunities when these are not "closed" by appropriate social and institutional controls. The reforms on the organisation of the economy and the reforms of decentralization were not accompanied by reforms of the accountability and control systems.

First, the reforms and the related social evolutions weakened the former system of social control. Generally speaking, we can say that a system of control has two dimensions: an institutional dimension (i.e. government bodies in charge of audits and controls, corresponding procedures, etc.) and a moral dimension (representations of society and of the state, values conveyed in public discourses, etc.).

At the basis of the institutional control system were the Communist Party of China (CPC) and its penetration into every aspect of society. It could be said to be a system of control by proximity (as opposed to external control). This system was complemented by tightly controlled discourses conveying communist ideals. For instance, private ownership and personal enrichment were condemned, so any ostentatious display of wealth would lead to unwanted attention and criticism.

The reforms weakened both dimensions of the control system. As the economic reforms created pockets of unregulated economic activity, they also contributed to the evolution of the control system as well as of the political system. The decentralization dimension of the economic reforms also contributed to the weakening of existing controls, as local controls were insufficient and their articulation with central powers uncertain. At the same time, following Deng Xiaoping's exhortations to enrich, it became acceptable once again to enjoy material comforts. Visible growing inequalities weakened the credibility of equalitarian discourses calling for individual sacrifices for the collective good.

Second, China has been slow in moving towards a modern system of accountability and control. Before the Communist regime, external supervision of the administration was weak, as in many developing countries with market economies. Contrary to the Western culture of political accountability, whose emphasis has long been placed on external checks and balances of power and the rule of law, in traditional Chinese society and the People's Republic of China (PRC) alike, there has been an over-emphasis on individual moral standards on the one hand and a serious lack of external checks of power on the other. Since the beginning of the economic reforms, the strengthening of other circuits of control has been very slow.

Recent newspaper articles, however, clearly indicate a new will of the leadership to strengthen the role of the China National Audit Office (CNAO).[3] In addition, several measures have been taken to institutionalize the control mechanisms and to a certain extent the checks and balances mechanisms internal to the Party structure.

1.3. Emergence of non-state actors

In the planned-economy regime, enterprises were productive units fulfilling the plan's targets. The notion of profit did not exist. As mentioned above, the means of exchange were limited as were spending opportunities too. Therefore "in the 60s and 70s in China, agents of the production or marketing units wined and dined the representatives of the supplier or buyer units and gave them free samples or products at below costs. (…) in the past, factory managers mainly had to keep their suppliers happy". After the beginning of the reforms, "[factory managers] had to please representatives from the licensing board, the power company, the water works, the telephone services, public security, the railroad company and any other units whose services they would need in their everyday operations. (…) To ensure smooth operation of their business, administrators had to please or bribe not one or two but a number of different clients" (Julia, 1997).

How can we explain this development? Enterprises were now seen as organisations generating profits, with the help and participation of a number of associated services which consider that they should receive a share of these profits. Of course they are remunerated for their services in the first place (either directly by the company or by the state), but it is as if the "price structure" was not accepted as such. These draw on the alleged profits of the company are considered as a way to adjust the existing price structure. So in a way, this could be explained both by the representation of enterprises and profits and by the shaping of an "acceptable" price and remuneration structure. Adjusting prices indeed takes time: the service provided by such or such a person may in fact be of considerable value for the activity leading to profit.

1.4. *New role for the state as an economic and social regulator*

The process of transition and economic development has increased the state's regulatory role in the economic and in the social sphere. Some of these regulations, such as environmental norms or labour norms, respond to issues that become more pressing with the development process and receive more attention. Previously, problems were solved locally, through trust-based relationships. The development process increases the flows of goods and people as well as the complexity of exchanges, and distends the link between the producer and the consumer. Therefore, risks increase and a need for regulations to protect consumers arises. The transition to a market-driven economy also creates a need for regulations that support the functioning of the markets (*e.g.* regulation of intellectual property rights or of competition). These regulations protect enterprises and their properties in a socially acceptable optimal manner.

These regulations compensate for market failures: *i.e.* individual behaviours co-ordinated via market mechanisms leading to a sub-optimal solution. These regulations therefore benefit society as a whole, but may induce free-riding behaviour from individuals who seek to take advantage of the situation.[4] The temptation to free-ride on the part of individuals exposes officials in charge of the enforcement of such regulations to corruption. Therefore, the implementation of these new norms, strongly pushed for by the international community, provides numerous opportunities of corruption.

In OECD member countries, the enforcement of such regulations is always based on a system which mixes, at varying degrees, state rule and enforcement and the involvement of advocacy groups or groups of interest that are committed to their enforcement. In China, for different reasons from one area of operation to another, and at varying degrees, this "intermediary layer of civil society" is still underdeveloped.

2. Sanctioning corruption in the People's Republic of China

Criminal and disciplinary sanctions are among the most commonly applied means to combat corruption worldwide. This is particularly true in China where these repressive instruments have been the primary means to address the problem of corruption. As in most countries, China for this purpose has established more than one sanction system: penal sanctions, which are applicable to any citizen, are complemented by disciplinary and other administrative and economic sanctions. Disciplinary sanctions target a limited scope of addressees and are used to enforce specific behavioural norms linked to their particular position and role. In China, such disciplinary mechanisms exist foremost for public employees and CPC members. In recent years, administrative and economic sanctions against legal persons were introduced on a trial basis in certain provinces as a third instrument to deter corrupt practices. As in most countries, penal, disciplinary and administrative and economic sanctions may be applied cumulatively in China if the respective conditions are fulfilled.

Three main actors share the task of enforcing these rules in China: The People's Procuratorate and Courts implement the criminal law; the Ministry of Supervision is responsible for the discipline of officials; and the CPC's Central Commission for Discipline

Inspection is in charge of enforcing the discipline of Party members. In addition, a number of other institutions have recently been set up, mostly tasked with combating corruption at specific administrative sub-levels or responsible for investigating certain types of corruption. Despite the distinctness of these law enforcement bodies at legislative and organisational levels, their operations and organisation are closely interwoven in practice. They share information, offices, and sometimes even staff, and their competencies and tasks sometimes overlap, the latter being a potential source of confusion or conflicting enforcement practice.

2.1. Criminal law

Chinese criminal law has covered certain forms of corruption for many years. Over the last few decades, these provisions repeatedly underwent reform. The rhythm of updating relevant statutes has recently accelerated with the broadening of the coverage of illegal acts and the introduction of new legislation aimed at making it more difficult to hide illegal gains.

2.1.1. Penal provisions directly tackling corruption

Penalization of corruption in modern China goes back to the Ordinance Regarding Anti-Corruption and Bribery, passed in 1952. Since then, the penal provisions regarding corruption have been repeatedly extended so that a dozen categories of corruption are today delineated in the criminal code and other legal provisions. Major reforms took place in 1979 with the enactment of the Criminal Law, and again in 1982 and 1988.[5] In 1993, the Law against Unfair Competition was passed, followed by other relevant statutes in 1995 and 1996.[6]

These reforms introduced new offences in reaction to emerging forms of corrupt behaviour and abuse of authority. They have thus contributed to the continuous expansion of the number of offences and have broadened the range of culpable behaviour; some provisions now exist in parallel in various statutes. Combined with the difficulties which arise in the context of economic transition with regards to the changing nature of what may be defined as a "public employee" under economic reform, the implementation of such provisions has become more complex, leaving wide leeway for interpretation, and creating opportunities for inconsistencies and loopholes.

Compared to policies developed by OECD member countries, these statutes considerably differ in three respects. These require the attention of the Chinese authorities in light of future reform efforts and their endeavour to comply with international anti-corruption standards, such as the UN Convention against Corruption or the ADB/OECD Anti-Corruption Action Plan for Asia-Pacific. First, the severity of the punishment for corruption in China, which has been successively increased by recent reforms, by far exceeds the standard in OECD member countries. Active bribery may be punished with lifetime imprisonment and passive bribery or solicitation of bribes in China may entail the death penalty (see below). For other forms of abuse of public authority, penalized under regulations on graft or embezzlement, penalties up to lifetime imprisonment apply.

Second, Chinese legislation penalizes passive bribery – i.e. the solicitation or acceptance of a bribe by a public employee or a Party official – much more severely than active bribery, i.e. the giving of bribes. For example, accepting RMB 5 000 (about EUR 450) in bribes is a crime, while twice the amount must be involved for the giving of a bribe to constitute a criminal act. Paying solicited bribes when involving small sums is even excluded from punishment under certain conditions. This uneven treatment of the two parties involved has been an expression of the commonly held view that those who bribe have no choice other than to do so. It is also the result of the peculiar circumstances of economic transition: there has been a prevalent belief that, for reasons of economic efficiency, standards should be stricter on Party members and state officials than on the emerging private sector. In this spirit, Chinese legislation foresees bribers who come forward and report their wrongdoing to be exempted from prosecution, at the exception of certain very serious cases (Li Jingrong, 2004). As a consequence, few bribery prosecutions in China have so far directly involved large multinationals or joint ventures with Chinese and foreign capital: an expatriate employee of a multinational accused of paying bribes can negotiate an exemption from prosecution in exchange for his co-operation in what local authorities deem the more important issue, *i.e.* the prosecution of the governmental official alleged to have received the bribes.

Third, the same holds true with regard to accounting standards that apply to the public and private sectors. Across public organisations, standards are stricter on public firms than on private firms. The offence of accounting violations is defined as corruption (*weifan caijing jilu*) when committed by public organisations and public firms and their executives, as such entailing particularly harsh sanctions; on the other hand, the same type of violation when committed by privately owned firms and their employees is not defined as corruption, thus less severe penalties apply. For sure, the confines of "public organisations" have expanded over time and the term now covers state and collective firms contracted to individual managers, joint-stock firms where the state or the collective has a major share, and Chinese-foreign joint ventures where the Chinese shares are owned by the state or by collectives. However, the offence does not cover all types of economic entities, thus leading to differences in the level of sanctions applicable to private firms on the one hand, and public organisations, on the other.

Recent reforms, including the introduction of criminal liability of legal persons and of administrative sanctions against legal persons on a trial basis in certain provinces (Jiangsu Province and Zhejiang Province in Eastern China; Chongqing Municipality and Sichuan Province in Southwest China; and Guangxi Zhuang Autonomous Region in Southern China), may however be a sign that the PRC is gradually focusing more on active bribery. Enterprises and even government units may now be fined for active bribery. Also, a representative of an involved company holding direct responsibilities may face criminal charges for the company's illicit action; sanctions include fines, detention or a prison term of up to five years.[7] A recent initiative to tackle bribery by means of blacklisting in the construction industry, which is thought to be the most corruption-prone sector in China, is also being considered by some policy makers in the state as well as the Party apparatus as a potential turning point in the fight against serious corruption in this sector.[8] Depending on the severity of the corruption case for which the company has been sanctioned, it may be temporarily or permanently debarred from access to the local construction market. However, to evaluate the effectiveness of this system, it will need to run for some time and would ideally need to be introduced nationwide and applied to other sectors as well.

2.1.2. Provisions that indirectly deter corruption

With a view to reinforcing the criminal provisions aimed at sanctioning corruption, China has regularly introduced new types of offences. While bribery is still a major target, it is no longer the main target of China's criminal law in the matter. New offences such as graft, illicit enrichment and money laundering, have been established to address more effectively the corruption problem.

Article 11(1) of the Supplementary Regulations on Suppression of Corruption and Bribery (1988) and Article 395(1) of the Criminal Code thus penalize the possession of unexplainable wealth: an official whose property or expenses obviously exceed his or her legal income must explain its sources. Unexplained excess property is considered to be illegally acquired and may be confiscated; the offence may further entail imprisonment of up to five years. The provision also covers so-called "expenses", a popular scheme of bribery in China that consists for instance of offering expensive education of an official's children abroad.

A new bill, which is to be passed in 2005, also aims at adding corruption as a predicate offence to money laundering. The massive flow of illegally gained assets out of the country is a major problem in China. An estimated USD 24 billion of illegally gained assets is laundered every year,[9] and the amounts brought secretly out of the country have kept rising. An important share of these assets has originated in corruption and embezzlement. Cases of clandestine departure of the suspects have raised particular concern, especially in light of an unprecedented exodus of Chinese officials who have brought embezzled assets out of the country over recent years. In the first half of 2003 alone, more than 8 300 officials supposedly fled the country and another 6 500 disappeared within China to escape prosecution for corruption and embezzlement; roughly two-thirds of the fugitives were senior executives of state-owned enterprises.[10] Between USD 8.75 and 50 billion were supposedly brought out of the country in recent years.[11]

According to analysts, this phenomenon is being facilitated by the Chinese financial environment which today still makes it relatively easy to transfer, hide and launder ill-gotten gains, and by an underground banking system, anonymous accounts, outdated accounting methods and the lack of record-keeping which impede effective supervision of financial transactions. Regulations that criminalize money laundering, contained in Article 191 of the Criminal Code, have indeed so far only applied to assets originating from narcotics trafficking, organised crime or smuggling – but not corruption. As a result of this debate, a new bill which is expected to enter into force in 2005 will add corruption as a predicate offence to money laundering. Furthermore, the Bank of China, which shares responsibility for banking supervision with the State Administration of Foreign Exchange and the China Banking Regulatory Commission, set up the Anti-Money Laundering Supervising and Analyzing Centre in July 2004. The establishment of a Financial Intelligence Unit is also planned. Under the present legislation, Chinese financial institutions are held responsible for handling suspicious financial transfers and for holding funds of suspicious origin in their clients' bank accounts.[12] Banks are obliged to report suspicious or large foreign exchange transactions. Since 2000, depositors must use their real names when opening bank accounts; there are yet no plans to apply similar rules to existing accounts. However, other financial institutions such as security firms and insurance companies are yet to be subjected to similar obligations.

2.1.3. Criminal law enforcement

Enforcement of the criminal law is mainly governed by the Criminal Procedure Law of the PRC and the Law on the Organisation of People's Procuratorates. The People's Procuratorates and Courts, organised at central and different local levels, are responsible for executing these statutes. This direct responsibility of the Procuratorates for the investigation of corruption cases constitutes an exception to the rule that investigations into criminal cases in China are conducted by the police organs organised under the

Ministry of Public Security. However, the procuratorates' anti-corruption and anti-bribery working bureaus are, for technically difficult investigations, supported by the Ministry of Public Security's specialized Economic Crime Investigation Department. For the investigation of major corruption cases or cases that involve senior government officials, the Supreme People's Procuratorate established the General Bureau against Corruption in November 1995. Such politically sensitive cases involving high-level officials or directors of state-owned enterprises are not handled by the People's courts, however. Although falling under criminal law, such cases are, after initial investigation, handed over to the CPC's Central Commission for Discipline Inspection. If sufficient evidence is found, the Central Commission for Discipline Inspection forwards them on to the Politburo Standing Committee of the CPC.

Very low conviction rates compared to the number of initiated investigations into corruption, and the stagnation of these numbers over the last decade, suggest that the current framework for law enforcement is still to some extent inadequate in effectively addressing corruption and bribery offences. Hu Angang of Beijing's Qinghua University estimates that only 10-20% of corruption cases are solved, and only 6.6% of Party officials who are disciplined for corruption receive any criminal punishment (Hu, 2001). According to statistics published by the Supreme People's Procuratorate, more than 42 000 cases of corruption involving officials were investigated in 2004, down from 64 000 cases in 1995. In the five years between 1998 and 2002, 83 300 cases led to convictions on corruption charges – roughly one conviction per 500 000 citizens per year.

A number of reasons have been given to explain the rather low effectiveness of the judiciary and law enforcement organs. Although the Criminal Procedure Law requires the authorities to investigate all alleged crimes, the decision whether or not the authorities take up investigations upon allegations of fraud and corruption appears in practice to depend on other, less reliable factors, including for instance the concerned officers' assumptions on potential support for the investigation from their superiors. This uncertainty and consequent reluctance is reported to be particularly strong when it comes to allegations of corrupt behaviour involving Party members or high-ranking officials.[13] Another reason ironically seems to be the existence of other sanction and enforcement mechanisms. For instance, investigations by the Party's Commission for Discipline Inspection and its subordinate commissions or by the government supervisory departments (see below) can warn the suspect and give him/her sufficient time to destroy evidence and cover up their tracks.

The international aspect of a growing number of corruption cases in China – nearly a third of the approximately 83 000 cases that led to convictions between 1998 and 2002 – represents another serious obstacle to criminal prosecution, as effective investigation and prosecution requires the involvement of foreign jurisdictions. Mostly, these cases involve officials who have fled the country with embezzled assets. Attempts to repatriate the offenders and the assets have met with little success. Although China has concluded agreements on extradition with 19 countries and on mutual legal assistance with 24 countries, no such agreements exist with Australia, Canada, the United States or other highly industrialized countries which represent the main destinations of higher ranking offenders. In 2003, China repatriated fewer than 600 suspects – 14 times less than the number that absconded in the same period.[14]

Consequently, improving the procedures for mutual legal assistance has become a key reform priority in China. China ratified the UN Convention against Transnational Organised Crime in September 2003 and signed the UN Convention against Corruption in December 2003. Both instruments place a strong emphasis on mutual legal assistance, extradition of suspects and repatriation of proceeds, and it is assumed that this aspect has been of central concern in the decision to adhere to these conventions.[15] China has further endorsed the Anti-Corruption Action Plan for Asia-Pacific in April 2005 in the framework of the ADB/OECD Anti-Corruption Initiative. Through the full membership in this Initiative, which brings together 25 Asian and Pacific countries, China aims to strengthen the exchange of experience and develop co-operation with countries from the region. Other recent reforms aimed at enhancing the effectiveness of law enforcement primarily tackle the lack of competence within the procuratorates and the courts and similar measures to enhance the professionalism and ethics of the judiciary.

Whether or not the enforcement of anti-corruption legislation bears fruit in the coming years will depend to a great extent on the concerned authorities' ability to react and rectify these shortcomings. As an indirect impact thereof, increased efficiency and ethical behaviour within law enforcement will also contribute to reducing the citizens' reluctance to report corruption cases.

Law enforcement appears to heavily depend on information from citizens, with about 80% of the investigations into corruption cases reportedly triggered by their allegations.[16] Corruption and Bribery Report Centres, established since 1979 to receive and handle such testimonies, along with more recently introduced 24-hour reporting hotlines, testify to the authorities' acknowledgement of the importance of public reporting for effective detection. Furthermore, several provisions aim to ensure the protection of reporters against retaliation, for instance by allowing them to request the confidentiality of their identity.[17] An additional regulation on whistle-blower protection relating to major infrastructure projects was enacted in 2001. The proper functioning of these mechanisms is dubitable, however. Both Chinese and international media frequently report about citizens who, having disclosed allegations and evidence of corruption, faced retaliation by the local or even the central government. Combined with the above-mentioned uncertainty about the likelihood of an actual follow-up to the report by the responsible authorities, these factors are not likely to encourage citizens to report their suspicions of corruption.

2.2. Enforcement of Party and public service discipline

While penal sanctions await any person who has committed a criminal offence, citizens holding public office are furthermore subject to rules of conduct related to this position. These rules usually set higher standards of conduct than the criminal law, and applicable sanctions can be added to potential penal sanctions. As in most other countries, the Chinese Government has enacted disciplinary rules and sanctions for officials. In addition, China runs a specific disciplinary regime for members of the CPC.

2.2.1. Disciplinary sanctions concerning officials

Codes of conduct and related disciplinary sanctions applicable to China's officials are laid down in a number of statutes and regulations on ethical conduct, embezzlement, income disclosure and gifts.[18] Violation of these rules may entail administrative warnings, the recording of a demerit or major demerit, demotion, dismissal from office or discharge. In the aim to further bolster respect of the codes, some cities and provinces have recently complemented these sanctions by financial incentives: pension schemes allow for the reduction or loss of pension if an official has been disciplined during his or her incumbency.[19]

Moreover, some segments of the public administration and the judiciary are subject to particular codes of conduct in addition to those applicable to officials in general. In June 2003, the Supreme People's Court issued a code of conduct for Chinese judges in order to strengthen corruption prevention in the judiciary. Corruption and unethical behaviour in the judiciary have been of growing public concern in the recent past and is seen to considerably hamper the effectiveness of law enforcement. The code prohibits corruption and bribe-taking as well as the involvement of judges in business for profits. To avoid conflict-of-interest situations, the code also proscribes the acceptance of gifts and private meetings with parties or lawyers involved in on-going legal proceedings. In light of their specific tasks and working environment, the establishment of such specific codes of behaviour for certain categories of public servants, in particular the judiciary, can prove necessary and useful. However, as explained in the section on corruption prevention, experience in OECD member countries shows that, in order to avoid contradictory and overlapping provisions, such measures are best embedded in a comprehensive ethical framework covering all sectors of the public service.

The enforcement of discipline regulations applicable to officials and the investigation of potential cases of misconduct fall mainly under the responsibility of the Ministry of Supervision and its subordinate bodies. The Ministry of Supervision is subordinate to the State Council and its responsibility for supervision work applies throughout the country. Its central body is directly in charge of exercising supervision over departments under the State Council and their officials and of staff of large state-owned enterprises. It is further responsible for supervising the governments of the provinces, autonomous regions and municipalities which fall under the direct control of the central government. The ministry has further dispatched supervisory bodies and personnel to various ministries, commissions and other government departments.

The investigative procedures, regulated since 1997 by the Law on Administrative Supervision, are quite similar to those applicable to investigations under penal law: a report system, including hotlines and public hearings, enables citizens to file charges against officials. Most forms of reports are accepted, including those submitted anonymously. The ministry is required by its statutes to follow up on every complaint that it receives and, if a preliminary inquiry produces sufficient elements of proof, to open a formal investigation. Citizens exposing major violations of laws and discipline to the ministry may be rewarded, and a law exists to protect them against retaliation. However, exposing such violations to the public may on the contrary entail repression, as various cases have testified.

In addition to reports from the public, the Ministry of Supervision itself inspects the due implementation of laws and the respect of disciplinary rules both on a regular basis and by means of unannounced checks. Investigative means at the disposal of supervisory organs embrace the access to information on bank accounts of investigated officials or departments. Supervisory organs may also request People's Courts to temporarily freeze deposits of suspected personnel at banks or other financial institutions in an effort to prevent the transfer of suspicious assets to foreign jurisdictions.

Unlike under the penal procedure that separates the investigative and judiciary functions, the Ministry of Supervision is empowered to inspect, investigate, judge and directly execute punishment of the official involved. Such an integration of investigative and judiciary functions in disciplinary procedures is an exception to the principle of an independent institution exercising the judiciary role, but similar schemes also exist in many other countries. Compared to these other countries, however, the disciplinary sanction system in China has particular weight.

2.2.2. Disciplinary sanctions concerning members of the CPC

Similarly to officials, members of the CPC are subject to specific disciplinary codes and sanctions, laid down in the CPC's Constitution and other statutes. In February 2004, the Regulations on Inner-Party Supervision of the Communist Party of China and the Regulations on the Punishment for the Discipline Violation of the Party updated the existing rules with a particular view to combating corruption. Violations of the above-mentioned rules can entail a warning, a serious warning, removal from Party posts, or probation within and expulsion from the Party.[20]

The enforcement of these regulations among Party members is the responsibility of the CPC's Central Commission for Discipline Inspection. The Commission reports to the National Party Congress – the CPC organ of supreme power – and works under the CPC Central Committee. Its set-up, competencies, and procedures are governed by the Constitution and other statutes of the CPC. Article 44 of the Constitution of the CPC explicitly assigns the Central Commission for Discipline Inspection to co-ordinate the Party's work against corruption.

Cases of minor violation of Party rules are usually dealt with by the general membership meeting of the concerned Party branch; cases considered to be important or complex, and cases which would entail the expulsion of a member from the Party, fall under the responsibility of the Central Commission for Discipline Inspection and must be handled at least at county level. Decisions with regard to disciplinary sanctions against a member of the Central Committee or of a local committee are subject to approval by the Party committee of one level above the concerned body so as to reduce conflict-of-interest situations or the abuse of the Party's sanction regime. In cases of serious violation of the criminal law by a member of the Central Committee, the decision is taken by the Political Bureau of the Central Committee.

The Central Commission for Discipline Inspection and the Ministry of Supervision co-operate closely; they share information that any of the offices has received, and at certain levels, also share offices and staff. Similar to the organisational structure of the Ministry of Supervision, the Commission for Discipline Inspection is organised hierarchically; subordinate commissions are set up at various levels of the CPC.

2.3. China's enforcement priorities and future challenges

Major corruption cases have been extensively publicised in recent years by the largely state-controlled media. However, it remains uncertain whether or not China's efforts to combat corruption and bribery bear fruit. Although prosecutors in China receive and investigate a large number of allegations of bribery, the conviction rate remains relatively low. Generally speaking, despite rather harsh rules and the continuous expansion of offences covering a wide range of culpable acts, corruption seems to remain widespread in China.

One explanation may lie in the fact that the supporting legal and regulatory framework for combating corruption in China is in rapid transition, as outdated legislation is replaced by new legislation with a view to better reflect the country's evolving market economy system. The reform process has also resulted in new laws broadening the range of individuals culpable for corruption and the range of culpable behaviour. More laws are in the making, including a bill that would establish corruption as a predicate offence for the purpose of implementing the anti-money laundering legislation. These changes represent an attempt to more effectively deter corruption of state and Party officials. However, the legislation may sometimes be inconsistent, both internally and with respect to other relevant legislation, often leaving wide leeway at the law enforcement level for interpretation as regards what constitutes corrupt behaviour.

Loopholes or provisions that may present potential for misuse can be observed as well. For example, while China's legislation sanctions the non-respect of accounting procedures by state-owned companies and joint ventures, there are no provisions clearly prohibiting company management from placing relatives in charge of book-keeping and financial disbursement. As managerial autonomy has extended to most personal appointments, the practice seems to have become common since the 1990s. Therefore, streamlining legislation addressing corruption and related offences such as those with regard to accounting, as done by OECD member countries over the last decade, would appear as a necessity.

Another explanation may lie in the two main considerations that guide China's enforcement policy, one of which is political, the other economic. First, corruption committed by public servants or the political elite is seen as seriously endangering the stability of the government and of the CPC. Second, while most countries' policies understand corruption itself to be a barrier to domestic and foreign investment, many policy makers in China still consider that the main barrier in this respect is in bringing charges against those who bribe state and Party officials and that such a policy may be a potential impediment to private sector development. Both considerations result in a strategy which seeks to crack down harshly on high-level public corruption cases, prioritizes repressive rather than preventive means, and prosecutes the receiver rather than the giver of the bribe.

The priority which is given to the sanctioning of officials rather than those that give the bribe in business related transactions, i.e. local and foreign business representatives and companies, is illustrated by the relatively larger number of laws, regulations and enforcement policies and institutions targeting the sanctioning of misconduct by officials as compared to similar rules governing the private sector. Furthermore, sanctions applicable to officials for accepting bribes are considerably higher than those applicable to a potential giver of a bribe. The predominance of sanctions handed down to officials and Party members is also expressed by the dominant role of the disciplinary mechanism in comparison to the criminal justice system. In practice, the role of the disciplinary mechanism is drastically reflected in the statistics: in 2003, about 175 000 officials were punished for lack of discipline – about 10 times the number of criminal convictions, and this including all Chinese citizens.[21] A similar relation exists between the number of cases handled by the Party Committees for Discipline Inspection and of those handled by the procuratorates.

Until the late 1980s, most OECD member countries followed a similar approach of prioritizing the prosecution of bribe takers rather than bribe givers in business-related transactions. Recognizing that a comprehensive and effective anti-corruption strategy needs, however, to pay equal attention to the giver and the recipient of the bribe, they have started to address both passive and active bribery through preventive and repressive tools. Reforms undertaken by OECD member countries in the framework of the OECD Convention on Combating Bribery of Foreign Public Officials in International Business Transactions of 1997 are illustrative of this trend. In China, in terms of repressive tools, the effective sanctioning of active bribery requires, on the one hand, a declared change in China's enforcement policy and, on the other, needs to be facilitated by the introduction and/or consequent implementation of a certain number of legal provisions, in particular the responsibility of legal persons for corruption. Also, preventive tools would need to focus on the emerging private sector and, as a priority, seek to deter bribery in public procurement by means of setting up transparent and accountable institutional structures and laws effectively prohibiting this type of bribery. The recent initiative to blacklist and exclude from public contracts in the construction sector companies that have been convicted of corruption is clearly an encouraging step in this direction.

Finally, in light both of China's serious concerns about the massive outflow of illegally gained assets to foreign jurisdictions and of China's rapidly growing role in international trade, China's fight against corruption would clearly benefit from a stronger involvement in a certain number of regional and international initiatives, including the OECD Convention on Combating Bribery of Foreign Public Officials in International Business Transactions and its related instruments, and the UN Convention against Corruption, as these instruments would allow China to better tackle the source of corruption and, by establishing close working relations with foreign jurisdictions in terms of mutual legal assistance in the OECD and Asia-Pacific regions, the outflow of assets. In this context, the Chinese Government's decision in April 2005 to endorse the Anti-Corruption Action Plan for Asia-Pacific in the framework of the ADB/OECD Anti-Corruption Initiative for Asia-Pacific can be viewed as a very positive development.

3. Preventing corruption and promoting integrity in the public service

3.1. *Prevention: an emerging issue*

Detecting and prosecuting corruption has been the centrepiece of China's anti-corruption policy to set an example and deter those inclined toward future corrupt practices. While China has developed a complex legal framework for criminalizing, investigating and prosecuting numerous forms of corruption, and also for disciplining misconduct, much less effort has been made to examine the sources of corruption and to develop preventative measures. However, more gradually, and particularly over the last five years, more attention has been paid to reviewing risk areas prone to corruption, and to creating conducive conditions and improving management arrangements that encourage ethical behaviour and make corruption harder to commit and easier to detect.

Prevention became an integral part of the anti-corruption strategy in the second half of the 1990s[22] and recent government actions have indicated that it can nowadays be considered as an equal priority.[23] Prevention measures have been included in a wide range of new policy initiatives, in particular promoting professionalism in human resources management,[24] reforming financial management (*e.g.* by separating the collection and spending of public money),[25] closing loopholes, particularly in risk areas such as public procurement and contract management, simplifying procedures on administrative licensing[26] as well as using new technologies to widen accessibility to public information.[27]

China has a long experience in developing and testing economic reform measures in selected cities and provinces and subsequently transposing successful initiatives to the national level. In line with this practice, dedicated measures for promoting integrity and preventing corruption have been gradually introduced in selected cities that played a "pilot" role. When proved successful, these measures have been rapidly applied in other cities and provinces across the country. The Chinese Government successfully used this method to test anti-corruption and integrity measures and to approve them by law.

Separate measures may not produce the expected results as illustrated by the experience of OECD member countries. In order to ensure consistency, comprehensive strategies in OECD member countries have integrated distinct integrity measures into solid building blocks of a sound "ethics infrastructure", that ensures the synergy between the institutions, systems and mechanisms for promoting integrity and preventing corruption in the public service.

Box 3.2. **Building an ethics infrastructure**

A well-functioning ethics infrastructure supports a public sector environment which encourages high standards of behaviour. Each function and element is a separate, important building block, but the individual elements should be complementary and mutually reinforcing. The elements interact to achieve the necessary synergy to become a coherent and integrated infrastructure. The elements can be categorized according to the main functions they serve – control, guidance and management – noting that different elements may serve more than one function:

- Control is assured primarily through an effective legal framework that sets basic standards of behaviour for officials and enforces them through effective accountability mechanisms, such as internal control and external audit; transparency mechanisms providing access to public information, facilitating public involvement and scrutiny; as well as arrangements for independent investigation and prosecution.

- Guidance is provided by strong commitment from leadership; statements of values and standards of conduct such as codes of conduct; and professional socialisation activities such as education, training and counselling to raise awareness and develop skills for the application of laws and standards in daily work.

- Management policies and practices create public service conditions that ensure fair and impartial selection, promotion and remuneration, and also contribute to social respect. A special dedicated body or existing central management body is often in charge of the systemic co-ordination in order to ensure consistency of the combination of separate actions and their constant integration into the overall public administration.

The ideal mix and degree of these functions will depend on the cultural and political-administrative environment of each country.

Source: Trust in Government: Ethics Measures in OECD Countries, OECD, 2000.

3.2. *Creating supportive conditions for integrity*

Transforming a traditional bureaucratic administration to a citizen-oriented public service requires a comprehensive vision and strategy that integrates all the key elements of the ethics infrastructure. Recent measures indicate the Chinese Government's increased efforts to develop distinct elements of the ethics infrastructure and advance reforms in key areas.

3.2.1. A critical shift in personnel management

Personnel management reform has intensified efforts to ensure the integrity and professional competence of officials by increasing transparency in the recruitment process, establishing criteria for integrity in the promotion of officials, providing incentives as well as requiring rotation in risk areas:

- Although highly competitive open examinations have been widely used to promote merit in recruitment for civil service positions at the national level[28] since the 1993 reform, exceptions to this general practice have been widely used by the central administration.[29] In sectors performing core state functions specific examinations have been used, for example, an exam for auditors to become a member of the CNAO, or the national judicial exam for procurators and judges organised by the Ministry of Justice. A professional evaluation system was also introduced for judicial staff in March 2002. At the local level, however, recruiting employees through examination has remained the exception rather than the rule, which widely facilitates corrupt practices such as the sale and purchase of positions.

- Integrity is a core criterion of the annual performance appraisal in the civil service. Colleagues, superiors and subordinates are requested to provide a 360-degree feedback on the performance and behaviour of the official concerned. New laws set ethics as explicit evaluation criteria.[30]

- Double-checks in susceptible procedures, security vetting and rotation of officials are commonly applied methods in vulnerable areas in OECD member countries and more and more recognized as a prevention measure in China. Recent proposals of the Supreme People's Procuratorate urge double-checks in the tendering process of infrastructure projects[31] and extend the rotation policy to chief procurators in charge of anti-corruption in grass-root procuratorates.[32]

Providing incentives for high standards of professional conduct is a major concern in human resource management. A special bonus (up to RMB 500) was introduced to reward those evaluated as excellent. Moreover, after three consecutive years of excellent ratings, officials could skip to the next salary category. However, even this exceptional increase in the salary level could have limited impact in at-risk areas without reasonable civil service salaries and pension schemes.[33] To improve the income level of government employees and discourage them from corruption, civil servants have received several pay rises since 1989, and they receive special allowances in cities such as Beijing, Shanghai and Shenzhen.

Recognizing the importance of appropriate remuneration, some local governments are considering offering their officials additional financial incentives to refuse incitements to corruption. For instance, Shenzhen is examining the introduction of a special bonus system for honest officials.[34]

Setting clear standards of expected conduct is an initial step towards an ethical culture in the public administration. However, rules could easily remain just words on paper without ever being implemented. Communication of standards through training is a popular instrument to raise awareness of existing laws and rules and to improve understanding of their application in daily work. For instance, the Ministry of Public Security provides standards both for official conduct[35] and procedures,[36] and has developed formal educational programmes and management plans as well as strengthened supervision and audit.

Police supervision and internal audit offices were set up for all public security organs above county level to review the functioning of systems, the monitoring of on-site law-enforcement activities and performance, and the organisational practice of how law enforcement bodies implement standards in handling individual cases. In line with similar efforts across the public administration, in the supervision and internal audit procedures special attention was paid to improving management systems in areas which are particularly exposed to corrupt practices, namely the administrative examination and approval system, as well as the financial and personnel management of the public security organs. The resulting proposals focused on a simplification of examination and approval formalities, on strengthening the control of examinations and approvals, as well as on standardizing procedures for financial management, appointments and promotion.

3.2.2. Conflict of interest: An emerging challenge of the transition process

Similarly to OECD member countries with long administrative law traditions, conflict-of-interest policy in China traditionally focused on family and personal relationships in administrative structures and procedures. The Criminal Law as well as specific laws and codes, for example for public procurators[37] and law enforcement officials,[38] provide a list of prohibited activities and positions for officials, their spouses and defined relatives. For example, in order to avoid conflict-of-interest situations, provisions prohibit policemen to accept gifts and money, to have a second job, to abuse their power by giving favours to relatives and friends running businesses, or to promote the sale of social security products. Laws also require the withdrawal from procedure when officials or their relatives have an interest in the matter.[39]

However, as described above, the economic transition process amplified the interaction between the public and business sectors, blurring the frontiers between the public and collective sphere on the one hand and the individual sphere on the other, and creating the potential for involving officials in business. Strict emphasis on individual moral standards became less satisfactory and new formal procedures have become necessary in the form of financial disclosures of private capacity interest.

A new policy imposed by CPC[40] rules targets the economic interest of employees. It does not allow employees of concerned companies to buy shares of their company or officials to buy shares of companies under their authority or involved in securities management. The new policy also requires regular disclosure from division director level and above, and has been extended on a trial basis to include the disclosure of children's wealth. Under a pilot scheme, officials at selected organisations in Hubei, Shanxi and Beijing must submit reports on the assets and income sources of their children living abroad.

3.2.3. Towards a comprehensive approach

Supportive personnel management and effective conflict-of-interest policies are necessary but not sufficient conditions for creating a favourable public service culture. A culture of integrity entails:

1. a clear mission for the public service that regularly updates public service values and standards to meet public expectations;
2. integrity measures that become an integral part of daily management practices;

> Box 3.3. **Managing Conflict of Interest in the Public Service: OECD Guidelines and Toolkit**
>
> Conflict of interest in both the public and private sector has become a major problem worldwide. The *OECD Guidelines for Managing Conflict of Interest in the Public Service** provide a unique international benchmark for developing and implementing a comprehensive conflict-of-interest policy. The Guidelines introduced a deliberately simple definition of conflict of interest and a principle-based approach to support public organisations review and modernise their policies and practices.
>
> In addition, a set of practical tools (*The OECD Toolkit*, OECD, 2005), such as checklists, self tests, model provisions and training materials were developed and tested to help managers in the daily application of the conflict-of-interest policy.
>
> * The Guidelines were approved in the form of a recommendation by the OECD Council in June 2003. The Guidelines and the Toolkit can be consulted at *www.oecd.org/gov/ethics/*.
>
> Source: *Managing Conflict of Interest in the Public Service: OECD Guidelines and Country Examples*, OECD, 2003; *Managing Conflict of Interest in the Public Service: A Toolkit*, OECD, 2005.

3. a forward-looking approach that anticipates a potential problematic situation that could weaken adherence to public service values and standards of behaviour, and also the preparation of suitable responses to prevent adverse effects;[41]

4. providing evidence on the implementation of measures by assessing their effectiveness, relevance and coherence with other elements of the ethics infrastructure.

Modern integrity management strategies adequately combine enforcement and prevention measures. However, there is a growing recognition in OECD member countries that increased attention to prevention reduces the need for enforcement. Furthermore, prevention is a less expensive investment in the long term, with a more positive impact on the public service culture and on the relationship between the public service and society at large.

The experience of countries in transition is particularly relevant in that context. During the 1990s, they gradually refined their legal framework for civil/public service standards, then upgraded management mechanisms to support putting values and standards into practice. In the transition process, control mechanisms, particularly external audit and independent government control, played a crucial role in ensuring compliance and identifying systemic shortcomings. The growing demand for transparency and mechanisms for public scrutiny has sustained the new relationship between society and the public service.

Demand for transparency is a major driving force in OECD member countries to ensure integrity in the public service. In China a critical step in the direction of transparency was taken by the Shanghai Municipal Government[42] to make available public information provided by 15 key government departments. After a six-month trial period, all the other departments followed the practice. Public information is also accessible on the municipal government's Web site.[43] Citizens could demand government information without giving reasons; exceptions are restricted to state and commercial secrets as well as personal privacy.

Expanded transparency is a precondition for public scrutiny that facilitates accountability. Increased transparency opens up the public service and makes urgent adjustment of institutional and procedural arrangements inevitable to ensure that officials are accountable for their conduct and performance.

A growing demand in OECD member countries exists not only for providing information on the implementation of integrity and corruption prevention measures, but also for providing evidence on impacts. Assessment is a key feedback mechanism on the outcomes and impacts of government actions that enables accountability by verifying whether policy objectives are reached. Assessment of policy measures in China could particularly support organisational learning and systemic adjustment, consequently central to designing and updating an overall strategy for modernising national integrity arrangements.

3.3. Supporting prevention: an emerging role for oversight bodies

Following its political recognition, corruption prevention has become one of the key functions of China's supreme oversight bodies: the Supreme People's Procuratorate, the Ministry of Supervision and the CNAO.

The general approach taken by these oversight bodies has been to identify specific sources of corruption in reviewed cases and make recommendations to improve procedural and organisational arrangements based on the information collected from particular institutions under review. Oversight bodies have paid particular attention to vulnerable areas and launched highly publicised campaigns across the country. The Ministry of Supervision and the CNAO are part of the government. However, in the exercise of their duties inspectors and auditors are requested to act independently according to the law.

3.3.1. Supreme People's Procuratorate

The Public Procurators Law[44] does not specify prevention amongst the core functions and duties of procuratorates. However, in daily practice corruption-related crime prevention has become an integral part of the oversight function along with investigation and prosecution of criminal cases. As an organisational consequence, procurator bodies established specific divisions in charge of prevention in the second half of the 1990s, such as the Corruption-related Crime Prevention Department (CCPD) of the Supreme People's Procuratorate at the national level. The CCPD has fulfilled an emerging role to co-ordinate the prevention efforts of procurator bodies at the sub-national levels and supply them with guiding documents such as the Recommendations on Corruption-related Crime Prevention issued by the Supreme People's Procuratorate.

Although effective and timely prosecution has remained the principal activity of procurator bodies, preventive measures have gained relative importance for identifying common sources of corruption by research, providing patterns/examples for organisational improvement and supporting a better understanding of the problem of corruption:

- **Preventive research** mainly focuses on analyzing sources, causalities and common features of corruption cases and also on reviewing their political, economic, social and cultural contexts. Investigation of individual cases also provides information for analysis on types of incentives and external conditions conducive to corruption.
- **Strengthening the institutional, management and legal frameworks.** Particular proposals aimed at strengthening the management and control mechanisms in specific targeted sectors and public organisations,[45] whereas systemic suggestions have been submitted to support the reinforcement of entire institutional and legal frameworks.
- **Awareness-raising** campaigns have been launched not only for officials working in the public administration, but also in schools, state companies and private enterprises, in order to underpin a supportive culture in society at large and to raise public awareness of existing laws and probable occurrence of corruption.

Reviewing and improving organisational and procedural arrangements in vulnerable areas has been the key focus in recent years to support compliance with regulations. When requested, procurator bodies have provided consultation to help the proper application of relevant laws. If necessary, they set up joint task forces and work out common recommendations on preventative measures related to the specific needs of organisations working in at-risk areas, such as tax and customs, or engineering projects. For example, in the case of large construction projects, such as highways, a joint notice was issued on the critical stages of the bidding process.[46] With the assistance of procuratorates, altogether over a 1 000 specific corruption-prevention units have been established across the country. Their prevention activities focused on major construction projects in the communication, energy and water conservation sectors.

3.3.2. Ministry of Supervision

As an executive arm of the State Council, the Ministry of Supervision not only carries out inspections of the application of laws, but also sets complementary standards of behaviour for officials across the public administration and supports their adequate application by socialisation:

- **Setting standards for officials.** The Ministry issued numerous regulations to set expected standards across the public administration in the past decade. Regarding gifts and benefits, for example, regulations have been developed against offering and accepting gifts in both domestic and foreign official activities, and against accepting and offering money and negotiable securities in official activities. Special attention has been paid to senior officials – deputy division director level and above – and managers to set an example.

  However, the standards that have been imposed by a set of explicit regulations such as the Code of Ethical Conduct for Senior Officials, the Regulations on Income Declaration by Leading Officials and the Regulations on Reporting Major Personal Matters by Leading Officials or the Regulations on Honesty and Self-discipline of the Managing Officials of State-owned Enterprises, are also expected to be applied across the whole public sector.

- **Supporting implementation of the regulations.** Socialisation by training and education focuses mainly on raising awareness of existing regulations and their accurate application in the daily process. Special attention has been paid to risk zones, such as business involvement of senior officials and receiving gifts.

- **Supervision.** As a critical component of the state control mechanisms, a principal function of the supervision departments is to inspect the application of relevant laws, in particular the exercise of discretionary power of officials within the executive branch. In addition to checking the legality of individual decisions in the public administration, more and more inspections focus on examining management practices, and result in proposals for modernising measures and improving their effectiveness in the future.

The numerous sources of standards make it difficult to locate the relevant, and sometimes conflicting, provisions. The complex legal language used in documents is also a barrier to effectively communicate the standards within the public administration and particularly to make the expected conduct of behaviour understandable for stakeholders dealing with the administration and the public at large. Integrating core values and basic standards into a single concise document, such as a Civil Service Code of Conduct or Ethics Code, is an emerging practice in OECD member countries. To achieve this it would require the review of all existing relevant provisions, their simplification, harmonization and re-grouping in a logically structured simple document. A single concise document written in plain language could substantially support the inculcation of expected standards in the public administration and facilitate internal control and public scrutiny.

3.3.3. China National Audit Office

The China National Audit Office (CNAO), established in 1983, primarily supervises public finance through auditing revenues and expenditures of government departments, state-owned banks, companies and undertakings, as well as the organisations of the CPC receiving funds from the central budget. One of its main tasks[47] is to promote clean and honest government by detecting irregularities, revealing systemic deficiencies, and identifying officials responsible for them. When auditors:

1. Find evidence of irregularities and the case falls within the jurisdiction of a specific audit institution, it can issue a decision letter or disposition letter with warning, impose fines or even confiscate illicit income as well as recommend provisions for systemic improvement. The management is obliged by the Audit Law to follow up these recommendations. However, recent practice shows insufficient compliance,[48] mostly explained by lack of resources.

2. Discover administrative irregularities and detect administrative wrongdoings, the Ministry of Supervision is notified.

3. Identify criminal activity, the case is transferred to police or procurators for judicial process.[49]

Ensuring integrity in the audit process has been a key concern for CNAO. The CNAO has strengthened relevant rules,[50] issued standards[51] and used extensive training and education as traditional methods to improve the professional quality of auditors and to ensure their impartiality. The CNAO introduced six implementation measures[52] to improve transparency, advance professional standards and prevent corruption in the audit process. These include: introduction of consultation processes, development of audit standards, liability of auditors, prohibiting potential conflict of interest, reinforcing internal financial management, establishing external feedback mechanisms and complaint procedures.

The CNAO at the national level and external audit organisations at the sub-national level also supervise the audit activities of internal audit units and provide them with professional guidance (for example on quality insurance) to improve their efficiency and effectiveness.

Reflecting the increased awareness generated by the media, recent audits in particular focused on areas exposed to high attention in society, such as the spending of SARS funds, construction of dams, as well as emerging risk areas (*e.g.* related to the stock exchange, the real estate market, and to post-employment practices in state-owned enterprises).

To contribute to the improvement of government transparency and accountability, the CNAO has published annual audit reports on the implementation of the central budget since 2001.[53] Furthermore, specific audit reports reviewing particular organisations and the use of public funds have also been made public since 2004, naming and shaming senior officials responsible for irregularities and corruption discovered by the auditors.

In spite of major achievements in discovering irregularities,[54] recognizing systemic deficiencies and initiating their adjustment, the shortcomings in the follow-up procedure reveal common deficiencies in the institutionalisation of accountability. As indicated in recent reports, the majority of central government and provincial units did not take timely steps to correct exposed irregularities and improve their anti-corruption mechanisms.

4. Conclusion

Despite significant efforts from the CPC and government leaders, corruption remains a serious problem for both citizens and businesses, particularly for foreign direct investment.[55] It continues to pose a significant political challenge as a particular feature of the transition process.

Over the past decade, China has developed a firm stance to combat corruption and declared this a priority in its efforts to modernize its economic structure. Important reforms of the institutional and legal frameworks to fight corruption have been undertaken, and further efforts in this respect are underway. Many challenges yet remain before corruption and bribery will be contained successfully.

Based on the experience of the OECD and its member countries in combating bribery, the present analysis suggests that a number of issues concerning anti-corruption legislation and law enforcement might require particular attention in the course of designing China's future anti-corruption policies.

China has undertaken laudable efforts to strengthen and consolidate its repressive instruments to deter and sanction corruption and related offences by redefining and extending a number of offences. In order to further improve the effectiveness of this framework, adjustments at the level of enforcement appear to be advisable. In this respect, OECD member countries' experience has shown that the deterring effect of sanctions depends foremost on effective and equal enforcement rather than on the severity of penalties. Given the actual state of the progress of reforms, effective enforcement of anti-corruption legislation would benefit from capacity building for prosecutors and judges. Prosecuting with comparable importance and severity all actors involved in corruption schemes in business related transactions, i.e. bribe payers as much as recipients of bribes, those engaging in the laundering of proceeds of corruption as well as legal persons engaging in corrupt business practices is likely to further improve the effectiveness of the fight against corruption. Sanctions applicable to natural persons and applied in all sectors and country-wide have proven to be an effective tool to prevent and deter corruption of officials in a growing number of countries. Given China's rapidly growing involvement in international trade and investment, China would further benefit from taking steps to criminalize and prosecute foreign bribery in line with the OECD anti-bribery standards. These modifications would allow moderating the existing penalties while rendering sanction mechanisms more credible and effective.

Further, in light of the growing exposure of China's economy to the international market and in light of the particular difficulty China is facing in the context of repatriation of officials that have absconded with embezzled assets, the current focus of China's anti-corruption strategy on domestic challenges would benefit from being complemented by a strong involvement in regional and international anti-corruption efforts. In this regard, the PRC's recent endorsement of the Anti-Corruption Action Plan for Asia-Pacific in the framework of the ADB/OECD Anti-Corruption Initiative is likely to facilitate the exchange of experience in matters related to both prevention and prosecution of corruption and as such bolster its domestic anti-corruption framework. It would further allow strengthening China's ties with both countries from the region and OECD member countries, including in matters related to international judicial cooperation, and it would assist in advancing the country's laudable efforts to implement the UN Convention against Corruption.

Gradually, and particularly over the last five years, more attention has been paid to reviewing risk areas prone to corruption, and to creating conducive conditions and improving management arrangements that encourage ethical behaviour and make corruption harder to commit and easier to detect.

A lot remains to be done to complete a national ethics infrastructure and ensure that it functions in an effective and consistent manner. In addition to adjusting existing mechanisms in the public service, key challenges include how to implement and co-ordinate the new policy instruments.

Notes

1. Section 1 of this chapter was written by Irène Hors, Public Sector Management and Performance Division, Public Governance and Territorial Development Directorate, OECD; Section 2 was written by Gretta Fenner and Joachim Pohl, Anti-Corruption Division, Directorate for Financial and Enterprise Affairs, OECD; Section 3 was written by Janos Bertok, Innovation and Integrity Division, Public Governance and Territorial Development Directorate, OECD.

2. See Chapter 10 for more information.

3. Formerly called the State Audit Administration.

4. For instance, the optimal situation for an entrepreneur would be that everyone else respects regulations protecting the environment while he does not bother about these regulations that would normally oblige him to properly handle waste from his firm's production process.

5. Decision Regarding the Severe Punishment of Criminals who Seriously Undermine the Economy, promulgated by the Standing Committee of the National People's Congress on 8 March 1982, and Supplementary Regulations on Suppression of Corruption and Bribery.

6. Decision Regarding Anti-Company-Law Offences, adopted by the Standing Committee of the National People's Congress on 28 February 1995, and Provisional Regulations Regarding Anti-Commercial-Bribery Practices, expanding the application of the Law against Unfair Competition.

7. Article 396 of the Criminal Code; Article 9 of the Supplementary Regulations on Suppression of Corruption and Bribery.

8. Ren Jianming, Head of the Office for Research on Corruption, Tsinghua University, cited in "Blacklist to Tackle Construction Bribes", by Li Jingrong in *China through a Lens*, www.china.org.cn, 14 June 2004.

9. According to IMF estimates, quoted in *China Daily*, 9 July 2004.

10. *Wen Wei Po* (Hong Kong, China), 30 January 2004, and *People's Daily*, 12 September 2003.

11. USD 8.75 billion according to Public Security Minister Zhou Yongkang, reported by china.org.cn on 15 June 2004. A report published by the Ministry of Commerce estimates the loss at USD 50 billion, according to a report by *China Daily*, 20 August 2004.

12. In 2003, 2.6 million suspicious and large-sum transactions were reported amounting to USD 600 billion, *China Daily*, 24 July 2004.

13. *The Economist*, 15 February 2002.

14. Jia Chunwang, Procurator-General of the Supreme People's Procuratorate claimed that 596 fugitive corrupt officials were brought back from overseas in 2003, (Xinhua News Agency, 24 March 2004); according to Public Security Minister Zhou Yongkang, in June 2004 more than 230 economic crime suspects have been repatriated since 1998.

15. Li Xuezhong, quoted by *People's Daily*, 18 September 2003.

16. *China Daily*, 12 March 2004.

17. Article 85(3), Criminal Procedure Law.

18. These include: the Code of Ethical Conduct for Leading Officials, the Regulations on the Responsibility System for Clean Government, the Interim Regulations on Administrative Sanctions against Government Functionaries who Committed Embezzlement or Bribery, the Regulations on Income Disclosure, and the Regulations on Declaration of Gifts.

19. Associated Press, 2 April 2004; *China Daily*, 26 August 2004.
20. Article 39 of the CPC Constitution.
21. Information released by the Supreme People's Procuratorate on 8 January 2004.
22. For example in September 1997, the 15th National Congress of the CPC recognized the need for "combining the crackdown on prevention and tackling both the symptoms and root causes" of corruption.
23. The report presented by President Hu Jintao at the Third Plenary Session of the Sixteenth Central Commission for Discipline Inspection underlines this shift. On the basis of summing up past experiences, President Hu Jintao put forward the aim of combating corruption by attaching "equal importance to preventative measures" (Xinhua News Agency, 12 January 2004).
24. Trends and measures are outlined in Chapter 1 on civil service reform in China.
25. More information on the budget management reforms can be found in Chapter 7.
26. Further details on the regulatory aspects and the reform of licensing practices and procedures can be found in Chapter 9 on regulatory management and reform in China.
27. For details see Chapter 4 on e-government in China.
28. For the classification of positions in the public service and the description of *nomenclatura* system see Chapter 1.
29. For example moving demobilized solders into the administration.
30. For example for procurement officials by Article 62 of Government Procurement Law.
31. Xinhua News Agency, 22 October 2004.
32. Xinhua News Agency, 15 November 2004.
33. For example, a pension scheme for police introduced in Jiangsu Province in 2003 halved corruption cases in a year (*China Daily*, 26 August 2004).
34. According to a proposal under discussion, the city government would offer bonuses worth up to RMB 2 million (EUR 200 000) at retirement.
35. The most prominent one is the Professional Code of Ethics of the People's Police.
36. For example the Procedures and Rules on Handling Criminal Cases by Public Security Organs, Rules on Assessing and Appraising the Quality of Law Enforcement of Public Security Organs, Code of Law Enforcement and Practice of Local Public Security Office.
37. Chapter VI, Article 18 of the Public Procurators Law on Posts to be avoided.
38. For example the Professional Code of Ethics of People's Police, Professional Code of Post-Responsibilities of Vehicle Control Office, Ten Forbidden Acts of Public Security Officials and Police Officers under Public Security Organs, Rules on Occupation of Family Members of Leading Cadre of Public Security Organs.
39. For example, in the course of supervision, as required by Article 14 of the Law on Administrative Supervision, Order No. 85 of the President of the PRC, promulgated on 9 May 1997.
40. Information provided by the Ministry of Supervision. Given the representation of Party members in the public service, particularly in senior positions, these new Party rules could play a significant role in changing attitudes and applying a stricter policy that includes the obligation of regular disclosures for senior officials.
41. An example is the approach of the Olympic Supervisory Committee – formed by senior decision-makers to support efforts for preventing corruption in all Olympic projects and ensure a "clean Olympiad"; the Committee pays special attention to support the development of corruption prevention mechanisms in the entire process of organising the Olympics, including big construction projects, involvement of private sector actors (*e.g.* in public-private partnerships), franchise, the distribution of tickets, etc.
42. The Regulation of Shanghai Municipality on the Release of Government Information came into effect on 1 May 2004.
43. May be consulted at *www.shanghai.gov.cn*, *China Daily*, 2 November 2004.
44. Chapter II, Article 6 of the Public Procurators Law promulgated by Order No. 39 of the President of the PRC of 28 February 1995.

45. For example, recent suggestions for relevant government departments to improve relocation rules in relation to the preparation of the Shanghai World Expo in 2010 (Xinhua News Agency, 21 January 2005).

46. Common notice issued by the Henan Province Procuratorate and Transportation Department.

47. Determined by the Audit Law, August 1994.

48. *E.g. China Daily*, 3 November 2004. Several other cases were reported by newspapers in late September 2004, for example AFP 24 September 2004.

49. The number of cases fluctuates around 1% of audits; for example, out of 145 713 audits, 1 456 cases were handed over to judicial organisations in 2000, an approximately 7% increase from the previous year.

50. For example in the Professional Ethics Codes for Auditors in Audit Institutions, the Rules for Auditors, Regulations for Building Clean and Honest Audit Institutions.

51. CNAO issued 38 auditing standards in 1996 to ensure efficiency and quality of audits across the country.

52. In line with the Instruction Measures to Root out Corruption issued by the Central Committee for Disciplinary Inspection of the CPC.

53. The annual audit reports have been submitted to the Premier of the State Council then to the National People's Congress since 1996.

54. Over RMB 20 billion was turned over to the central budget in 2000.

55. See section on corruption in Chapter 15.

Bibliography

Guo, Yong (2003), "Zhongguo gaoguan fubai de tedian he bianhua qushi yanjiu", mimeo.

Guo, Yong and Hu Angang (2004), "The Administrative Monopoly in China's Economic Transition", mimeo.

Hu Angang (2001), *Zhongguo: tiaozhan fubai (China: Fighting Against Corruption)*, Hangzhou, Zhejiang renmin chubanshe.

Kwong, Julia (1997), *The Political Economy of Corruption in China*, East Gate Book, M.E. Sharpe.

Li Jingrong (2004), "Blacklist to Tackle Construction Bribes", *China through a Lens*, www.china.org.cn, 14 June.

National People's Congress (1995), Public Procurators Law, promulgated by Order No. 39 of the President of the PRC of 28 February 1995.

National People's Congress (1996), Criminal Procedure Law of the People's Republic of China, adopted at the Second Session of the Fifth National People's Congress on 1 July 1979, and revised according with the Decision on Revising the Criminal Procedure Law of the People's Republic of China adopted at the Forth Session of the Eighth National People's Congress on 17 March 1996.

National People's Congress (1997), Criminal Law of the People's Republic of China, revised at the Fifth Meeting of the Standing Committee of the Eighth National People's Congress, Order No. 83 of the President of the PRC, promulgated on 14 March 1997.

National People's Congress (1997), Law on Administrative Supervision, Order No. 85 of the President of the PRC, promulgated on 9 May 1997.

National People's Congress (1988), Supplementary Regulations on Suppression of Corruption and Bribery, Order No. 63 of the President of the PRC, promulgated on 21 January 1988.

National People's Congress (2002), Government Procurement Law of the People's Republic of China, adopted at the 28th Meeting of the Standing Committee of the 9th National People's Congress on 29 June 2002, and effective as of 1 January 2003.

National People's Congress (2003), The Law of the People's Republic of China on Administrative Licenses, adopted at the Fourth Session of the Standing Committee of the Tenth National People's Congress on 27 August 2003, and effective as of 1 July 2004.

OECD (2003), *OECD Guidelines for Managing Conflict of Interest in the Public Service*, OECD, Paris, www.oecd.org/gov/ethics/.

OECD (2000), *Trust in Government: Ethics Measures in OECD Countries*, OECD, Paris.

OECD (2003), *Managing Conflict of Interest in the Public Service: OECD Guidelines and Country Experiences*, OECD, Paris.

OECD (2005), *Managing Conflict of Interest in the Public Service: A Toolkit*, OECD, Paris.

Pei, Minxin (2002), "The Long March against Graft", *Financial Times*, 10 December.

Zhang Siqing (1998), "Zuigao renmin jianchayuan gongzuo baogao", *People's Daily*, 2 March.

PART I

Chapter 4

E-government in China

Table of Contents

Summary 137

E-government in China 138

    1. Introduction 138

    2. The case for e-government 138

    3. E-government development and structure 140

    4. Barriers to e-government 142

        4.1. Legislative barriers 143

        4.2. Budgetary issues 144

        4.3. Security and surveillance 145

        4.4. Digital divide and wider social appeal 145

    5. The national e-government initiative 146

        5.1. Two networks 146

        5.2. One portal 148

        5.3. Four databases 148

        5.4. The Golden Projects 150

    6. Customer focus and information sharing 153

        6.1. Information provision 153

        6.2. Service delivery 155

        6.3. Public participation 157

        6.4. Data sharing and compatibility 157

    7. E-government programmes and reform of the public administration 158

        7.1. Efficiency and seamless service delivery 159

        7.2. Transparency and accountability 160

        7.3. Horizontal and vertical co-ordination 161

        7.4. Public management 161

    8. Key challenges/recommendations 163

Notes 165

Bibliography 165

Annex 4.A1. E-government Web Sites 167

List of boxes

4.1. Timeline 141
4.2. Shanghai Informatization Committee 143
4.3. Top Leadership Project in Nanhai 147
4.4. Suzhou's Public Supervision Bulletin Board System 157

List of figures

4.1. The growth of e-government resources in China 139
4.2. Types of information provided by China's e-government Web sites (%) 154
4.3. Online service deliveries by China's e-government Web sites (%) 156

Summary

E-government refers to the use of information and communication technologies, and particularly the Internet, as a tool to achieve better government. In China, the state of e-government reflects the transitional nature of contemporary Chinese society toward a "socialist market economy". The country's information society is inchoate with persisting digital divides, i.e. diffusion and access to information and communication technologies (ICT) are uneven and although Internet penetration has grown rapidly in wealthy urban areas, it remains fairly low in per capita terms.

Despite these drawbacks, China is committed to moving forward: Its leadership has adopted a "cyber-strategy" to reap the economic and social benefits of ICT and the Communist Party of China (CPC) has set out to promote e-government with an eye on its relationship with broader reforms in law, administrative institutions and macroeconomic management.

To a certain extent, the trajectory of e-government in China overlaps with general trends occurring in OECD member countries. E-government initiatives are moving from simply encouraging the adoption of ICT to promoting substantive reform in the public sector. The main challenge has shifted from putting more services online to improving the quality of information and services to drive user take-up, to improve interconnectivity in order to join up "islands of information", to promote collaboration in order to reduce redundancy and to establish national databases in order to meet shared data needs. In order to meet these challenges, the main actors are migrating from relatively peripheral positions to the very centre of institutional power in recognition of the crosscutting nature of e-government and the need for a whole-of-government perspective.

The success of e-government programmes is contingent upon progress in legal and administrative reforms that seek to codify fundamental concepts such as power-sharing, resource re-distribution or the standardization of operational procedures. These issues involve broader transformations, to which e-government can act as an additional catalyst.

E-government in China[1]

1. Introduction

E-government refers to the use of information and communication technologies (ICT), and particularly the Internet, as a tool to achieve better government. This chapter provides baseline information and policy assessments on e-government in China. Drawing upon more than 30 interviews with experts and focus group discussions with Chinese citizens, it reviews the state of e-government initiatives and analyzes the objectives and prospects for change.

Although some unique characteristics can be revealed, the study shows that Chinese e-government initiatives share a basic approach with similar projects in OECD member countries: E-government helps forward the public reform agenda, as it serves as a tool for reform, renews interest in public management reform, highlights internal inconsistencies, and underscores commitment to good governance objectives.

2. The case for e-government

Since China launched its first public Internet service in 1994, the growth of the use of ICT has been rapid. Within less than 10 years, China had the world's second largest Internet user population (80 million by the end of 2003) and the largest mobile phone user population (269 million) (Ministry of Information Industry, 2003). By 2003, the number of online computers in China had reached 31 million and nearly 600 000 Web sites were based on servers in the country (China Internet Network Information Centre, 1997-2004).

This rapid growth, however, stands in stark contrast to the low penetration rates of ICT across the total population base of 1.3 billion. Only 6.1% of the Chinese population can access the Internet and almost 60% of the population still does not have a landline or mobile phone. ICT distribution is disproportionately concentrated in urban areas along the coast. Moreover, many Internet users have never visited government Web sites. The reach of e-government in China, therefore, is still limited.

The coupling of high-speed growth with low per capita indicators of the use of ICT among ordinary citizens reflects the overall transitional nature of China's economy. Since 1978, the country has been experiencing "marketization" reform designed to fundamentally transform the planned economy. With its accession to the WTO in December 2001, China has also been increasingly integrated into the global market, which creates a pressing need for significant improvement of its business environment and a growing demand for information.

In this context, the Chinese Government has formulated and implemented a "cyber-strategy" to reap the economic and social benefits of ICT while minimizing its potential threats (Hachigian, 2001). One of the main components of this strategy is China's recent effort to develop e-government, which is expected to help sustain growth in the IT sector in the midst of the worldwide e-commerce slowdown.

China's e-government is burgeoning "on a scale without precedent among developing nations" (Kluver, 2004). One indicator is the number of registered domain names under gov.cn, which grew from 323 in 1997 to 11 764 in 2003 (CNNIC, 1997-2004). During this brief six-year period, the number of Chinese Internet users working in government and public management offices also rocketed from fewer than 6 000 to 6.4 million (ibid.).

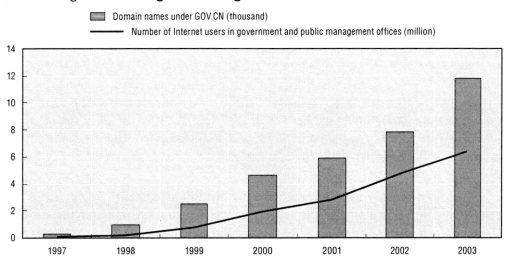

Figure 4.1. **The growth of e-government resources in China**

According to the National Conference on Government and the Informatization of Public Administration held in December 2003 (Xinhua, 11 December 2003), 97% of regional government bodies in China have established computer networks for internal usage. Seventy-five per cent of them have connected internal networks among their subordinate departments, bureaus, cities, and counties. Meanwhile, at the national level, 43% of ministry-level State Council offices have created their own intranets that cover subsidiary bodies throughout the country.

This rapid growth owes much to China's booming economy, WTO entry, and fledging information society. More immediately, within the government, it has to do with the official recognition of "informatization" (xinxihua) as a central strategy for modernization and, most importantly, the resolve of the Chinese authorities to advance public sector reform.

Although economic gains have been a main objective, for the Chinese Government the most fundamental benefits of e-government are the reform of the structure and procedures of government itself. E-government therefore has a potentially important role to play in China's current reform efforts which have set out to make the public sector more efficient, transparent and accountable (World Bank, 2003).

High-level policy makers in Beijing have reached a consensus that the ultimate purpose of e-government in China is to facilitate public sector reform. According to the Resolution of the Sixteenth National Congress of the Communist Party of China (CPC) held in November 2002, e-government is to be understood within the framework of "deepening institutional reforms in public sector management", as part of the efforts to "further change the functions of the government, improve the mode of management, promote e-government, enhance administrative efficiency, and reduce administrative cost in order to form an administrative management system with standardized procedures and concerted actions that are just, transparent, clean, and highly efficient" (translation by author).

E-government, therefore, has the potential to serve as a new anchor point that connects reform programmes in the realms of law, administrative institutions, and macroeconomic management. If successfully carried out, it will play an important role in the modernization of China's public sector, helping the Chinese authorities to "achieve better government", the ultimate goal identified in *The E-Government Imperative* (OECD, 2003).

3. E-government development and structure

Although the Chinese Government has been using computers for office work since the 1980s (see Box 4.1), the administrative structure for the country's e-government initiatives has yet to be completely established. In the context of fast economic growth and the furthering of marketization reform, the government launched the Three Golden Projects (Golden Bridge, Golden Gate and Golden Card) in 1993, aiming at the construction of basic infrastructure and the promotion of electronic transactions in both the public and private sectors. Since 2002, the Three Golden Projects have been superseded by a series of new programmes, which will be presented in Section 5.

In 1999, a few entrepreneurs affiliated with China Telecom, the country's largest telecom operator, initiated the Government Online Project. With help from the Information Centre of State Economy and Trade Commission, they enlisted more than 40 ministry-level offices in a drive to facilitate the utilization of Internet technologies in government bodies across the country (Government Online, 2003). The main Web site of the Government Online Project, *www.gov.cn*, is now a comprehensive portal for e-government Web sites in China. However, Government Online is a for-profit organisation that does not have a direct mandate from the central government to be a major e-government player.

Although the central government issued broad guidelines back in 1997, the current, better-developed administrative framework for e-government co-ordination did not come into being until after August 2001, when the State Council Information Leading Group (*Guowuyuan xinxihua gongzuo lingdao xiaozu*, hereafter SCILG) was established as the highest authority on matters regarding ICT.[2] Since then a national structure for e-government has gradually emerged, reflecting recent changes in the overall environment of public sector reform and the understanding of the role that e-government can play in reform efforts. This structure is outlined in the "SCILG Recommendations on the Construction of E-Government in China" (hereafter "State Council Document No. 17") issued in July 2002.

Before the promulgation of State Council Document No. 17, the relationship between e-government and public sector reform was unclear. Consequently, there was insufficient co-ordination of e-government initiatives by the central government and the majority of projects were conducted by sectoral and local authorities or propelled by commercial operations, producing a level of chaos with overlapping programmes in certain areas and many isolated "information islands" (*xinxi gudao*).

However, since the release of State Council Document No. 17, much progress has been made in clarifying the responsibilities for the development of China's e-government programmes. As Premier Wen Jiabao emphasized at the third SCILG meeting in 2003: "The foci of our work include transforming government functions, advancing e-government at faster speed, enhancing government capacities in economic regulation, market supervision, social management and public services, and increasing openness in the public sector." In

Box 4.1. **Timeline**

Mid 1980s – Computers entered Chinese Government offices during the country's first wave of "office automation" applications.

1993 – The initiation of the Three Golden Projects (Golden Bridge, Golden Gate and Golden Card) marked the formal beginning of e-government in China. Computers and databases started to be networked.

April 1997 – The National Informatization Convention announced China's guiding principles for informatization: "co-ordinated planning led by the state; unified standards built co-operatively; interconnected resources shared among the departments".

January 1999 – The Government Online Project (www.gov.cn) was launched by China Telecom and the Information Centre of the State Economy and Trade Commission, with support from more than 40 ministries and ministry-level offices.

October 2000 – China's 10th Five-Year Plan promotes a new overall strategy for economic and social development: "the utilization of informatization to propel industrialization" (yi xinxihua daidong gongyehua).

August 2001 – The State Council Informatization Leading Group (SCILG) was re-established, as was its standing administrative organ, the State Council Informatization Office (SCIO). SCIO and the State Commission Office for Public Sector Reform (SCOPSR) are now the two central co-ordinators for e-government in China.

July 2002 – The second SCILG meeting passed "the SCILG Recommendations on the Construction of E-Government in China". Also known as "State Council Document No. 17", it lays out the overall structure of e-government in China including "two networks, one portal, four databases, 12 Golden Projects".

November 2002 – The Resolution of the CPC Sixteenth National Congress called for "a major strengthening of e-government initiatives" within the framework of "deepening institutional reforms in public sector management" in order to "form a public administrative institution with standardized procedures and concerted actions that are just, transparent, clean, and highly efficient" (CPC, 2002).

April 2003 – The State Council Informatization Office, the Ministry of Science and Technology, and the Ministry of Information Industry jointly issued the "Technical Guidelines for E-Government Projects".

May-June 2003 – During the SARS epidemic, Beijing and several city governments initiated disease control information systems to centrally manage the SARS crisis. Some of these projects received financial and expert support from international organisations such as UNDP.

July 2003 – The third SCILG meeting passed "the Recommendation on the Strengthening of Information Security Protection", which was later promulgated by the State Council General Office as "Document No. 27".

order to realize this vision, the institutional structure for e-government projects will have to reflect new principles for public administration in the realms of transparency, accountability, anti-corruption, and the separation of decision-making and implementation.

Although the SCILG is the highest authority for ICT matters in China, it only convenes once a year. Hence, the central decision-makers for national e-government policies are the State Council Informatization Office (the standing office for SCILG, hereafter SCIO) and the

State Commission Office for Public Sector Reform (hereafter SCOPSR). Since 2003, SCIO and SCOPSR have been working closely to establish frameworks that will guarantee long-term development and the realization of reform outcomes in the public sector.

In addition, at the national level there are service-delivering bodies that help provide financial, technological, and personnel support for e-government projects in general, such as the Ministry of Information Industry, the Ministry of Science and Technology, the National Development and Reform Commission, and the Ministry of Finance. Moreover, from education to healthcare, from trade to public security, every government unit at the ministerial level has launched e-government initiatives in its specific domain of jurisdiction.

At the local level, however, e-government varies greatly. Not surprisingly, there is often stronger commitment among provincial and city-level authorities in wealthy regions such as coastal areas in the southeast. Higher financial capacities of these local governments facilitate this commitment. In many cases, rapidly expanding local businesses and burgeoning export industries in these areas also create strong demand for e-government. Some of the most forward-looking and creative e-government projects can thus be found at the provincial, city, or township levels.

The informatization offices (*xinxiban*) are the central sites for e-government co-ordination at the sub-national level, but the institutional position of local informatization offices differs from place to place. Some are built on the basis of previous "information centres" (*xinxi zhongxin*), which tend to have less administrative power. Others are located within local planning commissions that directly control development projects of all kinds. Still others draw on the political clout of local CPC propaganda divisions, science and technology bureaus, or telecom regulatory agencies. With the SCOPSR joining the decision-making process of e-government at the national level, local SCOPSR offices may also play an increasingly important role in the localities, as part of their oversight function for public management reform and public sector human resources.

Differences in the bureaucratic setup of informatization offices lead to a wide margin of maneuver among local government bodies, whose role often goes beyond the simple implementation of national policies. This is particularly the case because, during this era of reform, governance in China is centralized in principle but often decentralized in practice.

Hence, despite the differences in their institutional settings, local informatization taskforces are key players in China's e-government development. In many cases, especially in wealthier regions, local operations tend to be "one step ahead" and provide valuable lessons for the rest of the country. E-government initiatives in mega-cities such as Shanghai (see Box 4.2) and Guangzhou, as well as those in smaller cities such as Fuzhou, Qingdao and Nanhai, whose local experimentation dates back to the mid-1990s, have all informed national e-government programmes. These national projects also draw on local experiments covering diverse geographic regions, including less developed cities or provinces.

4. Barriers to e-government

Despite its booming economy and rapid IT growth, China faces multiple barriers in developing e-government due to its size, pre-reform institutional legacies, and the transitional nature of its state-society relationship. Most of these hurdles are not particular to e-government programmes but involve larger issues in the public sector and are due to the fact that China's information society is still in its initial phase of development. The OECD draws attention in particular to those barriers outside the scope of an individual IT project or

> Box 4.2. **Shanghai Informatization Committee**
>
> A notable development at the local level is the establishment of the Shanghai Informatization Committee (*www.shanghaiit.gov.cn*) on 1 August 2003. This is the first major experiment approved by CPC Central Committee and the State Council that uses institutional restructuring to enhance local e-government programmes. With its corresponding branches set up in all of Shanghai's urban districts and rural counties, the new Shanghai Informatization Committee – in terms of administrative ranks – is half a rank higher than most municipal bureaus. Such a change not only centralizes its functions in drafting local regulations, supervising telecom services and managing local infrastructures, but also gives the committee additional authority in e-government implementation across the municipality.

unit that set up the context within which e-government projects are taking place: "External e-government barriers often concern breakdowns, missing components or lack of flexibility in the government-wide frameworks that enable e-government" (OECD, 2003).

4.1. Legislative barriers

Legal system reform is central to e-government initiatives because progress in public sector reform is impossible without the modern rule of law. More specifically, the core prerequisite to implement e-government successfully is the clarification of power relationships between state and society and among different government bodies. In the past, Chinese laws and regulations tended not to restrict the political and administrative power of government officials regarding the handling of information, particularly regarding the regulation of online content and transactions (Harwit and Clark, 2002; Cheung, 2003). Hence officials or government bodies could choose to release very little information about their practices, especially with regard to wrongdoings. This behaviour, however, is inconsistent with the goals of transparency and accountability in e-government.

Aware of this challenge, China's top leaders have paid more attention in recent years to the creation of a legal framework that focuses on balancing the power of administrative bodies. At the Sixteenth CPC National Congress, former President Jiang Zemin called for "the restraining and monitoring of power" and "serious implementation of a system to publicize government information". Since then, legislative measures have established new parameters that restrict the government's power in the handling of information.

One major undertaking is the proposal of an Open Governance Act, designed to balance existing legislation such as the State Secrets Provisions and Measures for Managing Internet Information Services. Still under revision, the new Act for the first time defines "state secrets" in legal terms and requires government officials to obtain approval from a central body before withholding information. If passed and implemented, this will lead to a sea change in the Chinese Government in which all non-secret information will belong to the public domain and can be put onto the Internet.

Apart from the Open Governance Act, the future of e-government in China depends on a series of legal measures, some already issued and others still being drafted or revised. These include the Public Procurement and Bidding Act and Network Security Management Measures for the construction of e-government projects, the Privacy Protection Act for State-Citizen Relationship, and the Electronic Signature Act and Government Information

Registration Measures for everyday administrative routines. All these legislative efforts have spurred debates over the basic principles of e-government in China, among institutions and social groups with different policy priorities.

Despite recent legislative moves, China's e-government is still supported by a very inchoate legal system with insufficient measures to guarantee the healthy and sustainable development of e-government in the long run. The fundamental challenge is as much about clarifying nationwide goals and priorities as about setting up basic procedures that can be enforced at the local level. It is therefore not surprising that so far informal relationships remain important to the success of many e-government projects in China, which rely on the personal influence of key officials due to the lack of laws and formal regulations.

4.2. Budgetary issues

In 2002, China spent approximately RMB 30 billion (USD 3.6 billion) on e-government including RMB 23 billion on hardware and infrastructure, RMB 3.8 billion on software and RMB 3.2 billion on IT services. The total expenditure was estimated to grow 17% to reach RMB 35 billion in 2003 (CCW Research, 2002).

The size and speed of growth in the gross e-government budget, however, do not mean that a sound budgetary system is in place. On the contrary, several officials interviewed in the central government and local government bodies in Eastern China said that budgeting e-government projects remains a major problem throughout the country. Although a key Beijing official acknowledged that in recent years there was some improvement in budget control, he maintained: "No one knows how much money has been wasted."

E-government in China is currently financed in a variety of ways. Government bodies at the sub-national level provide much of the funding, since many e-government projects are local or regional experiments, although there are also a significant number of national projects funded directly by the ministries. Local initiatives sometimes receive subsidies from higher levels of government and sometimes utilize bank loans or investment from the private sector. However, local operations, especially those using private funds, tend to produce network redundancy and incompatible platforms. Therefore, the consensus since the SCILG conference of 2002 is that more co-ordination and supervision are needed to ensure structural optimization and maximum cost efficiency.

Even with this consensus, the budgetary system remains insufficiently structured, lacking formal rules or clear guidelines. In general, it allows for different government entities to share expenses, but guidance is often unclear when it comes to the budgeting of a specific project that involves multiple divisions at different administrative levels. At the national level, construction costs should be covered by the basic infrastructure funds of the central government, whereas operational costs should be included in the budgets of the corresponding ministries and co-ordinated by the Ministry of Finance. At the sub-national level, usually local governments are responsible for the construction and maintenance of their own e-government projects, although they may also receive subsidies from the central government in case of need.

Although national e-government decision makers are concerned about cost efficiency, the problem is sometimes neglected at the local level and in certain economic sectors. Many e-government projects are unnecessarily expensive, and a large portion of the budget is spent on hardware and infrastructure rather than on software and applications.

Often there is insufficient funding for system update and maintenance, leaving expensive equipment and network resources underutilized.

4.3. Security and surveillance

Another major challenge facing e-government in China is developing network security measures and surveillance mechanisms to oversee internal usage. Concerns about computer viruses and unauthorized intrusions are prevalent among government bodies, because in China the reliability of computer systems is much more jeopardized by the spread of viruses and worms than in most OECD member countries. Periodic hacker attacks have caused damage to thousands of government Web sites (Qiu, 2002a).

Many administrative and technological measures have been undertaken to prevent security problems, including the Golden Shield Project and the physical separation between internal and external networks as required in State Council Document No. 17. The interface between the e-government external network and the Internet is protected by passwords, firewalls, and virtual private networks (VPN), among other security technologies. Since 2003, there is also growing support for the use of Public Key Infrastructure (PKI), a system of *digital certificates* and Certification Authorities (CA) that verify and authenticate the validity of each party involved in an *Internet* transaction, in order to ensure the authenticity of user identity so that internal databases and documents will not be inappropriately accessed or modified.

There are, however, two inadequacies in the current modes of network security protection, both of which stem from old compartmentalized bureaucratic practices and insufficient central co-ordination (Ding, 2002). First, there is the problem of overlapping construction and lack of common standards. Since the first CA was established in 1998, China now has more than 70 CAs working in different realms using different standards. Many ministries and local governments have built or are planning to build their own CAs. However, there is no nationwide standard for electronic authorization using a common PKI.

Second, insufficient attention is paid to non-technical or low-tech solutions. Often network security is perceived to be a matter of technological sophistication rather than a set of institutional procedures. This mentality, particularly prevalent among members of local informatization offices, puts the responsibility for network security on programmers and devices, which only have a limited ability to ensure safety in an ever-changing technological environment.

It is therefore important to internalize such responsibilities and make them part of the operational routine in "a culture of security" that relies on "new ways of thinking and behaving" as much as on technology (OECD, 2003d). Standardized administrative practices would facilitate internal monitoring within the government and would be less expensive and more reliable than a technological solution. They would also contribute to the ultimate goal of government reform.

4.4. Digital divide and wider social appeal

The influence of e-government in China is also critically limited by the low level of development of the country's information society. As previously mentioned, new communication technologies have only diffused to a small percentage of the Chinese population. Reaching and serving the "digital have-nots", such as the peasants, migrant labourers, laid-off workers, and people with disabilities, will be a formidable task.

The most difficult challenge will be to launch and maintain e-government initiatives in the hinterland, in the vast, less developed regions where population density is low and information resources very limited (Qiu, 2002b). A survey in 2003 found that despite China's "Go West" campaign designed to alleviate poverty in the hinterland, the digital divide between the east and west regions is still increasing (*People's Daily*, 2003). According to Zhao Xiaofan, a high-ranking SCIO, official who supervised the survey, "the key to promoting informatization in the west is to improve computer and Internet literacy among the public" (*ibid.*).

It is clear that, in order for e-government to play a more active role in China, the Chinese Government must overcome the barrier of low computer literacy and Internet penetration rates. However, more access to ICT is a necessary but insufficient solution. E-government Web sites must also develop more broadly useful content and applications to appeal to the general public. Only then can the influence of e-government projects bring more benefits to Chinese society at large.

5. The national e-government initiative

One of China's major advantages in developing e-government is the commitment of its high-level political leaders to reform the public sector by using ICT in government operations. This has resulted in a comprehensive, nation-wide plan for e-government based on a coherent vision. The new leaders that emerged from the Sixteenth CPC National Congress in 2002 adopted the vision of previous leaders that informatization is central to the modernization of the Chinese Government. President Hu Jintao and Premier Wen Jiabao have both publicly reiterated the importance of e-government to China's reform agenda. In addition, numerous provincial governors, mayors, and general secretaries of local CPC committees have been active in promoting e-government at the sub-national level.

At the local level, political leadership is essential to the initiation and sustenance of e-government initiatives because the strongest resistance usually comes from those with vested interests in the *status quo*, such as middle-rank officials who fear losing power as a result of using ICT. So far, the prevalent way to counter such resistance has been to launch the so-called "Top Leadership Project" (*yibashou gongcheng*), i.e. the highest CPC or state official at the given administrative level would head the e-government leading group and then try to persuade reluctant stakeholders. This has been an effective strategy in most cases, for example, in Nanhai in South China (see Box 4.3).

Since 2002, the central government has put into place a common framework to guide and co-ordinate e-government projects throughout the country. According to State Council Document No. 17 (*i.e.* the NISG E-Government Recommendations), China's key nationwide e-government initiatives include "two networks, one portal, four databases, and 12 Golden Projects". This programmatic structuring signals that the core leadership of the central government has adopted a hands-on approach toward e-government. The purpose of this new framework is to clarify responsibilities at the national level around key government priorities, to ensure common standards for interoperability and to create a technical platform on which individual bodies and local government can develop their own services.

5.1. *Two networks*

The "two networks" refers to the "internal network" (*neiwang*) for use inside government offices (i.e. government to government, G2G) and the "external network" (*waiwang*) that reaches citizens and businesses (government to citizens, G2C, and government to business,

> **Box 4.3. Top Leadership Project in Nanhai**
>
> The local government of Nanhai was among the first in the country to launch major citywide e-government projects, starting in 1996 (Qiu, 2003). It offers a good example for the Top Leadership Project because high-ranking officials, including Nanhai CPC Secretary Deng Yaohua and Mayor Chen Zhongyuan, were active in promoting the application of Internet in government work. Under their leadership, an informatization leading group was formed that included chief directors of all major local government bodies. Special incentive mechanisms were established to reward progress with bonuses and promotions. In the face of resistance from middle-level officials, members of this committee insistently advocated e-government projects to their subordinates in both public gatherings and everyday work. To increase the impact, committee members were encouraged to "reiterate in all meetings, large or small, on a daily basis (*dahui jiang, xiaohui jiang, tiantian jiang*)".
>
> Major resistance came from the technophobia of older officials, who had little training in using computers or the Internet. The leading group thus decided to provide technical training for most of the local government employees by hiring, at competitive salaries, teachers and IT experts from around China. Following a classic model of public persuasion used in China since the early years of CPC, they also selected model students in these training programmes and gave them significant publicity. One such model student was "Uncle Fa (*fashu*)", a 55-year-old clerk with only an elementary school education. He was highly praised by the local government for his quick adoption of new technologies. "If Uncle Fa can do this", said the leader of a township, "there is no excuse for most of us younger people not to learn the new technology".

G2B). The new division of labour centered on these two networks indicates that China has passed the early development phase in which e-government was dominated by local experiments. A more streamlined co-operative relationship has started to take shape that allows the central government to play a more important role in both macro-management and the supervision of local operations.

This structure also demonstrates Chinese concerns about the security of its information systems. According to "the NISG Recommendations on the Strengthening of Information Security Protection" (hereafter State Council Document No. 27) released in 2003, the internal network is mostly for transmitting confidential information among central government bodies and 47 departments at or above the vice-provincial level. For security considerations, it is "physically separated" (*wuli geli*) from the external network and offices below the vice-provincial level. The internal network is also used for the transfer of data between ministries, for example, in large national G2G databases (i.e. the four databases discussed below), which play a major role in improving services for citizens and businesses throughout the country.

Local governments below the vice-provincial level are encouraged to concentrate on the construction and maintenance of the external networks or *waiwang*, whose main purpose is to provide services directly to the general public. These external networks are operated by local governments, usually by a set of local government bodies under the co-ordination of the corresponding city or provincial informatization offices. Information on the external networks can be accessed via the Internet ,but, as required by State Council Document No. 27, some of the contents are "logically separated" (*luoji geli*), meaning they are protected by passwords and firewalls.

5.2. One portal

Ministries and sub-national governments are encouraged to have one central portal for the public information, service applications, and interactive functions they provide. Information and services can be stored in a portal Web site directly operated by a ministry or a local government such as a province or a city. They can also be maintained by sub-divisions of the particular government body but include hyperlinks to the central portal. This is part of the effort to construct an efficient interface between the external network and the public. The portal is supposed to help users find information and services stored in different parts of the e-government external network or in non-government Web sites to which the portal may hyperlink.

This guideline has been in place since 2002 and with the exception of the Ministry of National Defence and the Ministry of Public Security, most ministries and ministry-level commissions of the central government have established "one portals" for themselves that are accessible to the general public. There is no single portal for the whole of central government, however, and little indication at the national level of who is actually responsible for building the one portal for the central government and whether it will be based on certain existing sites such as the one operated by Government Online.

At the sub-national levels, many local governments, especially those in wealthier regions, have already established their one-portal Web sites. According to the National Conference on Government and the Informatization of Public Administration held in December 2003, 85% of China's regional governments had established portals for citizens and businesses. In addition to local government and CPC offices, these also include portals for the People's Congress, the Political Consultative Conference and the Judiciary.

5.3. Four databases

The four databases (see below), as recognized by the State Council, are the pillars of e-government in China. They are designed to facilitate the storage, transmission and retrieval of information that is central to everyday government operations. Since these are nationwide databases involving exchanges among the ministries, a large amount of their information is transmitted via the G2G internal network. But these key databases also play an important role in back-office reforms by facilitating data-sharing across institutional barriers.

With the exception of the Basic Population Information Database (BPID), these databases are still at a very early stage of development. The main task is not only adding and processing data but also integrating fragmented data resources currently housed in individual government bodies. Once completed, they will provide a powerful tool for the Chinese Government to provide data-sharing services. While more common in the Nordic countries, large comprehensive national databases are more rare in other OECD member countries given legacy systems and concerns about privacy and government misuse of data. Achieving such a system requires a significant amount of central leadership and co-ordination. But it remains to be seen how these four databases will actually materialize, what level of data quality they will produce, and whether their construction will be slowed down due to old institutional barriers as well as new concerns about the privacy of individual citizens and the protection of information regarding business enterprises.

5.3.1. Basic Population Information Database (BPID)

Formally initiated in October 2002, the construction of BPID is led by the Ministry of Public Security (MPS) and jointly managed by the National Population and Family Planning Commission, National Bureau of Statistics, Ministry of Labour and Social Security, and State Administration of Taxation. It is the largest and most comprehensive database for storing basic information and providing unique identifiers for individual citizens in China.

Building on the existing population information system of MPS, the BPID has covered approximately 1.17 billion residents (i.e. 90% of the total population), of which 760 million entries can be remotely retrieved. As of December 2003, the BPID was still in its experimental stage when different technical solutions, models of funding and administrative frameworks were being tested in selected localities.

Phase One of BPID is to be completed by the end of 2006, with its main task being the construction of comprehensive databases at each level of administration and the integration of certain public management information resources. Phase Two will start in 2007 to integrate population information resources in different government departments and provide information services to the general public.

5.3.2. Basic Juridical Person Information Database (BJPID)

BJPID is designed to standardize the ways in which information about commercial entities and non-profit organisations are collected and exchanged. It is spearheaded by the State Bureau of Quality and Technical Supervision and jointly managed by the State Administration for Industry and Commerce, State Administration of Taxation, Ministry of Civil Affairs, State Commission Office for Public Sector Reform, and National Bureau of Statistics.

The first meeting on BJPID was convened in September 2002. By May 2003, the draft proposal for BJPID construction had gone through two rounds of revisions, and more comments from experts were being solicited. The plan is to spend the first three years developing database standards and inputting content. Then, during the following two years, the focus will be on developing networked application systems at the national, provincial and county levels.

5.3.3. Natural Resource, Space, and Geography Information Database (NRSGID)

This database is under the jurisdiction of the State Development and Reform Commission, which co-ordinates the Ministry of Land and Resources, Ministry of Water Resources, Chinese Academy of Science, State Oceanic Administration, National Bureau of Topography, State Forestry Administration, and China Meteorology Administration.

China has a complicated geography and very rich natural resources, which are currently managed by separate government bodies. The purpose of NRSGID is to develop a system with shared standards for all these resources that can be constantly updated and easily exchanged so that optimal resource management (e.g. of land) can be achieved. The project started in September 2002. The first draft of the project proposal was completed in July 2003. Its feasibility research is currently under way.

5.3.4. Macro Economic Information Database (MEID)

This initiative is led by the National Bureau of Statistics and also involves the National Development and Reform Commission, Ministry of Finance, State Economic and Trade Commission, People's Bank, State Administration of Taxation, Customs General

Administration, State Administration for Industry and Commerce and the State Bureau of Quality and Technical Supervision. Its goal is to establish a distributive economic information database to serve the needs of macroeconomic management, public service delivery and requests from international partners.

The first meeting on MEID was held in September 2002. The MEID Construction Project Proposal was drafted in December 2002. Comments are still being solicited.

5.4. The Golden Projects

According to State Council Document No. 17 of 2002, the first phase of e-government in China focuses on 12 professional systems known as the "12 Golden Projects". These include: *i)* core systems designed to strengthen supervision and enhance efficiency (*i.e.* Administrative Professional Resources System and Golden Macro); *ii)* projects designed to safeguard government revenue and rationalize government spending (*i.e.* Golden Tax, Golden Customs, Golden Audit, Golden Finance, and Golden Card); and *iii)* systems designed to ensure basic order in the national economy and social development (*i.e.* Golden Shield, Golden Quality, Golden Agriculture, Golden Water Conservancy and Golden Social Security). While some of these projects include front-office applications on the external network, most of them operate on the e-government's internal network with direct links to the main databases.

The 12 Golden Projects are as follows:

1. ***The Administrative Professional Resources System* (bangong yewu ziyuan xitong)** is under the direct co-ordination of the State Council. Unlike other Golden Projects, this is a comprehensive system that underlies e-government operations in all divisions of government work.

   The project has five components: *i)* a desktop video-conference system; *ii)* an electronic meeting announcement and registration system; *iii)* a State Council supervision management system; *iv)* an electronic document-transmission system; and *v)* a government crisis-management system. While some of these components continue earlier efforts in corresponding areas, all of them are expected to enter a new phase of development in 2004. Public records so far show no definite deadline for the completion of this project.

   SCIO serves as the main planner of the Administrative Professional Resources System, with MII being the implementer and the Ministry of Finance being the funding body. Several other ministries, such as the Ministry of Public Security and the State Secrecy Bureau, are also involved.

2. **Golden Macro (jinhong),** also known as the Macro Economic Management Information System, is directed by the National Development and Reform Commission and jointly led by the Ministry of Finance, the Ministry of Commerce, the People's Bank of China, the State-owned Assets Supervision and Management Commission, the Customs General Administration, the National Bureau of Statistics and the State Administration of Foreign Exchange. The main purpose of Golden Macro is to increase connectivity and information-sharing among government bodies in charge of macroeconomic management so that national economic policy-making can be more efficient, accurate and transparent.

3. **The Golden Tax (jinshui) Project,** led by the State Administration of Taxation, is intended to prevent tax evasion that uses counterfeit receipts and invoices. So far this is one of the most successful Golden Projects in promoting efficiency and accountability. Phase One of the Golden Tax Project was launched in 1994. Phase Two started in May 2000 with some adjustments in planning and implementation. By the end of 2002, it had covered approximately 600 000 units, i.e. about 45% of taxpayers nationwide. It had also integrated 3 835 taxation offices at or above the urban district or rural county level.
Phase Three of the Golden Tax Project began in December 2002 and will take four to five years. The new focus is on the China Taxation Administration Information System, a multi-functional platform that will provide secure and integrated information about taxation at national and sub-national levels.

4. **Golden Customs (jinguan),** also known as the Golden Gate Project, was one of the three Golden Projects initiated by the Chinese Government in 1993. It was formally launched in 2001 under the leadership of the then Ministry of Foreign Trade and Economic Co-operation (now Ministry of Commerce, MOFCOM). The Customs General Administration and 11 ministry-level departments were involved in the establishment of "electronic port centres", a centrepiece of the Golden Customs (see Box 4.6 for the Golden Customs' anti-corruption achievements).
The Project's current emphasis is on developing application systems for: *i)* quota and licences; *ii)* import/export statistics; *iii)* tax returns for exporting companies; and *iv)* international trade currency transactions. Its long-term objective is to facilitate the modernization of China's international trade and economic transaction system by using computer network technologies.

5. **The Golden Finance (jincai) Project** started in 1999 as the Ministry of Finance attempted to construct its Government Finance Management Information System. As part of the effort to modernize financial management within the Chinese Government, Golden Finance has two primary objectives: first, to integrate eleven existing sub-systems at the national level, from income and budgeting management to procurement and debt control; and second, to establish vertical networks that include provincial and municipal bureaus of finance.
By the end of 2002, the project had expanded to 38 national government bodies (762 budgeting units) and 25 provincial-level units. This included the payment of salaries for most government entities at or above the provincial level as well as the management of non-tax revenues.

6. **Golden Card (jinka)** is part of the overall Financial Supervision (*jinrong jianguan*) Project designated in State Council Document No. 17. Originally one of the three key informatization projects initiated in 1993, Golden Card promotes the use of electronic currency in Chinese society. By the end of 2002, the Project had extended to banks and department stores in more than 300 cities where more than 60 million debit cards and credit cards issued by financial institutions have been in circulation.
The central government reckons that the spread of electronic currency usage will not only enhance e-commerce but also allow government offices to improve the regulation of financial markets based on a unified payment clearance system. Effective supervision of financial exchange will enable public authorities at different levels to track and monitor transactions in public and private sectors, which also enhances anti-corruption efforts.

7. **Golden Audit (jinshen)** is under the National Audit Office. It was formally launched in November 2002 with an initial funding of RMB 50 million (USD 6 million). Its long-term goal is to establish a centrally organised electronic auditing system for government entities in China. By the end of July 2003, the Project was mainly focused on building infrastructure within the National Audit Office and its 18 subsidiaries nationwide. Meanwhile, the development of application systems and information databases was in progress and the Handbook for Audit Software R&D was compiled, which specified standard procedures, database structures, and ways to guarantee interconnectivity and information sharing.

8. **The Golden Shield (jindun) Project** was initiated by the State Planning Commission (now NDRC) and Ministry of Public Security in July 2001. Its goal is "the adoption of advanced ICTs to strengthen central police control, responsiveness, and crime combating capacity, so as to improve the efficiency and effectiveness of public security work". Two phases are planned, with Phase One (2002-04) focusing on building infrastructure and a common operation platform, and Phase Two (2005-06) emphasizing the development of applications.

   By the end of Phase One, the Project was expected to connect all public security units at or beyond the regional level and 95% of units at the county level. The National Public Security High-Speed Inquiry System (including the China Crime Information Centre) was also to be completed. In the meantime, the National Public Information Network Security Supervision Centre is also being set up, with the mandate to combat hacker attacks and computer viruses.

9. **The Golden Social Security (jinbao) Project** was launched in October 2002 during the National Conference on the Informatization of Labour Protection. The Ministry of Labour and Social Security spearheads the project, which has the long-term goal of setting up a unified national information system for labour protection and social security.

   In addition to recording and processing information about people and work units in the social security system, the Golden Social Security Project will also monitor changes in the labour market and provide policy recommendations to government offices at national, provincial and city levels. By April 2003, 29 provincial units had confirmed funding to support the project at local levels. Preparation for the nationwide networking of retirement insurance information systems was in progress. In September 2002, the Web site "China Labour Market" (*www.lm.gov.cn/*) was launched to provide job and employment information as well as national policies for labour market regulation.

10. **The Golden Quality (jinzhi) Project** has the goal of transforming quality supervision authorities into public service providers, enhancing transparency in administration and forming a standardized national network. The project is housed under the State Bureau of Quality and Technical Supervision. Until 2003, the project was mostly in the stage of feasibility research. A main challenge for its implementation is funding, particularly for local inspection units in less developed regions.

11. **Golden Agriculture (jinnong)** promotes the utilization of ICT for agriculture in China. Led by the Ministry of Agriculture, Phase One of the Project is attempting to build a monitoring and management information system that will connect government bodies in China's vast countryside. This phase is expected to last until 2005. Phase Two (until 2010) will expand the system to more realms of service delivery, such as agriculture adjustments and market supervision. The project will have three major

applications: *i)* a monitoring and alert system that will provide warnings for agricultural production and animal diseases; *ii)* an information system that will supervise the marketing of production materials; and *iii)* a service system that will provide science and technology information for agriculture production.

12. **The Golden Water Conservancy (jinshui) Project,** led by the Ministry of Water Resources, was launched in 2001. Its short-term goals include building basic infrastructures, increasing the supply of information, and enhancing the capacity for data sharing. In the long run, the project will provide more advanced specialized applications for government decision-making. Two central components of the Golden Water Conservancy Project were launched in 2003: one is the National Flood-Control and Draught-Relief Command System, and the other is the National Supervision Network for Water and Soil Conservation.

Overall, the 12 Golden Projects represent a comprehensive framework for co-ordinating and streamlining e-government initiatives at the ministerial level. While the Administrative Professional Resources System and Golden Macro are of fundamental significance to the general functioning of government bodies, the other 10 Golden Projects are expected to become the pillars of e-government application in their respective sectors.

The development of the Golden Projects, however, has been quite uneven. Some projects have gone through the first or second phase of construction already, whereas others are still at the planning stage or are just beginning to establish computer networks between relevant offices. In general, those projects dealing with economic management and law enforcement tend to be built up at a faster speed than those providing other services to the general public. This is in part because some projects were initiated earlier than others; it is also due to the different amount of resources controlled by the ministerial bodies, reflecting the priority placed on economy and security.

Other Golden Projects are not included in the 12 mentioned above. One is the Golden Bridge *(jinqiao)* Project started in 1993 to connect government offices, state-owned enterprises, and the general public. Since this is a basic infrastructure project led by China Jitong Telecom Inc., it does not count as one of the main e-government initiatives in State Council Document No. 17. The list of 12 also excludes several other Golden Projects sponsored either by individual ministries (*e.g.* Golden Hygiene, Golden Wisdom, Golden Trade, Golden Travel) or government bodies at lower levels (*e.g.* Golden Enterprise).

6. Customer focus and information sharing

The experience of most OECD member countries has been that, when properly deployed, e-government can help provide higher quality information provision, service delivery and citizen engagement (OECD, 2003a). The following section reviews these three aspects of e-government and demonstrates how new e-government projects have begun to promote a more customer-oriented approach in certain local government bodies and government sectors leading to more wide-ranging changes in government processes and government-citizen relations.

6.1. Information provision

By the end of 2003, most central government bodies in China had launched their Web sites for external usage among citizens and businesses. So had 85% of the regional governments (Xinhua News Agency, 11 December 2003). The quality of information provided from these Web sites, however, varies tremendously. While some provided comprehensive information for the public as discussed below, others were poorly maintained. An earlier study found that among China's 2 500 e-government portal sites, approximately one-third were "dead sites" that could not be opened (Yang, 2003). The problem may have improved since, because e-government leaders at all levels have been emphasizing the importance of Web site maintenance.

Among all the working Web sites, most contain general introductions about the public offices, government news, regulations and policy documents. A moderate number provide information about administrative procedures, announcements and other information needed by the industries and the general public. These are some of the main findings from the 2002 Quantitative Survey on Internet Information Resources in China conducted by the China Computer Industry Development Research Institute (CCID) and CNNIC under the supervision of SCIO.

The survey found furthermore that the "overall situation for the updating of government Web site information is not optimistic". Only a small number of the web-hosts update on a monthly basis their online statistics and reports (5.7%) and introductions about administrative procedures (5.2%). Other types of information are renewed more frequently, such as government news (57.5%), economic news for industries (54.3%), information for residents regarding housing, transportation, and so on (75.8%) as well as announcements (85.7%).

The predominant majority of Web sites do not support interactive exchange. Only 26.4% allow users to conduct an automated information search and a mere 10.7% accept inquiries from the public regarding the progress of particular administrative work.

Figure 4.2. **Types of information provided by China's e-government Web sites (%)**

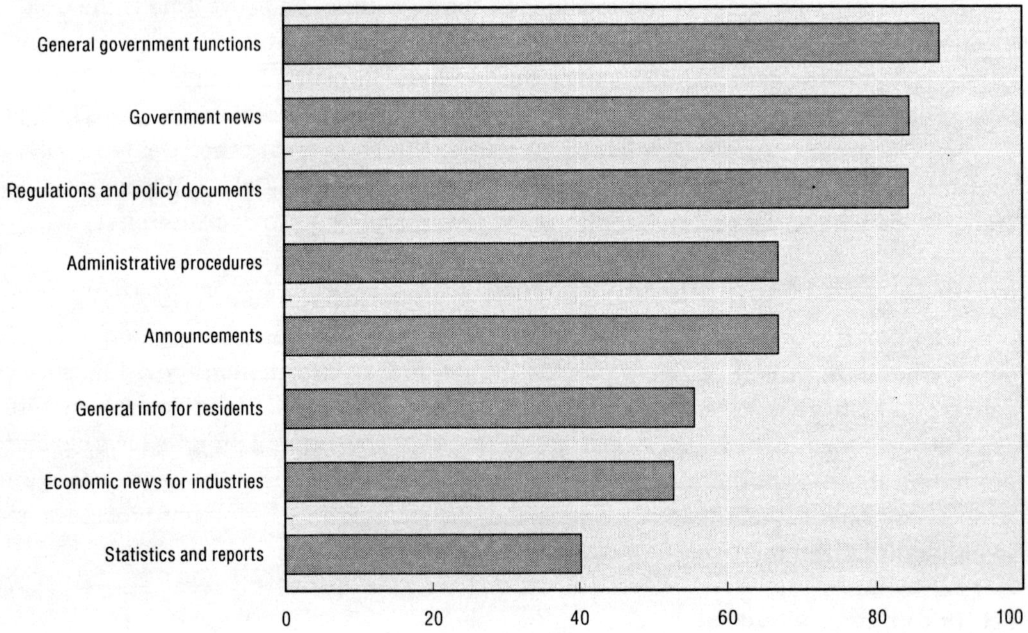

Source: CCID and CNNIC (2002).

A set of focus groups, carried out in 2002 in a medium-sized southern city found that e-government Web sites do not attract much attention from the general public because they have insufficient and often outdated information. Although more than RMB 100 million (USD 12 million) had been spent on local e-government projects over the course of several years, participants reported that they seldom visited the portal site of their city, because they did not think it provided very useful information or services. The few people who had visited the e-government Web site revealed that they found the content useful only for certain aspects of their professional work, but not for their everyday life. Nor did they find the Web site appealing in design or user-friendly in function.

These findings are confirmed in an earlier study based on log analysis, showing that very few people accessed government Web sites by the end of 2000 (Zhang, 2002). For example, in a city of 2.79 million, the daily click-through number for the main government Web site was only 18; in a smaller city of 440 000 residents, the number was three. The Web site of a major ministry-level body received about 32 hits each day. Although it is likely that the situation has significantly improved since 2000, a more recent survey in 2003 found that most e-government Web sites still function merely as "online brochures" (*People's Daily*, 2003). Improving information provision therefore remains an important task for e-government in China.

Finally, analysis of the languages in which Web content is presented reveal that officials developing e-government are aware that their sites may have users from outside of China, be they foreign investors, tourists or overseas Chinese. More than half of the Web sites (53.6%) have English versions, 10.4% have a Japanese version, while 22.3% have a traditional Chinese character version using BIG5 coding, the official standard in Chinese Taipei and Hong Kong, China. Although the foreign language and BIG5-coded Web pages often contain less information, the sizeable proportion they represent indicates that many e-government sites are indeed designed to meet the demand of foreign users.

6.2. Service delivery

Compared to the information provision function, there are significantly fewer e-government Web sites offering online service delivery to citizens. The Qualitative Study of Internet Information Resources in China (QSIIR, 2002) shows that in 2002 the more frequently offered services were filing complaints (27.6%) and downloading paperwork (20.1%). About one-tenth of the Web sites supported online bidding for government projects and Web-based government procurement of supplies. Only a small percentage provided online document submission (6.9%), job application (6.9%) or company registration (3.4%).

Shanghai Municipality, for example, is particularly active in promoting Web-based service delivery to citizens and businesses. The Web site of the Shanghai Informatization Committee (*www.shanghaiit.gov.cn*) provides 12 service links for the general public, allowing residents to apply for social security cards, join IT training schools and check scores for college entrance examinations. It has comprehensive functions to assist commercial enterprises including the downloading of 16 forms and 15 online application programmes as of March 2004. The Shanghai Administration of Industry and Commerce (*www.sgs.gov.cn*) also provides a series of online services for local and international entrepreneurs, who can fill in and submit most of the registration and licensing paperwork on the Internet.

Figure 4.3. **Online service deliveries by China's e-government Web sites (%)**

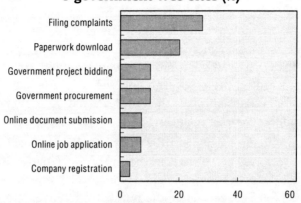

In addition to online services targeting Internet users, e-government may also bring about back-office changes that can improve services to those without Internet access who contact the government through more traditional channels. For instance, local governments in China are experimenting with innovative ways to blend online e-government applications with such traditional media as the telephone. The Haishu District Government of Ningbo City, Zhejiang Province, established the 81 890 Community Service Centre, which is both a Web site (*www.81890.gov.cn*) and a hotline. Using either mode of communication, residents can request a wide variety of services from plumbing to childcare to street repair. The system is supported by several databases that record not only service requests and appointment information but also customer feedback and ratings for service quality. By the end of June 2003, the centre had handled 142 518 requests since its inception in August 2001. Similar e-community services have been launched in Shanghai, Hangzhou (Zhejiang Province), and Jiangmen (Guangdong Province), using both the Internet and the telephone.

Innovative modes of G2G service delivery are also emerging at the local levels. In Nanhai, Guangdong Province, an online accountancy centre was established that centrally manages financial accounts for all public service units (PSUs) directly under the city government. This is a secured internal network system that gives high-ranking officials more access to financial information updated on a daily basis with data retrieved from the PSUs and their bank accounts. As a result, the PSUs no longer need to have their own accountants. Bookkeeping and funds allocation can all be done online.

At the national level, the capacity for service delivery to citizens and businesses has been rapidly increasing since 2002, especially with the launching of the 12 Golden Projects. The full impact of the Golden Projects, however, is not readily quantifiable as their full impact on back-office operations still needs to be studied. For instance, the Golden Tax Project simplifies the process of invoice verification, increases efficiency and reduces the possibility of corruption by enabling online supervision from the national to county-level taxation offices. By so doing, it not only guarantees government revenue but also shortens the process of filing taxes and getting tax returns. These reforms may not be apparent from the examination of Web sites on the external network, but their profound impact is not to be underestimated.

6.3. Public participation

According to the QSIIRC 2002 study, one-fifth of China's e-government Web sites have online public opinion polls or designated space to accept suggestions from the public. Since 2003, some national or local government bodies have begun to host online public opinion polls and solicit feedback on policy proposals. One example is the Web-based opinion collection for regulations issued by the State Administration of Industry and Commerce (SAIC). From March to July 2003, SAIC's China Foreign Investor Registration Network (http://wzj.saic.gov.cn) publicized five draft regulations and received 1 200 comments and suggestions, of which 41 were incorporated into the final documents. It remains to be determined, however, how widespread and how effective such efforts to consult foreign investors and other stakeholders are in practice.

The most outstanding experiment at the sub-national level is being carried out in Suzhou City, which has launched a Web site with a public forum (see Box 4.4).

Box 4.4. **Suzhou's Public Supervision Bulletin Board System**

Suzhou Online (www.suzhou.gov.cn) is a local experiment intended to increase citizen participation through ICT. Hosted by Suzhou City, Jiangsu Province, this portal allows the delivery of e-mail to the inboxes of city mayors, heads of district/county governments and directors of all city-level departments. It includes an "Open Government Affairs" (*zhengwu gongkai*) section on the Web site that publicizes regulations, shows administrative structure and introduces key national and local policies. An online bulletin board system (BBS) titled "Public Supervision" (*gongzhong jiandu*) enables individual citizens to share their concerns with related government bodies in an open public forum. In addition to the content of citizen-government interactions, this BBS also shows when an inquiry was first raised, which office was in charge, whether it replied, and if so, when.

By the end of February 2004, the forum had close to 1 000 posts, of which more than 900 received replies from specified government offices. One typical message was from an anonymous resident who expressed concern about the police's use of force during a car chase following a kidnapping incident. The City Bureau of Public Security posted a reply on the following workday reporting the result of a quick internal investigation, explaining that adequate precaution was taken and thanking the citizen for his/her concern. In another message, a Suzhou resident proposed to reduce bus noise by stopping the announcement of bus station names using loudspeakers. The City Bureau of Transportation responded within 24 hours, saying that it had asked bus companies to control noise in the evenings and that the situation would soon improve.

However, Suzhou has a population that is relatively affluent and well educated, and the city's geographic adjacency to Shanghai means it is more influenced by global market forces than elsewhere. Hence, it remains to be seen whether or not such examples of increased openness will spread to other parts of the country or to other spheres of state-society relationship such as NGOs, which are largely absent in the current e-government processes.

6.4. Data sharing and compatibility

Sharing information across institutional boundaries is among the most serious challenges. Before 2002, local governments, bodies led by the ministries and competing commercial enterprises initiated a large number of e-government projects. Neglecting the need for data-sharing with other e-government systems thus gave rise to a great number of "information islands" with incompatible formats and structures.

The NISG recognizes that the main challenges to China's e-government are: "*i)* separate operations in network construction that result in overlapping and/or incorrectly structured systems; *ii)* inadequate online platforms with limited scope of application and services; *iii)* slow utilization of information resources constrained by the lack of interconnectivity and sharing; and *iv)* incompatible standards, security risks, and legislative weaknesses" (2002).

State Council Document No. 17 thus outlined the common framework of "two networks, one portal, four databases, and 12 Golden Projects". While the internal and external networks are expected to provide the infrastructure for data sharing, the four nationwide databases are the most central to the effort of integrating separate information resources. Unconfined by sectoral and ministerial boundaries, the four databases under construction are structured to provide a material basis for data sharing about the management of individual citizens, juridical persons (non-profit or for-profit organisations), natural resources and the macroeconomy. While most of these initiatives are in progress, they are establishing common standards for a large number of state bodies at various administrative levels to work together in a shared framework.

However, the development of e-government standards is still at an early stage in China. Although official documents often call for more interconnectivity, they are seldom translated into actual operational procedures with the necessary level of specificity. One exception is the *Technical Guidelines for E-Government Projects* jointly issued by SCIO, the Ministry of Science and Technology, and the Ministry of Information Industry in April 2003. This document attempts to give operational instructions, but even so it provides mostly "guidelines" at the national level. Our interviews with local government bodies and IT industry players show that, while they appreciate the value of the *Technical Guidelines*, the need for more specific standards persists.

A tension exists: while lower-level officials and e-government contractors (*e.g.* programmers) demand more detailed guidelines, for example, about system standardization, leaders at higher administrative levels tend to be cautious and would like to see more experiments and more "natural selection" in the marketplace before the central government promotes any specific standard. This is understandable given the preliminary stage of e-government in China, and it will take some time to regularize interactions across the government and with the IT industry to produce a more inclusive framework of co-operation. In the meantime, local government officials do not have the authority to make formal decisions. Hence, without sufficient guidance, there is a real danger of a roadblock in terms of e-government policy and decision-making.

7. E-government programmes and reform of the public administration

According to the Proclamation of the Sixteenth CPC National Congress in November 2002, China has committed to reconfiguring its public administration into a new organism that is "just, transparent, clean, and highly efficient". To reach this goal, the general function of government is to be transformed from traditional top-down regulation focusing on service provision and management. E-government efforts can contribute to changes in administrative processes, working methods, and organisational culture. As former Premier Zhu Rongji reportedly said, the focus of e-government initiatives were not on the "e", but rather on the "government", "to improve the transformation of government in terms of management systems, management values, management patterns, and management methods" (Zhang and Gao, 2003).

Despite the early stage of transformation and the lack of indicators, positive organisational changes can be observed resulting from e-government developments in different geographic regions and different sectors. The main outcomes include the enhancement of efficiency, transparency and accountability, which all contribute to China's anti-corruption endeavours. Besides back-office G2G relations, the new, more transparent administration also encompass G2C and G2B connections to engage members of the growing civil society and private sector players.

7.1. Efficiency and seamless service delivery

E-government programmes can contribute to increasing the efficiency of government work. This is the objective of officials, IT entrepreneurs, and NGO representatives with regard to the specific tasks and projects they are engaged in. At the national level, the framework of "two networks, one portal, four databases, and 12 Golden Projects" explicitly encourages interconnectivity and content sharing within the government both horizontally and vertically. In so doing, it is creating a simplified structure across the nation that is expected to greatly improve administrative efficiency.

Meanwhile, the central government is promoting the standardization of operational procedures. Two kinds of procedures are affected: the processes of e-government construction (front office) and the applications of e-government in administrative work (back office).

Under such circumstances, local projects that aim at increasing efficiency have begun to emerge, especially since 2002. For example, on 1 January 2003 the Suzhou Industrial Park One-Stop Service Centre was established, where local businesses can obtain most of the services they need in one location. With five main offices and 24 counters, the Centre accommodates officials from various local government bodies, whose computer terminals in the building are networked with their central offices, such as the Bureau of Industry and Commerce, of Taxation, and of Land Resources. The Centre is equipped with a Web site (*http://ossc.sipac.gov.cn*) offering document downloading, online consultation and online application services.

The "one-stop" setup greatly enhances efficiency for both users and government. From the customer's perspective, applicants no longer need to travel back and forth among multiple office buildings to complete one task, such as setting up a new firm. It also simplifies work for government employees because, after visiting the Web site and getting consultation services, most business representatives walk in better informed about administrative procedures, and many of them have already completed their downloaded paperwork. By September 2004, the Centre had received more than 55 000 service requests, of which more than 54 000 were already processed.

With the progress of e-government, measures have also been taken in cities such as Beijing to consolidate previously separate procedures into so-called "one-form" services. In November 2002, the Beijing Administration of Industry and Commerce simplified its administrative process by consolidating eight different business enterprise registration forms into a single document. The Haidian District Committee of Zhongguancun Science and Technology Park launched one-form services in June 2002, so that only one document needs to be exchanged between business enterprises and the local government, while information is shared among relevant government bodies (Zhu, 2002). As a result of this restructuring, on average it now only takes three working days to approve a new domestic enterprise, as opposed to 15 working days in the past.

In Southern China, the People's Court of Nanhai (*http://fayuan.nanhai.gov.cn*) is using its Web site to provide services more efficiently to the general public. In addition, its local access network allows multiple offices to share data and automatically assign cases to judges following a random selection procedure. As a result, while it used to take about one week for the court to accept a case and put it on file for investigation and prosecution, it now takes just 30 minutes.

7.2. Transparency and accountability

By providing information about government structure and administrative procedures, e-government initiatives can increase official transparency and accountability both inside the government and in relation to the general public. Essential to this transformation are three measures taken by the central government: i) setting up standardized operational guidelines for public administrators; ii) reshaping the examination and approval system in the administrative structure; and iii) formulating specific measures to ensure openness and transparency (Wang et al., 2003, p. 21).

As discussed earlier, a key move that may lay the cornerstone for a more transparent government is the Open Governance Act, which is being revised. This development is crucial because, although many e-government experiments like the Public Supervision BBS in Suzhou (see Box 4.4) are taking place, they are only local projects yet to be elevated into formal rules of behaviour for all government employees.

One of the most notable changes in local-level administrative practice is in the procedures of e-government construction itself. Before 2002, given the predominantly local experimental nature of e-government at the time, few guidelines addressed the proper working methods for e-government projects. Contracts were therefore often given to companies that had personal connections to local decision-makers through an informal process that was neither transparent nor accountable, causing particular problems with meeting deadlines and controlling budgets.

Since 2002, new measures have been taken to transform the practice of government procurement and project bidding. According to the Government Procurement Act promulgated in June 2002, government bodies are now required to first release information to the general public about its future purchases. A formal process of bidding follows, after which a committee will choose the best bidder based on factors such as price, work quality and risk estimation. At the end of the selection process, the selected company must sign a contract specifying terms, including penalties if requirements or deadlines are not met.

These measures are carried out in many localities. By 2003 when most local governments had established their online presence, it was common practice to include pop-up announcements on their portals about government purchasing and future projects. Some large cities also launched special Web sites for this purpose, for example, the Shanghai Government Procurement Network (*www.ccgp-shanghai.gov.cn*). Interviews conducted in South, East, and North China showed that this open bidding system had greatly improved government procurement practices by significantly lowering costs and enhancing the work quality of contractors.

On another note, while some maintain that China's e-government initiatives are largely designed to increase surveillance over not only other governmental entities but also private citizens (Walton, 2001; Kluver, 2004), the growth of the external network is exposing an increasing amount of government activities to public scrutiny. There is certainly an enormous need to increase citizen engagement, as previously discussed. But as shown in the case of Suzhou's Public Supervision BBS (see Box 4.4), citizens and business firms may begin to hold government bodies accountable by subjecting them to the new online environment of open inquiries. From the city mayor to investors to ordinary residents, everyone can see which city government offices receive what kinds of queries and suggestions, how they respond and how long it takes for them to provide feedback. The formalization of measures to increase government accountability is still a pending issue, though, as progress is often made within the limited institutional context of a specific city or particular profession. But despite the limited scope, at least the process of transformation has begun in actual organisational practice, not as mere rhetoric.

7.3. Horizontal and vertical co-ordination

With the increase of transparency enabled by the internal network, it is now easier for officials to quickly retrieve information and distribute documents at and across administrative levels. This is particularly helpful for authorities at higher levels. According to Foster, Goodman, and Tan (2000): "in the interests of productivity, the government wants to decentralize decision making to the provinces and the markets, but wants to make sure that it is able to keep track of those decisions". Thus, as Hachigian (2001) observes, "the central government is using the Internet's infrastructure to improve its own administrative control over provincial and local officials" by acquiring a stronger capacity to monitor administrative procedures and results at the sub-national levels.

The experience of the Golden Customs Project helps to illustrate that a major function of e-government in China is to increase the capacity of the central government to step up internal monitoring of subordinate bodies (Hachigian, 2001; Kluver, 2004). Due to the lack of real-time interconnection within the customs system, illegal transactions frequently took place with support from government employees who accepted bribes. However, the Golden Customs Project implemented the "electronic port system" that networks 12 divisions, including customs, banks, import/export inspection, foreign currency management, foreign trade administration, and taxation. Using a model called "electronic base-record and online crosschecking", no transaction can be approved without positive feedback from all the networked databases. According to the Customs General Administration, the total amount of illegal transactions caused by official corruption was RMB 1.5 billion (USD 181 million) in 1997 and RMB 2.1 billion (USD 253.9 million) in 1998. The number decreased to RMB 313 million (USD 37.8 million) in 1999, the first year that the "electronic port system" was completed. Since 2000 it has become almost non-existent.

Although it remains uncertain how ICT-based anti-corruption measures can be implemented in sectors other than customs and procurement, e-government offers an opportunity to institutionalize transparent sharing of information and increased accountability embedded in specific technological mechanisms

7.4. Public management

A main promise of e-government in China is that it will enhance the government's capacity to manage public resources and provide services by using ICT. But to realize this goal, long-standing issues in the existing public management system must be resolved, such as the relatively low computer/Internet literacy among government workers, the traditional top-down approach to treating citizens and businesses, and the ambiguous relationship between the public and the private.

Compared to government workers in OECD member countries, state employees in China require more technical training because their competence in using ICT varies significantly. Although 65% of central government employees are college-educated, only 10% of those who work at the sub-national level have a college education (Wang et al., 2003). A large number of those who have not attended college have low computer literacy, which is particularly an issue in small cities and less-developed inland regions. It thus remains an urgent task to increase information management skills among average Chinese officials.

Besides increasing technological know-how, the Chinese Government faces a deeper problem because, in the existing administrative culture, officials tend to take a top-down approach in their management style when dealing with citizens and businesses. As Kluver (2004) points out, this is very different from most OECD member countries, in which technology is used to reinforce good existing government practices. In China, "in attempting to launch the e-government initiatives, the government is implementing procedures that are based on a set of assumptions about human behaviour that are largely untested".

An important task, therefore, is to transform the management style, or else e-government in China will not succeed. Certain officials would use ICT for their own personal benefit or for the sole purpose of social control, which contradicts the goals of cost reduction and transparency. Transforming the general management style obviously goes beyond the undertaking of e-government and may need much more time than the diffusion of technology. But it is critical because, after all, the essence of e-government is to overcome dysfunctional past tendencies to achieve better government.

Due to the influence of the previous socialist planned economy, the ambiguous relationship between state and non-state sectors poses another barrier to public management reform. As mentioned earlier, for-profit and private companies have played an important role in the early development of e-government in China, and they continue to be an indispensable driving force in the e-government market. These include a large number of telecom service providers, infrastructure builders, and software and hardware producers from both within and outside the country, whose relationship with government bodies is often contingent upon specific contexts and the informal personal connections of *guanxi*.

While it is understandable that the direct involvement of foreign companies is usually limited to the provision of hardware and some basic software for the protection of state secrets, the debate is ongoing regarding whether and how domestic private or for-profit companies should play a role in the e-government process. This is not an easy decision, because many commercial e-government operations, like the Government Online Project, were initiated with administrative support from certain government bodies. Many companies were also funded in part or in full by local governments, which adds to the situation's complexity. Although the recent Government Procurement Act standardizes the public-private relationship to some extent, the co-operative ties remain murky in many cases, indicating a need to enhance the public management framework when it comes to working with non-state organisations in e-government projects.

8. Key challenges/recommendations

China has made rapid progress in setting up a basic Web presence for the majority of government bodies, but without a more user-focused approach to improve the relevance of online services, take-up will remain low. China's approach to e-government seems to be in line with that of a majority of OECD member countries in terms of linking e-government with the broader reform of the public sector. This means, however, that e-government is more than simply about improving efficiency. As e-government in China continues to develop, the government will need to address how it can continue to improve the relationship between government and its users, including citizens, businesses and the civil society:

1. **Balancing the functions of social control and public service** – E-government is not meant to be an instrument for state surveillance and social control. Although the concern over electronic surveillance has been voiced in many societies, including most OECD member countries, there is relatively little discussion on this subject within the e-government policy-making community of China. The recent emphasis on service provision and customer focus is helping to restore the balance between service and control, although this subject requires attention in the long run because of its fundamental significance in the state-society relationship.

2. **Bridging the digital divide and promoting e-government in less developed regions** – National co-ordination is required to address this problem, which may benefit from China's "Go West" inland development strategy. So far there is no specific policy to encourage e-government in less-developed regions. As e-government continues to expand, however, access to electronic information and services will grow in importance as both an equity and a cost savings issue. Future steps need to include new policies for and investments in infrastructure building, training and technical assistance, as well as the research and development of new applications that would suit the needs of citizens and government bodies in these regions.

3. **Harnessing e-government for better citizen engagement and the involvement of NGOs** – Although some local government bodies are experimenting with e-government as a new way to spur citizen engagement, these trial efforts have not been systematically examined to draw broader lessons for the rest of the country. Moreover, there has been virtually no effort to include Chinese NGOs in the e-government policy process. Although state officials are not yet ready to work with NGOs on this matter, NGO representatives in Beijing have expressed their eagerness to facilitate the realization of China's e-government goals, if there is sufficient financial and technical support.

Achieving China's ambitious e-government programme will entail first meeting a number of implementation challenges, many of which are more general challenges for the Chinese administration such as the legal and budgetary framework and inter-agency collaboration. The current commitment to reform through e-government should be used to bear pressure on addressing these priority areas:

1. **Establishing basic legal parameters** – Legal parameters provide the most fundamental rules of the game, guaranteeing the long-term development of e-government in the country. Besides the Open Governance Act, a new set of rules needs to include more co-ordinated considerations for intellectual property rights, administrative simplification, network security and privacy.

2. **Improving budget allocation for ICT spending** – Determining and allocating funds remains a central issue in the planning and implementation of e-government projects. Most local governments have yet to institute a formal procedure to estimate cost, which has to do with the lack of formative research. Insufficient funding for software, application development and system maintenance is common, and the general budgeting problem is particularly challenging in less-developed regions. Improved cost and benefit estimation methodology will help to target scarce resources, and improved mechanisms are needed for sharing costs in order to promote inter-agency collaboration.

3. **Reshaping institutional frameworks** – Making one-stop service a reality requires more than electronic service portals. The Chinese Government will need to look at how it can streamline and improve the horizontal and vertical relationships within government in order to increase co-ordination and collaboration for seamless service delivery. Deeper back-office reform is needed in order to improve customer focus and data-sharing among bodies and to eliminate institutional barriers that lead to redundant systems and inconsistent programme rules. In addition to its guiding principles, China needs more detailed implementation plans that specify priority orders, procedures and ways of adjusting to a changing environment.

4. **Establishing interconnectivity** – While the lack of interconnectivity is also a common problem in OECD member countries, it reflects the specific path of institutional development in each country. A major challenge for the Chinese Government is integrating existing e-government "information islands" that use different platforms, standards and protocols. Connectivity and interoperability is a pressing issue nationwide. Meeting this challenge requires the elaboration of basic, open standards, for example for electronic identification and authentication, which will promote the interoperability of IT systems regardless of specific technology choices.

5. **Strengthening network security** – To solve the network security issue, Chinese authorities need better security technologies and more training, moreover, a comprehensive set of organisational rules and procedures has to be developed and implemented. The technical and non-technical measures for security protection should be incorporated in the plan for a common e-government framework.

6. **Clarifying the public-private relationship** – Debate continues over whether e-government taskforces should form co-operative ties with private and non-state IT enterprises, including domestic and foreign firms, especially the local IT companies that were founded in the first place to implement e-government experiments with state sponsorship. The promulgation of the Government Procurement Act is but a first step in clarifying the public-private relationship. It will be important to identify which form of collaboration is best suited to which type of e-government project; for example, network maintenance or the development of multi-functional platforms.

7. **Improving evaluation of e-government initiatives** – Measures of information and service quality provide a more balanced picture than the number of Web sites alone. The Chinese Government will also need to take into account user take-up of services in order to assess actual benefits realized.

Notes

1. This chapter was written by Jack Linchuan Qiu, Assistant Professor, School of Journalism and Communication, The Chinese University of Hong Kong, and Nina Hachigian, Senior Political Scientist and Director, The RAND Centre for Asia Pacific Policy, with the guidance of Edwin Lau, Innovation and Integrity Division, Public Governance and Territorial Development Directorate, OECD.

2. This body was first established in July 1996, but with the re-shuffle of IT-related ministries in 1998, it gradually lost its leadership functions in late 1990s. There was no formal dismissal, but it was not functioning by early 2001. Thus, then-Premier Zhu Rongji "re-established" it in August 2001.

Bibliography

Accenture (2002), *The Current State of E-Government in China: Building the Platform for Future Development.*

CCW Research (2002), "The Truth About Government Web sites in China" (in Chinese), available at *www.ccwresearch.com.cn/cn/news/0912_01.asp*.

Cheung, A. (2003), "The Business of Governance – China's Legislation on Content Regulation in Cyberspace", paper presented at the conference "China and the Internet: Technology, Economy, and Society in Transition", Los Angeles: 30-31 May.

China Computer Industry Development Research Institute (CCID) and China Internet Network Information Center (CNNIC) (2002), *Survey Report on the Quantitative Survey on Internet Information Resources in China* (in Chinese).

China Internet Network Information Centre (CNNIC) (October 1997 – January 2004), "Semi-Annual Survey of China's Internet Development" (in Chinese), available at *www.cnnic.net.cn/index/0E/00/11/index.htm*.

ChinaLabs (2002), *E-Government Research Report* (in Chinese).

Chinese Communist Party (2002), "Resolution of the Sixteenth National Congress of the Chinese Communist Party" (in Chinese), available at *www.china.com.cn/chinese/zhuanti/233872.htm*.

Damm, J. (2003), "China's E-Policy: Examples of Local E-government in Guangdong and Fujian", paper presented to the conference "China and the Internet: Technology, Economy, and Society in Transition", Los Angeles, 30-31 May.

Ding, X. L. (2002), "The Challenges of Managing a Huge Society Under Rapid Transformation", in J. Wong and Y. Zheng, (eds.), *China's Post-Jiang Leadership Succession: Problems and Perspectives*, Singapore, Singapore University Press, pp. 189-213.

Editorial Division for Computer Books (2003), *2003 China E-Government Yearbook* (in Chinese), Beijing, People's Telecommunications Publishing House.

Foster, W., S. Goodman, and Z. Tan (2000), "The Internet and E-Commerce in Greater South China ([Chinese Taipei], Hong Kong [China], Fujian and Guangdong)", INET 2000 Proceedings, The Internet Society, available at *www.isoc.org/inet2000/cdproceedings/7c/7c_1.htm*.

Gong, T. (2003), "More Than Mere Words, Less Than Hard Law", *Public Administration Quarterly*, Vol. 27, Issue 1/2, pp. 159-188.

Government Online Project Service Center (2003), "Introduction to the Government Online Project" (in Chinese).

Guo, L. (ed.) (2003), *Approaching the Internet in Small Chinese Cities*. Research Center for Social Development, Chinese Academy of Social Sciences.

Hachigian, N. (2001), "China's Cyber-Strategy", *Foreign Affairs*, March/April 2001, Vol. 80, No. 2.

Hachigian, N. and L. Wu (2003), *The Information Revolution in Asia*, RAND.

Harwit, E. and D. Clark (2001), "Shaping the Internet in China: Evolution of Political Control over Network Infrastructure and Content", *Asian Survey*, Vol. 41, No. 3, pp. 377-408.

Jiang, Q. (2003), "How to Utilize Technologies for Governance" (in Chinese), 3 December, available at *http://news.enet.com.cn/*.

Kluver, R. (2004), "E-Government in China: Empowering Citizens or Establishing Control?", paper presented to the conference "The Internet and Governance: The Global Context", Oxford Internet Institute, 8-10 January.

Ministry of Information Industry of the People's Republic of China (2003), "Operational Situations of Telecommunications Industry During January – December 2003" (in Chinese), available at www.mii.gov.cn/mii/hyzw/tongji/tongjifenxi200312.htm.

OECD (2003a), *The E-Government Imperative*, OECD, Paris.

OECD (2003b), *From Red Tape to Smart Tape: Administrative Simplification in OECD Countries*, OECD, Paris.

OECD (2003c), *Checklist for E-Government Leaders*, OECD, Paris.

OECD (2003d), *Implementation Plan for the OECD Guidelines for the Security of Information Systems and Networks: Towards a Culture of Security*, OECD, Paris.

OECD (2004a), *Promises and Problems of E-Democracy: Challenges of Online Citizen Engagement*, OECD, Paris.

OECD (2004b), *Managing Conflict of Interest in the Public Service*, OECD, Paris.

People's Daily (2001), "Resolution on the Making of the Open Governance Act", *East China News*, 8 March, p. 2.

People's Daily (Overseas Version) (2003), "Survey Shows China's East-West Digital Divide Growing", 17 July, available at http://english.people.com.cn/200307/17/eng20030717_120449.shtml.

Qiu, J.L. (2002a), "Chinese Hackerism in Retrospect", *MFC Insight*, September.

Qiu, J.L. (2002b), "Coming to Terms with Informational Stratification in the People's Republic of China", *Cardozo Arts and Entertainment Law Journal*, Vol. 20, No. 1. pp. 157-180.

Qiu, J.L. (2003), "The Model of E-Government: A Case Study of Nanhai", in Guo Liang (ed.), *Approaching the Internet in Small Chinese Cities*, Research Centre for Social Development, Chinese Academy of Social Sciences, pp. 1-19.

Quantitative Survey of Internet Information Resources in China (QSIIRC) (2003), *Survey Report* (in Chinese), The QSIIRC Working Group commissioned by State Council Informatization Office.

State Council Informatization Leading Group (2002), "Recommendations of the State Council Informatization Leading Group on the Construction of E-Government in China (State Council Document No. 17)" (in Chinese), available at www.china.org.cn/chinese/zhuanti/283233.htm.

State Council Informatization Office (2003), Ministry of Science and Technology, and Ministry of Information Industry, "Technical Guidelines for E-Government Projects" (in Chinese), available at http://61.138.108.226/tls/info/gzdt/gz3.htm.

Yong, J.S.L. (2003), "Enter the Dragon: Informatisation in China", *E-Government in China*, Singapore, Times Editions.

Walton, G. (2001), "China's Golden Shield: Corporations and the Development of Surveillance Technology in the People's Republic of China", International Centre for Rights and Democracy, available online: www.ichrd.ca/.

Wang, C., Y. Zhang, H. Xu, and X. Zhang (eds.) (2003), *Blue Book of Electronic Government: China E-Government Development Report No. 1* (in Chinese), Beijing, Social Sciences Documentation Publishing House, December.

World Bank (2003), *Reform of Public Service Units in China: A Concept note of a World Bank Study for SCORES*.

Zhang, J. (2002), "Will the Government 'Serve the People'? The Development of Chinese E-Government", *New Media and Society*, June, pp. 163-184.

Zhang, J. (2003), "Good Governance Through E-Government: Assessing China's E-government Strategy", paper presented to the conference "China and the Internet: Technology, Economy, and Society in Transition", Los Angeles, 30-31 May.

Zhang, Y. and Gao, H. (2003), "An Analysis of the Macro-Benefits of China's E-Government", *China Economic Times*, 10 January, available at http://online-edu.org/article/article/2755.html.

Zhou, X. (2003), "E-Government in China: A Content Analysis of National and Provincial Websites", paper presented to the conference "China and the Internet: Technology, Economy, and Society in Transition", Los Angeles, 30-31 May.

Zhu, R. (2003), "The Harvest of E-Government" (in Chinese), China Computer Industry Development (CCID) Network, 1 July, available at http://digital.zhongguancun.com.cn/zgc2/about0102.html.

ANNEX 4.A1

E-government Web Sites

Beijing Administration of Industry and Commerce	www.hd315.gov.cn/
Customs General Administration	www.customs.gov.cn
Government Online Project	www.gov.cn
Ministry of Civil Affairs	www.mca.gov.cn
Ministry of Commerce	www.mofcom.gov.cn
Ministry of Culture	www.ccnt.gov.cn
Ministry of Education	www.moe.gov.cn
Ministry of Finance	www.mof.gov.cn
Ministry of Foreign Affairs	www.fmprc.gov.cn
Ministry of Information Industry	www.mii.gov.cn
Ministry of Labour and Social Security	www.molss.gov.cn
Ministry of Public Security	www.mps.gov.cn
Ministry of Science and Technology	www.most.gov.cn
National Bureau of Statistics	www.stats.gov.cn
National Informatization Evaluation Center	www.niec.org.cn
Ningbo 81890 e-Community Service Center	www.81890.gov.cn
The People's Bank of China	www.pbc.gov.cn
The People's Court of Nanhai	http://fayuan.nanhai.gov.cn
The People's Government of Beijing Municipality	www.beijing.gov.cn
The People's Government of Guangdong Province	www.gd.gov.cn
The People's Government of Shanghai Municipality	www.shanghai.gov.cn
State Administration of Foreign Exchange	www.safe.gov.cn
State Administration of Industry and Commerce	www.saic.gov.cn
State Administration of Taxation	www.chinatax.gov.cn
State Development and Planning Commission	www.sdpc.gov.cn
State Economic and Trade Commission	www.setc.gov.cn
Shanghai Administration of Industry and Commerce	www.sgs.gov.cn
Shanghai Government Procurement Network	www.ccgp-shanghai.gov.cn
Suzhou Industrial Park One-Stop Service Center	http://ossc.sipac.gov.cn
Shanghai Informatization Committee	www.shanghaiit.gov.cn

PART I

Chapter 5

Institutional Arrangements for the Production of Statistics

Table of Contents

Summary 173

Institutional Arrangements for the Production of Statistics 174

1. Introduction 174
2. Main features of China's statistical system 175
   2.1. Institutional organisation of statistical data compilation 175
   2.2. Changes in data collection methods 183
3. Evaluation of institutional organisation and data compilation methods 184
   3.1. Historical legacies 184
   3.2. Central-local complications 185
   3.3. International standards 186
   3.4. Governance constraints 187
   3.5. Chinese reform proposals for the statistical system 190
4. Conclusions and recommendations 190

Notes 191

Bibliography 194

List of figures

5.1. Organisational chart of statistical work 176
5.2. Organisational chart of China's Statistical Authority 178

Summary

Chinese statistics have come a long way from a pure reporting system in a centrally planned economy to a system that increasingly relies on surveys and modern statistical techniques to service users, be they government or the public at large. Nonetheless, many challenges remain. In recent years, the quality of Chinese economic statistics, in particular the growth rate of real GDP and other data has been repeatedly questioned by several Chinese and western authors. Questions about data quality inevitably lead to questions about the institutional organisation of China's statistical authority and the methods of statistical data compilation in China.

Some of the governance issues affecting the production of statistics are specific to this policy context, while the majority can also be found in other policy areas. As described in this chapter on statistics, there is still a legacy of reporting via ministries that limits the scope of the data collected and that limits the influence that NBS should have on the conception and quality of data collections. Second, complications persist between the central and the sub-national level of the statistical system. Often, local statistical offices are closer to local governments than to the NBS (National Bureau of Statistics) and this may create incentives that are not conducive to the compilation of high-quality statistical information. Stronger line structures between NBS and statistical offices at the local level and better enforcement of the statistical laws at all levels of the administration should help to advance on this issue. Third, there is a need to establish functioning channels to address complaints against violations of the Statistics Law. Fourth, there is a welcome but still sluggish move from enterprise reporting to survey techniques.

Other issues relate to transparency. Further efforts should be made to enhance transparency about data collection methods, and statistical methodology in general. Not only information about methods and source, but data itself should also become more accessible to a broad range of users, for example through user-friendly Web sites with readily available, up-to-date statistics. Also, clear rules should be established on which data are available to the public for free and which data can be purchased through individual contact with the NBS. Transparent or at least standardized pricing for the latter would be desirable.

Finally, recognition of the desirability of a user-orientation of statistics is only in its beginnings. Further steps need to be taken to focus not only on data that reflect government priorities. Statistics are indeed an important tool for macroeconomic decision-making, but are also a fundamental input for individual decisions. Statistics become all the more important as China shifts towards a market economy. Productive debate and decisions – whether in local communities, the media, or the halls of government – require comprehensive, trustworthy and comprehensible information.

Institutional Arrangements for the Production of Statistics[1]

1. Introduction

Statistical data in China are compiled by a number of government departments. At the national level these include the National Bureau of Statistics (NBS, *guojia tongjiju*), the People's Bank of China (China's central bank), the Ministry of Finance, the State Administration of Foreign Exchange, the Customs General Administration, and dozens of other central government departments.[2] While the People's Bank of China is responsible for financial sector data including foreign exchange reserves, the Ministry of Finance for fiscal sector data, and the State Administration of Foreign Exchange and the Customs General Administration for external sector data, the NBS carries the responsibility for organizing, directing and co-ordinating the statistical work throughout the country.[3]

The NBS compiles real sector data, ranging from national accounts aggregates to price indices and labour market indicators, as well as various socio-demographic data covering such issues as population, health, education, and poverty. In its core publication, the annual *Statistical Yearbook*, it publishes data that it has collected itself as well as data obtained from other government departments; these include the financial, fiscal, and external sector data from the relevant departments, but also a wide variety of other data such as, for example, data on tourism obtained from the State Tourism Administration (supplemented with NBS survey data) or patent data obtained from the State Intellectual Property Office.

In recent years, the quality of Chinese economic statistics, in particular the growth rate of real GDP and other data has been repeatedly questioned by several Chinese and western authors.[4] Alternative guesstimates of China's real GDP growth rates suggest around 0% growth in 1998 and 1999 (compared to the original official, unrevised real growth rates of 7.8% and 7.2%), and approximately half the original, official unrevised real growth rates of 7.1% and 7.3% in 2000 and 2001. The official real growth rate of 2002 is accepted as correct if not an underestimate.[5]

In the late 1990s, the Chinese press carried numerous articles criticising the quality of official statistics. On 23 August 1995, Zhang Sai, then NBS Commissioner, in support of the 1996 revisions to the PRC Statistics Law argued that: "recently the phenomenon of false and deceptive reporting has spread in some localities and some units. The danger is large, the impact very negative". Reports on data falsification then became standard fare in the monthly NBS journal *Zhongguo tongji* [China Statistics]. The Chinese slogan of *jiabao fukuafeng* ("wind of falsification and embellishment") soon made the round.

Questions about data quality inevitably lead to questions about the institutional organisation of China's statistical authority and the methods of statistical data compilation in China. For example, the quality of locally collected data has a direct impact on the quality of nationwide GDP data in that the NBS makes (typically downward) adjustments to local data in the calculation of nationwide GDP. Thus, the more unreliable locally compiled data, the more difficult it is to make correct adjustments at the national level. But, as the critics of Chinese official data point out, these adjustments often lack transparency themselves and may cast doubt on the reliability of NBS data.

Holz (2004d) assesses the quality of GDP data at greater depth and concludes that however one may evaluate the allegations of data falsification in certain years, even the critics acknowledge that long-run growth trends are approximately correct. In many cases, the data problems reported are facts which are unlikely to be unique to China; other transition and developing countries experience similar difficulties.[6] The margins of error are inevitably larger than in developed countries, perhaps even uncomfortably large. More information about actual (rather than supposed or desired) data compilation methods would be of much help in evaluating the quality of specific data. In the absence of such information, the organisational underpinnings of data compilation may provide more perspective on data quality in China.

The present document describes therefore the organisational aspects of Chinese statistics and evaluates them in light of the perceived shortcomings in Chinese data identified above.[7]

2. Main features of China's statistical system

There are two organisational aspects to statistical data compilation. One is the institutional organisation of data collection, and the other the methods of data collection. These are described in the following sections.

2.1. Institutional organisation of statistical data compilation

The primary institution in charge of the compilation of statistics is the National Bureau of Statistics in co-operation with local statistical bureaus under its professional leadership (in total, the statistical bureaucracy, or statistical *xitong*). A second channel consists of statistical divisions within specific bureaucracies in charge of particular economic or social activities, for example, the Agriculture Ministry together with the local agricultural departments (the agricultural *xitong*).

2.1.1. Overview of the statistical system

Figure 5.1 summarizes the two different channels by treating the levels of provinces, municipalities/prefectures, and counties as one administrative level rather than three separate ones. The figure distinguishes between three different types of relationships between actors, namely administrative leadership (*xingzheng lingdao*), business (or professional) leadership (*yewu lingdao guanxi*), and business (or professional) guidance (*yewu zhidao*).

The State Council, as the Government of China, exerts administrative leadership over: i) central ministries, commissions, and other central government departments, which include the NBS as an organisation directly under the State Council; and ii) all provincial and provincial-level entities. Administrative leadership means that the State Council issues binding orders, appoints major personnel, and plays a crucial role in budget decisions (in the case of central government departments, it provides all budgetary funding). At the next level of administration, the central ministries, commissions, and government departments (in the following, altogether denoted "other government

I.5. INSTITUTIONAL ARRANGEMENTS FOR THE PRODUCTION OF STATISTICS

Figure 5.1. **Organisational chart of statistical work**

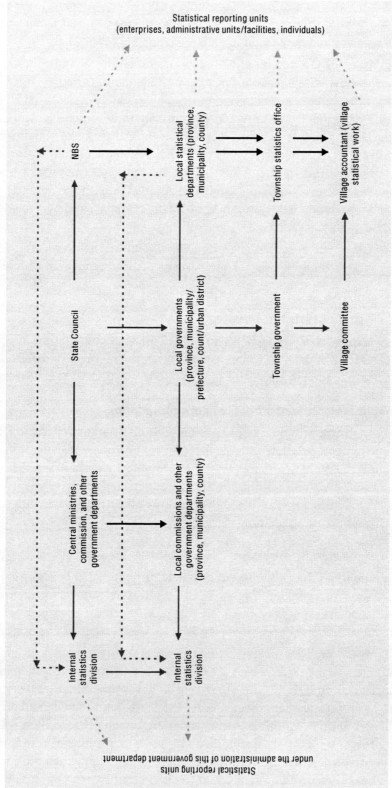

Source: Following Wang Qi (2000), p. 920.

departments") exercise administrative leadership over their internal divisions, while the provincial governments exercise administrative leadership over their government departments as well as the next lower-level government. As the NBS is directly subordinate to, or part of, the State Council, so local statistical bureaus are directly subordinate to, or part of, local governments.

The NBS is linked to local statistical bureaus through its business (or professional) leadership. In all matters related to statistical work, such as the definition of statistical variables, the classification of enterprises, or the standardization of report forms for statistical reporting units, the provincial statistical departments follow NBS rules. The NBS also has some influence on local appointment decisions and provides some funding to local statistical bureaus (further explored below). A similar relationship exists between other central government departments and their provincial counterparts. "Business leadership" typically characterizes the relationship among different tiers within one xitong.[8]

The NBS is far removed from the statistical divisions within other central government departments in that it has virtually no influence on their appointment decisions and funding, but does co-operate on, for example, the design of their report forms. For a variety of data the NBS relies on these statistical divisions within other central government departments, without being able to dictate the types of data to be collected or the precise collection method. Its authority is limited to "guidance". The same type of relationship is repeated at the lower level tiers, between the local governments' statistical departments and the statistical divisions in other local government departments. The relationship between internal statistical divisions at different administrative levels is also limited to business guidance.[9]

The NBS and local statistical departments collect data from statistical reporting units, which comprise enterprises, individuals, and administrative units (xingzheng danwei) or public service units (shiye danwei), with the latter two ranging from government administrative departments to universities and sectoral business associations. Data collection is regulated in the Statistics Law as a compulsory task for statistical reporting units.[10] The statistical divisions of other central government departments collect data from the statistical reporting units (for example, enterprises or banks) under their direct administration.

The various xitong typically extend down to the county level. In the case of the statistical xitong, statistical work is further supported at the township level by a township statistics office, often consisting of no more than one person (who may only work part-time on statistical issues), and at the village level by the village accountant.

2.1.2. The statistical system in detail

Figure 5.2 omits the State Council/local governments and the non-statistical xitong to focus in more detail on only the institutions involved in data collection. In this figure, all administrative levels are included, as is one representative of the various divisions within a statistical bureau (the national income accounts division). The central as well as local (provincial) survey teams are also included. The business leadership between statistical bureaus at different administrative levels is reproduced from Figure 5.1. Two special instances are the provincial and the county statistical bureaus in that their business leadership may not only extend to the next-lower tier but also to two tiers below. Thus, for example, a circular on some business matters issued by the provincial statistical bureau could go directly to the county statistical bureau, rather than only to the municipal/prefectural tier.

I.5. INSTITUTIONAL ARRANGEMENTS FOR THE PRODUCTION OF STATISTICS

Figure 5.2. **Organisational chart of China's Statistical Authority**

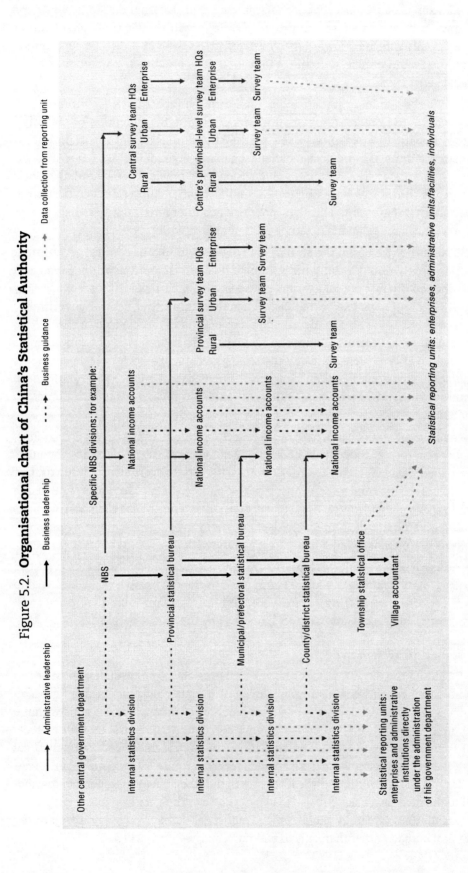

The statistical bureau at each level is fully in charge of its various divisions, such as, for example, the national income accounts division; the relationship consequently is an administrative leadership one. A division within the statistical bureau then exerts business guidance over the corresponding division at the next lower level government tier.

Divisions of the statistical bureaus at all levels may collect data from the statistical reporting units, although, in practice, most data collection occurs at the municipal and at the county level (or equivalent district level within municipalities). Traditionally, individual divisions within the statistical bureau at a specific government level would only collect data from statistical reporting units under the jurisdiction of this, or lower level governments. For example, a provincial-level statistical bureau would not collect data from enterprises located in this particular province but belonging to (being under the administrative leadership of) a central government department, unless the centre had agreed to such an arrangement. This has become more variable in the most recent years with a gradual transition to statistical data compilation based on geographic locality (*zaidi*) rather than administrative subordination.

The two types of survey teams, central and local, are subject to a direct subordination relationship (*chuizhi*). Central survey teams located at the county or municipal level report directly to the centre's provincial-level survey team headquarters, which in turn report directly to the centre's nationwide survey team headquarters (administrative leadership across all tiers). Local governments and local statistical departments supposedly have no influence over central survey teams at any level. A similar arrangement holds for the local (provincial) survey teams with regard to the municipal and county level governments and statistical bureaus. All members of the central survey team *xitong* are paid directly by the centre, and all appointment authority rests within the central survey team *xitong*.

Central and provincial survey teams tend to co-ordinate at the provincial level to avoid duplication, and they share information. Thus, for example, the centre's rural survey teams may collect a certain set of data in the counties they cover, while the province's rural survey teams do the same or fulfil a similar task in those counties they cover. The centre's provincial survey team headquarters relies primarily on its own data but usually has access to the local provincial survey team headquarters' data, and may report both sets of data to the NBS. The centre's provincial survey team headquarters, in turn, may share its findings with the local provincial survey team headquarters and the provincial statistical bureau.

2.1.3. Appointment authority and funding

The NBS as a national-level bureau is ranked half a rank below ministries and commissions, which implies that the NBS commissioner is appointed by the State Council (the Prime Minister).

At the provincial level, all leading appointments to the statistical bureau are a matter of the provincial Party Committee and government. When appointing the head and deputy-heads of the provincial statistical bureau, suggestions by the NBS need to be taken into consideration. This amounts to a *de facto* veto right for the NBS. The same pattern is repeated at the municipal and county levels; the suggestions of the next higher-level statistical bureau have to be sought before appointing the head and deputy-heads.[11] More recently, the implementation instructions to the Statistics Law (NBS, 2 June 2000, Article 29) even go a step further in that they stipulate higher level statistical bureau approval for appointments of all "mid-ranking" and higher statistical "special" and "technical" regular staff, although this may in practice not amount to much more than an advisory role.[12]

All appointment authority to central survey team organisations at any administrative level rests with the NBS. But with survey team staff at county and municipal level usually hired locally, the local statistical bureau is officially given an assisting role. In the case of internal statistical divisions of other government departments, all appointment authority rests within that *xitong*; the statistical *xitong* may make suggestions but has no veto power.

Official funding for statistical work at central to county level comes from three sources: central government budget, local government budgets, and various types of income received for services provided (such as surveys implemented on behalf of paying customers). The third type of income accounts for approximately 4% of total funding; the main sources of funding are central and local government budgets, each providing approximately one-half of total funding. These official funds are in all likelihood supplemented by a significant (but unknown) amount of informal funds collected through fees or various money-making undertakings.[13]

Central government budgetary funds are intended not only to finance the operations of the NBS but also to support statistical work at lower-level tiers. In principle, local statistical bureaus receive central funding to cover work-related costs (*shiye bianzhi de jingfei*), while local funding covers basic administrative costs (*xingzheng jingfei*), presumably costs such as offices, staff housing, and perhaps some salaries, or a basic salary for all employees. All local purchases of tangible assets are locally funded. Central survey teams are fully centrally funded. Internal statistical divisions of other government departments are funded by those government departments. Special tasks, such as censuses, are jointly funded by centre and province.[14]

When the NBS in its current form emerged from the Cultural Revolution in 1976 it had just 7 000 staff nationwide; by 1986 that number had risen to 67 360 staff at the county level and above.[15] Today, the total regular staff of the statistical *xitong*, depending on the source, numbers approximately 80 000 or 90 000.[16] Regular staff refers to formal positions determined in government regulations, with salaries guaranteed through government budget appropriations. The NBS has 280 regular staff in its administrative divisions. This number includes the commissioner, four deputy-commissioners, 36 division heads and deputy-heads, the chief statistician, chief economist, and chief accountant; it does not include the employees of the central survey teams (who are also regular staff). Nor does it include the staff of the NBS' administrative facilities, who are not "regular" staff.[17]

2.1.4. NBS internal organisation

Apart from the commissioner, the four deputy commissioners, the chief statistician, chief economist, and chief engineer, the NBS officially consists of 15 administrative divisions, 12 administrative facilities, and three survey team systems.

The 15 administrative divisions comprise five functional departments, such as the national income accounts division, and otherwise general departments, such as a division for policies and legislation. The particular arrangements of divisions and the particular functions of individual divisions undergo minor changes over time. For example, in 1998 the task of collecting data on furloughed labour of state-owned enterprises was transferred from the NBS (presumably from the NBS division in charge of population, social, science and technology statistics) to the Labour and Social Security Ministry.[18]

Administrative facilities reflect a fractional outsourcing of former NBS tasks. These tasks are not fully outsourced in that there is no competitive bidding by outsiders to fulfil these tasks, but neither are they completely internal to the NBS since the staff are not regarded as regular staff. However, the administrative facilities remain part of the NBS *xitong*, and funding by the NBS for some of them continues, possibly supplemented by cross-funding from administrative facilities.

The official organisational chart of the NBS is incomplete. For example, it does not include the "China Market Information Survey Association" (*Zhongguo shichang xinxi diaochaye xiehui*) founded in early 2004 (although a news item on this association is listed on the NBS Web site).[19] This association is a social organisation (*shehui tuanti*) approved by the State Council and registered with the Civil Affairs Ministry. A deputy commissioner of the NBS is association head and a deputy-head of the NBS statistical information service centre is the association secretary; the NBS commissioner is honorary chairman. Its tasks are to develop survey policies, to set standards for survey work, to supervise survey work, to provide education, and to serve as a bridge to similar institutions and associations in the West. Presumably, membership will be *de facto* compulsory for all organisations conducting survey work in China, and will come with regular fees. Similar associations will probably appear at the provincial level.

The association could fall into a typical pattern in China whereby government departments with excessive staff and short of funding create new organisations outside the official government realm to absorb excessive staff and to serve as (fee-charging) intermediaries between the government department and the public. In the best of circumstances these intermediaries serve as facilitators, while in the worst of circumstances they create a new level of fee-charging non-government institutions with quasi-government powers.

Another example of an NBS institution not included in the official organisational chart is the "China State of the Nation Research Society" (*Zhongguo guoqing yanjiuhui*), another social organisation under the NBS. On 30 March 2004 the NBS ordered a temporary halt to all activities of this society and its subordinate institutions due to, as the NBS claimed, poor internal administration and illegal activities by some outside elements under the name of this society or its subordinate institutions.[20]

At least in 1997, the NBS also ran two companies, the China Huaxin Information Technology Development Company (*Zhongguo huaxin xinxi jishu kaifa gongsi*) and the China Statistical Consulting Company Ltd. (*Zhongguo tongji zixun youxian gongsi*).[21] The statistical *xitong* also runs a statistics college in Xi'an Municipality (in Shaanxi Province) and a statistics school in Sichuan Province.

2.1.5. Interaction between the statistical xitong and other government departments

For the compilation of many statistics the NBS relies on other central government departments, such as the line ministries or their successors. This is largely a historical legacy. As long as state-owned enterprises and urban collective-owned enterprises are organised under line ministries extending from central to local tiers, the respective line ministry or its successor is likely to collect data on its enterprises.[22] The internal statistical division of a line ministry communicates directly with the relevant division of the NBS. In the case of industry, for example, statistical departments in industry-related line ministries and state companies (conglomerates) communicate with the NBS Division for Industrial and Transport Statistics. Dozens of other government departments contribute, in particular, to national accounts data (including GDP).[23] At the central level, the NBS probably receives data from approximately 100 different government departments, central companies and conglomerates (former line ministries), or associations.

The reliability of data obtained from other government departments in the collection of statistics varies from sector to sector. One of the most problematic is rural industry, where the Township Enterprise Bureau of the Agriculture Ministry collects detailed data on township-run and village-run collective enterprises, and basic statistics on co-operative enterprises, private enterprises and individual-owned enterprises. The NBS assists the Township Enterprise Bureau in the design of the statistical reporting forms, while the Township Enterprise Bureau collects the data and makes some of them regularly available to the NBS. The NBS relies on the Township Enterprise Bureau's data and has no independent regular reporting system for rural enterprises. The industrial census of 1995 revealed significant over-reporting by township and village enterprises, but in subsequent years the NBS continued to have no way of making meaningful adjustments to the Township Enterprise Bureau data.[24]

Another extreme example of the NBS's reliance on other government departments is the transport and communication sector. Gross output value data in the production approach to the calculation of value-added are collected by the Railway Ministry (Bureau), the Communication (Transportation) Ministry (Bureau), the Aviation Bureau, the Post and Telecommunications Ministry (Bureau), the Township Enterprise Bureau of the Agriculture Ministry, and the Industry and Transport Department within the Ministry of Finance. These departments do not cover the relevant sub-sectors in their entirety.[25] In the calculation of GDP, gross output value data on road and water transportation by transport and communication enterprises which are not part of these departments are guesstimated in the GDP calculations.

Although the NBS relies on other central government departments for much of the data it reports, its authority in relation to other government departments is weak. The NBS as a bureau directly under the State Council (government) is half a rank below that of central government ministries and provincial governments, with no authority to issue binding orders to either of the two. Consequently, the NBS, according to the Statistics Law, is only responsible for "directing and co-ordinating" the nationwide statistical work rather than for conducting it.

What the NBS has available are indirect channels through which to influence data compilation in other central government departments. Through its business guidance it can try to influence the work done in the internal statistical divisions of other central government departments. The NBS is in a stronger position when it comes to survey work conducted by other government departments. All statistical surveys conducted by central government departments or units under their jurisdiction must be reported to the NBS, and any survey that extends beyond the particular department requires NBS approval. As part of the approval/reporting requirement, a copy of the survey report form must be submitted to the NBS. If the government department publishes any of its findings later, a copy of the published findings must be submitted to the NBS no later than 10 days after publication. (The same pattern of authority is repeated at the local level; for example, the provincial statistical bureau enjoys the same authority in relation to other provincial government departments.) A separate set of regulations applies for surveys conducted by non-government units or foreign entities.[26]

At the central level, the NBS maintains a Web page where it lists approved surveys and (department-internal) surveys reported to the NBS by approximately 100 other government departments. Surveys in this context include regular reporting within the government department. The Web page gives the appearance of complete coverage of all surveys, but either the coverage is incomplete, or some government departments do not report (or seek approval) for all their statistical work. For example, the State Asset Supervision and Administration Commission requires that all state-owned and state-controlled enterprises file regular, detailed financial reports; yet a record of NBS approval for these reports does not appear on the NBS Web page.[27]

One further sign of the relative weakness of the NBS in relation to other government departments is that what could be considered part of the NBS's core work has been appropriated by China's central bank. Thus, the People's Bank of China in its quarterly statistical bulletin reports aggregate quarterly data on 5 000 main industrial enterprises; these data include detailed financial indicators as well as the results of a survey on business conditions. They are collected by the People's Bank of China, with approval of the NBS, even though the NBS itself has an administrative facility in charge of economic monitoring and economic analysis (with its Chinese name referring to "business conditions").[28]

Finally, even though the NBS is an organisation directly under the State Council, *de facto* it may well be subject to some form of guidance by the National Development and Reform Commission (the former State Planning Commission, or National Development and Planning Commission), which is the major administrative organ in charge of economic matters. For example, the NBS reports in the International Monetary Fund's General Data Dissemination Standard (GDDS) metadata homepages that access to the data produced and disseminated by the NBS before release is provided to senior officials of the State Development and Planning Commission, as well as to the (by now defunct and partly integrated into the National Development and Reform Commission) State Economic and Trade Commission; for official work, staff of the State Development and Planning Commission also have access to the tabulated data.[29]

2.2. Changes in data collection methods

Traditionally, line ministries collected data on their enterprises in the four non-agricultural production sectors, and the Agriculture Ministry collected agricultural data through the communes. All data collection occurred through reporting forms. The NBS served as little more than a repository of the data collected by different line ministries. In 1996, the revised Statistics Law (NPC, 15 May 1996) officially laid the foundation for major revisions to data compilation methods in that it stipulates that censuses and surveys are to provide the core statistical data, while regular reporting only plays a supplementary role: "Statistical investigation should collect and compile statistical material through regular censuses as the basis [jichu], routine sample surveys as mainstay [zhuti], and unavoidable [biyao de] statistical reporting, key [zhongdian] investigations, and comprehensive analysis as supplement [buchong]" (Article 10).[30]

The new "basis" of data collection since 1996 is censuses. China currently conducts five censuses, of which four every 10 years, and one every five years: population census, tertiary sector census, industrial census, agricultural census, census of basic statistical units. Also, a one-off "economic census" of industry and the tertiary sector was conducted in 2004.

In addition to censuses, the Chinese statistical system is increasingly relying on surveys. Surveys are not necessarily based on random samples. Most surveys involve some form of stratification, but the choice of samples within strata is usually not specified. Detailed information on surveys is scarce, especially on those introduced only recently, such as in industry and in commerce and catering.[31] By mid-2001, an employee of the NBS claimed that steady progress had been made in the use of sample surveys of small industrial enterprises (those not reporting directly to the statistical departments) for the compilation of GDP statistics, while, after four years of hard work, sample surveys of the wholesale and retail trade as well as the catering sector are finally in place across all 31 provinces.[32] One complication may well be that tertiary sector surveys tend to involve a number of other government departments, i.e. cannot simply be implemented by the NBS on its own.[33]

3. Evaluation of institutional organisation and data compilation methods

3.1. Historical legacies

China's institutional organisation of statistical data compilation has been transformed dramatically in the reform period, especially since the early 1990s. Nevertheless, some features of the pre-reform institutional arrangements persist. These include the involvement of a large number of other government departments in the collection of statistical data, the predominance of report forms, the poor coverage of tertiary sector activities, the duplication of data reporting tasks and reporting channels, and the choice of GDP calculation method.

3.1.1. Continued role of government departments other than NBS in data compilation

As a legacy of the planning system, a large number of government departments other than the NBS are collecting a vast amount of data, with a range probably exceeding data collection in developed economies. These data are of mixed quality. Most are likely to be of good quality since they form the basis for planning in these other government departments. But coverage is often limited to the specific tasks of the government department. For example, the Communications (Transport) Ministry may only collect data on freight transportation within its *xitong*, leaving the NBS to make guesstimates on total freight transportation in the country without necessarily having a (NBS) system in place to do so properly.

In other words, the choice, quality and coverage of specific statistics are dictated by the relevant government departments' data needs and departmental reach. The low rank of the NBS at deputy ministry level in comparison to other central government departments, combined with the limitation to the NBS's business guidance over internal statistical divisions in other central government departments, imply that the NBS does not have the authority to impose a unified framework within which data are to be collected across all government departments. In many instances, the NBS is likely to know little about exactly how the data were collected.

The low rank of the NBS may also prevent it from launching innovations in data collection and from co-operating with other government bodies on an equal footing. For example, the NBS appears to make no use of tax bureau data; the tax bureau belongs to the tax *xitong*, which in turn is associated with the fiscal *xitong*. Tax bureau data could be particularly helpful in the case of small enterprises on which the NBS has little reliable data.

3.1.2. Report forms and tertiary sector data

It is only since the passing of the 1996 revised Statistics Law that the focus has gradually shifted from regular reporting through report forms to surveys. Report forms still play a major role in many economic sectors, and are likely to continue to do so in the future. For example, in industry, the above-norm enterprises (annual revenues of more then RMB 5 million) regularly report to the statistical authority, and these data are likely to be of high quality. The intention is to capture the below-norm enterprises (annual revenues of less then RMB 5 million) primarily through surveys, and in industry these NBS sample surveys are in the process of becoming well established.

In the tertiary sector, sample surveys are still at an early development stage. The difficulties of collecting accurate data in some tertiary sectors are exacerbated by the fact that the NBS cannot rely on data collected by other government departments (there are often none, or none modelled on line ministries), and that the rank of the NBS may be too low for it to effectively collect high-quality data. One example is the real estate sector; no direct central government department exists with an interest in collecting detailed data on these units. The large differences between the sum of locally reported tertiary sector value-added and the nationwide aggregate figures compiled by the NBS attest to the continued difficulty of measuring tertiary sector value-added. The 2004 economic census may yet provide a benchmark for the design of future tertiary sector value-added measurement.

3.1.3. Duplication of data reporting and reporting channels

A side-effect of China's pre-reform statistical system as well as of the development of a new statistical system is the frequent duplication of statistical work. For example, some basic statistical reporting units (such as above-norm enterprises) report their data to their superordinate government department which passes them on to the next higher level within their particular *xitong*; the central government department of the *xitong* then may report some of the data to the NBS. Other basic statistical reporting units report to the local statistical authority. Yet others report to both, the superordinate government department and the local statistical authority.[34] The outcome is a multitude of reporting tasks and reporting channels. The NBS may receive statistics on the same set of enterprises from a central government department as well as from all provincial statistical offices; after the many layers of transmission, the two sets of data are probably no longer identical.

Many statistics, furthermore, are collected independently by the statistical authority and by other government departments, i.e. the reporting unit does not send one report form to two or more institutions, but the reporting unit is approached independently by the statistical bureau (or even statistical bureaus at different government levels) as well as various government departments (only one of which may be the superordinate government department of the *xitong* to which the reporting unit belongs) with separate requests for data.[35] As a consequence, reporting units are overstretched and have little interest in conscientiously fulfilling reporting tasks. The remnants of the pre-reform planning system and the continued strong bureaucratic involvement in the economy lead to what appears a higher data volume in China than in other economies. In contrast, the Statistics Law (Article 10) stresses the need to severely limit regular reporting tasks for basic reporting units and to rely as much as possible on sample surveys, focused (*zhongdian*) surveys, and administrative records.

3.2. Central-local complications

The gradually increasing discrepancy between the sum of provincial GDP and nationwide aggregate GDP reveals the margin of error inherent in official data. But it also attests to the willingness of the NBS to innovate, in that the lack of discrepancy in the years before 1997 is likely to reflect the inability of the NBS at that time to calculate GDP independently of provincial data, rather than a higher degree of accuracy in the earlier years. The willingness of the NBS as well as of local statistical bureaus to publish their own data, even if in contradiction to the other party's estimates, is a welcome change from the uniformity usually imposed in a centralized socialist system.

On the one hand, the discrepancy reflects the fact that local statistical bureaus even in business matters are more likely to listen to the local government than to the NBS. On the other hand, it also reveals the extent to which China today has, *de facto*, two statistical systems, a central one and a provincial one. The NBS in the calculation of nationwide GDP primarily relies on report forms from directly reporting (above-norm) enterprises in all economic sectors and on central sample surveys otherwise. The report forms are mostly collected locally, but the data on each enterprise are passed on individually to the NBS, i.e. aggregation can occur at the NBS itself. Unless local statistical bureaus flagrantly falsify individual enterprises' reports, which is unlikely, and unless enterprises misreport data, these data are as good as the accounting system within the enterprise. Surveys implemented by central survey teams then fill the gaps on the below-norm enterprises. Economy-wide, approximately one half of GDP is produced in directly reporting (above-norm) enterprises, and the other half in agriculture, below-norm enterprises, and administrative units/facilities.

The central-local dichotomy is also apparent in the establishment of two separate survey team systems, one under the authority of the centre, and the other under the authority of the province. While central and local survey teams may share information, and while central survey teams will probably never be able to operate perfectly independently of local statistical bureaus or other local government departments, in terms of formal appointment authority and funding the two systems are separate. This again raises questions about duplication: is there a need to have both a central and a local survey team in one county, or even a need to have just about every county in China covered by some survey team?

3.3. International standards

By international standards of statistical work, China scores well on some principles, but poorly on others. Among such standards are the 10 fundamental principles of official statistics identified by the United Nations. Similar principles are incorporated in the General Data Dissemination Standard (GDDS) of the International Monetary Fund to which China subscribed on 1 March 2002.

Going through the 10 fundamental principles of official statistics identified by the United Nations (see Holz 2004d), there is clearly room for improvement with respect to items: (3) information on methods, (7) public availability of laws and regulations, and (8) co-ordination among statistical agencies. The issue of co-ordination between the NBS and other central government departments as well as provincial statistical bureaus (Principle 8) has already been discussed above. Regarding the public availability of laws, regulations, and measures under which the statistical system operates (Principle 7), the Statistics Law and a very few NBS regulations have been published, but most rules and regulations regarding the statistical system are still considered internal.[36] Information on how the internal statistical divisions of other central government departments operate is not published. In the most recent years, some provinces have begun to publish the primary regulation covering statistical work at the provincial or municipal level, but all others of the presumably many hundred detailed regulations on the compilation of individual statistics are not available to the public.

Regarding information on methods (Principle 3), the NBS, let alone local statistical bureaus, rarely presents comprehensive information on the sources, methods and procedures of the statistics. The NBS in the *Statistical Yearbook* offers approximately one page of general explanations for each section (such as the industry section) on how the data in the particular section were compiled; each section also comes with a list of variable definitions. Yet the general explanations are often sparse, changes in compilation method over time are rarely made explicit, and the list of definitions tends to be highly incomplete; all too often, explanations and definitions appear to have simply been copied from the previous issue of the *Statistical Yearbook* and can occasionally be shown to not match the data or variables they claim to explain or define. Some of the richest information on the sources, methods and procedures of Chinese statistics can today be found on the Web pages of the International Monetary Fund's GDDS. Methodological information has also become available via documentation of a series of workshops on national accounts carried out with the OECD. The information provided on the NBS homepage is much scarcer, and there is no link on either the English or Chinese NBS homepage to the GDDS Web site.[37]

A similar picture emerges if China's statistical system is evaluated using the GDDS' four evaluation criteria: *i)* the coverage, periodicity, and timeliness of Chinese data are excellent, but questions about the reliability of these data loom large; *ii)* data quality is the weakest element, with dissemination of documentation on methodology, sources, component details, and reconciliations being incomplete and possibly reflecting a desired rather than actual state; *iii)* in terms of integrity, while confidentiality of households and enterprises in household and enterprise surveys appears highly trustworthy, little is known about the terms and conditions under which official statistics are produced. Internal government access to statistics is documented only in the GDDS, and even there probably not in full. Information about revisions is not provided reliably; information on revisions may disappear in later statistical publications even when the data which need explanation are reproduced; *iv)* the public has relatively ready and equal access to some data, but a large volume of data is collected only for government-internal use.

3.4. Governance constraints

The fact that Chinese statistics fare poorly when evaluated in light of information on methods, public availability of laws and regulations, or data quality can to a large extent be attributed to governance issues.

3.4.1. Limitations to statistical reporting and accountability

Some data remain of limited quality. For example, in spite of ongoing efforts to address this problem, data on official government revenues do not always include the extra-budgetary funds of government departments, nor the "little gold storage" (*xiao jinku*) of these departments. These funds are obtained through a wide variety of channels, ranging from various fees, often illegal, to dubious land transactions. Compared to the official government revenues, the undocumented funds could be of considerable size, perhaps even a similar size. Data on government revenues are collected by the fiscal departments. The NBS has no authority to collect these data, or to explain them.

Even when it comes to sensitive data, such as unemployment data, the NBS is constrained by institutional imperatives. This does not imply that the data it reports are false, but it implies that it is crucial to understand the fine print on, for example, coverage, except that this fine print often is not on offer. For instance, an economically meaningful measure of unemployment is not provided to the public. Other issues are the size of the black economy, or the extent of smuggling. The latter, for example, can wreak havoc on the meaning of the official import-export figures and create big inconsistencies between production-income approach GDP and expenditure approach GDP. But the NBS has no authority to publish data on these sensitive topics. As a consequence, it does not have the authority to explain why its data do not add up. In all likelihood, the NBS has even compiled data on these issues in internal survey reports for the Party and government leadership, and it may even use this information to (properly) adjust its GDP data, but then it cannot (is not allowed to) explain to the public how its GDP data are derived (and adjusted).

In other words, given these constraints, the NBS is not always able to fully explain particular statistics to the public. Individuals within the NBS have made repeated and highly laudable efforts to explain their statistics to the public, including to international organisations, and may be interested in sharing their experiences and in learning from other countries' experiences, but they always remain constrained by domestic political considerations. This also implies that nobody, except those individuals within the NBS who actually manipulate the data, has a chance to fully understand Chinese statistics (and the understanding of each of the specific individuals in the NBS is likely to be limited to their narrow specialisation).

3.4.2. Hierarchy structure and professionalism

Some constraints are directly built into the statistical institutional system. The Statistics Law states that "statistical personnel must seek truth from the facts, strictly abide by professional standards [*daode*], and have the necessary professional knowledge that qualifies them to do statistical work"; and "the leaders of localities, government departments, or other units may not order or ask statistical departments and statistical personnel to change or falsify statistical data" (NPC, 15 May 1996, Articles 24 and 7). In contrast, a NBS "work regulation" of 16 November 1995 explicitly states that the NBS is to implement "important decisions and instructions of the Chinese Communist Party Central Committee and the State Council".

At the local level, key data compiled by the local statistical bureau, such as GDP data, need approval by a local government leader before they can be reported up to the next higher-level statistical bureau.[38] This need for government leader approval of statistical data, calls into question the relevance of the published formal rules and regulations that include such statements as Article 7 of the Statistics Law, which requires that "the leaders of localities, government departments, or other units may not order or ask statistical departments and statistical personnel to change or falsify statistical data". While there is no written evidence of a similar approval pattern at the central level, the fact that the National Development and Reform Commission has access to NBS data before publication (and presumably the same holds for the State Council) suggests that channels for interference are plentiful.

The local government leader's approval authority of key data may create incentive mechanisms for local statistics officials that potentially conflict with professional statistical reporting. If a local government leader were to, in violation of the Statistics Law, "request" higher economic growth rates (perhaps to advance his or her promotion), the Statistics Law requires the local statistical bureau to refuse to co-operate with its immediate superior (the local government leader), and there the matter ends (Article 7). Such a refusal may, however, be unrealistic. The local statistical bureau could possibly report the local government leader to the next higher level statistical bureau. But the next higher level statistical bureau has no authority over the local government. It could inform the party disciplinary commission, which may act.[39] But it may be detrimental to the career of an official of a lower level statistical bureau to contact the local party discipline commission. Indeed the local government leader is likely to be the deputy head of the local party committee, which in turn also has some authority over the local party discipline commission. In the end, given these situations of potential conflicts of interest, statistics officials are unlikely to report on their government superiors since the chances of success are minimal and the likelihood of reprisals from these superiors is high.[40]

3.4.3. Regulations and control

The NBS and provincial statistical bureaus are to regularly publish statistical material "according to state regulations" (Article 14). But these state regulations appear to not be in the public realm.

National inspections of the NBS were conducted in co-operation with the Ministry of Supervision and the Bureau of Legislative Affairs of the State Council in 1987, 1989, 1994, 1997, and 2001. The latest inspection revealed 60 000 violations of the Statistics Law and led to punishment in 20 000 cases. Misreporting, predominantly by enterprises, accounted for almost 60% of the violations, with other violations consisting of enterprise refusals to report data, or late reporting, not of misbehaviour by statistics officials.[41] What may be under proper supervision, thus, is data reporting from basic reporting units to the statistical authority. No information about internal violations, i.e. violations within the statistical *xitong*, is available, even though statistical work of government departments was also supposed to be investigated. Perhaps the operation of the statistical system in China is as much scrutinised as are the reporting units, but, then, neither the investigations nor their results are made public. The little evidence that can be gleaned from reports in various sources suggests that regular supervision of statistical work in government departments may not happen at all, while the periodic inspection efforts, usually limited to exemplary inspections of selected work units, could be toothless.[42]

3.4.4. Statistics and the public

Zhang Sai (2001), NBS commissioner from 1984 through 1997, in the context of discussing the tasks of the statistical bureau vs. that of the statistical divisions of other government departments stated that: "the government statistical organisation primarily serves the needs of macroeconomic decision-making of party and government leaders at each administrative level, and is responsible to the party and government leaders at each administrative level". Not only is the statistical *xitong* at the service of party and government leaders, but this statement also implies that the NBS does not primarily serve the public.

Indeed, the Statistics Law lists as "fundamental task of statistical work" to conduct statistical examination of the implementation of the national economic and social development plan, to analyse the statistics, to provide statistical material and statistical advice and suggestions, and to supervise through the use of statistics (NPC, 15 May 1996, Article 2). Providing the public with statistics is not a fundamental task, nor does the Statistics Law make it an explicit duty.

According to the Statistics Law, the public is also supposed to supervise statistical work. "Statistical work should receive supervision by society and the public" (Article 6). This is unrealistic as long as the public is not given an opportunity to find out about the rules for statistical work.

There are new developments, however. In May 2004, NBS Commissioner Li (2004) put the consolidation of statistical legislation forward as an important objective for Chinese statistics. This includes raising public awareness of statistical laws and the improvement of law enforcement. For example, the NBS announced the launching of a publicity campaign, and training on statistical laws and regulation for statisticians.

3.5. Chinese reform proposals for the statistical system

3.5.1. Past proposals

Reform of China's statistical system has been under discussion for some time, usually with a focus on how to strengthen the NBS's authority. Proposals include the switch to direct central leadership over local statistical departments (*chuizhi*), the permanent dispatch of supervisors by the NBS to local statistical departments, and the establishment of a double system where provincial statistical bureaus as well as the NBS each have their own lower level tier statistical departments.[43] These proposals all appear inferior to the current arrangements. Due to the focus of governments at all levels on economic development and due to the evaluation of cadres according to their economic achievements, local governments have their own statistical needs and thus need some control over local statistical departments. Direct central leadership would also imply that all costs of maintaining the statistical system have to be borne by the centre. Dispatched central supervisors are likely to be co-opted by the locality over time. A double system appears wasteful of resources.

3.5.2. Recent proposals

More recently, and following a call by Premier Wen Jiabao in November 2003 to improve the statistical system and methodology, Commissioner Li (2004) stated several important development goals: reforming the management system, improving the operation mechanism and enhancing the legal framework and more generally to "establish a modern official statistical system […] to provide efficient and quality statistical services to the governments, the public and the international community". This orientation towards end-users is new and should inform the choice of data on which the NBS should focus in its own work, which may have implications for the choice of administrative divisions within the NBS and the type of survey work to be done.

Li (2004) also announced a reform of the management system of surveys to make NBS more independent in conducting surveys. There would also be more direct administration of higher-level statistical offices over those at local level. It is also planned that NBS will provide guidance and co-ordination of statistical work that is carried out in ministries: for example, surveys conducted by ministries will have to be reviewed by NBS. Finally, measures are announced to promote the role of non-governmental survey institutions.

The other cornerstones of the 2004 Strategy are the reform of statistical methodology and standards, the improvement of national accounts statistics, the development of the IT system for statistics, the consolidation of statistical legislation and the improvement of statistical services, including the promotion of wider public access to statistical information.

4. Conclusions and recommendations

Chinese statistics have come a long way from a pure reporting system in a centrally planned economy to a system that increasingly relies on surveys and modern statistical techniques to service users, be they government or the public at large. Nonetheless, many challenges remain. The present work has reviewed some of the central aspects of the institutional arrangements in Chinese statistics and the following key points have emerged.

First, there is still a legacy of reporting via ministries that limits the scope of the data collected and that limits the influence that NBS should have on the conception and quality of data collections. The role of NBS in co-ordinating and reviewing statistics produced by ministries needs strengthening.

Second, complications persist between the central and the sub-national level of the statistical system. Often, local statistical offices are closer to local governments than to the NBS and this may create incentives that are not conducive to the compilation of high-quality statistical information. Stronger line structures between NBS and statistical offices at the local level and better enforcement of the statistical laws at all levels of the administration should help to advance on this matter. Alternatively, if the role of NBS in relation to local statistical administrations cannot be strengthened, NBS may consider minimizing its reliance on local statistical bureaus or limit it to low-priority data.

Third, there is a need to establish functioning channels to address complaints against violations of the Statistics Law.

Fourth, there is a welcome but still sluggish move from enterprise reporting to survey techniques. Reporting requirements still appear very large both in the number of institutions that can order a reporting unit to report, and in the volume of data collected. The views of the reporting units on this matter and their compliance costs are not known. A systematic study would be helpful, and if reporting requirements were indeed excessive, mechanisms to reduce them should be explored.

Fifth, recognition of the desirability of a user-orientation of statistics is only at its beginnings. Further steps need to be taken to focus not only on data that reflect government priorities. Consultation with the public (for example domestic and foreign business associations, academia and non-government organisations) would be desirable.

Sixth, further efforts should be made to enhance transparency about data collection methods, and statistical methodology in general. Not only information about methods and source, but also about data itself should become more accessible to a broad range of users, for example through user-friendly Web sites with readily available, up-to-date statistics.

Seventh, clear rules should be established on which data are available for the public for free and which data can be purchased through individual contact with the NBS. Transparent, or at least standardized pricing for the latter would be desirable.

Notes

1. This chapter was written by Paul Schreyer, Prices and Structural Economic Statistics Division, Statistics Directorate, OECD and Carsten Holz, Associate Professor of Social Science, the Hong Kong University of Science and Technology.
2. Some government departments publish their data on the NBS Web site at *www.stats.gov.cn/tjfw/index.htm* (accessed on 22 June 2004). For an overview of the division of labour among the key Chinese data-collecting government departments see the International Monetary Fund's General Data Dissemination System (at *http://dsbb.imf.org/Applications/web/gdds*) on China, Table C on "Data Integrity and Access by the Public".
3. On the NBS responsibility see Article 4 of the Statistics Law (NPC, 15 May 1996).
4. See, for example, Gerard F. Adams and Chen Yimin (1996); Meng Lian and Wang Xiaolu (2000); Thomas Rawski (2001a, 2001b, 2003a, 2003b); *The Economist* (7 March 2001); and the *Asian Wall Street Journal* (22 November 2001).

5. These alternative growth rates are suggested by Thomas Rawski (2003a); in detail, he suggests –2 to +2% in 1998, –2.5 to +2% in 1999, +2 to +4% in 2000, and +3 to +5% in 2001. Also see Thomas Rawski (2001b, p. 349; 2003b, Figure 5.1).

6. Price issues in the derivation of real growth series have not been discussed at all. The official GDP deflator is frequently suspected of being too low, leading to an over-estimate of real GDP growth rates. For additional data complications also see Carsten A. Holz (2004b) and Carsten A. Holz and Yi-min Lin (2001).

7. A more extensive version of this assessment can be found in Holz (2004d).

8. The implementation instructions to the statistics law (NBS, 2 June 2000, Article 23) use the term "double leadership" (*shuangzhong lingdao*) for local statistical bureaus: in all professional matters, the next higher level statistical bureau exerts the main leadership. (Implicitly, otherwise, the local government exerts the main leadership.)

9. The relationship is "twice" removed from the core administrative leadership relationship between, say, central and provincial government. In a first step, the central, for example, Agriculture Ministry exerts business *leadership* over the provincial agricultural bureau (of the provincial government). In the second step, the statistical division of the central Agriculture Ministry exerts business *guidance* over the statistical division of the provincial agricultural bureau.

10. Wang Qi (2000), confusingly, also labels this relationship a "business guidance" relationship. But, contrary to a guidance relationship, in the interaction between statistical *xitong* and data reporting units all authority rests with the statistical *xitong*. The statistical reporting units have no choice but must report according to the requirements of the statistical *xitong*.

11. For the provincial level and below, in this and the following two paragraphs, see He Keng and Zheng Jingping (2001), pp. 40, 50.

12. The NBS does not have the authority to regulate on lower level government matters (such as appointment authority). The fact that the implementation instructions received the formal approval of the State Council provides the necessary authority, but the implementation instructions are unlikely to be taken as seriously by local governments as would have been a State Council circular or a National People's Congress law.

13. For example, all legal-person production units in China need to register with the statistical bureau – against a fee (NBS, 24 May 2000). This fee may well not appear in the formal budget of the statistical bureaus.

14. See He Keng and Zheng Jingping (2001), p. 50. In Shaanxi Province, 52% of central funding (*shiyefei*) received was passed on to statistical departments at the "basis" (*jiceng*), which probably implies county level and below (*Shaanxi Yearbook 2002*, p. 337).

15. On a history of Chinese statistics going back 2 000 years see Li Huicun and Mo Yueda (1993), with data on the NBS staff size on pp. 377, 399.

16. See He Keng and Zheng Jingping (2001), p. 45, *vs*. Zhang Sai (2001), p. 276. The latter source gives a number of 900 000, which appears mistaken by one digit.

17. See State Council (1998), p. 401.

18. See State Council (1998), p. 397. Lower level statistical bureaus comprise matching administrative divisions. For example, the Xi'an Municipality (of Shaanxi Province) statistical bureau has the same administrative divisions as the NBS except four (the Division for International Cooperation, the Division for Statistical Design and Management, the Division for Finance and Construction, and the Office of Retired Civil Servants), plus an extra division for rural social and economic statistics. (Xi'an Government, 28 May 2002).

19. See *www.stats.gov.cn/tjdt/gjtjjdt/t20040408_402142383.htm*, accessed on 9 April 2004.

20. No further details are provided. It would have been of interest to know which further institutions were operating under the umbrella of this society. The NBS note ordering the temporary halt to all activities of the society and its subordinate institutions was posted on the NBS homepage (at *www.stats.gov.cn*, accessed on 16 April 2004).

21. See *Statistical Work Yearbook 1998*, p. 338. A reviewer pointed out that the consultancy "was privatized in 2000 or 2001".

22. In recent years, many central line ministries were turned into companies (conglomerates) directly subordinate to the State Council. The principle of administrative leadership over central enterprises and possibly business leadership over lower level tier enterprises, however, still applies. Another possible successor to a line ministry is an association.

23. According to He Keng and Zheng Jingping (2001), p. 49, some of these departments providing rather comprehensive statistics related to the national accounts are the Ministry of Finance, the People's Bank of China, the Customs Office, the Ministry of Foreign Trade and Economic Cooperation, the Education Ministry, the Health Ministry, the State General Administration of Sports, the State Environmental Protection Administration, the State Tourism Administration, the Justice Ministry, and the Land and Natural Resources Ministry. OECD (2000) on national accounts in China includes references to individual other government departments throughout the text.

24. For further details see Carsten A. Holz (2002).

25. See NBS (1997), pp. 59-63. The Division for Industrial and Transport (or Communication) Statistics of the statistical *xitong* has an annual report form on transportation and freight as well as on post and telecommunications. It is unclear whether the statistical *xitong* collects data independently of the various other government departments, or whether this report is compiled by making use of the other government departments' data; this report appears to be used only in as far as it covers local (non-central) post and telecommunication services.

26. The relationship between the NBS and other central government departments is regulated in the Statistics Law, in a follow-up regulation specifically focusing on statistical work within these institutions located outside the immediate NBS *xitong*, and in the implementation instructions to the Statistics Law (NPC, 15 May 1996, Article 18; NBS, 27 Oct. 1999, Article 16; NBS, 2 June 2000, Articles 20, 29).

27. The NBS Web page is at *www.stats.gov.cn/tjgl/index.htm*, accessed on 15 April 2004. Two relevant State Asset Supervision and Administration Commission regulations on statistical reporting are the "Enterprise State Asset Statistical Report Measures" and the "Central Enterprise Financial Budget Report Administration Measures", both of 12 Feb. 2004, available in Chinese in *China Infobank*.

28. One possible explanation is that the People's Bank of China survey started in 1992, at a time when the stature of the NBS was perhaps lower than today, and the survey continues to be conducted by the People's Bank of China simply for historical reasons. The NBS now publishes its own business climate index (at *www.stats.gov.cn/english/statisticaldata/monthlydata/t20040120_137788.htm*, accessed on 15 April 2004). (The full name of the People's Bank of China publication is *The People's Bank of China Quarterly Statistical Bulletin*. NBS approval for the survey of industrial enterprises can be found at the NBS Web page *www.stats.gov.cn/tjgl/bmtjdcxmml/t20020401_16076.htm*, accessed on 15 April 2004).

29. See the General Data Dissemination Standard Web pages (for this particular information, see *http://dsbb.imf.org/Applications/web/gdds/gddscountrycategorydiapreport/?strcode=CHN&strcat=175*, accessed on 16 April 2004).

30. No such statement was included in the original 1983 PRC Statistics Law (NPC, 8 December 1983).

31. Surveys are also subject to limitations encountered in other countries; for example, most price data are limited to urban areas, comparable to the case of the United States where the Bureau of Labor Statistics only publishes an urban Consumer Price Index.

32. At the local level, the switch to sample surveys of industrial enterprises is more gradual. For example, Xi'an Municipality in Shaanxi Province in 2002 switched to sample surveys of industrial enterprises with independent accounting system and with annual sales revenue below RMB 5 million, but the other municipalities in Shaanxi are unlikely to already have made the switch (*Xi'an Yearbook 2002*, p. 216).

33. Shaanxi Province, for example, conducted an "emerging sector" survey of renovation and decoration, real estate administration and rental housing, news and consulting services, computer-related services, and urban district (*shequ*) services in 2002. This survey involved a large number of other provincial government departments (planning commission, economic and trade commission, finance bureau, information sector bureau, construction bureau, education bureau, civil affairs bureau, judicial bureau, and industrial and commercial administration). It was to be repeated in the future every five years. (See Shaanxi Government, 11 July 2002.)

34. According to He Keng and Zheng Jingping (2001), p. 61, double-reporting is the case particularly in industry and in wholesale and retail trade.

35. According to He Keng and Zheng Jingping (2001), p. 26, this is particularly common in the case of agricultural output statistics, township and village enterprise statistics, unemployment statistics, import-export statistics, and FDI statistics.

36. While the NBS every few years publishes a compendium of selected statistical regulations of previous years, complete with ISBN number, these compendia are not available to the public. Some of these volumes also carry a stamp "for internal use only" (*neibu*). A few regulations have appeared on the NBS Web site.

37. While each separate topic on which China provides information to the GDDS comes with a complete contact address (and name of a contact person) in the NBS, the NBS Web site, in contrast, carries no such information. The International Monetary Fund's GDDS can be found at http://dsbb.imf.org/Applications/web/gdds/gddshome/, and the NBS homepage is at www.stats.gov.cn.

38. See Pan Zhenwen and An Yuli (2003), p. 8.

39. A very few exemplary cases of punishment of a statistics official or local government leader were made public in the late 1990s.

40. The NBS provides a telephone number and an e-mail address on its homepage (www.stats.gov.cn) to which violations of statistical laws and regulations can be reported; nothing is known about the effects of such reporting.

41. For information on inspections see the China Web pages in the International Monetary Fund's GDDS (http://dsbb.imf.org/Applications/web/gdds/gddshome/) under the heading "Table C – Data Integrity and Access by the Public".

42. For details on the 2001 inspection also see www.stats.gov.cn/xwkj/tjdt/20010523002.htm, accessed on 8 Feb. 2002. The inspection explicitly included statistical departments at all administrative levels and internal statistical divisions of other government departments, but inspections may have been *a priori* limited to 5% of all relevant work units.
The NBS and at least provincial statistical bureaus also have an auditing office (*shi*), with the label indicating that it is part of one of the divisions (possibly the internal finance and construction division) rather than an independent division of its own (NBS, 1 March 1995). It focuses on internal financial issues.

43. See, for example, *Zhongguo tongji* No. 11/1999, 25, and No. 2/2001, 8f. Much earlier, the journal *Jingji yanjiu cankao ziliao* in its issue of 28 August 1988, devoted solely to China's statistical system, already raised such institutional questions. Zhang Sai (2001), former NBS commissioner, devotes one full chapter to possible reforms, without, however, promoting one particular overall reform programme.

Bibliography

Names which in the original are in Chinese characters are reported here in the same order as in the original, i.e. last name, followed by first name.

Adams, Gerard F. and Chen Yimin (1996), "Scepticism about Chinese GDP Growth – the Chinese GDP Elasticity of Energy Consumption", *Journal of Economic and Social Measurement* 22, No. 4 (1996), pp. 231-40.

China Infobank, Internet database with Chinese news and laws and regulations, at www.chinainfobank.com.

Dougherty, Sean (1997), "The Reliability of Chinese Statistics", *China Online*www.chinaonline.com/refer/statistics/secure/us_prc.asp, accessed on 22 June 2004.

Fujian shengzhi tongjizhi (Fujian Provincial Almanac, statistics volume) (2000), Beijing: Fangzhi chubanshe.

GDP 1952-1996, Zhongguo guonei shengchan zongzhi hesuan lishi ziliao (zhaiyao) 1952-1996 (Abstract of historical material on China's GDP 1952-1996) (1998), Beijing: Zhongguo tongji chubanshe.

He Keng and Zheng Jingping (2001), *Zhongwai zhengfu tongji tizhi bijiao yanjiu* (A Comparative Study of the Statistical System in China and Abroad), Beijing: Zhongguo tongji chubanshe.

Holt, Tim (1998), "The Fundamental Principles and the Impact of Using Statistics for Administrative Purposes", *Statistical Journal of the United Nations Economic Commission for Europe* 15, No. 3/4, pp. 203-12.

Holz, Carsten A. (2002), "Institutional Constraints on the Quality of Statistics in a Developing and Transitional Economy: the Case of China", *China Information* 16, No. 1, pp. 25-67.

Holz, Carsten A. (2003), "Fast, Clear and Accurate: How Reliable Are Chinese Output and Economic Growth Statistics?", *The China Quarterly* 173 (March 2003), pp. 122-63.

Holz, Carsten A. (2004a), "Deconstructing China's GDP Statistics", *China Economic Review* 15, No. 2, pp. 164-202.

Holz, Carsten A. (2004b), "China's Statistical System in Transition: Challenges, Data Problems, and Institutional Innovations", *Review of Income and Wealth* 50, No. 3, September, pp. 381-409.

Holz, Carsten A. (2004c), "China's Reform Period Economic Growth: Why Angus Maddison Got It Wrong and What That Means", Mimeo, Hong Kong University of Science and Technology/Asia-Pacific Research Center at Stanford University.

Holz, Carsten A. (2004d), "The Institutional Arrangements for the Production of Chinese Statistics", *OECD Statistics Working Paper*, OECD, Paris.

Holz, Carsten A. and Yi-min Lin (2001), "Pitfalls of China's Industrial Statistics: Inconsistencies and Specification Problems", *The China Review* 1, No. 1, Fall, pp. 29-71.

Huenemann, Ralph W. (2001), "Are China's Recent Transport Statistics Plausible?", *China Economic Review* 12, No. 4, pp. 368-72.

Keidel, Albert (2001), "China's GDP Expenditure Accounts", *China Economic Review* 12, No. 4, December, pp. 355-67.

Klein, Lawrence R. and Suleyman Ozmucur (2003), "The Estimation of China's Economic Growth Rate", mimeo, Department of Economics, University of Pennsylvania.

Lardy, Nicholas (2003), "Evaluating Economic Indicators in Post-WTO China", *Issues and Studies* 38/39, No. 4/38–1/39, December 2002/March 2003), pp. 249-68.

Li Huicun and Mo Yueda (1993), *Zhongguo tongjishi* (History of Chinese Statistics), Beijing: Zhongguo tongji chubanshe.

Li, Deshui (2004), "Statistics of China: Goals, Priorities and Measures", paper presented at the International Symposium on Reforms, Achievements, and Challenges: China and Its Partners in Statistical Co-operation, Beijing, May.

Maddison, Angus (1998), *Chinese Economic Performance in the Long Run*, Development Centre of the OECD, Paris.

Meng Lian and Wang Xiaolu (2000), "Dui zhongguo jingji zengzhang tongji shuju kexindu de guji" (An Evaluation of the Reliability of China's Statistics on Economic Growth), *Jingji yanjiu*, No. 10, October, pp. 3-13.

NBS (National Bureau of Statistics) (1 March 1995), "Guojia tongjiju guanyu tongji bumen neibu shenji gongzuo guiding" (NBS Regulation on Internal Auditing of Statistical Departments), in *China Infobank*.

NBS (National Bureau of Statistics) (16 November 1995), "Guojia tongjiju gongzuo guize (xiuding)" [NBS Work Regulation (revised)], in *Tongji gongzuo zhongyao wenjian xuanbian 1991-1995* (selected important documents on statistical work 1991-1995), Beijing: Zhongguo tongji chubanshe, 1996, pp. 1450-6.

NBS (National Bureau of Statistics) (1997), "Zhongguo niandu guonei shengchan zongzhi jisuan fangfa" (Method of Calculating China's Annual GDP), Issued by the NBS National Income Accounts Division. Beijing: Zhongguo tongji chubanshe.

NBS (National Bureau of Statistics) (27 October 1999), "Bumen tongji diaocha xiangmu guanli zanxing banfa" (Temporary Administrative Measures for Departmental Statistical Surveys), NBS Decree No. 4, in Zhonghua renmin gongheguo guowuyuan gongbao, No. 967, 10 February 2000, pp. 36-9.

NBS (National Bureau of Statistics) (24 May 2000), "Guojia tongjiju guanyu jiaqiang tongji dengji guanli gongzuo de yijian" (NBS Suggestions on Strengthening the Administration of Statistical Registration), in *Tongji gongzuo zhongyao wenjian xuanbian 1996-2000* (selected important documents on statistical work 1996-2000), Beijing: Zhongguo tongji chubanshe, 2001, pp. 839-41.

NBS (National Bureau of Statistics) (2 June 2000), "Zhonghua renmin gongheguo tongji fa shishi xize" (Detailed Implementation Instructions for the PRC Statistics Law), Revision of original regulation of 19 January 1987, approved by the State Council, in China Infobank.

NPC (National People's Congress) (8 December 1983), "Zhonghua renmin gongheguo tongji fa" (PRC Statistics Law), in *China Infobank*.

NPC (National People's Congress) (15 May 1996), "Zhonghua renmin gongheguo tongji fa" (PRC Statistics Law), Revision of original 8 December 1983 PRC Statistics Law, in *China Infobank*.

OECD (2000), *National Accounts for China: Sources and Methods*, OECD, Paris.

Pan Zhenwen and An Yuli (2003), "Yi wan yi de chaju cong he er lai: dui guojiaji, shengji hesuan shuju chaju de sikao" (Where is the One Trillion Difference From? Some Thoughts on the Difference between National and Provincial Accounts Data), *Zhongguo tongji*, No. 11, November, p. 8f.

Rawski, Thomas G. (2001a), "China by the Numbers: How Reform Affected China's Economic Statistics", *China Perspectives*, No. 33, January/February, pp. 25-34.

Rawski, Thomas G. (2001b), "What's Happening to China's GDP Statistics", *China Economic Review* 12, No. 4, December, pp. 347-54.

Rawski, Thomas G. (2003), "Economic Issues and the Future of China", mimeo, University of Pittsburgh.

Rawski, Thomas G. (2003), "SARS and China's Economy", mimeo, University of Pittsburgh.

Rawski, Thomas G. and Xiao Wei (2001), "Roundtable on Chinese Economic Statistics: Introduction", *China Economic Review* 12, No. 4, December, pp. 298-302.

Shaanxi Government (2002), "Shaanxi sheng renmin zhengfu bangongting zhuanfa sheng tongjiju guanyu kaizhan quansheng xinxing chanye diaocha yijian de tongzhi" (Shaanxi Province Government Office circular passing on the suggestions of the provincial statistical bureau on starting a province-wide emerging-sectors survey), 11 July, in *China Infobank*.

Shaanxi Yearbook. Shanxi nianjian (Shaanxi Yearbook), Xi'an: Shaanxi nianjian chubanshe, various years.

State Council (1998), *Zhongyang zhengfu zuzhi jigou* (Central Government Organisations and Institutions), Issued by the State Council General Office Secretariat and the Comprehensive Division of the Chinese Communist Party Central Committee Institutional Design Committee's General Office, Beijing: Gaige chubanshe.

Statistical Work Yearbook, Zhongguo tongji gongzuo nianjian (Statistical Work Yearbook of China), Beijing: Zhongguo tongji chubanshe, various issues.

Statistical Yearbook, Zhongguo tongji nianjian (Statistical Yearbook of China), Beijing: Zhongguo tongji chubanshe, various years.

Wang Qi (2000), *Xinbian tongji gongzuo shiwu quanshu* (New Compendium on Statistical Work), Beijing: Zhongguo tongji chubanshe.

Xi'an Government (11 April 2001), "Xi'an shi renmin zhengfu guanyu quxian an zaidi yuanze zuohao tongji gongzuo de tongzhi" (Xi'an municipality government circular on well performing statistical work according to the county and district geographical principle), *Xi'an zhengbao*, No. 8-9, pp. 31.

Xi'an Government (10 September 2001), "Xi'an shi renmin zhengfu bangongting zhuanfa shi tongjiju guanyu xi'an shi zaidi tongji gaige shishi yijian de tongzhi" (Circular of the general office of the Xi'an municipal government passing on the implementing suggestions of the municipal statistical bureau regarding the Xi'an municipal geographical statistics reform), Xi'an zhengbao, No. 18, p. 17f.

Xi'an Government (28 May 2002), "Xi'an shi renmin zhengfu bangongting guanyu yinfa xi'an shi tongjiju zhineng peizhi neishe jigou he renyuan bianzhi guiding de tongzhi" (Circular of the general office of the Xi'an municipal government passing on the regulation on the tasks, internal institutions, and staff of the Xi'an Municipal statistical bureau), Xi'an zhengbao, No. 15, pp. 16-18.

Xi'an Yearbook. Xi'an nianjian (Xi'an Yearbook), Xi'an: Xi'an chubanshe, various years.

Xu Xianchun (1999a), "Shijie yinhang gaogu zhongguo GDP shuju" (The World Bank Estimates China's GDP to be Higher), *Zhongguo guoqing guoli*, No. 1, January, pp. 7-10.

Xu Xianchun (1999b), "Shijie yinhang dui zhongguo guanfang GDP shuju de tiaozheng he chongxin renke" (The World Bank's Adjustments to China's Official GDP Data, and Later Acceptance), *Jingji yanjiu*, No. 6, June, pp. 52-8.

Xu Xianchun (2000), "Zhongguo guonei shengchan zongzhi hesuan zhong cunzai de ruogan wenti yanjiu" (Some Problems in the Calculation of China's GDP), *Jingji yanjiu*, No. 2, February, pp. 10-16.

Zhang Sai, (1995), "Guanyu 'Zhonghua renmin gongheguo tongjifa xiuzhengan (zao'an)' de shuoming" (Explanation of the (Daft) Scheduled Revisions to the PRC Statistics Law), 23 August 1995, in *China Infobank*.

Zhang Sai (2001), *Zhongguo tongji gaige fazhan zhanlue de lilun yu shijian* (Theory and Practice of China's Statistical System Development Strategy), Beijing: Zhongguo tongji chubanshe.

Zhongguo tongji (China Statistics), monthly publication of the National Bureau of Statistics.

PART II

Public Finance

PART II

Chapter 6

Governance in Taxation in China

Table of Contents

Summary 203

Governance in Taxation in China 205

   1. Overview 205

   2. The current Chinese tax system 205

      2.1. Tax authorities in China 206
      2.2. Chinese taxes 206
      2.3. Indirect taxes 207
      2.4. Direct taxes on income 209

   3. Challenges 211

      3.1. Key issues in tax policy 211
      3.2. Key issues in tax administration 212

   4. Direction of future reforms 218

      4.1. Going forward 219

Notes 219

Bibliography 219

Annex 6.A1. Tax Levels and Tax Structure (General Government) 1998-2003 220
Annex 6.A2. Tax Levels and Tax Structure (Central Government) 1998-2003 221
Annex 6.A3. Tax Levels and Tax Structure (Local Government) 1998-2003 222

List of boxes

6.1. Organisational structure of tax administration in OECD member countries 215

List of tables

6.1. GDP and tax revenue (1998-2003) 212

List of figures

6.1. GDP and tax revenue 213

Summary

With its transition to a market-oriented economy, China has gone through major tax reforms in the last two decades. Significant measures to improve governance in taxation were implemented, including unifying tax laws, equalizing tax burdens, simplifying the tax system, rationalizing the decentralized system and standardizing revenue allocation methods between the central and local governments. However, more needs to be done to improve China's tax system so that transparency, stability and the rule of law become the guiding principles.

Key issues in tax policy

In tax policy, a country's tax system should provide a level playing field to participants in its market so that the market works in the most efficient way while raising necessary revenue for the government. China's tax system was overhauled in 1994. After 10 years of operation, a number of issues have emerged, which call for a new round of reforms. The rapid transition to a market economy and China's accession to the World Trade Organization (WTO) also indicate the need for tax reform. These reforms will embrace, in particular, transforming the production-type value-added tax (VAT) to a consumption-type VAT, fine-tuning excise tax, unifying the two Corporate Income Tax Codes (one for domestic enterprises and the other for foreign-invested enterprises and foreign enterprises), reforming individual income tax, restructuring local taxes and streamlining agricultural taxes.

Key issues in tax administration

On the implementation side, any tax system is only as good as its tax administration. In China, more effective tax administration will make a significant contribution to improving governance, among other things, in respect of transparency, a level playing field and the rule of law.

Over recent years, there has been a consistent increase in the ratio of tax revenue to gross domestic product (GDP): the ratio rose from 11.6% of GDP to 17.5% in the five years from 1998 to 2003. This impressive upward trend can be attributed, in fact, to the major organisational reform in 1994 when the State Administration of Taxation (SAT) became independent of the Ministry of Finance. SAT was given a wider mandate and more resources, and considerable efforts were made to improve the efficiency and effectiveness of tax administration. While the 1994 reform led to improved governance in taxation with better oversight over local tax offices, the efforts to build a modern tax system are far from complete.

From the governance point of view, emphasis should be placed on the following aspects: First, the current organisational structure of tax administration, based both on "type of tax" and "function", could be flattened and streamlined through centralizing functions, merging replicated and overlapping functions. Second, communication and co-ordination between the central and local tax authorities should be improved. Third, tax authorities should aim at improving voluntary compliance instead of relying on revenue targets. Experience shows that better compliance would not only lead to more tax revenue but also to less tax-induced distortions. Fourth, administrative regulations in China should be simplified. Simplification of regulations could lead to a substantial reduction of compliance cost for taxpayers as well as administrative cost for tax authorities. Fifth, it is of vital importance for China to develop a unified computer system to integrate the varied functions of tax collection and administration. Last but not least, appropriate training should be given to those who deal with increasingly important and complex issues relating to multinational and large taxpayers. China has some new ideas about large taxpayer units to deal effectively with these taxpayers, and these ideas are still being carefully considered by local as well as head offices.

Going forward

With China becoming an observer on the OECD's Committee on Fiscal Affairs, it is expected that China will associate itself more closely with OECD work on taxation, and in doing so will benefit from the wealth of knowledge and experience of OECD member countries and *vice versa*.

Governance in Taxation in China[1]

1. Overview

Although China's tax system has only a short history, it has gone through major tax reforms in the last two decades. With its transition to a market-oriented economy, China has taken on board market-based approaches, as well as internationally accepted principles and practice. Though further reform is necessary, this has made significant contributions to China's economic transition and development.

Significant measures to improve governance in taxation were implemented, including the following:

1. unifying tax laws;

2. equalising tax burdens;

3. simplifying the tax system;

4. rationalizing the decentralised system; and

5. standardising revenue allocation methods between the central and local governments.

However, more needs to be done to improve China's tax system so that transparency, stability and the rule of law become the guiding principles. In setting tax policy, a country's tax system should aim to provide a level playing field for all market players so that the market works in the most efficient way, while raising the necessary revenue for the government. From this perspective, there are still major issues in China's tax system that need to be dealt with. For example, China still has a two-track system for corporate income tax, distinguishing between foreign and domestic companies. These systems need to be merged to come into line with the WTO national treatment rule. The current production-type VAT should also be changed to a broadly based consumption-type VAT so that China can avoid distortions in investment decisions arising from blocking input tax on fixed assets.

On the implementation side, any tax system is only as good as its tax administration. No matter what tax legislation is applied, a country cannot be said to have a good tax system if it lacks effective and efficient tax administration to implement such laws. In China, a more effective tax administration will make a significant contribution to improving governance, among other things, in respect of transparency, establishing a level playing field and the rule of law.

2. The current Chinese tax system

The present tax system, which dates back to 1994, is a revenue-sharing system, with the imposition of some taxes being central, others being local and still others being shared.[2]

2.1. Tax authorities in China

Taxation in China follows laws and regulations formulated by the National People's Congress, the State Council, the Ministry of Finance and the State Administration of Taxation. Tax legislation is centralized, *i.e.* local governments do not have tax legislative power.

The Ministry of Finance (MOF) is a government agency under the State Council, the highest administrative body in China, responsible for formulating development strategies, policies, mid- and long-term planning and taxation reform schemes. The State Administration of Taxation (hereafter referred to as SAT) is the headquarters of China's tax administration. As a ministerial level government institution it ranks under the direct leadership of the State Council. The functional offices at below headquarter level, called National Tax Service (NTS), are responsible for collecting taxes (including value-added tax, excise tax and corporate income tax) whose revenue is either for the use of the central government or shared between central and local governments. Local governments have their own tax administrations called Local Tax Services (LTS) that collect the remaining taxes and use the revenue thereof to finance their operations. NTS are subject to the leadership of the SAT headquarters in terms of business guidance (*yewu zhidao*) and administration leadership (*xingzheng lingdao*). SAT provides business leadership (*yewu zhidao*) over LTS and shares administrative leadership (*xingzheng lingdao*) with local governments. Customs duties, value-added tax and excise tax on imports are collected by the customs administration.

2.2. Chinese taxes

The system comprises 22 taxes, among which indirect taxes and income taxes constitute the principal classes. The tax system consists of the following taxes:

- Indirect taxes:
  - value-added tax (VAT);
  - excise tax;
  - business tax;
  - customs duties.
- Income taxes:
  - corporate income tax;
  - income tax for foreign-invested enterprises (FIEs) and foreign enterprises;
  - individual income tax.
- Resource taxes:
  - resource tax;
  - urban and township land use tax.
- Property taxes:
  - house property tax;
  - urban real estate tax (for FIEs).
- Special-purpose taxes:
  - city maintenance and construction tax;
  - farmland occupation tax;
  - land appreciation tax;
  - vehicle acquisition tax.

- Behavioural taxes:
  - vehicle and vessel usage tax;
  - vehicle and vessel usage license plate tax (for FIEs);
  - vessel tonnage tax;
  - stamp tax;
  - deed tax;
  - slaughter tax;
  - banquet tax.

2.3. Indirect taxes

2.3.1. Value-added tax (VAT)

VAT is a consumption tax levied mainly on goods on the basis of the value added in the course of commodity production, selling and taxable service provision. VAT taxpayers include enterprises, institutions, individual householders and other individuals engaged in sales of goods, importation, provision of taxable services, processing, repairing and replacement activities within the territory of the People's Republic of China. The VAT system is production-based, meaning that input tax paid on purchasing fixed assets is not creditable against output tax.

VAT is levied at a standard rate of 17%. However a reduced rate of 13% is applied to the following:

- agriculture, forestry, products of animal husbandry, aquatic products;
- edible vegetable oil and food grains duplicates;
- tap water, heating, cooling, hot water, coal gas, liquefied petroleum gas, natural gas, methane gas, coal/charcoal products for household use;
- books, newspapers, magazines (excluding the newspapers and magazines distributed by the post department);
- feeds, chemical fertilisers, agricultural chemicals, agricultural machinery and plastic covering film for farming;
- dressing metal mineral products, dressing non-metal mineral products and coal.

VAT payers whose annual turnover exceeds a certain threshold are required to register with the competent tax offices. Registered standard taxpayers enjoy input tax credit except for the purchase of fixed assets.

Small-scale VAT payers do not enjoy input credit and their liabilities are assessed with their turnover multiplied by a collection rate of 6%.

VAT is not chargeable on the following:

- agricultural production materials;
- self-produced primary agricultural products sold by agricultural producing units and individuals;
- imported goods being processed for exportation;
- self-use equipment imported as part of the total investment for projects with foreign investment or domestic investment which is encouraged by the state;
- contraceptive medicines and devices;

- antique books purchased from the public;
- instruments and equipment imported for direct use in scientific research, experiment and education;
- imported materials and equipment donated by foreign governments or international organisations;
- materials imported to support poverty relief and charity causes donated by overseas natural persons, legal persons and other organisations;
- articles imported directly by organisations for the disabled for exclusive use by the disabled;
- processing and repair services provided by individual disabled labourers.

Like in most other countries, Chinese authorities try to zero-rate exports. However, administrative deficiencies and other difficulties have restrained their ability to do so. After several revisions, exporters are entitled to VAT refunds at 17%, 13%, 8% and 5%, depending on the type of exported product.

VAT must be paid within 10 days of the end of each tax period. Registered taxpayers have to assess their own tax liability and submit their tax returns for each tax period, which varies according to the volume of turnover of each taxpayer. Tax credits can only be carried forward to the next VAT period and are not refundable.

2.3.2. Excise tax

Excise tax is chargeable when excisable products are manufactured, contract-processed or imported into China. Taxpayers of excise tax include all enterprises, institutions, household businesses and other individuals engaged in production, contract processing or importation of excisable products within the territory of the People's Republic of China.

Major tax exemptions and/or reductions include two situations:

1. Taxable consumer goods exported shall be exempt from excise tax if not restricted by the state rules.
2. Thirty per cent of excise tax may be credited if an enterprise produces and sells cars, cross-country vehicles and/or vans which meet the stipulated low pollution standards.

2.3.3. Business tax

Business tax is an indirect tax complementary to VAT. It covers provision of services excluded by VAT, transfer of immovable property and sale of intangible assets. Business tax is an important source of revenue for local governments, and is administered, in most cases, by LTS.

Business tax is assessed on business turnover, with no deduction allowed. Tax rates vary from 3% to 20%, depending on the services provided. However, the most common rate is 5%.

Services with the nature of public benefits can be exempted from business tax if they meet the requirements set by law. Another exemption is on the transfer of technologies. Transferors, both domestic and foreign, can apply for exemption if technologies are transferred to transferees in China.

2.4. Direct taxes on income

2.4.1. Corporate income tax

China has two Corporate Income Tax Codes, one for domestic enterprises and the other for foreign-invested enterprises (FIEs) and foreign enterprises, with similar structures but dramatic differences in concessions (for information on FIE also see Chapter 15). On the whole, FIEs enjoy more favourable treatment than domestic enterprises. FIEs, as Chinese-incorporated entities, are taxed on their worldwide income. Foreign enterprises are taxed on profits earned from trade or business activities carried out through an establishment or a place of business in China.

The nominal corporate income tax rate is 33%, the same in the two codes. However, the rate may be reduced to an effective 24% or 15% if the stipulated criteria are met. The tax is levied on taxable income, which is the net income in a taxable year minus costs, expenses and losses in that year. It is explicit in the codes that an accrual method of accounting be followed in assessing the taxable income, whilst tax adjustments are necessary in some cases. Taxable income includes all receipts and capital gains. Expenses are deductible to the extent that they are directly related to the trade or business activities generating the income. Investment proceeds obtained by FIEs, including inter-company dividends, can be excluded from the taxable income of the investing company. Accordingly, any expenses and losses incurred in the investment are not deductible from the taxable income. Foreign income is included in the taxable income, with a foreign tax credit allowed for income taxes paid on foreign-source income up to the limit calculated within Chinese tax laws.

Inventory is valued at cost. Taxpayers can choose methods from First In First Out (FIFO), Last In First Out (LIFO) or weighted average for inventory evaluation. However, approval from the competent tax offices must be obtained before changes can be made to the method of evaluation.

Fixed assets with useful lives of two years or fewer and items with a cost of RMB 2 000 or less can be deducted. Other fixed assets must be capitalized and depreciated in accordance with the depreciation schedule set in the codes. Depreciation is calculated using a straight-line method. Under special circumstances, an application may be filed with the tax authorities to use accelerated depreciation. The residual value is estimated at 10% of cost. Houses and buildings must be depreciated in no less than 20 years; trains, ships, machines, equipment and other facilities used in production in no less than 10 years; while electronic equipment, means of transportation other than ships and trains, furniture, fittings and other appliances in no less than five years. Enterprises engaged in petroleum exploitation can enjoy exceptional depreciation rules that are more favourable than for other enterprises.

A deduction is allowed for amortization of intangible assets, such as patents, proprietary technology, trademarks, copyrights and other intangibles. The amortization period of intangible assets is no less than 10 years. Organisation expenses incurred during the preparation period can be amortized over a period of no less than five years. Offshore oil projects can amortize exploration expenses over a period of no less than a year after commencement of commercial production.

Net operation losses can be carried forward for a period of no longer than five years, and no carry-back is allowed. Losses are computed in the same way as profits, and any losses realized must be declared in the tax return.

Royalties and interest payments by FIEs to foreign affiliates are tax deductible, provided they are charged on an arm's-length basis. Management fees paid to foreign affiliates are not deductible unless related to specific services.

Income tax and local surtax charges are not deductible in determining an enterprise's taxable income. Other taxes, such as irrecoverable VAT, excise tax, business tax, etc. are deductible in determining the taxable income.

No withholding tax is levied on business profits remitted overseas as dividends to foreign investors by FIEs. However, foreign enterprises without establishments or fixed places of business in China are subject to a withholding tax of 10% on the gross income from interest, rentals, royalties and other China-source passive income.

The taxable period for corporate income tax follows the calendar year. Tax payments must be made in four quarterly instalments, the amount of which being determined with reference to the following:

1. actual quarterly profits;
2. one-quarter of the tax paid in the proceeding year; or
3. other formulas approved by the directly responsible tax offices.

Final settlement must be made within five months after the end of each taxable year. No consolidation of returns for affiliates is allowed while the combination of profits and losses for different branches of a single legal entity is permitted.

2.4.2. Individual income tax

Resident Chinese individuals are subject to individual income tax on their worldwide income, and non-residents are subject to individual income tax on their China-source income. A resident is a person having a place of abode in China, or a person residing in China for more than one year though maintaining no place of abode therein. Foreign expatriates working in China and deriving income from an overseas employer with no permanent establishment in China will be exempt from Chinese individual income tax, provided they are not physically present in China, consecutively or cumulatively, for more than 90 days in a calendar year, or 183 days if a tax treaty is in place. For foreign expatriates residing in China for more than a year but less than five years, their foreign-source income not received in China is exempted from Chinese tax. Foreign expatriates who reside in China for more than five consecutive years will be subject to tax on their worldwide income from the sixth year onward.

Individual income tax is assessed on a scheduler basis, which is in contrast to the global basis used by most developed countries. Different items of income are treated differently under the current law. Salaries and wages are taxed at nine progressive rates scaled from 5-45%, with a standard deduction of RMB 800 per month. Foreign expatriates, including residents of Hong Kong, China, Macao and Chinese Taipei, are given an additional allowance of RMB 3 200 per month. Salaries of an individual include basic salary, bonus, foreign service premium, area allowance, cost-of-living allowance, housing allowance in excess of actual rental, local tax reimbursement, insurance and pension contributions, stock benefits, other cash benefits and benefits in kind received in compensation for dependent personal services. Individual income tax on salaries and wages must be paid monthly, and employers are required to withhold the tax and surrender it to local tax authorities.

Other income, including compensation for personal services, income from publication of articles, royalties, interest, dividends, incidental income and rentals, is taxed at a flat rate of 20%. Capital gains are treated as other income and are subject to tax in the same manner as the above-mentioned income. Special deductions are given to income from compensation for personal services, income from publication of articles, royalties, or income from the lease of property. A 30% tax reduction is applicable to income from publication of articles. Interest and dividends are taxed on the gross basis without any deduction. For sales of property, the original value of the property and the reasonable expenses incurred are deductible from the sales proceeds to arrive at the taxable income.

Additional tax may be assessed if the income received for services performed is deemed to be excessively high.

When paying taxable income to an individual, the employer, the institution or the person making the payment is mandated to act as the withholding agent to withhold the income tax due.

Self-employed individuals are also taxed under the Individual Income Tax Law, with different progressive rates and deductions. These individuals have to make monthly payments, with a final settlement within three months after the end of the tax year.

In the case of partnerships, individual income tax is assessed on the income of each partner on a transparent basis.

3. Challenges

3.1. *Key issues in tax policy*

China's tax system was overhauled in 1994. After 10 years of operation, a number of issues have emerged, which loudly call for a new round of reforms. From a governance point of view, the most important element in tax policy is to provide a level playing field to all the taxpayers concerned – i.e. treat different taxpayers on an equal basis and avoid distortions in economic decisions being caused by the tax system – in order to provide the most suitable economic environment for the efficient use of resources.

The rapid transition to a market economy also calls for a new round of tax reform, which will embrace, in particular, transforming the production-type VAT to a consumption-type VAT, fine-tuning excise tax, unifying the two Corporate Income Tax Codes, reforming individual income tax, restructuring local taxes and streamlining agricultural taxes. China's accession to the WTO prompted reform as well.

The first priority is to transform the production-type VAT to a consumption-type VAT. The current VAT system was designed in an inflationary period in which a production-type system was justifiable. However, as time goes on, the government sees a more urgent need to encourage capital investment so as to boost China's economic growth. The production-type VAT runs counter to this need. In addition, taxpayers with large volumes of non-creditable VAT on fixed assets, usually large and capital-intensive enterprises, have been complaining about the negative effect thereof. Therefore, the system needs transformation.

The second step is to unify the two separate Corporate Income Tax Codes. While China's accession to the WTO guarantees national treatment to foreign products and enterprises, the playing field for foreign and domestic enterprises is not level. Different treatment under corporate income tax, and in particular, uneven access to tax incentives, has put domestic enterprises in a much less favourable position than foreign companies.

Although better-than-national treatment of foreign investment is not against WTO principles, domestic enterprises have been urging the government to merge the two separate codes as quickly as possible.

The third priority is to reform the individual income tax. Currently, the total revenue from this tax is quite low. A large portion of it comes from withholding tax on salaries and wages. Taxpayers, the wage earners in this context, complain that the tax burden is high because of the low personal allowance and because of the discrimination against Chinese nationals. People believe in the pay-as-you-can principle, but those with the ability to pay are not properly and sufficiently taxed because of the 20% flat rate for **other income** and the malfunctioning of the present tax collection and administration system related thereto.

Proposals have been made to adjust personal deductions to take family situation into consideration, and for some of the income items to be jointly reported for the assessment of annual liability.

The fourth step is to fine-tune the excise tax system. The present list of excisable goods needs adjustment. Some goods are no longer luxury in nature, and therefore should be deleted from the list. Some goods are luxury and excisable in nature, or environmentally costly or unfriendly, and therefore should be added to the list.

The fifth challenge is to streamline the agricultural taxation system, which was designed under a planned economy system. The focus of the reform is to convert reasonable fees to taxes and to cancel unreasonable fees, to relieve the burden on farmers and bring the rural and urban tax systems closer into line with each other.

In addition, reforms are also necessary in taxation related to property and real estate, local taxation, and the tax power division between the central and local governments.

3.2. Key issues in tax administration[3]

Over recent years, there has been a consistent increase in the ratio of tax revenue to gross domestic product (GDP) (see Table 6.1 and Figure 6.1): the ratio has risen from 11.6% of GDP to 17.5% in the five years from 1998 to 2003. This increase in tax revenue has been double that of nominal GDP which has been growing at an exceptional rate of around 5-12% annually. The impressive upward trend can be attributed to the considerable efforts by tax authorities to improve the efficiency and effectiveness of tax administration. While tax authorities should be commended for their achievement so far, the efforts to build a modern tax system are far from complete.

Table 6.1. **GDP and tax revenue (1998-2003)**
Denomination: hundred million RMB

	GDP	Nominal GDP growth %	Real GDP growth %	Tax revenue	Tax revenue increase %	Tax buoyancy	Tax revenue as % of GDP
1998	78 345	5.2	7.8	9 093	10.5	2.0	11.6
1999	82 068	4.8	7.1	10 315	13.4	2.8	12.6
2000	89 468	9.0	8.0	12 665	22.8	2.5	14.2
2001	97 315	8.8	7.5	15 165	19.7	2.2	15.6
2002	105 172	8.1	8.3	16 997	12.1	1.5	16.2
2003	117 252	11.5	9.1	20 462	20.1	1.8	17.5

Source: National Bureau of Statistics, Ministry of Finance and State Administration of Taxation.

Figure 6.1. **GDP and tax revenue**

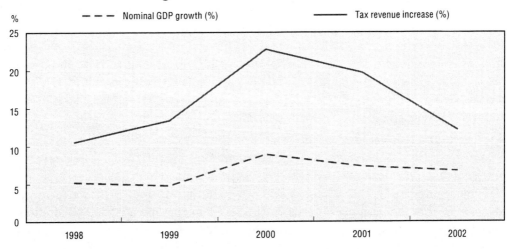

3.2.1. Organisational structure

In 1994, SAT became an independent ministerial-level organisation directly under the State Council. Before the 1994 reform, SAT was one of the departments within MOF. The MOF exercised business guidance (*yewu zhidao*) over the local offices of the tax service at different levels, but these were under the administrative leadership (*xingzheng lingdao*) of local governments (including funding, appointment of staff and supervisory functions). The reform was deemed necessary by the Chinese Government as proper oversight over the local offices – which was essential to ensure uniform and transparent application of tax laws – was very difficult from the central level without appropriate authority and resources. On becoming an independent institution, SAT was given a wider mandate, which enabled it to strengthen its grip over the local offices, as well as more resources.

It was made clear that only the central government has legislative power over tax: i.e. tax laws are legislated by the National People's Congress; regulations are made by the State Council in accordance with tax laws; MOF and SAT formulate departmental rules as well as draft tax laws and regulations. In other words, local governments do not have tax legislative power.

Moreover, the prior fiscal contracting system was changed to a nationwide tax-sharing system in 1994. Under the previous contracting system, a fixed target was negotiated between the central and the provincial governments, who could retain the tax revenue over the agreed target. There were very strong incentives for local governments to conceal local revenue from the central government as it was the basis for the negotiation. This had led to continuously deteriorating tax revenue, which was one of the main reasons for the 1994 reform. Under the tax sharing system, NTS collects "central taxes"[4] and "shared taxes",[5] whereas LTS collects "local taxes".[6] Taxes are now allocated in order to reflect the responsibilities of the central and local governments. Thus, local governments are no longer able to gain by collecting more than the amount agreed with the central government. Furthermore, the number of staff at the central level was increased significantly. With these changes, SAT's grip over the local offices has been strengthened considerably, which partly explains the increase in tax revenue after the reform.

Tax administration in China was designed in line with the political administration setup, which created many levels of administration. There are five levels of tax administration, corresponding to the five levels of government: the central headquarters level, the provincial level, the prefecture level, the county level and the lowest level, tax stations. The function of tax administration is split into NTS and LTS at and below the provincial level. In addition, both NTS and LTS have replicated offices at different levels. As a result, the system is hardly flat, and with a large staff of about 800 000 split equally between national and local officers, it is extremely difficult to manage.

Due to the requirements of the revenue sharing system, the function of China's tax administration is split between the national tax authorities and the local tax authorities at and below the provincial level. SAT controls SAT (including NTS at all levels) organisation, size, personnel, budget, and assists the provincial governments in the form of dual leadership[7] over the local tax bureaus (LTS). Shared and co-operative administration both vertically and horizontally allows independence while permitting administrative specialization. But a lack of co-ordination and communication between the state tax authority and the local tax authorities in carrying out their work has resulted in taxpayer complaints about the overlap of work and in considerable duplication of efforts, overlap, and unnecessary compliance costs for taxpayers as well as additional administrative costs.

Several possible measures to improve communication and co-ordination between the different levels of tax authorities have been identified: i) co-ordination of registration and administration for national and local taxes to ease business development and to facilitate communication between state and local administrations; ii) use of a single taxpayer identification number; iii) improved exchange of audit and other compliance data; iv) co-locating taxpayer services offices for both state and local tax purposes to the greatest possible extent; and v) co-ordinating payment mechanisms for central and sub-national taxes.

Another problem is that the present organisational structure follows the classification of taxes as well as the functional diversification of tax administration, which leads to far too many departments, divisions, sections and business groups with overlapping functions and business procedures. There is a general trend among OECD member countries to move from a tax-based to a function-based structure, and further to a structure based on type of taxpayer (see Box 6.1). The Chinese tax authorities are aware of the challenges and have already started moving in this direction.

3.2.2. Revenue target and voluntary compliance

At present, one of the most salient features of the Chinese tax system is the fixed revenue target for each level of tax administration, which is also the most important performance indicator for tax administration at different levels. Once the budget is drafted by the Ministry of Finance and approved by the State Council, the tax revenue estimate in the budget becomes a "target" for SAT to meet. The SAT headquarters then assign the amount of tax each province should collect during the course of the year based on the previous year's result, and each province in turn assigns the "targets" for municipality level offices, and so on. Although tax is collected according to law in China, setting quotas or revenue targets for local offices appears to have contributed to a less-than-optimal performance: Once a revenue target is met, there are fewer incentives to vigorously pursue the collection of tax/arrears as higher tax collection this year means a higher baseline for the next year. In addition, in order to meet the revenue targets, tax administrations might sometimes resort to measures which are not envisaged by law.

Box 6.1. **Organisational structure of tax administration in OECD member countries**

In general, over the last 20-30 years, there has been a clear trend among OECD member countries in the evolution of the organisational structure of national tax bodies: i.e. the organisational structure has been changed from one mainly (but not solely) based on "type of tax" – i.e. separate multilateral departments for each tax that are largely self-sufficient and independent of each other, to "function" – i.e. staff being organised principally by functional groupings (e.g. registration, accounting, information processing, audit, collection, appeals, etc.) and generally working across taxes, then to "type of taxpayer" – i.e. organising principally around segments of taxpayers (e.g. large taxpayers, small/medium businesses, wage earners, etc.). Typical problems with the "type of tax" model are that: it fails to deal with taxpayers' compliance problems in a co-ordinated "whole of taxpayer" manner (e.g. separate audit operations and collection actions); it impedes sharing of information; and it can result in different treatment across taxes. Therefore, the "tax type" model is less efficient because of its inherent duplication of functions (e.g. registration, accounting, audit, collection, training, information technology (IT), human resource management) and reduced flexibility in use of staff. It is also more burdensome for taxpayers as they have to deal with separate bodies on similar issues and suffer from uncoordinated administrative actions.

Many of the problems with the "tax type" model can be alleviated with the "function" model. The "function" model could provide: a single point of access for taxpayer inquiries; a common registration function and system; a single accounting framework, possibly integrated: "across taxes" enforced collections and audit actions; dedicated information processing operations; common support functions (e.g. human resource management, IT); and enhanced staff skills by working across taxes.

However, the "functional" model is not without its problems: it has a tendency to treat all taxpayers with a "one size fits all" approach; functional management is complicated by having to deal with different taxpayer segments who present different compliance issues/behaviours and may require separately tailored approaches; and issues may "fall through the cracks" due to a lack of focus and management complexity.

As a result, many OECD member countries have moved to the "taxpayer" model. Taxpayers are divided into different categories and then the organisational structure takes care of the different inherent risks of different groups.

OECD member countries do have revenue targets as well, but they are treated a little differently from those in China. The revenue targets derived from the budget process are used as milestones, with the understanding that deviations from the targets may inevitably occur depending on the actual performance of the economy. Typically, they will be broken down into monthly milestones (possibly by regions) and are used to track overall revenue collections during the course of the year. What is not done, however, is to break those goals down further to functional units as this leads to undue pressures on tax officials responsible for collections. Thus, revenue targets used in such a way in China would encourage arbitrary application of tax laws: tax officials might vigorously collect tax until they meet the target, but might not do so with the same intensity afterwards. This runs counter to the very basic rule of tax administration, i.e. fair application of tax laws. Instead, many tax administrations in OECD member countries have adopted better compliance as their mission. It is widely agreed that the primary goal of a revenue authority is to collect the taxes and duties payable in accordance with the law and to do this in such manner that will sustain confidence in the tax system and its administration. All the revenue authorities are appropriated a finite level of resources, invariably well short of what is required to ensure full compliance from each and every taxpayer as tax liabilities arise. This means that effective tax administration has to be about optimizing collection under the tax laws in ways that sustain community confidence in the tax authority and in ways that demonstrate that the system is operating correctly. According to the OECD *General Administrative Principles – GAP001 Principles of Good Tax Administration*[8] "[t]he main role of revenue authorities is to ensure compliance with tax laws. The promotion of voluntary compliance should be a primary concern of revenue authorities".

It is clearly indicated from the adoption of better compliance for their mission what direction the Chinese tax administration is heading for and what needs to be accomplished in the future. Three principles can be pointed out:

1. The main role of tax administration is to improve taxpayer compliance with tax law. In this respect, each tax official should strive to maintain and improve core business compliance by taxpayers, or taxpayers' willingness to observe their tax obligations as voluntarily as possible.

2. Dual effects can be expected from voluntary compliance by taxpayers with their tax obligations. Greater effectiveness will be gained from better observance of tax laws, which in turn means more efficiency for tax administration. As a result, the total tax revenue will increase in the long term, whereas the costs of collection will decrease.

3. Two elements of the mission of tax administration can be linked by compliance. Voluntary compliance requires fair and proper treatment of taxpayers. Improved compliance means better tax returns from taxpayers and therefore leads to optimum results.

Better compliance would not only lead to more revenue but also to less tax-induced distortions; it would lead to greater fairness in the tax system as more taxpayers begin to take up their part of the burden and in the long run raise taxpayers' confidence in the fairness of the tax system, which in turn will translate into more voluntary compliance.

3.2.3. Strengthening enforcement

Tax evasion is a worldwide problem, and discussions with the Chinese tax authorities have revealed that China is no exception. Some taxpayers ignore certain tax liabilities when the perceived risk of detection and cost of penalties are low. The tax administration will need not only to improve its abilities to detect and punish evasion, but it will also need to publicise its improved abilities. China's tax authorities have made considerable efforts to improve their capabilities in verifying tax liabilities, using new technologies to help deal with taxpayers who do not comply, as well as reinforcing collection of their liable taxes. But more needs to be done in China, especially in the area of sanctions and penalties.

A good system of sanctions and penalties is an indispensable tool for enforcing compliance. As part of the assessment of tax administration, China needs to evaluate the effectiveness of sanctions and penalties as well as the criminal prosecution system in encouraging taxpayers to voluntarily comply with their tax obligations.

3.2.4. Simplification of administrative regulations

Administrative regulations can put unnecessary burdens on taxpayers. The cumulative effects of many administrative regulations, formalities from multiple institutions and layers of tax authorities would be to slow down business responsiveness, divert resources away from productive investments, reduce transparency and accountability, and discourage taxpayer's compliance.

Simplified regulations could lead to substantial reductions not only in compliance costs for taxpayers but also in administrative costs for tax authorities. Simplification of administrative regulations in OECD member countries has primarily been driven by the desire to improve the cost-efficiency of tax administration. However, many of the tools and practices aimed at improving the cost-efficiency of tax administration have also led to, or are supported by, measures that will improve transparency and accountability.

China has taken first steps in the right direction by simplifying administrative regulations in the area of taxation both at the policy level and at the implementation level: *e.g.* one-stop shops (physical as well as electronic), simplification of procedures for permits and licences and time-limits for decision-making. Although commendable, more work should be done to further improve the efficiency of tax administration.

3.2.5. Optimising through e-government

As described in Chapter 4, advances in information technology have made it possible to carry out increasingly sophisticated electronic transfers of a wide range of information between government entities and different levels of governments (G2G), government and citizens (G2C), and government and business (G2B). The introduction of e-government is a way to reduce administrative burdens by improving the efficiency and effectiveness of the administrative process. SAT is fully aware of the necessity of introducing new electronic means to tax administrative procedures in order to improve taxpayer service, to simplify procedures and to reduce administrative and compliance costs.

The computerisation of tax administration has not proceeded in a smooth and timely manner, however. Because of great disparities between different regions as well as the lack of co-ordination among the regions, tax authorities at different levels and in different cities have developed different computer systems and software for their tax administration. The lack of compatibility has understandably resulted in inefficiency and overlap of work (see Chapter 4 on e-government).

Without a doubt, China needs to develop a unified system to integrate various functions in tax administration. To achieve this objective, there is a need for strong political will, a strategic focus and the adoption of consistent policy approaches across tax administration. Only if these elements are present, the maximum inter-operability of the systems and facilities can be assured. As the implementation of e-government initiatives necessarily involves close scrutiny of existing operational processes and procedures, it can also be considered as a driver for reduction of administrative burdens in itself.

Supported by the World Bank, SAT has developed a system called China Tax Administration Information System (CTAIS) that is intended to integrate and replace the systems developed separately in different localities. CTAIS, together with the ambitious computerisation project called Golden Tax III, is expected to integrate all the functions of the current systems, including functions of the SAT headquarters, national tax branches of SAT and all local tax functions.

3.2.6. Training

Tax authorities in China are keen to improve their capacities to deal with increasingly complicated tax issues, especially in the area of international taxation, by training its tax officials. After becoming the No. 1 recipient of foreign direct investment (FDI) in the world in 2002, actual FDI flowing into China reached USD 57 billion in 2003, a figure surpassed only by that of the United States. This has had a great impact on China's international taxation. Facing these challenges, China needs to give more tax officials, especially those who are responsible for dealing with multinationals and large taxpayers, appropriate training to tackle these issues.

For example, in the field of transfer pricing, tax authorities feel that potential tax avoidance through income shifting has become a serious threat to its tax base. China has recently been planning to reinforce its transfer pricing legislation. It now also needs to reinforce the administration of these rules. China needs more skilled tax officials to conduct effective investigations into overseas companies, which benefit from rich experience in avoiding paying tax under market economy conditions.

4. Direction of future reforms

To address the problems mentioned in Section 3, reform efforts have already begun. On tax policy, the general direction in which China is heading should be encouraged: transforming the production-type VAT to a consumption-type VAT, fine-tuning excise tax, unifying the two Corporate Income Tax Codes (one for domestic enterprises and the other for foreign-invested enterprises and foreign enterprises), reforming individual income tax, restructuring local taxes and streamlining agricultural taxes.

From the governance point of view, however, emphasis should be placed on the tax administration aspects. First, the organisational structure of tax administration should be restructured in line with the procedures of taxation such as taxpayer service, tax return processing and targeted audits, etc. The Chinese tax authorities are aware of the challenges and have already started moving in this direction. Efforts to flatten and streamline the system by means of centralizing functions where appropriate, merging replicated and overlapping functions, reducing the number of tax staff and ultimately generating simplicity and efficiency should be encouraged.

Second, in order to improve communications and co-ordination between the central and local tax authorities, necessary measures should be considered as mentioned in the section on organisational structure above.

Third, tax authorities should aim at improving voluntary compliance, instead of relying on revenue targets. Experience shows that better compliance would not only lead to more tax revenue but also to less tax-induced distortions.

Fourth, administrative regulations in China should be simplified. Further simplification could lead to a substantial reduction of compliance costs for taxpayers as well as lower administrative costs for tax authorities. China has moved in this direction, but more needs to be done.

Fifth, appropriate training should be given to those who deal with increasingly important and complex issues relating to multinational and large taxpayers. China has some burgeoning ideas about setting up large taxpayers units to deal effectively with these taxpayers, but these ideas are still being carefully considered by local as well as head offices.

Last but not least, it is of vital importance for China to develop a unified computer system to integrate the varied functions of tax collection and administration.

4.1. Going forward

Now that China has become an Observer on the OECD's Committee on Fiscal Affairs, it is expected that China will associate itself more closely with OECD work on taxation, and in doing so will benefit from the wealth of knowledge and experience of OECD member countries and *vice versa*.

Notes

1. This chapter was written by Kazutomi Kurihara, Unit for Co-operation with Non-OECD Economies, Centre for Tax Policy and Administration, OECD with assistance of Xinyu Chen, a visiting expert from China's State Administration of Taxation.
2. For figures on tax levels and tax structure see Annex 0.A1.
3. The following issues have been identified through policy dialogue between the OECD and China, including discussions leading to China's observer status on the OECD Committee on Fiscal Affairs which was formalised in May 2004.
4. Domestic excise taxes, customs duties, VAT and excise taxes on imports, and income tax on deposit interest.
5. Domestic VAT, business tax, enterprise income tax, income tax on foreign and foreign-funded banks, income tax on foreign and foreign-funded non-banks, resource tax, city maintenance and construction tax, securities tax.
6. Personal income tax, city and township land use tax, farmland occupation tax, fixed assets investment tax, land appreciation tax, house property tax, urban real estate tax, vehicle and vessel use tax, deed tax, slaughter tax, banquet tax, agricultural and animal husbandry taxes.
7. As mentioned previously, SAT provides business leadership (*yewu zhidao*) over LTS and shares administrative leadership (*xingzheng lingdao*) with local governments.
8. Issued: 25 June 1999, amended: 2 May 2001.

Bibliography

Liu Zuo Liu Tieying (2002), *China Foreign Tax Guide*, China Law Press.

OECD (2001), *General Administrative Principles – GAP001 Principles of Good Tax Administration*, issued 25 June 1999, amended 2 May 2001.

OECD (2002), "The Current Tax System and Priorities for Reform", Chapter 18 of *China in the World Economy*, OECD, Paris.

OECD (2003), *OECD Investment Policy Reviews – China*, OECD, Paris.

OECD (2003), *Model Tax Convention on Income and on Capital*, OECD, Paris.

OECD (2004), *Revenue Statistics 1965-2003*, OECD, Paris.

State Administration of Taxation of China (2003), *Tax System of The People's Republic of China*, China Taxation Press.

Onishi, Yasushi (2004), The Current Situation and Future of China's Fiscal and Tax System (in Japanese), Okurazaimukyoukai.

ANNEX 6.A1

Tax Levels and Tax Structure (General Government) 1998-2003

Denomination: hundred million RMB

	Consolidated general government revenue						In % of GDP						In % of TR (total R)					
	1998	1999	2000	2001	2002	2003	1998	1999	2000	2001	2002	2003	1998	1999	2000	2001	2002	2003
Total revenues	9 875.95	11 444.08	13 395.20	16 386.00	18 913.90	21 715.25	12.61	13.95	14.98	16.84	18.47	18.52	100.00	100.00	100.00	100.00	100.00	100.00
Tax revenues	9 092.99	10 314.97	12 665.80	15 165.47	16 996.56	20 466.14	11.61	12.57	14.16	15.59	16.6	17.45	92.08	90.14	94.55	92.55	89.86	94.25
VAT	4 301.94	5 032.14	6 149.32	7 090.77	8 141.18	10 096.25	5.49	6.13	6.87	7.29	7.95	8.63	43.56	43.97	45.91	43.27	43.04	46.59
Consumption tax	838.14	854.63	877.29	946.19	1 072.47	1 221.67	1.07	1.04	0.98	0.97	1.05	1.04	8.49	7.47	6.55	5.77	5.67	5.63
Business tax	1 608.03	1 696.53	1 885.70	2 084.65	2 467.63	2 868.87	2.05	2.07	2.11	2.14	2.41	2.46	16.28	14.82	14.08	12.72	13.05	13.31
Enterprise income tax	856.27	1 009.38	1 444.65	2 121.89	1 972.65	2 342.24	1.09	1.23	1.61	2.18	1.93	2.01	8.67	8.82	10.78	12.95	10.43	10.89
Income tax on foreign enterprises and foreign-invested enterprises	182.49	217.81	326.15	512.58	616.03	705.4	0.23	0.27	0.36	0.53	0.6	0.61	1.85	1.90	2.43	3.13	3.26	3.35
Individual income tax	338.65	414.31	660.37	996.02	1 211.07	1 417.33	0.43	0.5	0.74	1.02	1.18	1.27	3.43	3.62	4.93	6.08	6.40	6.63
Resource tax	61.93	62.86	63.65	67.11	75.14	83.11	0.08	0.08	0.07	0.07	0.07	0.08	0.63	0.55	0.48	0.41	0.40	0.38
City construction and maintenance tax	294.98	315.29	352.13	384.4	470.92	550.01	0.38	0.38	0.39	0.4	0.46	0.48	2.99	2.76	2.63	2.35	2.49	2.53
House property tax	159.85	183.53	209.58	228.59	282.4	323.86	0.2	0.22	0.23	0.23	0.28	0.28	1.62	1.60	1.56	1.40	1.49	1.49
Stamp tax	238.52	282.33	521.85	337.04	179.42	214.98	0.3	0.34	0.58	0.35	0.18	0.18	2.42	2.47	3.90	2.06	0.95	0.99
Vehicle and vessel usage tax	19.05	20.86	23.44	24.61	28.89	32.16	0.02	0.03	0.03	0.03	0.03	0.03	0.19	0.18	0.18	0.15	0.15	0.15

Source: Chinese Ministry of Finance and State Administration of Taxation.

ANNEX 6.A2

Tax Levels and Tax Structure (Central Government) 1998-2003

Denomination: hundred million RMB

	State revenue						In % of TR (total R)						In % of TR (tax R)					
	1998	1999	2000	2001	2002	2003	1998	1999	2000	2001	2002	2003	1998	1999	2000	2001	2002	2003
State revenues	4 892	5 849.21	6 989.17	8 582.74	10 388.64	11 865.27	49.53	51.11	52.18	52.38	54.93	54.64	–	–	–	–	–	–
State tax revenues	5 033.9	5 787.67	7 459.94	8 711.48	10 424.64	13 088.12	50.97	50.57	55.69	53.16	55.12	60.27	55.36	56.11	58.96	57.44	61.33	63.95
Export tax rebate	–436.33	–627.11	–810.02	–1 071.57	–1 259.35	–2 038.99												
VAT	3 369.8	4 031.93	4 982.44	5 727.64	6 572.34	8 260.93	34.12	35.23	37.2	34.95	34.75	38.04	37.06	39.09	39.34	37.77	38.67	40.36
Export tax rebate	–404.93	–578.92	–735.41	–929.64	–738.24	–1 419.05												
Consumption tax	838.14	854.63	877.29	946.19	1 072.47	1 221.67	8.49	7.47	6.55	5.77	5.67	5.63	9.22	8.29	6.93	6.24	6.31	5.97
Export tax rebate	–3.74	–6.38	–7.60	–7.28	–6.61	–10.87												
Business tax	258.43	236.03	257.42	233.72	171.3	101.23	2.62	2.06	1.92	1.43	0.91	0.47	2.84	2.29	2.03	1.54	1.01	0.49
Enterprise income tax	341.87	403.29	677.77	833.22	1 199.73	1 611.72	3.46	3.52	5.06	5.08	6.34	7.42	3.76	3.91	5.35	5.49	7.06	7.88
Income tax on foreign- invested enterprises and foreign enterprises	42.39	43.07	89.34	167.21	326.96	440.35	0.43	0.38	0.67	1.02	1.73	2.03	0.47	0.42	0.71	1.1	1.92	2.15
Individual income tax	0	0.83	149.48	279.24	605.97	850.71	0	0.01	1.12	1.7	3.2	3.92	0	0.01	1.18	1.84	3.57	4.16
Resource tax	0.00	0.00	0.00	0.00	0.00	0.00	0.00	0.00	0.00	0.00	0.00	0.00	0.00	0.00	0.00	0.00	0.00	0.00
City maintenance and construction tax	2.95	2.63	3.29	3.57	3.71	3.3	0.03	0.02	0.02	0.02	0.02	0.02	0.03	0.03	0.03	0.02	0.02	0.02
House property tax	0.00	0.00	0.00	0.00	0.00	0.00	0.00	0.00	0.00	0.00	0.00	0.00	0.00	0.00	0.00	0.00	0.00	0.00
Stamp tax	180.26	215.26	422.92	265.91	108.62	123.87	1.83	1.88	3.16	1.62	0.57	0.57	1.98	2.09	3.34	1.75	0.64	0.61
Vehicle and vessel usage tax	0.00	0.00	0.00	0.00	0.00	0.00	0.00	0.00	0.00	0.00	0.00	0.00	0.00	0.00	0.00	0.00	0.00	0.00

Source: Chinese Ministry of Finance and State Administration of Taxation.

ANNEX 6.A3

Tax Levels and Tax Structure (Local Government) 1998-2003

Denomination: hundred million RMB

	Local revenue						In % of TR (total R)						In % of TR (tax R)					
	1998	1999	2000	2001	2002	2003	1998	1999	2000	2001	2002	2003	1998	1999	2000	2001	2002	2003
Total local revenues	4 983.95	5 594.87	6 406.06	7 803.30	8 515.00	9 849.98	50.46	48.89	47.82	47.62	45.02	45.36	–	–	–	–	–	–
Local tax revenues	4 059.14	4 527.30	5 205.86	6 453.99	6 571.92	7 378.02	41.10	39.56	38.86	39.39	34.75	33.98	44.64	43.89	41.10	42.56	38.67	36.05
VAT	932.14	1 000.20	1 166.88	1 363.13	1 568.84	1 835.33	9.44	8.74	8.71	8.32	8.29	8.45	10.25	9.70	11.31	8.99	9.23	8.97
Consumption tax	0.00	0.00	0.00	0.00	0.00	0.00	0.00	0.00	0.00	0.00	0.00	0.00	0.00	0.00	0.00	0.00	0.00	0.00
Business tax	1 349.60	1 460.50	1 628.28	1 850.93	2 296.33	2 767.64	13.67	12.76	12.16	11.30	12.14	12.75	14.84	14.16	15.79	12.20	13.51	13.52
Enterprise income tax	514.40	606.09	766.87	1 288.67	772.92	730.53	5.21	5.30	5.72	7.86	4.09	3.36	5.66	5.88	7.43	8.50	4.55	3.57
Income tax on foreign-invested enterprises and foreign enterprises	140.09	174.74	236.81	345.38	289.07	265.05	1.42	1.53	1.77	2.11	1.53	1.22	1.54	1.69	2.30	2.28	1.70	1.30
Individual income	338.65	413.48	510.90	716.78	605.11	566.63	3.43	3.61	3.81	4.37	3.20	2.61	3.72	4.01	4.95	4.72	3.56	2.77
Resource tax	61.93	62.86	63.65	67.11	75.14	83.11	0.63	0.55	0.48	0.41	0.40	0.38	0.68	0.61	0.62	0.44	0.44	0.41
City maintenance and construction tax	292.03	312.65	348.85	380.83	467.21	546.71	2.96	2.73	2.60	2.32	2.47	2.52	3.21	3.03	3.38	2.51	2.75	2.67
House property tax	159.85	183.53	209.58	228.59	282.40	323.86	1.62	1.60	1.56	1.40	1.49	1.49	1.76	1.78	2.03	1.51	1.66	1.58
Stamp tax	58.27	67.07	98.93	71.13	70.79	91.11	0.59	0.59	0.74	0.43	0.37	0.42	0.64	0.65	0.96	0.47	0.42	0.45
Vehicle and vessel usage tax	19.05	20.86	23.44	24.61	28.89	32.16	0.19	0.18	0.17	0.15	0.15	0.15	0.21	0.20	0.19	0.16	0.17	0.16

Source: Chinese Ministry of Finance and State Administration of Taxation.

PART II

Chapter 7

Public Sector Budgeting Issues in China

Table of Contents

Summary 227

Public Sector Budgeting Issues in China 228

1. Introduction 228
2. The background to budget management reform 229
3. The reform package... 230
   3.1. Reforms in budget preparation – introduction of departmental budgets 231
   3.2. Reforms in budget implementation 233
4. A glass half full? The current status of public expenditure management 236
   4.1. The budget is still not comprehensive 237
   4.2. Extension of improved budgeting to the sub-national levels is limited 238
   4.3. Compliance with existing laws and regulations needs strengthening 240
5. Next steps? 241

Notes 242

Bibliography 242

Annex 7.A1 244

List of boxes

7.1. An in-year budget request.. 231
7.2. China's large extra-budgetary revenues and expenditures.................. 237

List of tables

7.1. Sources of revenue for major expenditures in Hunan Province (1999) 240
7.A1.1. China's expenditure decentralization in comparative perspective 244
7.A1.2. Expenditure assignments.. 245

List of figures

7.1. The "two ratios"... 229
7.2. Resources under central budget allocation............................. 229
7.3. Structure of government in China (2003)............................... 239
7.A1.1. Shares of sub-national expenditures (1999) 244

Summary

China has undertaken extensive reforms to its budgeting system over the past 10 years. These have encompassed the entire budgeting cycle: formulation, approval, implementation and audit. This chapter reviews each of these elements.

China has made crucial progress in this field. The early challenge was fundamentally to create the institutional infrastructure for a modern budget process where none had previously existed. In the planned economy, all resource allocation decisions were made in the plan with the budget serving essentially as a secondary accounting device.

China now has the basic budgeting infrastructure to build on. This chapter, however, argues that the budgeting system remains marred by key weaknesses that remain to be overcome.

The budget is still not complete in that important decisions are made outside of the budget process. The capital budget is made separately from the recurrent budget with key decisions made by the National Development Reform Commission (NDRC, the former State Planning Commission). Despite improvements over the years, off-budget expenditures continue to be large and unreported. The Ministry of Finance (MOF) still does not have comprehensive authority on spending. Staffing decisions, which have major spending implications, are made by the State Commission Office for Public Sector Reform with little consultation with fiscal authorities.

The greatest challenge, however, for China is its highly decentralized fiscal system. China consists of five levels of government – national, provincial, prefectural, counties and townships. The national government only accounts for about 30% of total government expenditure in China. The remaining 70% of expenditures is accounted for by the four sub-national levels of government with the third and fourth tiers accounting for the greatest share. For example, prefectures and counties account for nearly all expenditures for social security including old-age pensions, unemployment insurance, and other income support and welfare schemes. Moreover, the central government lacks effective control over the fiscal relations between provincial and lower level governments which is manifested by distinct differences across provinces.

With sub-national governments playing such a vital role, improvements in budgeting in China depend critically on associated changes being implemented at these levels. The achievements in budgeting have largely been at the national level and in the wealthier coastal provinces.

China is almost unique in having virtually no system of intergovernmental transfers that are designed to ensure adequate financing at the local levels for meeting national mandates in the provision of critical public services such as basic education, pensions and unemployment benefits.

Public Sector Budgeting Issues in China[1]

1. Introduction

In November 2003, the Sixteenth National Congress of the Communist Party of China celebrated China's remarkable economic achievements over some 25 years of transition to a market economy, but also called for some significant corrections. One clearly identified strand of correction aims to renew the Party's commitment to a more balanced growth that benefits all regions and sectors and stem the alarming growth in inequalities that has marred the achievements of the recent years. This was spelled out in more specific terms in Premier Wen Jiabao's Report to the National People's Congress (NPC) on 5 March 2004, when he called for:[2]

1. reorienting China's development strategy to one that emphasizes balanced, sustainable and "people-centered" growth;

2. strengthening social protection;

3. solving fiscal problems of the rural sector;

4. curbing corruption and government abuse;

5. putting China on a timetable to achieve a "*xiaokang* society" (a well-off society). Although the indicators for "*xiaokang*" are still being worked out, they will include socio-economic indices such as educational attainment, access to clean water and health care, etc. that closely mimic those used by international organisations to measure "human development".

What is notable about this call for a *xiaokang* society is that, for the first time, the government is explicitly focusing on targeting the **outcomes** of economic growth, shifting away from the traditional emphasis on the quantitative targets such as **rates** of growth and income levels. This new emphasis on outcomes will bring more scrutiny onto government performance, since the public sector is the primary provider of many of the services that are critical to achieving a "people-centered" growth. To achieve the goals set out will require improving public expenditure management and ensuring that government spending is more tightly linked to priorities, improving budget processes and execution, and holding government accountable for improving its performance. Indeed, in a speech during 2002, then-Vice Premier Li Lanqing called improving public expenditure management "an important guarantor for the achievement of *xiaokang* society"(Xiang and Lou, 2004). In sum, the pressure is on to improve public expenditure management.

This chapter discusses the main issues in public expenditure management in China. It provides an update on earlier OECD publications on the budget management system (OECD, 2002), focusing on the reform measures being implemented and their objectives, what improvements have been achieved, what obstacles these reforms face and why. Section 2 briefly explains the background to budget reform. Section 3 discusses the package of reforms being implemented. Section 4 reports on achievements to date and the problems in going forward. Section 5 provides a brief summary and conclusion.

2. The background to budget management reform

As noted in previous publications, reform of the budget management system has lagged behind other reforms in China.[3] This is an unsurprising feature of an incremental, gradual approach to reform that has, at least through the first decade, relied primarily on liberalization. While the gradual reduction of government control has worked wonders in the productive sectors by releasing pent-up energies and resources and improving allocative efficiency, the approach has worked less well in effecting change in the core economic institutions. By the early 1990s, the budget was weak – with the revenue mechanisms of the planned economy undermined by market forces, revenues had fallen to a low of 11% of gross domestic product (GDP). As part of its effort to mobilize revenue collection, the central government had turned over an increasing share of revenues to local governments. The result was that by 1993, the central share of revenues had fallen to just 22% of the total (see Figures 7.1 and 7.2). With central government finances in peril, it was not surprising that fiscal reform became an urgent agenda item in the early 1990s, or that the first efforts were focused on "raising the two ratios" – i.e. to increase the share of

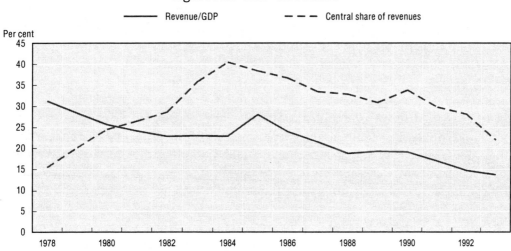

Figure 7.1. **The "two ratios"**

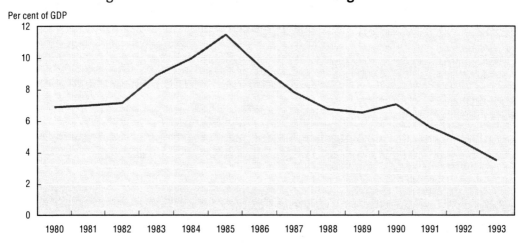

Figure 7.2. **Resources under central budget allocation**

revenues in GDP and the central share of total revenues. It was only in the late 1990s, with the upturn in revenue collection assured and with the central government regaining control over more than half of the revenues, that attention turned to improving the efficiency of public expenditures.

At the outset of budget reform, the weaknesses of China's budget system were explained by one senior official of the Ministry of Finance (MOF) as follows:

The budget submitted for examination and approval at the beginning of the year was a rough budget that was drafted by function only and did not show the budget allocations to departments. It did not reflect specific details of revenues or expenditures. There was no overall expenditure limit. It did not reflect all revenue and expenditure activities. The government's fiscal policy had only coarse control over the expenditure composition; our capacity to control and manage public expenditures was very weak (Chen, 2003).

Chen (2003) described the budgeting process as "chaotic", characterized by fragmented control under numerous bodies and departments, and lacking transparency and accountability over the management of resources. Within the MOF, numerous departments or bureaus were involved in budgeting, with each one in charge of one or more expenditure items, which were divided and allocated to many ministries or departments. For example, the department in charge of "capital construction expenditures" had to interact with all ministries and departments, thus limiting the amount of detailed budgeting that was possible. In turn, the spending units had to make budget proposals to many departments in the MOF. To add to the confusion, allocative authorities for capital expenditures rested mostly outside the MOF, in the (then) State Planning Commission and the Ministry of Science and Technology, to which spending units also had to apply. This budgeting process made it difficult to exert expenditure control over any ministry whose budget came from a number of ministries, commissions, departments and bureaus, and there were no set limits. For grassroots spending units the situation was murkier still: because reserves were set aside for contingencies at every level and doled out throughout the budget cycle as line ministries allocated their budgetary funds downward by line item and by project, bargaining for budget appropriations continued throughout the fiscal year. Moreover, the budget was not comprehensive, and many resources were outside the budget, in extra-budgetary accounts, a topic treated below in Section 4. It was also commonly accepted that new spending needs that could not be accommodated within the budget could provide justification for the introduction of new fees, a practice that further softened the budget constraint on spending units (see Box 7.1 for an illustrative example). As Chen (2003) noted, "[t]he drafting of the budget was very arduous and involved ongoing conflicts".

3. The reform package

Given this backdrop, it is easy to understand the MOF view that improving public expenditure management first required regaining control over the budget process. Since 1999, a broad package of reforms in budget management has been introduced, covering reforms in budget preparation, budget classification, treasury management, government procurement and installing new information systems.

> **Box 7.1. An in-year budget request**
>
> In 1997, two months after the budget passed, a line ministry approached the MOF for additional funding for a certain high priority function. To increase its capability in this function, the ministry asked for (in order of preference): *i)* a tax earmarked for this function; *ii)* a special fund for this function; *iii)* a rule to increase expenditures on this function by more than revenues; *iv)* to earmark the fines the ministry collects for this function; and *v)* a grants system to counties for the specific function.
>
> In an OECD member country, the MOF answer to the request could be as follows. First, the budget has just been passed, so the ministry would have to wait for next year's budget round. Second, if the function falls within the government's priorities, financing should first be sought within savings from the ministry's other, non-priority activities. If budgetary money were still needed, the proposal would have to specify the concrete activities planned for achieving the government's strategic goals. Furthermore, the line ministry should specify measurable indicators for success of the policy, and – in some OECD member countries – would be required to present an evaluation plan.
>
> Even if the final proposal were satisfactory and accepted during the regular budget round, it would rarely happen in an OECD member country that the line ministry would obtain earmarked revenues for the function. Rather, it would be funded from general revenues.
>
> *Source:* World Bank (2000), Box 4.1.

3.1. Reforms in budget preparation – introduction of departmental budgets

The centrepiece of the reform in budget preparation was the introduction of departmental budgets, which had several important objectives:

- **To improve transparency.** In the past, the budget showed appropriations by sector, and the sectoral amounts were cut up into pieces for different ministries and organisations. Therefore, it was hard to know how much education and training, for example, was performed by each ministry.
- **To improve budgeting.** Under the system prior to the introduction of departmental budgets, making budget proposals to multiple departments and organisations was a cumbersome and unpredictable process for spending units.
- **To harden the budget constraint for each spending unit.** The absence of a departmental breakdown in the budget approved by the NPC meant that there were no firm spending limits per line ministry. Instead, the sectoral budget was a common pool of funds for individual line ministries operating in the sector, and it opened the door for the ministries to lobby the MOF for more funding throughout the year for priority projects. With a departmental budget, approval by the NPC ends the negotiation for resources.
- **To improve accountability for spending.** With departmental budgets spelling out how much is being spent by each spending unit, the precondition now exists to hold each ministry responsible for delivering results.

In the 2000 budget cycle, four central ministries were chosen for piloting: the Ministry of Agriculture, the Ministry of Education, the Ministry of Science and Technology, and the Ministry of Labour and Social Security. On the basis of their experiences the MOF designed new budget proposal forms and software and began training and dissemination to the other line ministries. In the following year, 29 departmental budgets were presented. This system has been quickly adopted in some localities. In Hebei Province, one of the pioneers in budget reform, departmental budgets were already being prepared in 2000 for the first level budgetary units at the provincial level. At the next level of prefectures and municipalities, Wuhan reported that it began in 2000 by presenting departmental budgets for five units under four departments. By the following year, they were presented for all 115 municipal departments (Yang, 2002).

The introduction of departmental budgets has facilitated and sometimes necessitated other reforms, which include the following:

3.1.1. Detailed budgeting

Also in line with the objective of regaining control over the budgeting process is the trend toward specifying more line items in budgets, under the call to "change the practice of presenting budgets on a single piece of paper to presenting budgets as books". In the circular issued in 1999, Concerning Improvements in the Central Budgeting for the 2000 Budget, the MOF laid the groundwork for the detailed preparation of departmental budgets by requiring that all planned expenditures be listed in the budget proposals, with the proviso that those not listed would not be funded. Some localities have followed suit to such an extent that in January 2003, delegates to the Guangdong Province People's Congress were surprised and delighted to be presented with a 600-page provincial budget for discussion.[4] Following the trend to present detailed budgets, the municipality of Wuhan has similarly transformed its budget presentation from "two pages to two books" (Yang, 2002).

3.1.2. Comprehensive budgets

The circular on the 2000 budget also required each line ministry to include all extra-budgetary revenues and expenditures in their budget proposals. Since most fees and charges collected by line ministries had been approved under the rationale that they were needed to help finance identified new services, the MOF used the opportunity of formulating departmental budgets to require reporting on these extra-budgetary resources in order to present an integrated budget that reflects all resources and expenditures of the department.

This has proved to be a major side benefit of the introduction of departmental budgets. The information gathered has facilitated the process of reviewing, rationalizing and gradually reining in extra-budgetary revenues – a process that had begun a few years earlier. Under the slogan "separating revenues and expenditures into two channels", the MOF has begun to budget for expenditure needs separately from the department's own revenue situation. This is due to the fact that the information on extra-budgetary revenues has finally provided the precondition for enforcing the fiscal rule first announced in 1996 (State Council Document No. 29) that extra-budgetary resources are fiscal revenues subject to allocation by government, rather than the collecting body. If fully implemented, asserting this fiscal rule could bring extra-budgetary revenues under budget allocation, a major step toward improving the comprehensiveness of the Chinese budget.[5]

3.1.3. Renewed focus on "norms"

Paradoxically, in order to implement comprehensive budgets and to end the inequitable situation where departments that could levy fees and user charges had plentiful running costs while those with poor access to extra-budgetary revenues were starved for funds, the government has also focused on collecting cost information for line item expenditures and setting "norms" for budgeting. A pilot reform was introduced in ten central ministries and departments in 2003 with staffing "norms" and expenditure norms, including in the National Development and Reform Commission (NDRC), the Science and Technology Commission, and the then-State Economic and Trade Commission.

3.1.4. Prioritization of expenditures through zero-based budgeting

To move away from the passive, incremental budgeting based on past allocations, the MOF has also promoted the use of zero-based budgeting to review all expenditures including staffing levels.

3.1.5. Budget classification reform

To improve the informational content of budget presentations to facilitate analysis, the reform package has also included a reform of the classification system. Under the Soviet-type system adopted in the 1950s, budget categories were broad, and were a mix of organisational and functional divisions that did not allow government to disaggregate expenditures by sector or economic function – for example, it was impossible to know the personnel share of expenditures in any sector or department. To improve transparency and aid analysis, China is adopting a Government Finance Statistics (GFS) system with some modifications. Some changes have been introduced since 2002 and are used in budget preparation at both the central and sub-national levels. Even at the lowest tiers of government, the new GFS-based classification system that is in use shows expenditures by organisation and by economic function. A full rollout of a new classification system was scheduled for mid-2005.

3.1.6. Internal reorganisation of the MOF

In accordance with the new budget preparation procedures, in June 2000 the MOF undertook a major reorganisation of its internal structure to end the "chaotic" process described earlier, to strengthen its interface with spending units. Although several departments are still involved in budgeting – *e.g.* the culture and education department, the agriculture department, the industry and transport department, etc., each department now has comprehensive responsibility for overseeing preparation of the whole budget of spending units within their jurisdiction. This has allowed spending units to make budget proposals to only one "window".

3.2. Reforms in budget implementation

3.2.1. Treasury reform

At the heart of efforts to improve the government's ability to control and monitor budget implementation is treasury management reform. Prior to the current reforms, China had a highly decentralized system of treasury management that did not provide the information needed by the MOF to monitor and enforce budget implementation. Some functions – such as cash management – were not performed at all, whereas control over bank accounts was not effectively enforced. The system had the following features:

1. The legal basis for the treasury function was weak. The budget law did not put the MOF squarely in charge of government money, nor did it clearly define what government money is.

2. Line ministries and spending bodies had their own bank accounts and were responsible for their own payments.

3. Expenditure reporting from spending units to the MOF was *ex post*, and on a highly aggregated basis.
4. No reconciliation of spending reports and bank account statements took place until after the end of the budget year.
5. MOF controlled only the disbursement of funds from the general treasury account (in the People's Bank of China) to the line ministry account. While it was informed on the balance in this account on a daily basis, it had no information on the overall cash position of the government, nor could it use idle balances in the accounts of line ministries and spending units.
6. Line ministries and bodies had multiple extra-budgetary accounts which largely fell outside the oversight of the MOF, on which reporting requirements were lax.
7. The central bank's management system did not allow direct deposit from the central treasury account to regional accounts, nor did it allow direct deposit from one level of government to another without going through a time-consuming, elaborate process of interbank clearing.
8. Transfers of tax revenues from taxpayer to the central treasury were subjected to a similarly slow interbank clearing.

The treasury system resulted in a number of weaknesses:

1. Government had higher interest costs as large amounts of cash sat idle in spending units' bank accounts, while the central treasury was issuing debt to raise funds.
2. Government lacked information on the stance of fiscal policy, because no information on actual spending was available on a timely basis.
3. Government could not adjust aggregate spending at short notice, because line ministries could continue to spend from their budgetary and extra-budgetary bank accounts.
4. Government could not stop abuse of funds until after the fact, because the system did not allow for *ex ante* spending control.

The inefficiencies and lack of accountability inherent in this system are illustrated by the following example from the Ministry of Water Resources: budgetary appropriations for capital spending go through as many as seven layers before reaching the project entity. Because of delays *en route*, in 1999, there were undisbursed funds of RMB 4.6 billion at year end. During the first 10 months of 2000, in the aggregate there was an average balance of RMB 5.6 billion in the various bank accounts within the system (Xiang and Lou, 2004).

In July 2001, China began to implement treasury management reform on a pilot basis. The new treasury system would recognize five types of accounts:

1. A treasury single account at the central bank that manages all fiscal resources and is controlled by the MOF.
2. Special accounts at commercial banks set up either by the MOF or by spending units on authorization from the MOF, for small expenditures.
3. Extra-budgetary accounts controlled by the MOF and deposited at commercial banks.
4. Petty-cash accounts set up by the MOF on behalf of spending units at commercial banks to take care of miscellaneous transactions.
5. Special accounts set up by the MOF for earmarked, transitory activities under State Council or provincial government approval.

Under the new system, all fiscal revenues would enter directly into either the treasury account or one of the other special accounts, all of which are controlled by the MOF. No other bank accounts would be allowed for spending units.

The reform started cautiously. In 2001, a Treasury Disbursement Centre (TDC) was created at the central level to manage the budget general ledger and approve disbursement claims. Six central ministries and departments were chosen to pilot the new treasury system, including the MOF, the Ministry of Water Resources, the Ministry of Science and Technology, and the State Council Law Office. Together they accounted for RMB 17 billion in budgetary expenditures, equal to about 3% of central government budgetary expenditures net of transfers. A 38% share of their expenditures was directly disbursed through the TDC, and 62% was disbursed by spending units under delegation by the MOF. In addition to the pilot ministries, the TDC made direct disbursements on some earmarked funds including vehicle purchases from the Special Fund for Transport, grain storage facilities construction fund, and government procurements.

Some localities introduced treasury management pilot experiments at the same time. The province of Hainan has adopted direct disbursement on all government procurement. Tianjin has cancelled transit accounts and required all fiscal funds to be directly deposited in the treasury of fiscal special accounts. All government procurement and capital construction funds are directly disbursed by the municipal Treasury Single Account (Zhang, 2002). By far the most extensive reach of the new treasury system has been in the direct disbursement of civil service salaries, which has been introduced in many localities. Associated with the direct payroll disbursement has come much improved information flows: the MOF now boasts of having more than 20 items of personal information on every civil servant in the country, and it has access to information on the government's fiscal stance on a daily basis. By 2004, TDCs and disbursement offices have been set up in most localities all the way down to the county level.

3.2.2. Government procurement reform

The reform programme has also sought to improve cost efficiencies and to reduce the scope for corruption in government procurement by adopting many of the procedures of international organisations for tendering large-scale purchases of vehicles and equipment, as well as service contracts. A State Procurement Law was passed in 2002, with full implementation beginning in January 2003.

3.2.3. Government financial management information system reform

To meet the needs of treasury reform and improved budgeting, the MOF began work on a new government financial management information system in 2000 under the "Golden Finance Project" (see Chapter 4). The aim is to provide a system that permits information sharing and supports the operations of MOF departments concerned with budget formulation and monitoring, disbursement, cash management, payroll disbursement, debt management, government procurement, state asset management, revenue management and economic forecasting. The Golden Finance Project has also created a platform that unified data reporting standards throughout the fiscal system, with software provided to sub-national governments all the way down to the township level. As a result, the MOF is now able to obtain more timely information to support analytical capacity.

4. A glass half full? The current status of public expenditure management

If credit for the initiation of budget reform had to be attributed to a single event, it would be the China National Audit Office's (CNAO)[6] audit report of the central budget in 1999, which issued stinging criticisms of the 1998 budget implementation:

1. Authorizations for spending ministries were not made until one to five months into the fiscal year; some ministries did not receive their budgets until the fourth quarter.

2. Management of government funds was lax – in some instances funds were diverted to illegal uses, such as investing in companies and buildings; some were even sent to overseas accounts.

3. Reporting requirements for extra-budgetary funds (EBF) were routinely ignored – even the MOF failed to present final accounts for the EBF that are included in the budget.

4. Losses, failure to collect and diversion of extra-budgetary fees were rampant. Illegal uses included pension reserves that were invested in companies or used for speculation in the securities markets.

These criticisms prodded the NPC to demand some immediate changes in budgeting procedures. Among them:

1. spending ministries be given timely authorizations;

2. organisational budgets be introduced, to increase accountability for public funds;

3. standardized procurement procedures be implemented to cut waste and corruption;

4. public disclosure of all intergovernmental transfers by province;

5. greater consultation with the NPC, including more detailed presentation of the budget.

As described in Section 3, reforms implemented over the past four to five years have mainly been in response to these demands. The major effort has gone into the introduction of organisational/departmental budgets. At the July 2003 Central Government Work Conference on Departmental Budgets, Vice Minister of Finance Lou Jiwei noted that achievements from the introduction of departmental budgets included the following:

1. one budget for one department;

2. zero-based budgeting;

3. integrated budgets; and

4. establishment of internal budgeting rules for the MOF and central departments.

For 2004 and beyond, he stated that continuing reform would aim to move toward building a multi-year framework and an efficient performance evaluation system for spending programmes. In the meantime, he promised to continue improvements on norm-setting, budgeting procedures and building flexibility into departmental budgets (Lou, 2003).

With the reforms to date, China appears to be, step-by-step, putting in place the infrastructure necessary for building a modern system of budget management. Although some measures, *e.g.* detailed budgeting and norm-setting, appear to run counter to the trend in OECD reforms in budgeting, they can be understood as part of the process of regaining control over the basics. The 2003 report of the CNAO noted approvingly that since the 1998 audit, the government has drafted more than 400 measures to improve financial management. While "[t]he 1998 audit [had] identified violations amounting to RMB 16.4 billion by 2001 the amount of such violations had fallen ... to RMB 2 billion, with a pronounced reduction in major violations at the central-department level" (Li, 2003).

However, in spite of the many advances, the budget management system remains marred by some of the weakness noted in earlier studies.

4.1. The budget is still not comprehensive

First, the capital budget is made separately from recurrent budgets, and capital spending decisions are not required to co-ordinate with fiscal authorities even when these decisions create large recurrent costs downstream.[7] To some extent this reflects the continuing rivalry between the NDRC (then called the State Planning Commission) and the MOF, which is hindering co-ordination. Under the planned economy, resource allocation was made primarily by the plan – controlled by the State Planning Commission, with the budget playing only a supporting role in financing the plan. With the NDRC retaining control over the capital budget, it is still forcing the MOF to play an accommodative role.

4.1.1. Extra-budgetary expenditures remain large

While the introduction of departmental budgets has succeeded in incorporating fees and levies into budgetary accounts (Item 1 in Box 7.2), and improved budgeting and SOE reform have likely reduced the size of Items 2 and 3 in recent years, they have certainly not eliminated them. Activities in Items 4 and 5 remain large and unaccounted, and appear to have grown in the past few years.[8]

Off-budget government spending remains large and unreported. Despite progress on curbing extra-budgetary levies, governments and bodies continue to raise large amounts of "self-raised funds" – nearly all infrastructural investments are financed off-budget, in

---

Box 7.2. China's large extra-budgetary revenues and expenditures

In the 1990s China became increasingly dependent on using extra-budgetary resources to finance government, especially at the sub-national levels. For many local governments, these financed half or more of all expenditures of government, and they comprised:

1. Fees and levies collected by branches of government and spent off-budget.
2. Expenditures of branches of government that are not reported in budgetary or extra-budgetary accounts:

    a) Tax expenditures – tax incentives or tax credits

    b) Payments arrears – unpaid/deferred wages to teachers and civil servants, unpaid subsidies to the grain marketing system, unpaid interest subsidies to the banking system on policy loans, unpaid utility and telephone bills of government bodies, etc.

    c) Goods and services provided to government at less than full compensation.

3. Quasi-fiscal expenditures of state-owned enterprises and public service units – for the provision of schools, health care and housing, etc., as well as carrying surplus workers on payrolls (in lieu of unemployment payments by the government).
4. Quasi-fiscal expenditures of government – directed credit to state-owned enterprises (SOEs), uncollateralized loans to public service units and local governments through the banking system.
5. Commercial incomes or losses of government branches, and revenues from asset sales. In recent years, the sale of land leases and the use of land by local governments in development schemes have grown rapidly and are becoming a source of concern in the banking sector.

non-transparent ways and poorly tracked. The involvement of government and other public bodies in land and real estate developments has loomed as a major cause of overheating in the Chinese economy.

Policy makers continue to use tax expenditures whose costs are not reported in the budget. Most recent examples include: tax exemptions for industries and regions hard-hit by the epidemic of Severe Atypical Respiratory Syndrome in 2003 and tax preferences for the Northeast provinces to aid in "resuscitating" the rustbelt.

4.1.2. The MOF still does not have comprehensive oversight authority on spending

Staffing decisions, which have major spending implications, are made by the State Commission Office for Public Sector Reform and its local branches, with little consultation with fiscal authorities. Top political leaders still intervene too often to make policy unrestrained by budgetary vetting. For example, the decision taken by then-Premier Zhu Rongji to significantly increase civil service salaries greatly increased government financing requirements, but the MOF had little influence over the decision.

4.1.3. Co-ordination between central and local governments is improving, but remains weak

Policies made by central government usually have financing implications for local governments, but local governments are not always consulted before rollout. For example, most local officials reportedly learned of the salary increase for civil servants from TV broadcasts even though the costs were mostly borne at the local level. But improvements are clearly evident in consultation with local governments in recent years – for example, the recent reforms in rural fees and agricultural taxes have been worked out with local governments, but compensation remains only partial.

Many earmarked transfers arrive late in the year and in unpredictable amounts. The matching funds requirement means that local governments have to hold significant reserves of funds in the event that they are successful in getting projects allocated (World Bank, 2002).

4.1.4. Revenue forecasting remains weak

Revenue forecasting remains weak and pegged to directive growth targets, rather than economic fundamentals, and reporting on contingent liabilities is weak to non-existent.

4.2. Extension of improved budgeting to the sub-national levels is limited

Public expenditure management in China is complicated by the country's huge size and diversity, since policies formulated in Beijing have to filter through several layers of bureaucracy before reaching the public. How the signals are transmitted through these complex organisations, and what incentives lower level agents have to respond to these signals jointly determine the outcomes.

Several aspects of China's structure of government have important implications for its system of public expenditure management. There are five tiers of government and five levels of budgeting (see Figure 7.3). The Budget Law requires every level of government to make its own budget and have it approved by the People's Congress at that level.

Figure 7.3. **Structure of government in China (2003)**

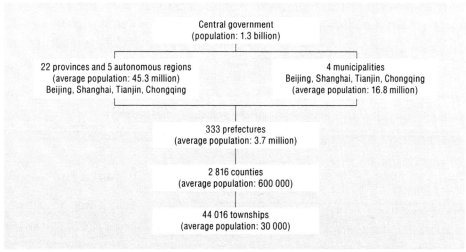

Note: The figures exclude Hong Kong, China, Macao and Chinese Taipei.

Compared to other countries, the organisational structure of the Chinese fiscal system is exceptional in two important respects. First, it is highly decentralized: the central government accounts for only 30% of total budgetary expenditures (see Table 7.A1.1 in Annex 7.A1). The rest is distributed among the four sub-national tiers, with 55% spent at sub-provincial levels. By comparison, sub-national governments account on average for only 14% of total budgetary expenditures in developing countries, and 32% in developed countries.[9]

This decentralization is even more notable because China is virtually unique among countries in the world in assigning responsibilities for providing vital social services such as social security, basic education, health care and public safety to local governments. Cities at the third and fourth tiers account for all expenditures for social security: pensions, unemployment insurance, and other income support and welfare schemes. Counties and townships (fourth and fifth tiers) are together responsible for providing basic education and public health for the rural populace – these two tiers account for 70% of budgetary expenditures on education, and 55-60% of expenditures on health.[10] Table 7.A1.2 (Annex 7.A1) shows that these expenditure assignments in China deviate significantly from those in other countries and helps to explain the high share of expenditures at the sub-national levels. With sub-national governments playing such a vital role, improvements in budgeting in China depend critically on associated changes being implemented at the grassroots levels.

The second exceptional feature of China's fiscal system is that decentralization occurred in an incremental and uncoordinated fashion, a process that left revenue and expenditure assignments significantly mismatched, with local governments largely self-financed, and provision of services to the local populace vulnerable to variations in local fiscal health. The problems of this intergovernmental fiscal system were examined in detail in the 2002 World Bank report, *China: National Development and Subnational Finance*, which came to the firm conclusion that the current intergovernmental arrangements were dysfunctional, and the shortage of revenues at the lower tiers and especially in poor regions constituted a bottleneck to national policy implementation.

Through the 1990s, revenue inadequacy was also a major cause of poor budgeting practices at the sub-national levels, which replicated most of the weaknesses at the central level. In fact, the rise of extra-budgetary revenues in the 1990s was in large part attributable to budgetary shortfalls and the exhortation by higher level governments for local governments to go out and "find local solutions" to fiscal gaps. Over the years, extra-budgetary revenues have been funding many needed services (World Bank, 2002; Wong, 1997, 1998; Fan 1998). This is illustrated in Table 7.1, which shows the extent to which key public services in Hunan province (a middle-income province) are financed from extra-budgetary funding, including salary payments for public employees.

Table 7.1. **Sources of revenue for major expenditures in Hunan Province (1999)**
Billion RMB

	Budgetary allocation	Actual expenditure	% financed by budget	Personnel costs	Personnel costs as % of budget allocation
Education					
Primary schools	1.44	3.33	43	2.45	170
Middle schools	1.73	3.55	49	2.45	142
Health	1.17	7.23	16	2.57	220
Agriculture	2.27	3.16	72	0.87	38
Urban Maintenance	1.28	1.55	83	0.5	39

Source: World Bank (2002), Table 5.2.

In recent years, as the central government has stepped up transfers to alleviate funding problems at the sub-national level, the nature of the problem has shifted somewhat, to issues of improving the mechanisms of transfer to achieve efficient outcomes.

To improve budgetary practice and the efficiency of public expenditures at the sub-national level, and to rein in extra-budgetary revenues and activities, will require some fundamental reforms of the intergovernmental fiscal system – a long and protracted process that has only just begun.

4.3. Compliance with existing laws and regulations needs strengthening

While the thrust of reform efforts has been to strengthen the framework for expenditure management, recent audit reports point to significant problems of non-compliance with existing rules and regulations by government bodies, starting with the MOF. For example, the 2003 audit report complained that despite rule changes to discourage in-year incremental budgeting and stipulating tougher rules on supplemental budgets, both the MOF and the NDRC released significant funds in the course of the fiscal year (Li, 2003). According to both the 2003 and 2004 audit reports, the use of tax expenditures for policy purposes continued apace and unrecorded. In 2002, the MOF used value-added tax and income tax refunds totaling RMB 1.36 billion to support the Three Gorges Dam construction and resettlement. In 2003, central ministries spent RMB 28.2 billion in tax rebates of various forms to compensate state-owned enterprises (mostly in nine enterprise groups) for their quasi-fiscal expenditures in providing education, health care, and social security. "These methods of handling the expenditures is not according to regulations […] and should have been reported as budgetary expenditures instead" (Li, 2004). Both the 2003 and 2004 reports also point to many instances of diversion of earmarked subsidies to unintended uses, local borrowing against regulation, and falsification of revenue and expenditures.

5. Next steps?

The current programme of budget reform comprises a large, complex and ambitious package of measures that are long overdue, and they will be crucial in moving China toward a modern budgeting system and a well-functioning public sector. However, these reforms are only just beginning, and they are focused at the central level.[11] Given the decentralized fiscal system, the reforms will have to be implemented at all levels of government, a process that promises to be protracted and difficult.

To date, the government has focused mainly on tackling technical issues:

1. revamping budgetary processes;
2. improving treasury management;
3. improving government procurement procedures;
4. introduction of new payroll systems to monitor and control payroll expenditures;
5. introduction of improved accounting and financial reporting on extra-budgetary funds, elimination of many fees and incorporation of others into the budget;
6. introduction of new debt management procedures to improve information and tracking of government debt and contingent liabilities;
7. introduction of a new government financial management information system to improve information flows within the MOF and linking up with provincial databases.

Reforms have shied away from significantly tackling areas that involve political challenges, such as:

1. redefining the role of government and refocusing budget priorities;
2. limiting policy initiatives outside the budgetary context to improve orderly prioritization; and especially
3. enhancing the role of civil society.

There has also been little public discussion of the need for a major realignment of the intergovernmental fiscal system in spite of the many changes underway since 2000 as a result of reforms in the rural sector.[12]

Judging from the recent audit reports of the CNAO, the many difficulties government faces in enforcement highlight its continuing inability to enforce fiscal discipline and hold spending units accountable for results. Strengthening accountability mechanisms and enforcing aggregate fiscal discipline constitute the critical challenges for reforms in the next phase, and these will require government to tackle some of the political challenges avoided thus far. Fortunately, the prospects look far brighter in 2005 than in the late 1990s when budget reform was first initiated.

The single most important advance has been the growing prominence of the CNAO, whose annual reports have kept up criticism of the MOF and other government bodies at the central and local levels. Beginning in 1999, the Auditor-General has appeared each year at the NPC Standing Committee Meetings in June to present the administration's report on the audit of the previous year's budget. In recent years, this has become a popular annual event that attracts a great deal of media attention and follow-up investigations by the press. This has generated continuing pressure to improve public sector management and provided support for budget reform through the NPC. More importantly, the new "scientific development" paradigm adopted under Hu Jintao and Wen Jiabao, which calls for a more balanced, inclusive and people-centered approach, should translate into support from the top leadership for continuing reforms in public expenditure management – the vital ingredient that was missing in 1998.

Notes

1. This chapter was written by Christine Wong, University of Washington, with the guidance of Jón R. Blöndal, Budgeting and Public Expenditures Division, Public Governance and Territorial Development Directorate, OECD.

2. Traditionally, the Premier appears at the annual NPC meetings in March to present a report on the work of the government. This report reviews the achievements of the past year and outlines the main undertakings for the coming year. It provides the occasion for presenting major new policies and changes in direction.

3. See OECD (2002), World Bank (2000) and World Bank (2002).

4. *Southern Weekend*, 23 January 2003. Even so, the review was, in the words of one delegate, "largely symbolic". Many delegates complained that it was impossible to conduct a thorough review since they received the budget only a few days prior to the meeting. They called for the establishment of a budget oversight committee within the legislature to review the budget in advance and in greater detail, before submitting it to the delegates (*China Law and Governance Review*, January 2004, No. 1).

5. In remarks at an OECD meeting in December 1998, Vice Minister Lou Jiwei spoke of government fees and charges equal to about 10% of GDP and "not entirely under the control of the budget". Since then, the size of these extra-budgetary revenues has declined as some fees and charges were reclassified as budgetary revenue or as business incomes of the government bodies and excluded from extra-budgetary accounts.

6. Formerly called State Audit Administration.

7. Blöndal (2002) cited the example of the decision to build the National Library, which was made without consultation with the MOF even though once built, the MOF was obliged to provide a substantial recurrent budget for the library's operation.

8. Some evidence for this was provided in the State Audit General's reports to the NPC in 2003 and 2004.

9. The sample comprises about 100 countries for which sub-national budgetary data is available from IMF, World Bank, OECD and other sources (Bahl, 2002).

10. For examples of shares of sub-national expenditures see Figure 7.A1.1 in Annex 7.A1.

11. The examples of Wuhan Municipality and Hebei Province cited above not withstanding, budget reform has been mostly a central government activity to date, with sub-national participation limited to a selected few. The rest of the country is little involved. This picture is strikingly similar to that for civil service reforms described in Chapter 1 of this study, with a modernizing core that comprises the central government and selected coastal areas, and a large unreformed "other" area.

12. Since 2000, reforms have been gradually rolled out to eliminate all fees and levies in the rural sector. Beginning in 2004, the government has also implemented a programme to eliminate the agricultural tax over a period of five years. These reforms are eliminating the bulk of the revenue base for governments at the township level and have necessitated some revisions to expenditure assignments between the county and the township, as well as a proliferation of transfers from higher levels of government to fill the fiscal gap. For public expenditure policies also see Chapter 8.

Bibliography

Bahl, Roy (2002), Presentation at the World Bank and State Council Development Research Center Conference on Rural Public Finance, December, Beijing.

Blöndal, Jón R. (2002), *Budgeting in China*, OECD, Paris.

Chen Shixin (2003), "Reforming Budget Preparation: The Introduction of Departmental Budgets", in Christine Wong and Wu Jinglian, Editors, *Reforming Public Finance in China: Current Program and Next Steps*, (in progress).

Fan, Gang (1998), "Market-oriented Economic Reform and the Growth of Off-Budget Local Public Finance", in Donald Brean (1998) (ed.), *Taxation in Modern China*, Routledge, London and New York.

Li Jinhua (2003), "Report on the Audit of the Implementation of the Central Budget and Other Fiscal Revenues and Expenditures in 2002", the Third Meeting of the Standing Committee of the 10th National People's Congress, 25 June.

Li Jinhua (2004), "Work Report on the Audit of the Implementation of the Central Budget and Other Fiscal Revenues and Expenditures in 2003", delivered to the 10th Plenary Session of the 10th People's Congress Standing Committee on 25 June.

Lou Jiwei (2003), "Doing a Conscientious Job of Budgeting Work for Central Departments in 2004", speech given at the 2004 Central Department Budgeting Work Conference.

Mountfield, Edward, and Christine Wong (2005), "Chapter 5: Public Expenditure on the Frontline: Towards Effective Management by Sub-national Governments", Roland White and Paul Smoke, Editors, *East Asia Decentralizes*, The World Bank.

OECD (2002), *China in the World Economy: The Domestic Policy Challenges*, OECD, Paris.

State Council (1996), Document No. 29, "Further Strengthening the Management of Extra-Budget Funds – Any Locality, Department Or Unit Should Not Have Their Fiscal Revenue Concealed and Unreported", *People's Daily*, 6 August, p. 1.

Wong, Christine (1997), Editor, *Financing Local Government in the People's Republic of China*, Oxford University Press, Hong Kong.

Wong, Christine (1998), "Fiscal Dualism in China: Gradualist Reform and the Growth of Off-Budget Finance", in Brean, Donald J.S. (ed). *Taxation in Modern China*, Routledge, New York and London.

World Bank (2000), *China: Managing Public Expenditures for Better Results*, Report No. 20342-CHA.

World Bank (2002), *China: National Development and Sub-national Finance, a Review of Provincial Expenditures*, April, Report No. 22951-CHA.

World Bank (2004), *World Development Report: Making Services Work for Poor People*, Oxford University Press.

Xiang Huaicheng and Lou Jiwei (2004), Editors, *Five Years of Budget Reform in China, 1998-2003* (in Chinese), China Financial Economics Press, Beijing.

Yang, Hao (2002), "Investigating Wuhan Municipal Departmental Budget Reforms (2 parts)", *Hubei Finance and Tax*, No. 3 and 4.

Zhang Tong (2003), "Research on the Reform of China's Treasury Management System", in Christine Wong and Wu Jinglian, Editors, *Reforming Public Finance in China: Current Program and Next Steps* (in progress).

ANNEX 7.A1

Table 7.A1.1. **China's expenditure decentralization in comparative perspective**

	Sub-national expenditure (as a percentage of national expenditure)
China 2002	70
Developing countries 1990s	14
Transition countries 1990s	26
OECD member countries 1990s	32
Other large countries 1990s	
Germany	40
India	46
Japan	61
Pakistan	29
Russia	38
United States	46

Source: Adapted from Mountfield and Wong (2005); Bahl (2002).

Figure 7.A1.1. **Shares of sub-national expenditures (1999)**

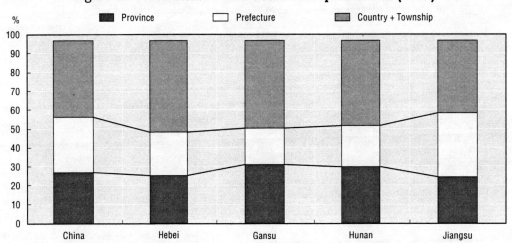

Source: MOF and provincial officials.

Table 7.A1.2. **Expenditure assignments**

	Defense	Foreign affairs	Environment and natural resources	Unemployment insurance	Industry and agriculture	Education	Health	Social welfare	Police	Highways
China	F	F	F, S, L	L	F, S, L	L	L	L	L	F, S, L
Vietnam (2004)	F	F	F, S, L	..	F, S, L	S, L	S, L	F, S, L	F	F, S, L
India[1]	F	F	F, S	F, S	F, S	F, S	S	F,S	S	F
India[2]	F	F	F, S	F, S	F, S	F, S, L	S, L	F, S	S	F
Japan[1]	F	F	..	..	L	F, L	F, L	F, L	L	..
Japan[2]	F	F	..	..	..	L	F, L	F, L	F, L	L
Malaysia[2]	F	F	L	..	F, S	F	F, S	F, S	F	F
	Assignment of constitutional powers									
Canada	F	F	F, S	F	C	S	S (F)	F, S	F, S	S
United States	F, S	F	F, S	F, S	S	S, F	S (F)		F, S	F, S
Switzerland	F	F	C	C	F, S	C, F, S	S, C	F, C	S	FS
Australia	F, S	F	F, S	C	S, C	F, S	F, S	C	S, F	F, S
Germany	F	F, S	C	C	C	C, S	C, F, S	C	C, S	C
Austria	F	F	F, S	F	F	F, S	C, F, S	C	F, S	F, S

Key:
1. Financing responsibility.
2. Provision.
F Federal/national.
S State/province.
L Local.
C Concurrent (shared).

Source: Adapted from Mountfield and Wong (2005), Table 2.

PART II

Chapter 8

China's Public Expenditure Policies

Table of Contents

Summary 251

China's Public Expenditure Policies 253

1. Introduction 253
2. Overview of issues 253
   2.1. The scope of China's public expenditures 254
   2.2. The allocation of public expenditure 256
   2.3. Official government spending has been growing rapidly. 257
   2.4. Government spending is exceptionally but unevenly decentralised 260
3. Regional fiscal disparities and their implications
   for China's expenditure policies 261
   3.1. Inequalities in public spending across provinces 262
   3.2. Differences in the absolute level of spending 265
   3.3. Reforms to reduce spending disparities 267
   3.4. Implications and policy options 268
4. Conclusion 270

Notes 271

Bibliography 272

List of boxes

8.1. Classifications and reporting on government spending ... 256

List of tables

8.1. Officially reported government expenditure 254
8.2. Shares of major expenditure categories in on-budget expenditure
     and by government levels in 2002 257
8.3. Major expenditure categories, their shares in GDP and average growth rates 259
8.4. Disparities in provincial per capita expenditures revenues
     and incomes in 1995-2003 263
8.5. Disparities across provinces in selected categories measured by the Gini
     and Theil indices in 2002 264

List of figures

8.1. Public and private education spending as % of GDP
     in selected countries in 2000 258

8.2. Relation of per capita expenditure and per capita GDP
at the provincial level in 2002... 263
8.3. Disparities in county level per capita expenditure by province 2001,
Theil index of inequality.. 265
8.4. Actual public spending by province relative to adjusted national average
spending 2001, % of actual spending 266
8.5. Actual county-level public spending by province relative to adjusted national
county-level average spending 2001, % of actual spending.................. 267

Summary

China's evolution from a centrally planned to a market-based economy has led to major transformations of its public expenditure policies. Significant progress has been made in raising spending on infrastructure to a level more in line with China's development needs, in improving mechanisms for expenditure budgeting and planning, notably by bringing some extra-budgetary accounts into the main budget. Nevertheless, significant problems remain.

General government spending needs to be allocated more efficiently

The allocation of public spending appears out of line with China's development needs and goals in at least three respects: public spending on education, science and health are still low by international standards. Notwithstanding recent reforms, the government remains overly exposed to extra-budget and off-budget activities, which make public expenditures difficult to plan and control and which impair their accountability and transparency. The analysis in this report suggests the following guidelines for further reforms to improve the effectiveness of China's public expenditure policies:

1. Improve allocative efficiency of public expenditures by raising spending on education, health, science and other social/development needs, as a share of overall spending and relative to GDP, to levels in line with China's needs.
2. Continue efforts to bring expenditures now off-budget onto the budget as part of broader efforts to subject all expenditures to more rigorous formulation, implementation, and accountability.
3. Improve transparency by reforming accounting systems for expenditures along functional lines, using international standards as a guide, so that amounts spent on key social, development and strategic needs can be clearly determined and assessed.

Spending disparities across regions and government levels should be reduced

Fiscal relations among different government levels in China are characterised by a comparatively high but also uneven degree of decentralisation. This system decentralises spending decisions but gives little freedom for localities to set tax rates in a way that matches revenues with local spending needs. As a result, a strong system of revenue transfers is needed to ensure that low-income areas do not have low levels of public spending. A revenue transfer system does exist but has not been able to prevent the emergence of marked variations in public spending across the country. It also gives rise to current substantial gaps between the expenditure responsibilities of sub-national governments and their resources. Such gaps have also been an important factor behind the growing resort to off-budget funds and illicit borrowing by local governments, and are partly responsible for the relatively low level of public outlays on education and other important development needs.

To increase the potential efficiency gains from the decentralised provision of public goods and services in China, the inter-governmental fiscal relations need to take more account of differences in resources across the country.

1. Reform fiscal relations between central and sub-national governments to bring expenditure responsibilities at each level of government into line with financial resources.

2. Improve accountability of sub-national governments by establishing more explicit criteria for performance in key areas such as education. Consideration might also be given to allowing local governments some greater discretion over the rates of certain taxes.

China's Public Expenditure Policies[1]

1. Introduction

China's public expenditure policies constitute one of the government's key instruments for promoting economic and social development. Policy makers have been facing major challenges in adapting these policies, and the institutions and institutional arrangements governing them, to the rapidly evolving economy.

This chapter examines issues concerning the macroeconomic aspects of China's public expenditure policies and the allocation of those expenditures in relation to official policy goals.[2] The analysis is based on information gathered at the sub-national level in a number of provinces as well as official statistics published by the central government. The first section examines the issues from a national perspective and the second provides an in-depth look at the current state, problems and policy options concerning expenditure relations among various levels of government.

As indicated in the following two sections, institutional mechanisms originally derived from the central planning era but which have adapted only imperfectly to the market economy are important factors behind the problems identified in these areas. The transparency, accountability and effectiveness with which policies are implemented are greatly hampered by the fact that a substantial amount of expenditure which the government controls or is ultimately liable for occurs outside of the formal budget. The lack of transparency is aggravated by China's antiquated systems for classifying expenditure statistics. Off-budget spending, particularly contingent liabilities arising from bank non-performing loans (NPL), are the most difficult to control and pose the greatest risks to fiscal stability.

Distortions in the fiscal relations among levels of government in China have been especially serious impediments to the effectiveness of China's expenditure policies. These have resulted in substantial gaps between the expenditure responsibilities of sub-national governments and the resources they have to finance these responsibilities, and have also created adverse incentives in expenditure decisions at the local level. These problems in turn have contributed to widespread disparities in public spending per capita among and within provinces. They have also been an important factor behind the growing resort to off-budget funds and illicit borrowing by local governments, and are partly responsible for the relatively low level of public outlays on education and other important development needs.

2. Overview of issues

Prior to the reform period, China's government effectively controlled most of the spending in the economy. The institutions and institutional arrangements governing China's public expenditure policies have evolved considerably since then, but they still bear important vestiges of the central planning era. While the distinction between spending carried out by the government itself and spending by entities outside the government has become progressively sharper over time, it remains somewhat blurred, and the administrative responsibility for spending is highly decentralised although the decisions about how spending is allocated remain highly centralised. Budget statistics are still substantially based more on administrative classifications from the central planning era than on their economic or social purpose. These vestiges are at least partly responsible for the relative lack of transparency in public expenditure, the fragmentation and unevenness in the mechanisms by which expenditures are planned and implemented, and the overall difficulty authorities have sometimes had in controlling the outlays for which the government ultimately bears the burden. They have also helped to distort the allocation of expenditures, both across categories and among regions, and between urban *versus* rural areas.

2.1. The scope of China's public expenditures

The actual scope of China's public expenditures is considerably larger than official statistics seem to suggest. In terms of percentage of gross domestic product (GDP), on-budget public expenditure in China was 20.7% in 2002 (see Table 8.1) compared to the OECD average of 43.9%.[3] China's ratio is lower than that of any OECD member country except Mexico (18.5%) and noticeably below that of Korea (25.3%), which has the second lowest ratio of expenditure to GDP.

Table 8.1. **Officially reported government expenditure**

	On-budget expenditure (billion yuan)	Share of GDP (%)				
		On-budget expenditure	Extra-budgetary expenditure	Social security funds expenditure	Total expenditure (budgetary data)	Total expenditure (National Accounts data)
1993	505.4	14.6	3.8	1.4	19.8	22.2
1994	615.9	13.2	3.7	1.4	18.3	21.2
1995	715.1	12.2	4.0	1.5	17.7	19.3
2000	1 616.5	18.1	4.0	2.7	25.1	24.6
2001	1 920.3	19.5	3.9	2.8	26.5	26.6
2002	2 231.3	20.7	3.6	3.2	27.7	26.4
2003	2 487.6	20.4	3.4	3.3	27.4	n.a.
2004	2 857.9	20.3	n.a.	3.3	n.a.	n.a.

Note: Total expenditure includes reported on-budget and extra-budgetary expenditures, expenditure of social security funds and local authority spending financed by the issue of bonds by the central government. The payments made to cover the losses of state-owned enterprises have been treated as expenditure in the above data, rather than as negative income as in the official statistics.

Source: Various issues of the *Finance Yearbook of China* and CEIC database.

The on-budget figures, however, exclude large amounts of outlays of public social security funds and extra-budgetary funds controlled by local governments. Social security fund outlays have been rising rapidly and amounted to 3.2% of GDP in 2002. Extra-budget accounts comprise a collection of individual funds used by local governments (or by other entities on their behalf) to carry out a wide variety of activities. The planning and control procedures for extra-budget accounts are typically distinct from those applying to on-budget spending. They are financed by legally sanctioned fees, surtaxes, user charges, and other levies specific to each account. Spending through these accounts increased somewhat during the 1990s, but not as rapidly as on-budget spending. Since 2000, such outlays have been edging down relative to GDP. This drop reflects ongoing efforts to consolidate government expenditure into the formal budget that have almost halved the importance of extra-budgetary spending relative to on-budget outlays as compared with the mid-1990s.

Overall, the exclusions from the budget add one-third to on-budget spending, bringing total outlays to 27.4% of GDP. For 2004, no data is yet available for extra-budgetary expenditure but given social security spending and on-budget outlays, total government spending is not likely to have shown an increase relative to GDP. Internationally comparable data on general government expenditure, derived from the national accounts, are only available with a considerable lag but confirm the spending levels implied by the addition of various budgetary accounts.

Official government expenditure is still only part of the spending that the government actually carries out. Taking government expenditure to include all activities that ultimately involve the financial liability of the government, and/or are directly mandated by the government, these non-official expenditure activities include the following three items:

1. First, China also has extensive off-budget expenditures that are not legally sanctioned and which are financed by illegal fees and charges, often on an *ad hoc* basis, for example levies imposed on various activities of farmers. While no official statistics on off-budget expenditures exist, estimates by Wong (2001) and Ma (2000) suggest that off-budget expenditures have risen from around 2% of GDP in the mid-1990s to around 4% of GDP in recent years. Adding estimated off-budget expenditures to official spending suggests a figure for China's general government spending (roughly in line with OECD definitions) of around 32% of GDP. This is well below the OECD average but more in line with or above those of other emerging economies at a comparable stage of development.

2. Second, there are substantial tax expenditures in the form of preferences or exemptions for certain businesses. Probably the most important are the extensive preferences enjoyed by foreign-funded enterprises, which typically are exempt from corporate income tax in the first several years of their operation and have also been exempt from tariffs on their imports of capital equipment and other inputs.

3. Third, the government has over time accumulated considerable implicit or contingent liabilities whose cost effectively amounts to substantial past unacknowledged spending. Chief among these contingent liabilities are the portion of non-performing loans incurred by financial institutions (in large part) as a result of the government's past use of the banking system to support unprofitable state-owned enterprises (SOE) or other non-commercial purposes.[4] Estimation of contingent liabilities is always difficult, but particularly so in China because data on conditions of financial institutions and (to a lesser degree) non-financial enterprises is relatively limited. However, various estimates suggest that the ultimate cost to the government from the NPL will amount to at least 20% and as much as 50% of GDP (see OECD, 2002). This amounts to unacknowledged past spending on the order of 1-2.5% of GDP annually over the past 20 years.

Overall, China's aggregate public expenditure does not appear to be obviously low given its level of development. However, the large amount of public expenditure falling outside of the formal budget greatly limits the transparency of expenditure policies. This lack of transparency is aggravated further by the way in which expenditure statistics are classified, compiled and reported (see Box 8.1). The reduction of expenditures now outside the formal budget is crucial to government efforts to improve the planning, control, and implementation of public expenditure policies. The authorities have been undertaking

> **Box 8.1. Classifications and reporting on government spending**
>
> Statements about the structure of Chinese Government spending are greatly complicated by the continued use of a classification system derived from the former central planning system. Expenditures are generally classified according to the (often formerly) responsible administrative units or by their line-entry into the government plan rather than by functional categories, so that spending on key activities is divided among official classifications. For example, spending on schools and other major educational facilities is included in infrastructure spending while operating expenses are included in the broad category of "culture, education, health and science".
>
> Expenditures for many activities are also carried out both on-budget and through the extra-budgetary funds. The difficulty of interpreting expenditure data is further complicated by the high level of aggregation of published expenditure statistics for China as a whole. The overall result is to seriously limit the transparency of government expenditure policies and thereby complicate the task of planning and control of those policies. Reforms to bring the classification and reporting of government spending more in line with international norms could thus yield significant benefits.

important initiatives in recent years to bring extra-budgetary accounts (and ultimately the social security accounts) onto the formal budget and to curtail illegal off-budget activities. Reducing the scope of contingent liabilities and increasing their transparency is also important but depends on progress on enterprise and financial reforms that are likely to take more time.

2.2. The allocation of public expenditure

While there are significant difficulties in determining from published data how China's expenditures are allocated (see Box 8.1), it appears that official public outlays are characterised by a relatively low portion spent on human resource development, science and technology, and social welfare; and by a relatively high portion spent on public investment and public administration including defence. On-budget expenditure on operating expenses of culture, education, public health, and science made up 18.6% of total on-budget expenditure in 2002 (Table 8.2), or 3.9% of GDP, and about 22% of official spending once outlays for these activities included in other categories are included.[5] This figure is well below the OECD average of 28.6% as well as the ratio for virtually all individual OECD member countries.

Despite a significant increase in recent years, overall official expenditure for education – including estimated outlays in other budget categories and in extra-budget accounts – was about 3.2% of GDP in 2002, noticeably below a long-standing government goal of 4.0% of GDP. Public education expenditure relative to GDP has been less than that of major developing countries such as Brazil and India (see Figure 8.1). (Total education expenditure relative to GDP, on the other hand, has been higher in China than in India or Brazil owing to the higher share of private financing in China.) The share of public health outlays in on-budget spending fell from 4.2% in 1994 to 2.8% in 2002. China's public spending on science and technology has also been relatively low by international standards.[6] Although growing rapidly, spending on pensions and other social relief make up a relatively low fraction of total government expenditure (11.8% of on-budget expenditure and 2.4% of GDP in 2002).

Table 8.2. **Shares of major expenditure categories in on-budget expenditure and by government levels in 2002**

In billion RMB and %

	Amount spent (billion yuan)	% of total on-budget expenditure	Central share in %	Local share in %
Current expenditure				
Administration	405	18.2	19.1	80.9
Defense	171	7.7	99.0	1.0
Culture, education, public health, science	415	18.6	10.8	89.2
Economic services	146	6.5	7.8	92.2
Pensions and social relief	264	11.8	22.7	77.3
Subsidies	90	4.1	35.0	65.0
Interest expense	68	3.0	100.0	0.0
Others	261	11.7	22.4	77.6
Capital expenditure				
Infrastructure	314	14.1	39.9	60.1
Development of production capacity of enterprises	97	4.3	24.6	75.4

Note: Payments to finance the losses of state-owned enterprises have been counted as subsidies. In Chinese budgetary data, they are counted as negative income rather than expenditure.

Source: *Finance Yearbook of China 2003*.

Low government spending on education and health has been partly made up for by a comparatively high portion of private spending on these activities. However this has also tended to accentuate disparities in available resources for education and health between wealthier and poorer provinces, and between rural and urban areas.

In contrast, the share of Chinese Government spending allocated to investment appears high by international standards, well above the OECD average and greater than in most individual countries with the notable exception of Korea. This relatively high level of infrastructure spending at least partly reflects the fact that China is a large developing country with a growing need for basic transport, power, and other capital intensive facilities. The level of capital spending has nearly doubled since 1998, due largely to the heavy infrastructure spending for western economic development.[7] The share of administration in China's official government spending, at 23% in 2001, is higher than in any OECD member country except Belgium and Italy and even the share of expenditure on administration in on-budget expenditure is well above the OECD average.[8] The portion of expenditure going to public administration is at least partly attributable to relatively high levels of staff on sub-national government payrolls.

The Chinese authorities have recognised the need to improve the allocation of spending by increasing spending on key social development needs that are currently under-funded. In particular, the government has been increasing its aid for education in poorer areas. However, given the constraints on aggregate public spending, the scope for improving its allocation will depend on the future trend in spending on public administration/defence and infrastructure.

2.3. *Official government spending has been growing rapidly*

China's official public expenditures have grown at a very rapid pace in recent years. On-budget expenditures grew at an average rate of 17.7% between 1995 and 2002, while official expenditures have increased at an average rate of 16.4%. These figures are almost

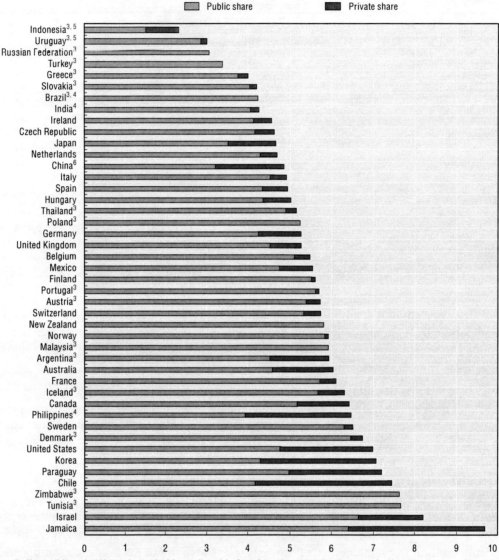

Figure 8.1. **Public and private education spending as % of GDP in selected countries in 2000**

1. Including public subsidies to households attributable for educational institutions. Including direct expenditure on educational institutions from international sources.
2. Net of public subsidies attributable for educational institutions.
3. Public subsides to households not included in public expenditure, but in private expenditure.
4. Year of reference: 1999.
5. Direct expenditure on educational institutions from international sources exceeds 1.5% of all public expenditure.
6. Year of reference: 2002.

Source: OECD, *Education at a Glance*, 2003.

double the annual average growth in nominal GDP (9.1%) over the same period. While government revenues have also grown rapidly, they have lagged behind spending, leading to a rise in the government (on-budget) deficit to 2.9% of GDP in 2002. Thus spending growth will almost certainly have to be slowed significantly in future years if it is to be sustainable.

The two biggest contributors to the overall growth in official expenditures have been in infrastructure spending and in administration/defence, each of which increased at average annual rates exceeding 20% between 1997 and 2002 (see Table 8.3). In contrast, spending on

Table 8.3. **Major expenditure categories, their shares in GDP and average growth rates**

In billion RMB and %

	1997	1998	1999	2000	2001	2002	Average growth 1997-2002
Administration and defense	2.7	4.0	4.5	5.3	6.4	7.3	22.0
Culture, education, public health, science	2.6	2.8	3.4	3.8	4.7	5.3	14.9
Economic services	1.1	1.2	1.3	1.4	1.6	1.8	9.9
Pensions and social relief	0.2	0.2	1.1	2.0	2.6	2.5	65.3
Subsidies	1.2	1.4	1.3	1.8	1.4	1.2	−0.2
Interest expense	0.8	1.0	0.8	1.0	1.1	0.9	2.8
Others	2.8	2.6	2.6	2.3	3.1	4.0	7.7
Infrastructure	1.4	1.9	2.8	2.8	3.4	3.9	23.7
Development of production capacity of enterprises	0.9	0.9	1.0	1.2	1.3	1.4	10.7
Memorandum: extra-budgetary items:							
Capital construction	0.7	0.5	0.7	0.6	0.5	0.3	−12.3
Operating and administrative	1.7	24.1	14.3	22.5	12.4	12.4	48.5
Social security fund: expense	1.8	2.2	2.8	3.2	3.7	4.6	21.0

Note: Average growth is calculated as compound average growth.
Source: Various editions of the *Finance Yearbook of China*.

culture, education, public health and science has grown less rapidly than overall on-budget expenditure (although more rapidly than GDP). Outlays for (on-budget) pensions and social relief more than doubled over the period, but from a very low base. The rapid growth in government infrastructure spending reflects the official goal of promoting development in western economic regions but has also been aimed at supporting China's aggregate GDP growth as aggregate demand slowed during the latter half of the 1990s. As a result, China's ratio of infrastructure spending to GDP now exceeds the target recommended by the World Bank (1997) in the mid-1990s, when infrastructure spending was judged to be too low relative to China's development needs. Much of the increase in spending on administration and defence as a share of total on-budget expenditure is attributable to two salary increases granted to government employees (in 1998 and 2002), which have more than offset extensive cuts in public sector workforces at the central and sub-central government levels.

The rapid growth of government spending since the mid-1990s can be viewed at least in part as a correction of the secular decline in the size of China's official government spending from the late 1980s to the mid-1990s, when spending fell to just above 17% of GDP.[9] Beginning with the 1994 tax reform, the authorities have placed a high priority on expanding the tax base and improving collection. These efforts, together with a recovery in business profits, have led to an increase in the ratio of official government revenues relative to GDP from a low of 17% in 1995 to 25.7% in 2002. This increase in revenue has allowed the authorities to increase spending to levels more in line with the economy's needs.

A number of factors are likely to act to slow official expenditure growth relative to GDP over the next several years.

1. First, given that the central government is committed to reducing the budget deficit (which on a national accounts base dropped to an estimated 0.9% of GDP in 2004), this implies lowering the growth of spending to below that of revenue. Moreover, revenue growth is likely to slow toward GDP growth as the means to improve collection and compliance become exhausted.

2. Second, growth in government infrastructure investment should be noticeably slower over the medium term, both because buoyant exports and non-state investment have made government fiscal stimulus unnecessary and because a growing portion of government infrastructure investment is being replaced by non-state sources.

3. Third, barring further major increases in salaries of government workers, spending on public administration is also likely to at least slow down, and could even fall relative to GDP, as efforts to cut government workforces are extended to lower levels of government.

The latter two of these factors could also facilitate efforts to raise the level of spending on education, health and science relative to GDP.

A number of risks surround the future growth of public spending. One uncertainty relates to government health spending that has fallen to low levels especially in rural areas. Another outbreak of the Severe Acute Respiratory Syndrome (SARS) and the longer term consequences of AIDS could boost outlays. There also are important uncertainties about the cost of social security obligations, particularly during the transition to a more universal system as it expands coverage to rural workers and those in urban areas that are now uncovered.[10] However, the pace of this expansion is subject to policy decisions of the central government.[11] The greatest risks to the outlook for China's public expenditures stem from contingent liabilities that are currently off-budget. In particular, past experience suggests that non-performing loans of financial institutions are perhaps the most important risk to the controllability of public expenditure, even though reforms have been undertaken in recent years which appear to have significantly improved credit quality. The loans necessary to finance these bad debts could raise interest payments by between one and three percentage points of GDP, depending on how large past NPLs turn out to be.[12] This cost could be raised further as the outlays necessary for further restructuring of SOEs are likely to take the form of debt write-offs financed directly or indirectly by the government.

2.4. Government spending is exceptionally but unevenly decentralised

Fiscal relations among different government levels in China are characterised by a comparatively high but also uneven degree of decentralisation that helps explain much of the distinctive characteristics of its government spending and contributes to a number of its problems. The central government is almost entirely responsible for spending on national defence, but most other major activities, including spending on education, health and social welfare, are largely the responsibility of sub-national governments. Infrastructure spending is shared between the central and sub-national governments. The division of responsibility for expenditures within provinces is less formalised, but typically sub-provincial governments bear the main responsibility for expenditures within their jurisdiction assigned to the sub-national level. The devolution of expenditure responsibilities to sub-national governments has been further accentuated by central-government imposed requirements to support workers laid off from SOEs (outside of the fledgling unemployment insurance system) and other un-funded mandates.

As a result of this expenditure assignment, China's provincial and local governments account for an unusually large share of total public outlays. The sub-national share of on-budget government expenditure rose by over 10 percentage points from the early to the mid-1990s reaching 68.4% in 2001. The sub-national share of general government spending, including extra-budget accounts and social security spending, would be even greater, in the mid-70% range.[13] These ratios are higher, generally considerably higher, than those of OECD member countries, including those with explicit federal structures, as well as the shares in Russia (whose sub-national share of public expenditure was 55.4% of GDP in 2002) and other major emerging economies.

China's fiscal revenues are also decentralised but substantially less so than expenditures. Sub-national governments accounted for nearly 47% and 60% of on-budget and total official government revenue respectively in 2003 – more than 10 percentage points below the corresponding expenditure shares. The greater centralisation of revenues compared to spending derives from the 1994 tax reform, which established explicit sharing formulas between the central and provincial governments for the main taxes and which substantially increased the central government's overall share of revenue. Transfers from the central to provincial governments to bridge this gap have risen substantially since the 1994 tax reform, and now account for nearly one-third of total central government outlays. However, as discussed in detail in the next section, the transfers only imperfectly make up for the gap between expenditure responsibilities and tax revenue resources, which have contributed to substantial disparities in spending capacity on key development needs across provinces.

While revenues and expenditure responsibilities are highly decentralised, the policies that govern them are largely determined by the central government. Sub-national authorities have virtually no discretion over rates applied for the major taxes or the tax bases, and the allocation and much of the regulations governing expenditure are also determined by the central government. Moreover, local government officials are appointed and their performances evaluated by government and Party officials at the national level.

While substantial decentralisation of expenditures is probably inevitable and necessary in a country as large and varied as China, the current system has engendered serious distortions. The most serious problem is the large (negative) gap between available financial resources and expenditure responsibilities/needs that prevails for many sub-national governments. These gaps have encouraged the resort to illicit off-budget spending and borrowing. They are also partly responsible for the relatively low level of overall spending on key development needs such as education and have reduced the efficiency with which such spending is allocated. These issues are discussed further in the next section.

3. Regional fiscal disparities and their implications for China's expenditure policies

The management of public expenditure requires a number of improvements in order to take advantage of the highly decentralised fiscal system in China. This system decentralises spending decisions but gives little freedom for localities to set tax rates in a way that matches revenues with local spending needs. Indeed, tax rates are set almost entirely by central government and so tax yields reflect the marked dispersion of economic activity that exists across provinces. As a result, a strong system of revenue transfers is needed to ensure that low income areas do not have low levels of public spending. A revenue transfer system does exist but has not been able to prevent the emergence of marked variations in public spending across the country. In addition, while the decentralisation of spending decisions might be expected to raise the efficiency of spending by achieving a better tailoring of public goods and services to local needs than could be achieved by a central administration, there are a number of adverse incentives inherent in the institutional system that result in spending not adjusting to local needs. Thus, both the equity and the efficiency of the current fiscal system could be improved. This section examines the types and source of disparities, describes the major forces driving them and attempts to identify measures to reduce disparities and increase efficiency.

3.1. Inequalities in public spending across provinces

There are large differences in economic activity and incomes across the different provinces in China. The interaction between the structure of these incomes and the tax system results in tax yields being even more unequally distributed geographically than income. As a result, the national government has put various mechanisms in place to moderate the differences in tax revenue that would otherwise occur. In 1994, a major change was made to the operation of the sharing agreement. The previous bargaining-based system was ended. In its place, a set of rules was introduced to determine the extent to which the yield from all forms of taxation would be shared between provincial and central governments. Moreover, the responsibility for the collection of certain forms of taxation was transferred from the provincial authorities to the national government. One of the objectives of this reform was to try to ensure that the share of central government in overall tax revenues rose over time, and this has been achieved. While the sharing arrangements between central and provincial governments are well determined, the central government provides only general guidelines as to how tax revenues should be shared within provinces.[14] As a result, provinces have considerable discretion as to whether or how they share taxes.

While revenue-sharing and the complete delegation of some taxes to lower levels of government give stability to revenue, these measures are incapable of generating the required degree of equality in spending. Therefore, a significant redistribution of revenue is made through transfers from central government.[15] The extent of central government transfers to lower levels of government, aside from the tax rebate transfer, has increased markedly since the reform of the revenue-sharing system. Two factors have been behind this growth. First, overall central government revenues have been very buoyant. Secondly, the growth of the tax rebate transfer has been much slower than the growth of GDP. These two movements have made room for a marked increase in all other central government transfers that rose to 4.8% of GDP in 2003 from 1.3% in 1994. As a result, the central government has gained considerably more leverage over provincial budgets, with the share of transfers (excluding the tax rebate component) in provincial revenue rising to just over one-quarter by 2003 from 10% in 1993. The tendency of tax rebate transfers to go to better-off regions is partly offset by transfers to regions with large shares of non-Han population, which are located mainly in poorer western provinces. Overall, there is a slight negative relative relationship between per capita transfers and real income – a relationship that is even more marked when transfers are related to provincial GDP.

As a result of the transfer system, there is markedly less dispersion of public expenditure at the provincial and lower levels of government than of the budgetary revenues of these levels of government. This conclusion holds whether the extent of dispersion is measured by the Theil index or the Gini coefficient (see Table 8.4). Moreover, with the gradual fall of the tax-rebate transfer relative to GDP, there has been little or no increase in expenditure dispersion since 1998, despite an increased extent of revenue dispersion in the same period. Not all inequality has been removed and there is still a positive relationship between income per head and public spending per person (see Figure 8.2). However, the relationship is sufficiently weak that the share of provincial income devoted to public expenditure is higher in low-income provinces than in high-income provinces.

II.8. CHINA'S PUBLIC EXPENDITURE POLICIES

Table 8.4. **Disparities in provincial per capita expenditures revenues and incomes in 1995-2003**

	1995	1996	1997	1998	1999	2000	2001	2002	2003
Total figures									
Theil – expenditure per capita	0.158	0.165	0.174	0.216	0.218	0.190	0.196	0.204	n.a.
Theil – revenue per capita	0.225	0.247	0.251	0.313	0.318	0.295	0.306	0.338	n.a.
Theil – GDP per capita	0.154	0.160	0.159	0.166	0.173	0.157	0.169	0.169	0.168
Gini – expenditure per capita	0.304	0.305	0.307	0.332	0.332	0.310	0.325	0.333	n.a.
Gini – revenue per capita	0.351	0.363	0.362	0.393	0.394	0.382	0.399	0.415	n.a.
Gini – GDP per capita	0.298	0.304	0.302	0.307	0.312	0.300	0.312	0.313	0.314
On-budget figures									
Theil – expenditure per capita	0.192	0.193	0.207	0.204	0.205	0.180	0.197	0.208	0.216
Theil – revenue per capita	0.300	0.311	0.329	0.333	0.348	0.334	0.387	0.409	0.413
Gini – expenditure per capita	0.331	0.326	0.334	0.331	0.331	0.310	0.330	0.338	0.341
Gini – revenue per capita	0.390	0.393	0.400	0.402	0.412	0.406	0.441	0.449	0.452

Note: Total provincial expenditures include reported on-budget and extra-budgetary expenditures, expenditures of social security funds and spending of central government bonds except for 2003, for which extra-budgetary data are not yet available. The payments made to cover the losses of state-owned enterprises have been treated as expenditure in the above data, rather than as negative income as in the official statistics.
Source: OECD calculation.

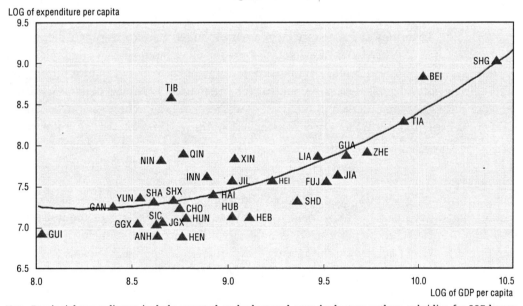

Figure 8.2. **Relation of per capita expenditure and per capita GDP at the provincial level in 2002**
In logarithmic form

Note: Provincial expenditures include reported on-budget and extra-budgetary outlays, subsidies for SOE losses, spending by social security funds and spending financed by central government bonds issued on behalf of local authorities.
Source: Various editions of the *China Statistical Yearbook*.

There are considerable variations in the extent to which different categories of public spending are spatially distributed. Spending on government administration, agriculture and social relief are relatively evenly distributed but capital expenditure per capita is very unevenly distributed (see Table 8.5). For capital investment, per capita outlays are

Table 8.5. **Disparities across provinces in selected categories measured by the Gini and Theil indices in 2002**

	Capital expenditure	Public health	Social relief	Education expenditure	Government administration	Agriculture	Total expenditure
Gini	0.50	0.37	0.28	0.34	0.28	0.26	0.33
Theil	0.48	0.25	0.13	0.25	0.15	0.11	0.20

Source: OECD calculation.

particularly high in a few eastern provinces and in the west where outlays have been boosted by earmarked financing of infrastructure projects under the aegis of the Western Development Programme (*xibu kaifa*) together with central bond financing of infrastructure projects. In central areas, infrastructure spending is very low. Also, a bias towards material investment may be a reflection of the continuation of the non-market orientation of the public sector and could also be related to the incentive system that has been in place to determine the pay and promotion of civil servants. The distribution of health and education spending is only slightly more uneven than that of total outlays but that masks a very uneven distribution of resources within provinces between rural and urban areas in the case of health care and between different levels and types of expenditure in the education sector. The distribution of both the number of and expenditure on teachers in primary and secondary education is quite even. The distribution of capital spending and outlays financed by supplementary taxes and levies, on the other hand, is extremely uneven with remarkably high Theil index of 0.85. Moreover, there are marked inequalities in the provision of higher education across provinces.

Spending disparities at the county level are even larger than at the provincial level. A decomposition of the Theil index of inequality for per capita spending shows that two-thirds of the disparities observed across counties are attributable to within-province differences, with between-province disparities accounting for the remaining third. The largest within-province disparities are observed in the poorest western and the richest eastern provinces, while in central and north-eastern provinces expenditures are more equal in per capita terms (see Figure 8.3). The high level of inequality within richer eastern provinces suggests that some provinces have not followed through the reform of national-provincial fiscal relations with their own reforms. In provinces where within-province income disparities are low, a larger portion of taxes could be shared and be allocated to the county level to provide stable revenue sources for their operations without generating further inequalities in spending. Transfers, on the other hand, should serve the purpose of reducing inequalities, and their size should depend on the extent of disparities. The approach towards the mix of revenue-sharing and transfers varies considerably across provinces. In provinces such as Jiangxi, Hunan, Hainan and Anhui, a high proportion of central government transfers are passed onto counties. Such transfers, coupled with the initially low level of income disparities, allow a relatively high level of revenue-sharing while still achieving an even distribution of expenditure as evidenced by within-province indices of spending inequality of less than 0.1, as measured by the Theil index. However, in a number of cases neither reducing the extent of revenue-sharing nor passing on a large share of central government transfers to counties would be sufficient to reduce spending disparities if initial income disparities are high (as in Shaanxi, Sichuan and Gansu). In these cases, the absolute level of central government transfers appears too low to correct spending disparities.

Figure 8.3. **Disparities in county level per capita expenditure by province 2001, Theil index of inequality**

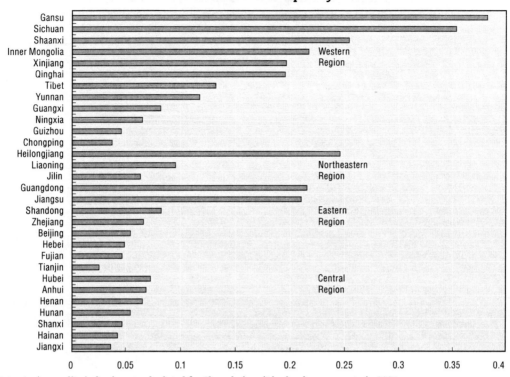

Note: An inequality index is not calculated for Shanghai, as it had only one county in 2001.
Source: All China Database.

3.2. Differences in the absolute level of spending

The positive relationship between spending and income levels, though weak, is sufficient to ensure that there are considerable shortfalls between national average expenditure and actual expenditures per capita in a number of provinces. However, a comparison of the provincial and national averages for per capita expenditure is an inadequate measure of the extent of the shortfall in expenditure because the distribution across provinces of the factors driving different categories of expenditure may differ from the distribution of population (see Figure 8.4).[16] After correcting for the spatial distribution of the factors driving seven categories of expenditure, 16 provinces have below average adjusted spending, with the mean shortfall being nearly 40% of current spending, or 7% of GDP in these provinces. Of the provinces with shortfalls, seven are located in the central region, six in the west and three are eastern provinces. The three largest proportionate shortfalls are exhibited in two central provinces (Henan and Anhui) and a western province (Guizhou). While the authorities have put in place a development programme to aid western regions, as yet the low level of spending in central provinces has not been addressed. Overall, the shortfall in adjusted expenditure in these 16 provinces represents slightly more than 3% of national GDP and 12% of total public spending.

Shortfalls in adjusted expenditure at the county level account for a significant part of the shortfall measured at the provincial level. When county level adjusted expenditure is aggregated to the provincial level, 13 of the 16 provinces with shortfalls still show below average expenditure at the county level (see Figure 8.5). The situation at the county level mirrors that of the province: disparities are large not only in western provinces, but also in

Figure 8.4. **Actual public spending by province relative to adjusted national average spending 2001, % of actual spending**

The adjustment redistributes national average spending in seven categories of outlays according to the spatial distribution of the factors that drive these expenditure categories

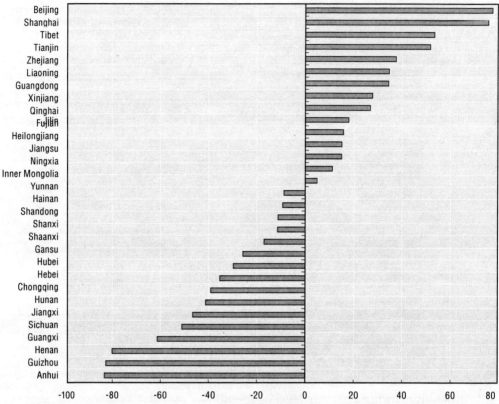

Note: A negative figure indicates that public spending in a given province is below national average spending, allowing for the spatial distribution of the factors that drive spending, such as the number of school-age children for education. A detailed description of the methodology used to calculate adjusted national average spending can be found in OECD (2005a).

Source: OECD estimation.

the central region. The provinces with below average county-level spending are equally distributed between the central and western areas of the country, with only one from the eastern area. Provinces having low within-province disparities in per capita expenditures and large expenditure shortfalls at the county level (such as Henan, Anhui, Chongqing, Hunan, Guizhou, Jiangxi, Shanxi and Hubei) may require greater transfers from the central government in order to boost overall spending in the province. On the other hand in Gansu, Sichuan and Shaanxi, where there are large within-province inequalities in spending but where expenditure shortfalls are low, disparities could be dealt with by, over time, reallocating of resources across counties. In addition, considerable scope for financing redistribution between counties would exist if certain types of expenditure, notably on public administration and capital investment were reduced (see below).

Figure 8.5. **Actual county-level public spending by province relative to adjusted national county-level average spending 2001, % of actual spending**

The adjustment redistributes national average spending in seven categories of outlays according to the spatial distribution of the factors that drive these expenditure categories

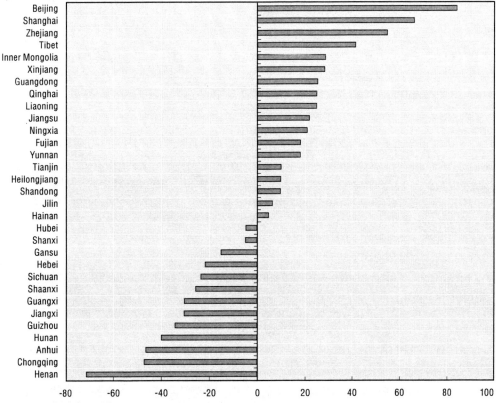

Note: A negative figure indicates that public spending in a given province is below national average spending, allowing for the spatial distribution of the factors that drive spending, such as the number of school-age children for education. A detailed description of the methodology used to calculate this indication can be found in OECD (2005a).
Source: OECD estimation.

3.3. Reforms to reduce spending disparities

Large dispersions of spending at the county level suggest that relations between sub-national governments need to be reformed in order to achieve more uniform spending levels within a province. The first step should be to introduce clear assignments of spending to each level of government. If adhered to, such an allocation would eliminate the tendency of upper-level governments to delegate expenditure mandates downwards and would also overcome the lack of accountability inherent in a system with unclear assignments. At present, there is a wide variation between provinces in the responsibilities and expenditure assignments of different government levels and in the layers of government that deliver goods and services as independent budgeting units. Even within a province, expenditure assignments can differ and even be overlapping as in the case of education and health. When there is downwards delegation of spending mandates without accompanying revenue, incentives are created for local officials to levy unauthorised fees and accumulate illegal debt. If, on the other hand, local authorities do not use such illegal financing methods, they are forced to prioritise spending according to the wishes of the higher authority rather than adjusting expenditure to local needs. In addition, excessive downward delegation results in the provision of similar services by too large a number of authorities. Diseconomies of scale are introduced into the delivery of basic public services as many townships are below the optimal size and as many prefectures have few activities other than administration. Several pilot projects suggest that the prefecture level can successfully be bypassed, though abolishing this level of government may be more difficult in provinces with low population densities and large distances between centres of population.

The structure of public spending at the provincial level also differs markedly from that in OECD member countries. The incentives in place have led to relatively high shares of physical investment and public administration total outlays. In part, the bias towards physical investment may have stemmed from the appraisal system for local officials that bases officials' promotion on the GDP performance of their localities. Many officials have had a demand-side approach to the determination of GDP that considers that outlays on physical investment will boost GDP in the short term during the construction phase and so favour infrastructure investment. Outlays on education or health are also profitable for economic growth but have been neglected in the past. The recent proposal to replace the present GDP-focused appraisal system with a more objective, indicator-based one may eliminate some of these adverse incentives. It is not clear, however, whether it will be sufficiently transparent and clearly tied to public sector outputs, given the large number of indicators used in the system.

China also allocates a much larger total of government expenditure to public administration than do most OECD member countries. At the provincial level, such expenditure is almost 15% of total outlays, rising to 20% at the county level. There are also marked variations geographically. At the township level, while no nationwide data are available, surveys show that a large part of total expenditure is spent on government administration.

The number of levels of government may need to be reviewed following China's decision to markedly reduce the tax receipts of the lowest level of public administration: the township.[17] The rural tax reform will entail the abolition of a number of agricultural-related taxes and the progressive reduction of the agricultural production tax. While the national impact of this change will be small (raising farmers' income by around 3-4% and lowering total tax revenues by 2%) it will have a much larger impact on townships that will lose revenue equal to nearly a half of their own income. In addition, levies and the obligation of farmers to work for the township without pay, when required, will be abolished. As a result, the tax system will become more transparent and revenue collection will become easier. Simultaneously, the central government will assist the townships with paying teachers' salaries, and counties are also expected to increase transfers, but compensation will remain only partial. Given the drop in revenues, township governments will be faced with the need to increase efficiency and reduce employment. That may call into question the need to keep townships as units that supply public services and maintain separate budgetary accounts.

3.4. Implications and policy options

Despite the significant increase in central government transfers to lower levels of government as the result of reforms over the past decade, there still exists considerable geographic inequality in public spending levels. Public expenditure per capita (corrected for the geographic distribution of the factors that drive the demand for spending) is particularly low in a number of low-income central provinces. These areas have been left behind in the drive to increase infrastructure spending in the west and to revitalise the north-east. A substantial increase in central government transfers of around 3% of GDP (around 12% of total central government spending) would be needed to eliminate differences between outlays in the worst-served provinces and the current level of per capita expenditure in the nation as a whole.

Just increasing transfers from the centre to the provinces would be an inadequate response to inequalities in spending across provinces, as most spending inequalities arise from differences within provinces between one county and another. Part of the problem arises from the absence of central control over the fiscal relations between provincial and lower level governments. The central government has set guidelines but they are neither sufficiently specific nor binding to influence behaviour. Arrangements for the sharing of revenues differ considerably across the country, as does the extent of transfer programmes.

In many OECD member countries, it has been argued that matching revenue-raising ability to expenditure is desirable in that it allows local preferences to be better taken into account and the willingness of the population to pay for given service levels to be better tested (Joumard and Kongsrud, 2004). However, there are limits to applying such a policy in China given the political context of limited local accountability. Consequently, more centralised control of spending through a more standardised province/prefecture/county revenue-sharing agreement may be needed. While such a system would give a degree of stability to local revenue sources, it would tend to result in spending inequalities that reflect existing income disparities and so would require the redesign of the intra-provincial system of transfers in a fashion that was more rule-based to overcome defects in the present systems. In any case intra-provincial agreements would need to ensure that lower level authorities have clear responsibilities allocated to them and that there is no overlap of responsibility between authorities. Such a system should also ensure that lower level authorities have sufficient revenue to adequately carry out the tasks assigned to them by higher level authorities – a necessity that has already been recognised in the area of education. In the absence of such a tying of revenue and expenditure tasks, new unfunded mandates are likely to emerge, thus moving local authorities away from locally-decided goals, a result that may lower the efficiency of public spending.

The finance for boosting expenditure in low income areas should not come exclusively from increased transfers from other layers of governments or from higher taxation. There is considerable scope for reducing the large share of total spending allocated to public administration. Several measures could be considered for curbing outlays in this area thereby freeing funds for use in priority areas such as education and health. These could include the merging of localities and the abolition of townships as a separate budgetary unit to take advantage of scale economies, simplifying the administrative system by eliminating prefectures in areas where the distances between the provincial capital and prefectures are relatively short. More generally, the number of administrative staff could be reduced substantially. A more transparent and priority-focused appraisal system for local officials could eliminate incentives to artificially boost demand and output in a given geographic area by increasing physical investment. Thus it is crucial that the current reform of the methods used to determine public service pay and promotions is implemented effectively.

4. Conclusion

China's evolution from a centrally planned to a market-based economy has led to major transformations of its public expenditure policies. Significant progress has been made toward bringing extra-budget accounts onto the main budget, in raising spending on infrastructure to a level more in line with China's development needs, and in improving mechanisms for expenditure budgeting and planning. Nevertheless, significant problems remain. The government remains overly exposed to off-budget activities, notably contingent liabilities, which make public expenditures difficult to rationally plan and control and which impair their accountability and transparency. The allocation of public spending appears out of line with China's development needs and goals in at least two respects: public spending on education, science and health are still low by international standards; and there are large disparities in public spending per capita in these areas among and within provinces. These problems are greatly aggravated by the problems in fiscal relations among levels of government discussed in the last section.

The analysis in this report suggests the following guidelines for further reforms to improve the effectiveness of China's public expenditure policies.

1. Continue efforts to bring expenditures now off budget onto the budget as part of broader efforts to subject all expenditures to more rigorous formulation, implementation, and accountability. Accurate and comprehensive reporting of all government expenditures should be required of all government levels. Over time and as conditions permit it would be desirable to include estimates of tax expenditures and of contingent (and other off-budget liabilities) as part of published budget reports.

2. Improve transparency by reforming accounting systems for expenditures along functional lines, using international standards as a guide, so that amounts spent on key social, development, and strategic needs can be clearly determined and assessed.

3. Improve allocative efficiency of public expenditures by raising spending on education, health, science, and other social/development needs, as a share of overall spending and relative to GDP, to levels in line with China's needs. In particular, public expenditure on education should be raised to 4% of GDP within the next several years, in line with the longer standing official goal. Strong efforts should be made to constrain the growth of spending on public administration by improving efficiency and eliminating waste. Consideration might also be given to simplifying the structure of the public administration system, for example by combining administrative units that are of sub-optimal scale, or eliminating the prefecture government level.

4. Reform fiscal relations between central and sub-national governments to bring expenditure responsibilities at each level of government into line with financial resources. Central government mandates that entail additional spending by sub-national governments should be explicitly accounted for in budget statements and wherever possible accompanied by transfers or other additional revenue. Among other specific reforms that might be considered are: the establishment of a graduated system of tax sharing under which poorer provinces would receive a higher portion of shared revenues than more wealthy provinces; and increases in transfers to poorer provinces (only) that are able to improve their tax collection.

5. Improve accountability of sub-national governments by establishing more explicit criteria for performance in key areas such as education. These should include not only aggregate targets but also, for higher levels of government, indicators of uniformity of

accomplishment across lower levels for which they are responsible. Recent initiatives from the central government to broaden criteria for evaluation of provincial and lower-level government officials to include indicators of progress toward key social goals are a useful step in this direction. Consideration might also be given to allowing local governments some greater discretion over the rates and other provisions of certain taxes, as part of a broader effort to improve incentives to improve the social pay-off to public expenditures by reducing the tendency to spend up to the amount of revenue gained. Mechanisms to include "bottom up" assessments by local bodies in the evaluation of local officials should be developed further.

Notes

1. This chapter was written by Margit Molnar and Charles Pigott, Non-member Economies Division, Economics Department, OECD.

2. The material here is based on a more detailed analysis of these issues in OECD (2005). The third broad set of issues concerning public expenditure policies (see Van den Noord, 2000), namely the technical efficiency with which they are planned, formulated and carried out, are not examined here. Some of these issues, notably those concerning China's budgeting mechanisms, are treated in Chapter 7.

3. Admittedly, care needs to be taken in comparing Chinese and OECD on-budget expenditure figures. In the OECD these typically cover all outlays of the central, state and local governments including social security (see www.oecd.org/eco/sources-and-methods), a significant portion of which are excluded from the on-budget figures in China.

4. In addition, local governments, although not legally permitted to borrow to cover their expenditures, have incurred substantial illicit debt to financial institutions, non-financial businesses and individuals. The amount of this debt that will ultimately have to be assumed by local or central governments is unclear, especially the portion owed to non-financial entities and individuals.

5. These other expenditures were about 25% of on-budget operating expenses in 2001. The estimates include amounts spent on this category in the off-budget funds. For a more detailed discussion see OECD, 2005a.

6. See "Technology Challenges for China's Industries", Chapter 6 of *China in the World Economy* (OECD, 2002).

7. The World Bank recommended an increase equivalent to 1% of GDP in China's infrastructure spending in its 1997 report, *China 2020*. Spending now exceeds the target suggested in that report.

8. It should be noted, however, that China's expenditure on administration as percentage of GDP does not appear to be high compared to OECD member countries (see OECD, 2005b).

9. This decline reflected the shrinking importance of SOEs – the main tax base – in the overall economy and their declining profitability, along with difficulties in collecting taxes due from non-state enterprises.

10. Government outlays to cover social security deficits could rise significantly as older SOE workers with generous pension rights retire and to the extent that local governments continue to be unable to fully finance obligations they are theoretically responsible for.

11. Recent statements by government officials indicate that authorities plan to increase the portion of total expenditure going to social security by more than one-half (from around 10-11% now to 17%), although the time horizon is not clear (*People's Daily*, 22 September 2004).

12. Various estimates suggest that the potential increase in public debt arising from resolution of non-performing loans (NPL), including debt now with the four bank asset management companies and NPL of the rural credit co-operatives is on the order of 20-40% of GDP. At the current interest rates on government debt, this implies a debt-service cost of 1-2% of GDP, and somewhat higher if this rate, which is now quite low, were to rise. See *China in the World Economy*, Chapter 14, on "Developing the Financial System", and Chapter 22 on "Macroeconomic Policy Priorities", Table 22.5, for estimates of the potential NPL burden and rough simulations of the resulting increase in government debt service.

13. Sub-national governments accounted for 76% of the total of on-budget, extra-budget and social security funds spending in 2002.
14. Lou, J. (2002) provides a description of these guidelines.
15. Certain transfer components such as minority transfers or the recent education transfer by the central government to poor counties reach directly the sub-provincial level, but most transfers are allocated by the province.
16. Capital spending was deducted for lack of details of its composition. A major caveat to this estimation is the assumption that the national allocation of spending across categories is unchanged. Total national expenditure was made equal to total expenditure needed, i.e. shortfalls and surpluses sum up to zero.
17. In general, townships are the lowest level with independent budgets in the government administration, though in a number of cases townships do not have independent budgets and are directly financed from the budget of the county above.

Bibliography

Asian Development Bank (2004), *To Serve and to Preserve – Improving Public Administration in a Competitive World*, Asian Development Bank, Manila.

Joumard, Isabelle and Per Mathis Kongsrud (2003), "Fiscal Relations across Government Levels", *Economics Department Working Paper No. 375*, OECD, Paris.

Lou, Jiwei (ed.) (2002), *Zhongguo Zhengfu Yusuan: Zhidu, Guanli Yu Anli*, (in Chinese) (*Chinese Government Budgeting: Structure, Management and Practise*), Zhongguo Caizheng Jingji Chubanshe, Beijing.

Ma, Jun (2000), "Off-budgetary Activities of China Governments Since Economic Reform", paper presented at Association for Budgeting and Financial Management 12th Annual Conference, Kansas City, 7 October 2000.

OECD (2002), *China in the World Economy – The Domestic Policy Challenges*, OECD, Paris.

OECD (2005a), *China's Public Expenditure Policies: An Analysis of Selected Issues*, OECD, Paris, forthcoming.

OECD (2005b), *Economic Survey of China*, OECD, Paris, forthcoming.

Qiao, Baoyun, J. Martinez-Vazquez and Y. Xu (2003), "The Tradeoff between Growth and Equity in Decentralisation Policy: China's Experience", *Department of Economics Working Paper*, Andrew Young School of Policy Studies, Georgia State University, Atlanta.

Van den Noord, Paul (2000), "Surveillance of Public Expenditure: A Framework for EDRC Reviews", ECO/CPE/WP1(2000)15.

Wang, Shaoguang (2001), "For National Unity: The Political Logic of Fiscal Transfer in China", *Department of Government and Public Administration Working Paper*, The Chinese University of Hong Kong, Hong Kong, China.

Wong, Christine (2001), "Fiscal Decentralisation in China: the Problematic Outcomes of Unplanned Changes in Transition toward a Market Economy", paper presented at Asian Development Forum, Bangkok.

Wong, Christine (2005), "Decentralisation and Governance in China: Managing across Levels of Government", paper prepared for the OECD, first draft, 3 April 2005.

World Bank (2000), "China: Managing Public Expenditures for Better Results", Country Economic Memorandum, Washington.

World Bank (1997), *China 2020*, World Bank, Washington.

Zhang, Gang (2002), "Technology Challenges for China's Industries", in OECD (2002), *China in the World Economy*, OECD, Paris.

Zhang, Xiaobo and R. Kanbur (2003), "Spatial Inequality in Education and Health Care in China", *CEPR Discussion paper Series No. 4136*.

PART III

Institutional Framework for Market Forces

PART III

Chapter 9

Regulatory Management and Reform in China

Table of Contents

Summary 279

Regulatory Management and Reform in China 280

1. Introduction 280
2. Potential benefits and challenges of regulatory reform in China 281
3. Recent efforts to improve regulatory quality 282
   - 3.1. Moving toward the rule of law 282
   - 3.2. The law-making process is becoming gradually more standardized 283
4. Regulatory transparency and accessibility 284
   - 4.1. WTO requirements as a key driver for improving regulatory quality 284
5. Public consultation 286
6. Assessing market impacts of regulations 287
   - 6.1. Assessment of regulatory impact in China 289
7. Building regulatory institutions 290
   - 7.1. SCOLA assumes roles similar to central regulatory reform offices in many OECD member countries 291
   - 7.2. Network industries 291
   - 7.3. Drawing on OECD experience 293
8. Reform of the administrative approval system 293
9. Reform of licensing practices and procedures 295
10. Improving the application and enforcement of regulations 296
11. Conclusions 298

Notes 299
Bibliography 300

List of boxes

- 9.1. Definitions 281
- 9.2. The OECD Principles on Regulatory Reform 283
- 9.3. Recent initiatives to improve regulatory quality 284
- 9.4. The law-making process in China at a glance (national level) 285
- 9.5. The OECD Reference Checklist for Regulatory Decision-making 288
- 9.6. Transitional and structural reasons for inadequate enforcement in China 297
- 9.7. Guiding principles for public administration in accordance with the law in China 298

List of figures

- 9.1. Phases of regulatory reform 289

Summary

China's potential benefits from regulatory reform are significant, as is the potential downside if a number of serious regulatory problems are not addressed. This chapter reviews China's recent efforts to improve regulatory capacities and to build a regulatory environment on the basis of the rule of law.

China has taken a series of steps to construct a framework of credible rules, legal systems, procedures and institutions needed for a market economy. Reforms to introduce and consolidate the rule of law, which were started in the late 1970s, have been accelerated and broadened since the late 1990s. Improving regulatory quality and promoting administrative and regulatory practices within the rule of law continues to be a high priority of the Chinese Government.

China is sustaining momentum in implementing these objectives. Recent initiatives, such as the reform of China's administrative approval system, which began in 2001, may mark a fundamental change in China's regulatory practices. These reforms have established explicit criteria and principles for regulatory interventions. In principle, they will transform previous practices based on *ex ante* licensing of most business activities into a system based on *ex post* control. Although reform is still at an early stage, China is also taking steps to standardize and improve regulatory consultation and transparency mechanisms, and to introduce assessments of the economic impacts of proposed regulation. To avoid dangerous market failures in the utility sectors, which are gradually beginning to operate under market conditions, China has moved toward establishing more autonomous regulators in order to prevent capture by vested interests and to avoid bias in decision-making.

A number of severe regulatory problems continue to weaken or threaten China's economic performance, however. China suffers high costs due to poor regulatory practices: insufficient law enforcement, over-regulation, under-regulation, inefficient and outdated regulation, and the abuse of discretionary regulatory powers. Moreover, co-ordination between levels of government in a context of significant regulatory powers delegated to provinces and regions constitute a separate and equally important challenge. Continued efforts to promote regulatory quality and reform are needed to address these challenges.

The Chinese Government realizes this. Commitments to improve regulatory quality and enforcement in accordance with the rule of law have been supported by a series of concrete measures. World Trade Organization (WTO) requirements have been an important driver behind improvements, but there is still reason to be cautious about their impact in the absence of further reforms. Among the most pertinent challenges is the excessive discretion accorded to civil servants in interpreting, issuing and implementing regulations, as well as the lack of appropriate resources and independence of the judiciary. Building appropriate capacities to develop and co-ordinate new regulations is another challenge, involving the development of institutions, procedures and criteria to prepare high-quality regulation.

Regulatory Management and Reform in China[1]

1. Introduction

China has taken a series of steps to construct a framework of credible rules, legal systems, procedures and institutions needed for a market economy. Reforms to introduce and consolidate the rule of law were started in the late 1970s and have been accelerated and broadened since the late 1990s. Improving regulatory quality and promoting administrative and regulatory practices within the rule of law continues to be a high priority of the Chinese Government.

China is rapidly moving forward in pursuit of these objectives. Recent initiatives, such as the reform of China's administrative approval system which began in 2001, may mark a fundamental change in China's regulatory practices. These reforms have established explicit criteria and principles for regulatory interventions. In principle, they will reverse previous practices based on *ex ante* licensing of most business activities into a system based on *ex post* control. Although reform is still at an early stage, China is taking steps to standardize and improve regulatory consultation and transparency mechanisms, and to introduce assessments of the economic impacts of proposed regulation. To avoid dangerous market failures in the utility sectors, which are gradually beginning to operate under market conditions, China has moved toward establishing more autonomous regulators. This also aims at preventing capture by vested interests and at avoiding bias in decision-making.

A number of severe regulatory problems continue to weaken or threaten China's economic performance, however. China suffers high costs due to poor regulatory practices: insufficient law enforcement, over-regulation, under-regulation, inefficient and outdated regulation, regulation with department interest orientation and the abuse of discretionary regulatory powers. Moreover, co-ordination between levels of government in a context of significant regulatory powers delegated to provinces and regions constitute a separate and equally important challenge. Continued efforts to promote regulatory quality and reform are needed to address these challenges.

The Chinese Government realizes this. Commitments to improve regulatory quality and enforcement in accordance with the rule of law have been supported by a series of concrete measures. Although the nature, pace and effect of regulatory and administrative reforms will continue to be shaped mainly by China's particular circumstances, the convergence with and application of OECD best practices in many areas is noteworthy.

The chapter is organised as follows: After having defined basic terms (see Box 9.1), Section 2 summarizes some of the benefits and major challenges of regulatory reform in China, while Section 3 provides an overview of some the recent initiatives to improve regulatory quality. The seven following sections look at efforts to improve specific regulatory practices, tools and institutions. Section 11 concludes.

Box 9.1. **Definitions**

Regulation refers to the diverse set of instruments by which governments set requirements on enterprises and citizens. Regulations fall into three categories: economic regulations intervene directly in market decisions such as pricing, competition, market entry or exit; social regulations protect public interests such as health, safety, the environment and social cohesion; and administrative regulations are paperwork and administrative formalities through which governments collect information, among other things, to monitor regulatory compliance and to inform other policy decisions.

Regulatory tools and institutions refer to the mechanisms by which governments promote regulatory quality, consistent with their underlying regulatory policies. Examples of regulatory tools include Regulatory Impact Analysis (RIA), consultation and communication mechanisms, simplification measures such as time-limits for decision-making, sun-setting and automatic review clauses. Regulatory institutions include central regulatory quality oversight units, external committees (established by government with the purpose to promote, propose or implement various regulatory quality measures) and independent regulators.

Regulatory policies are policies designed to maximize the efficiency, effectiveness, transparency and accountability of regulations based on an integrated and rational approach to the application of regulatory tools and institutions. Regulatory policies focus on creating the optimal framework for the process of producing and reviewing regulations, rather than on the material content of regulations *per se*.

Regulatory quality refers to the extent to which a regulatory system pursues its underlying objectives. These objectives involve the specific policy objectives which the regulatory tool is being employed to pursue and the efficiency with which those objectives are achieved, as well as governance-based objectives including transparency and accountability. To decide whether a system of regulation is of high quality, or in need of reform, it is necessary to be clear about the benchmarks that are relevant in such an evaluation. The OECD's Reference Checklist for Regulatory Decision-Making sets out 10 general criteria and principles for regulatory quality, which have been widely applied by OECD member countries in designing and implementing regulatory procedures (see Box 9.5).

2. Potential benefits and challenges of regulatory reform in China

Experience from OECD member countries shows that a comprehensive approach to regulatory reform can boost consumer benefits, reduce business burdens, improve competitiveness of industries and reduce vulnerability to external shocks, while maintaining and increasing high levels of regulatory protection in areas such as health and safety (OECD, 1997; OECD, 2002b).

An efficient and market-oriented regulatory environment can help China create the incentives in which trade, investment liberalisation and good governance will support longer term growth. Regulatory reform can help China meet its legal WTO obligations by removing barriers to trade and investment; by improving transparency, neutrality and due process; and by building new institutions and practices expected by international norms, such as autonomous regulators in utility sectors. In a wider sense, regulatory reform should be seen as a proactive strategy that complements trade and investment liberalization in boosting potential growth in China. As subsidies and monopolies for state-owned enterprises are eliminated, regulatory reform is also necessary as a defence against pressures on regulators to increase protection for incumbent firms.

However, China is facing a number of specific regulatory problems, which could undermine sustainable economic performance:

- **regulatory risks** are high, reducing investment and competition by increasing the cost of capital;
- **regulatory transactions costs** are high due to an overly-complex, multi-layered, often arbitrary and interventionist regulatory environment that is vulnerable to corruption;
- **regulatory barriers to market entry and competition** in many sectors are high. In other areas, regulation distorts incentives and misallocates resources;
- **under-regulation:** China suffers in many sectors from too little regulation, poor enforcement, and under-institutionalization. Insufficient regulatory safeguards reduce consumer and investor confidence in markets;
- **checks and balances,** such as an effective judiciary to ensure application of the rule of law and efficient dispute resolution procedures between the state and market entities, are weak. This reduces the capacity of outsiders to challenge market insiders;
- **infrastructure bottlenecks** raise production costs throughout the economy, partly due to the lack of market-oriented regulatory regimes.

There is no universal model for the right regulatory system. Appropriate solutions must be designed to fit both the specific circumstances of a country's values and institutions, and its stage of economic development. There is little doubt that the nature, pace and effect of regulatory and administrative reforms have been, and will continue to be, shaped mainly by China's particular circumstances.

On the other hand, international experiences and expectations for high-quality regulatory regimes can be a valuable source of information, not least given the emerging convergence and consensus on a range of regulatory quality principles. Moreover, since China is increasingly operating in the global economy under its WTO obligations and is itself evolving into a market economy, international experiences may serve as targets and benchmarks for reforms. Box 9.2 summarizes the OECD Principles of Regulatory Reform.

3. Recent efforts to improve regulatory quality

3.1. Moving toward the rule of law

The principal elements of a rule of law system include meaningful limits on the arbitrary exercise of state power, predictable and equal application of the law, transparency in the law-making process and an independent judiciary. China has made progress in building a legal infrastructure and has taken steps to provide checks on state actors and improve transparency. The Chinese Government has made the judiciary a primary focus of its legal reform effort.

In 1999, the Chinese Constitution was amended to emphasize the concept of rule of law. This is widely recognized as a change of significant symbolic importance. Subsequent laws such as the Administrative Litigation Law, the State Compensation Law, the Legislation Law and the Administrative Licensing Law have demonstrated the priority and importance of implementing these revisions into real-world effects. In 2004, the Constitution was amended again, with the adoption of explicit rules to protect private

> Box 9.2. **The OECD Principles on Regulatory Reform**
>
> - Adopt at the political level broad programmes of regulatory reform that establish clear objectives and frameworks for implementation.
> - Review regulations systematically to ensure that they continue to meet their intended objectives efficiently and effectively.
> - Ensure that regulations and regulatory processes are transparent, non-discriminatory and efficiently applied.
> - Review and strengthen where necessary the scope, effectiveness and enforcement of competition policy.
> - Reform economic regulations in all sectors to stimulate competition, and eliminate them except where clear evidence demonstrates that they are the best way to serve broad public interests.
> - Eliminate unnecessary regulatory barriers to trade and investment by enhancing implementation of international agreements and strengthening international principles.
> - Identify important links with other policy objectives and develop policies to achieve those objectives in ways that support reform.
>
> *Source:* OECD (1997), *Report on Regulatory Reform*, OECD, Paris.

property rights, and in May 2004 the State Council issued a detailed guideline – the *Guideline for Advancing Administration in Accordance with the Laws* – intended to provide a framework and roadmap for the next decade's efforts to build a rule of law-based society.

However, legal restraints on the arbitrary exercise of government power often remain weak in practice, due to various context-specific factors such as shortcomings in the legislative system, weak courts, poorly trained judges and lawyers, corruption, a low level of legal consciousness among government officials and the citizenry, and the fragmentation and overlapping of authority that have resulted from the transition to a more market-oriented economy. Therefore, although significant initiatives have been launched, the sheer size of the challenge will make the change to a rule of law based regulatory regime incremental.[2]

3.2. The law-making process is becoming gradually more standardized

As part of the Chinese Government's efforts to consolidate the rule of law, a range of laws, regulations and guidelines have been enacted to make the law-making process more standardized, transparent and coherent (see Box 9.3). The 2000 Legislation Law and procedural rules for administrative regulations effective from 2002 are among the most important initiatives.

The Legislation Law is intended to regulate China's law-making process (see Box 9.4) and to more clearly define the boundaries of legislative power in China. The Law clarifies that only the National People's Congress (NPC) and in some cases its Standing Committee can pass primary legislation.[3] The State Council, government ministries and commissions, and the People's Congress at local level can pass administrative regulations or local laws accordingly. The Legislation Law also provides more concrete frameworks for the State Council's rule-making power by defining relevant authorities, procedures and interpretations on legislative affairs concerning laws, administrative ordinances, regulations and notices at various levels of government.

> **Box 9.3. Recent initiatives to improve regulatory quality**
>
> Administrative Litigation Law (1989).
>
> State Compensation Law (1994).
>
> Administrative Penalty Law (1996).
>
> Administrative Supervision Law (1997).
>
> Amendment of the Constitution to emphasize the concept of rule according to law (1999).
>
> Resolution on Advancing Administration in Accordance with the Law (1999).
>
> Legislation Law (2000).
>
> Resolution on Rectifying and Standardizing the Market Economy Order (2001).
>
> Procedural Rules for the Enactment of Administrative Regulations (2001).
>
> Procedural Rules for the Enactment of Regulatory Rules (2001).
>
> Administrative Licensing Law (2003).
>
> Amendment of Constitution adopting explicit rules to protect private property rights (2004).
>
> Outline for Advancing Administration in Accordance with the Law (2004).*
>
> * The guidelines are a follow-up to the State Council's 1999 resolution to promote administration in accordance with the law.

The *Procedural Rules for the Enactment of Administrative Regulations* set out rules for the drafting and publication of administrative regulations and departmental rules. Under the new rules, the creation of administrative regulations must be subject to a series of preparatory stages intended to allow for better scrutiny and transparency.

4. Regulatory transparency and accessibility

Transparency is essential for regulatory quality. In an operational sense, transparency is the capacity of regulated entities to express views on, identify and understand their obligations under the rule of law. Transparency is an essential part of all phases of the regulatory process – from the initial formulation of regulatory proposals to the development of draft regulations, through to implementation, enforcement, review and reform, as well as the overall management of the regulatory system.

China has been making gradual progress in improving regulatory transparency and accessibility, driven by strong political commitments and WTO requirements, as well as by increasing demands from the public. China's accession to WTO and the implementation of the obligation of notification under the WTO agreements gave impetus to improve regulatory transparency of government bodies. E-government initiatives (see Chapter 4) have also contributed to make the regulatory process of ministries more transparent. However, significant results seem to be hampered by a number of factors, including the absence of an overall strategy to implement the WTO transparency obligations.

4.1. WTO requirements as a key driver for improving regulatory quality

In the WTO process, China has made extensive commitments to improve transparency measures as well as to establish judicial review mechanisms for administrative actions relating to trade matters.[4] Increasing awareness of the importance of WTO compliance has served as the motivation for a number of reform efforts by national and local government

> Box 9.4. **The law-making process in China at a glance (national level)**
>
> At the beginning of each year, the State Council issues a notice on legislation planning, outlining the tasks for issuing or revising laws or administrative rules. It then delegates the drafting of the administrative regulations to one of its functional departments or its legal affairs department (the State Council's Office for Legislation Affairs, SCOLA).
>
> The responsible ministries or commissions usually carry out the preparatory work. In the course of the drafting, the responsible department can solicit opinions and views from relevant government departments and the general public. Such solicitation will be conducted through seminars, expert meetings, hearings and other similar forums.
>
> After the drafts are prepared, they will be sent to SCOLA for review and examination. The review process will in particular aim to resolve whether the proposed administrative regulations are in conformity with the Constitution and the laws of the state. SCOLA also reviews whether relevant parties have been consulted on the draft and may circulate it among relevant government ministries for additional comments. Where the administrative regulations are of general importance, the State Council will publish the draft for public opinion before it finally adopts the regulations.
>
> Following co-ordination and consultation between ministries, the draft laws are submitted by the State Council (formally vetted by SCOLA) to the National People Congress (NPC) for reading and approval.
>
> Within the NPC, the relevant parties include the Special Committee, the Legal Committee and an administrative body of the Standing Committee. There are usually closed door meetings with the committee members, or relevant experts from outside the drafting group may be called upon to comment on matters considered relevant to the legislation. The NPC approves or rejects the law, usually through a voting procedure with the general meetings of the Standing members.
>
> For **administrative rules and regulations**, drafts are reviewed by the Standing Committee of the State Council and approved by the State Council. The administrative regulations are published after approval and signature by the Prime Minister. They are effective 30 days after publication unless otherwise stated. Administrative regulations are required to be filed with the Standing Committee of the NPC for record.
>
> **Departmental rules and administrative notices or guidance** (*xingzheng guizhang*) can be issued by ministries, commissions, the People's Bank of China, the Bureau of Auditing and other regulatory agencies directly under the State Council. While these rules are not "law" *per se*, they provide administrative and regulatory guidance on specific areas of the administration. Departmental rules must undergo a drafting process similar to administrative rules and regulations. Departmental rules enacted in violation of these rules are invalid.

bodies throughout China. China's transparency commitments under the WTO have also been cited as justification for launching other types of reform.

Many observers have noted that the Chinese Government is demonstrating a serious commitment to meeting its WTO obligations. Some observers note that there have been significant changes in regulatory frameworks and practices as China has prepared to enter into the WTO, and that more can be expected.

More government bodies have made their laws and regulations available to the public through publication in gazettes and on Web sites. Following the integration of a number of trade functions with the Ministry of Commerce (MOFCOM), transparency and accessibility to trade measures may be improved, as MOFCOM will publish a single gazette compiling Chinese trade measures that were once published in the gazettes of several different government agencies. MOFCOM is also the sole channel to transfer notifications of domestic regulations related to trade initiated by different government bodies to the WTO. While publication of enacted laws and regulations has become more regular, no uniform procedure yet exists for making draft legislation available for comment before implementation.

The full application of the transparency provisions under the WTO Agreement on Technical Barriers to Trade (TBT) and the WTO Agreement on the Application of Sanitary and Phytosanitary (SPS) Measures can serve as an example for improved regulatory quality. The National WTO/TBT Enquiry Point and the National WTO/SPS Enquiry Point, established within the General Administration of Quality Supervision, Inspection and Quarantine (AQSIQ) are in charge of notifying trade-related technical measures proposed by any government body via MOFCOM. From the accession to WTO until the end of 2004, 77 TBT notifications and 87 SPS notifications were made.

Despite positive developments, there is reason to be cautious about the immediate impact of WTO obligations in the absence of further reforms. Trade partners have complained that compliance with WTO commitments have been limited in scope, uneven and incomplete, in particular due to localism. United States Congressional analysts have argued that China's compliance with its WTO obligations has been "hampered by resistance to reforms by central and local government officials seeking to protect or promote industries under their jurisdiction, government corruption, and lack of resources devoted by the central government to ensure that WTO reforms are carried out in a uniform and consistent manner".[5]

5. Public consultation

Public consultation is a vital support for analytically based decision-making, since it is not only a cost-effective source of data but also provides information on issues such as the acceptability of different policies, which can be essential in determining their practicability and designing appropriate compliance and enforcement strategies.

Traditionally, the concept of open access to government legal drafts has not been widely accepted by the Chinese administration. Access has been limited to special interests with good contacts inside the administration. Consultation – if carried out at all – has occurred too late in the policy process to assess market impacts, alternative approaches and the need for regulation. This increases market uncertainties and the costs of mistakes.

Sometimes, consultations are external. China's legal framework for new forms of public consultation is slowly developing, most notably since the Law on Legislation of 2000. An implementing by-law promulgated in November 2001 and enacted in 2002 – Procedural Rules for the Enactment of Regulatory Rules – clarifies that during the process of designing regulations, relevant government organisations and the relevant public should be consulted through workshops, meetings, or other forums. The Legislation Law also permits the NPC and its Standing Committee to seek outside opinions on its legislation. The NPC increasingly relies on scholars, private-sector lawyers and other outside experts during the legislative process.

Despite these formal changes, public participation in the regulatory process remains limited. The current framework and practices for regulatory consultations are often not providing business and citizens with a *de facto* possibility to effect change. This is due in part to the design of the consultation procedure. It does not set standards for the public consultation process or the involvement of major affected interests, nor for the time period of consultation and treatment of comments from the public. It does not set sanctions or remedies for failure to consult, nor does it establish any oversight of compliance. Another reason for the limited participation in consultation mechanisms may be the need for stakeholders to familiarize themselves with the consultation procedures. Moreover, capacities for making consultation documents physically available and accessible to businesses may also play a role.

In 2002, the OECD recommended that China should move toward more standardized consultation procedures that are more open and systematic (OECD, 2002a, p. 373). Given the need for a flexible approach and taking into account that regulatory issues differ in impact and importance, a consultation system with (legally defined) minimum standards has several advantages. First, minimum standards provide clear benchmarks to all parties as to whether consultation has been properly undertaken, thus protecting all interests. Second, consistent procedures enhance participation by a wider variety of stakeholders. Because the procedures are more widely understood, opportunities for input are less likely to be missed. Third, adopting a consistent process permits better co-ordination for regulatory initiatives across policy areas. Where potentially important stakeholders are known to be harder to reach or less able to participate, specific efforts may be required to actively seek and ensure their input.

6. Assessing market impacts of regulations

Regulatory Impact Analysis (RIA) is perhaps the most important regulatory tool available to governments, as its aim is to ensure that the most efficient and effective regulatory options are chosen. It has been the most valuable tool to improve regulatory quality in OECD member countries, and may be equally useful in transition and developing countries. RIA is a decision tool, a method of: i) systematically and consistently examining selected potential impacts arising from government action; and of ii) communicating the information to decision-makers. Most of the *1995 OECD Reference Checklist* relates to RIA good practice (see Box 9.5), and the OECD *Report on Regulatory Reform* (1997) recommended that governments "integrate regulatory impact analysis into the development, review, and reform of regulations".

Policy makers in most OECD member countries and an increasing number of other countries use RIA to measure the benefits, costs and risks of public laws and regulations on consumers and the economy. RIA allows them to assess economic and social trade-offs and consider alternatives to proposed regulations. RIA can be incorporated in the process for developing proposed rules and can also be used by the government to assess existing legislation and regulations.

Emerging evidence suggests that RIA is also a valuable tool in developing and transition countries.[6] RIA can strengthen the transparency, accountability and positive economic impact of regulatory decision-making. Introducing a RIA system takes time and involves learning by mistakes. However although the design and processes are not first-best, once introduced, RIA may also have a "self-correcting" quality effect by making the reasoning behind public decisions clear and public. As for other regulatory tools and institutions, RIA is not a "one-size fits all" tool and must be introduced or adapted in an appropriate manner to the government's capacities and sequenced to the current stage of a country's regulatory reform activities.

Box 9.5. **The OECD Reference Checklist for Regulatory Decision-making**

The checklist reflects principles of good decision-making that are used in OECD member countries to improve the effectiveness and efficiency of government regulation. In many OECD member countries, RIA guidelines require regulators to address all or most of the Checklist's 10 questions:

1. Is the problem correctly defined?

The problem to be solved should be precisely stated, giving evidence of its nature and magnitude, and explaining why it has arisen (identifying the incentives of affected entities).

2. Is government action justified?

Government intervention should be based on explicit evidence that government action is justified, given the nature of the problem, the likely benefits and costs of action (based on a realistic assessment of government effectiveness), and alternative mechanisms for addressing the problem.

3. Is regulation the best form of government action?

Regulators should carry out, early in the regulatory process, an informed comparison of a variety of regulatory and non-regulatory policy instruments, considering relevant issues such as costs, benefits, distributional effects and administrative requirements.

4. Is there a legal basis for regulation?

Regulatory processes should be structured so that all regulatory decisions rigorously respect the rule of law; that is, responsibility should be explicit for ensuring that all regulations are authorized by higher-level regulations and consistent with treaty obligations, and comply with relevant legal principles such as certainty, proportionality and applicable procedural requirements.

5. What is the appropriate level (or levels) of government for this action?

Regulators should choose the most appropriate level of government to take action, or if multiple levels are involved, should design effective systems of co-ordination between levels of government.

6. Do the benefits of regulation justify the costs?

Regulators should estimate the total expected costs and benefits of each regulatory proposal and of feasible alternatives, and should make the estimates available in accessible format to decision-makers. The cost of government action should be justified by its benefits before action is taken.

7. Is the distribution of effects across society transparent?

To the extent that distributive and equity values are affected by government intervention, regulators should make transparent the distribution of regulatory costs and benefits across social groups.

8. Is the regulation clear, consistent, comprehensible and accessible to users?

Regulators should assess whether rules will be understood by likely users, and to that end they should take steps to ensure that the text and structure of rules are as clear as possible.

Box 9.5. **The OECD Reference Checklist for Regulatory Decision-making** *(cont.)*

9. Have all interested parties had the opportunity to present their views?

Regulations should be developed in an open and transparent fashion, with appropriate procedures for effective and timely input from interested parties such as affected businesses and trade unions, other interest groups, or other levels of government.

10. How will compliance be achieved?

Regulators should assess the incentives and institutions through which the regulation will take effect, and should design responsive implementation strategies that make the best use of them.

The *1997 OECD Report on Regulatory Reform* suggests that regulatory reform comes in three phases, with RIA arriving in the middle phase. The first is primarily deregulatory with a focus on eliminating regulations that impede competition and trade, reducing the number, burdens and costs of regulations. The second phase – here labelled regulatory quality improvement – focuses on improving the regulatory processes, including the use of RIA. The third phase takes a long-term systemic focus, concerned with institutions and performance (*cf.* Figure 9.1).

Figure 9.1. **Phases of regulatory reform**

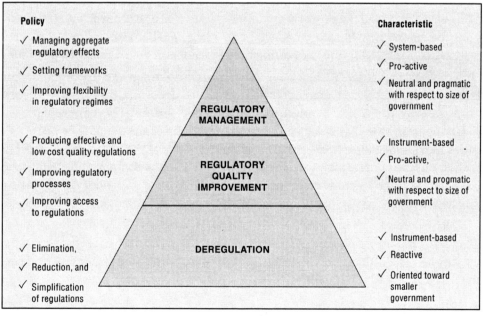

Source: Adapted from OECD (1997).

6.1. *Assessment of regulatory impact in China*

The capacity to assess market impacts is particularly important in China. In the current transition phase, when market needs are changing quickly, the risk of making bad regulatory decisions is high.

Several mechanisms already exist through which potential regulatory impacts are assessed on an *ad hoc* basis. The National Peoples' Congress evaluates the quality of proposed laws, mostly through the debates of its relevant committees. Independent economists and analysts often write papers and reports for the State Council on new proposals for regulations. The State Council may, for example, organise investigating teams to assess reforms, as was done for the banking system. The practice of allowing local governments to draft and test regulations at local levels, and to report their results to the central government, is a form of market testing that can reduce the risks of failure later. For example, the reform of China's Company Law began with pilot projects at local levels. Based on their successes, local regulations were published and revised at the ministry level and extended to national law.

The Chinese Government seems to acknowledge the potential benefits of a more systematic approach to RIA and to incorporate those assessments into public consultation procedures, while also recognizing the need to take a gradual approach as regulatory capacities develop.

The State Council has endorsed basic principles supporting evidence-based assessments of draft regulation. In the State Council's *Outline for Advancing Administration in Accordance with Laws* published in May 2004, government agencies are encouraged "to actively explore the using of cost-benefit analysis in administrative legislation, especially in making laws and regulations for economic affairs. Government's legislation has to take into account not only the cost of the rule-making process, but also the enforcement costs and social cost of the rules to be implemented".[7]

These commitments should be followed up by training, guidance and an appropriate targeting of RIA efforts. If not properly organised, sequenced and scoped, RIA requirements may only be complied with as a bureaucratic formality at the very end of the regulatory process, instead of framing and supporting the regulatory process as early as possible.

After accession to the WTO, a new mechanism of consultation and co-ordination, called "inter-ministry co-presence conference", was introduced. Presently, three such conferences are approved by the State Council. In July 2003, 17 ministries, commissions and administrations organised a "National Inter-ministry Co-presence Conference on Technical Measures" (TBT and SPS) to Trade. AQSIQ was the convener of the co-presence conference. From then on, the conference met, albeit irregularly, to consult important matters with common interests and to co-ordinate positions. The conference itself does not stipulate any rules or decisions, but has an important role in the regulatory process of each participant; it even has some influence on the State Council concerning the issues it covered.

Though regulatory reform is in progress in China, most regulation-makers or policy-makers have little or no knowledge of the concepts of good regulatory practice, of regulatory quality or RIA methodology, etc.

7. Building regulatory institutions

Promoting regulatory reform requires that institutional drivers charged with the promotion, co-ordination and implementation of policy objectives be put in place. This section examines China's recent efforts to establish regulatory institutions responsible for general regulatory oversight, and institutions responsible for regulatory implementation and enforcement in economic sectors. In OECD member countries, two of the most widespread types of institutions of modern regulatory governance are: 1) regulatory oversight bodies at the centre of government promoting regulatory quality and coherence; and 2) so-called independent regulators or autonomous agencies responsible for implementing and enforcing regulation in economic sectors such as utilities and financial services. As this section will show, China is progressively building regulatory institutions of type similar to those found in many OECD member countries.

7.1. SCOLA assumes roles similar to central regulatory reform offices in many OECD member countries

The allocation of specific responsibilities and powers to agencies at the centre of government is often seen as necessary to promote regulatory reform over years, across levels of government and across multiple institutions.

In China, the State Council's Office for Legislation Affairs (SCOLA) assumes a key role in planning and co-ordinating the law-making process.[8] SCOLA (see Box 9.4) acts as a gatekeeper for draft regulations on their way to cabinet approval, and it has significant advisory and advocacy functions in terms of regulatory quality, not least due to its role of producing guiding material to ministries and commissions on how to prepare regulations. SCOLA is charged with checking the constitutionality of all draft regulations at the central level[9] and to examine their accordance with the Law on Legislation and subsequent ordinances. SCOLA often redrafts regulatory proposals from ministries and commissions, and carries out (additional) internal co-ordination if deemed necessary. The decision to forward draft laws to the State Council rests with SCOLA's minister.

In addition to SCOLA, the State Council's General Office has been taking a leading and co-ordinating role in relation to the implementation of the Administrative Licensing Law and the Guideline for Administration in Accordance with Law.

7.2. Network industries

China is in the middle of a number of large-scale reforms of its network industries, prompted by demands from rapidly growing markets and commitments made under free-trade agreements. The results of reforms in the network industries will be largely determined by the quality of the regulatory institutions set up to guide the reform process. Transforming the structure of a network-based industry, such as electricity and telecommunications, from monopoly to competitive markets requires a sophisticated and evolving regulatory structure. The Chinese Government has taken several steps toward establishing more autonomous regulators.

Until the late 1990s, the restructuring of the network industries was piecemeal. Since then, the restructuring, in particular of the electricity industry, railways and telecommunications has accelerated.[10] Aspects of the regulatory frameworks for network industries and the financials sectors are summarized in the following paragraphs.[11]

As part of a complete restructuring of China's power industry in 2002, the Chinese Government established the State Electricity Regulatory Commission (SERC). SERC was not established by law, but by a State Council statute. SERC is charged with promoting and ensuring competition and with further implementing and developing electricity reforms. Powers to regulate market entry and pricing as well as to improve large projects still rest with the National Development and Reform Commission (NDRC). In May 2004, the State Council approved a plan for SERC to establish six regional offices to promote the development of regional electricity markets. The sharing of regulatory powers between

SERC and local pricing bureaus is not yet settled. A revision of the Electricity Law is currently underway, among other things to establish a clearer legal framework for SERC and regulation of the electricity sector.

In China, the rail industry is owned and operated by the state. The Ministry of Railway executes the state's functions as owner, operator and regulator. In the early 1990s, entry regulation was relaxed to allow non-state capital to invest in building tracks for the rail system. The lack of separation of the state's regulatory, policy and operational functions is believed to have discouraged new entrants. As a result, potential new entrants were organised as joint-stock companies with local governments, believed to have more bargaining power with Ministry of Railway. According to recent statistics, around 30 railway branches have been built with funding provided by entities other than the Ministry of Railway. The Chinese Government is currently drawing up a reform plan, which is expected to separate the regulatory and policy functions from enterprise functions.

China's gas sector was restructured in 1998, whereby regulatory and policy functions were separated from the two largest state-owned companies, China National Petroleum Corporation (CNPC) and China Petroleum and Chemical Corporation (SINOPEC), and transferred to the State Economic and Trade Commission (SETC) in October 2000. With the abolition of SETC in 2003, NDRC assumed the policy-making role for the development of China's gas market. There is no specific law governing China's gas market. This creates uncertainties for investment and causes difficulties in conducting business related to gas transportation and distribution. There have been widespread calls for China to produce a "Natural Gas Law", but there still does not seem to be a consensus about the urgency and necessity for such a law. Lack of competition due to the monopoly structure of the gas industry and the lack of transparent and unified regulation are considered key constraining factors in China's gas market development.

In 1998, the Chinese Government merged the Ministry of Posts and Telecommunications and Ministry of Electronics Industries to form a new Ministry of Information Industries (MII). Subsequently, China Telecom, the country's monopoly carrier, was divested from MII as part of an effort to separate government from enterprise. MII is both a policy body and a regulatory body for China's information industry, which includes all sectors of information and communications technologies and services (broadcasting excluded). It also allocates spectrum, licenses network access equipment and develops standards. The regulation of market entry remains the authority of the State Council. Moreover, NDRC has to be consulted and reported to on any key decisions on price regulations. There is an increasing appreciation of the possible benefits of an autonomous regulatory authority for the telecom sector. Article 4 of the Telecoms Regulations promulgated by the State Council in 1998 states that the supervision and regulation of telecom services shall abide by the principles of "separating government from enterprise, breaking up of monopoly, encouraging competition, and promoting development" and "openness, fairness and impartiality". A report prepared by a MII study group in 2002 recommended the creation of an independent regulatory organisation for the telecoms industry, similar to the China Insurance Regulatory Commission. As for gas, some of China's trade partners have argued that the absence of a specific telecom law and independent regulatory authority adds unnecessary uncertainty to market operators.

China's securities markets developed in the late 1980s, at first without any specific regulatory framework. The State Council Securities Commission (SCSC) was established in 1992 to regulate the securities markets, with the China Securities Regulatory

Commission (CSRC) as an "executive branch" responsible for the supervision and regulation of the securities markets. Although in principle a regulatory body with some resemblance to regulatory authorities in other developed market economies, the absence of clear rules or appropriate checks and balancing mechanisms rendered CSRC ineffective. The SCSC and the CSRC were merged in April 1998 to form one ministry rank unit directly under the State Council, and the power and functions of the CSRC have been strengthened. The primary task of CSRC is to secure the healthy development of China's still fledgling securities and futures markets. The enactment of China's Securities Law in July 1999 has brought some clarity to China's securities and futures market, as well as to CSRC functions, defined in Chapter 10 of the Securities Law. On several occasions, CSRC's regulation decisions were challenged in courts by regulated companies, illustrating the gradual development of check and balance mechanisms. CSRC's experience served as inspiration in the subsequent establishment of China's Insurance Regulatory Commission (CIRC) in 1998 and China's Banking Regulatory Commission (CBRC) in 2004.

As the preceding paragraphs show, China has made some progress in reforming the public utility sectors, but much remains to be done. In sectors such as gas, rail and telecommunications, reforms still rely largely on marginal changes to regulatory institutions and regimes created for state-provided services. Although new or reorganised state-owned companies were meant to be independent of the ministry, they have frequently retained close ties. The policy interests of the state are not separated clearly enough from the interests of commercial entities. Administrative agencies frequently use their regulatory power to benefit the companies in which they have an interest.

7.3. Drawing on OECD experience

There is no single right institutional model for these regulatory authorities. Institutional designs must be contextual, and based on flexibility and responsiveness.

In OECD member countries, independent regulators have most often been introduced in connection with the privatization of former state-owned enterprises and competition in formerly monopoly-based industries. Independent regulators have been established with the objective of keeping market interventions at arm's-length from political interference and improving transparency, expertise, and commitments to explicit long-term policy objectives.[12]

China must seek to establish regulatory authorities that match the country's particular circumstances and needs. However, as argued in OECD (2002a), an over-emphasis on the independent regulator is a mistake. The task of establishing a market-oriented regulatory regime should include all institutions with significant influence on policy design and implementation. This will help avoid any unhealthy focus on single components of the system, to the exclusion of others. No single aspect of autonomy is the litmus test for success. Rather, the key question is whether the checks and balances built into the overall system are sufficient to prevent capture and bias in decision-making contrary to the core mission of long-term consumer welfare.

8. Reform of the administrative approval system

Most economic and social activities in China have traditionally been subject to *ex ante* administrative approvals. As a legacy of the old planned economy, administrative approvals are pervasive in most aspects of economic and social life in China. Until the recent reforms, there were more than 4 000 activities requiring separate administrative approvals or licences, just at the national level. The administrative approval system has long been recognized as a major source of corruption and a significant regulatory barrier to doing business, given the scope of activities requiring approval through complicated procedures, combined with the significant discretion left to civil servants, the lack of transparency and weak accountability mechanisms. Many local and departmental administrative licensing practices have been utilized as a tool for localism. The drawbacks of this system have become very obvious in the context of opening and rapidly developing markets.

In recent years, reform of the administrative approval and licensing system has become a high priority of the Chinese Government, leading to a range of legal, organisational and policy changes. If well-implemented, changes to the administrative approval system could mark profound changes in regulatory practices in China. First, the changes reverse the current control of many business activities from *ex ante* approval to *ex post* control. Second, the reforms set out explicit quality criteria to be adhered to when making and reviewing administrative approval. Third, and partially as a consequence of the above, the reforms are groundbreaking in trying to establish clear boundaries between the market and the state, and in pushing national and local government agencies to abandon direct interference in economic and social activities.

In 2001 the State Council issued a decree to guide ministries' reforms of their administrative approval practices.[13] The decree requires government ministries and agencies at all levels to adhere to the following principles for issuing new and reviewing existing administrative approvals:

- **Legally sound:** All administrative approval requirements must be in line with the law and compatible with the overall legal system. The Legislation Law must be observed.
- **Proportional and reasonable:** All administrative approvals must be beneficial to economic development and social progress in a socialist market economy.
- **Cost-effective:** Administrative approvals should be cost-effective and administrative approval authorities should be properly divided, procedures simplified and "one-stop-shops" introduced.
- **Responsible:** There must be internal control mechanisms to make sure that government departments carry out administrative approval procedures in a timely and proper way.
- **Accountable:** Laws, rules and transparent procedures should be in place to make government departments accountable to the administrative approval they make.

Since 2001, a special State Council Leading Group for Administrative Approval System Reform located within the Ministry of Supervision has been charged with promoting reforms of the administrative approval system.

Government ministries at the central government level have been asked to review all their existing administrative approvals according to the above-mentioned principles. The reviews have been carried out in consultation with affected ministries and co-ordinated by the State Council's Administrative Approval Systems Reform Office. Three review rounds in June 2002, November 2003 and May 2004 have led the 65 central government ministries, commissions, bureaus and other bodies to abolish around 1 795 administrative approval items. This corresponds to almost half of the total items requiring administrative approval at the central level. Another 100 items have been given over to industrial associations and other intermediary agencies. The reviews showed that a large number of the existing administrative approvals had been established without any basis in existing laws and regulations.[14]

9. Reform of licensing practices and procedures

Administrative licences which primarily relate to business activities constitute an important sub-category of items subject to administrative approval. Efforts to reduce and standardize criteria for administrative approvals were given additional impetus with the Administrative Licensing Law approved by the NPC in 2003 and enacted on 1 July 2004. The law specifies the rules for the establishment and implementation of administrative licensing, including the scope, procedure and appeal mechanism for administrative licences.

As a general principle, the law mandates that administrative licensing can only be applied in one of six exclusive situations:

1. Activities that directly concern national security, public safety, macroeconomic adjustment and control, ecological and environmental protection, and that directly relate to individual health, safety of life and properties.

2. Activities relating to the development of scarce natural resources, allocation of public resources and market entry in specific industries that directly concern public interests.

3. In professions that provide services to the public with direct impact on public interests and social welfare, items concerning professional qualification that require special credibility, special conditions, and special skills require administrative licensing.

4. For important equipments, utilities, products and other objects that are directly related to public security, human health, safety of lives and properties, items that require approval by verification, testing and quarantine inspection in accordance with technology standards and technology regulation require administrative licensing.

5. Items that require validation of the qualification of entities such as the creation of enterprises and other organisations.

6. Administrative licence requirements can also be created for other items that are required by relevant laws and administrative regulations for licensing.

In cases where one of these criteria is fulfilled, the law specifies that administrative licensing may not be necessary if self-regulation, market mechanisms or *ex post* supervision are considered to be better alternatives.[15]

The Administrative Licensing Law states that only the NPC, the State Council and the local people's congresses have the right to determine whether an activity needs an administrative licence. Licences not covered by the above six criteria will not have any legal status. Under the law, citizens or businesses ordered to obtain and pay for illegal licences will be able to take legal action against relevant administrative bodies.

The Administrative Licensing Law specifies that all administrative approvals not in line with the law were to be abolished automatically by 1 July 2004. The Chinese Government prepared the implementation of the Administrative Licensing Law by issuing a State Council notice in September 2003.[16] Another notice was issued by the General Office of the State Council in December 2003, detailing the arrangement for special training courses of ministers, provincial heads, mayors and other government officials at all levels in order to prepare for the implementation of the law.

Having come into force on 1 July 2004, it is still too early to say much about the effect, pace and consistency of the implementation of the law. However, the efforts to train civil servants and policy makers and to inform public agencies and organisations of their (fundamentally) new obligations under the law indicate that long-term dynamic effects may be significant.[17]

10. Improving the application and enforcement of regulations

Adopting a rule is easier than implementing it. To be effective in achieving policy objectives, regulation must be adequately applied and enforced, and regulated entities should have appropriate rights to redress regulations and regulatory decisions. Poor enforcement and low regulatory compliance threatens the effectiveness of policy reforms and can undermine confidence in the rule of law.

The quality of the Chinese law enforcement system is improving, as the national government takes steps to ensure fair and equitable enforcement, most notably in those policy areas where investors have the greatest interest.

The judiciary system's lack of independence and resources is often at the centre of concerns with regulatory enforcement in China. Historically, the Chinese courts have not had the power to strike down legislation that is inconsistent with the Constitution. In practice, however, the Supreme People's Court has pushed the limits of its delegated authority, issuing a number of interpretations of key laws (Peerenboom, 2002, p. 317). Several recent legal reforms and events suggest that China is taking tentative steps toward more robust mechanisms of constitutional enforcement (CECC, 2003, p. 70).

Together with the Administrative Litigation Law and the State Compensation Law, the Administrative Licensing Law provides a set of legal mechanisms through which citizens can challenge state action when these judge that laws or regulations have not been properly enforced. Under the Litigation Law, citizens have the right to petition the NPC Standing Committee for review of administrative regulations that they believe contradict the Constitution or national laws. Under the Administrative Licensing Law, as mentioned in the previous section, a citizen arbitrarily denied a licence by an administrative agency can challenge such decisions in court. Courts also have the power to grant compensation to claimants. In practice, however, litigants face a number of obstacles in using the available mechanisms to challenge administrative decisions. The scope of both the State Compensation Law and Administrative Litigation Law do not enable citizens to challenge acts or administrative decisions with general applicability. Moreover, official resistance and procedural defects have been reported as important obstacles (*cf.* CECC, 2003, p. 72). China's judiciary continues to be subject to a variety of internal and external controls that significantly limit its ability to engage in independent decision-making.

There is still considerable scope for improvement. Complaints about poor enforcement – inconsistent, too little, or too much – are widespread. Some of the main reasons for the inadequate enforcement practices are listed in Box 9.6.

Recent efforts to improve judicial review and administrative appeal mechanisms are important and necessary, but it may take a long time before significant results are apparent. China's judiciary continues to suffer from complex and interrelated problems, including a shortage of qualified judges, pervasive corruption, and significant limits on judicial independence. As mentioned, the Chinese Government has made progress in its efforts to improve the capacity, efficiency, and competence of its judiciary, but progress is likely to be incremental due to the breadth and complexity of problems, limited resources and limited concepts of judicial independence.

Two recent initiatives launched by the Chinese Government to control excessive administrative discretion may prove to be very helpful in resolving some of the interlocked institutional and structural weaknesses undermining legal enforcement. First, reform of the administrative approval and licensing system, as discussed in Sections 8 and 9, in

> **Box 9.6. Transitional and structural reasons for inadequate enforcement in China**
>
> *Co-ordination and consistency problems of multiple-layered government.* Local governments have regulatory and enforcement powers in most policy areas. China's regulatory enforcement system is highly decentralized and poses formidable co-ordination and consistency issues. Almost all of the staff who inspect and enforce regulations are employed at provincial, county or municipal levels, having little accountability to the national ministries for their actions. Many local inspectorates are funded locally.
>
> *Localism and capture of the enforcement process.* These managerial and financial links to the local level create a favourable ground for localism and capture of the enforcement process. It appears that powerful, sometimes corrupt, interests at local levels may influence regulatory enforcement decisions affecting competitors.
>
> *Inadequate checks and balances on enforcement actions.* A major problem is excessive discretion at national and sub-national levels of administration. Provincial, county and municipal levels of administration may exercise powers of interpretation of regulatory requirements, a discretion not controlled by the Legislation Law. China's administrative procedure laws do not define the rights of citizens affected by regulatory decisions with respect to disclosing compliance interpretations in advance, explaining decisions publicly, and limiting delays.
>
> *Lack of effective judicial review.* As a result of still partly ineffective judicial review mechanisms, China's enforcement personnel are often not constrained by external judicial accountability under principles of administrative law. Courts are not empowered to interpret administrative regulations – ultimate authority over the interpretation and application of such rules rest with the issuing agency. Court judgments are not always enforced. Local actors are able to exert influence on judges because local authorities control judicial salaries and court finances and also make judicial appointments.
>
> *Lack of adequate sanctions and penalties.* Sanctions are sometimes disproportionately low compared to the profits of violating the law.
>
> *Intrusive and excessive regulation.* Inspectors in most policy areas have a wide range of opportunities to intervene in business decisions. Business licences, for example, are sometimes given for very short periods, perhaps six months to a year. The frequent use of permissions and approvals rather than general regulations expands the enforcement problems, because these regulatory instruments inherently increase discretion, particularly when the criteria for these decisions are not clear and independent checks are not available.
>
> *Source:* OECD (2002a); CECC (2003).

many respects goes to the root of the problem. By reducing and simplifying the vast number of existing rules, bad regulation subject to potentially poor enforcement will be reduced. Moreover, the newly established criteria for making and reviewing administrative approvals may enhance regulatory predictability and accountability.

The Chinese Government's broad and general push to improve administration in accordance with the rule of law is also likely to enhance regulatory predictability and accountability. The "Guideline for Advancing Administration in Accordance with the Law", published in April 2004, sets out six basic requirements for rule of law based administration (see Box 9.7) and includes a range of specific guidelines on administrative decision-making and enforcement as well as on conflict resolution and administrative monitoring mechanisms.

> **Box 9.7. Guiding principles for public administration in accordance with the law in China**
>
> **Legality.** All administration has to be conducted in strict accordance with laws, regulations and other administrative rules. No executive branches are allowed to make decisions violating the rights of citizens, legal persons and other organisations or increasing burdens and obligations to them.
>
> **Proportionality.** Administrative bodies must conduct administrations according to the principles of fairness and justice. They should be unbiased and non-discriminatory. Administrative discretion should be exercised in line with laws, independent of irrelevant factors. Means should be justified as necessary and appropriate.
>
> **Transparency.** With the exception of activities concerning national security, state secrets, commercial secrets and individual privacy protected by laws, all administrations should be conducted in an open and transparent way, and citizens, legal persons and other organisations should be consulted. The administration should be conducted in accordance with the legal procedure as mandated by laws and regulations so as to safeguard the rights of stakeholders to be informed, to participate and to seek aid.
>
> **Efficiency and customer-orientation.** Administrative bodies must carry out administration in an effective and efficient way. The time limit should be observed and high quality service assured. Administration should be carried out in a way that is convenient to citizens, legal persons and other organisations.
>
> **Credibility and integrity.** Information disclosed by administrative bodies should be comprehensive and accurate. Administrative decisions should not be revoked without resorting to proper legal procedure. Losses incurred to any affected bodies resulting from changes of administrative decisions for the sake of national or public interests should be compensated.
>
> **Accountability.** Administrative bodies will be empowered by laws and regulations to conduct administrative activities and implement administrative rules. Administrative bodies should be also made accountable for any wrongdoings. The aim is that administrative bodies be empowered by laws, power go with responsibilities, power be monitored and checked, violation of laws be made accountable and violation of legal rights be compensated.
>
> Source: State Council's Guideline for Advancing Administration in Accordance with Law, published on 20 April 2004 (unofficial translation).

11. Conclusions

This chapter has reviewed some of China's recent efforts to improve regulatory capacities and to build a regulatory environment on the basis of the rule of law. China's potential benefits from regulatory reform are significant, as is the potential downside if a number of severe regulatory problems are not addressed.

Among the most pertinent challenges are the excessive discretion accorded to civil servants in interpreting, issuing and implementing regulations, as well as the lack of appropriate resources and independence of the judiciary. Building appropriate capacities to develop and co-ordinate new regulations is another challenge, involving the development of institutions, procedures and criteria to prepare high-quality regulation.

China has taken a series of steps to construct a framework of credible rules, legal systems, procedures, and institutions needed for a market economy. China is gradually moving toward a system based on the rule of law. Law-making processes are becoming gradually more standardized and co-ordinated. WTO requirements have been an important driver behind improvements in regulatory quality, but there is still reason to be cautious about their impact in the absence of further reforms. Reform of the administrative approval and licensing system could mark a fundamental change of regulatory practices by – to a large extent – abolishing *ex ante* licensing, by making very clear criteria for regulation making, and by establishing similar criteria for regulatory reviews.

Moreover, the training of regulation-makers and regulatory participants to conduct regulatory reform will be crucial for the success of China's regulatory reform. For this purpose, the theory and concepts of good regulatory practice and RIA could be disseminated pervasively and the RIA methodology could be publicized to regulation-makers and regulatory participants.

Although recent reforms are extremely promising and dynamic, a full endorsement and realization of the rule of law will eventually require solutions to some of the institutional and structural weaknesses characteristic of the relations across levels of government, and to reinforce co-operation among the actors and bodies in charge of regulatory enforcement.

Notes

1. This chapter was written by Peter Ladegaard, Regulatory Policy Division, Public Governance and Territorial Development Directorate, OECD. An important contribution to the chapter was provided by Shiji Gao, Deputy Director for Research, Institute of Economic Systems and Management, National Development and Reform Commission.

2. As noted by Peerenboom (2002), rule of law does not require that discretion afforded to administrative officials is eliminated, just that it is limited by law. Peerenboom argues that administrative officials in China may actually need more discretionary authority to deviate from existing (bad) rules to meet the demands of a rapidly changing economy: "China's legal reformers face a dilemma. They can either: i) provide administrative officers with sufficient discretion […]; or ii) pass laws that give administrative officials less discretion than is optimal" (Peerenboom, 2002, p. 413).

3. Beginning in the early 1990s, the role of the NPC has gradually changed towards exercising more control over the legislative and policy agenda in accordance with its constitutional mandate (Tanner, 1999, quoted in CECC, 2003, p. 57).

4. Commitments include: Only those laws, regulations and other measures that are published shall be enforced; all laws and regulations shall be publicly available before they are enforced; an official journal must be designated for the publication of these laws and regulations; there must be "reasonable periods" for comment before implementation of laws and regulations; establishment of enquiry points where any interested party can obtain all information on all laws and regulations; requests for information should be answered within 30 days (in exceptional cases within 45 days); China must establish independent, disinterested tribunals and procedures for prompt review of all administrative actions relating to implementation.

5. "China-US Trade Issues" (2003), quoted in: CECC (2003), p. 68.

6. See for example, Kirkpatrick *et al.* (2004).

7. "Outline for Advancing the Administration in Accordance with Laws", Section 17.

8. Since 1998, SCOLA has ministerial status. For a detailed description of SCOLA's functions, see *www.chinalaw.gov.cn/jsp/contentpub/browser/contentproe.jsp?contentid=co1059687381*.

9. China has no Constitutional Court.

10. See Feng (2001) for a review of reforms of China's network industries.

11. *Cf.* IEA (2002); Gao and Qin (2004); and USITO.

12. Independent regulators can be defined as public organisations, created by legislation, with regulatory powers operating at arm's-length from ministries. Set out in public law, independent regulators are organisationally separate from ministries and have more or less narrowly defined

regulatory functions in areas of policy implementation free of direct ministerial oversight. In certain cases they may exert in a limited sphere joint legislative, judicial and executive functions. Independent regulators are always subject to different kinds of control by elected politicians and judges. Many OECD member countries have moved towards independent regulators, establishing separate "agencies" at arm's-length from the political system, with delegated powers to implement specific policies in one or more sectors of the economy. This trend has accompanied the deregulation and privatization process experienced in OECD member countries since the 1970s.

13. State Council Decree No. 33 (2001), endorsing the Directives on the Implementation Plan for Administrative Approval System Reform, jointly issued by Ministry of Supervision, SCOLA, State Council Office for Restructuring Economic Systems (SCORES), and State Commission Office for Public Sector Reform (SCOPSR).

14. Examples of activities that no longer need central approval include: urban infrastructure construction projects, agricultural, forestry and water reservation projects not requiring central government investment/funding, real estate development and construction projects, and "social projects" undertaken and funded by local governments and enterprises: *www.china.org.cn/English/2003chinamarket/79439.htm*.

15. Gao and Qin (2004) referring to the Administrative Licensing Law, Section 13.

16. State Council Notice 23 (2003): Resolution of the State Council on Implementing the Administrative Licensing Law, referred to in Gao and Qin (2004).

17. The State Council notice required that all civil servants be trained at special training courses on the law before the end of June 2004, including all vice-ministers and vice-governors in charge of legal affairs (*People's Daily Online*, 1 July 2004). Moreover, "millions of civil servants […] have taken […] tests on the law prior to its implementation date", according to Chinese newspaper *China Daily*, quoted in China Economic Net*http://en.ce.cn/national/law/2004040701_1164869.shtml*). In Zhejiang Province alone, more than 220 000 civil servants attended an examination in the Law in April 2004.

Bibliography

CECC (United State's Congressional-Executive Commission on China) (2003), *Congressional-Executive Commission on China Annual Report 2003*, US Government Printing Office, Washington, D.C.

Feng, Fei (2001), "Reforming China's Monopolized Industries", in Wang Mengkui (ed.) *Globalization and the Government's Role*, People's Press, Beijing, pp. 177-191.

Gao, Dr. Shi-Ji and Dr. Hai Qin (2004), *Regulatory Governance in China: Understanding the Issues and Reporting Progresses*, paper prepared for the OECD (forthcoming).

IEA (International Energy Agency) (2002), *Developing China's Natural Gas Market. The Energy Policy Challenges*, Paris.

Kirkpatrick, Colin et al. (2004), *Regulatory Impact Assessment in Developing and Transition Economies: A Survey of Current Practice*, University of Manchester.

OECD (1997), *OECD Report on Regulatory Reform: Sectoral Studies*, Paris.

OECD (2002a), "An OECD Perspective on Regulatory Reform in China", prepared by Scott Jacobs, in *China in the World Economy*, Paris.

OECD (2002b), *Regulatory Policies in OECD Countries. From Interventionism to Regulatory Governance*, Paris.

State Council (2004), *State Council's Guideline for Advancing Administration in Accordance with Law*, 20 April 2004.

Peerenboom, Randal (2002), *China's Long March toward the Rule of Law*, Cambridge University Press.

United States Information Technology Office (USITO), *www.usito.org/uploads/112/independent_regulator.PDF*, *www.usito.org*.

United States' Congressional-Executive Commission on China (2003), *Annual Report 2003*, available via *www.cecc.gov*.

PART III

Chapter 10

Reforming State Asset Management and Improving Corporate Governance: The Two Challenges of Chinese Enterprise Reform

Table of Contents

Summary 305

**Reforming State Asset Management and Improving Corporate Governance:
The Two Challenges of Chinese Enterprise Reform** 308

   1. Introduction 308
   2. Reforming the governance of state-owned assets 309
      2.1. Background 309
      2.2. Expected role and functions of the SASAC 309
      2.3. Challenges for the SASAC 312
      2.4. Improving the legal and regulatory framework for state
          asset supervision 313
   3. Improving corporate governance of listed companies 314
      3.1. Background 314
      3.2. Proposed measures to improve the situation 314
      3.3. Recent initiatives to improve corporate governance 315
      3.4. The key issue of enforcement 317
      3.5. Clearly defining the role of the regulatory bodies 317
      3.6. Policy options: legislation, regulation or self-regulation? 318
   4. Concluding remarks 319

Notes 320

Bibliography 321

List of boxes

10.1. Simulating markets: A gradual move towards autonomy, corporatisation
      and partial flotation 310
10.2. Summary of the Shanghai Stock Exchange proposals to reform corporate
      governance of listed companies 315
10.3. Corporate governance topics being considered in the pending
      Company Law reform 316

Summary

Enterprise reform in China is facing two main but interwoven challenges: on the one hand, to establish the state as a full or part-owner of enterprises rather than as a manager, and on the other hand, to improve corporate governance in general, and of listed companies in particular.

Reforming management and control of state-owned enterprises

The reform of state-owned enterprises (SOEs) has proceeded in several phases, each of which could be characterized as seeking to introduce modern management and market mechanisms. More recently, policy has turned to diversifying ownership through corporatisation, or partial privatisation, to domestic (including local governments) and foreign shareholders.

Corporatisation has clarified central and local governments as *de jure* owners, but by doing so it has also allowed multiple interference at different levels. The state is represented by different ministries and administrative bodies at different levels of government. There has been no clear indication regarding the resolution of potential conflicts between different state entities or agencies. This increases the capacity for insiders to abuse and divert state assets.

Setting priorities for State-owned Assets Supervision and Administration Commission of the State Council (SASAC)

The Guiding Principles for State-owned Assets presented by the Sixteenth National Party Congress of the Communist Part of China (CPC) in 2002 and the creation of the State-owned Assets Supervision and Administration Commission of the State Council (SASAC) are important steps towards reinforcing the role of the state as an owner and shareholder. The fundamental idea underpinning SASAC is to exercise ownership rights in a centralized and unified manner, while complying with the Company Law. The objective of state supervision has shifted from direct intervention in enterprise management to capital oversight.

At this stage, several policy priorities appear key for the development of SASAC: i) creating and enhancing the role of boards in SOEs; ii) improving recruitment procedures for SOE board members as well as performance evaluation; and iii) restricting irregular behaviour by the state as a shareholder. Upon its establishment in 2004, SASAC obtained the right to nominate boards. However, most board members were appointed before it received this authority. SASAC is currently carrying out a pilot project on board nomination in seven SOEs. In doing so, SASAC should consider international best practice.

To improve state asset management, it is also necessary to further improve the legal and regulatory framework regarding: i) its coverage; ii) its completeness; and iii) its consistency.

Improving corporate governance standards of listed companies

The *China Corporate Governance Report 2003* recognizes a number of corporate governance weaknesses deriving from the strong but distorted development path of the Shanghai and Shenzhen stock markets. The stock markets have been used more to support SOEs than to allow the development of private business. The resulting ownership structure of listed companies has created challenges which need to be tackled by the policy makers, including: *i)* a low free float; *ii)* an excessive concentration of non-tradable shares; *iii)* a highly dispersed ownership of tradable shares; and *iv)* a lack of a robust institutional investor base.

Issues identified by the *China Corporate Governance Report 2003* are concerned primarily with limiting abuse by controlling shareholders (usually an SOE) and with improving minority shareholder rights. In addition, it mentions the poor quality of information disclosure by listed companies, which is regarded as emphasizing form over substance. This is due to the lack of proper internal control systems and the lack of effective legal sanctions for poor disclosure.

Priorities for legislative and regulatory reform initiatives...

The Company Law is due to be amended shortly and the opportunity should be used to address fundamental issues. The Company Law (together with other legislation and regulation) forms the legislative basis for corporate governance of listed companies in China. According to the CSRC, the objective of this legal framework is to protect the interests of investors based on the principles of "transparency, fairness, and justice". This objective is not in line with the rationale behind the original Company Law (*i.e.* the specific circumstances of the state sector prevailed rather than drafting an enabling framework for the private sector) so that updating is required in line with new challenges.

Most recent reform proposals have one thing in common: they all focus on the internal governance of listed companies. In order to make the (proposed) reform measures work, the emphasis needs to be on proper implementation and enforcement.

Institutional investors may play an active role in enforcement in China. They are expected to have doubled their investment in the stock market in 2004. The China Securities Regulatory Commission (CSRC) is actively encouraging this trend. It recently introduced the Qualified Foreign Institutional Investor scheme, which provides for opening (under certain restrictions) the market for foreign direct institutional investments in a wider range of securities. The scheme may contribute to diversifying ownership.

... should include better enforcement

Considering the (recent) reforms to the legislative and regulatory framework it should be noted that these initiatives do not secure proper enforcement. Enforcement in corporate governance can be pursued in three ways: administrative, civil or criminal enforcement. For administrative enforcement to function well, responsibilities should be distributed functionally and transparently among the stock exchanges, the CSRC and other market parties. The state predominance in each of these institutions is a source of potential conflict.

Regarding civil enforcement, shareholder activism may be the obvious tool to be used by investors to improve corporate governance practices. However, in China this may not yet be the most effective path for corporate governance improvement, given that the state still owns more than two-thirds of the shares of all listed companies.

Effective enforcement starts with the need for both national and local authorities to commit to the rule of law. In addition, regulatory and judicial capacity needs to be expanded and procedural barriers for private enforcement need to be reduced.

Regulatory bodies need to be accountable

The accountability of regulatory agencies needs to be clarified and the division of responsibilities between them needs to be clearly identified. The division of responsibilities between the SASAC and the CSRC is of particular importance. In the end, both the SASAC and the CSRC report to the state, but this does not necessarily make them accountable. The accountability of the CSRC, rather than just their reporting lines, needs to be clearly defined. A transparent division of responsibilities between the CSRC, the stock exchanges and other self-regulating organisations needs to be implemented. Such clear delineation of responsibilities may benefit the efficiency and effectiveness of administrative enforcement.

The debate on corporate governance in China would benefit from policy makers being transparent about the approach followed regarding reforms as well as the rationale behind them. This would enhance the efficiency of the legislative and/or regulatory drafting process.

Reforming State Asset Management and Improving Corporate Governance: The Two Challenges of Chinese Enterprise Reform[1]

1. Introduction

Reform of the Chinese enterprise sector is now at a critical juncture. Previous methods of enterprise control have continued to show weaknesses and signs of abuse, while more market-based instruments of corporate governance, including effective commercial banks,[2] financial discipline of enterprises, effective shareholders and more widespread competition[3] are still developing. The challenge for the Chinese authorities is to negotiate the transition to a new system of corporate control with its associated checks and balances as quickly as possible.

The present situation arises in part from the programme for partial flotation of large-scale state-owned corporations and the ensuing expansion of equity markets which has taken place since 1990-91. This has left the state as a dominant shareholder in many listed firms. But the objective to improve corporate governance at the same time has not been fully accomplished. Corporate governance issues are thus becoming of critical importance for the success of enterprise reform and further capital market development that will also include the private sector. Meanwhile, the majority of enterprises and banks remain under full state ownership. This results in tensions between this sector and partially privatised or fully private firms which need to be resolved.

The authorities have been active in undertaking reform measures over the past two years. With respect to corporate governance, the Code of Corporate Governance for Listed Companies in China (CCGLC) was issued by the China Securities Regulatory Commission (CSRC) and the State Economic and Trade Commission (SETC) in January 2002. This Code is based on the *OECD Principles of Corporate Governance*, and the authorities have been taking steps to enhance its implementation through special inspections. A first report on corporate governance, published by the Shanghai Stock Exchange in 2003, highlights not only the progress to date but also the significant challenges that remain. China's accession to the World Trade Organisation (WTO) in 2001 also underpins the need for continued enterprise reform since competition is expected to intensify in a number of sectors.

In parallel, in late 2002 the Sixteenth National Congress of the Communist Party of China (CPC) concluded that better management of state-owned assets would be one of the top priority areas for the current government in order to curtail continued managerial abuse of power, which could challenge the political legitimacy of the reform programme. It also reflected the decision that full privatisation will take quite some time and that the state will remain active, if not dominant, in a number of sectors and enterprises. A commission was set up in 2004 to manage state-owned assets, the SASAC.[4] This represents a crucial step in separating the ownership function from the regulatory one within the administration.

Enterprise reform in China is thus now facing two main but interwoven challenges: on the one hand, to establish the state as a full or part-owner of enterprises rather than a manager, and on the other hand, to improve corporate governance in general, and of listed companies in particular. This chapter will give an overview of main issues and trade-offs with respect to these two major challenges. It will first discuss the reform of state asset management, underlining the challenges faced by the SASAC in defining the state's ownership role. The chapter then considers the current situation in the corporate governance of listed companies and examines some priority areas for improvement of practices, which are all the more necessary given the need to further reduce state ownership. The chapter closes with some concluding remarks and recommendations.

2. Reforming the governance of state-owned assets

2.1. Background

The reform of SOEs has proceeded in several phases, each of which could be characterized as seeking to improve or to introduce modern management, and to simulate market mechanisms (see Box 10.1).

More recently, policy has turned to focusing state control on four main types of firms, while "diversifying" ownership through partial privatisation to domestic and foreign shareholders. Diversification, or partial privatisation, it was thought, would lead to greater market discipline of management. These reform steps, while moving in the right direction, have been on reflection disappointing. In the words of one observer, "instead of state sector enterprises being made more efficient by being forced to follow the rules of the private sector enterprises (the original ambition), potential private sector enterprises are hamstrung by having to follow rules that make sense only in a heavily state-invested economy" (Clarke, 2003), and which are themselves not effective.

Corporatisation has clarified central and local governments as *de jure* owners, but it has also further blurred the lines of responsibility, while at the same time allowing multiple interference at different levels. Such state intervention has been especially heavy in personnel issues. It is important that the state take on the responsibilities of real owners in a market if the reform programme is to be internally consistent. This is even more important given the government's goal to reduce the proportion of state-owned shares in enterprises from 68% to 30% in two stages. The authorities have therefore taken the timely action to set up SASAC.

2.2. Expected role and functions of the SASAC

Whatever the scale and speed of the announced partial or full privatisation of state assets, it is realistic to assume that the state will remain a dominant or at least significant shareholder of many companies for the foreseeable future. The crucial challenge is thus how the corporate governance of SOEs can be enhanced. When exercising its role as an owner and shareholder, the state usually faces two challenges. On the one hand, it should avoid being a passive shareholder but rather act as an owner, making its views about the governance and objectives of the enterprise known. On the other hand, the state should also avoid using its considerable powers to interfere unduly in the day-to-day management of SOEs.

Corporatisation in the 1990s has reinforced the status of the central and local governments as *de jure* owners. However, combined with the more general decentralization of state administration, it has also resulted in a complex scheme for the effective exercise of

Box 10.1. **Simulating markets: A gradual move towards autonomy, corporatisation and partial flotation**

The main steps in enterprise reform in China since the 1980s have been:

A) The **Contract Responsibility System** developed in the second half of the 1980s was aimed at giving responsibility for profits and losses to SOEs. It resulted for a while in increased efficiency, but also in rent-seeking behaviour and short-term opportunism due to imbalances in residual risks, to the high costs of supervision and to asymmetries in information. Administrative and political interference remained strong, including the selection by the state of SOE management. Following these mixed results, many small firms were sold, leased or even closed.

B) In the 1990s, the reform of state enterprises was pursued and deepened by transforming the status of large SOEs through "**corporatisation**". The objective was to create a "modern enterprise system" by transforming SOEs into corporate entities that would behave like privately owned corporations, subject to the newly adopted Company Law, while maintaining state ownership and oversight. Other objectives included the need to raise equity capital for SOEs and the expansion of state control in some sectors through leverage. By the end of the 1990s, more than half of the SOEs had been transformed into joint stock companies, reinforcing in the process the status of the central and local governments as *de jure* owners. The results of corporatisation in terms of management autonomy and the introduction of new corporate checks and balances were disappointing. Corporatised SOEs remained subject to extensive day-to-day state intervention while increased autonomy allowed managers to more easily expropriate the state as an owner, sometimes in collusion with the supervisory and administrative authorities, especially at the local government levels. SOE boards were filled by local politicians with no business experience or other relevant expertise and thus did not act as a check on management (Chen, Fan and Wong, 2003).

C) Another crucial step in transforming SOEs was the decision by the State Council in 1996 to promote the **public issuance of SOE equities** and the development of stock markets. This move aimed at mobilizing private savings to finance resource-poor SOEs, while at the same time instilling "market" discipline to improve their efficiency through public listing. Another underlying concern was also to ease the pension funding problem. A frequent approach has been to "corporatise" former SOEs into two parts, a parent and a subsidiary. Typically, the subsidiary acquired the productive assets and was incorporated as a joint-stock company and listed. The parent retained the debts and non-productive assets, including redundant staff, and either remained a traditional SOE or was also corporatised. It thus has had every incentive and the possibility to expropriate the minority shareholders in the listed firm.

D) A new approach to state control was finally developed and approved in 1999. It was decided to **concentrate state control** on four main types of enterprises (state security, natural monopolies, important goods and services, high and new technology industries), while withdrawing progressively from other areas. Moreover, a diversification of ownership was approved for enterprises over which the state decided to maintain control. This diversification of ownership was also called "**partial privatisation**" as private domestic and foreign shareholders were becoming shareholders of "corporatised" SOEs, along with the state and state-controlled bodies.

Source: OECD (2002), *China in the World Economy, The Domestic Policy Challenges.*

this state ownership. The state has been represented by a multitude of different ministries and administrative bodies at different levels of government. There has been no clear indication regarding the resolution of potential conflicts between claims emanating from different state entities or agencies, which significantly increases the capacity for insiders to abuse and divert state assets.

The effectiveness of the corporate governance of SOEs depends both on the organisational set-up upstream, i.e. of the state as an owner and thus of the SASAC in the Chinese case and its relations with SOEs, and on the organisational set-up within SOEs, i.e. the relationships and distribution of power among the company organs.

The Guiding Principles for State-Owned Assets presented by the Sixteenth Party Congress in 2002 and the creation of the SASAC have marked a crucial turn and an important step towards reinforcing the role of the state as an owner and shareholder. The setting-up of a centralised ownership entity is usually considered as instrumental in reinforcing the ownership function within the state administration. This is the case in developed market economies where this centralisation has been carried out recently in a number of countries, including France, the Netherlands, Sweden and the United Kingdom. In the Chinese case, with a different scale of state ownership, the centralisation under the SASAC authority is a very impressive and crucial step in separating more clearly company management from the ownership and the regulatory responsibilities of the state. Centralization by itself can also lead to a more uniform approach to the exercise of ownership rights and thereby improve the effectiveness of asset management.[5]

This decision has also been accompanied by adjustments and a redistribution of state-owned assets. The SASAC is to oversee the largest and centrally owned non-financial SOEs, a total of 189 entities. Local supervisory bodies were established to oversee locally-owned SOEs. By February 2004, 12 provinces and municipalities had established such agencies and other provinces or cities were expected to do so before the end of 2004.

The SASAC is under the direct authority of the State Council, and its main duties are defined as follows: i) to carry out its responsibilities as investor and to guide and promote the reform and reorganisation of the SOEs; ii) to represent the state on the supervisory boards of some large enterprises; iii) to appoint, dismiss and assess senior executives and to assign rewards and penalties on the basis of performance; iv) to monitor the extent to which SOE value is maintained or enhanced; v) to draft laws and regulations on the administration of SOEs and set related rules and regulations; vi) to direct and supervise the administration of SOEs under local ownership in conformity with the law (Ling, 2004). Finally, for SOEs without boards, the SASAC will have also to supervise the audit process and financial disclosure.

The fundamental idea underpinning SASAC is to exercise ownership rights in a centralized and unified manner, and according to the Company Law. One breakthrough is that the objective of supervision has shifted from direct intervention in enterprise management to capital oversight, although objective 3 above could prove quite intrusive and counterproductive, as discussed below. The SASAC and its regional and local affiliates have the objective to "fulfil the functional responsibilities of capital investors", which means a clear separation of ownership from management, a focus on investment returns, and the use of legal means and mechanisms for shareholder intervention, as defined in the Company Law (Chen, 2004).

2.3. Challenges for the SASAC

The SASAC has yet to elaborate a clear policy on how it will exercise its ownership rights, and on how it will behave as an institutional investor acting as a fiduciary for the Chinese people. Three priorities for action by the SASAC should be as follows:

2.3.1. Creating and enhancing the role of boards in SOEs

The SASAC has first to set up boards in the largest wholly state-owned companies in strategic sectors, which may still have a "managing director responsibility system".[6] Establishing boards will be a critical first step in curbing insider control and decreasing power concentration. Until now, only a quarter of the 189 SASAC enterprises have boards, but up to 80% of second- and third-tier enterprises[7] have been transformed into the corporate form. As long as SOEs do not have boards, the SASAC remains responsible for the audit process and for the integrity of financial reporting. It is only once they have their own board that enterprises set up audit committees which become responsible for this critical pillar of good governance.

Furthermore, once SOEs have boards, empowering and giving them the full responsibility for strategic guidance and monitoring of management will be a central element of reforming the governance of SOEs, as evidenced both within OECD member and non-member countries (OECD, 2005a). The SOE Code mentions that the board should have an active role in guiding the company and in selecting management. This will imply also letting SOE boards fulfil one of their critical functions, i.e. nominating and eventually dismissing the CEO and top management.[8]

However, the promotion and compensation of managers in key state-owned and state-controlled enterprises, whether or not they are corporatised and listed, remains largely under the control of the CPC at the central, provincial and municipal levels. The Company Law formally transferred the power to appoint or remove, as well as reward and punish managers to the boards of directors. However, it remains vague regarding the formal Party rights[9] and powers in enterprises and "provides local party committees with a certain leeway to continue their involvement and interventionist activities" (Opper, Wong and Hu, 2002). Moreover, "the tendency toward persistent party control at the firm level is further reinforced by the central leadership's insistence on upholding the CPC's political authority" (Wong, Opper and Hu, 2004), and shareholders and managers still have strong incentives to co-operate or maintain good relations with old local elites due to the quasi-market institutional environment. Consequently, "the formal constraints of the Company Law are not likely to induce a complete withdrawal of the local Party committees from enterprise decision-making processes" (Opper, Wong and Hu, 2002). This is evidenced in a survey carried out by the Shanghai Stock Exchange which investigates power persistence of the local Party committees in China's listed companies. It shows that local Party committees stayed involved in all enterprise decisions and that this interference concentrates on personnel policy issues such as recruitment, evaluation and dismissal of key managers (*idem*; Wong, Opper and Hu, 2004).

2.3.2. Improving recruitment procedures for SOE board members as well as performance evaluation

Once boards are created and given their full authority, establishing a well-structured and transparent board nomination process becomes a critical function of the ownership entity. Decree No. 378 (2003) of the State Council gives authority to the SASAC to nominate boards, but most board members were appointed before it received this authority. Consequently, the SASAC is currently carrying out a pilot project on board nomination in seven SOEs, and is reviewing its criteria for board member selection. In this regard, it should adopt international best practice, *i.e.* base this selection on competency and experience criteria, while ensuring a necessary degree of independence with the presence of both non-executive and fully independent board members, including in relevant cases foreigners. The Chinese SOE Code recommends the nomination of independent directors and the separation of the chairman from the role of the CEO. The SASAC is also developing codes of good behaviour for SOE board members, as well as guidelines for SOE boards. It should also undertake a major training effort.

In many SOEs without boards, SASAC will also continue to appoint managers and is currently elaborating plans to reform the nomination, evaluation and remuneration process for top management of SOEs.[10] However, such actions should remain restricted if boards are to develop.

2.3.3. Restricting irregular behaviour by the state as a shareholder

The state is by far the most important controlling shareholder in China. Moreover, under the Company Law it has important powers as a controlling shareholder and this does not change with partial privatisation. It is therefore crucial to eliminate abuses by the state as a controlling shareholder. This will not only determine its future capacity to sell further shares on the market, but it will also set the tone for corporate governance practices in the business sector. Once SOEs do have outside minority shareholders, it is critical that the state applies fully the provisions of the Company Law regarding the protection of minority investors.[11] To improve the protection of minority shareholders' rights, together with the CSRC, the SASAC issued in August 2003 a Notice on Certain Issues Relating to "Standards for Regulating Listed Companies" Dealing with Related Funds and External Guarantees Offered by Listed Companies. Chinese SOEs could thus, following international best practice, aim at applying the more comprehensive protection provided by the Code for Listed Companies regarding the protection of minority shareholders rights.

2.4. Improving the legal and regulatory framework for state asset supervision

Finally, to improve state asset management, the legal and regulatory framework needs further development regarding its coverage, completeness and consistency.

Firstly, SOEs under SASAC supervision are not all covered by the existing legal and regulatory framework regarding corporate governance. The Company Law and Decree No. 378 apply to all SOEs, while it is not clear at which point the "provisional" SOE Code[12] is binding on all SOEs. Moreover, most SOEs are not covered by the Code for Listed Companies. Indeed, none of the 189 companies directly under the SASAC control and only a minority of their partially owned subsidiaries are listed.

Secondly, regarding consistency, Decree No. 378 specifies that the SASAC should act as an investor to represent the interests of the state, and its function should be clearly separated from those of the management. However, as discussed above, the same Decree includes conflicting provisions giving the SASAC quite significant decision-making powers and leverage on many critical issues, including selection of managers and auditing and disclosure for non-board SOEs.

Finally, regarding completeness, the SOE Code does not cover a number of issues which are deemed critical for the corporate governance of SOEs such as, for example, which responsibilities should be exercised by SOE boards and the SASAC respectively. The SOE Code should be significantly revised and refined. Alternatively, a new code for unlisted companies could be drafted, bearing in mind that its provisions should remain globally consistent with the Listed Company Code, as many unlisted companies will eventually be listed.

3. Improving corporate governance of listed companies

3.1. Background

The Shanghai and Shenzhen stock markets have developed strongly[13] but are distorted since they have been used more to support SOEs than to allow the development of private business. Consequently, they are dominated by state-controlled listed firms,[14] and only one-third of shares issued by SOEs (*geren gu*) are publicly issued and freely tradable by individuals and institutions.[15] The ownership structure resulting from these series of reforms is problematic as it is characterized by a low free float, an excessive concentration of non-tradable shares, combined with a highly dispersed ownership of tradable shares and a lack of a robust institutional investor base. These weaknesses are well described in the Shanghai Stock Exchange's *China Corporate Governance Report 2003*. The largest shareholder is in general an SOE. At the end of 2002, 41% of listed firms had as their largest shareholder almost always a legal entity (*i.e.* an SOE), holding more than 50% of their equity, and there was another third where the dominant shareholder controlled between 30% and 50% of the equity.

The market has been extremely narrow, dominated by small retail shareholders and short-term speculative trading, with valuations considered as grossly inflated. There have been many instances of malpractice and abuse in initial public offerings (IPOs),[16] combined with poor disclosure and transparency standards that have led to markets being perceived as sometimes even "worse than a casino" (Greene, 2004). These problems of the Chinese stock markets have been characterized as resulting from "ownership without constraint", and have resulted in huge losses for individual shareholders in recent years. The most widespread abuse is asset stripping by controlling "legal entity" shareholders at the expense of the firm itself and its minority shareholders through abusive related party transactions among firms of the same group, intra-group lending or guarantees, and excessive cash dividends. Indeed, the parent company will typically transfer productive assets to its listed subsidiary, retaining liabilities and redundant staff, while remaining an SOE (Green, 2004). This makes it almost inevitable that, lacking a proper fiscal system to socialise such burdens, the parent company will exploit the subsidiary to meet its commitments.

The evidence regarding the performance of listed firms is thus mixed (Wang, Xu and Zhu, 2004),[17] as an effective regulatory framework has been slow to develop. The oversight previously exercised by line ministries has declined with listing, while new oversight bodies such as the CSRC have been slow in establishing an effective regulatory framework. Moreover, there has also been a marked divergence of interest between local and central governments, and effective enforcement is underdeveloped.

3.2. Proposed measures to improve the situation

Under these circumstances it is hardly surprising that the *China Corporate Governance Report 2003* identified a number of issues concerned primarily with limiting abuse by

> Box 10.2. **Summary of the Shanghai Stock Exchange proposals to reform corporate governance of listed companies**
>
> - Improve conditions which restrict the exercise of minority shareholders' rights.
> - Introduce a system of compulsory cumulative voting.
> - Representatives nominated by holders of tradable shares to serve on board of directors.
> - Independent directors to be banned from concurrently holding a position of independent director at more than two listed companies.
> - Non-executive directors to make up more than half the number of board members.
> - Strengthen the board of directors' function of collective decision-making.
> - Restrict the chairman of the board from also being the managing director.
> - Introduce audit, remuneration and nomination committees within the board.
> - Tighten the obligation of controlling shareholders, directors and the senior managers to act in good faith.

controlling shareholders and with improving minority rights including controversial proposals to ensure their representation on the board (see Box 10.2).[18] Another main corporate governance problem underlined by the report is the poor quality of information disclosure which is regarded as emphasizing "form over substance". This is due to the lack of proper internal control systems and of effective legal sanctions for poor disclosure.

3.3. Recent initiatives to improve corporate governance

The Company Law, together with the Securities Law, the Securities Investment Fund Law and the Labour Law, form the legislative basis for corporate governance of listed companies in China. According to the CSRC, the objective of the legal framework is to protect the interests of the investors based on the principles of "transparency, fairness, and justice". Legislation is supplemented by other regulations, administrative rules, listing requirements, departmental rules, guidelines and codes.[19]

Since its implementation in 1993, the Company Law has not been amended substantially. Reflecting concerns at the time, the Law was written with the specific circumstances of the state sector in mind rather than as an enabling framework for the private sector. An update is clearly necessary including serious reconsideration of the role of the supervisory board which has proved generally superfluous, apart from allowing some form of employee representation. The authorities are now considering necessary amendments to the Company Law in order, among other things, to introduce a more appropriate framework for proper corporate governance (see Box 10.3).

With respect to the regulatory framework, the CSRC has recently published draft rules on transferring more power to minority shareholders. In particular, the draft rules propose that listed companies will need prior approval from a majority of independent directors for any related-party transactions. In addition, it is proposed that only investors owning traded shares will have voting rights on both new share issues and major strategic decisions. This would result in an expropriation of state shareholder rights, but at the end of the day may strengthen weak market incentives and favour improved corporate governance.

> Box 10.3. **Corporate governance topics being considered in the pending Company Law reform**
>
> - Improving corporate governance by clearly describing the duties of the different corporate bodies and stakeholders.
> - Securing self-determination rights for companies, among other things in drafting their constituent documents (articles of association and shareholders agreement).
> - Strengthening shareholder rights with respect to information, dividends and derivative suits and/or class actions.
> - Clearly defining the role of independent and non-executive directors.
> - Strengthening the position of the external auditor and improving company accounting.
> - Strengthening exit possibilities, *e.g.* liquidation liability in case of dissolution or bankruptcy.
> - Defining the role of public servants in their capacity as board directors or supervisory board members of listed companies in representing the state.

The above-mentioned proposals for legislation and regulation have at least one thing in common: they all focus on the internal governance of listed companies, *i.e.* the interaction between the different corporate bodies such as the shareholders' meeting, the board of directors, the supervisory board and the employees. However, in order to make the proposed measures work, they need to be properly implemented and enforced.

Experience in other transition economies indicates that the method of privatisation and the associated regulatory environment are crucial if corporate governance is to be improved. One method being pursued in China is negotiated sales, which are being pursued slowly but surely. Not all of these sales result in a change in control to the benefit of private owners, but an increasing number do so. By the end of 2003, 250 listed firms were controlled by private shareholders. Many of these sales may be motivated by the strengthening of regulation and enforcement by the CSRC. Controlling legal person shareholders (*i.e.* SOE) are increasingly limited in their ability to strip assets from the listed firms, and consequently may prefer exit and raise cash. Since private firms are still largely excluded from the IPO market, such purchases of listed firms gives them access to financing on the secondary market.

There is, however, a downside to such developments. A number of these deals may also be aimed at manipulating market prices, as has been evidenced in a few cases in 2003. Indeed, most transactions are one-to-one deals, without a transparent or competitive bidding process. However, here again the CSRC has reinforced its oversight of takeovers,[20] but a new global framework or regulation should be developed and should make mandatory that sales of non-tradable shares are done in open and transparent auctions. The first necessary step towards a constructive role for private shareholders is indeed to enable control to be held in the market by legal rules and/or private ordering mechanisms that protect shareholders from stealth acquisitions of control (Coffee, 2000).

A recently announced strategy aims at allowing listed blue-chip companies to begin selling their state shares on the basis of negotiated agreements with existing shareholders. A variety of methods are being developed or tested including selling, writing-off or giving away state shares. As any sales of state shares would have a large impact on share prices and on the ownership structure of listed enterprises, this programme will most probably take time to evolve and is likely to be implemented only progressively.

Institutional investors are becoming apparent, and closed and open-ended funds are rapidly expanding. These funds are expected to double their investment in the stock market in 2004, to reach 15 to 20% of market capitalization. The CSRC is actively encouraging this trend, both by licensing new funds and by working with other relevant regulators to encourage insurance companies and pension funds to invest in stocks. The recently introduced Qualified Foreign Institutional Investor (QFII) scheme is a "partial and measured opening of the market", allowing foreign institutional investors who meet certain criteria to apply for approval to the CSRC in order to invest directly in a wider range of securities. A number of challenges and complex legal and regulatory issues lie ahead, but this scheme is expected to contribute to improving the situation with regard to ownership diversification (Yeo, 2003).

3.4. The key issue of enforcement

Although the basic legal framework has been established over the past decade, it does not by itself secure proper enforcement. In general, enforcement in corporate governance matters can be pursued in three ways: administrative, civil or criminal enforcement. For administrative enforcement to function well, responsibilities should be distributed functionally and transparently among the relevant players, including in any event the stock exchanges and the regulator (i.e. the CSRC). Given the predominance of the state in each of these institutions, a number of difficulties will need to be resolved.

For civil and criminal enforcement, a solid and independent judiciary is needed. The challenge will be to diminish and even prevent or abolish state (or local) government interference. In addition, training of the judiciary on corporate governance issues should be considered. Specialized company courts have been used in other jurisdictions to tackle the lack of in-depth knowledge of corporate governance matters by attributing company law disputes to the competence of specialized judges and prosecutors.

For civil enforcement, shareholder activism is the obvious tool to be used by investors to improve corporate governance practices. However, in China this seems to be not yet the most appropriate and effective path for corporate governance improvement given that the state still owns more than two-thirds of the shares of all listed companies. Some empirical research on securities market laws suggest that the impact of private sector-led mechanisms to enforce minority shareholders rights and disclosure is greater than the use of public (i.e. administrative and criminal) enforcement mechanisms (Berglof and Claessens, 2004). Having said that, it appears that China cannot afford to rely solely on private sector-led enforcement mechanisms for corporate governance at this stage of development of its capital markets. Public enforcement of corporate governance remains crucial for the time being, and will need the further development of administrative enforcement via regulatory bodies such as the CSRC.

3.5. Clearly defining the role of the regulatory bodies

As a starting point for effective enforcement, the national and local authorities need to commit themselves to adhering to the rule of law, including the regulations set by the regulatory agencies. Regulatory and judicial capacity will also need to be expanded (Berglof and Claessens, 2004). However, perhaps of even greater importance, the accountability of regulatory agencies and the division of responsibilities between them needs to be clearly identified.

The division of responsibilities between the SASAC and the CSRC is of particular importance. For example, if one of the 189 SOEs currently under the control of the SASAC applies for an IPO on one of China's stock exchanges, it will have to comply with CSRC rulings. In such cases, both state agencies might have strong incentives to defend their respective positions which might not be necessarily aligned. It might be the case, for example, that the SOE concerned would tend to overstate disclosed revenues to attract more investors. In the end, both the SASAC and the CSRC report to the same ultimate beneficiary, the state, but this does not necessarily make them accountable. The accountability of the CSRC, rather than just their reporting lines, needs to be clearly defined. The mere fact of being publicly accountable increases transparency and improves the incentives for rational decision-making and policy development.

In addition, the enforcement functions of the CSRC should also be enhanced including broadening the range of incentives and sanctions currently available to meet policy objectives. For example, the Securities Commission in Malaysia has established a system including incentives such as protection for whistle blowing, a green lane scheme (which means faster approval for corporate proposals and less stringent conditions of approvals for companies with good records of corporate governance) and recognition of good corporate governance through annual awards. Sanctions include enforcement actions against those who breach securities laws and listing requirements as well as a "merit/demerit" scheme, which means that the Securities Commission will investigate listed companies with poor governance practices. Such investigations may result in slower approvals for corporate proposals. In some jurisdictions, a blacklist of the worst performers is published and has proved very effective.

Finally, a transparent division of responsibilities between the CSRC, the stock exchanges and other self-regulating organisations needs to be implemented. Such clear delineation of responsibilities may benefit both the efficiency and the effectiveness of administrative enforcement. In other jurisdictions, the securities market regulator (i.e. CSRC equivalent) is often positioned as the enforcement agency with powers to investigate and take administrative actions. The role of the stock exchange is to enforce compliance with the listing rules and any corporate governance code. The enforcement power is embedded in its right to suspend, or even de-list companies, to issue formal warnings and to impose fines. The role of self-regulating organisations such as associations of directors or of stockbrokers is to regulate the conduct of their members, as well as to provide education and training services.

3.6. Policy options: legislation, regulation or self-regulation?

What to include in legislation and what to include in other regulation or even in market-based corporate governance codes is an important decision for policy makers in their efforts to ensure good corporate governance (Hopt, 2004). Chinese policy makers are confronted with similar difficulties as in other jurisdictions, although the initial conditions they face are quite different.

China may need to consider several ways of addressing corporate governance challenges relating to the internal functioning of listed companies. Currently, a two-way approach is being pursued with substantial amendments of the Company Law on the political agenda for 2005, while the CSRC just issued last September its proposal to grant minority shareholders more substantive rights. However, it may add even more substance to the debate on corporate governance in China if policy makers communicate explicitly what approach will be followed as well as the rationale behind it. This would enhance the transparency of the legislative and/or regulatory drafting process. This in turn may be beneficial to investors, who can then more clearly assess the policy approach and include that in their respective investment decisions.

Although it has been argued that sound self-regulation by securities exchanges and professional associations in transitional economies can close much of the gap between "advanced" Western markets and those of transitional economies (Coffee, 2000), it seems that there remains an important role to be played for the legislator in this context. In particular, regarding the need for a transparent division of responsibilities among the CSRC, the stock exchanges and other self-regulating organisations, effective legislation, rather than self- (or market) regulation, seems to be the natural option at this particular stage of the transition.

4. Concluding remarks

China has introduced laws, regulations and codes for better corporate governance that are comparable with those in some developed countries. It has also implemented major steps in reforming the management of its state-owned enterprises with the creation of a central agency, the SASAC. Furthermore, there have been initiatives by the regulators to enhance the enforcement of those laws and regulations, for example, through special comprehensive inspections in 2002. But the fact remains that the state is the dominant player and thereby has to undertake several functions at once, each associated with strains, tensions and the possibility for conflicting decisions.

Several major challenges need to be addressed in a timely manner. First, regarding the management of state-owned assets, China should further reduce state ownership while at the same time clearing the way for informed and effective private owners. The newly-created SASAC needs to clarify its role and function, and to implement significant measures to "fulfil the functional responsibilities of the capital investor" in an effective way, without interfering in the day-to-day management of SOEs. To this end, the SASAC might give priority to creating and enhancing the role of SOE boards and encourage them to improve the recruitment and evaluation of managers. It should also strive to control the behaviour of the state as a controlling shareholder and reduce the abuse of minority shareholders. Finally, the legal and regulatory framework for state asset supervision requires further improvement regarding its scope, completeness and consistency.

Second, as far as the corporate governance of listed companies is concerned, the key challenge for China lies in implementation and enforcement, as is often the case with many emerging market economies and developed countries. Good corporate governance requires not only proper laws and regulations but even more their effective enforcement. Company law is in need of reform but more effective sanctions and incentive mechanisms also need to be developed. A clear and transparent division of tasks among state regulatory bodies, stock exchanges and SROs is needed. Their independence and capacity should also be strengthened, and they should be granted sufficient financial and human resources as well as legal authority. However, while strengthening the enforcement capacities of regulators, it is also important to enhance their accountability in parallel.

Another challenge for implementing effective corporate governance will be to prevent box-ticking exercises and "form over substance" behaviour. Although both specific and detailed legislation on corporate governance and more flexible, principle-based codes might well lead to the same outcome in the end, this may not be the case for China. This is due to its unique shareholding basis in listed companies, its relatively short history in dealing with corporate governance matters, and above all the encompassing role of the state as (often) the ultimate decision-maker and also beneficiary in all relevant aspects involved in the corporate governance debate.

China is at a critical point in transforming its economy, with old methods of corporate control showing signs of stress while new systems are not yet effective. In such a situation, the potential for distortions is great. It is thus extremely important to move quickly and resolutely to establish a new system, something that the authorities understand well and which needs support from the international community.

Notes

1. This chapter was written by Louis Bouchez and Mathilde Mesnard, Corporate Affairs Division, Directorate for Financial and Enterprise Affairs, OECD.
2. For governance of banks in China see Chapter 13.
3. For competition issues see Chapter 12.
4. Decree of State Council of the People's Republic of China (N°378) "Interim Regulations on Supervision and Management of State-Owned Assets of Enterprises", 27 May 2003, provided the SASAC with its basic mandate.
5. "To achieve a clear identification of the ownership function, it can be centralised in a single entity, which is independent or under the authority of one ministry. This approach would help in clarifying the ownership policy and its orientation, and would also ensure its more consistent implementation. Centralisation of the ownership function could also allow for reinforcing and bringing together relevant competencies by organising 'pools' of experts on key matters, such as financial reporting or board nomination. In this way, centralisation can be a major force in the development of aggregate reporting on state ownership. Finally, centralisation is also an effective way to clearly separate the exercise of ownership functions from other activities performed by the state, particularly market regulation and industrial policy" (OECD, 2005b).
6. Under the "management responsibility system", the responsibility is vested in one individual, the managing director. Large, solely state-owned Chinese companies either have no board of directors, being registered under the Law on Enterprises, and implement the managing director responsibility system; or they do have a board, being registered under Company Law. However, in this case the board does not necessarily exercise its functions and there is *de facto* a "board chairman responsibility system", the chairman being the legal representative of the company (Chen, 2004).
7. Subsidiaries and subsidiaries of subsidiaries of centrally SASAC-supervised SOEs.
8. "One key function of SOE boards should be the appointment and dismissal of CEOs. Without this authority it is difficult for SOE boards to fully exercise their monitoring function and feel responsible for SOEs' performance. In some cases, this might be done in concurrence or consultation with the ownership entity… Regardless of the procedure, appointments should be based on professional criteria. Rules and procedures for nominating and appointing the CEO should be transparent and respect the line of accountability between the CEO, the board and the ownership entity" (OECD, 2005b).
9. Article 17 of the Company Law states that "the activities of the local party committees of the CPC in a company shall be carried out in accordance with the constitution of the CPC". This article was apparently added in the last minute to avoid too much resistance from the Party local officials (Opper, Wong and Hu, 2002).
10. In November 2003, the State Council issued a Decree detailing the criteria by which the SASAC should appraise executive performance and determining their remuneration. (Decree of SASAC of the State Council No. 2, "Provisional Procedures on the Business Performance Appraisal of the Central Enterprises Executives", 25 November 2003).
11. "It is in the state's interest to ensure that, in all enterprises where it has a stake, minority shareholders are treated equitably, since its reputation in this respect will influence its capacity of attracting outside funding and the valuation of the company. It should therefore ensure that other shareholders do not perceive the state as an opaque, unpredictable and unfair owner. The state should on the contrary establish itself as exemplary and follow best practices regarding the treatment of minority shareholders" (OECD, 2005b).

12. The Fundamental Code on the Modern Corporate System Establishment and Management of State-Owned Large and Medium Enterprises, 27 October 2000. This Code includes a strong commitment to grant SOEs autonomy and to provide recommendations regarding board independence.

13. The two Chinese stock exchanges, having been formally created in 1990 and 1991, have a market capitalization that rose to 57% of gross domestic product (GDP) in 2000. If only tradable shares are taken into consideration, however, the market remains relatively small, at under 17% of GDP by the end of 2003.

14. 95% of the 1 300 listed firms at the end of 2003 are former SOEs and remain largely controlled by the state. The non-state sector has been *de facto* almost excluded.

15. SOEs which have been "corporatised" issued three types of shares: one-third are legal person shares (*faren gu*) owned by other SOEs having contributed to the capital before the IPO, typically the parent companies. These cannot be traded on the exchange but can be exchanged among legal persons. Another third are state shares (*guojia gu*), non-listed and non-tradable, their transfer being subjected to multiple approvals. Thus, only one-third (*geren gu*) is publicly issued and freely tradable by individuals and institutions. These are in turn divided into three types, A, B, and H/N shares. A and B shares are respectively held by mainland private individuals and institutions, or by foreign individuals and institutions and domestic individuals in China. H and N shares are listed abroad, in Hong Kong and New York.

16. Malpractice has frequently occurred in the presentation of the accounts in the underwriting process. Underwriters, established by SOEs or by government organs, have disguised the firms' accounts with the assistance of local officials in order for the firm to meet the CSRC requirements and thus get listed (Greene, 2003).

17. Firstly, the listed firms were all from the most problematic economic sector in terms of profitability (the state-owned sector), even though those selected to be listed were the best in their class. Some argue that listed firms compare favourably both to unlisted Chinese firms and to their foreign peers (Tong, 2003). But more convincing and opposite evidence shows that the performance of listed firms, in terms of profitability, efficiency and sales, has declined after listing. Return on equities and earnings per share all declined in the 1990s, except for the utilities, transport and finance sectors.

18. Parts of the report have been discussed during the "Policy Dialogue on Corporate Governance in China" hosted by the Shanghai Stock Exchange and the OECD in February 2004, in co-operation with the Enterprise Research Institute/Development Research Centre. The proceedings of this meeting are available at the OECD Web site, *www.oecd.org/document/32/ 0,2340,en_2649_34795_31173536_1_1_1_1,00.html*.

19. The framework includes the CSRC and SETC Code of Corporate Governance for Listed Companies (CCGLC), CRSC Guidelines for the Introduction of Independent Directors to the Board of Directors of Listed Companies, CSRC Guide to Articles of Association of Listed Companies, and the CSRC Standardisation of Shareholders Meetings. For an extensive summary of the legal framework describing the different types of shares and their respective characteristics, see OECD, 2002.

20. For example by limiting the number of times large blocs of legal persons shares may be traded, or by fixing a minimum price floor at the net asset value. However, this latter measure may have negative consequences, by blocking the sale of non-performing assets and by making it easier for local officials to strike deals just above the minimum, but still well below the real market value.

Bibliography

Berglof, Erik and Stijn Claessens (2004), "Corporate Governance and Enforcement", *World Bank Research Working Paper No. 3409*, September.

Chen, Fan and Wong (2003), "Do Politicians Jeopardize Professionalism? Decentralization and the Structure of Chinese Corporate Boards", March, Working Paper.

Chen Xinyuan (2004), "Overview of Corporate Governance Research in China", presentation for the China Research Incubator.

Chen Qintai (2004), "State Shareholders Should Become an Active Force in Promoting and Establishing Effective Corporate Governance", China/OECD Policy Dialogue on Corporate Governance, 25-26 February, Shanghai.

Clarke, Donald C. (2003), "Corporate Governance in China: An Overview", Working Paper, University of Washington School of Law, July.

Coffee, John C. (1999), "The Future as History: The Prospects for Global Convergence in Corporate Governance and Its Implications", *Columbia Law School Center for Law and Economic Studies Working Paper No. 144*, February.

Coffee, John C. (2000), "The Rise of Dispersed Ownership: The Role of Law in the Separation of Ownership and Control", *Columbia Law and Economics Working Paper No. 182*, December.

CSRC and Trade Commission (2002), "Code of Corporate Governance for Listed Companies in China", January.

CSRC (2004), "China's Securities and Futures Markets", *Global Proxy Watch*, 1 October.

Green, Stephen (2003), "China's Capital Market, Better than a Casino", *World Economics*, Vol. 4, No. 4, October-December.

Green, Stephen (2004), "Enterprise Reform and Stock Market Development in Mainland China", *China Special*, Deutsche Bank Research, 25 March.

Hopt, Klaus *et al.* (2004), "European Corporate Governance in Company Law and Codes", paper prepared for the European Corporate Governance Conference of 18 October 2004.

ISI Publishers (2004), *Practitioner's Guide to Corporate Governance in Asia*.

La Porta, Rafael, Florecio Lopez de Silanes, Andrei Shleifer, and Robert W. Vishny (1999), "Investor Protection and Corporate Governance", *Working Paper Series*, June, http://ssrn.com/abstract=183908.

La Porta, Rafael, Florecio Lopez de Silanes and Andrei Shleifer (1998), "Corporate Ownership Around the World", *Harvard Institute of Economic Research Paper No. 1840*, August, http://ssrn.com/abstract=103130.

Ling Shao (2004), "Policy Dialogue on Corporate Governance in China" China/OECD Policy Dialogue on Corporate Governance, 25-26 February, Shanghai.

OECD (2002), *China in the World Economy, the Domestic Policy Challenges*, OECD, Paris, http://new.sourceoecd.org/.

OECD (2003), "White Paper on Corporate Governance in Asia", OECD, Paris, www.oecd.org/dataoecd/48/55/25778905.pdf.

OECD (2004), "OECD Principles of Corporate Governance", OECD, Paris, www.oecd.org/dataoecd/32/18/31557724.pdf.

OECD (2005a), "Comparative Report on Corporate Governance of State-Owned Enterprises in OECD Countries", OECD, Paris.

OECD (2005b), "Guidelines on Corporate Governance of State-Owned Enterprises", OECD, Paris.

Opper Sonja, Wong Sonia M.L. and Hu Ruyin (2002), "Party Power, Market and Private Power: Chinese Communist Party Persistence in China's Listed Companies", *The Future of Market Transition*, Vol. 19, pp. 105-138.

Perkins, Dwight H. (2004), "Corporate Governance, Industrial Policy, and the Rule of Law", in *Global Change and East Asian Policy Initiatives*, edited by Shahid Yusuf, M. Anjum Altaf and Kaora Nabeshima.

Shanghai Stock Exchange Research Center (2004), *China Corporate Governance Report 2003*.

Siow Kim Lun (2004), "Regulatory Enforcement: The Malaysian Experience", speech presented at the China /OECD Policy Dialogue on Corporate Governance, 25-26 February, Shanghai.

Tenev, Stoyan and Chunlin Zhang, with Loup Brefort (2002), *Corporate Governance and Enterprise Reform in China*, published by The World Bank and the International Finance Corporation.

Tong Daochi, (2003), "Current Conditions, Problems of Listed Companies and How to Exercise Regulation", Working Paper.

Wang Michael, Xu David and Desvaux Georges (2004), "Spurring Performance in China State-Owned Enterprises", *The McKinsey Quarterly*, Special Edition: *China Today*.

Wang Xiaozu, Xu Lixin Colin and Zhu Tian, (2004), "State-Owned Enterprises Going Public", *Economics of Transition*, Vol. 12(3) 2004, pp. 467-487.

Wei, Yuwa (1998), "A Chinese Perspective on Corporate Governance", *Bond Law Review*, No. 10.

Wong Sonia, Opper Sonja and Hu Ruyin (2004), "Shareholding Structure, Depoliticization and Firm Performance, Lessons from China's Listed Firms", *Economics of Transition*, Vol. 12(1), pp. 29-66.

Yeo, Stephen (2003), "The PRC Qualified Foreign Institutional Investors Market", *China Economic Review*, 14, pp. 443-450.

PART III

Chapter 11

Labour Protection: Challenges Facing Labour Offices and Social Insurance

Table of Contents

Summary 327

Labour Protection: Challenges Facing Labour Offices and Social Insurance 329
   1. Introduction 329
   2. Extending the reach of formal employment institutions. 330
   3. Labour Law and administrative resources 331
      3.1. Administrative networks 332
      3.2. Merging urban and rural labour markets: a desirable but distant goal 333
   4. Employment services and related programmes 336
      4.1. The urban unemployed and the laid-off remain a priority... 337
      4.2. ... while there are many other potential clients 338
   5. Labour inspection. 339
   6. Social insurance administration 340
      6.1. Extending the coverage to new groups of workers 341
      6.2. Issues concerning the pension system. 342
Notes 345
Bibliography 347

List of boxes

11.1. The household registration (*hukou*) system and its reform 335
11.2. The public pension system 343
11.3. Social insurance on special conditions for rural migrants: Two examples 344

List of tables

11.1. Employed persons by main labour market segment 330
11.2. Workers enrolled in social insurance. 342

Summary

One of the key institutional outcomes of China's economic reforms has been to create a new role for employers that is separate from the state and allows enterprises to concentrate on their business. To protect workers, the government has set up public institutions for many social and administrative functions that until recently pertained to work units (*danwei*) or did not exist. This chapter focuses on three such functions for which the 1994 Labour Law makes the government responsible: employment services, labour inspection and social insurance.

OECD experience has potential interest for China on many specific points, for example in the administration of social insurance funds or in ensuring adequate co-ordination between "passive" income support and "active" job-search assistance for the unemployed. A more fundamental problem, however, is that all formal labour market institutions in China – as in other developing countries – have limited application outside the most developed part of the economy, which consists mainly of urban formal enterprises. Implementing labour law and social insurance is generally difficult in the less productive rural and informal segments of the labour market. But real incomes are rising in most parts of the economy, and the present scale of rural-urban migration and economic interdependence makes it urgent to reduce institutional inequity as far as possible.

Administrative controls on migration have for a long time exacerbated the division between urban and rural labour markets. This division persists but it has become less rigid, as the household registration system (*hukou*) has been partly liberalized and restrictions on the recruitment of migrants have been abolished. Social insurance is gradually extended to rural migrants and workers in "flexible" forms of employment. These developments enhance both efficiency and social equity, but they need to be consolidated and followed up by further reforms in the same direction.

The public functions studied here fall under the Ministry of Labour and Social Security at national level, and under Bureaus of Labour and Social Insurance (commonly called Labour Bureaus) at lower levels. This structure appears to permit the co-ordination that is needed to achieve a coherent focus on selected priority goals, such as the promotion of formal employment contracts and enrolment in social insurance. Specialized office networks have been developed in urban areas, but much less so in rural areas. Insofar as the traditional client groups in the urban formal economy are concerned, the office networks appear relatively well equipped by international standards. Clearly, however, any future policy to extend formal employment institutions to rural areas would require major further expansions of administrative resources.

Concerning employment services, both OECD and Chinese experience suggests that the counselling and monitoring of unemployed job seekers who receive public support (unemployment benefits or special support of the laid-off) must have high priority. As more and more workers adhere to unemployment insurance, the numbers of registered benefit claimants will also increase and this will put pressure on the administration. But in addition, Labour Bureaus have an important role to play as an intermediary between rural migrants and urban employers. Recruitment efforts that target migrants are often large in scale, and so give limited room for paying attention to each individual; but some individual services should, as a rule, be afforded to those who demand it when resources permit. It is no longer appropriate to discriminate between clients according to their *hukou* status.

The Labour Inspectorate cannot monitor all enterprises, but it frequently takes action in response to individual complaints. By making this service relatively accessible and effective, the inspectorate has become a safety valve that may be particularly important in China, where other possible channels for workers' complaints, such as trade unions, are not independent of political powers or enterprise management. As a further concern of special importance in China, the country needs to remove grounds for suspicion that it tolerates poor labour standards in order to attract foreign investment. This appears to require more inspections of working time and wage payments. Foreign actors and non-governmental organisations (NGOs) can play a complementary role in putting pressure on some enterprises, but they cannot replace an effective labour inspectorate.

The governance of social insurance involves many decentralized decisions about contribution rates and benefit levels. In contrast to most OECD member countries, which standardize these decisions at national level, China's size and diversity impose flexibility. The national government encourages provincial governments to harmonize the system and to centralize the pooling of social insurance funds in each province. But contribution rates are often reduced for certain groups, especially rural migrants and workers in small private firms, who may also be offered a choice between alternative insurance packages. While such differentiation is justified, it may not be sufficient to attract rural migrants unless the accumulated entitlements are portable. The social insurance system as a whole needs to be revised with a view to actual mobility patterns in the labour market. The pension programme, in particular, is unsuitable for migrants because it requires 10 contribution years in the same locality. This limit should be abolished, and the administration should be equipped to take account of all contributions made by an individual during his or her lifetime, regardless of where they were paid. A more centralized administration might facilitate this, but with good co-ordination it should also be possible in a decentralized system.

Labour Protection: Challenges Facing Labour Offices and Social Insurance[1]

1. Introduction

China's economic reforms have established a new relationship between enterprises, workers and the state, placing the public administration at arm's-length from most decisions in the economy. The Enterprise Law and the Labour Law, both dating from 1994, assign employers a new role, which is separate from government and permits enterprises to concentrate on their business activities. Many administrative and social responsibilities have therefore been removed from what until recently was called work units (*danwei*), while the state is facing the need to develop a variety of institutions that previously did not exist or had different functions. This process is well underway but much remains to be done. The problems encountered are still partly related to China's peculiar heritage, but the principal goals and policy constraints are comparable to those found in many developing market economies.

This chapter focuses on public institutions for employment services, labour inspection and social insurance. A starting point is provided by Chapter 16 in *China in the World Economy: The Domestic Policy Challenges* (OECD, 2002), which reviewed the principal issues of labour market and social policy. Several of its recommendations concerned the need to overcome labour market segmentation, especially between urban and rural workers and between formal and informal employment, and to extend social insurance to a bigger part of the workforce. Analysis of labour mobility suggested that the urban formal economy was still marked by low mobility by OECD standards, notwithstanding many lay-offs, while, by contrast, many informal jobs were too unstable to generate much on-the-job learning or adequate income.

Some governance issues of relevance mainly in China's urban areas are comparable to those in developed OECD member countries, making it pertinent to draw on their experience. These concern, for example, the relationship between administration of unemployment insurance and "active" measures to promote job search, and, in social insurance, questions about fund management and how these are linked with other policy decisions. These questions are briefly considered under the respective headings below. But the principal governance problem to which this chapter is devoted is that formal employment institutions in general are difficult to apply outside the most developed parts of China's labour market.

The chapter is based on an OECD mission to Beijing, Sichuan and Fujian in March 2004. Information collected on this occasion was complemented by research and the exchange with Chinese experts. The next section considers the scope for policies to promote a gradually wider use of relevant institutions. This is followed by a discussion of legislation, administrative resources and recent efforts to bridge the urban-rural divide. The last three sections look in turn at each of the selected functions of public administration.

2. Extending the reach of formal employment institutions

Protecting workers' rights is intrinsically difficult in a situation of labour surplus. With rural under-employment estimated at 150 million people or more, and net rural-urban migration flows amounting to perhaps 10 million people per year, China's labour market will remain for the foreseeable future a "buyer's market" where most job seekers have a weak bargaining position. This is bound to influence wages and other negotiable employment conditions, and it limits the scope of what can realistically be achieved by means of legal regulation of the labour market. Even so, workers have a legitimate claim on basic labour standards, an orderly and predictable application of the law and adherence to contractual agreements.

A key challenge of public governance is therefore to develop institutions that can pursue such objectives under the varying conditions that prevail in different parts of the economy. Existing labour market institutions, as reformed over the past few decades, are largely similar to those of more developed economies, but their impact – in China, as in many low- and middle-income countries – remains highly concentrated in a "formal" segment of the urban job market. Judging from the coverage of pension insurance, for example, this market segment can be considered to include around 150 million workers or one-fifth of total employment (two-fifths of non-agricultural employment). It primarily concerns employees in public institutions and large and medium-sized urban enterprises, along with some of the workers in small firms known to urban business registers, but few rural workers. Table 11.1 shows the relative size of the main labour market segments.[2] As discussed further below (cf. Table 11.2), efforts to extend the social insurance coverage have until now mostly targeted urban workers, but rural migrants and some other groups have attracted increasing policy attention. Similar limitations apply, albeit with many variations, to the enforcement of most provisions in labour legislation.

Table 11.1. **Employed persons by main labour market segment**
Estimated percentage distribution at the end of 2003

Urban formal employees[1]	15
of which:	
Government, state-owned enterprises and urban collectives	*11*
Shareholding, jointly-owned enterprises etc. and foreign-owned firms	*4*
Self-employment and employees in small private firms, registered in urban areas	7
Other employment in urban areas[2]	13
Off-farm jobs in rural areas	17
of which: Small private firms and self-employment	*5*
Agriculture (mostly self-employment)	49
Total	**100**
(Total, million persons)	744

1. Reported "staff and workers" (14 percentage points) and a few others.
2. Approximate estimate, including many rural migrants.
Source: China Statistical Yearbook, 2004, various tables.

To some extent, it is inevitable that the spread of formal employment institutions across the labour market will follow, rather than precede, the development of the economy. Nevertheless, the present scale of rural-urban migration and economic interdependence makes it important to reduce institutional inequity as far as possible. This will require a sustained effort over many years, which should aim to gradually achieve a more equal treatment of the principal groups of employees, especially with respect to the use of formal labour contracts and participation in social insurance.

OECD experience suggests that governments in general have good reason to promote a "formalisation" of informal jobs (OECD, 2004, Chapter 5). This requires an effective enforcement of labour law, social insurance and taxation of wage income and profits. It may also motivate measures to limit red tape and to reduce taxes and social contributions, so that the cost of formal employment does not become too high relative to the potential benefits for workers and employers. For society as a whole, such policies can enhance both efficiency and equity, because informality tends to be associated with several undesirable job conditions. The short duration and casual nature of many informal jobs make them unlikely to motivate sufficient investment in job-specific human capital. In addition, employers who hire workers informally are often informal themselves, a situation known to limit their access to legitimate business contacts, formal credits and legal protection, e.g. against fraud and corruption. All these factors tend to reduce the chances of business expansion and productivity growth in informal firms.[3]

To promote the above-mentioned objectives in the near future and in a longer term perspective, a three-pronged approach appears justified with the following elements:

- Develop administrative capacity and front-line offices for employment services, labour inspection and social insurance so that they can cover gradually larger parts of the urban and rural labour force.

- Promote the use of formal employment contracts and extend social insurance to additional groups in the labour market. Priority groups in the near future should include workers in small firms, rural migrants in urban areas and selected groups in rural areas.

- Inform all workers about their rights and insist that the minimum wage, working time and safety rules apply even in the absence of formal contracts.

3. Labour Law and administrative resources

The 1994 Labour Law aims to "protect the legitimate rights and interests of labourers, readjust labour relationships, establish and safeguard a labour system suited to the socialist market economy, and promote economic development and social progress" (Chapter 1 of the Law). Articles 2 and 3 specify that the Law as a whole applies to all employers ("enterprises and individual economic organisations") and their employees, and that workers have "the right to be employed on an equal basis".

The rules about individual labour contracts resemble those in OECD member countries on essential points (Chapter 3 of the Law). Contracts must be established in writing and follow "the principles of equality, voluntariness and unanimity through consultation". They can be fixed-term or flexible (indefinite), but after 10 years with the same employer the worker has a right to a flexible contract. An employer who terminates a contract must give 30 days' notice and pay severance benefits according to separate regulations. Children under 16 must not be employed. Normal working time is up to eight hours per day and 44 hours per week, while overtime is possible at higher pay within the limits of three hours per day and 36 hours per month (Chapter 4 of the Law).

The rules about collective bargaining also resemble those in OECD member countries to some extent, but here there is a bigger difference in practice due to the official nature of China's trade unions. The Labour Law does not regulate the establishment of trade unions.

This is an area where the key role pertains to the All-China Federation of Trade Unions – a "mass organisation" with close relations to the political leadership. Where trade unions exist, the Labour Law's Article 33 gives them an exclusive right to conclude collective agreements. As an exception, elected representatives of staff and workers can conclude collective agreements with an enterprise "where the trade union has not yet been set up". Once concluded, a collective agreement must be registered with the local government.

The state's responsibilities according to the Labour Law fall upon the Bureaus of Labour and Social Insurance (commonly called Labour Bureaus) of central, regional and local governments down to the county level. These responsibilities mainly concern the following:

1. *Promotion of employment.* Chapter 2 expresses a general policy commitment towards employment and economic and social development, and it calls for the provision of employment services. Local governments' Labour Bureaus mostly organise these services themselves, but they also promote and standardize job agencies run by other bodies.

2. *Regulatory powers.* Local governments give detailed rules about working time and holidays (Chapter 4) and set minimum wages (Chapter 5), following national and provincial norms. Governments at various levels issue rules about the employment of youth aged 16-18 and women (Chapter 7). They also regulate vocational training, which they may sponsor "where conditions permit", although employers carry the main responsibility (Chapter 8).

3. *Social insurance* (Chapter 9). Workers have a right to public social insurance covering retirement, illness, occupational injury and disease, unemployment and maternity. Labour Bureaus must set up agencies to administer these programmes and their funds.

4. *Arbitration Committees* (Chapter 10), appointed to resolve labour disputes, gather representatives of workers, employers and the Labour Bureaus. The latter are also responsible for supervision and administration.

5. The *Labour Inspectorate* (Chapter 11) has a wide remit to check that employers follow the law, along with powers to stop unlawful practices.[4] However, this does not concern the inspection of occupational health and safety which, according to recent legislation, falls under the Ministry of Health, although the Labour Law's Chapter 6 contains general rules.[5]

3.1. Administrative networks

The policies considered here fall under the Ministry of Labour and Social Security (MOLSS) at national level and under Labour Bureaus at province and city/county levels. Social insurance is generally managed in separate departments within the Labour Bureaus, called Social Insurance Agencies, which enjoy a degree of independence and have their own budgets. Other departments cover employment services, training and labour inspection (also called employment security supervision). The respective office networks are largely new and well developed in urban areas, but much less so in rural areas.[6]

Further rapid development is expected with gradually better coverage of the territory, more specialized offices and more qualified staff for the different functions. Organisational structures vary, but as a rule, the government of any territorial unit encompasses most areas of public policy. If there is no specialized office, the public may ask for the corresponding services in a multi-purpose office. Many localities, including four prefecture-level cities visited by an OECD team in March 2004, have specialized job centres and social insurance outlets in cities and/or city districts, while the existing offices at lower administrative levels are less specialized (in urban areas: street communities and neighbourhood communities). Street community offices visited had some staff members devoted to employment services, paid by separate budgets, while others represented different branches of government (e.g. social assistance, services to the elderly, civil affairs and police).

The reported number of office outlets for employment services was 26 000 at the end of 2003, of which 18 000 were run by governments at various levels and the rest by other bodies. The staff numbers probably exceeded 100 000 in 2004. For the social insurance administration, the total staff number in 2004 was estimated at nearly 100 000, of which around 50 000 were for pension insurance and 30 000 for health care insurance. The Labour Inspectorate was reported to have about 43 000 staff members, organised in somewhat more than 3 000 inspection units (also called labour security supervision organs). The Arbitration Committees for labour disputes numbered about 3 200 at the end of 2001, with nearly 20 000 full-time or part-time arbitrators.[7]

The expansion of these administrative networks is expected to continue at a rapid pace. For social insurance, in particular, information provided by the MOLSS suggests that the staff numbers may double over the next five years. This will raise difficult questions about staff qualifications, training and auditing because it requires an increasing use of dedicated offices and specialized staff at local level. Many new offices will be needed at low administrative levels, i.e. in street communities and towns, and, as an even greater challenge, in rural townships.

3.2. Merging urban and rural labour markets: a desirable but distant goal

Given that the Labour Law applies to all employers and employees (Article 2 of the Law), the present limitation to urban labour markets of such key functions as employment services and social insurance is hardly compatible with the law. In any case, the Law puts pressure on the government to extend these institutions as far as possible. In the meantime, there is some legal room for different treatment of various labour market groups, e.g. Article 71 stipulates that the level of social insurance "shall be in proportion to the level of social and economic development and social affordability".[8]

The 2002 National Congress of the Communist Party of China set broad guidelines and the 2004 National People's Congress endorsed a series of reforms to facilitate economic activity in rural areas, including the phasing out of several rural taxes and regulatory controls.[9] A similar shift of emphasis can be observed in labour market and social policy in the past two years, as gradually more attention is being paid to rural poverty and rural workers' labour market conditions. Furthermore, as discussed below, the role of China's household registration (hukou) system as a basis for different treatment of urban and rural workers has been much reduced.

To some extent, these policy changes in favour of rural workers must be understood against the background of the recent substantial downsizing of state-owned enterprises (SOEs) in urban areas, culminating in 1998 when the government issued its "two guarantees": subsistence income for the laid-off and old-age pensions. The urgency of these urban problems made it inopportune in the eyes of many, at least for a while, to exacerbate competition for urban jobs by changing too rapidly the existing institutions that gave urban workers a privileged position. From now on, however, the expected incidence of further lay-offs in the urban formal sector is moderate. Indeed, statistics show that China's urban formal enterprises in general have low labour turnover by OECD standards (OECD,

2002; China Statistics Press, 2003), while the opposite undoubtedly holds for informal and rural workers, although statistics are not available for them. At the same time, the gap between urban and rural wages has widened.[10]

Officials in all localities visited[11] expressed a commitment to the goal of "merging urban and rural labour markets". Mentioned priority groups generally included rural migrants and poor people in rural areas as well as the urban unemployed and the laid-off. There was also a widespread recognition of the principle of equal treatment and of the need to make the labour market more efficient by removing institutional distortions. The specific problems of urban labour markets were acknowledged to still be important, but the situation of rural workers had emerged as another policy challenge, raising questions of public governance in many policy areas. Three different but related problems can be distinguished in this context:

1. The precarious situation of rural migrants in urban areas. The *hukou* system combined with other adverse factors, notably poor education, has for a long time prevented low-skilled migrants from becoming fully integrated into urban labour markets, leading to a pattern of excessive mobility between mostly unattractive jobs.

2. Different public institutions in rural and urban areas. Some difference may be justified or inevitable due to economic conditions, but institutions should not exacerbate inequality or distort competition.

3. Obstacles to labour mobility. It is difficult to determine to what extent the *hukou* system has reduced rural-urban migration – but it clearly has *diverted* large parts of it towards a limited segment of urban job markets. It can also make it difficult for urban workers to move from smaller to bigger cities. The resulting loss of economic opportunity affects most workers, but especially the rural poor.

Several on-going reforms focus on the first problem, amounting to a major effort to reduce discrimination against rural migrants in urban areas and to provide them and their families with better public services, as noted below. On the other hand, no systematic extension of the present urban employment institutions to rural areas has been envisaged at national level, although this is being done to some extent in advanced regions. More limited steps in this direction are frequently mentioned, such as the extension of social insurance to workers in state farms or the provision of urban *hukou* status to farmers whose land is affected by urban expansion. Regarding office networks, it must be kept in mind that the territories served by offices in cities and their subdivisions frequently include rural areas. Nevertheless, MOLSS officials have underlined[12] that the lack of an appropriate rural office network remains a key obstacle to any extension of social insurance to rural areas.

The third problem – mobility barriers – is closely related to the *hukou* system and its reform (see Box 11.1). This system is administered mainly by public bodies other than Labour Bureaus. As explained in Box 11.1, several reforms have reduced the importance of an individual's *hukou* status, while other reforms have made it easier to change *hukou*. Small and medium-sized cities generally give urban *hukou* to persons who have been living and working there for a year. But most big cities are more restrictive, with the result that 20% or more of their actual population are still subject to discriminatory treatment in several areas of public service, notably education.

Labour Bureaus played a role in enforcing migration controls until 2003, when they were relieved of the duty to check that newly recruited workers in urban enterprises had the appropriate *hukou* status for the job category, as regulated by each city (see Box 11.1).[13] This reform was certainly welcome to many officials as it removed a cumbersome control

Box 11.1. **The household registration (*hukou*) system and its reform**

Main features

Chinese citizens must carry a household register card, called *hukou*, issued in the locality of residence. There are two main categories:

- Agricultural (rural) *hukou*, giving a right to a small piece of land and a duty to cultivate it.
- Non-agricultural (urban) *hukou*, giving a right to urban public services in the locality concerned.

Migrants can apply for temporary registration where they live. But permanent *hukou* changes are accorded only under specific conditions that can be difficult to fulfil, especially for low-skilled and poor persons.

In practice, over 20% of most big cities' inhabitants have a rural *hukou*, and thus do not enjoy full rights to public services. For example, their children's education often takes place in special schools that are less attractive than other schools in urban areas.

Important reform steps have been taken

- Regional pilot experiments began in the 1990s and encompass several provinces since 2001, principally the eastern coastal area, but also Sichuan and Anhui. In these provinces, rural citizens can obtain *hukou* in a city if they have permanent work and residence there. Some localities are particularly liberal while others, including most big cities, are partly exempted.
- From October 2001, all towns and cities with up to about 100 000 inhabitants should give urban *hukou* to residents with fixed jobs and homes (State Council Circular No. 6).
- In January 2003, the State Council's Notice on the Management of and Services for Rural People Coming to Work in Cities gave many new instructions to public officials, including the following:
    i) Abolish administrative controls (notably by Labour Bureaus) of enterprises hiring rural workers; remove restrictions concerning the job categories in which rural workers can be hired; simplify procedures; abolish procedures and fees that have been imposed only on rural workers.
    ii) Enterprises must sign labour contracts with rural workers and give them all rights stipulated by the Labour Law. On dismissal, employers should pay them a lump-sum compensation. Labour Bureaus should reinforce their inspection of rural workers' labour contracts.
    iii) Rural workers should have work injury insurance. If conditions permit, local governments can set up health care insurance for them. Training of rural workers should be organised. Rural workers' children should be guaranteed education at no extra fees, and poor families should be exempted from part of the fees.
- In June 2003, the State Council issued the notice Administrative Measures on Assistance and Administration of Poor Urban Vagrants and Beggars. It replaced a previous regulation from 1982 about "arresting and evicting" the same groups, which had been considered to justify frequent identity checks by police. According to the new regulation, beggars and other poor rural citizens in cities should no longer be arrested and evicted, but advised to visit help centres. These centres, to be set up by city authorities other than the police, should provide food, accommodation and assistance, including tickets home or to find jobs.

function with little relation to the other objectives of labour market policy.[14] It has been underlined by Labour Bureau officials[15] that they did not check the *hukou* status of individuals, neither on recruitment nor in other situations, as for example when they selected participants in various programmes. (As noted below, other regulations still require Labour Bureaus in sending and receiving localities to organise migration, and employers who recruit migrants are expected to use these services. But individuals can also move and seek jobs for themselves.)

The envisaged "merger" between urban and rural labour markets is evidently at an early stage, and its completion is a distant goal. The obstacles are largely economic, as illustrated by the gap between urban and rural wages, which has tended to widen. In 2001, the average wage in rural enterprises (township and village enterprises) was only 54% of the urban average wage, and the difference in labour costs was even greater, because urban enterprises must pay social insurance contributions. Assuming that the difference in productivity is similarly great, it would hardly be possible to finance social insurance and other public programmes on a basis of completely equal treatment in the short term. It is therefore important to design the programmes so that they can respond to different needs and varying financing capacity, as the Labour Law's Article 71 has foreseen concerning social insurance.

4. Employment services and related programmes

As noted above, most employment services and related programmes have been developed to meet the needs of the urban unemployed and the laid-off (*xiagang*), but Labour Bureaus have also for a long time been engaged in efforts to manage the flows of migrant workers. These policies differ in many ways, but recent developments have raised the prospect of a gradual integration within a general employment service framework. The following paragraphs consider the main issues from an administrative perspective.

In the labour market policies of urban China, as in OECD member countries, a principal governance problem concerns the need to co-ordinate "passive" income transfers – where they exist – with "active" measures to promote job search. OECD reviews of the public employment service in numerous countries have pointed to the crucial role of job counselling and monitoring of individuals' job-search activity.[16] Such procedures should be mandatory for recipients of unemployment insurance benefits. As a general rule, administrations of unemployment insurance have been found to be most efficient where they involve a combination of effective controls – checking that beneficiaries seek jobs – and job-search assistance, with the possible addition of further measures such as training and wage subsidies. The job-search control function was weak or non-existent in some Chinese localities visited by the OECD in 2004,[17] and previous studies in China have found that laid-off and unemployed workers often delayed their formal-sector job search in order to continue drawing benefits, while perhaps working informally (OECD, 2002; MOLSS, 2001).

The counselling and monitoring of unemployed clients is inevitably time-consuming, and it requires well-trained and committed staff if it is to be effective. The services provided to other groups of job seekers and employers are typically less staff-intensive, and not necessarily free of charge. Many OECD member country governments therefore allocate staff resources to local job centres in proportion to registered unemployment, and especially to the numbers of recipients of unemployment insurance benefits. Although the problems and constraints are partly similar in urban China, the country does not seem to apply any automatic rule to link staff allocations with unemployment statistics.

However, China differs from developed countries in that most of its poor and underemployed citizens are not covered by unemployment insurance. For most rural households, the chances of improving their living standards depend mainly on the off-farm labour market.[18] In response to this, some Labour Bureaus have adopted the target of providing off-farm work for at least one member of every rural household.[19] On average, approximately one person per rural household in China (with on average three adult members) already has off-farm employment – but these job opportunities are unevenly distributed. Worse, it is often difficult for rural job seekers to obtain reliable information about jobs available to them, which frequently are informal and of short duration, with the result that many travel long distances without knowing much about their job chances.

In sum, the employment service faces the need to serve a national labour market much bigger than the urban formal sector for which most of its resources were dimensioned. Its role in this broader labour market context is bound to be modest, but still potentially important, considering the need to improve the matching of labour supply and demand. A further reason for Labour Bureaus to play an intermediary role in labour migration, while respecting the individual freedom to move and seek jobs, is that they can and should use this role to promote an orderly application of labour law.

4.1. The urban unemployed and the laid-off remain a priority...

At the end of 2003, there were about eight million registered unemployed persons and around six million *xiagang*, or altogether about 14 million "priority" job seekers.[20] Most of the registered unemployed are beneficiaries of unemployment insurance, who must have contributed for at least a year, while some are first-job seekers who can register after a waiting period although they get no benefits. Registered persons receive Certificates of Entitlement to Preferential Employment Policies, giving a right to free job information, placement services and subsidised training. Similar rights apply to the *xiagang*. (By contrast, rural workers must pay for job information in many localities [Li, 2003].) The preferential policies also include fiscal advantages for up to three years to employers who hire such workers, or to the workers themselves if they start up a business. SOEs are frequently placed under pressure to recruit the unemployed or to set up subsidiaries to employ them, also with tax subsidies.

The special measures for *xiagang* represent a temporary programme, implemented since the mid-1990s, but especially from 1998, when the State Council obliged SOEs to create re-employment service centres. Those concerned receive monthly income for up to three years, higher than benefits of unemployment insurance, but lower than the previous wage.[21] The programme had been abolished in seven coastal provinces by 2004, while elsewhere its phasing-out is foreseen within a few years. This contributed to an increase in registered unemployment by about two million since 2000, and a further rise by nearly one million is expected in 2004. However, the unemployment insurance scheme still covers barely one-half of the labour force in urban areas, or a little over 100 million workers. A continued expansion in coverage is needed, not least in view of the changing structure of urban labour markets, with many job losses occurring in small as well as bigger firms.

To assess future staff requirements, it can be assumed that the number of the registered unemployed will increase with the number of adherents who contribute to unemployment insurance. As in many OECD member countries, benefit recipients must come to the labour office once a month. These appointments should ideally involve job counselling, but, in the offices visited by the OECD, they were often a mere formality. Judging from OECD experience, a systematic provision of monthly counselling sessions might require about one qualified staff member per 100 registered unemployed persons. The actual client-to-staff ratio appears moderately higher than this target, as in many OECD member countries. (With approximately 100 000 employment service staff members and 14 million unemployed and *xiagang* clients, the ratio is around 140; counting only qualified staff it is higher.) Labour Bureaus also offer numerous training courses, concerning as many as four million of their clients in 2004. Courses are procured from different providers including vocational schools, certified private schools, trade unions and large employers.[22]

By and large, the resources available for employment services and training appear quite impressive if compared only with the current numbers of unemployment insurance and *xiagang* clients. Until now, the development of a decentralized and relatively well-equipped office network for these clients has been facilitated by the previous existence of administrative structures at the level of street communities and neighbourhood communities. In localities visited, street community offices could handle some administrative matters concerning the unemployed and provide local job information. But those who needed more qualified services were sent to district-level job centres. Street communities also co-operated with neighbourhood committees (the lowest level) which organised activities for the unemployed, including temporary jobs subsidised by Labour Bureaus.[23]

All told, the urban unemployed have access to a variety of services at local level. The more expensive programmes are generally reserved for the registered unemployed and the *xiagang*. But basic services such as information about vacant jobs are also provided to other groups. Previous regulations that excluded rural *hukou* holders from many jobs have been repealed, as mentioned above, and the impression gained during the mission was that employment service staff increasingly regard it as inappropriate to discriminate between clients according to their *hukou* status.

4.2. ... while there are many other potential clients

Young urban job seekers looking for their first jobs, numbering nearly 10 million per year, often use the employment service although most of them find jobs without registering as unemployed.[24] The number of newly arrived rural workers in urban areas is also almost 10 million per year. The MOLSS expects the annual migration flows to increase, but such projections are extremely uncertain because the population groups that can be considered as potential migrants are very large. Furthermore, among previous migrants who already have urban work experience, there are probably millions of *de facto* jobless persons who are not registered as unemployed because they lack unemployment insurance. In China as a whole, the number of rural *hukou* holders susceptible to losing their jobs or seeking a change in the near future can be counted in hundreds of millions, given the present low productivity in farming and the insecure employment conditions experienced by rural workers in other sectors.[25]

In the localities visited in Sichuan and Fujian, special employment services for rural migrants were organised at city or district level, often as "job fairs" where large numbers of job seekers were gathered and employers could meet and interview them on the spot. Migrants arriving in the cities were required to attend courses about the Labour Law, given in classrooms receiving many hundreds of participants at a time. Labour Bureaus also helped enterprises organise large-scale recruitment efforts. For example, a visited enterprise in Xiamen that intended to hire 50 unskilled workers received 600 rural applicants for interview from the employment service.

Many measures of this nature will undoubtedly be needed in the near future. Available resources give limited room for individual treatment of job seekers in the large groups not eligible for unemployment benefits. As far as possible, however, labour offices should offer at least some basic information and job-search assistance to those who demand it.

5. Labour inspection

The Labour Inspectorate, part of Labour Bureaus, consists of about 43 000 officials whose task is to enforce the Labour Law (excluding occupational health and safety). A 1994 MOLSS directive regulates the appointment of labour inspectors, their decision powers and measures to ensure their qualifications and probity. They must undergo training and examination every three years.

Provincial governments organise the labour inspection in teams, operating at provincial and lower levels. Judging from discussions with officials in Sichuan and Fujian, the Inspectorate's position as part of the Labour Bureaus is regarded as advantageous, because it permits a co-ordination with other functions. This favours a consistent promotion of written labour contracts and social insurance – a national priority – and it facilitates the professional treatment of many complaints and disputes.

Individual complaints are a chief preoccupation, and on average about 60% of them are resolved in favour of the workers. All complaints are to be considered. By making this service relatively accessible, transparent and effective, the Labour Inspectorate has become a safety valve that appears particularly important in China, where other possible channels for workers' complaints, such as trade unions, are not independent of political powers or enterprise management. The Inspectorate has no formal link with trade unions but it often co-operates with them on specific matters.[26]

Inspectors in the visited localities also conducted annual inspections of enterprises and routine controls of new labour contracts. However, as in most countries, it is not possible to conduct routine inspections in all enterprises, so in practice most inspections are motivated by complaints. In Sichuan, inspectors reportedly reviewed 380 000 labour contracts during 2003 and urged employers to register 330 000 workers for social insurance (mainly migrant workers in private industry); 288 illegal firms were closed. As a complement to such law enforcement, Labour Bureaus organise publicity campaigns among employers, and, as noted above, offer courses in labour law for rural migrants.

A strategic goal for the MOLSS is to improve the social insurance coverage of the labour force, and a special priority in the short term is to extend at least work-injury insurance and unemployment insurance to rural migrants. Inspections in enterprises must therefore focus to a large extent on the establishment of labour contracts that give a right to social insurance, and, once this has been achieved, on checking the contribution payments and imposing penalties in cases of delay. It can then be difficult to place sufficient emphasis on other serious problems, such as excessive working time, below minimum wages and delayed wages. This makes it all the more important for the inspectorate to pay attention to individual complaints on such questions.

Despite their limitations, existing forms of inspection permit many interventions in matters of wages and working time. Faced with numerous disputes about wage arrears, the authorities have frequently responded by strengthening the inspection of wage payments. In Fujian, working time has been a particular preoccupation leading to additional inspections. According to officials interviewed, most inspected firms were then found to follow the working-time rules; but the issue remains sensitive, partly as a result of international interest in the situation in foreign-owned firms in the province.

Chinese authorities face the need to remove possible grounds for suspicion that they tolerate poor labour standards in order to attract foreign investment.[27] Foreign-owned companies in China are often subject to particular attention from the media and the general public in their home countries, concerned with the risk of "unfair" competition for jobs. Several NGOs, including foreign trade unions, also play a role in monitoring labour standards. But such attention is unevenly distributed between the foreign enterprises, so its impact on actual conditions is likely to vary. Inspectors in Fujian considered that the labour standards of some of the more well-known foreign firms were so high that it was unnecessary to inspect them.

Chinese trade unions are not independent in relation to political decision-makers and they are often too connected with enterprise management to be effective as worker representatives. Trade unions can only be set up by the All-China Federation of Trade Unions, but where no union exists, the workers may elect a Staff Assembly, requiring a two-thirds majority.[28] The Labour Law contains rules about collective bargaining, foreseen at enterprise level in firms with at least 25 workers, but until recently it has seldom concerned wages.

Against this background, it must be noted as a positive sign that the MOLSS has expressed its intention to develop the collective bargaining system during 2004. It is questionable if such an objective can be achieved without giving workers more freedom to choose trade union representatives. But policy makers appear to recognize that a more market-oriented wage-setting system is needed for economic as well as social reasons.[29] In April 2004, the government organised the China Employment Forum in co-operation with the International Labour Organisation, proposing to collaborate with this body in order to develop its international co-operation concerning collective bargaining.

6. Social insurance administration

For China's social insurance system, the past ten years have been a period of institution-building. Five contribution-based programmes with "socialised" management – no longer controlled by employers – are now in place, but their implementation in practice has been gradual. After several pilot experiments, they are currently promoted nationwide according to basic regulations from the years shown in brackets:

- maternity insurance (1994);
- work injury insurance (1996);
- pension insurance (1997);
- medical insurance (1998);
- unemployment insurance (1999).

Each programme is financially separate, but Labour Bureaus and their social insurance agencies co-ordinate the administration. Visited local outlets of these agencies covered the first four of the above five programmes, usually with separate desks for each of them. Concerning unemployment insurance, administrative arrangements can differ at local level, but the employment service always has a key role in certifying unemployment. Varying practices are also found with respect to the collection of employer and employee contributions, a task carried out in some provinces by Labour Bureaus, elsewhere by tax authorities.[30]

Key governance issues concern fund management and decisions about contribution rates and benefit levels, which are partly decentralized. As discussed in more detail below with respect to pension insurance, these responsibilities often fall on city governments, especially at prefecture level,[31] and sometimes on provincial governments.

The existence of some local discretion about contribution rates and benefits may seem to suggest a high degree of decentralization by OECD standards, although it must be seen against the background of China's size and regional diversity. National law and supervision limit the range of local variations and make them depend on objective criteria. For example, the maximum benefit of unemployment insurance must fall between the minimum wage and the minimum living standard (used for means-tested social assistance), and these two parameters also follow mandatory rules, taking account of local prices. The contribution rate for each branch of social insurance can vary around a national standard, recommended by the central government, from which most deviations have probably been motivated by the respective funds' financial positions.

A full harmonization of contribution rates and benefits at national level does not appear to be on the policy agenda for the near future, perhaps mainly due to the financial responsibilities this would place on the central government. However, the central government encourages provincial governments to centralize the pooling of social insurance funds and to harmonize the system in each province. The central government has also authorised a differentiation of contribution rates and other conditions within each locality in order to facilitate an extension of the coverage to new groups of workers, especially rural migrants.

6.1. Extending the coverage to new groups of workers

Social protection was previously limited to workers in SOEs, and not even all of them were covered. But since the early 1990s, it has been gradually extended to other urban formal-sector employees, first in collective firms and then in many enterprises with shareholding, mixed or foreign ownership. In principle, social insurance is now compulsory for urban employees and voluntary for the self-employed. But only from about 2003 has it been a national policy to promote the enrolment of rural migrants.

The coverage of the total population remains low by international standards. Pension insurance, with the highest number of contributors, covered only 16% of the employed in 2003, or 21% including civil servants, followed by unemployment insurance (14%), medical insurance (11%), work injury insurance (6%) and maternity insurance (5%) (see Table 11.2).[32] Expressed as a percentage of employment in urban areas (including rural migrants), both pension insurance and unemployment insurance had similar or slightly lower coverage in 2003 than in 1995, while only medical insurance of the three biggest programmes increased between 2000 and 2003.

Social insurance coverage is modest in most developing countries.[33] For example, the ratio of pension insurance contributors to total employment in 2000 was only 11% in India and it is similarly low in most of Sub-Saharan Africa, but around 45% in Mexico and Brazil and a little more than 50% in Malaysia. A principal explanation is clearly the informal nature of employment, combined with the fact that the incomes of large groups of the population are too low for them to afford to pay contributions, while most of the existing programmes were designed for a relatively well-off part of the population. This situation appears comparable in many developing countries, although the relative size of the formal

Table 11.2. **Workers enrolled in social insurance**
Millions and per cent of employment

	Pension insurance[1]				Unemployment insurance			Medical insurance		
	Million contributors	% of total employment	% of employment in urban areas	% of employment in SOEs	Million contributors	% of total employment	% of employment in urban areas	Million contributors	% of total employment	% of employment in urban areas
1994	85	13	46	63	80	12	43	4	1	2
1995	87	13	46	63	82	12	43	7	1	4
1996	88	13	44	63	83	12	42	8	1	4
1997	87	12	42	62	80	11	38	16	2	8
1998	85	12	39	73	79	11	37	15	2	7
1999	95	13	42	75	99	14	44	15	2	7
2000	104	14	45	80	104	14	45	29	4	12
2001	108	15	45	..	104	14	43	55	7	23
2002	111	15	45	..	102	14	41	69	9	28
2003	116	16	45	..	104	14	40	80	11	31

1. Civil servants' pension plans, not shown, covered an additional 38 million workers in 2003 (5% of total employment, 15% in urban areas).

Source: *China Statistical Yearbook*, 2001 and 2004.

labour market is greater in for example Mexico, Brazil and Malaysia than in China or India. As an additional factor, there is no doubt that China's legacy of institutional segregation between urban and rural workers has exacerbated the problem of informal employment.

For several years after the reforms of the 1990s, the expected growth of social insurance enrolment was held back, and temporarily even reversed, by the downsizing of SOEs. Thus in 1998, when SOE downsizing culminated, social insurance enrolment declined in absolute numbers even though it increased as a percentage of SOE workers. The subsequent years saw moderate growth of pension and UI enrolment, led by the "formal" part of the urban private sector – mostly large firms, often privatised or jointly-owned – whose adherence to pension insurance reached 60% by 2000. In smaller private business, often informal, it is probably still much lower.

From now on, a more rapid expansion of enrolment in China's principal social insurance schemes should be a realistic objective as the previous labour market segmentation gives way to a gradually more integrated labour market. All forms of social insurance should be promoted in the urban private sector, although, in China as elsewhere, it may prove impossible to collect contributions from all the self-employed. But the government's decision in 2003 to promote the extension of social insurance to rural migrants represents a more strategic policy shift. It will probably lead to a significant expansion of enrolment already in 2004, especially for medical insurance, work-injury insurance and unemployment insurance.

6.2. Issues concerning the pension system

While most OECD countries seek to implement uniform public pension systems, China's size and its economic and social disparity impose flexibility. Some basic parameters have been harmonized across the country, but benefits vary because first-tier pensions depend on the average wage in each locality (see Box 11.2). Contribution rates are generally high in old industrial regions where there are many retired SOE workers (especially the Northeast) and low in regions that until recently were less urbanised (for example, Fujian).

> Box 11.2. **The public pension system**
>
> **Urban workers**
>
> For urban workers there are three pension tiers. The first two are mandatory for employees in all enterprises, but voluntary for the self-employed. Transitional rules exist for those who contributed before 1997.
>
> *First tier: A pay-as-you-go defined-benefit programme*
>
> *Financing:* Employer contributions vary around a national standard of 20%, of which 17 percentage points for the first tier. The pooling occurs mostly at city level, sometimes by province or by county.
>
> *Benefits:* After at least 15 years of work, the benefit is 20% of the local average wage. The pension age is 60 for men and 50 for most of the women. No first-tier benefits can be drawn with under 10 contribution years.
>
> *Second tier: A defined-contribution programme with individual saving accounts*
>
> *Financing:* Employee contributions, now usually accounting for 7% of the wage, are to be raised to 8%. In addition, three percentage points of the employer contribution go to the individual accounts.
>
> *Administration:* The government can either invest the money, mostly in bank accounts and bonds, or use it on a pay-as-you-go basis. In the latter case, which is most common, the government pays a certain rate of interest to the notional accounts.
>
> *Benefits:* Benefits amount to 1/120 of the fund as accumulated on retirement. Thus, the programme assumes an average life expectancy of 10 years on retirement, but pensions are paid until death.
>
> Workers who stop contributing after less than ten years in a locality (pooling unit) can withdraw the individual accounts. But they receive no first-tier pensions.
>
> *Third tier: Voluntary pension saving*
>
> The third tier comprises mostly enterprise pensions for employees.
>
> **Rural workers**
>
> The pension of rural workers is entirely based on voluntary savings, possibly with some support from communities. Benefits can be drawn according to the accumulation on individual accounts.

The recent transfer of the pension administration from enterprises to the state has been broadly successful, with a reported "socialisation rate" of over 99% by the end of 2002. But this would apparently not have been possible without subsidies. Provinces are in theory required to subsidise pension funds in cities that are in deficit, but in practice the central government – which gave former SOE workers the above-mentioned "two guarantees", one of which is pensions – has found it necessary to cover most of these subsidies (RMB 130 billion in 2003, with 10% matching funds from the provinces).

With the present limited resources available for subsidies or transfers via the central government, no rapid harmonization between provinces appears to be on the policy agenda. But a pooling of pension funds at province level, favoured by the MOLSS where possible, can reduce the need for central government subsidies insofar as some cities in each province report a surplus on their funds. Seven provinces currently apply such pooling, which permits a harmonization of contribution rates and benefits at province level. This should also facilitate intra-provincial mobility.

Another technical question concerning the pension system's governance concerns its second tier, consisting of individual accounts. It was designed as a funded programme, a model the MOLSS now aims to introduce gradually. But its current application is limited and mainly concerns North-Eastern China, where the ministry supports it as an experiment. As in other countries with similar systems, it requires the fund administrations to resolve many institutional problems, an effort that according to its proponents can be useful for the development of capital markets in the long term. However, most local governments now run the second pension tier as a notional defined-contribution scheme. In other words, they keep individual records and promise to pay out the notional funds as pensions, but instead of saving contribution revenues they spend them on a pay-as-you-go basis, just as under the first tier. The acceptability of this approach in the long run would seem to depend, in large part, on the extent to which the general public is confident that local governments will honour their pension debts.[34]

To facilitate the coverage of new participant groups, especially rural migrants, the government has authorized the use of differentiated contribution rates (see Box 11.3). This

Box 11.3. **Social insurance on special conditions for rural migrants: Two examples**

Chengdu (Sichuan Province) introduced an optional low-cost insurance package for migrants in March 2003, covering second-tier pension insurance, work injury insurance and basic medical insurance (hospitalisation).

Flexible contributions are calculated on a "base wage", defined as the previous year's average wage in the city times one of the following multiples: 60%, 70%, 80%, 90%, 100%, 120%, 150%. The employer chooses a multiple for each worker, with effects on benefits as well as on contributions. The contribution rate, applicable to the chosen "base wage", is 14.5% for the employer and 5.5% for the employee. For the self-employed, it is 20%. At the end of 2003, this scheme covered 84 000 workers, or 10% of the rural migrants in Chengdu.

Note that for urban workers in Chengdu, the standard contribution rates for pension, work injury and medical insurance are, respectively, 20%, 0.6 to 2% and 7.5% for employers and 8%, 0% and 2% for workers. In other words, rural migrants and their employers contribute at about half of the rates that apply to urban workers.

Chengdu also gives employers in the urban private sector a three percentage point rebate on their pension contributions, down to 17%. This affects the city's revenues to the pay-as-you-go first tier, not the individual accounts. Such workers get the full insurance package despite the rebate.

Xiamen (Fujian Province) offers reduced contributions to rural migrants and their employers in the standard social insurance. Contributions are then calculated on the basis of the city's minimum wage, and employers are offered an 8 percentage point rebate on the pension contribution rate, down to 6% compared with Xiamen's standard rate of 14%. The employee contribution rate (for second-tier pensions) is the same as for urban workers: 8%. The rebate only affects the city's revenues in the first-tier pay-as-you-go pension scheme.

most often involves a rebate on the employer's contribution rate to the first pension tier. But in addition, as in Chengdu, rural workers may be offered a choice between alternative insurance packages, with a variation in benefits as well as in contribution rates.

To the extent that a lower contribution rate can persuade more workers and employers to join the system, it can be financially advantageous to the pension fund, even if the workers concerned receive full pension rights (which is sometimes the case, but not always; see Box 11.3 and further below). Under realistic assumptions, the first-tier pension system's contribution rate (national standard: 17%) is substantially higher than needed to finance the future first-tier pensions of young workers now entering the system (*cf.* OECD, 2002). This rate appears to have been chosen in order to support the relatively generous pensions now paid to retired SOE workers, which follow transitional rules. A further circumstance that can be considered to motivate a lower contribution rate for rural workers, at least in the near future, is that few of the current elderly members of rural households receive any pensions.

Some flexibility in contribution rates and other conditions will probably be needed for many years to come. However, this does not exclude that harmonization may be desirable as a long-term goal. In principle, a uniform system can be justified both on grounds of equity and solidarity and to facilitate labour mobility. But to fulfil the latter objective, pension rights should above all be portable, not only between employers – which is essentially the case already – but between localities and provinces, requiring more administrative co-ordination.

The present pension system also has other features that make it unsuitable for workers who move frequently. Someone who leaves a job after less than 10 years and then stops contributing to the pension insurance in the city (sometimes, the province) will lose the first-tier pension rights, while any second-tier pension savings are then paid out as a lump sum. This may have limited importance for urban workers, given their traditionally low mobility. But rural migrants stay on average only three to five years in jobs, and a significant group move every year. According to Labour Bureau officials encountered by the OECD mission, migrants often want the lump-sum payments, and this may even contribute to their excessive mobility. Where this is the case, the programme cannot be said to fulfil the objectives of a pension system.

In sum, the emergence of a more integrated labour market will require further adjustments in the pension programme. Pension conditions need not be identical for all workers, but they should be transparent and individual entitlements should be portable. The present mobility patterns justify abolishing the 10-year minimum limit for contributions periods. Moreover, the pension administration should be equipped to take full account of all contributions made by an individual during his or her lifetime, regardless of where they were paid. A more centralized pension administration might facilitate this, but with good co-ordination it should also be possible in a decentralized system.

Notes

1. This chapter was written by Anders Reutersward, Non-member Economies and International Migration Division, Employment, Labour and Social Affairs Directorate, OECD. Contributions were made by Mrs. Sylvie Mouranche, Delegate of France to the Employment, Labour and Social Affairs Committee (section on labour inspection), and Ms. Hiroko Uchimura of the Development Centre (section on pensions).

2. The overall employment distribution across different parts of the labour market can be estimated only approximately, because it requires a combination of data from different sources (*cf.* OECD, 2002, Chapter 16). Table 11.1 uses official estimates of total employment and the agricultural share, based on surveys of population changes and more detailed data from separate official sources for urban and rural areas.

3. Such negative effects of informality in OECD economies, reviewed in the 2004 *Employment Outlook*, were observed, for example, in Central and Eastern Europe (Belev, 2003), various EU countries (Avignon Academy, 2002) and Mexico (Winkler, 1997). Informality has also been found to contribute to low productivity growth and uneven economic development in Brazil and other Latin American countries (Gonzaga, 2004 and McKinsey&Company, 2004, quoted in *OECD Economic Surveys: Brazil*, 2005).

4. A separate directive, also from 1994, introduced certain safeguards to prevent inspectors from abusing their powers.

5. The 2001 Law on Occupational Diseases Control and the 2002 Safe Production Law.

6. The terms "urban area" and "rural area" refer to the grassroots level of 680 000 villages with village committees and urban neighbourhood committees (number not known).

7. The government does not publish precise data about staff resources in these office networks. The cited approximate figures were obtained from MOLSS officials and white papers (Information Office of the State Council, 2002 and 2004a).

8. The OECD (2002) has also recommended some differentiation of social insurance in order to make it affordable for various groups. *Cf.* below.

9. The Minister in charge of the National Development and Reform Commission said that the government aimed to increase the rural net per capita income by 5% in 2004 by following the principle of "giving more, taking less and loosening control" (speech by Minister Ma Kai, second session of the National People's Congress, March 2004).

10. The ratio of average wages in the urban formal sector compared with township and village enterprises has increased from about 1.5 in 1999 to nearly 2, reversing a previous trend of convergence (OECD, 2002, Chapter 16; *China Statistical Yearbook* and *TVE Statistical Yearbook*, various editions). The ratio of urban to rural per capita incomes is even greater, rising from 2.6 in 1999 to 3.5 in 2002.

11. During the OECD mission to China in March 2004.

12. In discussions with the OECD mission team.

13. In practice, cities allowed recruitment of outsiders only for two very different types of work: high-skilled jobs for which there was a shortage of qualified applicants and low-skilled and unattractive jobs that urban workers did not want (OECD, 2002).

14. These *hukou* controls on recruitment have become increasingly ineffective. A competitive business climate combined with new forms of enterprise governance made it more and more difficult for the authorities to influence enterprises' choices of workers (OECD, 2002, Chapter 16).

15. During the OECD mission in March 2004.

16. OECD reviews of the public employment service in various countries were summarised in OECD (1996). More recent reviews concerned Greece, Ireland and Portugal (1998), the Baltic countries (2000) and Australia (2001a). *Cf.* Struyven and Steurs (2003) concerning the Netherlands.

17. Chengdu and Leshan (both Sichuan Province), Fuzhou and Xiamen (both Fujian Province).

18. In 2003, rural households received 54% of their reported incomes from sources other than their own primary sector activity. This comprised 35% wages, 12% non-primary self-employment and 6% transfers (*China Statistical Yearbook 2004*, Tables 1-20).

19. For example, the Labour Bureau of Fujian had recently adopted this policy target at the time of the OECD visit in 2004.

20. The reported unemployment rate was 4.3% of the urban labour force at the end of 2003. In general, however, Chinese unemployment statistics must be used with caution because the urban labour force is not well defined, and *hukou* reform makes it increasingly blurred.

21. A laid-off worker who does not find a job within three years can claim unemployment insurance benefits afterwards, raising the maximum benefit duration to altogether five years. Experience shows that many find jobs although the elderly and the low-educated often face difficulties. There have been indications that workers often delay their search for formal jobs and work informally in order to receive the benefits (OECD, 2002).

22. This training often targets older workers (women older than 40, men older than 50), with special priority for former SOE workers. For the young, in contrast, the main priority is regular education.
23. Such jobs often seem to concern the cleaning of parks and care of elderly persons. A visited neighbourhood committee in Fuzhou also functioned as a half-commercial temporary-job agency, dispatching unemployed people for work in restaurants.
24. Some special policy concern is devoted to college graduates, among whom an estimated 30% have difficulties in finding work. However, most of them are not considered as unemployed but as persons waiting for specialized jobs or further education.
25. In 2003, 145 million employees appear to have worked without fixed hours, wages or other conditions. Only 10% of them had signed employment contracts with their employers and only 14% earned over RMB 500 (USD 60) per month (China Internet Information Centre, 2004).
26. By contrast, trade unions, employers and Labour Bureaus act formally together in labour dispute committees. The task of these committees is to resolve conflicts of interest, as opposed to conflicts of right under the Labour Law which are handled by the Labour Inspectorate.
27. See, for example, annual reports of the United States Congressional-Executive Commission on China.
28. Judging from the experience of some foreign-owned enterprises, Staff Assemblies are allowed to operate independently but they cannot call themselves trade unions (Trade Union News from Finland, 2004; *United States Congressional-Executive Commission on China*, 2003, p. 25).
29. The exceptionally strong real-wage growth in SOEs – up by 68% between 1999 and 2003, compared with 46% in private and mixed-owned enterprises – appears to strengthen the case for more market-driven wage setting (*China Statistical Yearbook 2003*, Tables 5-21).
30. MOLSS officials encountered by the OECD mission regarded it as preferable for Labour Bureaus to collect contributions because this put them in a good position to control the legality of employment and wage conditions. Where tax authorities collect contributions, there is apparently a need to improve co-ordination and to provide Labour Bureaus with more detailed and timely information about contribution payments.
31. The average prefecture has around four million inhabitants, of which one-third in urban areas.
32. The cited enrolment data for work injury and maternity insurance were quoted from the Information Office of the State Council (2004). A voluntary pension saving scheme for rural workers had about 60 million contributors in 2003 according to the same source, but it is unclear to what extent it involves significant saving.
33. See OECD (2002), Table 16.8. Concerning Brazil, *cf.* (OECD, 2001b).
34. If the second tier continues to be managed on a pay-as-you-go basis, the chances that local governments will be able to pay the promised pensions can probably be enhanced for a considerable time by an upward trend in the number of contributors. But from about 2030 onwards, population ageing is set to put the pay-as-you-go system under increasing pressure.

Bibliography

Avignon Academy (2002), Undeclared Work: Empirical Evidences and New Policy Issues at European Level, *www.academyavignon.net/undwork.htm* accessed 16 October 2004.

Belev, B. (ed.) (2003), *The Informal Economy in the EU Accession Countries: Size, Scope, Trends and Challenges in the Process of EU Enlargement*, Centre for the Study of Democracy (in partnership with the World Bank and the Bertelsmann Group) (*www.csd.bg* – publications), pp. 139-174.

China Internet Information Centre, *www.china.org.cn* accessed 18 July 2004.

National Bureau of Statistics, *China Statistical Yearbook*, various editions, Beijing.

Gonzaga, G. (2003), "Labor Turnover and Labor Legislation in Brazil", in *Economía*, Latin American and Caribbean Economic Association (LACEA), Rio de Janeiro.

Information Office of The State Council (2002), *Labour and Social Security in China*, white paper, http://news.xinhuanet.com/ accessed 28 October 2004.

Information Office of The State Council (2004a), *China's Employment Situation and Policies*, white paper, http://news.xinhuanet.com/ accessed 28 October 2004.

Information Office of The State Council (2004b), *China's Social Security and its Policy*, white paper, http://english.people.com.cn/200409/07/eng20040907_156193.html accessed 4 November 2004.

Li, Bingqin (2004), *Urban Social Exclusion in Transitional China*, Case Paper 82, London School of Economics.

McKinsey and Company (2004), *Eliminando as Berreiras ao Crescimento Econômico e à Economia Formal no Brasil*, São Paulo.

Ministry of Labour and Social Security (MOLSS) (2001), *Issues on Perfecting Social Security System and Re-employment of Laid-off Workers*, Beijing.

OECD (1996), *The OECD Jobs Strategy: Enhancing the Effectiveness of Active Labour Market Policies*, OECD, Paris.

OECD (1998), *The Public Employment Service: Greece, Ireland, Portugal*, OECD, Paris.

OECD (2001a), *Innovations in Labour Market Policies: The Australian Way*, OECD, Paris.

OECD (2001b, 2005), *Economic surveys: Brazil*, OECD, Paris.

OECD (2002), *China in the World Economy: The Domestic Policy Challenges*, OECD, Paris.

OECD (2004), *Employment Outlook*, OECD, Paris.

Struyven, L. and G. Steurs (2003), *The Competitive Market for Employment Services in the Netherlands*, Occasional Paper, OECD Directorate for Employment, Labour and Social Affairs, OECD, Paris.

Trade Union News from Finland (2004), "Clothing Chain H&M Seeks Progress in China", www.artto.kaapeli.fi/unions/T2004/h07 accessed 4 November 2004 (also in *Asian Labour News*, 17 March 2004, www.asianlabour.org/archives/001226.php).

United States Congressional-Executive Commission on China (2003), *Annual Report*, Washington, D.C.

Winkler, R. 1997, "The Size and Some Effects of the Underground Economy in Mexico", in Lippert, O. and M. Walker (eds.), *The Underground Economy: Global Evidence of its Size and Impact*, The Fraser Institute, http://collection.nlc-bnc.ca/100/200/300/fraser/underground/index.html accessed 16 October 2004.

PART III

Chapter 12

Competition Law and Policy in China

Table of Contents

Summary 353

Competition Law and Policy in China 355

  1. Introduction 355

  2. General considerations 356

    2.1. The operation and benefits of market competition 356

    2.2. The roles of competition law and competition policy 357

  3. How systematic use of competition principles in policy-making
can contribute to China's economic reform 358

    3.1. The applicability of competition policy to governance issues
in China today 359

    3.2. The applicability of competition policy to policy-making in China today 360

    3.3. Competition policy and China's infrastructure monopolies 361

  4. China's need for a general competition law 362

    4.1. China's vulnerability to anti-competitive conduct by enterprises 362

    4.2. China's vulnerability to anti-competitive actions by local government
officials and bodies 364

    4.3. Misconceptions that may have delayed China's adoption
of a competition law 364

    4.4. The substance of China's competition law 365

    4.5. The structure of China's competition law enforcement system 366

  5. Conclusion 367

Notes 367

Bibliography 368

List of boxes

12.1. Steps in pro-competitive infrastructure reform 361

Summary

This chapter focuses on two issues, namely: *i)* the **enactment of a general competition law** that would provide a coherent basis for combating localism and other "monopolistic" conduct by enterprises and local governments; and *ii)* the **adoption of a "national competition policy"** calling upon all parts and levels of government to incorporate competition policy into all aspects of proposed and existing laws and policies that affect market conduct. These two issues were identified in the 2002 OECD study *China in the World Economy: The Domestic Policy Challenges* and will here be discussed from a governance perspective.

The competitive process is recognized as key to economic efficiency. In this regard, it is important to note that "economic" efficiency does not only refer to efficient use of enterprises' resources ("productive" or "technical" efficiency). It also includes the optimal development of new processes and products ("dynamic" efficiency), and the best use of society's overall resources ("allocative" efficiency), thereby maximizing the overall welfare of society. In addition, competitive markets promote economic opportunity and macroeconomic stability. By giving firms incentives to adjust to internal and external shocks, competition reduces the macroeconomic cost of adjustment.

There are two main threats to competitive markets: anti-competitive conduct by enterprises and government regulation that imposes undue restrictions on enterprises' ability to enter, exit, or otherwise respond efficiently to consumer demand. In general, **competition law** bans anti-competitive conduct by enterprises, whereas **competition policy** refers to a general approach to government regulation whose essence is that laws and regulations should not contain restrictions on competition and consumer choice that are not necessary to achieve their goals. It is important to stress that ***competition policy promotes economic efficiency in order to maximize aggregate welfare; it does not seek to maximize competition or economic efficiency regardless of the consequences***.

Systematic use of competition principles in policy-making can contribute to China's economic reform in a number of ways.

1. Competition policy can help identify and analyze problems related to **government ownership**, either by reducing government ownership or taking intermediate steps to remove particular distortions.

2. Competition policy supports **market framework regulation** necessary to permit markets to operate efficiently, such as those providing for the rule of law, the clear definition of property rights, the enforceability of contracts, the prevention of fraud and corruption, and the prevention of anti-competitive activity.

3. Competition policy affirmatively supports **industry-specific government regulation** that is necessary to deal with **market failure**, like the regulation of "natural monopolies" in infrastructure sectors. Other examples of market failure, where competition policy may

play an important role, include markets where participants' activities impose significant cost on parties outside the market, and areas such as health care, where consumers cannot be expected to have enough knowledge to prevent exploitation.

In many ways, China's overall reform programme in recent decades has reflected an implicit competition policy approach through the reduction of formal entry barriers and other unnecessary restrictions on market activity. However, there has been no call for the national government, its ministries and other bodies, or local government to include competition policy principles in their policy-making and regulatory activity. Thus, China could realize substantial benefits by requiring systematic consideration of whether proposed and existing laws and policies contain restrictions on enterprise activity that are not needed to deal with market failure or to achieve some other specific policy goal. And competition policy also provides guidance on how to regulate markets that are natural monopolies.

Whereas competition policy provides **guidance** for government entities to use in analyzing policies, laws, and regulations that affect market activity, competition law sets forth **binding prohibitions** of anti-competitive conduct. The absence of a general competition law has left China vulnerable to anti-competitive enterprise conduct and to such problems as localism. The OECD recommends the rapid adoption of a competition law. This process would highly benefit from the experience of other countries, which has been analysed by the OECD and the Asian Development Bank.

In such consultations, OECD experts could discuss relevant issues like: i) how the law could best address China's vulnerability to anti-competitive conduct by enterprises; ii) how the law could best address China's vulnerability to anti-competitive actions by local government officials and bodies; iii) the substance of China's competition law; and iv) the structure of China's competition law enforcement system.

Competition Law and Policy in China[1]

1. Introduction

A leading theme of the 2002 OECD study *China in the World Economy: The Domestic Policy Challenges* and its chapter on competition in particular, is that having made great strides towards the opening **of its borders**, China should focus greater attention on governing market activities **within its borders**. The 2002 competition chapter recommended a number of specific laws and policies:

1. First, it recommended **enactment of a general competition law** that would provide a coherent basis for combating localism and other "monopolistic" conduct by enterprises and local governments. Such conduct was and is obstructing the economic integration and efficiency that China desires in order to promote growth and improve its citizens' standard of living.

2. Second, it recommended a **competition policy approach to regulating infrastructure monopolies**, explaining how this approach could introduce efficient market competition where feasible and improve government regulation where necessary. Based on the experiences of both OECD member countries and developing economies, the chapter offered specific comments concerning China's policies concerning electricity, natural gas, telecommunications and railways.

3. Third, it recommended the **adoption of a "national competition policy"** calling upon all parts and levels of government to incorporate competition policy into every aspect of proposed and existing laws and policies that affect market conduct. Without interfering in any way with governments' ability to restrict market activity in ways that are considered necessary, such a policy would help ensure that China's social, economic and other laws and policies realize their goals without imposing unnecessary costs.

This chapter endorses all of the 2002 recommendations, but its focus is different. The 2002 chapter contained an extensive discussion on using competition principles to regulate infrastructure monopolies – the second of the above-listed recommendations. Given that discussion, and because Chapter 9 of this study already addresses China's progress in reforming its infrastructure markets, this chapter focuses on the first and third of the above recommendations, and discusses them from a governance perspective. In other words, it focuses on how competition law and policy can assist China in "perfect[ing] a modern, integrated, and competitive market economic system under its national conditions and circumstances" (Hu, 2004). After a general discussion of core principles, the chapter looks at how the systematic application of competition policy principles would benefit policy-making in China, and why and how China should establish a competition law enforcement system.

2. General considerations

2.1. *The operation and benefits of market competition*

To understand competitive markets' benefits and how they are created, it is useful to view competition as the process by which enterprises seek to discover and satisfy consumer demand. Competitive markets, then, may be seen as those in which enterprises have incentives and freedom to develop, produce, market, and sell goods and services as efficiently as possible.

In such markets, buyers and sellers are in a dynamic and constantly evolving relationship, with sellers' innovations shifting consumer demand, while changing buyer preferences suggest new directions for sellers to explore. Moreover, markets produce much of the information that market participants need to operate efficiently. If the price for one product goes up, this acts as a signal to buyers to consider existing alternatives, and alerts both current and potential sellers that they may have a business opportunity. If buyers' demand shifts away from a product, increasing inventories and falling prices warn sellers to reduce production and either improve or replace the product.

By rewarding enterprises that efficiently respond to consumer demand and punishing those that fail to do so, the competitive process creates economic efficiency. In this regard, it is important to note that "economic" efficiency does not only refer to the efficient use of enterprises' resources (*i.e.* "productive" or "technical" efficiency). It also includes the optimal development of new processes and products – "dynamic" efficiency – and the best use of society's overall resources – *i.e.* "allocative" efficiency. Thus, economically efficient markets tend to produce products and services that reflect the quality, quantity, and cost and price levels that make the best use of society's resources. Stated differently, the economic efficiency that results from competition maximizes the overall welfare of society.

This welfare-enhancing process is distorted by restrictions on both entry and exit. Restrictions on entry, it should be emphasized, include not only barriers to initial "entry" but also restrictions on efficient methods of production, marketing, distribution, and other activities. Although government restrictions of this sort can be appropriate in some markets to deal with market failure or to pursue governments' social or other legitimate goals, unnecessarily broad restrictions on entry clearly reduce the overall welfare of society.

Barriers to exit interfere with the efficient operation of markets both by creating entry barriers (since investors are more reluctant to enter markets from which exit is difficult) and by distorting the market in other ways. For example, the exit of unsuccessful enterprises may be a signal that new entry into a particular market may not be warranted. When exit barriers are combined with soft budget constraints, as is often the case with enterprises owned by local governments in China, the distortion is greatly increased. The result (as in some of China's consumer electronics markets) can be "destructive competition" in which all producers price below marginal cost.

In addition to economic efficiency, competitive markets promote economic opportunity and macroeconomic stability. Halting cartels and eliminating special treatment of protected businesses gives more citizens a chance to contribute to and benefit from the resulting economic growth. In addition, competition provides firms with incentives to adjust to internal and external shocks, thereby reducing the macroeconomic cost of adjustment to shocks.

2.2. The roles of competition law and competition policy

There are two main threats to competitive markets: anti-competitive conduct by enterprises and government regulation that imposes undue restrictions on enterprises' ability to enter, exit, or otherwise respond efficiently to consumer demand. Both anti-competitive conduct and unduly restrictive government regulation harm efficiency, create economic waste, and generally reduce the overall welfare of society by restricting output (thereby creating artificial shortages), raising prices, and reducing enterprises' incentive and ability to discover what consumers want and find innovative ways to supply it. The principal goal of competition law and policy is to promote economic efficiency by addressing these two threats.

In general, **competition law** bans anti-competitive conduct by enterprises. Especially in developing and transition economies, it sometimes also prohibits anti-competitive conduct by government officials and government regulations or policies that place unwarranted and unauthorized restrictions on enterprises.

As used in this chapter, the term **competition policy**[2] refers to a general approach to government regulation – an alternative to central planning, *laissez-faire* and command-and-control – whose essence is that laws and regulations should not contain restrictions on competition and consumer choice that are not necessary to achieve their goals. Competition policy in this sense is distinct from competition law, but complements it by addressing the costs to society of government policies and laws that impose unduly restrictive rules on market activity. Thus, competition policy is closely related to the regulatory impact analysis that is recommended in the OECD Regulatory Reform Programme. In governance terms, competition policy provides an organising principle for all policy making that affects market activities (see *e.g.* Crampton, 2004).

The basic principle of competition policy is that governments should not restrict market activity any more than is necessary to achieve their social and other goals. Systematic application of this principle can assist all governments to meet their regulatory goals as efficiently as possible, thereby maximising the overall welfare of society.

It is important to stress that competition policy promotes economic efficiency in order to maximize aggregate welfare; it does not seek to maximize competition or economic efficiency regardless of the consequences. Thus, competition policy seeks the elimination of unjustified restrictions on competition, but does not oppose restrictions that legislatures or duly authorized government bodies find necessary to meet social or other goals such as helping needy citizens, providing for the public's health and safety, or protecting the environment. Competition law does not apply to such restrictions in any way; competition policy actually provides a tool for policy makers to use in pursuing their various policy goals as efficiently as possible.

It is important here to emphasize that competition policy opposes only those government laws and policies that unnecessarily restrict competition, because in many developing economies, especially in Asia and including China, policy makers sometimes express concern that adopting a competition policy approach would mean putting competition above other social goals – that markets should be deregulated (and competition maximized) without regard to other policy considerations. This concern is misplaced. Unlike *laissez-faire* economics, a competition policy approach to regulation recognizes that both market failure and social or other goals can justify laws and policies that restrict market activity. As set forth in the *OECD 1997 Policy Recommendations on*

Regulatory Reform (see OECD, 1997) and the 1999 APEC Principles to Enhance Competition and Regulatory Reform[3] competition policy has a central role to play in the assessment of such laws and policies, and indeed in **all** regulatory analysis.

Examples may help illustrate how competition policy contributes to analyzing laws and policies that implement social and other policies.[4] A simplified example involves the manner in which governments regulate products that present safety hazards. Possible approaches include banning the manufacture of products that do not meet certain safety standards, restricting the sale of hazardous products to buyers who are deemed qualified to use them safely, and permitting products to be sold only if they have warning labels. Each of these approaches has different market effects that can and should be considered in policy-making. Some products may be so dangerous that bans or elaborate restrictions are necessary, but for products that are safe unless used in a particular way, the use of mandatory warning labels may be a "less restrictive alternative" that maximizes the overall welfare of society.

In addition, competition policy principles can help governments choose the most efficient mechanism to assist citizens who are too poor to buy the products or services they need. For example, price controls can benefit the needy, but they are costly because they also benefit those who are not needy. Moreover, the existence of price controls distorts markets in undesirable ways, reducing the incentive of firms to make needed investments. Competition policy principles show that direct subsidies to the needy can often provide assistance that is more targeted and does not distort the market in ways that waste societies' resources.

3. How systematic use of competition principles in policy-making can contribute to China's economic reform

A 2002 paper of the Development Research Centre of the State Council (DRC) on governance issues in China[5] identified two key reasons for China to improve governance. First, China should "restructure the government organisation and transfer its function" – a transfer reflecting the fact that market participants will make many decisions previously made by government. Second, China wants its government to reflect "the principles of the modern market economy as well as Chinese practice". From this perspective, the central questions facing China include the following:

1. To what extent should governments own enterprises, and how should ownership rights be structured?

2. What sectors or activities should be specifically regulated by the state, and how should they be regulated?

3. What sectors or activities should be left to the market subject to general regulatory provisions such as bans on fraud, anti-competitive activity, etc.?

As noted above, both OECD and APEC reports suggest that competition policy should be incorporated into all policy-making that may affect market activities. This section first discusses how competition policy addresses these questions in China and elsewhere, and then turns to issues that have been raised concerning the application of competition policy in China in light of its history and current conditions.

3.1. The applicability of competition policy to governance issues in China today

3.1.1. Government ownership

In China and elsewhere, government ownership of enterprises has a tendency to distort markets because it results in opportunities and incentives to confer preferential treatment and soft budget constraints. Competition policy helps identify and analyze these problems, and seeks to deal with them by either reducing government ownership or taking intermediate steps to remove particular distortions. In the case of China, where extensive government ownership is still considered important, competition policy necessarily focuses on how to minimize the resulting distortions.

3.1.2. Market framework regulation

Competition policy supports generally applicable laws or policies that are necessary to permit markets to operate efficiently, such as those providing for the rule of law, the clear definition of property rights, the enforceability of contracts, the prevention of fraud and corruption, and the prevention of anti-competitive activity. Such laws and policies may be viewed as preventing market failure, but are perhaps better seen as necessary to provide a "framework" for market activities. They may restrict market activity to some extent, but if not overbroad they are pro-competitive.

The relationship of competition law to anti-corruption activities is particularly notable. Much government corruption consists of acts that illegally favour one business over another or are otherwise anti-competitive (*e.g.* the sale of an exclusive license; see Chapter 3 on fighting corruption in China). There are two ways in which competition law enforcement complements anti-corruption enforcement.

1. In Russia and many other transition countries, competition law has successfully been used to void government acts that illegally favour one firm or group of firms; this can be done even if there is no evidence of a bribe, so long as the preponderance of the evidence shows that the action was discriminatory. Thus, competition law can deprive the bribing entity of its illegal gains even in cases when the evidence would not support a criminal conviction.

2. Bid-rigging (collusive tenders) is a specific area in which competition law complements anti-corruption laws. In many bid-rigging cases, the participating enterprises not only agree among themselves concerning the bids they will submit, but also involve a government official in their illegal conspiracy in order to be more secure that the conspiracy will succeed.

3.1.3. Industry-specific regulation to address market failure

Competition policy affirmatively supports industry-specific government regulation that is necessary to deal with market failure. The clearest example of such failure, perhaps, is the case of "natural monopoly" – where the cost structure in some element of an industry is such that efficiency requires having only one provider. In that situation, it is generally accepted that the provider should be regulated to prevent it from abusing its monopoly.[6] China has already moved towards taking a competition policy approach to regulation of some infrastructure monopolies. Given the importance of infrastructure sectors to China's citizens and its overall economy, the cost savings realizable by promoting competition in infrastructure sectors could be substantial.

Markets in which participants' activities impose significant costs on parties outside the market are another example of market failure. Such "market externalities" are the market failure on which environmental regulation is generally based. Competition policy has played an important role in the development of environmental policies in OECD member countries, and can be equally useful in China.

In areas such as health care, where consumers cannot be expected to have enough knowledge to prevent exploitation, "information asymmetries" produce market failure. In general, this form of market failure leads to the licensing of health care providers and to establishing safety standards for medication.

Where market failure exists, competition policy seeks to limit government intervention to that which is necessary to deal with the market failure. Thus, the existence of a natural monopoly element previously led to government regulation or ownership of entire industries, but the focus now is on seeking to permit competition where possible and to regulate only the natural monopoly element.

3.1.4. Other industry-specific regulation

Except where market failures exist, competition policy generally prefers that specific sectors and activities be left to the market, subject to generally applicable laws and policies. Although competition policy recognizes that some sectors and activities may be regulated for social or other reasons that do not amount to market failure, it advocates that such regulations interfere with market forces no more than necessary to achieve their goals.

3.2. The applicability of competition policy to policy-making in China today

In many ways, China's overall reform programme in recent decades has reflected an implicit competition policy approach, in that China has taken dramatic steps to reduce formal entry barriers and other unnecessary restrictions on market activity. However, there has been no call for the national government, its ministries and other bodies, or local governments to include competition policy principles in their policy-making and regulatory activity. Given the extensive market reform that China has been pursuing, and the unfamiliarity of most Chinese officials with competition policy principles, China could realize substantial benefits by requiring the systematic consideration of whether proposed and existing laws and policies contain restrictions on enterprise activity that are not needed to deal with market failure or to achieve some other specific policy goal.

As noted above, competition policy analysis is very closely related to the kind of regulatory impact analysis that the OECD has recommended in its Regulatory Reform Programme.[7] Some have argued that these approaches are not appropriate for China today because of: i) China's heavy reliance on the exercise of administrative discretion by line ministries; and ii) its relative lack of independent bodies that engage in *ex ante*, rules-based regulation of enterprise conduct. This argument misconceives the role of competition policy as merely a discipline for regulatory decision-making by independent entities, rather than a general approach to all policy-making, legislation and regulation that affects market activities. China's National People's Congress, the State Council (and its Office for Legislation) and ministries can and should use competition policy in making policy judgments and exercising discretion, and it is recommended that China also require local government entities to apply this approach.

China's relative unfamiliarity with competition policy principles is not a reason to refrain from requiring systematic use of competition policy as a tool to policy-making. Competition policy analysis of some issues can be very complex, but it begins with the simple but important step of asking whether a policy, law, regulation or other action is designed to achieve its desired goals (health, safety, environmental protection, etc.) without interfering with market mechanisms more than necessary. By adopting a national competition policy or otherwise requiring government entities to consider this question in making policies or decisions that affect market activity, China could reduce the likelihood of unwarranted restrictions while at the same time increasing awareness of competition considerations without interfering with governments' ability to adopt the policies they consider necessary.

3.3. Competition policy and China's infrastructure monopolies

Although competition policy provides a guide to all policy-making that restricts market conduct, it is useful to note specifically its application to infrastructure industries. In this respect, competition policy begins by taking a sceptical approach to claims that a market has natural monopoly elements. Moreover, bearing in mind that natural monopoly markets can and do become potentially competitive over time, competition policy advocates regular reviews to determine whether markets stop being natural monopolies because of new technologies, new sources of supply, etc.

Competition policy also provides guidance on how to regulate markets that are natural monopolies. In this regard, much of competition policy consists of an analysis of how alternative rules are likely to affect the behaviour of the regulated firm and of the firms with which it deals.[8] The key reform steps that face China are described in Box 12.1. China has made some progress in reforming some of its infrastructure sectors, but, as is further discussed in Chapter 9 of this report, much remains to be done.

Box 12.1. **Steps in pro-competitive infrastructure reform**

- Define the boundaries between commerce and the state, and the respective roles of commercial enterprises to operate and the state to regulate. Competition is hampered where the division between state and commerce is unclear, because potential competitors to state-owned enterprise fear a "tilted playing field" and will hesitate to enter. Further, the separation means that government policy decisions must be made explicit in order for the commercial operator to carry them out.

- Establish state regulatory institutions that have the powers and the resources necessary to regulate commercial infrastructure enterprises so as to ensure that they achieve efficiency and other regulatory goals. These institutions will use regulations to create incentives for commercial entities by, for example, reducing regulatory barriers, ensuring fair and efficient access to essential facilities, and ensuring that regulation is predictable. Thus, a market environment requires regulatory institutions that make decisions that are neutral, transparent and not subject to day-to-day political pressures or capture.

- Put into place corporate governance systems to ensure adequate control and incentives for commercial infrastructure enterprises.

- Use competition principles to specify the structures of the sectors and the regulations that will be applied to ensure that they are efficient and will meet universal service objectives.

4. China's need for a general competition law

Whereas competition policy provides **guidance** for government entities to use in analyzing policies, laws, and regulations that affect market activity, competition law sets forth **binding prohibitions** of anti-competitive conduct. In most OECD member countries, the competition law applies to enterprises, including state-owned enterprises, but the competition laws enacted by many transition and developing countries include binding prohibitions on unauthorised, anti-competitive actions by government officials or bodies.

Like laws banning corruption and regulating natural monopolies, competition law is increasingly understood to be a necessary part of the framework for governing a market economy. Competition laws have been adopted by virtually all transition and many developing countries, and the record clearly shows that competition law enforcement can play an important part in the market reforms of such countries.

The absence of a general competition law has left China vulnerable to anti-competitive enterprise conduct and to such problems as localism. It therefore recommended that China move quickly to finalize and adopt a competition law. This recommendation was based on close co-operation between the OECD and China's "drafting group", which prepared an amendment of the competition legislation, during the 1997-2001 period. The OECD co-sponsored seminars to discuss draft laws and the Secretariat submitted detailed comments and suggestions on several occasions.

Despite much good work by China's anti-monopoly law drafting group, past drafts of the law have raised a significant number of issues concerning what private conduct is banned, how China will address anti-competitive abuses of government entities' administrative monopoly, how the law will treat market definition and the assessment of market power, what kind of evidence will be necessary to condemn particular practices as abuses of dominance, how allegedly anti-competitive horizontal and vertical agreements will be assessed, and how the merger review process will operate. In May 2005 the Legislative Affairs Office of the State Council held an important international conference to consider a new draft that addresses these issues in constructive ways. An OECD Secretariat representative attended the conference, and the OECD's Competition Division is providing comments on the new draft.

The discussion below addresses the following major topics: China's vulnerability to anti-competitive enterprise conduct and to unauthorised anti-competitive actions by local government officials and bodies, misconceptions that may have delayed China's adoption of a competition law, the substance of China's competition law, and the structure of China's competition law enforcement system.

4.1. China's vulnerability to anti-competitive conduct by enterprises

Because the 2002 OECD China Study focused on the domestic policy challenges to China's trade and investment liberalization, its competition chapter focused on the fact that none of China's competition-related laws provided a means to halt exclusionary conduct that obstructs the new entry that trade and investment reforms were intended to produce. China's vulnerability to such conduct continues today and remains the most important reason for the prompt enactment of a competition law.

Two points merit re-emphasis. First, some policy makers and scholars consider competition law a relatively low priority, arguing that since China's industrial concentration (the percentage of production, sales, or some other measure accounted by the leading enterprises) is relatively low, monopoly or market power is not a current problem in China. This argument is flawed, because concentration is not a meaningful indicator of competitiveness unless it reflects conditions in economically defined "product markets" and "geographic markets". Available reports of concentration in China, however, are generally based on statistical product categories and administrative boundaries; such reports are not reliable and are often very misleading. Given China's size, transportation problems and localism, national concentration ratios clearly understate actual market concentration in China.

Second, some policy makers and scholars have suggested that competition law is less important in China than in some other countries, because China has a problem of "administrative monopoly", rather than "enterprise monopoly". This argument is also flawed. It is true that preferential treatment by government is often the source of enterprises' power, and it is important to seek to eliminate the laws and policies that create or protect this power. However, government policies are a major source of enterprises' market power in all countries, and there is no policy reason for permitting abuses by enterprises that derive their power in this way.

A recent report by China's State Administration for Industry and Commerce (SAIC) focused on China's need for a competition law from a somewhat different perspective – China's vulnerability to anti-competitive conduct by foreign enterprises. The report's allegations against particular firms were not documented and remain unconfirmed, and some of the report's analysis was unclear or questionable. For example, the report appeared in some places to suggest that multinational firms have a dominant position merely because they have greater assets or experience than domestic competitors, whereas mainstream competition analysis finds dominance only when a firm has the power to behave substantially independently of its competitors in a relevant market.[9] Nonetheless, the report is certainly correct in saying that China's lack of a competition law exposes it to anti-competitive conduct by foreign enterprises as well as domestic ones.

As implied by the SAIC report, the competition-related measures China has taken since 2002 do not protect it against exclusionary or other anti-competitive conduct. In 2003, the State Development and Planning Commission (now the National Development and Reform Commission) issued *Provisional Regulations on Prohibiting Price Monopolistic Conduct*. The rules were a step forward, but they merely implemented the existing prohibitions and did not reduce China's vulnerability to anti-competitive conduct.

Also in 2003, China's Ministry of Foreign Trade and Economic Co-operation (now the Ministry of Foreign Trade and Commerce [MOFCOM]) issued Provisional Regulations on the Merger and Acquisition of Domestic Enterprises by Foreign Investors. These regulations may give China some protection against anti-competitive acquisitions, but they also could be improved. The regulations establish separate pre-merger notification thresholds for foreign investors' onshore and offshore acquisitions of equity or assets of domestic enterprises. (Mergers involving foreign firms are not covered by these regulations, but rather by a different regulation that has no pre-merger notifications system.) Improvements to the regulations could include: *i)* consistency concerning whether "foreign-invested enterprises" are "domestic enterprises"; *ii)* definitions of "onshore" and "offshore" transactions; *iii)* clarification of the standards for the disapproval of proposed transactions; *iv)* clarification of the respective roles of the two "relevant antitrust authorities" (the SAIC and MOFCOM); *v)* the creation of a clear deadline for the antitrust authorities to make a decision; *vi)* the application of "national treatment"; and vii) revision of a provision empowering a domestic competitor or trade association to request a pre-merger notification not otherwise required by the law.

At least some of the issues with the proposed "merger and acquisition" regulations have apparently been acknowledged by Chinese officials (see Tao, 2004). The existence of these issues, all of which relate to only one of the many topics that should be covered by China's competition law, illustrate the benefits that could come from further consultations with international experts to discuss the draft and any concerns Chinese officials have with incorporating international "best practice" standards into its competition law.

4.2. China's vulnerability to anti-competitive actions by local government officials and bodies

China's desire to create a more integrated economy is well known. Some of the obstacles to such integration are simply a reflection of its size, but the task of integration is made much more difficult by localism. Local governments are generally authorized to regulate commerce in various ways in order to protect the health and welfare of their citizens, but in many cases local governments in China have taken unauthorised, anti-competitive actions to prevent entry by new firms or products, thus protecting local enterprises at the expense of their citizens. Examples of such conduct were discussed in the 2002 competition chapter and are presented in various other chapters of both the 2002 China Study and this Report on Governance in China.

China's Law Against Unfair Competition[10] prohibits "administrative monopoly", which includes but is not limited to the unauthorized use of governmental power to impose protectionist policies. This law is enforced by the SAIC, and its enforcement has had some success in challenging localism. However, the SAIC has had significantly less success in challenging local government restraints than that achieved in the comparable activities of, for example, the competition bodies of the European Union, Russia, and Peru. There appear to be two reasons for China's relative lack of success. First, the local Administrations of Industry and Commerce are part of the local governments they are charged with policing, whereas the successful programmes use a central competition authority. Second, unlike most competition laws applicable to local government conduct, the Unfair Competition Law does not authorize the SAIC either to rescind illegal decisions or agreements, or to impose fines or other sanctions.

In order to deal more effectively with localism and other unauthorized, anti-competitive actions by local governments, China should include a ban on administrative monopoly in its competition law. Moreover, the law should authorize the competition authority to rescind illegal decisions or agreements and impose sanctions for violations. Finally, as discussed further below, the extent to which local governments are responsible for anti-competitive activity in China means that the competition law should be enforced by a central competition authority whose local offices are not dependent on local governments.

4.3. Misconceptions that may have delayed China's adoption of a competition law

In the past, some policy makers and scholars have opposed China's adoption of a competition law on the grounds that competition law enforcement would: i) prevent Chinese firms from merging to achieve minimum efficient scale, or ii) interfere with China's "industrial policy" initiatives, including in particular the creation of "national champions". Neither of these objections is sound. Competition law does not prevent mergers to achieve minimum efficient scale or in any way reduce a country's ability to create national champions or pursue other forms of industrial policy.

4.4. The substance of China's competition law

The substance of China's competition law can and should reflect both China's current conditions and international best practice. China's legal, cultural and other conditions will undoubtedly affect the enforcement structure it chooses, but they should not influence the core substantive provisions of the law. As in other countries, the law should ban abuse of dominance, anti-competitive agreements, and mergers and acquisitions that substantially lessen competition or create or maintain a dominant position. Moreover, the law should make it clear that except perhaps for cases involving hard core cartels or other conduct that is clearly anti-competitive and lacking any efficiency justification, all competition cases require: i) the definition of relevant product and geographic markets; and ii) the assessment of market power.

Despite much good work by China's anti-monopoly law drafting group, past drafts of the law have raised a significant number of issues concerning what kind of private conduct is banned, how China will address anticompetitive abuses of government entities' administrative monopoly, how the law will treat market definition and the assessment of market power, what kind of evidence will be necessary to condemn particular practices as abuses of dominance, how allegedly anti-competitive horizontal and vertical agreements will be assessed, and how the merger review process will operate. In May 2005 the Legislative Affairs Office of the State Council held an important international conference to consider a new draft that addresses these issues in constructive ways.

In addition to assuring that its competition law provides an efficient way of addressing anti-competitive conduct, China should – for "good governance" reasons – eliminate overlaps between the competition law and other laws. For example, China's Price Law bans monopolistic pricing, and its Provisional Regulations explain that this ban extends to output restrictions. At the same time, China's draft competition laws have consistently included "monopolistic pricing" and "output restrictions" as abuses of dominance. Such conduct is a harmful exploitation of market power. Although, at least in developed economies, it is increasingly believed that it is counter-productive to try to halt the conduct since: i) assessing whether pricing (or reduced output) is monopolistic is very difficult; and ii) halting such conduct is likely to prolong the monopoly, whereas permitting it encourages entry which can eliminate the monopoly. Assuming that China wants to continue to ban such conduct, it would be sensible to remove the bans from the draft competition law and keep them in the Price Law, which is enforced by an body whose price regulation responsibilities give it skills and tools that China's competition authority is unlikely to have.

On the other hand, some provisions of the Price Law – Articles 14.1 (collusion), 14.2 (predatory pricing) and 14.5 (price discrimination) – relate to conduct whose assessment requires the core skills and tools of a competition authority. Since it would be inefficient and very confusing to have two different bodies enforcing similar but non-identical provisions using different procedures and applying different sanctions, it is recommended that the competition law explicitly repeal these provisions of the Price Law. For the same reason, it is recommended that the competition law explicitly repeal Articles 6 (tying by statutory monopolists) and 11 (predatory pricing), and the first sentence in Article 15 (collusive tenders) of the Unfair Competition Law.

4.5. The structure of China's competition law enforcement system

How China will structure its competition law enforcement system is a vitally important issue. The discussion below therefore provides a comparatively extensive discussion of the considerations China might take into account in deciding the kind of competition authority it wants.

Some countries have competition policy departments in a number of ministries and bodies, and some give competition policy responsibility to a particular ministry, but it is generally accepted that an effective competition law enforcement system requires that the competition authority be free from undue influence by ministries, other government entities and other stakeholders. The importance of this independence was affirmed at the OECD Global Forum on Competition (GFC) in February 2003, which devoted considerable attention to the optimal design of competition authorities.[11] Those discussions noted that independence is not simply a matter of the formal organisational status of the authority or its place in the government administrative structure, though institutional and budgetary independence are clearly useful in protecting competition law enforcement decisions from being subordinated to other government objectives.

Despite the need to go beyond formal measures of dependence or independence, it may be useful to note that of the competition authorities that responded to a Secretariat questionnaire in connection with the 2003 GFC meeting, about 35% considered themselves as independent of government. Another 20% or so were independent of ministries but considered themselves in some way as responsible to government. Approximately 45% were part of a ministry.

Of course, no competition authority can be completely independent from the government structure of which it is a part. The authority's leadership is nominated or appointed by a government officer – often the President or the Prime Minister – though many countries provide a check on the appointment power by setting forth the necessary qualifications and/or requiring that nominees be reviewed by the legislature or some other independent body. Some countries also legislate that appointees may be removed only for cause. Competition authorities' need for government funding generally provides another opportunity for government to influence their actions. This opportunity is sometimes abused, but it is partially protected from abuse if restrictions imposed by the budget process are a matter of public record.

On the other hand, even competition bodies that are part of a ministry can be given substantial independence, at least with respect to their law-enforcement decisions. In countries with long traditions of competition law enforcement, this independence may be a matter of custom rather than law, but legal protection of independence is also common. For example, Germany's competition authority is organisationally part of the Ministry of Economics and Labour, but the independence of its decision-making process is subject to numerous legal protections. The ministry may become involved in competition cases only after the authority has completed a proceeding and prohibited a merger or cartel, at which point it can issue a public ministerial authorisation. Even this limited ministerial "override" could undermine competition enforcement, but it has not done so in Germany because the override has very rarely been used.

Although it is possible to provide the necessary independence for a competition authority that is part of a ministry, many countries prefer to create their competition authorities as independent entities, often multi-member commissions whose members are appointed for fixed terms and are removable only for cause. Other countries prevent their competition authorities from being subordinated to any particular ministry by making the authority directly responsible to the council of ministers or the Prime Minister.

Thus, another alternative that China could consider is the creation of a new national competition authority that is independent from China's ministries and whose local offices are independent from local governments. China does not have many independent bodies, and its national bodies tend to operate in local areas through the local governments. Nevertheless, China has taken some steps in this direction, and it could consider this alternative with respect to competition law enforcement because this is a field in which the need for independence is widely recognized.[12]

5. Conclusion

China's national government has implicitly applied competition policy principles in much of its recent policy-making, and by requiring a more systematic application of those principles by all national and local government entities, China could reduce the extent to which laws and policies waste resources by imposing unnecessary restrictions on legitimate market activity. A competition law is one of the key frameworks of a market economy, and China's lack of such a law reduces its ability to halt ongoing anti-competitive activity by enterprises and local governments.

Notes

1. This chapter was written by Terry Winslow, Consultant, with the guidance of Lennart Goranson and Bernard Phillips, Competition Division, Directorate for Financial and Enterprise Affairs, OECD.
2. The term is sometimes used as a synonym for competition law and sometimes to refer to a set of policies of which competition law is a part.
3. See *www.oecd.org/dataoecd/48/52/2371601.doc*.
4. The competition chapter in OECD (2002a) provides a more extensive description of situations in which OECD member countries have used competition policy principles in deciding what policies to pursue in infrastructure monopolies and in other kinds of policy analysis.
5. DRC (2002).
6. For a time, New Zealand sought to deal with natural monopoly sectors merely through its general competition law and the possibility of direct regulatory intervention, but in recent years it has increasingly taken a more regulatory approach.
7. Also see Chapter 9 on regulatory reform and management in China.
8. For a detailed discussion see OECD (2002a). Since then, the OECD Competition Division has pursued these issues by holding a seminar with China's Development Research Centre on promoting competition as part of railway reform in China (see OECD 2002b), and participating in relevant OECD and other conferences in China.
9. Moreover, the report's list of abuses discussed various forms of conduct as abuses without discussing whether the conduct had efficiency justifications that rendered it pro-competitive on balance. It discussed exclusive dealing, for example, as if it were always anti-competitive when engaged in by a dominant firm.
10. The current Law Against Unfair Competition does not meet the requirements of a general competition law, based on internationally recognised principles on anti-competitive behaviour.
11. See OECD (2004), which contains a summary of those discussions (and other matters considered during the first three meetings of the GFC. Both this summary and the background materials for the discussions are available at *www.oecd.org/competition*.

12. A particular aspect of institutional design was discussed in the 2005 meeting of the GFC, i.e. the relationship between competition authorities and sectoral regulators. China attended this event and submitted a written contribution [DAF/COMP/GF/WD(2005)9].

Bibliography

Bruce M. Owen, Su Sun and Wentong Zheng (2004), *Antitrust in China: The Problem of Incentive Compatibility*, AEI-Brookings Joint Center for Regulatory Studies, available at *http://aei-brookings.org/admin/authorpdfs/page.php?id=1052*.

Crampton, Paul (2004), *Competition Policy and Efficiency as Organising Principles for All Economic and Regulatory Policymaking*, IADB Working Paper, Series No. 2, January, prepared for the first meeting of the OADB/OECD Latin American Competition Forum. The report is available at *www.oecd.org/dataoecd/43/26/2490195.pdf*.

DRC (2002), *Governance Research in DRC*.

Hu Angang (2004), *Perfecting the Market Economic System, Meeting The Challenges of Economic Development*, Chinese version of *China in the World Economy*, Tsinghua University Press, China, 2004.

OECD (1997), *OECD Report on Regulatory Reform: Summary*, OECD, Paris.

OECD (1999), *The APEC Principles to Enhance Competition and Regulatory Reform*, available at *www.oecd.org/dataoecd/48/52/2371601.doc*.

OECD (2002a) *China in the World Economy: The Domestic Policy Challenges*, OECD, Paris.

OECD (2002b), *Railway Reform in China: Promoting Competition*, OECD, Paris.

OECD (2004), *Global Forum on Competition: Preventing Market Abuses and Promoting Economic Efficiency, Opportunity, and Growth*, OECD, Paris, available at *www.oecd.org/competition*.

OECD (2005), "The Relationship between Competition Authorities and Sectoral Regulators", DAF/COMP/GF/WD(2005)9.

Tao Jingzhou (2004), "China's Emerging Antitrust Regime", *The China Business Review*, May-June, at pp. 60-63.

Washington University Global Studies Law Review (2004), Vol. III, No. 2, Symposium: Chinese Antimonopoly Law. The entire symposium may be found at *http://law.wustl.edu/Publications/WUGSLR/volume_3_2.html*.

PART III

Chapter 13

Governance of Banks in China

Table of Contents

Summary 373

Governance of Banks in China 375

  1. Introduction 375
  2. Governance in the banking sector........................ 376
     2.1. The role of financial institutions in a market economy.... 376
     2.2. Special characteristics of banking...................... 376
     2.3. Governance and banking supervision...................... 377
     2.4. Internal risk management and the credit culture......... 377
     2.5. Market discipline 379
     2.6. Shareholders and bank governance 379
  3. Governance of banks in China............................ 380
     3.1. Historical legacy....................................... 380
     3.2. The present situation in the banking sector 380
     3.3. The institutional structure of the banking system 382
  4. Renewed efforts to reform the banking system after 2003 385
     4.1. Reforms in bank supervision 386
     4.2. Changing patterns of ownership.......................... 387
     4.3. Improving the framework for corporate governance in banking 390
     4.4. Transparency and exposure to markets 393
     4.5. Expanded foreign competition............................ 393
  5. Rehabilitation programme for the SOCBs................... 394
     5.1. Projected ownership changes............................. 394
     5.2. Internal governance of the pilot SOCBs 396
  6. Summary and conclusions................................. 397

Notes 399

Bibliography 400

List of boxes

13.1. Internal governance and banking supervision............ 378
13.2. Chinese banks under central planning 381

Summary

The conceptual framework for governance in banking reflects the special role of banks in a market economy. In order for the bank to act as a profit-oriented corporation, it must have genuine owners and the corporate governance regime should enable the owners to hold the management accountable for achieving a competitive return at acceptable risk. At the same time, banks have fiduciary obligations to depositors and also perform many "public good" functions such as acting as repository of savings, supplying currency and allocating resources in the real economy. Therefore, banks operate in a regulated environment.

There is a very close link between governance and supervision. The supervisors retain the right to determine whether their governance system, including their system of risk management, is appropriate. The modern paradigm of financial supervision relies on the bank's internal governance as the first "pillar" of bank oversight. The other two "pillars" are: i) surveillance by the market; and ii) official banking supervision.

With the economic reform begun in the late 1970s, Chinese banks have been moving way from their passive role under central planning. However, owing to unclear ownership structures and a history of support of regional and industrial policy, most Chinese banks have a governance regime that is not well adapted to the active role in resource allocation of banks in a market economy. This is particularly true for the four large state-owned commercial banks (SOCBs) which account for the predominant share of bank assets. Lacking profit-oriented owners to monitor bank management, the SOCBs have historically functioned as extensions of the government, with senior executives named by the party and approved by the State Council.

Part of the problem is that with their poor quality assets, the banks are financially weak. In 1998-99, a significant effort to strengthen SOCB balance sheets was undertaken with the sale of a large portion of non-performing loans (NPLs) to government-owned asset management companies. While resources committed to bank restructuring amounted to more than 16% of GDP, the results were nonetheless disappointing. The financial quality of the big four SOCBs remained rather poor, with low earnings, inadequate capital, and continued high levels of NPLs. The authorities concluded that further attempts at rehabilitation of the SOCBs had to address the issue of bank governance.

In contrast to the SOCBs, the second largest category of banks, the 11 Joint Stock Banks (JSBs), have stronger earnings and better balance sheets. The JSBs, which are owned partly by the government and partly by other interests, do not have the historical legacy as instruments of supporting government policy and their management has a stronger commitment to profitability.

The key elements of the most recent phase of the reform, which began in 2003, are:

- improved ownership structures of SOCBs;
- government support for two "pilot" SOCBs, conditional upon improvements in governance;

- heightened competition between the SOCBs and other kinds of domestic banks;
- increased transparency and exposure of all Chinese banks to scrutiny by the market;
- an expanded foreign presence partly linked to Chinese WTO membership and partly linked to a desire to benefit from foreign competition.

Ownership diversification, public listing and expanded foreign presence are designed to subject all banks to higher standards of transparency and disclosure, with more intense scrutiny by banking counterparties, investment analysts, institutional investors and rating agencies. At the same time, measures to improve bank supervision were accelerated with the formation of a specialized independent agency for bank supervision (the China Banking Regulatory Commission or CBRC) and the enactment of a series of laws and regulations pertaining to bank supervision.

In December 2003 a special entity (Huijin) was set up to assume the state's ownership interest in the SOCBs. The "pilot" SOCBs will first be transformed into joint stock companies with the state as the sole owner and will receive cash injections to increase capital to adequate levels and build reserves against NPLs. The pilot banks are expected to find domestic and international strategic investors to assume ownership positions and play an active role in corporate governance while Huijin represents the state's interest. The SOCBs will select their own management, which will be accountable for meeting the most commonly used benchmarks for earnings and balance sheet quality as well as targets for improvement in internal governance.

The JSBs have already been gaining market share in recent years and now have an opportunity to expand their share of the banking market yet further. To make further gains, the JSBs will raise capital by: i) domestic or international equity; ii) issues of subordinated debt; and/or iii) strategic investments by foreign banks. This will lead to changes in ownership structures and more intense market scrutiny for the JSBs.

While the programme is bold, there are doubts about how bank restructuring will proceed. On the one hand, competition may lead to a further contraction of the share of SOCBs in total lending, which could make the problems more manageable. On the other hand, it is not certain whether planned reforms are sufficient to make the SOCBs operate as market-based institutions. Continued majority state control of SOCBs with dispersed minority stakes may not result in effective monitoring of bank performance. The banks may be seen as "too big to fail"; they may still be perceived as benefitting from government support and therefore may not be exposed to full market competition. Ownership diversification and public listing thus far have generally not led to markedly improved performance for Chinese companies and thus their impact on banks is uncertain. Despite these uncertainties, the changes already introduced are such that there is no serious option of reverting to the old patterns of behaviour.

Governance of Banks in China[1]

1. Introduction

This chapter analyzes the special governance issues facing banks in China. Owing to their poor financial quality and their substandard governance systems, the major Chinese banks have been operating in ways that run counter to market-based rules of economic conduct. Since the onset of the reform in the late 1970s, awareness of the need to reform banks has grown. But banks have been slow to adapt their ways to the economic paradigms of a market economy and continue to lend to support state-owned enterprises, especially those that enjoyed the support of local government.

Efforts to change patterns of bank behaviour accelerated in the late 1990s, when the government sought to address the problem through providing funds to the banks for recapitalisation and for the removal of impaired assets from bank balance sheets. However, it soon became obvious that these measures were insufficient in scope to address the balance-sheet problems of banks and in any case the provision of funds provided no incentive to prevent the banks from reverting to earlier patterns of lending.

Since 2003, efforts to reform banks have been accelerated, with one of the express objectives of the present reform being an improvement in bank governance practices. While most of these policy changes have been under discussion for several years, taken together, the measures to reform the banking system represent a major step in the direction of a market-based financial system. Specific reform measures include further upgrading of supervisory techniques in line with international practices as well as significant opening and liberalization of the banking system.

Since this study focuses on issues of governance, it will focus on those particular parts of the banking system where reforms aimed at improving governance are explicit policy aims. As a result, the note will not be a full analysis of the situation in the banking system. Measures specifically aimed at improving governance include a change in the ownership of commercial banks, an enlarged possibility for banks other than those entirely owned by the state to compete, improved internal control systems, greater transparency and market discipline, and more competition from foreign owned banks. The aim of these measures is to strengthen incentives for bank management to operate the bank in the interests of financial return rather than in response to a mix of financial and non-financial considerations, some of which may be inconsistent.

This chapter first considers the question of why the governance of financial institutions, and particularly banks, requires a special framework of analysis, and some of the distinctive governance issues that characterize banks. Subsequently, the specific issues facing the Chinese banking system will be addressed.

2. Governance in the banking sector

2.1. The role of financial institutions in a market economy

Financial institutions (banks, securities companies, pension funds and investment management companies) occupy a unique place in market economies. Financial institutions gather the savings of the public, exchange and analyze information about prospective users of financial resources, price risk, balance risk against return, and channel resources to those entities in the economy that seem most profitable while encouraging change in those where performance is deficient. To the degree that the behaviour of financial institutions deviates from this pattern, the economy will have difficulty in operating according to market signals.

Financial institutions operate in a highly regulated environment. All governments have decided that it is permissible to carry out financial business (banking, securities, insurance or pensions) only through a defined legal and regulatory framework and have devised formal arrangements that stipulate the conditions under which it is permissible to solicit the savings of the public for various financial activities.

While financial institutions are expected to operate inside the normative framework that covers all corporate entities,[2] the governance structure of financial companies must also address some issues that are peculiar to the financial sector. Financial institutions typically utilize only small amounts of their own funds (capital) and instead deploy funds entrusted to them by the public. Financial institutions control large pools of assets and it is extremely difficult for the individual saver to monitor the ways in which financial institutions use those funds. Persons inside the institution, such as the management, brokers, traders, or money managers may not act in the interests of the client. Moreover, financial institutions frequently have ownership and control linkages to other key actors, such as allied industrial companies, governments, and local communities as well as their own management and workers. These linkages raise the risk of conflicts of interest and agency problems. Indeed, in emerging markets it is fairly common for these institutions to be "captured" by some group of outside parties. The governance regime has to build robust structures to protect the interests of parties to whom the institution owes a fiduciary duty.

Supervision and regulation are parts of the governance systems of the financial institution in a way that differs from non-financial institutions. Provisions in laws and regulations typically define products and prices, and licenses are required to engage in financial business. Furthermore, the supervisory authorities reserve the right to pass judgment on the adequacy of the governance of the institution.

2.2. Special characteristics of banking

The basic framework for governance of financial institutions has certain specific characteristics when applied to banking. Banks have special responsibilities regarding the issue of currency and the conduct of monetary policy. In most OECD member countries, a regime of deposit insurance guarantees that at least smaller depositors will be made whole even if the bank in which the deposit is made is unable to honour its commitments. By extending such guarantees, the authorities in effect remove the incentive for insured depositors to monitor banks, thus enabling banks to obtain funds without paying a risk premium fully commensurate with their risk profile. Systemic bank failures can have powerful negative effects on household wealth and on economic performance more generally. Furthermore, official rescues of failed banking systems are often very costly. For all these reasons, the authorities of most countries have decided that the banking supervisors may exercise higher degrees of control surveillance of the process whereby banks assume risks than is exercised over most companies and over other financial institutions.

2.3. Governance and banking supervision

While banking supervision entails a higher degree of control than other financial supervision, a process of deregulation has been occurring in finance over the past few decades. With deregulation, banking has become a highly competitive market-driven activity. In current conditions, banks are devising new product mixes and undertaking mergers and acquisitions and strategic alliances, frequently eroding the earlier lines of product segmentation. In current conditions, banks are allowed to compete much more freely than in the past and, at least in advanced markets, are under intense pressures to produce value for shareholders. The supervisory authorities are much more inclined than in the past to allow banks to determine their own risk preferences and to devise their own expansion strategies. Thus, the methods of bank supervision have evolved.

When a bank is adequately capitalised, the management places the capital of the owners at risk and the owners' investment is the first line of defence in maintaining financial integrity. It is plainly in the interest of the bank's shareholders to assure that high standards of profitability and financial soundness are maintained, since any deficiency on these scores ultimately falls on the bank's owners. The supervisor's main concern is to make sure that the bank operates within these parameters and does not experience a deterioration in financial condition that would shift the burden for risk-bearing to the public sector, by triggering government deposit insurance or by requiring intervention to assure the continuing operation of the bank or to prevent a disorderly bank failure that may cause systemic disturbances. Instead of the multiplicity of objectives and tight restrictions they faced in the past, banks are now expected: i) to earn adequate rates of return; ii) to observe high prudential standards and to maintain high quality risk management systems; and iii) to protect the interests of depositors.

Rather than criticising the bank's loan portfolio in detail, banks supervisors now see their role as one of engaging in dialogue with the directors of the bank and senior management about the risks the bank is taking, the quality of the bank's balance sheet and the systems that are in place to deal with those risks. Bank supervisors have systems under which they use a variety of quantitative and judgmental indicators to score banks under their own supervision.

2.4. Internal risk management and the credit culture

In order to protect the owners' investment and satisfy the requirements of supervisors, banks require strong internal "credit cultures" consisting of a strong in-house capability to analyze credit risk coupled with in-house systems to monitor the granting of credit and the assumption of risk. In competitive markets, the ability to characterize and price risk is a crucial determinant of whether the bank will survive and prosper. Credit analysts assign each proposed transaction a risk rating, and based upon this rating a cost of credit is assigned. Only deals that clear the bank's profit hurdles are approved.[3]

The internal audit function assures that information disseminated internally and externally is accurate and protects the integrity of the disclosure process. The audit committee of the board of directors is the ordinary means by which the attention of the board is kept focused on the audit process. The responsibilities of this committee include

Box 13.1. **Internal governance and banking supervision**

The relationship between the supervisory system of financial institutions and the internal governance of the institution has evolved significantly with deregulation. Previously, bank supervisors expended considerable effort validating financial accounts and examining individual loans, balance sheets and lending practices to check conformity with rules. These examinations often tended to occur at discrete time intervals. In the 1990s, however, banks began to innovate and to accept new kinds of risk. Many of these newer risks were not amenable to traditional examinations at discrete time intervals, since risk profiles changed rapidly within time periods. Simultaneously, the authorities have increasingly concluded that the responsibility for risk oversight must ultimately be the responsibility of the individual bank. The full process of oversight of banks consists of three elements: i) risk management and governance systems within the institution; ii) surveillance by the market; and iii) prudential oversight by the supervisory authorities.

As the nature of bank supervision evolved, supervisors increasingly insist on sound corporate governance inside the bank as the foundation of bank supervision. One aspect of bank governance is that the bank's directors and senior managers are responsible for seeing that banks have adequate risk management systems, including an internal audit function.[1] The revised global framework for banking supervision, commonly known as Basle II, places enlarged responsibility on the risk management systems of banks and establishes the accountability of bank boards and management for the adequacy of such systems.

The philosophy of banking supervisors with respect to the importance of corporate governance is spelled out in a statement by the Basle Committee on Banking Supervision, the international grouping that brings together banking supervisors from all major countries. This document highlights the crucial role that the board and senior management play in corporate goals and strategies, selection and appraisal of management, operations of risk controls and audit while building safeguards to minimize the risk of bank failure and to protect the interests of depositors.

The role of the board is crucial. The board is accountable to the shareholders, but also the supervisory authority. It names, monitors, compensates and, if necessary, removes the management. The board is responsible for the development of in-house systems to identify, quantify and manage risk.[2] The board is also responsible for the adequacy of the company's risk management and reporting systems.

While there is nearly universal agreement that the internal governance structure of the bank is the first line of defence in banking supervision, the exact specification of the role of the internal governance system differs in some degree among banking supervisors. The Governor of the Reserve Bank of New Zealand (RBNZ) states that "the ultimate responsibility for ensuring that risks are properly identified, monitored and controlled, lies in the boardroom and not with the supervisor". The RBNZ stresses the responsibility of bank directors in ensuring that a sufficient number of independent directors are on the board and that the board and senior management be accountable for devising strategies for the bank to thrive and earn adequate income while maintaining adequate internal systems for risk control.[3]

In an analysis specifically keyed to the situation of emerging Asian markets, Dr. Estanislao, President of the Institute of Directors of the Philippines, defines building board oversight capacity as an urgent priority for bank supervisors, especially in emerging markets which are often characterized by histories of government directed lending and of linkages between the banks and industry and government. The need to sensitise directors to their role in providing oversight to management and to defending the interests of minority shareholders

Box 13.1. **Internal governance and banking supervision** (cont.)

is especially important in emerging markets. In order to do this, banks are required to provide prospective training to directors to explain their responsibilities and also to require minimum numbers of independent directors and specialized committees on audit, risk oversight and governance. The majority of directors of these committees should be independent. Estanislao also emphasizes the need to develop rigorous definitions of independent directors and to use various tools to asses the quality of bank governance, such as the balanced scorecard approach.[4]

1. Bies (2002), pp. 1-2.
2. Basle Committee (September 1999).
3. See Bollard (2004).
4. See Estanislao (2004).

communications, selection and oversight of external auditors, safeguarding risk management and internal controls, oversight of accounts, and communications with and oversight of external auditors.

2.5. Market discipline

Banks and their operations are expected to be under constant surveillance by the capital markets, where they issue bonds and equities, and by rating agencies who assess their creditworthiness. Banks engage not only in funding and lending to final customers, but also in a variety of operations, such as interbank lending and borrowing, foreign exchange dealing and trading of various assets in which they act as counterparties. The institution is expected to disclose reliable data that enable interested parties, such as depositors, investors and prospective counterparties, to reach an informed judgment about the creditworthiness of the institution. One routine operation of banks is to assess the creditworthiness of other institutions that are active participants in the market and modify the conditions under which they are willing to deal with other institutions. In performing this task, banks are typically assisted by credit-rating agencies and other suppliers of financial information.

A loss of credit standing is likely to be a leading indictor that a bank is encountering financial difficulty. Any lessening of the willingness of other banks to engage in credit activities, or increases in risk premiums charged for engaging in such activity would make it impossible for banks to function competitively. An increase in the cost of borrowing due to a perceived decline in creditworthiness is one of the principal ways in which market discipline is exerted over banks, and the judgment of the market is imposed on banks.

2.6. Shareholders and bank governance

The concept underlying the governance paradigm for banks is that the owners of the bank have placed their own capital at risk and the institution is to be operated, at least in very large part, in order to protect the investment of the owners and to produce a competitive yield to investors. Shareholders are entitled to the residual profits of the bank. Thus, if the bank should be especially successful, its owners will obtain most of the benefits. Conversely, the owners' funds equity (or capital) acts as a buffer in cases where the institution sustains losses due to inadequate earnings and/or losses on loans and investments. Thus, the shareholders have an important stake in maintaining adequate systems to monitor the management of the bank. The board of directors of the financial institution is charged with ensuring that the management is acting in the interests of the owners. It is important that the bank have a group of owners who actually behave in accordance with this paradigm and that the owners have effective means to monitor.

Banks in major industrial countries can generally be relied upon to act in accordance with this model. In emerging markets, however, experience shows that it is difficult to assemble a group of investors who can perform the normal monitoring roles of shareholders. Domestic capital markets have not developed to the point that dispersed groups of domestic investors can act as effective monitors. Domestic strategic investors often have links to domestic industrial groups and hence the risk that the bank may be captured by domestic industry is always present. As a result, many emerging markets have found that efforts to reform bank governance require an expanded presence by foreign strategic investors. (This issue will be considered at length in the discussion of the Chinese case.)

When banks have no real owners, when the bank's capital is inadequate (or can be made to appear adequate only with regulatory forbearance), there is a likelihood that the management will engage in dysfunctional behaviour. Banks may take on excessive risk or they may engage in adverse credit selection in order to enable weak borrowers to maintain payments. Thereby, they increase their exposure to poor credits and conceal the true state of their balance sheets.

3. Governance of banks in China

3.1. Historical legacy

China's experience is distinctive inasmuch as between the early 1950s and the 1980s the economy functioned as a centrally planned socialist economy, with a system based upon state ownership in which a central authority issued directives that lower echelons executed.[4]

With the introduction of market reforms around 1980, a partial modification of the pattern of financing occurred. Some separation of commercial banking from the central bank took place, with the PBC focusing on its role as central bank. The banking system was expanded and diversified to meet the needs of the reform programme. New budgetary procedures permitted state enterprises to retain profits and to remit to the state only a tax on income and to seek investment funds in the form of bank loans. Between 1979 and 1985, the volume of deposits nearly tripled and the value of bank loans rose by 260%. Meanwhile SOEs became dependent upon bank loans rather than budget transfers for external finance. Further institutional reforms were accelerated in 1994, when the policy execution function of banks was separated from the commercial banking function, with new specialized "policy banks" being formed. In theory, the commercial banks were expected to act in accord with market-based principles of finance, but owing to conflicting motivations of bank management, banks have been slow to change patterns of behaviour.

3.2. The present situation in the banking sector

After two decades of partial and at times contradictory reform, the banking system shows some prominent characteristics:

1. China has a very high savings rate, with savings averaging about 40% of national income. The public holds the preponderant share of its savings in the form of bank deposits.

2. The post-1994 series of reforms, designed to subject the state-owned enterprises (SOEs) to greater market discipline, have been only partly effective. The formal financial

> Box 13.2. **Chinese banks under central planning**
>
> Under central planning, financial institutions played a passive role and were expected to check on conformity of lower-level actors with the objectives and directives of the plan. The Ministry of Finance exercised firm control over the banking system, credit, and the money supply. The People's Bank of China (PBC) essentially functioned as the "monobank" characteristic of centrally planned economies. As the central bank, the PBC had sole responsibility for issuing currency and controlling the money supply. It also served as the government treasury, the main source of credit for economic units, the clearing centre for financial transactions, the holder of enterprise deposits and the national savings bank. As a result, the skills of credit assessment and the use of financial tools to guide the conduct of enterprises did not develop.
>
> There were some specialized banks alongside the monobank. The Bank of China (BOC) handled financial transactions with foreign firms and individuals as well as all operations in foreign currency. The Agricultural Bank provided financial support to agricultural units, issuing loans, distributing state appropriations for agriculture and overseeing the operations of the rural credit co-operatives. The China Construction Bank (CCB) managed state appropriations and loans for capital construction. It checked the activities of loan recipients to ensure that the funds were used for their designated construction purpose. Money was disbursed in stages as a project progressed.
>
> Rural credit co-operatives were small, collectively owned savings and lending organisations that were the main source of small-scale financial services at the local level in the countryside. They handled deposits and short-term loans for individual farm families, villages, and co-operative organisations. Subject to the loose direction of the Agricultural Bank, they followed uniform state banking policies but acted as independent units for accounting purposes. Urban credit co-operatives began appearing in the mid-1980s. As commercial opportunities grew in the reform period, the thousands of individual and collective enterprises that sprang up in urban areas created a need for small-scale financial services that the formal banks were not prepared to meet.

system, (i.e. banks and securities market institutions) has had only limited success in instilling discipline in the SOEs. Many SOEs operate at a loss, partly because the SOEs have limited flexibility to control the size of their labour forces and still undertake many operations that are not closely related to their basic economic functions. This situation has been ameliorated somewhat by reforms in the SOE sector after 1997, but pressures from SOEs and local governments remain strong.

3. The private sector, which has been the source of the economy's dynamism over the past two decades, has been obliged to use informal finance for its expansion.

4. The financial quality of Chinese banks, especially the state-owned commercial banks (SOCBs), is rather poor, with low earnings, inadequate capital, and high levels of non-performing assets. Indeed, most SOCBs would probably be insolvent if their balance sheets were subjected to careful scrutiny using strict loan classification standards.

5. A process of adverse credit selection is at work in which one of the main motivations of the banks is to extend enough credit to weak but privileged borrowers to stave off bankruptcy. There is a certain symbiosis between the SOEs and the banks which have some motivation to continue lending to weak SOEs in order to avoid report credits to such SOEs as non-performing.

6. As currently structured, the governance system of Chinese banks is not well suited to operating as profit-seeking institutions under which the bank aims at providing a competitive yield to shareholders and maintain high prudential standards. This is particularly true of the major state-owned commercial banks (SOCBs). The banks do not have clear owners. The management of the banks is not conducted by professional managers with a clear mandate to return value to shareholders, but by government officials whose goal is to achieve a balance of economic and non-economic objectives.

3.3. *The institutional structure of the banking system*

The system contains five levels of banks. These banks differ in terms of their ownership structures, client base, governance structures and their balance-sheet quality.

3.3.1. *State-owned commercial banks (SOCBs)*

The four big SOCBs were created in their present form in 1994 with the passage of the Commercial Banking Act. This Act separated the commercial banks, which were supposed to operate in accordance with market criteria, from the policy banks, which were expected to execute government policy. The four SOCBs are the Bank of China (BOC), the Industrial and Commercial Bank of China (ICBC), the Agricultural Bank of China (ABC) and the China Construction Bank (CCB). These banks have extremely large nationwide branch networks, large numbers of employees and a workforce of some 1.7 million.

At the end of 2000, the SOCBs accounted for some 75% of banking assets, but their share has been declining in recent years as credit has expanded rapidly and other banks have been able to gain a market share. By the end of the first half of 2004, data from the CBRC showed that their share had fallen to about 55% of total bank assets, as well as 57% of deposits and 55% of lending, but SOCBs still handled 80% of payments and settlements. By volume of assets, the SOCBs are among the 50 largest banks in the world and the 10 largest in Asia.

Even on the simplest organisational level, the SOCBs lack the basic attributes of profit-making banks. In mid-2004, these banks had not yet been transformed into a corporate form and have not been fully separated from the Ministry of Finance (MOF). The banks do not have identifiable owners, boards of directors, or any of the specialized organs generally considered necessary for monitoring management, and are not subject to the governance rules that apply to independent banks. Like all Chinese companies, these banks have an external board of supervisors that is designed mainly to monitor conformity of bank acts with regulations and policies, but has no role in the governance or oversight of the management of the bank. Disclosure requirements are minimal. The bank is accountable only to the government, *i.e.* the MOF or the CBRC.

The management has traditionally been selected from inside the ministerial system, approved by the State Council, and subject to the close control of the Communist Party. The general manager (or chief executive officer, CEO) traditionally is subject to few checks and balances inside the bank. Senior managers tended to be from the civil service and to move between assignments in the banks and those in government ministries. The presidents of the SOCBs have the rank of vice-ministers. Bank management is not under a clear mandate to return value to the owners of the company or even to protect the interest of the owners, but instead responds to a variety of pressures from within the bureaucracy or the Communist Party, or from local governments.

Control over the operations of regional branches of the SOCBs has been a problem. Many local branches are subject to the influence of local industry, governments and the party. The traditional commitments of SOCBs are to distribute credit among regions and to support state-owned enterprises (SOEs), which in turn are responsible for maintaining employment and for making payments to retired workers as well as maintaining facilities such as schools and hospitals. Some progress has been made in relieving SOEs of the responsibility of supporting non-essential activities and in assuring payments for retired workers. In addition, the SOCBs have been given more autonomy in credit decisions. Nevertheless, local governments still have a considerable say in how bank credits are distributed.

The SOCBs have traditionally had poor credit assessment and control systems, and in any case they were not structured to exercise credit discrimination. The SOCBs have serious problems of asset quality, earnings inadequacy, inadequate capitalisation and balance sheet quality. Earnings tend to be low, due to high costs, low margins on lending and failure to develop non-interest sources of income. Data indicate that the return on assets of SOCBs is in the range of 15 basis points. Internationally, a return norm of 100 basis points is considered adequate, and many emerging markets have far higher rates.

The large volume of non-performing loans (NPLs) in China is concentrated in the SOCBs. CBRC data indicate that at the end of 2003, NPLs of the SOCBs accounted for 80% of NPLs in the banking system and that the NPL ratio was 20% compared to 8% for the joint stock banks and 17% for the policy banks. Furthermore, reserves against NPLs are insufficient, with BOC and CCB having reserves adequate to cover 10-20% of NPLs and the two other SOCBs having lower coverage ratios. Banks in other East Asian countries have NPL coverage ratios averaging around 75%. The SOCBs as a group do not have sufficient capital to meet the minimum 8% capital assets ratio. (However, as will be explained below, the two "pilot" SOCBs now have ratios in excess of 8%.)

Although the balance-sheet quality of SOCBs is already poor using existing data, there is a clear suspicion that reported data give a misleadingly positive picture of the financial state of the SOCBs. There are strong incentives for the management of banks to misclassify assets, since reporting of high NPLs would expose the bank to sanctions from the authorities and it is uncertain whether any benefits would result from more accurate reporting.

The authorities have recognized the poor earnings and balance-sheet quality of the SOCBs for several years. At first, the authorities tried to address the problem with cash infusions to strengthen the bank balance sheets. In 1998, capital of RMB 270 million (3% of GDP) was injected into the four SOCBs. In 1999, the government purchased NPLs for RMB 1.4 trillion (about 20% of the outstanding loans and 15% of GDP) from the SOCBs (as well as some assets from China Development Bank) at face value.[5] As these figures suggest, expenditure on rehabilitating the banking system has already been very significant. The government also lowered reserve requirements and allowed the SOCBs to invest the funds deducted from reserves to purchase special non-negotiable 30-year government bonds, with coupon rates of 7.2%. Simultaneously, the banks were warned to cease lending to poor customers and to adapt their internal credit systems.

Despite this significant support in the form of public resources, bank behaviour did not change sufficiently. True, banks cut back on lending to some borrowers of doubtful creditworthiness. The financial performance of the banks still remained substandard while SOCBs still functioned as appendages of the state rather than as true financial intermediaries. The authorities concluded that any further support should only be extended in circumstances in which SOCBs had strong incentives to focus on financial performance. Therefore in the most recent round of restructuring in 2003-04, efforts to strengthen the balance sheets of the banks have been tied to efforts to modify the governance regime of the SOCBs.

3.3.2. The policy banks

Three "policy banks" (the Agricultural Development Bank of China, the Development Bank of China and the Export Import Bank of China) were created in 1994 to assume the state-directed lending previously undertaken by the commercial banks. The policy banks accept few deposits and are funded mainly by government deposits and guaranteed bond issues. These banks are expected to fund infrastructure and development projects. The policy banks accounted for 14% of banking assets at the end of 2003. Their NPL ratios were lower than those of the SOCBs.

3.3.3. Joint stock commercial banks (JSBs)

There are 11 banks which have been operating in the corporate form for several years. (The first JSBs were formed more than 10 years ago.) The equity of these banks is partly owned by the state and partly by other interests, such as state-owned enterprises, private enterprises and minority investors. One bank, China Minsheng Bank, is entirely owned by non-state entities.[6] Since they are organised as corporations, they are required to have shareholder meetings and boards of directors and to produce accounts. As explained below, the JSBs are subject to additional governance requirements established by the banking supervisors. Five of these banks are listed on domestic stock exchanges in China and thus have additional disclosure requirements. All of these banks have some foreign owners, but until recently the foreign share in ownership has been small.

Although some JSBs were partly organised to further the objectives of local government, the JSBs do not have the same historical legacy as the SOCBs of having been formed mainly to support the objectives of central planners. The management of these banks has a clearer commitment to shareholder value. Their share of lending has been rising considerably in the past few years. They accounted for 14% of banking assets at the end of 2003. The JSBs have lower NPLs ratios, better capitalisation and more adequate provisions against NPLs than the SOCBs.

The JSBs have been seeking to introduce innovative products and to upgrade their internal risk management and credit procedures. Many JSBs have relied on international consultants and/or agreements with external partners in order to obtain access to the best international techniques. Among the improvements in credit procedures instated at the JSBs are the requirement for the management to articulate an overall lending strategy and to have written credit policies and procedures. All of the JSBs have now separated loan origination and loan approval and established limits on individual customers as well as regions and industries. JSBs are also developing databases on their lending portfolios. However, databases on consumer credit are not well developed and the JSBs do not have credit scoring models – a tool that has proven effective in minimizing loan losses from retail lending in many countries. While some of the SOCBs have been taking similar measures to introduce enhanced credit systems, the JSBs are generally seen to have acted more rapidly and to have advanced farther.

3.3.4. City commercial banks

There are more than 1 000 city commercial banks, which are owned by municipal governments. These banks accounted for about 5% of the total banking sector. They originated in the consolidation of urban credit co-operatives under the guidance of local authorities and are organised as joint stock companies. City commercial banks have been tightly controlled by local government and enterprises, which hold significant shares in the banks and often receive low-interest loans from them. Unlike SOCBs, they have multiple shareholders with representation on the board.

This group is very disparate with widely varying standards of governance. Some of the city commercial banks are simply financing appendages of local governments, but a few of the larger banks have governance structures and business plans that are comparable to those of the joint stock banks.

3.3.5. Rural credit co-operatives (RCCs)

There are 38 000 rural credit co-operatives which collectively account for 10% of total banks assets. With the reform of banking, the SOCBs have largely withdrawn from rural finance. (A partial exception is the ABC which retains a leading role in the rural sector.) As a result, the rural sector has been financed either from government banks, mainly ABC, some local commercial banks and rural credit co-operatives. The RCCs have succeeded in attracting large amounts of deposits but have been unable to expand lending to keep pace with demand, leading to rising dependence on informal money-lenders.

The RCCs have weak governance structures and very weak balance sheets. Indeed, the RCC sector is reportedly the weakest sector in the banking system, with major problems of governance and large stocks of NPLs. The RCC sector is benefiting from government policies that distribute rural credit at subsidised rates, but a more comprehensive long-run reform aimed at strengthening balance sheets in RCCs and improving their governance regimes is advisable.

4. Renewed efforts to reform the banking system after 2003

Since the 1990s, the authorities have been considering the basic elements that should be included in a transformation of the banking system. These elements included the corporatisation of the banks with the objective of public listing, the adoption of more sophisticated asset classification systems and an enlargement of the independence of the bank vis-à-vis local government. Taken as a whole, these reforms signify that the authorities have decided to change the nature of Chinese banking from a relatively opaque system with limited competition and limited foreign presence, where banks were protected by government guarantees, to a system based on more global standards of transparency and competition. Eventually banks should rely less on the protection of government guarantees and more on their own risk management capability.

In 2003, the process of bank reform advanced considerably as the authorities decided to step up attempts to translate these ideas, which had been under debate for more than a decade, into concrete action. The Sixteenth Congress of the Communist Party endorsed accelerated efforts to restructure the banking system. In the light of the limited progress made after the 1998-99 financial injections, it was recognized that attempts to repair the balance sheets by pumping additional funds into the banks would remain ineffective without changing the basic framework of incentives inside which the banks operate.

Future reforms had to address issues such as the ownership of the bank, the incentives of the bank's owners and managers, the market signals which the banks receive and the degree of competition in the market.

Since that time, the authorities have been articulating a doctrine as to how the governance system in banks should change. In the case of the SOCBs, this change will be linked to an attempt to strengthen the banks' balance sheets through additional financial support.

The key elements of the policy are:

1. A reform of ownership structures of banks in order to find owners capable of monitoring bank performance effectively.
2. Upgrading supervisory practices in line with international norms.
3. A strengthening of the legal and regulatory framework for bank governance.
4. Increased transparency and increased exposure of Chinese banks to scrutiny by the market.
5. An expanded foreign presence in the banking system partly linked to Chinese WTO membership and partly linked to a desire to benefit from foreign competition.

These measures apply to all banks. Simultaneously, a special programme is being launched for the SOCB sector, in which two "pilot" SOCBs, BOC and CCB, will be subjected to radical restructuring and in which access to public funds will be conditional upon reforms undertaken by the banks. The programme for the two pilot SOCBs is discussed below.

4.1. Reforms in bank supervision

Supervision of banks has been evolving along with the reform of the banking system since the late 1970s. The People's Bank of China (PBC), which functioned as both a lending institution and as the central bank under the central planning system, was designated as the nation's central bank and charged with the functions of all central banks, such as the conduct of monetary policy and lender of last resort, as well as responsibility for all financial supervision. The supervisory responsibilities of the PBC have been progressively diminished, with responsibility for insurance and securities being transferred to specialized bodies during the 1990s. Until 2003, however, bank supervision remained its responsibility.

The PBC had ongoing difficulties in providing effective bank supervision for several reasons. There was an inherent difficulty in supervising banks that still functioned as quasi-governmental agencies. While aware of the need to enforce prudential norms, government officials also responded to other considerations, such as the need to keep enterprises functioning in order to support employment and social benefits. The effectiveness of the PBC as banking regulator was further limited by the fact that local offices reported to the local government as well as to PBC headquarters in Beijing. Since local governments typically supported local enterprises that provided local employment and social services, there was a serious conflict between the PBC role as banking supervisor and its role as an arbitrator of the regional distribution of credit (Cai, 1999).

Despite these problems, the PBC made gradual progress in upgrading banking supervisory practices during the 1990s. Significant strides were made in building capacity and developing supervisory techniques based upon international norms. However, the PBC lacked the means of sanctioning banks that were unable to meeting prudential norms and were protected by local government or party interests. There were problems with the old loan classification system inasmuch as in the past loans were classified under four headings: normal, overdue, idle (more than 180 days overdue), and bad. Banks were not required to provide for NPLs, although they were required to set aside 1% of assets as a general provision each year. In 1999, the PBC proposed a more rigorous system of loan classification and provisioning. The new system contained five categories with progressively higher requirements for provisions: *i)* pass (1% provisioning requirement); *ii)* special mention (2%); *iii)* substandard (20%); *iv)* doubtful (50%); and *v)* loss (100%). The new system was, in principle, based upon forward-looking criteria and assessments of repayment capability rather than upon delinquency history. While some of the banks experimented with the system, few banks actually adopted it.

With the decision to accelerate banking reform in 2003, supervisory responsibility was transferred to the newly formed China Banking Regulatory Commission (CBRC). This decision reflected the thinking in many advanced countries that the central bank should focus on monetary policy and issues of systemic stability while actual supervision of banking institutions should be performed by a separate entity. At the same time, the PBC as central bank and lender of last resort will have significant responsibility for the soundness of the banking system as a whole.

The CBRC is now attempting to align its domestic activities with best international practices. The CBRC will be more centralized and its local offices will be insulated from local pressures. Three new laws on commercial banking, banking supervision and the PBC were enacted at the end of 2003. A series of directives and rules have been issued, covering a wide-range of issues related to supervision. The CBRC stated its intention of moving from the earlier compliance-based methods of supervision to the newer risk-based system. The five-tier loan classification system previously proposed by the PBC was made mandatory. The CBRC began building institutional capability to conduct on-site and off-site inspections and imposed a large number of sanctions for infractions of rules. The CBRC initiated a self assessment of its own compliance with the Basle Core Principles of Banking Supervision, the recognized global standard for banking supervision, and prepared a medium-term plan for improving compliance.

In February 2004, the authorities introduced a new risk assessment system that will be used in evaluating the JSBs. This system will be similar to the systems used in other markets. Banks will be scored for capital, asset quality, management competence, liquidity and profitability. The system will be used in interacting with the banks senior managers and board.[7]

Since late 2003, the CBRC has been articulating a strategy to reform the banking system based upon accelerated introduction of market-based principles of corporate governance in the banks as well as special programmes to rehabilitate the SOCBs.

4.2. Changing patterns of ownership

In the past, the lack of identifiable owners has been one of the reasons that the banks have operated in a systemic vacuum. The authorities have accepted that a different ownership structure for banks is needed to support a sound governance regime and thus are seeking to diversify present ownership patterns.

Investors can be sought for several reasons: *i)* to bring new capital into the bank; *ii)* to rectify a deficiency in governance by acting as genuine owners and active monitors; *iii)* to assist in the transfer of relevant skills into the bank. Various categories of owners can make different contributions to the bank. To find the appropriate mix of new owners is a critical challenge.

Clearly, a large share of equity will be owned by domestic interests. Domestic industrial interests may have some capital to contribute and may regard their investment in the bank as an "arm's-length" financial investment. Moreover, given the lack of a strong domestic institutional investor community, they may represent the category of domestic investor that is best able to act as a monitor. Most of the JSBs, the category of domestic bank most focused on shareholder value, have large investments from domestic industry. However, a very large presence in bank ownership raises the possibility that the industrial companies will seek to use the bank for connected lending. On balance, the possibility of conflicts of interest between banking and industrial interests suggests that such ownership linkages should be limited.

Domestic retail and institutional investors are an additional source of new owners, and there will be significant domestic ownership of banks by dispersed groups of Chinese investors. With large numbers of Chinese citizens holding sizeable stakes in the banks, a definable constituency should emerge for sound banking practices that will give boards and management a strong incentive to produce competitive returns and to avoid action that would result in diminution or loss of value of shareholders equity. On the negative side, neither domestic retail investors nor institutional investors have historically shown strong capabilities or inclination to monitor companies in which they are shareholders, and neither has tended to place pressure on the corporate sector to raise standards of transparency and disclosure or to respect the rights of minority investors. At this time, the Chinese capital market does not have a strong infrastructure of rating agencies and securities analysts who will engage in rigorous analysis, demand higher standards of performance and disclosure from companies. On the other hand, domestic investors will clearly benefit if the degree of professionalism in the Chinese investment market increases as a result of better governance standards and a more active presence by foreign investors. On balance, domestic portfolio investors can help improve bank performance, but they are likely to be most effective if they act in partnership with other kinds of investors. In any case, the enhancement of the monitoring capability of domestic institutional investors should be a long-term objective of the authorities, not only for the banking sector but throughout the entire capital market.

Foreign investors can plainly contribute to the improvement of governance in banks, and the Chinese authorities have decided that increased foreign presence will help to effect the desired transformation of the banking system. Foreign equity investors will demand better disclosure and will measure the performance of Chinese banks by the same criteria that other companies are measured. To the degree that foreign equity investors cannot be convinced that Chinese banks are producing value for investors, the share price will decline. Moreover, the listing of Chinese banks on overseas stock exchanges will oblige banks to observe stock exchange rules about disclosure organisation, governance and investor protection, which are more rigorous than in the domestic market.

Foreign strategic investors can make a sizeable contribution to the transformation of the banking sector. Foreign strategic investors are likely to be major banks from major OECD member countries or other financial centres that have developed significant banking-related skills in areas such as credit assessment and risk control, and they are likely to have state-of-the-art knowledge in banking. Such skills are abundant in the major, more advanced countries of the world but are still relatively scarce in many emerging markets. Many banks have developed strategies of expansion to key emerging markets where banking skill is less abundant. The pattern of bank rehabilitation making use of foreign strategic partners has been the basis for successful rehabilitation of banks in Central Europe, some Latin American countries and in the Republic of Korea.

China offers huge attractions to foreign banks pursuing global expansion strategies because of the size of the market, the high levels of savings and the low current levels of products and services. For example, the Chinese consumer and mortgage markets are largely underdeveloped, and skills in assessing the creditworthiness of smaller and private enterprises are not well developed. These activities are currently being financed through parallel markets that could be made highly profitable if they were brought within the formal financial system. Foreign banks would thus have an opportunity to have strategic investment in Chinese banks that would have the potential to grow as the bank moves toward global levels of competence.

At this time, the effort to change ownership structures is focused on two categories of banks: i) the joint stock banks where the ownership/governance structure is already more favourable than in the remainder of the banking system; and ii) the two pilot SOCBs which aim to transform their ownership structures as part of the reform.

The JSBs are in the process of broadening their ownership structures. The JSBs have already been gaining a significant market share and now have an opportunity to expand their share of the banking market yet further. In order to gain market share, however, it will be necessary to increase their capital without recourse to official support. The JSBs have been increasing their assets rapidly, so their capital adequacy ratios are consequently only marginally sufficient.[8] The JSBs will seek to raise their capital by: i) public equity issues on domestic or international exchanges, including rights issues; ii) issues of subordinated debt; and/or iii) strategic partnerships with foreign banks. At this time only five banks are publicly listed, but further domestic and international listings are expected.

Several JSBs have already included foreign entities such as Citibank, Hang Seng Bank, the IFC or the ADB as strategic investors, but thus far their positions have been rather small. Under the WTO rules accepted by China, foreign institutions will be authorized to own as much as 20% of total bank capital, with the share scheduled to rise to 49% in 2007.

There have been several highly publicised cases of large-scale foreign strategic acquisitions in recent months. In May 2004, Newbridge Capital, a US-based private equity firm that has a record of successful turnarounds of banks in other Asian countries, bought a 19% stake in Shenzhen Development Bank. In July 2004, the Hong Kong and Shanghai Banking Corporation (HSBC) announced its intent to acquire 19% of the Bank of Communications, the largest JSB in the country. This investment will give HSBC access to a network of 2 700 branches in 139 cities and a customer base. It may well set a pattern for other banks seeking to enter the Chinese market. The HSBC investment follows an increase in capital provided by the Chinese bank's existing shareholders and is also expected to lead to an overseas listing in the next two to three years. With increased capital and with increased transfer of foreign banking skills, the JSBs will aim to expand their market share further. The inclusion of foreign investors in the ownership structure is likely to facilitate the transfer of skills, the upgrading of risk controls and closer alignment of governance practices in the Chinese banking system with those in global markets. In fact, in some investment agreements, specific provisions are made for the foreign partner to devote resources to building up skills in the Chinese partner, usually in areas such as risk management, consumer finance or marketing.

Since there are only a limited number of opportunities for strategic partnership with JSBs, there may be some possibilities to forge partnerships with city commercial banks as well, especially some of the larger banks with a more commercial orientation. A few alliances of this kind have already been launched and more are reportedly under consideration.[9]

At the same time, many major international banks have strong reservations about participating as small minority investors in the SOCBs. This represents a major challenge for the authorities in implementing a change in ownership of the SOCBs in order to effect an improvement in bank governance.

4.3. Improving the framework for corporate governance in banking

The authorities have been seeking to improve the corporate governance framework, both for banks and for the non-financial corporate sector, during the past decade. Many laws, regulations, codes and standards necessary for a complete system of governance have been enacted. Efforts have been undertaken to ensure that those who will hold key positions under the new governance framework have sufficient training and experience. Simultaneously, enforcement efforts have been stepped up.

The legal and regulatory framework governance is not identical for commercial banks and for non-financial enterprises. Some instruments, such as the Company Law, are binding on banks and non-banks alike, so long as the entity is organised in the corporate form. State-owned enterprises (SOEs), other than banks, are also subject to an additional instrument.[10] On the other hand, banks are subject to several special laws and other instruments that create more stringent obligations than those applied to SOEs.

The main instruments affecting the corporate governance framework for banks are: i) the Company Law; ii) the Banking Law; iii) the Law on Banking Supervision;[11] iv) the Guidance on Corporate Governance for Joint Stock Commercial Banks; and v) the Code of Corporate Governance for Listed Companies (CCGLC).[12] The Company Law and the CCGLC apply to financial and non financial companies, but the other instruments only apply to banks. The CCGLC applies only to publicly listed companies, i.e. five JSBs, but a growing number of banks are expected to be listed eventually. As will be explained below, the two pilot commercial banks are subject to additional instruments.

The Company Law stipulates that all SOEs must have a board of directors with a chairman and vice chairman, and a general manager. The general manager, who is accountable to the board, may also be a member of the board. The Law limits the size of the board for a joint stock company to between five and 19 members. In addition, the Company Law also specifies the responsibilities of boards, which are generally in line with those accepted in international practice, but the Law does not provide board members with clear guidance on how they are to exercise their responsibilities.

The Banking Law of 1994, amended in 2003, contains many provisions concerning the corporate governance of banks such as the role of various organs of the company and the requirements regarding transparency and disclosure.

A number of laws and regulations impose further requirements on banks. In 2002, the PBC issued Guidance for Joint Stock Banks (the Guidance) which is aimed at giving more precise guidance to banks over and above the obligations specified in the Company Law and the Banking Law. This document specifies the framework for decision-making inside the bank, with specific roles with necessary checks and balances for the shareholders meeting, the board of directors, the board of supervisors and senior management and also stipulates that banks have an obligation to establish an adequate system of reporting and disclosure. These requirements go beyond those in the Company Law. One of the aims of the Guidance is to define means to protect the interests of shareholders and depositors and specifically establishes an obligation on the part of controlling shareholders to respect the rights of non-controlling shareholders and depositors. The obligation of directors to defend these interests is specified. Various prohibitions are established regarding related party transactions.

In order to promote the effectiveness of the board as an independent check on management, various persons having borrowing relationships with the bank are disqualified from serving as directors. The directors of banks have the right to obtain all information needed to monitor the operations and financial situation of the bank. Executive directors shall constitute between a quarter and one-third of all directors. In addition to non-executive directors, the board must have fully independent directors, i.e. those with no relationship to the bank or its shareholders that may raise conflicts of interest. Independent directors are specifically mandated to take into account the interests of smaller shareholders and depositors. Independent directors also have the duty to report any violations of laws or regulations to the banking supervisor.

There are some ambiguities concerning the concept of independent directors. In general, the term "independent directors" is used to mean a non-executive director, i.e. someone who is not an employee of the company. There is another definition of independent meaning free from other connections to the company and conflicts of interest arising from those connections. The connections may be personal (i.e. individuals having personal or family ties to the company or its executives), or they may be commercial (i.e. those affiliated with an entity that deals with the bank), thus posing the risk of conflict of interest. However, there has been some tendency in China to nominate fully independent directors, usually from universities or professions such as law and accounting.

One of the obligations of the board of directors is to disclose the assessments by the banking supervisors and in cases where remedial action is mandated to describe plans to correct shortcomings. The Guidance also mandates the separation of the chairman and the CEO of the bank, and the board is required to establish specialized committees including Related Party Transactions Control, Risk Management, and Remuneration.

The CCGLC further stipulates that the audit committee, the nomination committee and the remuneration and appraisal committee shall be chaired by an independent director, and independent directors shall constitute the majority of these committees. At least one independent director from the audit committee shall be an accounting professional. The main duties of the corporate strategy committee are to conduct research and make recommendations on the long-term strategic development plans and major investment decisions of the company.

Under the Guidance and under Chinese practice generally, the audit process is somewhat different than is generally recommended in international practice. The Guidance does not require the board to form an audit committee, and it also specifies that the internal audit report to the president of the bank rather than the board. Instead, the audit procedure is closely linked to the supervisory board which plays a distinct role in Chinese companies. The Bank Guidance also gives the senior management relatively strong protection from interference from the board and strongly discourages the board from replacing the senior management before the expiration of their term.

It is specified that the banks shall comply with disclosure requirements of the supervisor, but the specific items that must be disclosed are not spelled out. One of the obligations of the board of directors is to disclose the assessments by the banking supervisors in cases where remedial action is mandated and to describe plans to correct shortcomings.

Like all Chinese companies, banks are required to have a board of supervisors. Unlike the supervisory board in systems with two-tier board systems, the Chinese board of supervisors does not form part of the governance hierarchy. The board of supervisors is an entity that operates outside the decision-making hierarchy and with the function of overseeing compliance with laws and regulations. The supervisory board is composed of outside supervisors appointed by the state as well as some representatives of the workers. The supervisory board is responsible for: i) monitoring compliance of the company with laws, regulations and rules; ii) examination of the financial statements of the SOE; iii) inspection of business performance; and iv) evaluation of the CEO. The supervisory board engages the outside auditor. An audit is performed at least once a year and when the CEO changes. The supervisory board reports to the president and presents its finding to the shareholder meeting. Many analysts have argued that the board of supervisors does not represent an effective contribution to a set of checks and balances needed to establish clear lines of accountability from management to board to shareholder. In this context it has frequently been recommended that the role of the board of supervisors be re-evaluated as part of the general effort to align Chinese and international practices.

Overall, the basic set of instruments that form the governance framework for banks are in line with those in other countries. Given China's limited experience of the use of market-based governance tools, it would be desirable to devote significant resources to deepening understanding among those who will play significantly expanded roles under the new governance regime. For example, written guidance concerning the duties of bank directors would be helpful. This could be part of a general code of conduct for company directors or more specifically directed at bank directors. Many countries have such codes which may be formulated by the regulatory authorities, self-regulatory organisations, or by individual companies. Institutes of directors, which often engage in training for directors, often assist in formulating such codes and in promoting their use. Finally, difficulties in enforcement of laws and regulations remain a serious obstacle to improved corporate governance in China.

Since only a few banks have been corporatised and even fewer have been listed, for the most part banks have not been obliged to operate inside the formal corporate governance framework in China. At the same time, it is widely agreed that corporate governance in China needs to move closer to world standards. Specifically, it is generally agreed that corporatisation and public listing have not succeeded in improving the financial performance of listed Chinese companies and has not obliged listed companies to pursue shareholder value as an overriding corporate objective. Therefore, the goal of improving bank governance by subjecting Chinese banks to the same corporate governance framework to which listed Chinese companies are already subjected can only succeed if that framework itself improves significantly. To some degree the banking supervisors can impose stricter practices on Chinese banks than are imposed on other corporate entities. Thus, banking supervisors can be stricter regarding disclosure than is required by stock exchange rules for listed companies and the supervisors can require each bank to bring its system of corporate governance up to minimal norms. However, the entire system of corporate governance in

China will have to improve in order for the policy of requiring banks to operate in the corporate governance for listed companies to have its intended effect.

4.4. Transparency and exposure to markets

Under the new governance environment, banks will be required to observe far higher standards of transparency and will be subject to much more intense market oversight than in the past. Banks will be scrutinised by other banks, both domestic and foreign, be subjected to more intense coverage by the financial press and constant scrutiny of the capital market. As Chinese banks seek to raise capital through equity and subordinated debt issues, many foreign investment banks are undertaking analyses of the Chinese banking system and making recommendations concerning equity investments. In order to meet the expectations of new investors, Chinese banks will have to increase the quantity and quality of data disclosed and also to perform in line with market expectations. The CCGLC will add further disclosure requirements, and those banks that list on foreign stock exchanges will be subjected to additional requirements.

In addition to assessments by equity markets, the debt and interbank markets will place Chinese institutions under growing scrutiny. At this time, credit-rating agencies rely heavily on official guarantees in assigning ratings to Chinese banks, but as relationships become more complex, banks that can establish credibility with rating agencies and counterparties based upon their own financial strength will gain competitive advantage. In addition, Chinese banks will be engaging in an increasingly complex range of operations with foreign institutions. Each Chinese institution will have to take pains to convince prospective counterparties of its creditworthiness. On the strength of these ratings and their own assessments, investors and other financial institutions will be deciding whether, and at what cost, they are prepared to engage in various kinds of operations with Chinese intermediaries. The decision to accept market discipline means that in the long run the banks will be under growing pressure to persevere in restructuring. Thus, in order to raise new capital while borrowing on competitive terms, banks will have to meet market expectations by raising earnings to competitive levels, to bring costs under control and to reduce NPLs. The pressure from the market to make progress on these indicators will supplement the pressures from the banks' directors and from the banking supervisors.

4.5. Expanded foreign competition

As noted above, the foreign presence in the market will expand as a result of foreign participation in the equity of Chinese banks. Foreign participation in the market will also expand as the scope for foreign banks to compete directly in the domestic market through branches and subsidiaries increases and as foreign banks gain greater access to domestic currency operations. Previously, China imposed strict limitations on the operations that foreign banks could undertake and particularly limited operations in domestic currency. Largely as a result of these restrictions, foreign banks accounted for only 1% of total banking assets at the end of 2003. Most foreign banks operated in a few large cities and confined themselves to foreign currency loans, mainly to foreign businesses. With liberalization, this share is expected to grow significantly. By the end of 2006, all geographic restrictions on operations in Chinese currency will be lifted.

The Chinese authorities are unlikely to open their market to the same extent that countries in Latin American and Central Europe did when dealing with failed banking systems. In many of those cases the majority of capital in domestic banks eventually passed into the hands of foreign banks. First, the Chinese, with their huge stock of domestic savings, do not need foreign resources to recapitalise their banks. Second, the Chinese authorities are undoubtedly not prepared to accept such a degree of foreign ownership at this time. Nevertheless, the opening to foreign competition, through ownership in Chinese institutions, foreign-controlled branches and subsidiaries through cross border competition, has to be significant enough for foreign competition to have a visible impact on the Chinese market.

The experience of the Republic of Korea may be of relevance for China. Until the 1997 crisis, the Korean authorities limited foreign equity participation in Korean banks to very small amounts. At the same time, foreign bank branches and representative offices were restricted to a narrow range of activities which differed significantly from those permitted to Korean banks. After the 1997 crisis, the Koreans opened their banking system and encouraged foreign investors to acquire sizeable strategic positions in domestic banks with the objective of improving the governance of banks. Simultaneously, the authorities removed remaining capital controls and moved toward a policy of national treatment regarding foreign banks. While the foreign presence in the banking system was measured, it was markedly larger than in the years before 1997. The decision to accept an enlarged foreign presence was instrumental in effecting the improvement in bank governance and the successful restructuring of the banking system in ensuing years.[13]

5. Rehabilitation programme for the SOCBs

The preceding section discussed the framework for corporate governance of all banks that are organised in the corporate form. While most of the reform measures currently being implemented will apply to the SOCBs, the authorities have decided to concentrate reform efforts on two "pilot banks" the China Construction Bank (CCB) and the Bank of China (BOC). Based upon experience in rehabilitating these two target institutions, the programme may be extended or modified in coming years. The programme involves both the commitment of significant sums of money and an effort to change the incentives and governance systems in the banks.

In March 2004, the CBRC issued guidelines explaining their strategy for the BOC and CCB.[14] These Guidelines were the first concrete steps in a policy designed to produce a significant change in the two pilot banks by the end of 2007. Within that time frame, the banks are expected to operate profitably while maintaining adequate capitalisation, good internal controls, sound business operations and high quality services. In order to strengthen the balance sheets of the pilot banks, some USD 45 billion equivalent of resources from the country's international reserves was injected into these banks (USD 22.5 billion for each bank). The banks are expected to dispose of remaining NPLs through provisioning or through sale at a discount to face value to the AMCs. In June 2004 the pilot banks sold an additional RMB 279 billion (USD 34 billion) of NPLs to the AMCs. These two banks have also been engaging in sales of NPLs to foreign investment banks.

5.1. Projected ownership changes

The lack of identifiable owners and the resulting lack of a commitment to the shareholders are at the heart of the governance vacuum in the SOCBs. Unlike the JSBs, which are already operating as independent banks, the SOCBs were still not separated from the state in early 2004. The first step in changing the ownership structure was taken in December 2003 when a special state entity, the Central Huijin Investment Company

(Huijin), was set up to assume formal ownership of the SOCBs.[15] Huijin will operate under a Task Force for Pilot Joint Stock Reforms of State Owned Banks under the State Council. To some degree, the position of Huijin is comparable to that of the State-owned Assets Supervision and Administration Commission of the State Council (SASAC) which has the mission of assuming the role of state ownership of SOEs and promoting governance reform in the non-financial sector (see Chapter 10).

While there will be additional owners for the SOCBs, Huijin is likely act as the majority owner for the foreseeable future. Huijin will have the task of representing the state's ownership interest. The state's supervisory interest in the banks will be represented by the CBRC while it is hoped that the government will pursue its regional, social and industrial policy objectives using traditional tools such as tax and expenditure policy.

The ownership transformation process is expected to pass through three stages:

1. Coporatisation. In August-September 2004, the banks were transformed into joint stock companies with the state as the sole owner.
2. Ownership Diversification. While the state acting though Huijin will remain the majority owner, other entitles will become owners of minority stakes.
3. Public Listing. The banks will be listed on domestic and international exchanges.

At this stage, the state has no intention of relinquishing its controlling interest in the SOCBs. Most OECD member countries and most non-members with dynamic financial sectors have eventually decided to privatise their banks. One of the basic uncertainties overhanging the reform is whether the SOCBs can be transformed into profit-oriented entities while a commanding share of bank capital remains under the control of the state.

As noted above, domestic industrial interest or portfolio investors do not have a strong history of effectively monitoring investments in pursuit of shareholder value. Nevertheless, it is useful to give domestic investors experience in monitoring investments alongside international investors. Moreover, the commitment of savings by domestic retail investors and institutions will build a constituency in favour of pursuit of shareholder value by management.

It is part of the official strategy of the Chinese authorities to solicit participation by foreign banks as strategic partners in the SOCBs. Chinese policy makers insist that they are not seeking investment by foreign banks in order to obtain capital – which is comparatively abundant in China. Rather they are seeking to gain access to the monitoring capability and banking techniques of foreign banks.

There are reasons why foreign banks may hesitate to become strategic partners in SOCBs. In particular, even for banks that are committed to expanding in the Chinese market, many banks would find other means of entering the market, such as ownership stakes in JSBs or expansion of branch or subsidiary networks to be more appealing. Foreign banks are likely to be wary of a strategic partnership with SOCBs where the lack of history of operation as a profit-making entity represents a heavy burden. Furthermore, the SOCBs face a long period of restructuring and down-sizing, and are saddled with a large stock of NPLs. Foreign banks may well hesitate to be drawn into visible positions as strategic investors in which they will suffer the risk of financial loss and loss of reputation but over which they can exercise little control. Foreign banks may only be willing to take a minority position in order to promote their business with the SOCB in a specific area (e.g. credit cards), or to gain official support for their expansion into other, more lucrative areas of the banking sector through branches, strategic alliances or cross-border operations. Thus, the commitment of the foreign partners to improved governance may not be sufficient to produce the needed changes. On balance, foreign strategic investors are vital to the success of the effort to rehabilitate the SOCBs, but the authorities face an uphill struggle in persuading foreign institutions to participate as minority strategic partners.

Many market participants believe that the two pilot banks will seek to be publicly listed in 2005 and both banks are keen to achieve listing, but no deadline has been set for public listing.

5.2. Internal governance of the pilot SOCBs

The authorities aim to transform the SOCBs into entities that have a distinct legal identity with identifiable owners who have a stake in the financial performance of the bank while building governance structures designed to protect the interests of the owners. By assuming the corporate form, the pilot banks will become subject to the Company Law and the Bank Guidance as well as the specific measures aimed at the pilot banks. Overall, these instruments require the formation of a shareholder committee, board of directors, supervisory board and executive management with established functions for each organ. The two pilot banks are expected to find domestic and international strategic investors to assume ownership positions in the banks and to nominate directors and to take part in meetings of the shareholder committees. Huijin will nominate directors to represent the state's interest as an investor. Presumably these directors will include both those having very close ties to the government as well as some fully independent directors. The exact modalities by which Huijin will represent the state's interest are still under discussion.

The pilot banks will be expected to articulate strategies to achieve business targets and to set annual targets while assessing progress in meeting these targets. In order to be able to meet these targets, systems of human resource management are to be revamped. A quantitatively-based system to evaluate management performance is to be instituted and reported quarterly to the banking authorities.

The banks will have greater freedom in choosing their own management and in implementing personnel policy. In July 2004, the two banks each named their CEOs who will be separate from the chairmen of the bank. CCB chose an outsider who had been vice-chairman of a major financial institution controlled by the government, while BOC chose a governor of a province.[16] Moreover, both banks are engaging foreign consulting firms in upgrading skills such as risk management.[17] Beginning in 2004, the pilot banks applied the CBRC five category loan classification system to their entire portfolios including their off balance sheet items.

The pilot banks are expected to meet specified targets for the most commonly used benchmarks for earnings and balance sheet quality. In particular, return on assets should rise to 60 basis points by the end of 2005 and subsequently to internationally competitive levels. Return on equity should rise to 11% by the end of 2005 and to at least 13% by 2007. The cost income ratio should be held within a range of 35-45%. At all times the capital adequacy ratio shall be at least 8%.[18] NPLs will be held in the range of 3-5%. The pilot banks are expected to make continued progress in resolving NPLs and to identify any irregularities that occurred during the process under which loans became delinquent. By the end of 2005, provisions for NPLs shall be increased to 60% for the BOC and 80% for CCB.

The CBRC will evaluate progress in implementing corporate governance reforms and in improving financial indicators, through inspections and surveillance reports. The results of these reports will be transmitted to the Task Force for Pilot Joint Stock Reforms of State Owned Banks under the State Council.

6. Summary and conclusions

Banking in China is now entering a new historical phase. Following the decision to launch the economic reform in 1978, the authorities have been seeking to redefine the role of the banking system from its passive position under the old system of central panning to an active position in credit and resource allocation. The changes over the years have included the separation of the central bank from commercial banks, as well as a series of measures designed to encourage banks to act as independent monitors over the enterprise sector.

Through the late 1990s, the results were disappointing. The banks, particularly the state-owned commercial banks, lacked the identity of independent profit-seeking entities. Thus, the management continued to operate the banks as appendages of the government and continued to subordinate the financial soundness of the banks to a variety of political, social and economic considerations. Easy access to bank credit removed the incentives for enterprises to take action to become more efficient. One of the results of this adverse credit selection was very poor quality in bank balance sheets. Even with the commitment of significant resources to strengthen bank balance sheets in 1998-99, banks persisted in their earlier patterns of behaviour.

Observing the unsatisfactory results of these earlier efforts, the authorities concluded that any further use of public resources to strengthen bank balance sheets had to be linked to improvement in the governance regime of the banks. Following the decision at the 2003 Party Congress to press ahead with banking reform, the authorities introduced the most ambitious set of reform plans undertaken to date. The specific measures that were included in the programme had been under discussion for several years. Nevertheless, taken as a whole, the programme represented the most serious effort to date to change the behaviour patterns of banks. The key elements of the reform are:

1. a reform of ownership structures of banks in order to find owners capable of monitoring bank performance effectively;
2. upgrading banking of supervisory practices in line with international norms;
3. a strengthening of the legal and regulatory framework for bank governance;
4. increased transparency and increased exposure of Chinese banks to scrutiny by the market;
5. an expanded foreign presence in the banking system partly linked to Chinese WTO membership and partly linked to a desire to benefit from foreign competition.

In addition to these measures that will affect all banks, the authorities have committed USD 45 billion to support financial restructuring in two "pilot" state-owned commercial banks, contingent upon the implementation of governance reform by these banks.

The reform programme, which is very bold in its aspirations, reflects a striking willingness on the part of the Chinese authorities to relinquish direct control over banks and to allow the banks to be subjected to market pressures. Previously, the Chinese banking system operated under a system that was under the close control of the authorities and where efforts were made to minimize the influence of the global financial market on China. This set of policy changes represents a significant narrowing of the differences between the Chinese banking system and the world banking system.

The new policy postulates that, with ownership and governance changes, the boards and management of the banks will have to respond to the interests of their owners rather than act as agents of state policy. The enlarged flexibility to select and remunerate their managers should increase their independence. By encouraging stock exchange listing and enhanced transparency, the banks should ultimately rely less upon the guarantees of the government and more on their own standing with the market. Banks will be under great pressure to meet the expectations of financial markets, especially as they will be seeking to raise large sums in the capital markets both domestically and internationally.

While the present policy is the boldest introduced since the beginning of reforms two decades ago, there are still limits to the moves that the authorities have been willing to make. In the first place, the projected reform covers only the two smallest SOCBs and to a lesser degree the JSBs. This study, which is focused on governance issues, has concentrated on those sectors where governance reforms are expected to be centred. Other categories of lending institutions, such as the remaining SOCBs, the city commercial banks, and the rural credit co-operatives (RCCs), where the problems of solvency are more acute, are not targeted for reform at this time, but their problems may well continue to grow, even if some progress is made in the targeted groups of banks.

With respect to the two pilot SOCBs it is not obvious that the planned change in ownership structure, in which the state will retain its controlling share indefinitely, represents a viable model for governance. Additionally, if prospective foreign strategic partners are restricted to very small holdings, it is uncertain whether they will be interested in participating or whether their participation can be effective under these conditions. Furthermore, the SOCBs are extremely large and indeed they may be so large that they produce diseconomies of scale, particularly for banks that are only marginally solvent and that are troubled by serious flaws in governance.

It is not possible to foresee how the banking reform will proceed. For example, if the efforts to reform the "pilot" banks are encouraging, the programme might be extended to other SOCBs. Conversely, if the results are unsatisfactory, the authorities may have to consider more drastic measures, such as breaking up the state-owned banks or simply closing them.

Given the country's history of partial economic reforms and the lack of depth in the legal and institutional infrastructure, the problems to be overcome are formidable. The country lacks a cadre of experienced corporate directors and guidelines for directors are unclear. Public listing thus far has generally not led to markedly improved performance for Chinese companies. Therefore, the effect of market discipline will be felt only if improvements in the entire framework for corporate governance, for financial and non-financial companies, are made. Despite all the uncertainties, it is clear that, given the magnitude of the changes already introduced and those to be introduced shortly, there is no serious option of reverting to the old patterns of behaviour, especially since the reform is taking place in the full view of the Chinese population and the international financial community.

Although there are serious questions of whether the reform will succeed in its present form, there are some recommendations that can be made to maximize the chances for success. Many of the recommendations for improved bank governance are similar to those that would be made for the entire corporate sector. Some of the more salient of these recommendations concerning the corporate governance of JSBs and pilot SOCBs are:

1. Domestic industry will be permitted to have some ownership stakes in the pilot SOCBs. In view of the potential conflicts of interest between banking and industrial interests, such ownership linkages should be limited.

2. Foreign banks should be allowed to expand their presence in the market to the extent that they provide serious competition to domestic institutions.

3. Efforts should be enhanced to develop adequate regulatory frameworks for institutional investors and to enhance the capability of domestic institutions to act as monitors for the corporate sector.

4. The role and responsibilities of independent directors should be clarified. Codes of conduct for directors and specialized training have been used in other countries.

5. The means whereby Huijin will exercise the ownership rights of the state should be clarified and aligned with international practice.

6. Special programmes tailored to the needs of bank directors should be considered.

7. The Guidance on Corporate Governance for Joint Stock Commercial Banks of 2002 should be reviewed to assure that it adequately covers the situation of the pilot SOCBs.

8. The authorities should study the effectiveness of boards of supervisors in the context of corporate governance to determine whether fundamental changes are needed.

Notes

1. This chapter was written by John Thompson, Directorate for Financial and Enterprise Affairs, OECD.

2. The international standard for corporate governance of both financial and non-financial companies is the OECD's Principles of Corporate Governance.

3. In addition to the traditional credit risk that banks have historically assumed, many banks are now becoming involved in innovative transactions that involve other kinds of risk, such as market risk and exchange rate risk. Additionally, as banks began to engage in longer term, over-the-counter operations, often in unfamiliar products, counterparty risk, liquidity risk, settlement risk and legal risk assume greater significance. A complete risk management system requires that the bank develop adequate systems to identify each one of these risks and to quantify the amount of risk that is undertaken in each transaction. A strong internal compliance function should assure that all policy areas actually being implemented. The Risk Management committee of the Board typically approves the risk policies of the bank and seeks to ascertain that systems to ensure compliance are adequate.

4. In addition to characteristics stemming from China's history as a centrally planned economy, the Chinese financial system shares many characteristics with those of other Asian countries. In many Asian countries financial resources were not allocated on market-based criteria. Instead, the assets held by banks and other financial institutions tended to be used by governments, allied industrial groups and other well connected groups to further national industrial and social policy objectives. As a result, there was a subordination of prudential considerations to the interests of the banks' controlling shareholders and to the aims of national industrial policy. Consequently, financial supervisors did not attain the independence or the technical capacity to pose a counterweight to the pressures of industrial ministries within the decision-making structure. After the 1997 crisis exposed the risks of this pattern of intermediation, most Asian countries have identified the need to build capacity in financial supervisors and to change the governance regimes of financial institutions as a key task in their reform effort. China has followed this general pattern.

5. The assets that were removed from the balance sheets of the banks were transferred to four state asset management companies (AMCs) which had the mission of resolving the impaired assets of banks and recovering value from imparted assets. These AMCs were modelled on similar institutions that were formed in the Asian crisis countries to purchase impaired assets from banks, thereby allowing banks to concentrate energy on improvements in the institutions. Meanwhile the

AMCs were expected to focus on recovery of value from impaired assets. The four AMCs in China have made less progress in loan recovery than many of their counterparts in other Asian countries such as Korea or Malaysia.

6. For some useful insights, see "Building a Transparent Private Bank in China", *China Daily*, 23 February 2004.

7. "The CBRC introduces a Provisional Risk Assessment System for Joint-Stock Commercial Banks", *China Daily*, 22 February 2004. Also see: "New Banking Risk System Lauded", *China Daily*, 23 February 2004.

8. According to analyses of Morgan Stanley, the tier one capital as a share of assets of the four listed JSBs is the lowest of any group of banks in the East Asia region.

9. For example, the Bank of Shanghai has formed an alliance with Citibank with equity participation, while the Nanjing City Commercial Bank has a similar agreement with the IFC.

10. Interim Regulations on Supervision and Management of State-Owned Assets of Enterprises (27 May 2003).

11. Law of the People's Republic of China on Banking Regulation and Supervision (27 December 2003).

12. The Code of Corporate Governance for Listed Companies of the CSRC and the State Economic and Trade Commission (7 January 2001).

13. See OECD, *Annual Surveys of Korea*, 1998-90.

14. CBRC, Guidelines on Corporate Governance Reforms and Supervision of Bank of China and Construction Bank of China (11 March 2004).

15. Several options for the ownership transformation were considered such as forming a Committee under the State Council with the responsibility for bank rehabilitation, transferring ownership to the CBRC or creating a special bank rehabilitation agency with a limited life.

16. "China Moves to Improve Bank Boards", *Financial Times*, 29 July 2004.

17. "Bank of China Grooms Itself for Public Offer", *Wall Street Journal* (30 March 2004).

18. Although 8% is the international standard, the banking supervisors in other Asian emerging economies are now setting higher standards for their domestic banks.

Bibliography

Basel Committee for Banking Supervision (1999), *Enhancing Corporate Governance for Banking Organizations*, September.

Bies, Susan S. (2002), "Banking Supervision and its Application in Developing Countries", speech to World Bank Finance Forum, June, *www.federalreserve.gov/ boarddocs/speeches/2002*.

Bollard, Alan (2004), "The Role of Directors: A Reserve Bank Perspective", *Boardroom: The Journal of The Institute of Directors in New Zealand*, May.

Bu, Yongxiang (2004), "The Regulatory Framework and Government's Role in Improving Corporate Governance in the Banking Sector", paper presented at the APEC Finance and Development Programme Workshop on Improving Governance within Financial Institutions, National Shanghai Institute of Accounting, May.

Cai, E-sheng (1999), "Financial Supervision in China: Framework, Methods and Current Issues", *Strengthening the Banking System In China: Issues and Experience*, IS Policy Papers, Basle, Bank for International Settlements.

Chen, Kathie and Lora Western (2004), "Bank of China Grooms Itself for Public Offer", *Wall Street Journal Europe*, 30 March.

China Banking Regulatory Commission (CBRC) (2004), "Guidelines on Corporate Governance Reforms and Supervision of Bank of China and Construction Bank of China", 11 March.

China Securities Regulatory Commission (CSRC) (2001), "Guidelines for Introducing Independent Directors to the Board of Directors of Listed Companies", 16 August.

China Securities Regulatory Commission/State, Economic and Trade Commission (CSRC/SETC) (2001), *Code of Corporate Governance for Listed Companies of the CSRC and the State Economic and Trade Commission*, issued 7 January.

Dingmin, Zhang (2004), "New Banking Risk System Lauded", *China Daily*, 23 February.

Dolven, Ben, Howard Winn and David Murphy (2004), "HSBC Bets Big on China", *Far Eastern Economic Review*, 19 August.

Estanislao, Jesus (2004), "The Regulatory Framework and Government's Role in Improving Corporate Governance within the Banking Sector", paper presented at the APEC Finance and Development Programme Workshop on Improving Governance within Financial Institutions, National Shanghai Institute of Accounting, May.

Ferri, Giovanni (2003), "Corporate Governance in Banking and Economic Performance: Future Options for PRC", Asian Development Bank Institute Discussion Paper, 7 August.

Liu, Minkang (Chairman of the CBRC) (2004), "Setting a New Stage in China's Banking Supervision and Regulation", speech, 11 March.

Mellor, William (2004), "Building a Transparent Private Bank in China", *China Daily*, 23 February.

OECD (1999), *OECD Economic Surveys: Korea 1998/99*, OECD, Paris.

People's Bank of China (PBC) (January 2002), "Guidance on Corporate Governance for Joint Stock Commercial Banks".

People's Bank of China (PBC) (April 2002), "The Guidance on Internal Control of the Commercial Bank, Proposal".

People's Republic of China, Company Law of the People's Republic of China, Promulgated on 24 December 1994 and Amended on 25 December 1999.

People's Republic of China, Fundamental Code on the Modern Corporate System Establishment and Management of State-Owned Large and Medium-sized Enterprises (Provisional) of 27 October 2000.

People's Republic of China, Law of the People's Republic of China on Banking Regulation and Supervision (27 December 2003).

Slater, Dan (2004), "Bank of China Desperately Searching For Strategic Investors", Finance Asia.com, 10 September.

State Council of the People's Republic of China (2003), "Interim Regulations on Supervision and Management of State-Owned Assets of Enterprises", *Decree of the State Council of the People's Republic of China*, No. 378, 27 May.

Young, Harrison (2004), "Suggestions for Bank Directors", *The Age* (Melbourne), 21 May.

PART III

Chapter 14

Intellectual Property Rights in China: Governance Challenges and Prospects

Table of Contents

Summary 407

Intellectual Property Rights in China: Governance Challenges and Prospects 409

   1. Introduction 409

   2. IPR and economic development 410

      2.1. Definition and economic rationale for IPR 410

      2.2. The impact of IPR on economic growth in developing countries 411

   3. IPR policy and drivers of growth in China 412

   4. An overview of the IPR system in China 414

      4.1. The regulatory framework 414

      4.2. The institutional framework 415

   5. Governance and enforcement issues 417

      5.1. Governance issues 417

      5.2. Infringement 421

   6. How to improve enforcement? 424

      6.1. Actions taken by the Chinese Government 424

      6.2. Towards a multi-dimensional enforcement strategy 426

Notes 428

Bibliography 430

List of boxes

14.1. The main types of intellectual property rights 411
14.2. Infringement and safety 421

Summary

Today, top leaders in the Chinese Government have become aware of the importance for China to build a sound intellectual property rights (IPR) system. While accession to the WTO has opened new opportunities for the Chinese economy, it has also exposed Chinese firms to greater international competition under the WTO rules, including Trade-Related Aspects of Intellectual Property Rights (TRIPS). This means that the government and Chinese industry need to learn as quickly as possible how to play by the new "rules of the game". Indeed, Chinese leaders are realising that the protection of intellectual rights is crucial not only as a condition for foreign investment and technology transfer, but also for promoting Chinese innovation, which will determine China's future competitiveness in the global knowledge economy. China has thus, over the past two decades, quickly developed a set of IPR laws and regulations that are today basically in conformity with international practice and standards. The main challenge for the coming years is to improve upon the governance of the legislative, administrative and enforcement systems in order to make the existing laws more effective in stimulating innovation and protecting IPR.

The elaboration of the IPR system takes place in the broader context of building an institutional framework for market forces. This also means that the institutional environment that should support the IPR system is not fully in place. For instance, China has yet to introduce an anti-trust law which is needed to curb abuse of IPR. The recent amendments to China's Constitution on the protection of private property will consolidate the legal basis for intellectual property. More generally, efforts made to improve the rule of law will benefit the management and protection of intellectual rights.

Within the IPR field, which is an extremely complex and highly technical domain, challenges nevertheless remain numerous. Rather than looking at all of these, this paper highlights and analyses some important governance issues that affect the effectiveness of the Chinese IPR regime in terms of stimulating research and innovation, and the enforcement of IPR.

This study finds that on the one hand China's IPR system has not fully played its role in stimulating Chinese research efforts. On the other hand, in spite of efforts taken to improve IPR enforcement, infringement of IPR in China has been growing in recent years. This chapter identifies the main governance weaknesses underlying these two interrelated phenomena. These include the weaknesses in the regulatory framework, the lack of financial and human resources, the inefficient governance of the interface between research and patents, the weak deterrent effect of sanctions administered, the problem of localism, *i.e.* giving preference to local actors, and the complexity of the administrative organisational structure. The Chinese Government has taken a number of measures to address these challenges. This paper suggests three supplementary directions of action that could contribute to improve the effectiveness of the IPR system in China: *i)* to give full play to civil society actors; ii) to take measures to consolidate the political will for IPR enforcement locally; and iii) to reform the organisational structure of the administrative enforcement channel.

In summary, despite significant progress in the development of IPR policies and enforcement, China faces further short- and long-term challenges to improve and enforce its IPR legislation. Fundamentally, the challenge is to design and adapt IPR policies to accommodate changing needs and requirements. IPR policies will need to support not only foreign direct investment and transfers of foreign technologies, but also encourage domestic research and development (R&D) and innovation, and technology diffusion. The large size of the Chinese economy and the still low and uneven levels of economic development, coupled with a very weak awareness of IPR by government officials, enterprises and the vast Chinese population make it difficult for the government to meet these challenges. Steps to improve governance of the IPR system and in general will be important for China to meet challenges in both the short- and the long-term.

Intellectual Property Rights in China: Governance Challenges and Prospects[1]

1. Introduction

Today, top leaders in the Chinese Government have become aware of the importance for China to build a sound intellectual property rights (IPR) system. Indeed, Chinese leaders are realising that the protection of intellectual rights is crucial not only as a condition for foreign investment and technology transfer, but also for promoting Chinese innovation, which will determine China's future competitiveness in the global knowledge economy. China has thus, over the past two decades, quickly developed a set of IPR laws and regulations that are today basically in conformity with international practice and standards. The main challenge for the coming years is to improve upon the governance of the legislative, administrative and enforcement systems in order to make the existing laws more effective in stimulating innovation and protecting IPR.

The elaboration of the IPR system takes place in the broader context of building an institutional framework for market forces. This also means that the institutional environment that should support the IPR system is not fully in place. For instance, China has yet to introduce an anti-monopoly law to curb abuse of IPR. The recent amendments to China's Constitution on the protection of private property will consolidate the legal basis for intellectual property. More generally, efforts made to improve the rule of law will benefit the management and protection of intellectual rights.

Within the IPR field, which is an extremely complex and highly technical domain, challenges nevertheless remain numerous. Rather than looking at all the challenges facing China's IPR system, this paper highlights and analyses some important governance issues that affect the effectiveness of the Chinese IPR regime in terms of stimulating research and innovation (insofar as innovation can be measured by numbers of patents), and the enforcement of IPR.

This study finds that on the one hand China's IPR system has not fully played its role in stimulating Chinese research efforts. On the other hand, in spite of efforts taken to improve IPR enforcement, infringement of IPR in China has been growing in recent years. Our analysis has identified the main governance weaknesses underlying these two interrelated phenomena. These include the weaknesses in the regulatory framework, the lack of financial and human resources, the inefficient governance of the interface between research and patents, the weak deterrent effect of sanctions administered, the problem of localism, i.e. giving preference to local actors, and the complexity of the administrative organisational structure. The Chinese Government has taken a number of measures to address these challenges. This paper suggests three supplementary directions of action that could contribute to improve the effectiveness of the IPR system in China: i) to give full play to civil society actors; ii) to take measures to consolidate the political will for IPR enforcement locally; and iii) to reform the organisational structure of the administrative enforcement channel.

The paper is structured as follows. First, before analyzing IPR governance issues, we present some key concepts and the nature of IPR in Section 2, go on to discuss why China needs to have a strong IPR system in Section 3 and review the *status quo* of IPR legislation and enforcement in Section 4. We then analyse the governance weaknesses that reduce the effectiveness of the IPR system in Section 5. Finally, we review the measures taken by the Chinese Government to address these challenges and propose some further complementary measures in Section 6.

2. IPR and economic development[2]

Before we proceed to discuss governance issues of China's IPR system, it may be useful to introduce the definition of IPR, its nature, the economic rationale for IPR protection, and the principal relationships between IPR protection and economic development in the particular context of developing countries.

2.1. Definition and economic rationale for IPR

Intellectual property rights are commonly defined as the rights awarded by society to individuals or organisations principally over creative works. They give the creators the right to prevent others from making unauthorized use of their property for a limited period. The main categories of intellectual property (IP) include industrial property (functional commercial innovations) and artistic and literary property (cultural creations), as well as some recently emerging hybrids of the two referred to as *sui generis* systems, such as integrated computer circuits, plant breeders' rights, database protection, etc. Box 14.1 provides a concise description of the main types of IP and the mechanism through which protection works for each type.

One person's use of knowledge does not exclude another's, often at very low marginal costs and not limited by national borders.[3] From the point of view of society, the more people use the available stock of knowledge the better off the society will be, in the sense that more people can gain something at little or no cost. However, the other side of the coin is that if knowledge were available to everyone free of charge, there would not be sufficient economic incentive for private investment in the creation of knowledge, leading to an underinvestment with detrimental effects on society in the long run.

The economic rationale for protecting IPR is the need to address the failure of the market in ensuring sufficient private investment in the creation of new knowledge. This is done by granting temporary market exclusivities to IP owners to allow them to recoup the costs of private investment and to make a profit, which works as an incentive to encourage knowledge creation and technological innovation. Thus, IPR are policy instruments that confer economic privileges to individuals and institutions for the purpose of contributing to the greater public good. In other words, IPR protection is a means to an end, but not an end in itself.

At the same time, IPR protection comes at a cost to society. One part of the cost resulting from market exclusivities is the static cost to consumers in the form of pricing above marginal production cost. Other costs incurred by individuals and by society as a whole include the duplicative investments in research and development (R&D) due to the

Box 14.1. **The main types of intellectual property rights**

Industrial property

Patents: A patent is an exclusive right awarded to an inventor to prevent others from making, selling, distributing, importing and using their invention, without licensing or authorisation, for a fixed period of time (TRIPS stipulates 20 years minimum from the date of filing). In return, society requires that the patent applicant disclose the invention in a manner that enables others to put it in practice. Patents applications are examined and granted by applying the criteria of *novelty, non-obviousness and utility/industrial applicability*. *Utility models* are similar to patents, but in some countries confer rights of shorter duration to certain kinds of small or incremental innovations.

Trademarks: Trademarks provide exclusive rights to use distinctive signs (such as symbols, colours, letters, shapes or names) to identify the producer of a product, and protect its associated reputation. In order to be eligible for protection, a mark must be distinctive of the proprietor so as to identify the proprietor's goods and services. The main purpose of a trademark is to prevent costumers from being misled and deceived. Duration of trademark protection can vary, but a trademark can be renewed indefinitely.

Trade secrets: Trade secrets consist of commercially valuable information about production processes, business plans, clientele, etc. They are protected as long as they remain secret by laws which prevent acquisition by commercially unfair means and unauthorised disclosure. However, there is no exclusive right to the process if it is discovered by fair means, such as reverse engineering (Maskus, 2005).

Artistic and literary property

Copyright: Copyright grants exclusive rights to the creator of original literary, scientific and artistic works. Copyright begins, without formalities, with the creation of the work and lasts (as a general rule) for the lifetime of the creator plus 50 years (70 years in the United States and European Union). It prevents unauthorised copying, reproduction, public performance, recording, broadcasting, translation, and adaptation, and allows the collections of royalty for authorised use. It prevents copying, but not independent derivation, nor fair-use for scientific and educational purposes. Computer programs are protected by copyright in most countries.

Source: CIPR (2002).

---

race to secure a patent, and substantial enforcement costs associated with asserting and defending IPR (Maskus, 2005). As such, questions should be asked about what constitutes an optimal level of IPR protection, how it should be structured, and how the optimal structure may vary depending on sectors and levels of economic development.

2.2. *The impact of IPR on economic growth in developing countries*

The links between IPR protection and economic growth is extremely complex, and evidence of the benefit of IPR protection for the economic growth of developing countries is far from clear. The Report by the Commission on Intellectual Property Rights (CIPR, 2002) draws the following conclusions on the main dimensions of the relationship:[4]

- IPR, Innovation and Growth: Based on the experiences of developed and newly industrialised economies which suggest that the strength of IPR protection increases with economic development after countries have reached quite high income levels, the main conclusions of the Report are: *i)* for those developing countries that have acquired significant technological and innovative capabilities, there has generally been an association with "weak" rather then "strong" forms of IP protection in the formative period of their economic development; *ii)* in technologically advanced developing countries there is some evidence that IP becomes important at a certain stage of economic development, but that stage is not reached until a country is well into the category of upper middle-income developing countries.

- IPR, Trade and Investment: With a distinction made between the impact of IPR on developing countries, and on the exports and investment from developed countries, the Report concludes that: *i)* there is some evidence that trade inflows into developing countries are influenced by the strength of IPR protection,[5] particularly in IPR sensitive high technology industries, but the evidence is far from clear; *ii)* for technologically more advanced developing countries, IPR may be important in facilitating access to protected high technologies, by foreign investment or by licensing;[6] *iii)* it may be difficult to achieve a right balance for countries such as China and India where some industries have the potential to benefit from IP protection, but the associated costs for industries that were established under weak IP regimes as well as for consumers are potentially high.

3. IPR policy and drivers of growth in China

IPR protection is an important condition for China to pursue its development strategy based on openness to and integration into the global economy and technology upgrading and innovation. The quality of the IPR regime will indeed affect positively two drivers of China's growth, foreign direct investment (FDI) and R&D.

As a developing country, China needs to attract foreign investment and is dependent on the access to foreign technology for the modernisation of the Chinese economy. Various forms of foreign investments have been the major channel of transferring foreign technology into China in the past.

Since the 1980s, China has succeeded in attracting large amounts of FDI, and it was the largest FDI recipient in the world in 2002. To a large extent, its past success could be attributed to important factors such as the low labour cost for manufacturing industries and the huge size of the Chinese domestic market. The so-called "market for technology" policy, which attached technology transfer as a condition for approving foreign investment projects, played an important role in leveraging technology transfers in the past (OECD, 2002). Such a policy is no longer a feasible option since China's entry into the WTO. At the same time, as China is aiming to attract high quality FDI, measured by the technological content of investment projects, improving IPR is of greater importance than in the past. Clearly, the strength of IPR protection is a crucial factor for foreign firms' decision on what types of technology to bring to China. Firms, especially those in IPR sensitive industries such as pharmaceutics, will only bring the latest technology and production process into a country if they are confident that the country can provide secure and adequate protection for IPR, including trade secrets (see Chapter 15).[7]

In addition, China needs a strong IPR system to promote R&D and innovation. IPR issues are of growing importance to China, as it continues to modernise its science and technology system, on which future economic performance depends. Since the government adopted the strategy of "revitalising the nation through science and education" in 1995, China has paid increasing attention to improving its national innovation system as part of the country's overall development strategy. R&D expenditures have grown rapidly over the past decade, with gross domestic expenditure on research and development (GERD) reaching 72.1 billion in purchasing power parity (PPP) dollars in 2002 (OECD, 2004), up from 12.5 billion PPP dollars in 1991.[8] GERD as a share of gross domestic product (GDP) rose from 0.60% in 1995 to 1.23% in 2002. While this level is significantly below the average of OECD member countries, i.e. 2.26% in 2002, it exceeds that of some upper-middle income OECD members, such as Greece and Mexico.

The protection of intellectual property is a key consideration for multinational enterprises, whose R&D investment and activities can actually play an important role in filling the gaps in R&D resources, scientific knowledge, and transferring tacit know-how and expertise in research methodology and management. The Ministry of Science and Technology (MOST) estimated that R&D funding by overseas companies, including those from Hong Kong, China and Macau, China, and Chinese Taipei, accounted for between 15-20% of business R&D expenditures in China in the past year. Although FDI in R&D and technology services accounted for only 0.4% of accumulated contractual value of FDI until 2002, the increasing number of foreign-invested R&D facilities – from just a handful at the end of the 1990s to some 600 in 2004 – indicates that foreign R&D investments have grown quickly since China's entry into the WTO. Interviews with managers of foreign companies revealed a widespread reluctance to locate R&D facilities in China in the recent past (Maskus, 2005). Thus, a system of adequate IPR protection will further encourage foreign investments in R&D, helping China to participate in and benefit from the globalisation of R&D.

As Chinese industries become more technology-intensive and as business accounts for a growing share of R&D, IPR protection is increasingly important to domestic firms as well.[9] Promoting business R&D has been an important government innovation policy since the mid-1990s. Consequently, there has been a trend of increasing R&D spending by Chinese enterprises, which accounted for 57.6% of total R&D expenditure in 2000. The share of R&D performed by the domestic business enterprise sector[10] has also increased from 40% in 1991 to 61% in 2002 (OECD, 2004). However, innovative Chinese firms are particularly affected by trademark infringements, making significant impacts on the growth of this type of enterprise (Maskus, 2005).

Parallel to increasing R&D spending, the Chinese Government has carried out reforms of public research organisations (PROs), established high-technology development zones, successively developed several national plans for science and technology and created a number of key national laboratories such as those under the Chinese Academy of Sciences. Government measures have also been introduced to enhance R&D spending, innovation capability and appreciation of intangible assets, notably intellectual properties by Chinese enterprises. To facilitate technology transfer from public research to the private sector as well as co-operation between PROs and enterprises, China amended the Patent Law and promoted the creation of technology transfer centres and technology markets.

Increasing R&D expenditure combined with systemic reforms have led to a steep rise in the number of patents applications in China, which almost tripled, from slightly more than 100 000 in 1996 to more than 300 000 in 2003. Yet, more than three-quarters of the patents by Chinese inventors were not invention patents *per se*, but design and utility patents, reflecting their weak innovative capabilities (see Box 14.1). In contrast, invention patents accounted for the majority (85%) of foreign applications. Patent statistics also indicate low efficiency in Chinese enterprises' R&D activities: for example, the enterprise sector accounted for performing 60% of China's total R&D expenditure in 2001, but received only 17% of the invention patents granted to Chinese inventors that year. Low awareness of the importance of patents was considered an important reason for such a low level of patents owned by Chinese firms (MOST, 2002).

China aims to become a technologically advanced nation in the 21st century. To realize this objective it is critical that the government puts in place appropriate incentives for innovation and technology development and encourages broad diffusion of and access to scientific and technological advances. In this context, a good IPR system, which not only provides incentives for innovation but also promotes technology diffusion, is called for.[11] Furthermore, with significant public spending on R&D, publicly funded research forms the backbone of China's national innovation system. It is particularly important for China to adopt the right IPR policies for communalisation of public research in order to boost its contribution to social and economic development.[12]

Towards the end of the 1990s, it was already observed that at the highest level, the Chinese Government recognized the need for a workable IPR system (Maskus et al., 2005). Initially, the government's recognition of the importance of IPR protection was mainly prompted by China's need to improve investment conditions for FDI and to access advanced foreign technologies. This recognition has progressively evolved into a fuller understanding of the ultimate importance of IPR protection in the context of fostering China's domestic innovation capability. This marked a very important strategic shift in the government's thinking at the top level, which does not see IPR policies as an instrument for protecting "other's rights" in return for access to foreign capital and technology, but as part of the fundamental strategy that will determine China's long-term competitiveness in the global economy. However, this understanding has yet to be adopted by governments at all levels and among the Chinese enterprises.

4. An overview of the IPR system in China

4.1. The regulatory framework

Over the past two decades, China has made great strides in developing a comprehensive system of IPR legislation (Yang, 2003). China's current IP legal framework basically consists of three laws: the Trademark Law (1982, revised 1993 and 2001), the Patent Law (1984, revised 1992 and 2000) and the Copyright Law (1990, revised 2001). These laws are complemented by regulations such as those on the Protection of Computer Software (1991, revised 2001), on the Protection of New Plant Varieties and on the Protection of Lay-out Designs of Integrated Circuits (2001). Furthermore, the Anti-Unfair Competition Law promulgated in 1993 is used to provide a legal basis for protection of trade secrets and business know-how.[13] These laws and regulations have established the legal notion of intellectual property rights in China. The recent amendments brought to China's Constitution on the protection of private property consolidate the legal basis for intellectual property.

China has also progressively accepted its international obligations for the protection of IPR. It joined the World Intellectual Property Organization (WIPO) in 1980, ratified the Paris Convention for the Protection of Industrial Property in 1985 and the Madrid Agreement concerning the International Registration of Marks in 1989 as well as signed the Integrated Circuits Treaty the same year. China became a signatory country of the Berne Convention for the Protection of Literary and Artistic Works and of the Universal Copyright Convention in 1992, the Geneva Convention in 1993, the Patent Co-operation Treaty (PCT) and Budapest Treaty in 1994. Finally, with its WTO membership in 2001, China accepted the obligation to adhere to the Trade-Related Aspects of Intellectual Property Rights (TRIPS) Agreement of the WTO.

Accession to the WTO has motivated considerable strengthening of IPR protection in China. China revised its intellectual property laws and regulations, promulgating new regulations and abolishing old ones in an effort to bring the scope and strength of IP protection into conformity with the TRIPS Agreement. By the end of the first year of its transitional period, the WTO Council formed a positive opinion towards China's fulfilment of its obligations, including with respect to the TRIPS clauses. In 2003, China continued the effort by introducing a number of regulations and administrative protection measures, such as the regulations on customs protection of IPR, and implementation measures on copyright administrative sanction, and those on compulsory patent licensing and on the administration of patent agencies.

4.2. The institutional framework

4.2.1. Institutional framework at the national level

Under the State Council, there are several administrations involved in the protection of intellectual property, each specialised in a different kind of right. The State Intellectual Property Office (SIPO) is in charge of patents (including integrated circuit layout design); the State Administration for Industry and Commerce (SAIC) of trademarks; the National Copyright Administration of China (NCAC) of copyrights; the Ministry of Agriculture and the State Forestry Administration of new plant variety rights; the Ministry of Culture and the State Administration for Radio Film and Television of copyrighted works in the audio-video market and in the broadcasting, television and movie sectors, respectively.

The State Intellectual Property Office (SIPO) (previously the Chinese Patent Office) is also responsible for the co-ordination of foreign-related intellectual property affairs. SIPO represents China in WIPO and in the TRIPS Council reviews.

In 2003 SIPO became part of the State Council Leading Group for National Rectification and Standardisation of Market Economic Order (NRSMEO, *guowuyuan zhengdun he guifan shichang jingji zhixu lingdao xiaozu*).[14] Some 30 government bodies are represented in this leading group. Fighting against counterfeit production and sales, and the protection of intellectual property more generally are priorities on its agenda.[15]

The National Office for Rectification and Standardisation of Market Economic Order (or in short *zhengguiban*) is the Secretariat of this leading group. It is located in the Ministry of Commerce and led by a vice minister. This Office develops policy proposals to improve the market order; it co-ordinates rectification motions in specially targeted areas and supervises the investigations of cases of significant importance. It also instructs the relevant government bodies to research and draft policies, laws and regulations concerning cracking-down on the local blockades and sectoral monopolies.

In 2004 China set up an IPR Protection Leading Group, led by Vice Premier Wu Yi.

4.2.2. Institutional framework at the sub-national level

SIPO, SAIC, NCAC and the other administrations involved in the protection of IPR have local branch offices at the provincial, prefecture and municipal levels. National-level administrations are responsible for policy making and nation wide policy implementation, as well as for the examination, granting and registration of IPR, and for the handling of infringement cases of major importance (*cf. infra*). Sub-national administrations are responsible for the implementation of national policies, the making of local policies and regulations and for the administration and administrative enforcement of IPR in their jurisdictions. National-level administrations are also mandated to guide the work of their local offices, and represent China in international co-operation and relations in their fields of responsibility.

The central government does not have a policy for a uniform IPR administrative structure at local levels: local governments can decide what organisational structure the local IPR administration should have in their jurisdictions. The density of these agencies' local organisation is influenced by a number of factors, primarily by the level of economic development. SIPO has branches in all 29 provinces, autonomous regions and directly controlled cities. But in some provinces, such as Hebei, Shangdong, Hubei, Hunan, Guangdong and Sichuan, there are more than ten sub-provincial branches in each province, while in Liaoning, Heilongjiang, Fujing, Jiangxi, Henan, Guizhuo, Gansu and Xingjiang, there are only a few sub-provincial branches. In the remaining Chinese provinces, there is no sub-provincial SIPO branch office at all. The set-up of the sub-provincial judicial system for hearing IPR related litigations shares the same feature: the numbers of intermediate courts that are specialised or authorized to judge IPR cases vary greatly from one province to another, and from one autonomous region to another, and among cities in terms of secondary and basic courts.[16]

4.2.3. Institutional set-up for enforcement

China has a two-track system for the enforcement of IP rights, which is known in China as "two ways, synchronously operating" protection system (*liangtiao tujing xietiao yunzuo*). Under this system, the responsibility for IPR enforcement is shared between the Court and Procuratorate bodies, and the Ministry of Public Security on the one hand, and the State Council IPR administrations mentioned in the above section on the other. The latter also have the power to handle infringement cases through an administrative enforcement mechanism.

When their rights are infringed or harmed, IPR holders can turn to the responsible administrative authority for settlement.[17] This administration will investigate the complaint, and if infringement is found, it will order the infringing party to stop the infringing act, confiscate infringing goods and impose fines. If right owners are dissatisfied with decisions made by administrative authorities, they may seek redress by filing an administrative litigation against the settlement decision at court, which has the final say.

The alternative to this administrative enforcement channel is to launch either a civil or a criminal lawsuit with the judicial system. Broadly defined, China's judicial system consists of three parts: People's Court System, People's Procuratorate System, and the Public Security System. China's Court System consists of four levels of courts: the Supreme Court, High Courts, Intermediate Courts and Basic Courts. The Procuratorate System has the role of a "state organ for legal supervision", which reviews and monitors the conducts of the public security forces and of the Court System. The Public Security System is part of the administrative system, which carries investigation, detention, preliminary hearings and arrest.

China has been progressively establishing a system of specialised IP tribunals. Since 1993, dozens of High Courts and Intermediate Courts in some cities have established intellectual property tribunals. In 1996, the Supreme People's Court set up the Intellectual

Property Tribunal, whose role is to handle major IP cases and provide guidance for and supervision of IP cases tried across the country. Currently, all High Courts of the 31 provinces and Intermediate Courts situated in the provincial capitals, in the cities under the direct authority of the State Council, and in the capitals of autonomous regions have established specialised tribunals for the civil judgment of IPR cases. A few Basic People's Courts in large cities such as Beijing and Shanghai which receive significant IP litigation have also set up IP tribunals.

Another important enforcement actor is the General Customs Administration, which has been playing an increasing role in detecting, investigating and stopping the flow of infringing goods, according to the Regulations on the Customs Protection of Intellectual Property.

5. Governance and enforcement issues

As is the case in all policy areas, it is one thing to adopt a text that defines the general orientations of a country's policy, and quite another to see how these orientations are put into practice on the ground. Indeed, the definition of IPR and their protection involve a whole spectrum of actors, from the top, where the IPR laws are designed and passed, to local offices, closer to the field and to other interests: organisations with varying levels of resources, different mandates and powers, etc. The purpose of this section is to take a closer look at a selected number of aspects of the Chinese "IPR state machinery" mobilised for the development and maintenance of the IPR regime in China, and to show how its weaknesses contribute to shaping this regime in practice.

It first discusses the weaknesses in the governance set-up, and then takes the problem from the other end by looking at the problem of IPR infringement in China in the light of governance weaknesses.

5.1. Governance issues

In the following, several governance weaknesses are identified and analyzed successively, showing the impact that the regulatory framework, organisational structures, human and financial resources, and management practices have in the implementation of IPR.

5.1.1. Consultations in the regulatory-making process

Chinese enterprises and other institutions have complained that the competent intellectual property administrations did not extensively solicit opinions and comments when working out laws, regulations and policies (Lu, 2004). This insufficient public participation has led in some cases to inadequate protection standards. For instance, the TRIPS Agreement does not prescribe clearly the requirement on end-users of computer software; it allows WTO members to make their own provisions on the responsibility of end-users in accordance with their actual economic development. Yet the newly amended Chinese software regulations prescribe unnecessarily high protection standards for end-users – higher than those in Japan or in Chinese Taipei. The lack of public participation in the regulatory-making process also affects enforcement. If actors judge the system unfair, they will be less inclined to endorse its rules. Participation also allows actors to better understand why certain decisions are taken.

Consultation not only with parties affected but also with other government departments and bodies can contribute to ensuring the coherency of the IPR regime with other policy fields. Indeed, the IPR regime's design, implementation and enforcement are influenced directly or indirectly by the policies adopted in such fields as science and technology, competition and trade policies, foreign direct investment and access to foreign technology. Since China has a dual economic structure with both a modern sector (*e.g.* R&D and modern industry) and an underdeveloped traditional sector, IPR policies have to meet the different needs for IP protection and work in harmony with policies that support the development of different sectors. In many OECD member countries, such as the United States, regular consultations with rights holders and others affected by intellectual property rights are key to achieving and maintaining the coherency of the IPR regime with other policy fields (OECD, 2005).

5.1.2. Competition and IPR

Competition policy is a policy field which overlaps with IPR, and the immaturity of the competition regulatory framework in China today affects the IPR regime. Issues that arise at the interface between competition and IPR include the interdependence between competition and IPR laws and policies, competition issues in the context of bilateral and multilateral licence agreements, and the potential abuse of IPR when firms with significant market power refuse to grant competitors access to its IPR. As part of China's transition to a market-based economy, dealing with competition issues, in particular the adoption of an antitrust legislation, has become a priority concern.

Another dimension relates to the fact that the offence of unfair competition cannot be referred to in cases that are close to IPR infringement, as is generally the case, for instance, in European countries. China adopted a law on unfair competition in 2003, but judges as well as the authorities refer to it only if the facts of the case correspond exactly to one of the 13 or 14 cases mentioned in the law. In Europe, such a law is useful for instituting legal proceedings against any company that would, for instance, propose products very close to those produced by another company (same shape, same colour but not exactly the same product), thus trying to benefit from the latter's reputation.

5.1.3. Regulatory framework at the local level

Local regulations are designed to implement national policies and legislation and/or to complement them as the following example shows. The Chinese Patent Law states in general terms that a government official can be prosecuted for criminal liability for abuse of power or malfunction. The Regulations for the Protection of Patent Rights adopted by the People's Congress in the Xinjiang Autonomous Region for instance specify four types of situations: *i)* covering up or turning a blind eye to the falsification of patents; *ii)* in the patent dispute mediation process, taking sides to favour one party, while violating the legitimate rights and interests of the other party; *iii)* leaking litigant's technical or business secret; and *iv)* using their position to demand or receive bribery from other people.

Local regulations are in principle more concrete, implementable, and adapted to local social and economic conditions. Even if these are normally based on national legislation and central government policies, local regulations are sometimes in conflict with central government regulations. The National People's Congress and the State Council should normally play a supervisory role, but the large volume of sub-national legislation makes this task difficult to achieve.

There is also a lack of transparency in the regulatory framework at the local level, as noted for instance by the United States Government who reports that many local Chinese authorities are reluctant to provide copies of their local rules or regulations regarding IPR as well as any local enforcement decisions (WTO, 2003b). China committed to "make available to WTO members, upon request, all laws, regulations and other measures pertaining to or affecting trade in goods, services, TRIPS or the control of foreign exchange before such measures are implemented or enforced".[18] Yet the Chinese Government argues that providing such information is in itself a huge task, given the quantity of legislation (WTO, 2003c). It should be noted that Chinese firms and citizens are confronted with this lack of transparency just as much as foreign firms.

5.1.4. Prosecution and sanctions

Today, it is very difficult to launch a criminal lawsuit. Access to the criminal prosecution channel is not easy and the process is very long. A large percentage of criminal cases are based on referrals from administrative agencies. But the decision on orientation to the criminal channel is based on a financial threshold which is loosely defined, thus leaving important discretion to the administrative officers.[19] In addition, it is not always easy to prove that the moneys involved are higher than a certain amount, especially when the case starts with the seizure of only one lot of products. In addition, experience shows that the local police rarely take on cases of counterfeiting without strong support from the Ministry of Public Security in Beijing. In a recent case for instance, officials from the Ministry of Public Security came from Beijing for a criminal procedure to be initiated in Guangzhou, leading to the arrest of several persons.

Criminal prosecution, if successfully pursued, can indeed result in higher sanctions with a stronger deterrent effect than civil prosecution. Civil prosecution leads to the condemnation of legal persons, with rather low fines. It is not very difficult to declare bankrupt the company accused of counterfeiting, while moving the production lines to another company. It happens that businessmen caught once for infringement don't stop there; fines become another tax-like cost for doing business. Reasonable condemnations of real persons can be more dissuasive, as criminology shows that when the risk becomes too high, wrongdoers turn to other activities. For instance, in France, counterfeiters can be prosecuted at the same time in a civil and a criminal tribunal, leading sometimes to very dissuasive sanctions.

5.1.5. Organisational structure of the administrative enforcement channel

One of the weak points of the administrative enforcement channel is the complexity of its organisational structure and the lack of a well-functioning co-ordination mechanism. Indeed, cases of infringement often present several dimensions: for instance patent and trademark. But, as described previously, patents and trademarks are dealt with by separate government bodies. This organisational separation inevitably wastes resources and affects the efficiency of administrative enforcement efforts. In the United States, one single office, the Patent and Trademarks Office, covers both patents and trademarks; the same applies in Russia, with the Federal Service for Intellectual Property, Patent, and Trademarks.

Another weak aspect of the organisational structure is the overlapping authority and lack of co-ordination among various administrative enforcement bodies. For instance, in the context of brand protection, these include the Administration for Industry and Commerce (AIC) Trademark Division, the AIC Economic Supervision Division, the Technical Supervisory Bureaus (TSBs), Customs, the Public Security Bureaus (PSB) Social Order Divisions, the PSB Economic Crimes Investigation Divisions (ECIDs).[20] This complex and overlapping structure makes work more complicated on the one hand, and contributes to create loopholes in protection, on the other. One common example of the resulting problems is the difficulty in promptly transferring criminal cases from the TSBs to the ECIDs, notwithstanding the fact that the relevant standards for criminal investigation and prosecution have clearly been met.

5.1.6. *Financial and human resources*

The judicial bodies and administrative authorities for intellectual property administration and protection have insufficient financial and human resources. The significant increase in the number of IPR registered in China (*cf. supra*, growth rate around 20-30% per year) has put further pressure on resources. This lack of resources particularly affects the local level.

Financial resources of local IPR administrative authorities are allocated by the provincial government. Most of the local IPR administrative authorities have an operational budget but no funds for law enforcement. There are only a handful of provinces in which local governments give high attention to intellectual property protection and thus allocate resources to the administrative entities for law enforcement. Yet, even in these cases, resources are only provided in a provisional manner. In this context, administrative fines sometimes become important resources for local administrations. This therefore creates an inbuilt incentive for administrations to keep cases in their enforcement channel.[21]

The lack of competent human resources for IPR has also become a serious bottleneck that affects the quality of intellectual property administration and law enforcement. This problem also has a strong regional dimension: the administrative authorities of poorer regions have less capacity. It thus often happens that cases are not properly handled or prosecuted because the administrators or judges in charge do not really understand the litigation procedures. In addition, the capacity of judicial bodies for law enforcement is limited in some localities.

5.1.6.1. Management of research

Weak links between research management and IPR management impede making the most of research efforts in terms of the creation of IPR.[22]

Government administrative departments in charge of science and technology planning, as well as universities, public research institutions and enterprises, all lack IP management systems and agencies. Researchers and programme managers are not used to taking advantage of the IP system and protecting the legitimate rights and interests of the investors and their organisations. To create incentives for research results, the management of public research programmes traditionally relied on an award system, rather than encouraging the application and exploitation of patents. Indeed, personnel management systems in universities and scientific research institutions link professional titles and salaries to the number of publications and awards. As a result, research efforts are directed towards publication and the pursuit of awards, rather than towards the production of applicable and independent intellectual property rights. Let us note though, that it is only recently that OECD member countries have been reforming their IPR policies related to universities and public research organisations, to better connect science to innovation and IPR.[23]

On the private-sector side, some Chinese companies give up patent applications because they have little confidence that their rights will be protected. Others do not know clearly how to make full use of their own intellectual property rights and protect their legitimate rights and interests. This lack of awareness and capacity contributes to weakening the IPR system overall.

5.2. Infringement

The governance weaknesses described above affect not only the protection of IPR, but also the production and use of new knowledge. In this sub-section, we approach the problem from the other side and focus on the problem of IPR infringement.

5.2.1. Scope

Despite government efforts, the effect of criminal and administrative enforcement is insufficient to deter IPR infringement activities in China.[24]

All types of IPR are vulnerable to infringement. But counterfeiting (*i.e.* copying of trademarks and design) is the most frequent form of infringement. Almost all types of products are subject to counterfeiting in China: batteries, razors, medicines, shampoo, cigarettes, auto-parts, industrial valves, vision wear, apparel, air compressors, portable tools, power strips, extension cords, footwear, etc. In most cases, the counterfeited product does not present the same quality as the original. This may create serious health or safety hazards in the case of products such as medicine or windshields (see Box 14.2).

Box 14.2. Infringement and safety

Reports by the China Consumer Association (CCA, 1997; 2004) revealed that cases involving serious bodily harm and death to consumers caused by counterfeits occurs to a devastating degree. For example, 672 cases of serious injury were reported in 1997, and 1 214 cases in 1998. Some 35 cases in 1997, and 70 in 1998, involved permanent injury, and cases involving death increased from 19 to 33 between these two years.* It should be noted that the majority of the above cases were counterfeits of Chinese domestic products. For example, of the 33 deaths and 1 214 serious injuries reported in 1998, 27 deaths and 1 000 injuries can be traced to counterfeit rice wine in Shanxi Province in North China (QBPC, 2000). A recent assessment of the food safety standards by the CCA revealed that on average 76.6% of food products checked during 1999 and 2003 by the quality control agency met the quality standards. Manufacturing of fake products and counterfeiting were identified as the main threats to food safety.

* See China Consumer Association 1997 Report, p. 2; China Consumer Association 1998 Report, p. 4.

The potential losses from counterfeit and piracy and the resulting economic impact can be significant, although their exact magnitude are difficult to assess. According to a survey conducted by the Development Research Centre of the State Council in 2001, the value of counterfeit goods in market circulation in China was estimated to be between 160 and 200 billion RMB (*i.e.* 19 to 24 billion USD). The survey also revealed that Chinese firms, especially those with well-known brand names, were the victims of 80% of the IPR infringement cases. A survey of members of the Quality Brand Protection Committee (QBPC) conducted in mid-2003 revealed that, despite obvious progress on many fronts in anti-counterfeiting efforts, QBPC members viewed the problem as having remained the same or deteriorated over the past few years. According to this survey, counterfeits account for an average of 25% of the markets inside China for QBPC members' brands (QBPC, 2004).

A large proportion of counterfeit and pirated goods are exported and sold on foreign markets. The QBPC survey confirms that exports of counterfeit products from China are increasing, and over 80% of QBPC members characterized their problems with such exports as "serious". Data from seizures at foreign borders indicate that China is the world's leading source of counterfeit and pirated goods. For instance, the United States Department of Homeland Security's Bureau of Customs and Border Protection reported the seizure of 2 056 shipments from China containing counterfeit and pirated products, with a value of over USD 62 million. These statistics for fiscal year 2003 name China as the top source of infringing goods stopped at the United States border (IACC, 2004, p. 11). Other sources predict that China's share of the world's trade of counterfeit and pirated goods will continue to increase annually (WTO, 2003a).

The International Intellectual Property Alliance (2005) estimated that the losses due to piracy of the United States copyright based industry (CBI) in China, including motion pictures, records and music, business software, entertainment software and books was in the order of USD 2 860 million in 2003, compared to USD 1 085 million in 2000. According to this source, except for books, which had an estimated piracy level of 40%, piracy levels of all the other US CBI sectors were above 90% in the respective Chinese markets.

5.2.2. Analysis

To analyse the problem of infringement in China, as in other contexts, it is interesting to distinguish between different types of infringement. Governance weaknesses and the resulting ineffective enforcement system create opportunities for potential infringers of IP. Infringers of IP are not all the same: they may have different motivations, different business profiles and different types of links with the local business authorities. As we will further develop in Section 6, responses to these various infringement situations should differ accordingly.

In the following paragraphs, we introduce ways of distinguishing between different types of infringement situations, thus decomposing the infringement problem into several sub-problems.

In some situations, the infringer is not aware of the rights of the owner and naïvely uses the property without being conscious of infringing a rule. There can be two reasons for this "naïve infringing". The infringer may not be aware of the IPR system. By essence, IPR define an individual property, a notion intimately linked to market systems. The idea that a useful innovation or even that a brand's image or label cannot be used freely is not obvious and straightforward for most ordinary Chinese people. Moreover, the IPR system is sometimes opposed on the basis of the elements of Chinese culture, according to which, as only the great is copied, it is an honour to be copied and a petty reaction to feel offended.[25]

The other reason is when property or the related rules are not clearly defined. Indeed, rules always leave a margin of interpretation. Therefore an irreducible zone of situations exists in which the implementation of the rule will not be straightforward. In addition, defining precisely when patent abuse starts is a regulatory problem that is difficult to solve in any country.

In all other situations, the infringer is aware of infringing a property, but assesses that the costs and/or the risks of sanction are negligible in view of the benefits. Infringers thus take advantage of possible regulatory loopholes (for instance, a Chinese car manufacturer had put on the market a product borrowing for its front the design of a certain foreign brand car, and for its rear the design of another foreign brand car, thus taking advantage of a regulatory loophole on partial design) or of the ineffectiveness of the enforcement system. The different governance weaknesses discussed above – loopholes in the regulatory framework, the administrative organisational structure, the lack of resources, the lack of integration of IPR objectives in research and company business policies – all contribute to this ineffectiveness of enforcement efforts.

Infringement sometimes takes place with the more or less active complicity of local leaders. Indeed, while Chinese leaders at the top are convinced of the need to develop a sound IPR regime, in practice, some actors at the local level do not always adhere strictly to these views. In such situations, local officials may turn a blind eye on infringing practices or even interfere with the enforcement of IPR regulations to protect local enterprises involved in infringement. To give an example, the Japanese government reported in the framework of the WTO review of the TRIPS agreement that when some Japanese companies had requested the seizure of counterfeit goods, local authorities had refused to seize them because they had been produced by a major local company (WTO, 2003c).

The main motivations driving local officials to tolerate IPR infringement can be of different types. The loose compliance of local officials with national IPR laws and regulations can be related to the pressure on the local government to meet economic growth targets, the fulfilment of which is still an important determinant in the evaluation of local officials' performance and for their career promotion. The local official's interest in protecting infringing local firms can in some cases be related to corruption where protection is extended for a return of personal interest.

But this loose enforcement can also be guided by collective interests, when local officials judge that the local, short-term benefits of a strict IPR enforcement exceed the costs. Several situations can be envisaged:

- In situations of "localism", local officials seek primarily to develop the local economy and to maintain local employment, against competitors based in other provinces. This leads, for instance, to situations in which local leaders will influence court rulings in favour of the local defendants.
- Local officials may consider that the competitiveness of Chinese export companies based on low labour costs is reduced, or even lost, when these companies have to pay high licensing fees for foreign technologies or other royalties. Technological transaction cost increases can affect technology use, transfer and dissemination. As the credit system and the credit environment are still under construction, it is difficult for companies to overcome the barriers thus created. These short-term observations create incentives to free ride and fail to implement IPR policies efficiently.
- Local officials may consider that a company producing goods of similar quality and at cheaper prices, copying an original product, serves the interest of local consumers. A typical example of such a company would be, for instance, a company founded by local government 10 years previously, which has a fully formal facade and pays taxes, but that will combine perfectly legal operations with operations on the margins of legality in terms of obeying the IPR regulations.
- Local officials may also consider that the protection of property rights related to foreign culture products is not a priority in the Chinese context. They would thus not mobilize much effort to nail down the "fly by night" types of companies that usually provide copies of DVDs, software, etc. operating on a small scale, with few fixed assets.

Weak enforcement at the local level is a result of the organisational and resources structure at the local level: as described earlier, local administrative entities in charge of enforcement are dependent on the local government through their budget and career management of the staff. The judicial entities are not independent either. As links often exist, through Party structures, between enterprises and local government officials, the IPR enforcement system is vulnerable to the influence of local government interventions. The overlapping mandates of different executive administrations involved in IPR enforcement and the confusion that sometimes results also contribute to creating opportunities for interference.

6. How to improve enforcement?

6.1. Actions taken by the Chinese Government

The Chinese authorities acknowledge the need for stronger enforcement, and have been taking various measures for this purpose. Quoting SIPO's Commissioner Wang Jingchuan: "Protecting intellectual property is not only necessary for China to comply with its promises made in its accession to WTO, but also the needs of expanding, opening-up and introducing foreign investment and advanced technologies. Above all, it is also the inherent demand of the country in its economic development and comprehensive social progress" (Wang, 2004).

China recently revised its major IP laws and regulations, such as the Patent Law (2000), the Trademark Law (2001) and the Copyright Law (2001). It also formulated and promulgated the Regulations on Protection of the Layout Design of Integrated Circuits. Those laws and regulations expand the scope and force of protection of intellectual property. They also increase the rights of right holders and intensify the force of judicial and administrative law enforcement.

In 2003 a number of regulations and administrative protection measures were promulgated to increase protection, such as the Regulations on Customs Protection of Intellectual Property Rights, the Implementing Measures on Copyright Administrative Sanction, the Measures on Implementation of Compulsory Patent Licence and Measures on Administration of Patent Agencies. In addition, China has also amended or abolished some other regulations or rules not consistent with WTO rules.

As mentioned previously, an important step was the entry of SIPO in the National Office for Rectification and Standardization of Market Economic Order in 2003. Combating counterfeit production and sales, and protection of intellectual property became a priority on the work agenda of this leading group in 2004. A further step taken in this direction was the creation of State Council IPR Protection Leading Group later in 2004.

Also, on the occasion of the 2004 "World Intellectual Property Day", nine Chinese governmental agencies under the State Council (including the Ministry of Public Security; the Ministry of Culture; SIPO; SAIC; the General Administration of Quality Supervision, Inspection and Quarantine; NCAC and the Customs General Administration) jointly launched a week-long nationwide campaign in April 2004 to raise awareness of IPR protection.

The government is also well aware that the further enhancement of enforcement necessarily calls for a greater role to be played by the judiciary channels. In view of this, the government is taking the necessary steps to lower the threshold for criminal penalties in the judicial execution of the IPR laws. The Supreme People's Court and the Supreme People's Procuratorate issued a new judicial interpretation in the latter half of 2004 which will effectively clarify and relax the criteria for transferring IPR cases to judicial channels for enforcement.

China's Government has also taken various measures to address the shortage of qualified personnel. First, on-the-job training programmes for IP management and enforcement staff at various levels of government have been organised, sometimes through co-operation with international organisations or bilaterally with foreign governments (see examples in OECD, 2005). In addition, Chinese officials and professionals have been sent abroad for study visits. Particular attention has been attached to enforcement personnel, notably through exchange of experience with counterparts in the United States and the European Union. Second, training efforts have also been developed towards enterprises. For instance, to provide guidance to enterprises for their IP management and to foster their awareness of IP, various IP administrative departments and industry associations have co-organised workshops for enterprises. Third, more than 70 universities and colleges in China are now doing intellectual property research or offering IP courses. A complete intellectual property degree education mechanism, including combined-degree, master degree and PhD degree education, has taken shape, providing a competent and specialized workforce.

To improve the governance of the interface between research and patents, the government made two major amendments to the Patent Law to give public research organisations the legal status to own the IP generated by their research, and then to grant researchers the right to own the IPR of their research through contractual arrangements with their institutions. However, lack of understanding of the importance of IPR and shortages of the skills required for IP management and technology transfer resulted in an inadequate implementation of the government IPR policies in Chinese PROs and universities.

To address this situation, several other steps were taken by SIPO. In 2001, SIPO launched the Promotion Project for the Implementation of IP Strategy. IP demonstration programmes are presented in cities, science and technology parks, enterprises and industrial sectors. SIPO has approved 28 cities for the city IP system pilot programme, five pilot zones for the high-technology IP system, six pilot bases for industrial patent projects, 60 pilot enterprises, and 73 pilot projects for the commercialisation of patented technologies. For example, enterprise experimental work should mainly start by strengthening IPR administration and protection, guiding enterprises to establish patent management frameworks and to perfect management institutions. This mainly includes setting up the IPR management bodies, effective allocation of personnel and organisation, utilising patent information, and putting official innovation policies into practice. SIPO has also promulgated relevant documents, such as Guiding Principles for City Patent Demonstration Work to Promote Technological Innovation and Administrative Regulations for Enterprise Patent Work. Also, the Long-term and Mid-term Plan for Science and Technology under promulgation includes IPR policies.

Enforcement statistics confirm that progress has obviously been made on many fronts. In 2003, the number of trademark counterfeiting and infringement cases investigated and prosecuted by the trademark authority increased by 13% over 2002, the number of patent falsification cases investigated by SIPO increased by 67% and 41%, respectively, over 2002, the number of copyright infringement cases dealt with by the copyright authorities increased four-fold over 2001, and the number of IPR infringement cases detected by the Chinese customs increased by 32% in 2003 over the previous year. The number of IPR cases heard by the judiciary system also increased in recent years.

Yet, in spite of this progress, many Chinese and foreign enterprises included in the DRC survey on counterfeiting (DRC, 2003) considered that the problem had remained the same or had deteriorated over the past few years. The following sub-section will discuss how to improve the current situation, through governance changes.

6.2. Towards a multi-dimensional enforcement strategy

Enforcing IPR could be compared to a bout of arm-wrestling between the state and those that benefit from infringement. The state exerts efforts of control and sanctions against the interests of infringers. This simple comparison leads to three basic conclusions for the efficiency of IPR protection in China.

The stronger the interests linked to infringement, the more efforts authorities will have to put into enforcement. It is likely that the pressure stemming from infringing interests decreases with economic development. Not because the gap between static costs and dynamic costs related to IPR decreases with economic development – that would be difficult to say. But rather because economic development brings more alternative possibilities for development. In addition, other reform measures that have the effect of reducing the immediate costs of IPR protection for companies and consumers can also contribute to facilitating protection, as it would then be easier for these actors to stay within the system. For instance, policies to strengthen the credit system that would support licensing of technologies go in that direction.

An enforcement strategy should remain closely related to the ultimate goals of IPR protection, differentiating the different types of intellectual property in the process. The idea is not to pursue a strong IPR regime *per se*, but to serve particular purposes, *e.g.* fostering research and development, to nurture literary creation, etc. for economic and social development. In this respect, the approach should be tailored to the current Chinese context. If, in theory, IPR protection contributes to fostering R&D, in practice, in the current Chinese context, IPR protection will not lead to a spectacular increase in research results overnight. Enforcement targets should therefore be adapted to feasible objectives. For instance, it might be advisable to pay particular attention to the protection of utility models. It could also make sense to think sector by sector and to link IPR policies to other policies aimed at creating an enabling environment for businesses. This should not mean that IPR protection should be neglected in some sectors and ensured only in those where China is an IPR producer. Rather the idea is to build progressively an IPR culture and an IPR system.

In this arm-wrestling situation, the state will be stronger if it manages to solicit support from allies, *i.e.* those groups that benefit from IPR protection. This includes of course IPR owners but maybe more importantly the consumers that benefit from the existence of new knowledge, or the reliability of trademarks.

Industrial associations can be crucial allies. Chinese enterprise associations are beginning to play a role, one which should be further strengthened. Industrial associations can fulfil three types of functions: First, they can work as self-disciplinary organisations by soliciting member companies to sign intellectual property protection agreements. Such agreements call for the adoption of internal rules, encouraging both innovations geared towards IPR creation and respect of existing IPR. For example, the Wenzhou Lighter Association and the Shunde Furniture Association in Guangdong organised local firms to establish an IPR protection treaty. Second, industrial associations can help solve intellectual property disputes. For example, under the authorization of some local enterprises, the Chinese Audio and Video Association negotiated with foreign owners of IP rights on patent licensing fees. Third, industrial associations can serve as a bridge between government and enterprises, bringing information on the latest regulatory developments to members and providing guidance in the regulatory and decision-making processes.

Foreign chambers of commerce, associations and law firms have been extremely active in advocating for strong IPR protection and in providing support to companies and sometimes to the government. The Chinese Government has already been working very closely with the Quality Brand Protection Committee, and this relationship should be continued, while co-operation with the Chinese Government should be expanded to local levels as well.

As already mentioned, other civil society associations could also play an important role in enforcing IPR policies. This is especially true in the fight against situations of criminal infringement (cf. Box 14.2), i.e. when consumers are deceived about products and that this puts them in danger. For instance, consumer associations can provide support to building political will locally for the protection of IPR. Associations could even play a role in educating citizens on how to check whether products are original or fake, through simple quality tests.

State authorities can try to maximize this leverage effect of allies by supporting the creation of non-governmental associations around special interests. It is indeed important that the governance structure allows the expression of different interest groups and that checks and balances prevent local leadership from being captured by a group of actors benefiting from infringement. In the area of patents, further valorising the results of public research would also contribute to creating interest groups in support of IPR protection. Moreover, consultation with stakeholders should be encouraged in the policy and law-making processes. Recently, Beijing Municipal Government set a good example in this respect by holding hearings with Beijing citizens on the new traffic regulations and subsequently revising some clauses of the new regulation based on the results of the hearing. This practice should be adapted to the IPR rule-making processes.

Economic development is likely to facilitate the enforcement of IPR also in the following respect: as more Chinese firms become IPR owners, they will increase the pressure for stronger protection and the resulting political will.

This is well reflected by the fact that, in recent years, some local governments in relatively developed regions and high-technology industrial parks have come to realise the importance of IP protection for development. These rely on enhanced IP protection and management to promote their local brands, improve the investment environment and sharpen local competitiveness. They encourage patent application and have adopted various measures to strengthen enforcement, including increasing the resources allocated to IP administrative departments for that purpose.

But localism continues to pose serious obstacles to IPR protection, as noted for instance by the QBPC in its 2003 annual review (QBPC, 2004). In its response to criticisms on this issue from other member countries in the WTO TRIPS Review Mechanism (WTO, 2003c, Paragraph 51), the Chinese Government stressed that it has always been engaged in fighting localism. To this end, in April 2001 the State Council adopted the Provisions on Prohibiting Regional Blockage in Market Economic Activities. QBPC encouraged the government "to examine new ways to tackle protectionism and create a more stable foundation for enforcement work", including "the targeting of 'black spots' for anti-corruption investigations and the establishment of hotlines that will allow IPR owners and members of the public to report suspected cases".

The organisational structure of the administrative enforcement channel contributes in fact to sometimes loose enforcement at the local level. Indeed, as described previously, the administrative departments and the courts in charge of enforcement lack independence from local authorities and are therefore vulnerable to their interferences. This is primarily a matter of financing and of human resources management. The complex organisational structure of the administrative departments involved in IPR protection also contributes to this problem. Indeed, the resulting co-ordination problem reinforces the role of the local leadership as the only entity capable of solving problems that may arise.

Therefore, a possible solution could be to reorganise the administrative enforcement channel, by creating an enforcement agency that would deal with all types of IPR. While this agency would still be funded by local governments as part of the local administration machinery, it should be made relatively independent by having it placed directly under the supervision of the highest local government leader. This would solve the co-ordination problems between departments; it would clarify the funds budgeted for enforcement; and it would also make it easier to strengthen the weight of enforcement bodies and increase their independence in relation to local pressures. Such a restructuring option could be considered as an important policy research topic in the context of further strengthening IPR protection in China.

Notes

1. This chapter was written by Irène Hors, Public Sector Management and Performance Division, Public Governance and Territorial Development Directorate, OECD and Gang Zhang, Science and Technology Policy Division, Directorate for Science, Technology and Industry, OECD.

2. This section draws primarily on CIPR (2002). See also Barton (2004).

3. See also Jones (2004) on this issue.

4. The Report makes clear distinctions between the least developed countries and technologically sophisticated developing countries, including China. The conclusions of the Report cited here are those specifically related to technologically sophisticated developing countries.

5. For example, using affiliate-level data on US-based multinational firms, Branstetter et al. (2004) find that collectively, improvements in IPR result in real increases in technology transfers by multinational enterprises. Similarly, Park and Lippoldt (2003) find that intellectual property rights (as described by an IPR strength index positively influence FDI and moderately influence trade, with some variation by industry, depending on the risk of imitation and the importance of such factors as the market scale.

6. See Barton (2004) for a cautious view on the relationship between patent protection and transfer of technology to developing countries, where he concludes: "Strengthening of developing nation patent system will probably strengthen technology transfer through FDI and possibly through licensing – but only in certain industries and in nations that have appropriate complementary capabilities."

7. As made clear by the business representatives during the "High-level Workshop on IPR and Economic Development in China: Meeting Challenges and Opportunities Following WTO Entry, Beijing, China", 20-21 April 2004. See the summary proceedings of this workshop and a related event, in OECD (2005). See also Maskus (2005) on the hesitation of foreign companies in China to transfer advanced technologies into China because of their concern about the effectiveness of IPR protection.

8. It is possible that GERD in PPP dollars may overstate the magnitude of China's R&D effort. See Schaaper (2004) for a methodological note on the measurement issue and a comparison between GERD in PPP and in current US dollars. Extension of the statistical scope for business R&D expenditure in 2000 explained part of the dramatic growth of China's R&D expenditure before and after 2000.

9. Approximately 80% of IPR violations cases affected Chinese firms according to a study by the Development Research Council [(DRC) 2003].

10. It should be noted that the composition of the business enterprise sector in China is considerably different from that of OECD member countries, where private business unities constitute the majority of business entities. Most Chinese enterprises that conduct R&D activities are state-owned companies, where research is funded by public resources in that sense.

11. IPR protection is one of the policies required to improve China's innovation capacities. See OECD (2002) and Maskus et al. (2005) for discussions on what other policy measures would be needed to boost the level of innovation activity by Chinese industries.

12. The importance of IPR protection to China's social and economic development, and the issues related to the IPR policies on public research were addressed by the two OECD-China events on IPR organised on 20-21 and 22-23 April 2004, respectively in Beijing. See OECD (2005) for a summary of these events.

13. It should be noted that the Chinese Anti-Unfair Competition Law is not the same as an antitrust law, which has not yet been passed (see Chapter 12).

14. According to the International Anti-Counterfeiting Coalition (IACC, 2004), this leading group also involves leaders from the Department of Market System Development in the Ministry of Commerce, the Industry Department of the National Development and Reform Commission, the Supervision and Inspection Bureau of the Ministry of Finance, the Legal Enforcement Supervision Office of the Ministry of Supervision, the Department of Turnover Tax of the State Administration of Taxation, the Department of Public Roads of the Ministry of Communication, the Ministry of Public Security, the Department of Market Standardization Management of the State Administration for Industry and Commerce, the Department of Legal Enforcement and Supervision of the State Administration of Quality Supervision, Inspection and Quarantine. See the State Council's announcement of the creation of this leading group and the composition of the group at: *www.cas.ac.cn/html/Dir/2001/04/06/5744.htm*.

15. This reflects the increasing importance that the central government attaches to IPR enforcement. The 2003 Annual Governmental Report called for government agencies to "further strengthen intellectual property protection, combat and punish piracy and law infringement". See Wang (2004).

16. The difference in the number of IP courts across Chinese provinces, regions and cities is not only a matter of institutional design, but it is also determined by the number of local courts that are judged to have adequate professional competence to handle IP cases.

17. IP administrations may also decide to investigate certain cases without the complaints by the right holders. This is referred to as "active enforcement" in China.

18. China's transparency commitments appear in Part I (General Provisions), Section 2 (Administration of the Trade Regime) of the draft protocol of accession, the latest (and presumably final) version of which is in WTO document WT/ACC/CHN/49 dated 1 October 2001. China's draft protocol has additional special provisions in it.

19. See reply of the Chinese Government in WTO (2003c), Paragraph 46.

20. See Quality Brand Protection Committee (QBPQ, 2004).

21. If theoretically an administrative punishment does not preclude a subsequent criminal enforcement for the same act, in practice it is infrequent that criminal enforcement comes after administrative punishment. See response of the Chinese Government, WTO (2003c), Paragraph 55.

22. The productivity of research efforts in terms of patents is also affected by the fact that there is often duplication of work between research programmes, and that these are not sufficiently focused on really innovative topics at the frontier of knowledge.

23. See OECD (2003) and also OECD (2005), Part 2.

24. See QBPC (2004), DRC (2003), and Maskus (2005).

25. Of course, it is difficult to draw the line between situations where infringers would really be naïve about IPR, and situations in which infringers would be putting forward contextual or cultural arguments to minimize their fault.

Bibliography

Barton, John (2004), "Patents and the Transfer of Technology to Developing Countries", Chapter 21 in *Patents, Innovation and Economic Performance: OECD Conference Proceedings*, OECD, Paris.

Branstetter, Lee G., Raymond Fisman and C. Fritz Foley (2004), *Do Stronger Intellectual Property Rights Increase International Technology Transfer? Empirical Evidence from US Firm-Level Panel Data*, World Bank Policy Research Working Paper No. 3305.

China Consumers' Association (1997), "China Consumers' Association Annual Report", accessed at *http://eng.cca.org.cn:801/page/browseinfo.asp?db=xwyhd&order=20*.

China Consumers' Association (2004), "China Consumers' Association Annual Report", accessed at *http://eng.cca.org.cn:801/page/browseinfo.asp?db=xwyhd&order=20*.

China Customs General Administration (2003), "Statistics on IPR Cases Dealt with by Customs 1996-2003", accessed at *www.customs.gov.cn/ipr/ipr2001c/special.asp*.

Commission on Intellectual Property Rights (CIPR), (2002), *Integrating Intellectual Property Rights and Development Policy*, London.

Development Research Centre (DRC) of State Council (2003), *Survey on the Effects of Counterfeiting on the National Economy*, Abstract.

International Anti-Counterfeiting Coalition (IACC) (2004), "Special 301 Recommendations".

International Intellectual Property Alliance (2005), "2005 Special 301 Report for the People's Republic of China", *www.iipa.com/*.

Jones, I Charles (2004), *Growth and Ideas*, National Bureau of Economic Research (NBER), Working Paper No. 10767.

Lippoldt, Douglas (2005), "Can Stronger Intellectual Property Rights Boost Trade, Foreign Direct Investment and Licensing in Developing Countries?", in *The Intellectual Property Debate: Perspectives from Law, Economics and Political Economy*, Meir Perez Pugatch (ed.), Edward Elgar Publishing, Ltd. (2005).

Lu Wei (2004), "China's Intellectual Property System, Challenges and Policy Trend", background report prepared for the OECD-SIPO-DRC workshop on "Intellectual Property and China's Economic Development", 21-22 April 2004.

Lu Wei, *et al.* (2004), *Intellectual Property Right System: Challenge and Countermeasure*, Beijing, Intellectual Property Press.

Maskus, Keith E. (2005), "Intellectual Property Rights in the WRO accession Package: Assessing China's Reform", in Bhattasali, Deepak and Shantong Li, William J. Martin (eds.), *China and the WTO: Accession, Policy Reform and Poverty Reduction Strategies*, pp. 49-68, World Bank and Oxford University Press.

Maskus, Keith E., Kamal Saggi and Thitima Puttitanun (2004), "Patent Rights and International Technology Transfer through Direct Investment and Licensing", prepared for the Conference on "International Public Goods and the Transfer of Technology after TRIPS", Duke University Law School, 4-6 April 2003; revised paper dated 28 June (as cited in Lippoldt, 2005).

Maskus, Keith, E. Sean, M. Dougherty and Andrew Mertha (2005), "Intellectual Property Rights and Economic Development in China", in Carsten Fink and Keith E. Maskus (eds.), *Intellectual Property Rights and Economic Development*, Oxford University Press and World Bank (2005).

Ministry of Science and Technology (MOST) (2002), *China Science and Technology Indicators*, Beijing.

OECD (2002), "Technology Challenge for China's Industries", Chapter 12 in *China in the World Economy: The Domestic Policy Challenges*, OECD, Paris.

OECD (2003), *Turning Science into Business*, OECD, Paris.

OECD (2004), *Main Science and Technology Indicators*, Vol. 2004/1, OECD, Paris.

OECD (2005), *Promoting IPR Policy and Enforcement in China: Summary of OECD-China Dialogues on Intellectual Property Rights Policy and Enforcement*, OECD, Paris.

Park, Walter G. and Douglas Lippoldt (2003), "The Impact of Trade-Related Intellectual Property Rights on Trade and Foreign Direct Investment in Developing Countries", *OECD Papers: Special Issue on Trade Policy*, Vol. 4, No. 11, Issue 294.

Park, Walter G. and Douglas Lippoldt (2004), "International Licensing and the Strengthening of Intellectual Property rights in Developing Countries", *TD/TC/WP Document Series*, OECD, Paris.

Qu, Sanqiang (2002), *Copyright in China*, Beijing, Foreign Languages Press.

Quality Brand Protection Committee (QBRC) (2004), "Annual Review of Counterfeiting Developments", 12 January, accessed at *www.qbpc.org.cn/*.

Reisman, Arnold (2004), *Illegal Transfer of Technologies: A Taxonomic View.*

Scotchmer, Suzanne (2004), "The Political Economy of Intellectual Property Treaties", *Journal of Law, Economics and Organization*, Vol. 20, pp. 415-437, October.

Shaaper, Martin (2004), "An Emerging Knowledge-based Economy in China? Indicators from OECD Database", *OECD STI Working Papers 2004(4).*

State Intellectual Property Office, Statistics on IP Enforcement 2002, accessed at *www.sipo.gov.cn/sipo/tjxx/statisticannuals/default.htm.*

Trademark Office, State Administration of Industry and Commerce, China, "Statistics on Cases of Violating Trademark Rights", accessed at: *http://sbj.saic.gov.cn/tjxx/tjxx.asp.*

Wang, Jingchuan (2004), "Speech at the Press Conference – 2004/04/14", accessed at: *www.sipo.gov.cn/sipo_English/gftx_e/zyhd_e/t20040414_28096.htm.*

WTO (2003a), "Transitional Review Mechanism of China – Communication from the European Communities", Council for Trade-Related Aspects of Intellectual Property Rights, 12 November, IP/C/W/413.

WTO (2003b), "Transitional Review Mechanism of China – Communication from the United States", Council for Trade-Related Aspects of Intellectual Property Rights, 12 November, IP/C/W/414.

WTO (2003c), "Transitional Review under Section 18 of the Protocol on the Accession of the People's Republic of China – Report to the General Council by the Chair", Council for Trade-Related Aspects of Intellectual Property Rights, 10 December, IP/C/31.

Yang, Deli (2003), "The Development of Intellectual Property in China" in *World Patent Information*, 25(2003).

PART III

Chapter 15

The Governance Challenges of Foreign Investment Policy in China

Table of Contents

Summary 437

The Governance Challenges of Foreign Investment Policy in China 438

1. Introduction and summary 438
   - 1.1. China has attracted large quantities of FDI, but its record is uneven 438
   - 1.2. The legal framework for FDI has been further developed in recent years 438
   - 1.3. A separate law for each category of FIE 439
   - 1.4. Further liberalisation has resulted from WTO accession 439
   - 1.5. Regional FDI policy continues to evolve 440
   - 1.6. Co-ordination of government agencies in formulating investment policies could be improved 441
2. The FDI project approval process and remaining ownership restrictions 442
   - 2.1. Streamlining the project approval process 442
   - 2.2. The Catalogue for Guidance of Foreign Investment Industries 444
   - 2.3. Further ownership constraints 446
3. FDI incentives policies 447
   - 3.1. Tax incentives 447
4. State-owned enterprise reform and FDI 448
5. Corporate governance 451
6. Accounting standards and regulations 453
7. Cross-border mergers and acquisitions 454
8. Rule of law and foreign investment 455
9. Legal recourses 457
10. Intellectual property protection and foreign investment 459
11. Corruption and foreign investment 461

Notes 461

Bibliography 462

List of boxes

15.1. Incentives for foreign investment in the central and western regions 449

Summary

Foreign investment has played a major part in economic development and economic growth in China. When economic reforms commenced in the late 1970s, there was no framework for foreign investment. Thus, existing government structures were adapted and legislation created anew in the form of separate legislative enactments for each form of foreign-invested enterprise (FIE). China has subsequently received large quantities of foreign direct investment (FDI) in the past quarter of a century, rising to nearly USD 55 billion in 2004.

However, substantial challenges remain. China's absorption of FDI is low in per capita terms. The impact in the vast hinterland is limited – 80% of FDI goes just to the eastern region – and it is not bringing in as much high technology as the authorities would like. FDI from OECD member countries tends to be under-represented compared with sources such as Hong Kong, China.

Regional FDI policies have evolved towards a more even geographical FDI balance. The initial strategy in the 1980s was to "let some areas get rich first". From 1993 onward, the government switched to a policy of actively attempting to divert resources towards the central and western regions. In mid-2003, the authorities decided to refocus their regional economic development policy more towards North-East China.

Attracting more and better FDI to China may be achieved by further relaxing formal restrictions, a process that has been accelerated by commitments made in China's WTO accession agreements. Equally important is to tackle and overcome the impediments constituted by public governance weaknesses: the lack of nationwide effective judicial and enforcement systems, poor corporate governance, inadequate protection of intellectual property rights (IPR) and corruption.

These problems can be overcome by adopting policies to create a more open and transparent investment environment and by increased interdepartmental co-ordination which contributes to further improving the investment climate.

The Governance Challenges of Foreign Investment Policy in China[1]

1. Introduction and summary

1.1. China has attracted large quantities of FDI, but its record is uneven

China has made significant progress in providing a business environment conducive to foreign direct investment (FDI) since 1978 and FDI has consequently played an important role in the country's economic development for nearly a quarter of a century. Inward FDI reached a record USD 54.9 billion in 2004. However, in terms of FDI inflows per capita China continues to lag behind most OECD member countries and even many developing countries. If economic and geographical characteristics are taken into account, China's performance compares quite modestly with that of other developing countries (Chen, 2002).[2]

Although an increasing proportion of FDI flowing into China is sourced in OECD member countries, the latter tend to be under-represented compared with sources such as Hong Kong, China, which has supplied nearly half of cumulative FDI inflows to China and continues to provide nearly 40% of the annual inflow.[3] Moreover, the spatial distribution of realised FDI has been skewed towards the eastern coastal areas throughout the period of economic reform.

1.2. The legal framework for FDI has been further developed in recent years

In the 1990s, the patchy legal framework governing FDI was refined and expanded so that by the end of the decade a body of FDI law and regulations was in place. Experience gained in the 1980s enabled the authorities to expedite the process of examination and approval of foreign investment projects. In the 1980s, manufacturing foreign-invested enterprises (FIEs) were encouraged to export and not attempt to serve the domestic market, not merely by export performance requirements but also by restrictions such as those on distribution of products and the provision of after-sales service within China. During this period, FDI was largely concentrated in the five Special Economic Zones (SEZs) in South-East China and most of the rest of the country was officially closed. By the mid-1990s, most of the coastal region was open to FDI.

In the 1980s, FDI was largely concentrated in joint venture labour-intensive export manufacturing. As a result of the more favourable climate for FDI in the 1990s, a growing proportion of FIEs were set up as wholly foreign-owned enterprises (WFOEs), oriented to the expanding domestic market as well as to overseas markets. Moreover, a number of large, relatively high-technology projects initiated by multinational enterprises from OECD member countries began to appear.

1.3. A separate law for each category of FIE

China's laws relating directly to FDI take the form of separate legislative enactments for each form of FIE, together with some laws which apply to all FIEs. The advantage of such multiform legislation is that foreign investors can be certain of the rules governing the particular form of investment in China that they have chosen. For example, an investor wishing to establish a WFOE (see below) may consult the relevant law secure in the knowledge that it deals only with this form of FIE. The disadvantage is that this legislative division produces a compartmentalisation that makes it difficult to co-ordinate the activities of different enterprises. For instance, merging enterprises of different forms is made excessively complex. As a result of China's accession to the WTO, a number of requirements had to be removed from these laws and future relaxation of restrictions on foreign investment will presumably necessitate further changes. Ultimately, the Chinese Government has the option of integrating FDI law into domestic company law so that FIEs are treated on a par with domestic enterprises.

In the initial phase, FDI inflows were limited to joint ventures between foreign companies and Chinese entities, usually state-owned enterprises (SOEs). This form suited both the Chinese Government and foreign investors. Starting from an economy in which all major enterprises were state-owned, it would have been difficult politically for the government to accept entirely foreign-owned private enterprises at the outset. Foreign investors needed Chinese partners to help them understand and deal with an unfamiliar and uncertain operating environment.

Joint ventures took two general forms: equity joint ventures and contractual (also translated as co-operative) joint ventures. In July 1979, the National People's Congress (NPC) adopted a law on Sino-foreign equity joint ventures. This was followed in 1988 by a law on Sino-foreign contractual joint ventures. This sequence was the reverse of the developments on the ground: contractual joint ventures predominated in the first half of the 1980s before equity joint ventures gained dominance. The law also permitted the signing of joint exploitation contracts between a foreign company and a Chinese entity for projects involving joint exploration for both inland and offshore oil and gas, or other mineral resources.

There is a third form of FIE in China, the so called wholly foreign-owned enterprises, where there is no Chinese partner. A WFOE is a limited liability company or other form of organisation established in China by foreign investors exclusively with their own capital. The term explicitly excludes branches of foreign companies in China. The law governing wholly foreign-owned enterprises was passed in April 1986. More recently, China has permitted the establishment of foreign-invested companies limited by shares and foreign-invested holding companies, as well as build-operate-transfer infrastructure projects.

1.4. Further liberalisation has resulted from WTO accession

On 11 December 2001, China acceded to the WTO. Bilateral agreements signed with other WTO members as part of the accession process were weighted in favour of market-opening concessions by China.[4] The main focus of the agreements was on opening Chinese markets to imports by curtailing trade barriers.

However, increased market access is also being accelerated by opening a number of sectors, service sectors in particular, far wider to foreign investment within periods generally varying up to five years from accession. FDI in the financial sector is being greatly liberalised, as are the wholesale, retail and distributive sectors. Business services and consumer services are also being further opened to foreign investment.

China's WTO commitments are also widening the scope of operation of FIEs in the non-services sectors, especially manufacturing. Liberalisation of trading and distribution rights will eventually enable FIEs to import and export on their own behalf and to distribute and service their products throughout China. All FIEs will enjoy national treatment in such matters as the pricing and availability of production inputs and discrimination against them in the business activities of the government and state-owned enterprises will not be permitted.

As part of its WTO accession agreements, China is committed to implementing the WTO Agreement on Trade-Related Investment Measures (TRIMs) in full from the date of accession. As a result, trade performance, trade balancing and local content requirements imposed on FIEs have been removed from laws and regulations pertaining to FDI. Foreign enterprises are accorded treatment no less favourable than that accorded to domestic individuals and enterprises throughout the production process.

Another FDI investment liberalisation initiative was the revision in 2002 of the catalogues for guiding foreign investment industries that had been promulgated at the end of 1997. Similarly as a result of WTO accession, new foreign bank licensing regulations were promulgated by the People's Bank of China (PBC) in February 2002 covering market access rights of foreign banks.

FIEs were previously denied full rights to import and export goods (except for machinery and production inputs for their own use and their own products) by the imposition of such requirements as export performance, trade or foreign exchange balancing and prior experience as criteria for obtaining or maintaining the right to import and export. Since accession to the WTO, such import and export restrictions have been largely lifted.

Discrimination against FIEs or against imports in the making of purchases and sales by state-owned and state-invested enterprises is not permitted, nor may the Chinese Government influence, either directly or indirectly, commercial decisions of such enterprises, including decisions on quantity, value or country of origin of any goods purchased or sold, in a manner inconsistent with WTO rules.

Finally, as part of its WTO accession agreements China is committed to implementing the WTO Agreement on Trade-Related Intellectual Property Rights (TRIPs) in full from the date of accession. China already has legislation in place governing copyrights, patents and trademarks; modifications were made to these laws in line with TRIPs. This legislation has a major bearing on FDI because China is more likely to attract FDI embodying technology transfer if intellectual property rights are effectively protected.

1.5. Regional FDI policy continues to evolve

The initial strategy towards FDI in the 1980s was to maximise FDI inflows to the whole country, initially to experimental zones remote from the capital but then to any areas favoured by foreign investors, without attempting to ensure even geographical distribution. This policy was encapsulated in the slogan "let some areas get rich first", i.e. initially disregarding the regressive effects of economic growth on wealth and income distribution. It was therefore acceptable to the central government that the coastal region, starting with the SEZs, would benefit from FDI inflows while other regions received relatively little.

By the mid-1980s, representatives of hinterland provinces were complaining in the NPC that they were not benefiting from rapid economic growth and that they were falling further behind the coastal provinces. From 1993 onward, the government responded increasingly to such calls by attempting to divert resources towards the central and western regions. As well as commencing major infrastructure initiatives, the government encouraged foreign investments in the western and central regions.

In mid-2003, the authorities decided to refocus their regional economic development policy towards rejuvenating the old industrial areas in North-East China, while retaining policies aimed at developing the western and central regions. North-East China is more industrially developed than these other regions, but contains a high proportion of state-owned enterprises, many of which are loss-making and are in the process of being restructured. Foreign investment is now seen by the authorities as playing an important role in such restructuring.

To the extent that the investment incentives available to FIEs are the same as those on offer to domestic enterprises, the policy of attracting capital investment to the western and central regions is consistent with the principle of national treatment. However, such incentives do not constitute a sufficient condition for increased investment in those regions. If the Chinese Government wishes to redirect investment westward, it may prefer to put the main emphasis on improvements in the business environment. The current policy of allocating state funds to infrastructure construction in the western and central regions can be considered part of this effort. Institutional development is also necessary, in particular an initiative to raise the standard of investment promotion and investment approval in these regions to that prevailing in the open coastal zones, which are generally much more flexible in their interpretation of FDI laws and regulations. More officials in the western and eastern regions may, for example, be encouraged to visit their counterparts in SEZs and other open zones to experience and understand the procedures that have been so successful in attracting investment there.

1.6. Co-ordination of government agencies in formulating investment policies could be improved

Several government agencies are involved in making decisions on the fundamental direction of policy relating to foreign investment in China. The Ministry of Commerce (MOFCOM) is responsible for foreign investment in that it collects and publishes detailed statistics on FDI and drafts legislation and regulations governing the establishment, operation and treatment of FIEs in China. However, since foreign investment policy touches upon issues such as property rights and sovereignty, major initiatives must necessarily be approved by the Communist Party leadership, by the State Council and by the National Development and Reform Commission (NDRC). NDRC, formerly the State Development Planning Commission (SDPC), clearly retains a dominant position in relation to the other economic ministries despite the loss of its original central planning function. This is due to the fact that it is competent to make a decision that encompasses both foreign and domestic investment (for example, the announcement in July 2004 that most investment projects will no longer be subject to approval at national level). However, it contributes to bureaucratic inertia to the extent that officials in MOFCOM who have to deal more directly with foreign investors are unable to formulate and implement policy innovations until a strategic decision has been taken at a higher level to which they may not have regular access. Typically, decisions that require a high degree of interdepartmental co-ordination tend to be delayed until intervention occurs from a higher authority.

In other areas of policy, this problem has been to some extent overcome by setting up *ad hoc* working groups, including leading groups (*lingdao xiaozu*). In the case of foreign investment policy, the development of legislation and regulation, as well as their coherent implementation require a long-term approach. Therefore, a more effective arrangement would be the establishment of an interdepartmental committee charged with co-ordinating policy towards foreign investment across all the ministries and other government bodies that contribute to and have a direct interest in it.

This committee could act as a clearing house for proposals for legislative and regulatory changes submitted directly to the committee by a wide range of stakeholders. Specific proposals could be communicated both horizontally (among ministries and other government agencies at the same level) and vertically (upward from subordinate units of ministries and other government agencies and from other stakeholders – such as foreign-owned enterprises and domestic or foreign NGOs – and downward from the State Council and other central authorities above the ministry level). The committee could also prepare action plans for the development of legislation and regulations involving several ministries and other government agencies and recommend changes in overall policy towards foreign investment to the State Council. It could develop a schedule for implementing recommended changes in policy relating to foreign investment to ensure correct sequencing, especially as this concerns the division of labour between different government agencies. Finally, the co-ordinating committee could establish mechanisms for monitoring and overseeing co-ordinated implementation of policies towards foreign investment at provincial and sub-provincial levels.

2. The FDI project approval process and remaining ownership restrictions

2.1. Streamlining the project approval process

The procedures for examining and approving FDI projects involve a large number of administrative steps. These typically include lodging documents with local branches of a number of different authorities, such as the State Administration of Industry and Commerce (SAIC), the State Administration of Foreign Exchange (SAFE), the Customs Authority and the National Bureau of Statistics (NBS).

In July 2004, the foreign investment project approval process was streamlined to some extent by the Decision of the State Council Concerning the Reform of the Investment System. This Decision applies to large-scale fixed asset investments in infrastructure, transport and manufacturing. Its main features are the combination of several verification stages into a single application report and a greater delegation of project approval powers to local authorities. The Decision also included measures to liberalise the approval of domestic investments. Implementation regulations (not yet published) will clarify the scope and application of the Decision.

A problem understood to have arisen in the recent past is the co-existence of two sets of rules governing the approval process. National laws and implementing regulations are available to foreign investors, though not always in an instantly accessible form. These are described by Chinese officials as *gongkai* (public) rules. Accompanying these have been other rules, characterised by Chinese officials as *neibu* (internal) rules that are not published. This latter category includes rules used by local authorities to decide whether or not a project will be approved. It remains to be determined to what extent, if any, such *neibu* rules persist.

Where internal rules grant benefits in addition to those to which an enterprise is entitled according to the published rules, the problem is less serious, provided such benefits are available to all qualifying enterprises (if they are only available selectively, or on a discretionary basis, then this amounts to discrimination). It is, however, likely that some of the internal rules are more restrictive than the published rules, to the detriment of potential investors that have done their best to meet approval requirements on the basis of publicly available information.

The application to establish an FIE must be submitted for examination and approval by MOFCOM or by other authorities in charge of foreign economic relations and trade designated by the State Council. The examining and approving authority must make a decision on whether or not to grant approval within 90 days of receipt of the application in the case of a wholly-foreign-owned enterprise, three months in the case of an equity joint venture and 45 days in the case of a contractual joint venture. In all three categories of FIE, the foreign investor must then apply to the authorities in charge of industry and commerce for registration and a business licence within one month (30 days) after receiving a certificate of approval.

The cut-off point between approval by central and local authorities is a project size of USD 100 million (raised from USD 30 million in July 2004) in the case of projects in the permitted and encouraged catalogues of the Catalogues for Guiding Foreign Investment and USD 50 million in the case of projects in the restricted catalogue (which had all been subject to central approval before July 2004). (The catalogue regime is explained in the next section of this chapter.)

The practice of allowing encouraged projects to be approved at local level and merely notified to local offices of the State Council above the cut-off point will no longer be permitted. Projects valued at more than USD 100 million (or USD 50 million in the case of restricted category projects) must be submitted for approval to MOFCOM at national level and they will then be considered by NDRC.

Prior to July 2004, projects with a value exceeding USD 100 million had also to be submitted to the State Council for approval; it remains to be determined whether or not this requirement has been retained.

Projects below USD 100 million may be approved by government departments (currently MOFCOM and NDRC) at provincial level, including the governments of municipalities like Beijing and Shanghai directly under the State Council and autonomous regions such as Tibet.

This division of authority is open to abuse in that it encourages local authorities to split projects valued at over USD 100 million into smaller segments to avoid having to submit them to national level authorities, a practice which is in clear breach of the rule. A project which is submitted only to local, not national, approval is more likely to be approved, as local authorities seek to maximise revenue and employment creation of FDI projects, while the national authorities have to take into account other factors (such as the perceived need to avoid localised overcapacity and overall macroeconomic considerations) which may cause approval not to be granted.

This stratagem of local authorities indicates the existence of real bottlenecks in the approval process. Local authorities complain that if a project is submitted to a central government department, the approval process will be delayed. While this delay generally averages about six months, in some cases it may be as long as three years, in which case the market for the product to be produced by the FIE may have changed and the project may no longer be viable. Another violation of the rules that may occasionally occur is that an FIE may go into operation before it has obtained approval to do so, evidently with the tacit, if not explicit, connivance of the local authority. This practice is another indication that project approval times tend to be too long.

To obviate unnecessary delays in the approval process, the Chinese Government may wish to consider further measures such as the following:

1. Fast-tracking the national-level approval process by allocating more resources, including staff, to it.
2. Shortening the time limits for decisions on approval by the examining authority or authorities.
3. Reclassifying projects from restricted to permitted or from permitted to encouraged, as appropriate, to ensure that they are submitted for approval at local, not national, level. (Unless the catalogues for guidance of foreign investment industries are further liberalised, as suggested in this report.)
4. Further standardizing and simplifying the whole approval procedure.
5. Making all changes transparent, for example by putting them all on the MOFTEC Web site in both Chinese and English as early as possible.

2.2. The Catalogue for Guidance of Foreign Investment Industries

The Catalogue for Guidance of Foreign Investment Industries classifies sectors of the economy in terms of their openness to foreign direct investment and is the basis for decisions on treatment by the authorities of applications for foreign investment projects. It was promulgated on 11 February 2002 and came into force on 1 April 2002. A new Catalogue incorporating minor revisions was issued at the beginning of 2005. As with the end-1997 revised catalogue that preceded it, the kinds of projects remain fourfold: encouraged, permitted, restricted and prohibited foreign investment projects. Only three catalogues are published, those for encouraged, restricted and prohibited projects. Projects that do not fall into the classifications listed in these catalogues can be presumed to be permitted.

The main benefit of investing in a project listed in the Catalogue of Encouraged Foreign Investment Industries (hereafter referred to as Encouraged Catalogue) is that, apart from any preferential terms accorded it in other laws and regulations, it may enlarge its scope of business with approval, if it is engaged in the construction and operation of infrastructure facilities, such as fuel and power, transport networks or waste disposal, that require a large amount of investment and a long pay-off period. Projects in encouraged sectors may also benefit from lower income tax and value-added tax (in the form of rebates), may import capital equipment duty free, and may be allowed to borrow more than restricted-category investments. Other forms of encouragement are reportedly being considered.

The main disadvantage of investing in a project listed in the Catalogue of Restricted Foreign Investment Industries (Restricted Catalogue) is that approval authorisation may not be delegated to lower level authorities and may therefore take longer and run a greater risk that the project will not be approved. According to the Chinese authorities, the submission of restricted-catalogue projects to higher level organs for approval should not lengthen the approval process and does not involve an increased risk of non-approval. The Chinese authorities are also of the opinion that the approval process for restricted catalogue projects is identical to that used for other project categories and is conducted according to identical principles.

The number of types of projects included in the 2002 Encouraged Catalogue was increased to 262 from 186 in the 1997 Encouraged Catalogue. Encouraged industries include those using new or high technology; those in key sectors such as agriculture and infrastructure; projects that help meet both domestic and export demand; projects in central and western regions. Major changes in the 2002 Encouraged Catalogue include prospecting for and exploiting oil, natural gas and coal.

The number of types of projects included in the 2002 Restricted Catalogue was reduced to 75 from 112 in the 1997 Restricted Catalogue. This Catalogue includes projects that use dated technology, that are perceived as wasting resources or are harmful to the environment. It also includes industries which are being opened gradually to foreign investment.

The number of types of projects included in the 2002 Catalogue of Prohibited Foreign Investment Industries (Prohibited Catalogue) is similar to that of the 1997 Prohibited Catalogue. Prohibited projects include those that endanger the safety of the state or damage social and public interests; those that pollute the environment, destroy natural resources or impair human health; those that occupy large amounts of arable land and are unfavourable to the protection and development of land resources; those that endanger the safety and performance of military facilities; and those that adopt unique Chinese craftsmanship.

The revised catalogues represent a major step forward in FDI regime liberalisation. The Chinese authorities should keep up their efforts to achieve further liberalisation by removing more categories of projects from the catalogue of prohibited foreign investment industries. The inclusion of sectors where national control is considered desirable, such as projects that endanger the safety and performance of military facilities, is plausible; where not self-evident, an explanation of the reasoning involved would be helpful.

It is not clear that there is any benefit in maintaining an extensive catalogue of restricted industries that effectively raises the approval hurdle higher for a wide range of industries and services, including, it is important to note, most of the services sectors that are being opened as a result of WTO accession. The existence of the restricted catalogue necessitates the reference of a project approval decision to a national authority (usually the NDRC). The national authority then decides on approval on the basis of criteria regarding national economic policy or other considerations which are opaque because they are not precisely specified in such a way that a foreign investor can make a reasonable effort to comply with them.

Abolition of the Restricted Catalogue in its entirety could be considered, at a time when the Chinese authorities judge further opening to foreign investment to be appropriate to the stage of development of the Chinese economy, as part of the next phase of liberalising the FDI catalogue regime.

Unlike the other two published catalogues, the Encouraged Catalogue does not restrict FDI in any way. The future of this catalogue will be largely determined by the Chinese Government's policy regarding FDI-attracting incentives. One reason for questioning the need for the continued existence of the Encouraged Catalogue is the increasing length and complexity that has resulted from successive liberalisations and that will undoubtedly be exacerbated by further liberalisation. The list is now so detailed that many of the items are likely to become rapidly obsolete as a result of technological progress.

A clearer presentation of the permitted range of foreign investment activities could be achieved by replacing the catalogue regime with a single short list of sectors that are barred to foreign participation, supplemented by a clear explanation of the grounds for selection. All projects not on the list would then be permitted. As a transitional step towards wholesale reform of the catalogues, the prohibition of foreign investment could be reconsidered where the intention of controlling specific activities may be more effectively achieved in other ways, such as prudential regulation. The result would be the publication of a smaller Prohibited Catalogue containing only items which it is international practice to restrict or which China has a special and understandable reason for restricting.

As for prohibition, China currently prohibits FDI in a few traditional crafts. The intention of this prohibition is presumably to ensure the continued existence of these activities because they are considered to be part of the national heritage. If this is the case, then the prohibition of inward financial flows supporting such activities would appear to be an inappropriate means of achieving such an aim. The objective might more effectively be pursued by other measures, for example by increasing the resources available for education and training in these fields. The 2002 Encouraged Catalogue retains from the 1997 Encouraged Catalogue a final clause which includes permitted foreign-invested projects whose products are to be wholly exported directly. Since the inclusion of a proposed foreign investment project in either the permitted or the restricted foreign investment list can determine whether or not it is approved, this stipulation may be regarded as effectively imposing an export performance requirement on such projects.

2.3. Further ownership constraints

China has committed itself to a major opening of the banking sector to foreign participation. However, the resulting regulations promulgated by the PBC in February 2002 stipulate such high capital requirements for setting up branches in China. Therefore, only the largest foreign banks will be able to take advantage of the new market access opportunities. While the requirements for opening a representative office are relatively modest, those for establishment are much stricter.[5] Considering that the regulations also include reasonable stipulations requiring foreign banks to be governed by adequate supervisory systems in their home countries and to possess adequate internal control systems, such high capital requirements appear disproportionate to guarantee stability and are interpreted by some representatives of foreign banking institutions as protectionism.

According to the Code of Liberalisation of Current Invisible Operations agreed by OECD member countries, the total amount of any financial requirement imposed for the establishment of a branch or agency of a non-resident enterprise engaged in banking or financial services shall be no more than that required of a domestic enterprise to engage in similar activities. Furthermore, the total of the financial requirements to be furnished by all the branches and agencies of the same non-resident enterprise shall be no more than that required of a domestic enterprise to engage in similar activities. The minimum capital requirements in the foregoing paragraph apply only to foreign, not domestic, banks. Assessing the extent to which this might be considered as discriminating against the establishment of foreign banks in China is complicated by the lack of a firm basis for comparison, since there are very few private banks in China and state-owned domestic banks are the subject of a different set of regulations.

Greater opening of the banking sector to foreign participation could be achieved by lowering the capital requirements for branches and subsidiaries of overseas banks to less discouraging levels, in accordance with OECD and other internationally recognised standards.

3. FDI incentives policies

China is a unitary state whose policies towards FDI are determined by the central government. However, administration has been greatly decentralised during the reform period. As a result, implementation varies widely between the various provincial-level units and also within provinces between smaller administrative units such as municipalities and SEZs. Insofar as there are major differences in policy between regions, these are a result of national policy to shift FDI, along with domestic investment, towards the less-developed hinterland.

FDI attraction measures have taken a number of forms, including tax incentives, low land-lease charges in comparison with other FDI target locations, provision of low-cost labour and the development of physical infrastructure. The initial aim of policy makers was to convince foreign investors that it could be worthwhile investing in China despite the history of discouraging foreign investment before the reform period and despite subsequent deficiencies in the operating environment. Though it has offered labour at wages lower than those in FDI source economies, China does not appear to have concentrated on engaging in bidding wars to divert investment away from competing FDI recipients.

3.1. Tax incentives

Tax legislation regarding FIEs consists of a complex tax incentive system as a tool of the government to attract FDI in pursuit of national development priorities. Most of these incentives are not available to Chinese enterprises. Currently, 14 taxes relate to foreign investment, including corporate income tax, personal income tax, value-added tax (VAT), business and consumption taxes (see Chapter 6). Fees are also imposed by local governments. Other compulsory payments include social security contributions, mainly to pension funds and health insurance schemes. VAT is the largest single source of revenue. The Chinese tax system therefore differs from tax structures in OECD member countries, where personal income tax is the largest single revenue source, followed by social security contributions.

The 33% corporate income tax rate may be reduced to 15 or 24%, depending on the geographic location and the type of foreign investment. Generally, the 15% rate is applicable to FIEs located in SEZs, high-tech companies located in special technology zones and companies engaging in specifically designated industries in the western and central regions. The 15% rate can also be applied to production-oriented FIEs located in open provincial or port cities, provided the enterprises are engaged in high-tech industries. The 24% rate applies to production-oriented FIEs located in open coastal economic zones or in port cities. Therefore, in the case that an FIE has affiliates in different locations, each branch might be taxed differently, at the rate applicable in that particular location.

China offers FIEs a five-year preferential tax regime that consists of two years of tax exemptions followed by a 50% reduction of the general corporate income tax rate for three years. However, this holiday is applicable only to FIEs engaged in production-oriented activities for at least 10 years. The five-year concessional period starts to run from the first profitable year and continues for five consecutive years, regardless of subsequent profitability. A tax holiday may additionally be available for investments such as those in export-oriented enterprises, technologically advanced enterprises, or investments in port and wharf development. This entitles the FIE to a further tax reduction after expiry of the initial five-year concessional period. The standard concessions for a company thus include a top income tax rate of 15% which only comes into effect in a company's sixth full year of profit-making after a two-year tax holiday and three years at 7.5% income tax.

The Chinese Government has since 1994 been carefully studying the question of whether the two separate tax regimes for domestic and foreign enterprises should be merged. Discussions have intensified in the light of WTO accession. The government has indicated that income tax for foreign-funded and domestic firms would be unified in 2006, although officials appear to be unsure that the unification can be implemented by then. The standard rate of tax that will then apply has not yet been made public. The authorities have indicated that it is likely to be in the 25-30% range. It is understood that existing arrangements based on preferential tax rates will be grandfathered.

The current tax regime has been in operation without major alteration during most of the reform period and the approaching unification of rates has been officially announced well in advance (though not yet in detail). Investors have thus been able to make business plans with some certainty regarding their future tax liability.

However, this certainty is undermined by the proliferation of local practices in granting fiscal incentives, some of which may go beyond the regional incentives listed below, which make tax obligations less predictable. In some cases investors report that a full explanation of applicable tax rules is not available in English at the start of a project. It is also not clear that the tax authorities always and everywhere pursue payment by domestically-owned enterprises with the same thoroughness with which they enforce tax payment by foreign-invested enterprises. Greater transparency of the tax regime would reduce financial risk for FIEs and therefore contribute to improving the business climate for large-scale, long-term investments.

4. State-owned enterprise reform and FDI

The competitive environment for both FIEs and domestic enterprises in China is still evolving, as is explored in more detail in Chapter 12, while Chapter 10 examines institutional arrangements for the management of state assets. In this section, we look at how the reform of state-owned enterprises (SOEs) is changing the competitive environment within which FIEs operate.

China's accession to the WTO and its international commitments to open and transparent FDI policies more generally are providing an impetus to remove barriers to competition. These have hitherto been acute as local authorities, industry ministries and large SOEs have been able to use administrative monopolies to exclude foreign investors. In particular, China can achieve sustained economic growth from foreign participation in the process of restructuring its inefficient SOEs. For this to happen, the regulatory and informational environment will have to be further improved so that foreign investors are able to gauge accurately the profitability of domestic enterprises and, if appropriate, participate in some form of merger and acquisition (M&A) activity with them.

Box 15.1. **Incentives for foreign investment in the central and western regions**

From the mid-1990s, the government has encouraged FDI flows into the central and western regions in order to spread the benefits of economic development to China's vast interior. In 1996, the government raised the project approval limit of provincial authorities in the western region to USD 30 billion to bring it in line with that of the open coastal areas. Additional incentives to direct FDI more positively to the western region began in 1999.

Incentives are provided to attract FDI to both the central and western regions, but more incentives are available for the west than for the centre. While specific incentive provision is made for the western region as a whole, the central region is understood to be covered mainly by provincial-level measures.

In addition to the national catalogues for guiding foreign investment industries, the government has published a Catalogue of Advantageous Sectors for Foreign Investment in the Central and Western Regions. Projects included in this catalogue enjoy the same treatment as those in the Encouraged Catalogue.

A major emphasis of policies designed to attract FDI to the western region is on the construction of basic infrastructure facilities. Foreign investors are encouraged to invest in infrastructure projects in agriculture, water conservancy, ecology, transport, energy, municipal administration, environmental protection, minerals, tourism and resource development.

FDI is also encouraged to contribute to the development of services sectors in the western region. A 2000 regulation outlining the opening of banking, retail and foreign trade, initially only to pilot projects, has, however, been largely overtaken by the WTO commitments, which specify a more comprehensive opening of these sectors nationwide.

Restrictions on the operation and financing of FIEs are less strict in the western region, but the terms of relaxation have been left vague in the relevant regulation. The forms of foreign investment in the western region may now include build-operate-transfer and transfer-operate-transfer, though initially only on an experimental basis. Foreign-invested projects may be partly financed in RMB, and financing by initial public offering (IPO) is encouraged if the projects concerned are qualified to do so. Equity holding restrictions on foreign-invested projects in infrastructure construction and priority industries in the west "will be relaxed", though the precise form of this relaxation is not specified in the regulation.

SOEs, though no longer dominant, retain a major role in the Chinese economy. The private sector, however, was virtually nonexistent at the beginning of the reform era, but is increasingly firmly established as an important provider of goods, services and employment.

Since the mid-1990s, SOEs have been transformed into corporations of various kinds. Large-scale SOEs generally acquired autonomy from the state by transmuting themselves into listed companies, while small and medium-sized enterprises were disposed of in various ways that removed them, together with their financial obligations, from local government account books. (The overwhelming majority, 72%, of firms owned by local governments were in the red in 1995.)

While wholesale privatisation of SOEs has been ruled out by the government, privatisation of small and medium-sized SOEs in accordance with the principle of "grasping the big and releasing the small" (*zhua da fang xiao*) started in the mid-1990s and has gathered pace in recent years. According to the State Economic and Trade Commission

(SETC),[6] quoted in a recent World Bank study of corporate governance (Tenev and Zhang, 2002), over 80% of small and medium-sized SOEs had by 2000 been "transformed" in that they had been restructured, merged, leased, contracted, turned into joint stock companies, sold or been declared bankrupt. Most of these were in fact bought by managers and/or employees, a solution that was more ideologically acceptable than outright privatisation or sale to foreign investors. While the dispersion of ownership may initially have provided an incentive for the workforce to improve the performance of the firms in which they worked and in which they had acquired a direct interest, in the longer term there appears to have been excessive dividend distribution. This resulted in inadequate capital investment and a failure to strengthen performance monitoring and participation in decision-making. The diffused ownership structure gave inadequate control rights to employees who had power over key resources such as technology. Many such employees left to form their own enterprises, sometimes taking the technology with them.

The perceived failure of employee buy-outs has led local governments and enterprise managements to attempt a second wave of restructuring aimed at concentrating shareholding in the hands of managers and key employees. To the extent that this has succeeded, it has replaced the problem of excessive diversification with that of insider control, which may threaten the rights of minority shareholders.

An important feature of SOE reform in China is that the government intends to create 156 internationally competitive industry groups ("national champions") by merging existing enterprises into large diversified groups capable of cross-subsidising their operations to support large-scale investment in export manufacturing capacity and high technology. This strategy is largely modelled on the Korean Government's nurturing of the *chaebol*. To the extent that less profitable or unprofitable SOEs are merged with highly profitable SOEs, this policy is likely to give new life to soft budget constraints. It also threatens to stifle competition in markets dominated by the new groups. Taking into consideration the difficulties facing merger and acquisition attempts by FIEs and also the lack of "trust busting" or other competition laws, this process of domestic industrial agglomeration may appear to constitute a form of effective protectionism.

SOE reform offers interesting opportunities to foreign investors. Foreign investors will play an increasingly important role in the restructuring of SOEs, increasingly by acquiring such companies, in whole or in part, or their assets. Doing so promises benefits such as increased access by foreign investors to market sectors hitherto dominated by SOEs.

The reform of state-owned industry and the development of private sector forms of enterprise necessitate improvements in corporate governance and accounting standards which are also supported by the correction of defects in the banking system and the development and opening up to foreign investors of capital markets. As these improvements take shape, foreign investors will benefit increasingly from greater transparency in their dealings with joint-venture partners and other entities with which they do business.

The business environment has already benefited greatly from the removal of the main mechanisms of central planning such as price and output controls. SOE monopoly power persists in some sectors, but in others it has been eroded by the entry of FIEs and private enterprises. Provided the government fulfils its WTO accession obligations in this respect, foreign investment will suffer less from uncompetitive practices such as subsidies to domestic producers.

5. Corporate governance

If foreign investors are to play a full part in the restructuring of Chinese industry by developing relationships with existing domestic corporations, whether privately-owned or state-owned, improvements in corporate governance practices are necessary. The Chinese Government has established a framework of laws and regulations designed to ensure sound corporate governance. In strengthening corporate governance in China, a better implementation of existing rules is perceived as a key factor, however. Foreign investors are particularly interested in progress in the areas of transparency and disclosure and in reducing state interference in corporate affairs.

The corporate governance system is based on the Company Law that was promulgated on 29 December 1993 and amended on 25 December 1999, on the Code of Corporate Governance for Listed Companies in China (CCGLC) adopted on 7 January 2001 and on regulations and guidance documents issued by government bodies including the China Securities Regulatory Commission (CSRC), SETC and the Ministry of Finance (MOF). The other major piece of legislation whose provisions have some bearing on corporate governance is the Securities Law promulgated on 29 December 1998.[7]

The CCGLC was issued jointly by CSRC and SETC on 7 January 2001.[8] The Code, which is inspired by OECD principles, applies to all listed companies within China and is used as a standard to measure corporate governance performance by the CSRC, making it a major determinant of whether or not a company fulfils listing requirements on China's stock exchanges. A special inspection was introduced in 2002 to check companies' compliance with the Code.

CSRC issued a Guideline on the Management of Listed Companies on 7 January 2002. The aim of the Guideline is to encourage domestically listed companies to establish and develop a modern enterprise system; to regulate the operations of domestically listed companies; and to promote the healthy development of the securities market. The Guideline lists the basic principles on the governance of domestically listed companies, the measures needed to protect the interests of investors and the behaviour and professional ethics of the directors, members of the supervisory committee and managerial staff of listed companies.

A number of serious problems with corporate governance of limited liability and joint stock companies have been identified by regulators and by outside commentators.

Boards of directors usually consist largely of executive directors, with very few independent directors. The board of directors is thus subject to "insider control" (*neibu kongzhi*) and is unable to monitor the company's executives effectively. Boards of supervisors may report to shareholders' meetings, but their role is effectively nullified if the shareholders' meetings are dominated by the controlling shareholder (usually the state), who may also control the board of directors. It is, therefore, vital to enhance the role and independence of boards and ensure that minority shareholders are represented on boards of directors.

Guidelines for Introducing Independent Directors to the Board of Directors of Listed Companies were issued by CSRC on 16 August 2001. These Guidelines required at least one-third of board members to be independent directors by June 2003. Independence in this context is defined as being independent of management and of relatives of the management, of the controlling shareholder (which is usually the state) and of persons providing financial, legal or consulting services to the company. Candidates must be verified by the CSRC in each case before a director can be considered for appointment as an independent director. Candidates must declare their independence publicly and the declaration must be published in the newspapers. The Guidelines also stipulate that listed companies must provide adequate working facilities for independent directors and that they cannot dismiss independent directors without good cause (such as failure to attend three consecutive board meetings).

By the end of June 2002, 2 327 independent directors had been appointed by shareholders' meetings; 80% of the 1 084 companies concerned had at least two independent directors on their boards (not too far short of the interim target of 100% set for that date in the Guidelines), and 70% had at least one accounting professional as an independent director. In 2001, classes to train independent directors began in Beijing and Shanghai; in the 10 months to the end of June 2002, these programmes had trained 5 000 candidates for independent director positions. The Shanghai and Shenzhen stock exchanges are also mounting courses for existing directors. By 2005, all directors will have attended training classes. Training programmes for investors are also being organised in major cities and on the Internet.

The state still holds at least half the shares of all listed companies (some estimates range much higher) and the largest shareholder, usually the state, tends to hold about 45% of the shares of each listed company. It is often not clear who represents the state and who has control over state-owned assets, since state control of the original pre-corporatisation SOEs was vested in various levels of government. State control is also linked to the influence of the Communist Party. Communist Party committees in listed companies are also reported to retain influence that is not always wholly transparent, for example in regard to controlling membership of boards of directors. Large state shareholdings also require a clear distinction between the state's two roles as shareholder and regulator.

Recent research findings suggest that company performance would be likely to improve if state shareholdings were gradually replaced, including by large institutional shareholdings (Xu and Wang, 1997). Reducing the role of the state in corporate affairs in this way is difficult at present, as only about one-third of shares are traded on the stock exchanges, the rest consisting of non-tradable shares. The development of institutional shareholder involvement has been a slow process in OECD member countries and may take some years in China. Institutions have to be careful with their choice of good quality financial products and therefore demand high standards of corporate disclosure and transparency. It is thus not surprising that institutional investors, most of them held wholly or in part by the state, currently hold a mere 2.3% of market capitalisation. Institutional investors can play a vital and independent role in stimulating improvements in corporate governance, but only if they are fully empowered to do so in a system that provides full rights to shareholders. The entry of foreign institutional investors, which is permitted under a regulation promulgated in 2003, can be a major catalyst for change in this regard.

Related party transactions between the company and the controlling shareholder, or the holding group to which the company belongs, are common, often against the interests of the company and minority shareholders in particular. One OECD study of corporate governance in China identifies related party transactions as the "key threat to shareholder value" (OECD, 2002). They are aggravated by the need to maintain a vast array of social assets and services at the parent level and by politicised resource allocation decisions. Such practices may be concealed and exacerbated by the lack of transparency alluded to below.

Since the state controls many companies, it also appoints and controls their executive managers. Since managers are routinely regarded as civil servants, managerial salaries tend to be low and unrelated to performance. There is therefore little incentive for managers to improve. This problem is particularly acute in poorer hinterland areas where it may be difficult to consider the possibility of paying a manager more than the local officials who may be involved in appointing him or her. Stock options can not be substituted for incentivised salaries as they have as yet no legal basis. This situation is set to change, though, as provision for stock options is expected to be included in future legislation.

Information is not generally disclosed accurately, on time or in a form understandable by shareholders. The statistical system of SOEs was designed to produce information on the fulfilment of output plans. During the reform period it has metamorphosed into a system that is intended to supply data for the calculation of enterprise income tax. Managers of both listed and unlisted companies therefore have little or no practical experience of the type of financial information that should be provided to shareholders and the public (i.e. potential investors). There are also strong incentives to distort and manufacture information, often stemming from the loyalty of management to parent companies. These may be benefiting from related party transactions which entail a diversion of funds that may in some cases be detrimental to the profitability of the company concerned.

The problem is equally severe on the demand side. Shareholders tend on the whole to be unfamiliar with such techniques as ratio analysis of listed companies. One reason for this is inexperience: Chinese stock markets are still in their infancy, there are few experienced professional analysts, and institutional investor involvement remains minimal. Another reason is that investors tend to expect, not entirely without foundation, that share values will be supported by the state. The stock market at present tends to fall somewhat short of the task of providing a wholly objective standard by which to value companies. This lack of transparency may tend to weaken the use of stock market valuation as an incentive to optimise company performance. One study has even shown that IPOs by SOEs are more likely to worsen than improve the performance of the enterprises concerned (Chen and Shih, 2001). This is because companies tend to submit inflated figures in the financial statements they are required to provide, concealing their real situation until well after they have secured a financial listing.

6. Accounting standards and regulations

China has made enormous progress in developing accounting systems and standards that conform increasingly to internationally recognised standards. The opening of the accounting sector to foreign participation is likely to stimulate further improvements.

The Accounting Law of the People's Republic of China, adopted in January 1985 and amended in December 1993, provides the main legal basis for accounting, but not in excessive detail (it consists of 30 articles). The law lacks precision on some counts, for example in stipulating that accounting personnel must have "necessary professional knowledge", without mentioning any specific vocational qualifications.

Under the law, the Division of Administration of Accounting Affairs (DAAA) of MOF is responsible for setting accounting standards that all companies must follow. The first such standard, the Basic Accounting Standard (BAS), based on the International Accounting Standards issued by the International Accounting Standards Board, was promulgated in 1992 and implemented formally in 1993. In the same year, MOF set out a new uniform accounting system in line with the BAS to replace the existing Soviet-type accounting system. In 1993, the DAAA published the Accounting Standards for Business Enterprises (ASBE) and has since been developing specific accounting standards and regulations under the ASBE. In 1998, an Accounting Standards Department, which is responsible for developing accounting standards subject to approval by the Ministry of Finance, was established in the DAAA.

The Chinese Institute of Certified Public Accountants (CICPA) was established in 1988 under the Ministry of Finance and now has 135 000 members. Since 1997, CICPA has been a full member of both the International Federation of Accountants (IFAC) and its regional offshoot, the Confederation of Asian and Pacific Accountants. Through membership of these bodies, CICPA works to harmonise China's accounting practice with internationally recognised standards. CICPA works under the joint guidance of MOF and the National Audit Office. Like similar bodies in other countries, it sets standards, organises training and the national certified public accountant (CPA) examinations and registers CPAs. The CICPA promulgated its first set of Independent Auditing Standards in 1995. It also decides on the admission of foreign accounting firms into China and supervises and regulates them after admission. CICPA members must state in their audit reports whether or not the company being audited has complied with the ASBE.

The seven-member Chinese Accounting Standards Committee, which advised MOF on issues related to the promulgation of accounting standards, was inaugurated in 1998.

Initially the government allowed ministries and enterprises to set up their own accounting firms to fill the vacuum. Then from 1992 onward it forced accounting firms to separate from their parent organisations and merge into larger groupings.

MOF is continually upgrading China's accounting systems and standards in line with international practice, which is itself also being continually improved. Future tasks in this regard will include the elimination of existing inconsistencies between different standards and regulations.

7. Cross-border mergers and acquisitions

Global cross-border M&A flows have been increasing rapidly since the 1980s and have since the mid-1990s become the main form of FDI flow between developed countries. However, cross-border M&A flows continue to play a very small part in China's FDI inflows, despite the rapid development of domestic M&A in China.

The regulatory framework governing cross-border M&A is in principle that of existing foreign investment legislation, together with competition laws and regulations and laws governing the ownership and disposal of state-owned assets.

At the end of December 2003, the Chinese Government announced regulations which govern foreign acquisition of SOEs. The Provisional Regulations on Administration of the Transfer of Enterprise State-owned Assets, issued jointly by the State-Owned Assets Supervision and Administration Commission of the State Council (SASAC) and MOF, came into force on 1 February 2004. These regulations facilitate and render more transparent the transfer of the assets of SOEs, whether to domestic or foreign buyers. They do not apply to the transfer of state-owned assets of financial companies, offshore enterprises or of state-owned shares of publicly-listed companies. It remains to be determined to what extent the new rules succeed in their intention to facilitate and render more transparent the privatisation of state-owned assets.

All M&A activity, whether or not it involves a foreign investor, is regulated by a number of government organisations, each of which must be consulted before a particular merger or acquisition can be completed. Mergers and acquisitions involving state-owned enterprises or collective enterprises must be approved by SASAC. Local industry and commerce bureaux are responsible for registering the business scope and registered capital of the new legal person entity and for deregistering the old legal person entity. Local tax bureaux have to decide on the continuation or otherwise of entitlement to favourable tax treatment and other taxation matters. It is up to the customs administrations to decide on the continuation or otherwise of entitlement to duty-free status on imported machinery and equipment of the old legal person entity by the new legal person entity. Local labour bureaux need to be consulted and informed about what happens to the workforce after a merger or acquisition takes place. After obtaining approval from relevant government departments, the entity acquiring a company must then obtain the consent of the target company itself, as well as its main stakeholders, including the workforce, creditors and bondholders, and major suppliers and customers, with whom formal agreements must be signed.

A major problem with current M&A procedures involving foreign investors is that they are unclear. At the national policy level, there is uncertainty over the precise nature of policy in this field, although it is quite clearly aimed at gradually facilitating more cross-border M&A activity as a stimulus to improvement in company performance. At local level, this uncertainty is manifested by a lack of clarity with regard to M&A procedures. In particular, it is not clear in all cases how many agencies must agree before approval is obtained. The addition of yet more powers of examination and approval has in this regard not been consistent with the government's programme of administrative reform.

Although M&As involving foreigners and FIEs are possible in principle, in practice they have so far been rare. A major factor in this regard is protectionism. Some government bodies and representatives of domestic industry maintain that foreign investors use M&A to establish foreign investor control of a sector, causing Chinese firms to lose control of it, so they oppose cross-border M&A activity and refuse assent if it is in their power to do so. Protectionism is also common at local level. This is largely because of taxation arrangements. When two or more enterprises situated in different local government jurisdictions merge, tax liability is no longer shared and must be concentrated in the headquarters of the merged enterprise. Local governments are therefore likely to withhold approval for any merger or acquisition which would result in such a loss of tax revenue.

8. Rule of law and foreign investment

Laws relating to FDI have, especially since the early 1990s, become increasingly precise and focused. Codes of law tended in the past to be brief and vague, allowing maximum room for interpretation by officials. The rationale for this practice was that officials should not be restricted by inflexible rules when dealing with concrete local situations, but should be able to judge according to specific circumstances. The system was therefore generally weighted in favour of maximum flexibility. During the reform period, however, national leaders have postulated an overall goal of moving from the "rule of man" to the "rule of law" which, if it is to be achieved, will necessitate more precise framing of legislation and more consistent and transparent implementation and enforcement.

A major feature of the reform process since 1978 has been the devolution of policy implementation and legal enforcement to local level. This has enabled enforcement to become more thorough than if it had remained dependent on central initiatives, and it has also allowed more adaptation to local conditions – a consideration that has traditionally been important in China. On the other hand, localised enforcement can be less consistent than national, and it is also more likely to be subject to pressure from local officials to conform to local vested interests. Since 1985, the central government has attempted to ensure more regular application of national policies and regulations at local level by introducing an element of accountability to the local population in the form of a system of local elections.

A larger body of qualified legal personnel should, in principle, be better able to resist pressures from outside the legal system, but they will only be able to do so if the political system embodies respect for the principle of judicial independence. A crucial test of judicial independence is the existence or non-existence of judicial review of government action. If a court may rule a government action illegal, overturn it, and enforce that action, such a judgment demonstrates strong judicial independence. China's legal system has been characterised by its lack of independence, but regulations are now in place which do provide the possibility of judicial review of official decisions. It is of particular importance following WTO accession that judicial independence be strengthened and that administrative review become entrenched.

As for the law-making process, consultation does take place, but to a lesser extent than in many OECD member countries. Moreover, it seems to be at the behest of the officials in charge of drawing up the law; those consulted have no automatic right to make representations on their behalf, even if they belong to a constituency directly affected by a new law. FIEs are occasionally invited to participate in consultations when a law is being drafted, but they are sometimes consulted without seeing or without being able to review at leisure a written draft of the law or regulation. According to government officials, a major criterion used to decide which companies to invite is whether or not the company has a dominant position in a particular market or industry. However, some FIEs complain of having been left out of the list while, they allege, other companies with a lesser claim have been asked to attend and proffer advice. Consequently, a company taking part in a closed consultation session is likely to feel that it has been granted a special privilege denied to those not invited; if the session is open, however, it may decide not to make too many of its comments public and its advice is therefore likely to be of less practical use.

Laws are not freely discussed by a wide range of stakeholders before promulgation, and they frequently contain elements that are incomplete, inappropriate or inaccurate. After these imperfections have been drawn to the government's attention, a set of implementing regulations is drafted to fill the gaps, elaborate the details and rectify blatant errors. Until the implementing regulations are published it is often difficult to apply the original law because its detailed terms remain uncertain. Publication is not automatic; implementing rules are often circulated internally for some time, so that they are not available to the public. Advance publication would increase transparency regarding legislation and would also have the effect of forcing officials to explain the specific public purposes intended to be served by laws and regulations.

A large number of foreign law firms set up representative offices in China in anticipation of the opening up of the legal sector to foreign participation following WTO accession. The "one firm, one office" rule that limited foreign law firms to a single office in China was lifted in 2000, permitting foreign law firms to service clients who have business operations in several cities.[9] However, foreign law firms still report a number of difficulties in both establishment and operation. Some foreign law firms, including law firms based in Hong Kong, China, report that they have had to wait up to five years before being granted a licence to operate on the Chinese mainland. The agreed-upon lifting of restrictions on the location and number of foreign law firms which was implemented in regulations promulgated in January 2002,[10] appears to be heavily qualified by regulations that took effect in September 2002.[11] These give the Ministry of Justice the right to decide whether to allow the opening of new offices on grounds of local social, economic and legal-services development. Foreign law firms may not hire locally qualified lawyers and may not invest in local law firms. Lawyers qualified in other legal jurisdictions may not practise Chinese law. This limits the services foreign law firms may offer their clients. The September 2002 regulations further restrict the activities of foreign law firms by prohibiting them from dealing directly with any Chinese Government department and from acting on behalf of foreign companies in arbitration cases.

Current efforts to improve the functioning and independence of the judicial system[12] could be intensified by such measures as training and appointing legally-qualified judges to all courts; raising the pay of judges and other key legal personnel to reduce their vulnerability to offers of bribery; enhancing the status of judges in relation to local government and party officials; and establishing at national and regional level mechanisms to guarantee the execution of court judgments.

Current efforts to establish a more transparent and accountable process of formulating legislation and regulations could be expanded. All legislation and regulations could be published on a single, comprehensive, up-to-date and easily-navigable Web site in both Chinese and English. A mechanism similar to that of the US Federal Register or equivalent systems in other OECD member countries may be introduced to publish draft laws and regulations and obtain public feedback on them as early as possible before promulgation. The scope of stakeholder consultation with regard to FDI-related legislation could be expanded and regularised.

9. Legal recourses

The Chinese legal system contains an element of conciliation that is not present in many other jurisdictions. Although litigation is becoming more common in Chinese society, usage of such conciliation procedures remains popular, since it offers a quicker, cheaper and less vituperative method of dispute resolution. Local mediation committees handled over five million civil disputes in 2000.

A more specific conciliation procedure is available for disputes relating to the economy, trade, finance, security, investment, intellectual property, technology transfer, real estate, construction contracts, transport, insurance and other commercial and maritime business. In 1987, the China Council for the Promotion of International Trade (CCPIT) and the China Chamber of International Commerce (CCOIC) set up the CCPIT Conciliation Centre in Beijing for this purpose. In the 1990s, this was expanded to form a national network of over 30 conciliation centres. Such centres are not restricted to cases involving foreign investors or enterprises. Cases are accepted by the centres in accordance with a conciliation agreement between the parties, or, in the absence of such an agreement, on application by one party with the consent of the other party. Cases taken to the conciliation centres are expected to reach "an amicable settlement agreement" by the free will of both parties (CCPIT and CCOIC Conciliation Rules, 2000). The number of cases referred to the centres has not been great (some 2 000 by the end of 1999), presumably because disputes that are capable of easy resolution can be handled without recourse to outside conciliation, but the CCPIT states that the success rate is about 80%. The CCPIT

Conciliation Centre has signed co-operation agreements with similar centres outside China, including the Hamburg and New York centres. In 1995, it joined the International Federation of Commercial Arbitration Institutions (IFCAL), and in 1997, it joined the London Court of International Arbitration.

When foreign partners in Sino-foreign joint ventures find themselves in disagreement with their Chinese partners over such matters as the interpretation of the provisions of a joint venture agreement, contract or articles of association, they are first expected to resolve the dispute through consultation or mediation, for example via a conciliation centre. If this fails, there are several avenues for dispute resolution, including arbitration within China, arbitration abroad and litigation within China. Litigation is increasingly being used, but arbitration remains the preferred option, especially as enforcement of court judgments is largely left to the Public Security Bureaux, who do not regard it as their top priority. The Chinese authorities do not share the view that public security organs are the executors of court judgments. A dispute may be taken to the China International Economic and Trade Arbitration Commission (CIETAC) or, if appropriate, to the Chinese Maritime Arbitration Commission (CMAC).[13]

Disputes are accepted on the written application of one of the parties to the dispute in accordance with the arbitration clause in the contract or other written agreement signed between the parties. They are handled by arbitration panels selected by CIETAC from among Chinese and foreign persons with professional knowledge and experience in various fields. The tribunal must render an arbitral award within nine months from the date of formation of the tribunal. Arbitration tribunals are empowered to combine conciliation with arbitration. This means that an arbitration tribunal may, with the consent of both parties, help the parties to reach a voluntary amicable agreement and make a consent arbitral award, saving time and expense that would otherwise usually be necessary for an ordinary arbitral award. As would be expected from the more complex procedures involved in arbitration as compared with those of conciliation, CIETAC fees are slightly higher than those charged by the CCPIT Conciliation Centre. For example, for disputes relating to claims of between RMB 10 million and RMB 50 million, CIETAC charges RMB 210 000 plus 1% of the amount above RMB 10 million while the Conciliation Centre charges between 0.5% and 0.75% of the claimed amount.[14]

With the mutual consent of the parties concerned, arbitration can also be carried out through an arbitration agency in the country where the sued party is located or through one in a third country. The availability of an enforceable arbitration procedure outside China allows foreign investors to avoid the current shortcomings of the legal system in China in many cases. China has been a member of the International Centre for the Settlement of Investment Disputes (ICSID), so that arbitral awards by the ICSID in disputes involving China and the 135 other contracting states can be enforced under the terms of the United Nations Convention on the Recognition and Enforcement of Foreign Arbitral Awards, which China joined in 1987 (for commercial disputes only).

The option of taking arbitration to centres outside China has been taken by many foreign joint-venture partners in recent years. The main centres involved are the Stockholm Chamber of Commerce, the London Court of International Arbitration, the International Court of Arbitration of the International Chamber of Commerce and the Hong Kong International Arbitration Centre. Bilateral treaties signed by China with many countries include detailed provisions for the formation of arbitration tribunals chaired by a third-country national to make binding judgments regarding unresolved disputes between nationals of the two countries concerned. Such mechanisms are an important addition to domestic dispute resolution procedures because they remove any element of bias perceived to exist in the domestic court system of either country. It should be borne in mind that enforcement of an international arbitral award in China is still the function of Chinese courts and is not automatic, as it is possible for a Chinese court to challenge the status of such an award. Cases in which awards have been overturned on such grounds have occurred.

In addition, local centres established under such bodies as municipal service centres for foreign investment and municipal foreign economic and trade committees deal with complaints against government departments and suggestions for improving the FDI environment. These appear to be becoming more systematic. For example, in March 2001, a set of measures for handling FIE complaints was promulgated in Beijing designating the Beijing Centre for Handling Complaints Lodged by Foreign-Funded Enterprises within the Beijing Foreign Investment Service Centre. Under this system, local governments down to county level are charged with setting up centres to handle complaints from FIEs and report them to the municipal centre within three days of receiving them. The municipal centre must then reply to all questions that it can answer within three days and transfer those that it cannot answer to the handling department within three days and inform the complainant of the transfer. The handling department must then contact the department being complained about to verify the related information and inform the complainant of the result within 15 days.[15]

10. Intellectual property protection and foreign investment

The development of measures to protect intellectual property rights is described and analysed in Chapter 14. This section considers only the application of relevant legislation to the protection of intellectual property rights (patents, brand names, copyrights) of FIEs in China.

According to Article 1 Paragraph 3 of the TRIPS Agreement, WTO members must accord the treatment provided for in the TRIPS Agreement to the nationals of other WTO members; Article 3 Paragraph 1 further states that each member shall accord to the nationals of other members treatment no less favourable than that it accords to its own members with regard to the protection of intellectual property. There is no requirement to extend this treatment to non-WTO-member nationals. However, since the majority of economies are already WTO members and some of the remainder may accede to the WTO during the period of operation of current legislation, compliance with this requirement can be ensured by providing a wholly non-discriminatory framework of IPR protection legislation, which China has done. In addition to providing protection guaranteed by bilateral treaties, Chinese laws explicitly stipulate that all FIEs enjoy the same rights as domestic companies and individuals with regard to trademarks and patents.

Foreign investors continue to raise concerns about instances of intellectual property rights violations which are not always dealt with effectively by the courts. The main task ahead is to improve enforcement of existing laws on a regular rather than a sporadic basis and at the same time develop a public culture which respects intellectual property rights at all levels of society and the economy. Doing so will benefit domestic companies and individuals by protecting their trademarks, copyright and patents, and will also help attract more high-quality FDI to China. As Maruyama (1999) puts it: "China cannot realistically hope to attract foreign direct investment, secure transfers of cutting-edge foreign technology or foster world-class research and development if foreign firms are not convinced that their IPR will be adequately protected" (Maruyama, 1999).

While maximum penalties and damages are specified in the patent, trademark and copyright laws, there are no minima. The deterrent effect of the law is therefore not inherent in the law itself, but in the stringency with which it is applied, which may vary with time and place. It is also unclear how serious a violation of IPR must be before it can be brought to court. The laws do not clearly explain the procedure for taking IPR cases to the courts. Although a framework of IPR legislation in accordance with World Intellectual Property Organisation (WIPO) standards has been constructed, examples of IPR violations are still clearly visible in cities all over China. The existence of at least one large wholesale market which engages mainly in the distribution of copies of products of well-known global brands indicates that some local governments have not yet managed to deal with the problem. The government is itself unable to prevent counterfeiting of products produced by government monopolies, such as the tobacco industry, which lose large sums of money each year from lost sales. The Chinese Government's inability to protect itself against counterfeit manufacturers raises doubts about its ability to protect the intellectual property rights of foreign investors.

A further problem is that the sale of copies is not restricted to China. Large quantities of counterfeit products are being exported from China to both OECD member countries and to emerging markets. The consumer of such products suffers both from a lack of quality control and of after-sales service. A serious danger is that these insufficiencies can cause actual physical harm to purchasers or to third parties and thus will lead to product liability disputes. Chinese producers of food products, for example, suffered lost sales because of reports of health risks from copies of their products made in China and sold abroad.

Despite education campaigns, there is insufficient public respect for IPR. As Zhou Lin, deputy director of the Centre for Intellectual Property under the Chinese Academy of Social Sciences, put it: "Many people have little idea that intellectual property rights are just like a TV, a VCD and a house, that they are owned by somebody, and, if you want to use them, you should ask the owner first" (*People's Daily*, 2 May 2001). Although no sales figures are available, there is no doubt that many businesses and individuals regularly purchase counterfeit software, undermining sales of the genuine article. One indication of this is the very low ratio of sales of computer software to sales of computer hardware, which in other countries is usually near 1:1. The widespread purchase and open use of unlawful products at all levels of society bespeaks a public tolerance of IPR violation that makes successful prosecution of infringement difficult. The practice of forging qualifications, for example, is widespread: the 2000 population census recorded over 600 000 more higher education certificates than had actually been awarded. These cases are of crucial importance to foreign investors who wish to hire skilled personnel and need to be able to trust documentary evidence of educational qualifications.

While confidence in the patent application process appears to be strong, judging by the number of applications, concerns are frequently heard about the length of time taken before an application is examined and granted (or refused). This complaint is partly borne out by the magnitude of the discrepancy between the number of applications filed and the number granted. For example, in 2000, 170 682 applications were filed, while only 105 345 were granted. To some extent this discrepancy is explained by the 18-month time lag and by the rapid increase in applications, but this is not a complete explanation, as there were already 134 239 applications in 1999.[16]

11. Corruption and foreign investment

Corruption remains a general governance problem, as explained in Chapter 3. It can be a deterrent to FDI because it imposes a cost on the FIE for which there is no corresponding benefit.[17] The damage done to trust in official institutions by the existence of systematic corruption and the higher cost suffered by honest companies that refuse to pay such bribes should also be taken into account.

There is an extensive and growing exposure of OECD-based enterprises and their foreign subsidiaries to the sensitive Chinese business environment. It is clear that the volume of FDI entails the exposure of OECD companies and their subsidiaries to corrupt practices and the solicitation of bribes, especially since FDI include a large number of government contracts (government procurement and construction projects are among the sectors most afflicted by corruption),.

It is sometimes suggested that it is difficult for an executive to separate corrupt from non-corrupt patterns of behaviour when attempting to adapt to a genuinely different cultural environment, entailing confusion about the correct behaviour to engage in. For example, gift-giving is a deeply embedded part of Chinese culture, so it is difficult to refuse all gifts from actual or potential business partners or, on the other hand, to refrain from giving gifts to them. However, it is quite possible to work within the confines of a gift-giving culture without indulging in corrupt behaviour, as there is nothing inherently corrupt in the practice of making gifts. Such gifts are only corrupt if they lead to the granting of an advantage which would otherwise have been withheld.

The existence of systematic corruption in the Chinese economy affects FIEs even when they do not appear to be directly involved. For example, even if an FIE is not approached for bribes, it may encounter problems that result from the payment of bribes by domestically-owned competitor companies if those companies benefit from favours from bribed officials. In the next few years, FIEs are likely to be increasingly involved with domestic companies as M&A starts to play a larger role in FDI in China. They will therefore have to cope with any corruption that may occur in such companies as well as any corrupt practices indulged in by competing FIEs.

OECD-based enterprises are accustomed to operating in a legal and administrative framework that eschews corruption. Adapting to a business environment characterised by systematic corruption involves a cost to multinationals, whether this is in the form of corrupt payments actually made or in the form of revenue lost by refusing to make such payments.

Notes

1. This chapter was written by Kenneth Davies, Investment Division, Directorate for Financial and Enterprise Affairs, OECD.
2. The variables used in the econometric study include: market size (gross domestic product, GDP), per capita GDP, GDP growth rate, efficiency wage, labour quality, accumulated FDI stock, economic distance and trade and investment regime.
3. It is important to bear in mind that FDI from Hong Kong, China includes components such as investment from the Overseas Chinese diaspora and "round-tripping" investment from China itself [routed via Hong Kong, China to take advantage of FDI incentives such as tax reductions] which are inherently difficult to measure. Back in 1992, according to one estimate, 13% of China's total FDI intake stemmed from round-tripping; a contemporary World Bank estimate put the 1992 figure at 25%. Opinions differ as to whether the practice has grown or diminished since then.
4. The accession documents are available on the WTO Web site *www.wto.org*.

5. The parent bank must have USD 20 billion in total assets to open a branch and USD 10 billion to open a subsidiary. There are six levels of bank offices, with corresponding minima for operating funds in the case of branches and capital in the case of subsidiaries, in each case varying from RMB 100 million to RMB 600 million, or foreign currency equivalent.

6. The SETC was abolished and its functions and staff incorporated into the new Ministry of Commerce in the March 2003 government reorganisation.

7. The Securities Law is available in both Chinese and English on the CSRC Web site *www.csrc.gov.cn*.

8. The Code is available in both Chinese and English on the CSRC Web site *www.csrc.gov.cn*.

9. In December 2003 it was officially announced that China had approved the establishment of representative offices of 115 law firms from 16 foreign countries to set up representative offices on the Chinese mainland, and that 12 of them had opened their second representative offices on the Chinese mainland along with four law firms based in Hong Kong, China.

10. Regulations on Representative Offices of Foreign Law Firms in China, promulgated by the State Council as its Order No. 338 on 22 December 2001 and put into force on 1 January 2002.

11. Stipulations of the Ministry of Justice Concerning the Enforcement of the "Regulations on the Management of Representative Offices set up by Foreign Law Firms in China", Order No. 73, by the Ministry of Justice of the People's Republic of China.

12. China has a four-level court system. The Supreme People's Court is the highest judicial organ. It is responsible to the NPC or its Standing Committee and sits in Beijing. Higher People's Courts sit in the provinces, autonomous regions and municipalities directly under the State Council, such as Shanghai. Intermediate People's Courts sit at the prefecture level and also in parts of provinces, autonomous regions and municipalities directly under the State Council. There are also basic People's Courts in counties, towns and municipal districts. Special courts handle matters affecting military, railroad transportation, water transportation, and forestry. The court system is paralleled by a hierarchy of prosecuting organs called People's Procuratorates; at the apex of this structure stands the Supreme People's Procuratorate.

13. The CIETAC has its headquarters in Beijing and also has branches in Shanghai and Shenzhen. Other large cities also have their own arbitration centres which can handle disputes involving foreign partners as well as purely domestic disputes. CIETAC handles international or "foreign-related" disputes; disputes relating to Hong Kong, China, Macao (China) and Chinese Taipei; disputes between FIEs or between an FIE and a Chinese legal person; disputes arising from project financing, invitations to tender and bidding submissions, project construction and other activities conducted by a Chinese legal person and other persons or economic organisations that use capital, technology or services from foreign countries, international organisations, or from Hong Kong, China, Macao (China) or Chinese Taipei; and any other disputes that the parties have agreed to arbitrate by CIETAC. (CIETAC Arbitration Rules, revised and adopted by the China Council for the Promotion of International Trade and the China Chamber of International Commerce on 5 September 2000, effective from 1 October 2000).

14. CIETAC Arbitration Fee Schedule and CCPIT/CCOIC Conciliation Fee Schedule.

15. Measures Governing the Handling of Complaints Lodged by Foreign-funded Enterprises in Beijing, promulgated by the Beijing Foreign Economic and Trade Commission on 16 March 2001.

16. All the figures in this paragraph are from the *China Statistical Yearbook*, 2001.

17. It is sometimes argued that corrupt practices such as bribing officials to circumvent unnecessarily lengthy bureaucratic procedures can produce an efficiency gain. Two commentators even suggest that it also provides an effective inducement to local officials to promote economic reform (Fan and Grossman, 2001).

Bibliography

Chen, Chien-Hsun and Hui-Tzu Shih (2001), *Initial Public Offering and Corporate Governance in China's Transitional Economy*, Chung-Hua Institution for Economic Research, Chinese Taipei.

Chen Chunlai, "Provincial Distribution of Foreign Direct Investment in China", research paper to the MOFTEC/OECD co-operation programme on FDI, cited in OECD (2002), *China in the World Economy: The Domestic Policy Challenges*, "Foreign Direct Investment: Prospects and Policies", p. 339.

China Council for the Promotion of International Trade (CCPIT) and China Chamber of International Commerce (COIC) (2000), Conciliation Rules.

China Securities Regulatory Commission (1998), Securities Law of the People's Republic of China, available at *www.csrc.gov.cn*.

China Securities Regulatory Commission (2001), Code of Corporate Governance for Listed Companies in China, available at *www.csrc.gov.cn*.

Fan, Chengsze Simon and Herschel I. Grossman (2001), "Incentives and Corruption in Chinese Economic Reform", *Journal of Policy Reform*, Vol. 4, No. 3.

Maruyama, Warren H. (1999), "Five US-China IPR Negotiations: Trade, Intellectual Property, and the Rule of Law in a Global Economy" in Mark A. Cohen, A. Elizabeth Bang and Stephanie J. Mitchell (eds.) (1999), *Chinese Intellectual Property Law and Practice*, Kluwer Law International, Boston.

Ministry of Commerce, *www.fdi.gov.cn*.

Ministry of Justice (2002), Stipulations of the Ministry of Justice Concerning the Enforcement of the "Regulations on the Management of Representative Offices set up by Foreign Law Firms in China", Order No. 73, available at *www.doj.gov.hk/eng/topical/pdf/setup_law_firm_e4.pdf*.

National Bureau of Statistics (2001), *China Statistical Yearbook, 2001*, China Statistics Press.

OECD (2002), *China in the World Economy: The Domestic Policy Challenges*, "Establishing Effective Governance for China's Enterprises", OECD, Paris.

OECD (2003), *Investment Policy Review of China: Progress and Reform Challenges*, OECD, Paris.

OECD (2004), *International Investment Prospects*, OECD, Paris.

People's Daily (2001), "Experts Press for Tightened Control of IPR Infringements", 2 May.

State Council (2001), Regulations on Representative Offices of Foreign Law Firms in China, promulgated as Order No. 338 on 22 December 2001 and put into force on 1 January 2002.

Tenev, Stoyan and Chunlin Zhang (2002), *Corporate Governance and Enterprise Reform in China*, World Bank and International Finance Corporation, Washington, D.C.

World Trade Organisation (2001), the accession documents are available on the WTO Web site *www.wto.org*.

Xu, Xiaonian and Wang, Yan (1997), *Ownership Structure, Corporate Governance, and Firms' Performance: The Case of Chinese Stock Companies*, Amherst College and the World Bank.

PART III

Chapter 16

Institutional Framework for Effective Agricultural Policy: Current Issues and Future Challenges

Table of Contents

Summary 469

**Institutional Framework for Effective Agricultural Policy:
Current Issues and Future Challenges** 471

   1. Introduction 471
   2. Key decision-making and advisory bodies 471
   3. Laws, documents and decisions 474
   4. Central bodies under the State Council 474
       4.1. Bodies with broad responsibilities 475
       4.2. Operational ministries and administrations 477
   5. Grain market organisation system 478
   6. Ambiguous institutional and legal framework: the case of land tenure 478
   7. Future challenges 482

Notes 484

Bibliography 484

List of boxes

16.1. China's grain administration system as of the beginning of 2004 479
16.2. The distribution of land rights across levels of authority 481

List of figures

16.1. Central institutions with oversight over China's agro-food sector 473

Summary

Since reforms began in 1978, China's agricultural sector has been transformed from a centralized system of commune-based farming into a household-based system. China's leaders are de-emphasizing formal planning and are increasingly accepting allocation by markets. However, agriculture remains a sensitive area and is subject to intervention. This chapter describes the main institutions dealing with agricultural policies, with some suggestions for next steps in the reform process.

Policy takes shape through a sequence of institutions and decision-making bodies: *i)* senior leaders articulate national policy objectives and provide guidance; *ii)* a layer of staff, "leading groups", research centres and institutes link leaders to the formal bureaucracy, providing turnkey analysis and advice; *iii)* State Council commissions and ministries with overarching mandates co-ordinate the activities of line ministries and provinces; *iv)* other ministries, provincial governments and government-held corporations are charged with the implementation of the government agenda.

Top leadership. The President and the Vice-President, senior leaders of the Communist Party of China (CPC), high-ranking members of the State Council and members of CPC "leading groups" perform most of the leadership functions within China's governing apparatus – determining broad government policies and directions.

Legislation and rule-making. Laws are passed by the National People's Congress (NPC), China's official legislative body. During the legislative process, the NPC receives substantial contributions from various ministries, advisory groups and CPC organs. Many "documents", however, are issued by individual ministries. For cross-cutting issues, a "decision" statement may be released jointly by several ministries or, occasionally, by the General Office of the State Council or the CPC. In 2004, the CPC and the State Council jointly released the No. 1 Document "The Suggestions of the Central Committee of the Communist Party of China and the State Council on Policies for Boosting Growth in Farmers' Income".

Administration. Institutions falling under the State Council serve as the administrative arm. They can be divided into those having broad responsibilities and those taking care of day-to-day operations and the practical implementation of agro-food and rural policies.

Some suggestions arise from our review of China's agri-food governance.

1. Government processes must continue to evolve from a top-down hierarchical approach to one that enables, is service-oriented, responsive and accountable.

2. Remove institutional fiefdoms. Farmers and retailers are handicapped by transportation bottlenecks, jurisdictional fiefdoms of input suppliers and value-chain intermediaries.

3. Problems must be properly diagnosed. Focus on causes rather than symptoms. For example, the persistence of often-persecuted informal rural credit institutions is really an indication of the failings of the formal financial sector. "Symptoms" may actually be solutions in the making.

4. Don't pick winners. Few people are omniscient, whether in the public or private sector. Continue taking steps to "level the playing field", creating circumstances that allow winners to emerge.

5. While the creation of new institutions may be helpful, it may be better to focus on appropriate incentive systems rather than "bricks and mortar" approaches. Institutions can develop their own vested interests and even perpetuate problems (and their own mandate) rather than resolve them.

Institutional Framework for Effective Agricultural Policy: Current Issues and Future Challenges[1]

1. Introduction

Although the importance of agriculture in the Chinese economy has fallen, it is still one of the key sectors accounting for 15% of GDP and providing above 40% of employment. About 60% of China's population continues to live in rural areas. Since the reform process started in 1978, agriculture has been transformed from a tightly controlled, centralised system of commune-based farming into a household-based system increasingly driven by markets rather than plans and targets fixed by the government (OECD, 2002). In response to this change, agricultural production surged and incomes increased, thus helping to alleviate a large part of rural poverty. Currently, China's agriculture supplies food for 1.3 billion Chinese citizens and contributed to the annual net exports of agro-food products at about USD 3-4 billion between 2000 and 2002.

China's leaders are now de-emphasizing formal economic planning and allocation by command, and are increasingly accepting allocation by markets, but the agriculture sector remains a sensitive area and subject to central guidance – especially for food staples. China's official policy of encouraging a "socialist market economy" implies that production of and trade in commodities considered of strategic importance will continue to be managed, with state-linked enterprises still playing an important role (Gilmour and Brink, 2001). This dual approach to the basic regulatory mechanisms of the economy contributes to the creation of a complex organisational framework supporting the implementation of agricultural policy goals and measures. This "spider web" of institutions has been evolving – at varying speed and sometimes with unintended consequences. Often, new institutions have been added or appended to existing ones. As a result, their roles often overlap and are sometimes in conflict. This being said, important strides have been made during the latest reorganisation, with the number of redundancies and conflicts in mandate being reduced, and improvements made in accountability and professionalism in decision processes.

This chapter's main objectives are to provide an overall organisational structure of Party, state administration and parliamentary institutions dealing with agricultural policies. We also examine China's grain policies and land tenure system. These cases indicate that the complexity of grain policy measures and the ambiguity of land ownership rights sometimes make the achievement of policy objectives difficult. The last section provides some recommendations for the next steps in the ongoing reform process.

2. Key decision-making and advisory bodies

Agricultural policy takes shape through a sequence of institutions and decision-making bodies: i) a core of 25-35 senior leaders articulate national policy objectives and provide guidance and direction; ii) the layer of staff, "leading groups", research centres and institutes link the elite leaders to the formal bureaucracy, providing turnkey analysis and advice; *iii)* State Council commissions and key ministries with overarching mandates ensure cohesion and co-ordinate the activities of line ministries and provinces; *iv)* other ministries, provincial governments and government-held corporations are charged with the implementation of the government agenda (see Figure 16.1).

To a degree, the President and the Vice-President, senior CPC leaders within the Politburo, high-ranking members of the State Council and members of CPC leading groups perform the leadership functions within China's governing apparatus – determining broad government policies and directions and ensuring integration and consistency of effort across government activities and bodies.

The Chinese Communist Party (CPC) purports to represent the population at large and interprets and expresses the will of the people. Communist Party officials and institutions are thought to outrank officials and institutions that are part of the formal state apparatus. Through its extensive network, the CPC solicits input and advice from a broad cross-section of society over matters of concern, providing guidance and direction to the formal state apparatus. The top 25-35 senior leaders meet in several overlapping decision-making bodies, including: the CPC Politburo, the CPC Secretariat, the Standing Committee of the State Council and the Central Military Commission.

Senior leaders are informed and advised in their decisions by CPC "leading groups". Leading groups are typically made up of well-respected and influential specialists in the areas of focus and concern. These specialists are often senior-ranking CPC members or respected professionals from within the formal civil service, academia and other parts of society that have been invited to serve. Leading groups serve as multi-purpose instruments. Members within leading groups can serve as technical secretariats to China's senior leaders, including the president, the Prime Minister and the State Council. They can also provide analysis and advice directly to senior leaders. They act as catalysts, overseers and co-ordinators of analysis, advice, and implementation relating to the work of the government and directives of senior leaders. Because of their ties and rank, leading group members can ensure that the activities of commissions and ministries within the formal state apparatus are consistent with the direction and approach of senior leaders. Under each leading group there is a working office responsible for, among other things, preparing documents for both the CPC and the State Council and for providing advice for the top leaders. For example, under the leading group dealing with financial and economic issues is the "Office of Central Financial and Economic Leading Group". This office ranks at the ministry level. Normally, a deputy in this office is responsible for agricultural and rural affairs and plays a leading role in refining agricultural policy directions, with a rank roughly equivalent to that of a minister (Zou, 2004; *www.china.org.cn/english/features/state_structure/*).

The ascendancy and formalization of the role of different leading groups has been critical in the development of more cohesive policies and in expediting decision-making, including in the agro-food sector. However, the deliberations of the leading groups fall under the supervision of the CPC rather than within the state apparatus and are not open to the general public or subject to significant scrutiny.

Policy options are fed into the leading groups from many sources, including research institutes and think tanks. Several think tanks have been particularly influential, including the Development Research Centre of the State Council (DRC), the CPC Central Policy Research Centre Office, and the Institute of Economic Research of the National

III.16. INSTITUTIONAL FRAMEWORK FOR EFFECTIVE AGRICULTURAL POLICY: CURRENT ISSUES AND FUTURE CHALLENGES

Figure 16.1. **Central institutions with oversight over China's agro-food sector**

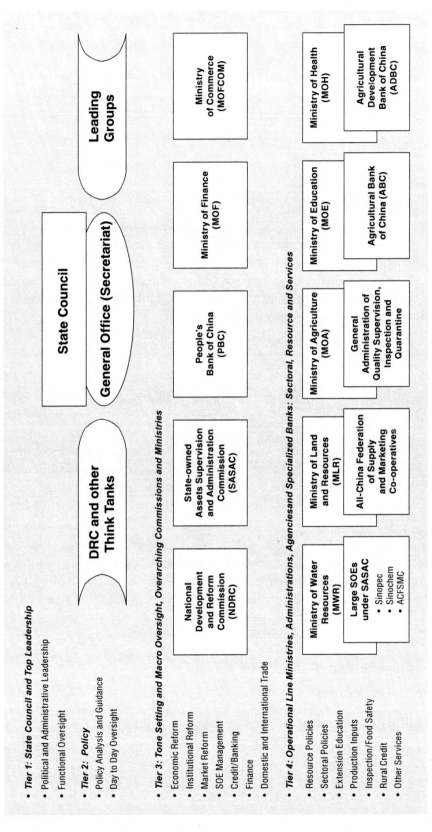

Development and Reform Commission (NDRC) (ADB, 2002). Other important government think tanks include the Chinese Academy of Sciences (and its Centre for Chinese Agricultural Policy), the Chinese Academy of Social Sciences (and its Rural Development Institute), the Ministry of Agriculture's Research Centre for the Rural Economy and the Institute of Agricultural Economics of the Chinese Academy of Agricultural Sciences. Some university, non-governmental and private think tanks have also been increasingly effective in informing policy discussion. These include the China Centre for Economic Research at Peking University, the National Economic Research Institute-China Reform Foundation, the Tianze Institute of Economics and the College of Agricultural Economics of Nanjing Agricultural University.

3. Laws, documents and decisions

The laws are passed by the National People's Congress (NPC), the legislative body in China. Within the NPC, the Committee on Agricultural Work is responsible for agricultural matters. During the legislative process, the Committee receives substantial contributions from various ministries (*e.g.* the draft Agricultural Law was prepared by the Ministry of Agriculture, MOA) and benefits from assistance from various above-mentioned advisory institutions. Generally speaking, the role of the NPC is still relatively weak, but in recent years it has progressively begun to assert its power.

While the CPC leading groups and their offices play a decisive role in policy formulation, most of the "documents" or "decisions" (policies to be implemented) are issued by individual ministries. Occasionally, for those across-ministries issues/policies, the "decision" is made (or document released) jointly by several ministries and occasionally by the General Office of the State Council (*Guowuyuan bangong ting*) or by the General Office of the CPC (*Zhonggong zhongyang bangong ting*).

For the top priority issues, documents are issued under the responsibility of the CPC. For example, in 2004, the No. 1 Document[2] "The Suggestions of the Central Committee of the Communist Party of China and the State Council on Policies for Boosting Growth in Farmers' Income" was issued by the CPC (*zhong fa*). This document addresses the Party and government organs (ministries, departments) at various levels.

Despite some progress in recent years, the transparency of the process of document preparation is still a problem in China. Usually, draft documents are not open to public debate. Experimental or informal policies and draft regulations are still regarded as internal matters and access to them remains tightly controlled by the government. Another complicating factor is that laws and regulations in China tend to be more general in nature than in other countries, allowing for flexible interpretations and inconsistency.

4. Central bodies under the State Council

Institutions falling under the State Council serve as the administrative arm of the government. They can be divided into those having broad responsibilities, overseeing macroeconomic issues and co-ordinating activities of other ministries, and those taking care of day-to-day operations and the practical implementation of agro-food and rural policies and directives (see Figure 16.1).

4.1. Bodies with broad responsibilities

4.1.1. National Development and Reform Commission (NDRC)

The NDRC and its predecessors have historically played a crucial role in the management of China's economy. The NDRC sets broader targets for annual plans as well as the core tasks for the medium and long-term plans. NDRC relies on a network of planning organs embedded in central ministries and provincial governments to perform its role. It also consults extensively with the Ministry of Finance (MOF) over China's financial situation, the Ministry of Commerce (MOFCOM) regarding trade, and the People's Bank of China (PBC) over monetary and fiscal policies.

As the institution under the State Council with the broadest mandate and the most cross-cutting powers, the NDRC oversees and co-ordinates activities across many areas of importance to the agro-food sector and to China's rural citizens. It is regarded as the key co-ordinating body overseeing the implementation of agricultural and rural policies in China (Han, 2003). For instance, it studies and co-ordinates activities focusing on major issues in agriculture and rural development, co-ordinating regional (and rural) planning, and policy development and implementation. It is responsible for guiding industrial and commercial development in both rural and urban settings. It also proposes strategies and major policies and measures relating to rural-urban disparities and urbanization.

NDRC monitors, studies and analyses domestic and international market situations, taking the lead in managing the trade balance and control of major commodities. It drafts, co-ordinates, and oversees the implementation of import and export strategies for major agricultural and industrial products. It manages the reserves and stocks of key materials and commodities such as grain, cotton, sugar, petroleum and drugs and makes proposals for modern logistics development.

NDRC also drafts and organizes the implementation of industrial and commercial pricing policies, drawing up and revising plans and prices for commodities and services controlled by the state. This includes the "guidance" of prices for many inputs, products and services of importance to the agro-food sector: grain, oilseeds, cotton, seeds, fertiliser, silkworm cocoons, irrigation water, transportation services, interest rates and banking fees.

The NDRC Department of Rural Economy covers such areas as agriculture, fishery, forestry, water management, livestock production, poverty reduction, etc. It oversees areas under the responsibility of the Ministry of Agriculture, the State Forestry Administration, and the Ministry of Water Resources. Being responsible for the infrastructure investment in rural areas, it co-ordinates budgetary allocations from the MOF and investments financed by banks operating in rural areas. The NDRC supervises directly the State Grain Administration and the State Administration for Tobacco.

4.1.2. State-owned Assets Supervision and Administration Commission (SASAC)

State-owned enterprises (SOEs) used to fall under the jurisdiction of several ministries. In 2003, the SASAC was created and empowered by the State Council to represent the government as the shareholder in SOEs, in accordance with the Company Law of the People's Republic of China and other administrative regulations (Chen et al., 2003). The creation of SASAC retains the central government's hand in the operations of the SOEs. The challenge for the SASAC will be to make the relationship between the government and the SOEs more transparent and less easy to manipulate. Increasingly, emphasis is being placed on market orientation and business performance, with office holders and corporate board members being held accountable. Being a major shareholder, SASAC is responsible for governance and oversight relating to business operations and conduct of several SOEs of direct interest to the agro-food sector, most notably the China National Cereals Oils and Foodstuffs Corporation (COFCO); Sinochem dealing e.g. with production and trade in fertilisers, herbicides and pesticides; Sinopec being China's leading supplier of major petrochemical products, including fertilisers; and the China National Tobacco Company.[3]

4.1.3. People's Bank of China (PBC)

The PBC is China's central bank and reports directly to the State Council. The PBC is in charge of formulating and implementing monetary policies and exercises macro-control of the monetary sector. Among other things, it supervises rural financial institutional systems, including rural credit unions and two banks specialized in extending loans for agriculture and rural businesses: the Agricultural Development Bank of China (ADBC) and the Agricultural Bank of China (ABC). The PBC is the main source of loans for the ADBC for the procurement of major crops such as grains, cotton and oilseeds.

4.1.4. Ministry of Finance (MOF)

Among other functions, the MOF is officially responsible for overseeing and administering all central financial expenditures. Technically, this means that any official expenditures in the agro-food sector made by central bodies or by their subordinate bodies at the provincial or sub-provincial level should in some way be accounted for in MOF reporting. The MOF has 20 departments, including departments specifically dedicated to economic trade, public expenditures, (primary) agriculture, international affairs, capital construction, state-owned capital administration, state-owned capital statistics, property appraisal and agricultural and rural development.

The Department of Rural Finance within the MOF is responsible for the drafting of policies supporting agriculture, participating in the formulation of agricultural development plans, allocating and managing financial funds on agriculture, participating in the allocation of the poverty reduction funds, etc. Even if the MOF is just the implementing body of the government plan and policy, in reality it plays a more important role. As various policy measures tend to be general in nature, allowing for rather flexible interpretations, and are not always assured by the sufficient allocation of funds, this leaves ample room and liberty for the MOF with regard to the actual distribution of funds. Therefore, the implementation of agricultural policy (like direct payments to grain farmers in the producing areas announced in Document No. 1/2004) depends to a large extent on the effectiveness of the allocation and delivery of funds from the MOF and its branches at local levels to the targeted population. Moreover, while all expenditures at various levels of government administration should be accounted in MOF reporting, it is difficult to verify whether this is the case. Publicly available budgetary data, including on expenditures related to agricultural policy, tend to be strongly aggregated, not allowing for a precise assessment of the amounts actually spent on various policy measures and for the evaluation of their effectiveness.

Within the MOF, there is an Office of National Agricultural Comprehensive Development, an agency with its own organisational structure. This agency is responsible for the drafting of the agricultural development projects and for managing and arranging corresponding funds (more than RMB 5 billion spent annually for this purpose). These projects involve not only many ministries at the central level, but also co-ordination with bodies at the provincial and local levels.

4.1.5. Ministry of Commerce (MOFCOM)

MOFCOM supervises domestic and international trade and international co-operation. It manages imports and exports of agricultural products and deals with WTO issues (with the Ministry of Agriculture involved in the agricultural trade negotiations). In 2003, MOFCOM took over from NDRC the responsibility for the implementation of Tariff Rate Quotas (TRQ) on agro-food imports established within China's WTO commitments. But for grain products such as wheat, rice and corn, the implementation of TRQs is still administered by NDRC.

4.2. Operational ministries and administrations

4.2.1. Ministry of Agriculture (MOA)

Nominally, the MOA is responsible for a broad range of issues related to primary agriculture, rural areas, and rural economic development and assumes wide responsibilities including: *i)* drafting the agricultural development strategy and organizing the implementation of such strategies once they are approved; *ii)* drafting the agricultural sector's policy to guide agricultural structural adjustment; *iii)* proposing opinions on the reform of the rural economic system; *iv)* drafting the development plan for the marketing system of agricultural produce; *v)* making suggestions and recommendations regarding policies for agricultural prices, tariffs, rural credit, taxation, fiscal support and the distribution of bulk agricultural products. The MOA oversees China's formal extension network and handles day-to-day work relating to the State Council's Leading Group for Poverty Relief and Development.

However, it is considered that the actual influence of the MOA on agro-food and rural policies is rather limited, in particular compared with institutions presented in the previous section. However, it may be expected that with further market and service orientation of China's agro-food sector, and the diminishing role of planning and institutions rooted in the centrally planned economy, the MOA will be given a stronger co-ordinating role in this sector.

4.2.2. Ministry of Water Resources (MWR)

The MWR is responsible for formulating policies, regulations, and development strategies and plans for water conservation. It has a mandate that extends from the construction and supervision of hydroelectric projects to flood control, irrigation, drainage and sometimes transportation. As water resources are critical to agricultural production, but are not always well-used, the role of the MWR is increasingly important.

4.2.3. Ministry of Land and Resources (MLR)

The MLR is responsible for the investigation, planning, management, protection and rational utilization of natural resources – including land, mineral and marine resources. The responsibilities of the MLR also include the protection of the lawful rights and interests of the owners and users of land and other natural resources, including mediating and coming to decisions regarding major disputes over rights. The ministry's 14 departments include an arable land protection department, a land registration department, a land use department, a law enforcement department, an international co-operation department and a science and technology department. The land tenure system in China remains very unclear (see Section 6).

4.2.4. Other ministries and co-ordination problems

Many other ministries, administrations and government-held institutions also deal with agriculture and rural development issues. They include *e.g.* the All-China Federation of Supply and Marketing Co-operatives (AFSMC), the State Forestry Administration, the Ministry of Science and Technology (MOST), the Ministry of Health (MOH), the Ministry of Education (MOE), the Ministry of Civil Affairs, the Ministry of Labour and Social Security (MOLSS), the General Administration of Quality Supervision, Inspection and Quarantine (AQSIQ), the State Food and Drug Administration, the ABC and the ADBC. Their responsibilities vary from the supply of agricultural inputs (*e.g.* AFSMC) and the provision of social services in rural areas (*e.g.* MOH, MOE and MOLSS) to the supply of preferential credits for agricultural and rural businesses (*e.g.* ADBC).

In general, horizontal co-ordination of policy implementation across ministries should be assured by the higher ranking commission/ministry and the vertical co-ordination by a selected ministry having its branches and offices at different vertical levels. However, in practice, co-ordination is very complex as the whole agro-food management system is a mixture of institutions still carrying characteristics of the planned economy and those charged with the implementation of policy measures based on market principles. Quite often their functions are over-fragmented and overlapping. It is generally believed that in total 14 ministries and commissions are directly involved in governing agriculture and its upstream and downstream sectors. Among them eight are involved in the management of the quality and safety of agro-food products, eight are responsible for agricultural investment, six for processing and allocation of farm products and five for the provision of inputs (Liang, 2003).

5. Grain market organisation system

Despite the overall trend towards liberalization, grain production, pricing, marketing, and distribution continue to be subject to a large amount of government control through the state procurement system, minimum purchase pricing and state trading. Moreover, while the government tends to preserve some functions which are characteristic of the command economy, *e.g.* the management of grain balances, it applies other policy measures such as minimum prices and, most recently, direct payments for grain producers. Therefore, each time a new policy measure is introduced, a new institution for its implementation is added or the existing ones are charged with additional functions. It makes the administrative framework supporting the grain policy of China's government particularly complex (see Box 16.1). For example, in mid-2004, the government issued a new regulation liberalizing grain marketing in China by allowing qualified non-state firms to purchase, sell, store and process grains. If this regulation is effectively implemented, a large part of the administrative framework presented in Box 16.1 would need to be dismantled. However, the government wants to maintain the "provincial governor grain-bag responsibility system", first introduced in 1995, which makes the governors of provinces responsible for securing local balances of grains and to contribute to the national balance of grains. To secure these balances, the governors will in all likelihood tend to preserve the current grain administration system with state-linked enterprises playing a key role.

6. Ambiguous institutional and legal framework: the case of land tenure

China had an active land market in the early 1950s, but land tenure practices have undergone several major transformations since then. The lack of incentives and the

Box 16.1. **China's grain administration system as of the beginning of 2004**

Planning and management strategies. The NDRC manages China's grain balances. The State Grain Administration (SGA), falling under the NDRC umbrella, is in charge of the national grain procurement and distribution system, guides the national grain sector and administers China's central grain reserves. It also works out plans for the construction of national grain distribution, storage and processing facilities. The provincial governments administer the regional grain supply and demand balances.

Grain management laws, policies and guidelines. The MOA is responsible for initiatives related to grain production, including guidance on the readjustment of crop production and its allocation. The SGA drafts plans, laws and reform programmes for the national grain distribution and grain reserve system and supervises their implementation.

Grain prices. The NDRC technically has oversight over grain purchasing and marketing prices. The SGA proposes a framework for grain purchasing prices, including minimum guaranteed purchasing prices for rice. The Grain Bureaus implement them.

Trade. The NDRC fixes grain export and import plans. MOFCOM is responsible for grain trade negotiations, dispute settlement and import quota allocation. COFCO is the state trading company responsible for the implementation of the government trade policies for agricultural products, including grains. The MOA suggests policies related to major imported farm products and to import duties. It is responsible for exports and imports of seeds, including grain seeds.

Grain reserves. The SGA supervises the management and maintenance of grain reserves and makes proposals as to the appropriate level and distribution of grain reserves together with plans for procurement, marketing, import and export of the central grain reserves. Subsequently, it supervises the implementation of the plans agreed upon by NDRC and other central bodies as well as inspecting the central grain reserves' stock for its quantity, quality and safety. The SGA also drafts and implements reform proposals for the national grain distribution system and provides guidance to the China Grain Reserves Corporation (Sinograin) and regional and local Grain Bureaus. Sinograin is responsible for the purchase, storage, delivery, processing, and import/export operations for the central grain reserves. The Grain Bureaus manage domestic marketing of grains at provincial, prefecture and county levels. The Agricultural Development Bank of China (ADBC) relies on loans from the People's Bank of China (PBC) to supply on preferential terms funds destined for Grain Bureaus for the purchasing, storage and marketing of grains.

Grain quality control. The SGA works with the General Administration of Quality Supervision, Inspection and Quarantine (AQSIQ) to manage grain quality standards. It formulates technical standards for grain storage, handling and transportation, and oversees their implementation. The AQSIQ is responsible for the implementation of quality standards, inspection and quarantine of grains and grain products as well as for the sanitary supervision of grain imports and exports. The MOA drafts laws and regulations on plant quarantine and monitors their implementation.

Grain marketing and processing. The NDRC and the MOA are responsible for building the farm produce market system. The NDRC is also responsible for food processing policy, while the Light Industry Association provides services and advice to the value-added industries and enterprises.

> Box 16.1. **China's grain administration system
> as of the beginning of 2004** (cont.)
>
> **Input supply.** The NDRC prepares overall plans for input supplies. Several enterprises under the SASAC (including Sinopec, Sinochem and the All-China Federation of Supply and Marketing Cooperatives [AFSMC]) are involved in the distribution of inputs. AFSMC is responsible for the management of supplies of agricultural inputs, including for grain production. The MOA is responsible for the organisation of quality supervision, inspection and registration of chemical fertilisers, pesticides and seeds. It is also responsible for the examination and approval of crop seeds. The MOA also draws up regulations on farm mechanization, industrial policies and technical standards for mechanized operations in agriculture.
>
> **Research, vocational training and extension.** The MOST manages key agricultural science and technology research programmes and demonstration projects, including those linked with grain production. While the MOA oversees the formal agricultural extension system, the SGA also provides vocational training, guides and promotes technological adoption, and is active in related agricultural extension work.

difficult management burdens inherent in the collective system (1958-78) ultimately gave way to reforms that restored the farm household as the main unit of production. Currently, farmland is *de facto* owned by village collectives, which extend land lease contracts to individual farm households.

Between 1978-84, the first round of lease contracts was granted for periods of 15 years in the framework of the household responsibility system. To maintain the egalitarian access to land which was a hallmark of the collective system, households were generally allocated rights to land on a per capita basis (some villages also took the number of workers into consideration). A new round of leases, typically for 30 years, was completed at the beginning of the 2000s. Farmers pay for their leased land with a proportion of their production or with a cash equivalent. The 1984 directive sanctioning the household responsibility system, explicitly extended to farm households the right to rent their land to other households, and most villages now allow households to exercise this right. A growing land rental market has developed, but land rental arrangements between farmers tend to be very informal and short-term.

Within this general framework there are many regional differences. In fact, surveys indicate that land-tenure rights differ from village to village, even within one county or township area, and that local government officials have an important influence in determining local land tenure regulations (OECD, 2002; Krusekopf, 2001). In general, as ownership rights to land are not clearly defined, these rights are diluted across various levels of authority and leave considerable scope for arbitrary decisions to be made by local leaders (see Box 16.2). This can lead to conflicting situations between village leaders and farmers, both in cases of administrative reallocations of land and when local leaders at the township, village or *xiaozu* level, assuming the role of landowners, decide to lease land to external investors without consensus from local farmers and without proper compensation for lost access to land.

The egalitarian distribution of land use rights led to a very fragmented land use pattern in China with an average farm operating on just 0.5 hectares. The government continues to make statements about the need to rationalize farms and achieve the (presumed) benefits of

> **Box 16.2. The distribution of land rights across levels of authority**
>
> **National government.** The central government establishes national land laws and directives that provide guidelines for local policy makers.
>
> **Provinces.** The implementation of general laws differs across provinces. For example, while the central government's policy is to extend the length of lease contracts to 30 years, some provinces strongly support such policy and discourage reallocation activity, but others have been less supportive and allow for the frequent reallocation of plots of land among households.
>
> **Counties.** County governments are responsible for the overall planning of land utilization within their respective jurisdictions. Their duties also include issuing Land Contract Certificates to farmers, ratifying the conversion of farmland to non-agricultural uses. It is only at the county level and above that land can be approved for conversion to non-agricultural uses, with the approval level required increasing progressively in accordance with the area of land being considered for conversion.
>
> **Townships.** In some areas, townships may influence village land policies, including village-wide land reallocations. A township district contains roughly 10-20 villages.
>
> **Villages.** China's villages typically comprise between 300 and 500 households. Village leaders usually have ultimate authority on land allocation, but often delegate some or all of this authority to *xiaozu*.
>
> **Xiaozu.** These are groups of 30 to 40 households (remnants of production teams of the collective era). *Xiaozu* are often the *de facto* collective owners of the land, but generally work with village leaders on land allocation. *Xiaozu* leaders may periodically reallocate land among member households, usually to provide land for new households at marriage but occasionally based on births and deaths in households. Such reallocations occur every three to five years, but currently they are less frequent in more developed villages, which may be less attached to egalitarian rules.
>
> **Households.** Households are allocated rights to use land, usually several non-contiguous small plots. Specific rights on each plot may vary, but are mainly the right to farm the land for a finite period and to keep or sell the produce. Individuals do not have rights to the land, but farm the land allocated to their household. Farmers take most of the production decisions on their land, but the land must stay in agricultural production. Villages sometimes impose compulsory planting requirements on some of the land allocated to farm households. For example, households are required to produce and deliver a fixed amount of grain to the state, although the grain delivery obligation has not been enforced in many provinces in the last few years. More recently, some villages have sought to promote the cultivation of specific cash crops, and have imposed compulsory planting requirements on some plots. Some villages allow land to go fallow, but others enforce fallow taxes.
>
> Source: Lohmar et al. (2002).

"scale farming", but as the current system leaves limited room for land market transactions, it substantially slows the natural process of concentration of land resources in the hands of most effective farmers. Further growth in land rental transactions may be constrained by ambiguity over land tenure rights. Moreover, the collective's right to reallocate land introduces tenure insecurity since households cannot count on being allocated the same land in the future, thus undermining their investment incentives.

7. Future challenges

Continued reforms in China's agro-food sector will entail further liberalization of production, pricing, and input and output marketing policies, stronger government support to a market environment and renewed government emphasis on the provision of services and infrastructure. China's WTO accession has stimulated reforms undertaken so far and provides a firm basis for reforms that need to be undertaken in the future. However, to support reforms, there is a need for a new organisational structure to design and implement agricultural policies. While this structure needs to be streamlined to avoid overlapping and to ease the decision-making process, the institutional reform should not be guided by the accumulation of all existing functions in the hands of a smaller number of institutions or just one, as it is sometimes suggested. The reform process should rather focus on the redefinition of the role of government and a clear definition of agricultural policy objectives. Only then can an appropriate organisational framework to accomplish stated policy objectives be defined.

In particular the notion of the "role of government" needs to be re-examined. It is important to determine on **when to assist, when to enable, and when to simply get out of the way** – allowing farmers, rural citizens, and agro-rural enterprises to make their own decisions. In particular, the government needs to de-emphasize its **planning** activities and focus more on **enabling** activities. Therefore, government processes and psychology must continue to evolve from a top-down hierarchical "we know what is good for you" paternalistic approach to one that is service-and-needs oriented, responsive and accountable. For example, as discussed in the previous section, "economies of scale" and "economies of specialization" in farming cannot be imposed from above. The circumstances in which they exist must be discovered and exploited by farmers themselves, but it is the government's role to allow land markets to function.

Self-disciplining incentive systems are preferable to "bricks and mortar" institutions. Creating and building new institutions can be an important contributor to "getting governance right". However, it is often better to reflect and focus on appropriate incentive systems rather than a "bricks and mortar" approach to establishing institutions. Institutions can develop their own vested interests and sometimes even perpetuate problems (and their own mandate) rather than resolve them. If carefully constructed, incentive systems can create an environment where firms and enterprises discipline themselves, without need of additional outside intervention or guidance.

Government bodies at all levels must continue their efforts to be more service oriented. In the past, many government bodies focused on production and capital. Line ministries typically had commercial enterprises under their umbrella. With the past emphasis on achieving goals set out in a central plan, the management style was top-down and focused on meeting specific output and physical capital objectives rather than meeting the needs of consumers, citizens and society. Line ministries must now re-calibrate their efforts and focus more on "enabling" the agro-food sector and rural economy. They must become more "client-focused" and service-oriented, and pay more attention to the needs, bottlenecks and challenges facing their clientele (farmers, the agro-food sector, rural enterprises and rural citizens). A wide-range of public service institutions – such as a rural education system; an agricultural research and extension system for farmers; an agricultural price information system; a sound, scientific, consistent and transparent system to determine the risks of pest and disease; agricultural and food product quality standards and institutions enforcing their implementation, to name just a few – are needed to improve the standard of living of rural populations and to allow China to be more competitive on international markets.

Correspondence principle. Governments must make greater efforts to establish a more level playing field between rural and urban interests, across regions and across ownership types. Failure to do so undermines incentives, efficiency and productivity. Between levels of government and localities, greater efforts must be made to establish a correspondence between authority, accountability, responsibility and resources available (including financial). The current trend is toward off-loading and increasing local-level responsibility without the commensurate transfer of funds and other resources. This increases off-budget and extra-budgetary activities, undermines transparency and accountability and increases opportunities for corrupt or opportunistic behaviour. In this respect, the role of government in terms of the delivery of public goods and services at the local level is in need of serious review, taking care to ensure consistency across jurisdictions and that the responsibilities do not exceed the resources available.

Problems must be properly diagnosed, focusing on causes rather than symptoms. For example, the persistence and success of often-persecuted informal rural credit institutions is really an indication of restrictive finance policies and of the failures and lack of flexibility and responsiveness within the formal financial sector. In this context, the incidence and magnitude of informal financial transactions suggest that these activities play a positive role in improving the lives and prospects for China's farmers and rural households (Tsai, 2002; OECD, 2004). Another example is the spontaneous farmer associations which, in spite of limited resources, have managed to fill gaps in services which formal institutions charged with agricultural extension, agro-food marketing and other services have not addressed. Rather than being suppressed, these symptoms may actually be solutions in the making.

Don't pick winners. Create circumstances that allow winners to emerge. Few people are omniscient, whether they are in the public sector or in the private sector. Rather than being prescriptive and attempting to "pick winners" with respect to the forms and scale of institution, enterprise, firm or farm deemed desirable or appropriate, it may be more advisable to continue taking steps to "level the playing field" and allow winners to emerge.

Promoting competition: eliminating institutional fiefdoms in the agro-food value chain. China's primary agriculture and retail sector are increasingly responsive. But farmers and retailers have been handicapped by transportation bottlenecks, jurisdictional fiefdoms of input suppliers and value-chain intermediaries. This taxes producers, retailers and consumers alike, reducing what producers receive and increasing consumer prices, while also lowering choice (Gilmour and Cheng, 2004). Empirical analysis and historical experience, both in China and elsewhere, show that sectors and enterprises that have been protected or coddled as a result of being designated a pillar of the economy are less efficient and responsive than those that are not afforded such protection (Phillips and Shen, 2003; Gilmour and Cheng, 2004). Managers of protected enterprises, including in the agro-food chain, do not always focus on efficiency and profits but, instead, are distracted by communal, social and political considerations. Overall, efforts to promote choice for producers and consumers and encourage competition across geographic boundaries and institutional jurisdictions will foster growth and improve welfare.

Notes

1. This chapter was written by Andrzej Kwiecinski, Agricultural Policies in Non-member Economies Division, Directorate for Food, Agriculture and Fisheries, OECD and Brad Gilmour, Agriculture and Agri-Food Canada.

2. The No. 1 Document is roughly equivalent to the State of the Union address in the United States.

3. For a more in-depth view on the role of SASAC see Chapter 10 on corporate governance in China.

Bibliography

Asian Development Bank (2002), *The 2020 Project: Policy Support in the People's Republic of China*, Manila.

Chen, X., W. Zhang and Z. Li (2003), "Some Views and Proposals on the State Asset Management System", *China Development Review*, 5(1), State Council Development Research Centre, pp. 21-42, Beijing.

Crook, F., S. Langley and F. Tuan (2002), *An Analysis of PRC Government Involvement in Domestic and Foreign Trade of Wheat, Rice, Corn and Soybeans and Soybean Products*, USDA-ERS, Washington.

Gilmour, B. and L. Brink (2001), "China in the WTO: Implications for International Trade and Policy Making in Agriculture", in *China in the Global Economy. China's Agriculture in the International Trading System*, OECD, Paris.

Gilmour, B. and G. Cheng (2004), "Enabling China's Agri-Food Sector: Responding to Challenges with Foresight, Infrastructure, Institutional and Enterprise Reform", in Tso, T.C. et al. (2004), *Dare to Dream: Vision of 2050 Agriculture in China*, Ideals Institute and Chinese Academy of Science.

Han, J. (2003), "Suggestions on Policy Issues Concerning Current Agriculture and Rural Economy", *China Development Review*, 5(1), State Council Development Research Centre, pp. 63-73.

Krusekopf, C.C. (2001), "Diversity in Land Tenure Arrangements Under the Household Responsibility System in China", Has China Become a Market Economy?, International Conference on the Chinese Economy, Clermont Ferrand, 17-18 May.

Liang Tiangeng (2003), "Reform of the Agricultural Administration System at the New Stage", Proceedings of the International Workshop on Agricultural Administration, China Agricultural Science and Technology Press, Beijing.

Lohmar, B (2002), "Market Reforms and Policy Initiatives: Rapid Growth and Food Security in China", *Special Report: Food Security Assessment*, USDA-ERS, Washington, pp. 21-32.

Lohmar, B., A. Somwaru and K. Weibe (2002), "The Ongoing Reform of Land Tenure Policies in China", *Agricultural Outlook*, USDA, September.

Phillips, K and K. Shen (2003), *What Effect Does the Size of the State-Owned Sector Have on Regional Growth in China?*, David M. Kennedy Center for International Studies, Brigham Young University, April.

OECD (2002), *China in the World Economy*, "The Domestic Policy Challenges", OECD, Paris.

OECD (2004), *China in the Global Economy*, "Rural Finance and Credit Infrastructure in China", OECD, Paris.

State Council (2004), "The Suggestions of the Central Committee of the Communist Party of China and the State Council on Policies for Boosting Growth in Farmers' Income", Beijing.

Tsai, K (2002), *Off Balance: The Unintended Consequences of Fiscal Federalism in China*, John Hopkins University, Department of Political Science, Baltimore.

Zou Lan (2004), "The Influence of China's Think Tank on Government's Policy Formulation in Financial and Environmental Arena as Well as Management of Public Crisis", *China Strategy*, Center for Strategic and International Studies, Washington, 30 January.

PART IV

Ensuring Sustainable Development

PART IV

Chapter 17

Environment and Governance in China

Table of Contents

Summary 491

Environment and Governance in China 493
  1. Background and purpose of the report 493
  2. Good governance and environment 494
    2.1. Key elements of good governance in environmental policies 494
    2.2. Why is good governance needed in China's environmental policy? 495
  3. Description of the framework for environmental policy 496
    3.1. Environmental policy planning 496
    3.2. Institutional framework 498
    3.3. Regulatory framework 501
  4. Governance challenges 504
    4.1. Environmental policy planning 504
    4.2. Institutional framework 507
    4.3. Regulatory framework 512
  5. Access to environmental information and public participation
     in environmental decision-making 516
    5.1. Provision of, and access to environmental information 517
    5.2. Public participation in environmental decision-making 519
    5.3. Suggestions for promoting access to information
        and public participation 523
  6. Conclusions and recommendations 525
    6.1. Progress in developing and implementing environmental policies
        and key challenges 525
    6.2. Contradicting responsibilities at different levels 528
    6.3. Recommendations for better governance in environmental policies 528

Notes 531

Bibliography 532

List of boxes

17.1. Government bodies involved in environmental management in China 500
17.2. Involvement of administrative and sectoral units in environmental
      protection at sub-national level 502
17.3. Regulatory instruments applied in China's environmental policy 503
17.4. Water management in Sichuan Province 506
17.5. China Council for International Co-operation on Environment
      and Development 509

17.6. China's discharge permit system 513
17.7. Environmental campaigns by the Chinese Government 515
17.8. Weekly and daily environmental reporting 518
17.9. Environmental information disclosure and performance rating in China 520
17.10. Forms of public participation in environmental decision-making in China..... 522
17.11. Key non-governmental actors 524
17.12. Examples of international instruments on strengthening the use of environmental information and public participation in decision-making ... 526

List of tables

17.1. Examples of environmental targets and indicators in the Tenth Five-Year Economic and Social Development Plan (2001-05) 498

Summary

China has made remarkable progress in sustaining high economic growth rates, raising incomes and lengthening life expectancy. However, the pattern of economic growth, rapid industrialization and urbanization has not been environmentally sustainable. These processes have generated high pressures on the environment, including surface and ground waters, air in urban areas, land and natural resources. This in turn has adversely affected human health and the productivity of natural resources. If the state of the environment continues to deteriorate, these problems will intensify and the potential for maintaining economic growth may be undermined.

China's policies and the institutional setting for environmental protection have undergone several transformations over recent decades. The late 1990s and the beginning of the new century witnessed an important acceleration in the development of a comprehensive regulatory and institutional framework for environmental management and more public participation in environmental policy-making. While there is some evidence that these policies have had some effect, there is still considerable scope for strengthening good environmental governance, drawing on international practices.

1. The current declarative character in environmental planning lacks realism and could be more targeted. This implies strengthened efforts in setting explicit but realistic objectives and targets, evaluating progress in achieving them, providing feedback to policy makers and adjusting priorities on the basis of "results of the ground" and lessons learned. Such an approach requires the participation of relevant stakeholders, including the general public. Analysis of the costs of achieving environmental goals, combined with a robust analysis of possible funding sources, could assist environmental protection authorities in their discussions with other relevant government bodies over the measures, including resources, for environmental improvement.

2. Given that most issues related to sustainable natural resource use and environmental management cut across lines of administrative responsibilities, effective ways are needed to co-ordinate the work of different bodies, to reduce overlaps and contradictions, maximize synergies and adjust problems. The elevation of the State Environmental Protection Administration (SEPA), which is the main government body responsible for the environment, to the full status of a ministry and full membership of the Cabinet could be one important step. This could be accompanied by the creation of a high-level co-ordination and communication mechanism for integration of environmentally-related decision-making within the whole government.

3. Taking account of China's size and complexity, a thorough review of relations across levels of government with regard to environmental protection policy could help identify ways to make the system more vertically and horizontally integrated. This could include assigning more regulatory authority over all but the smallest industrial enterprises to provinces and municipalities and away from counties, and increasing the supervision of

lower levels by higher levels through performance audits and public reporting. There is also a need for strengthened capacities of the staff of environmental bodies and aligning responsibilities with funding. The SEPA and the Environmental Protection Bureaus (EPBs) should concentrate their efforts on "core" public functions and a smaller number of priority issues, and focus on problems which are potentially solvable.

4. Environmental laws and regulations could be made more consistent, transparent and non-discriminatory. The Chinese authorities should launch a review of environmental legislation to eliminate important discrepancies and gaps between the principal laws and executive regulations. The legislative and rule-making processes should be made more transparent to build better relations between regulating bodies, the regulatees and the public. Regulatory impact analysis (RIA) applied in a number of OECD member countries can improve the quality of legislation by eliminating contradictions between various regulations, reducing the costs and enhancing effectiveness.

5. Promoting public participation in environmental decision-making should continue to be one of the key objectives of the state and local environmental administration. By enhancing environmental awareness, encouraging environmental associations, and providing training, the public can be mobilized to contribute constructively to policy development and implementation. The government could consider how barriers to the development of environmental non-government groups could be removed. Studying mechanisms for public participation in OECD member countries can help to apply the best approaches and procedures in a way that is adapted to the Chinese context.

Environment and Governance in China[1]

1. Background and purpose of the report

Rapid economic growth, stimulated by a policy of reform and opening-up, has helped China to increase the wealth of the population and provided employment and development opportunities. However, the rapid growth has not come without a price: natural resource depletion and environmental pollution of air, water and soil have been unintended, but significant, side effects.

Chinese society and decision-makers have increasingly realised the seriousness of environmental problems and the related economic and human health costs. In a variety of official government statements, Chinese leaders have accorded priority status to environmental protection. As the General Secretary of the Communist Party of China (CPC) Hu Jintao stated: "China needs the growth which balances development between urban and rural areas, between the regions, between social and economic aspects, between human and nature, and between domestic and international policy development."[2] A reduction of environmental pollution and better management of natural resources have become priorities for state policies.

Environmental protection and sustainable development have been proclaimed among the "major tasks and important targets" in five-year plans since the 1970s, while the most significant changes in environmental governance occurred in the second half of the 1990s and the first years of the new millennium. The narrow approach of maximizing gross domestic product (GDP) growth without considering other costs, including environmental, is being replaced by government policies at the central and local level that aim at a more balanced growth. This development was stimulated by the adoption of the Ninth (1996-2000) and then theTenth (2001-05) Five-Year Plans for Social and Economic Development of China and then the promotion of the "new development strategy"[3] by the central government. The strategy called for a comprehensive, co-ordinated and sustainable approach to economic development; an approach that takes social and environmental aspects seriously into account. The implementation of the strategy has been supported by important changes in environmental governance structures, the introduction of many new environmental laws and regulations, institutional capacity building and raising environmental awareness among society.

However, the reform of environmental governance is still a work in progress. Many obstacles must be overcome to strengthen the role, effectiveness and efficiency of environmental institutions and policies. This includes creating an effective enforcement system, based on an impartial judiciary, and providing for a greater role for civil society in environmental decision-making.

This chapter aims to identify areas where further efforts to design and implement environmental policies that promote economic development should be made while at the same time enabling social and environmental objectives should be met. The chapter is divided as follows:

- Section 2 examines relations between good governance and environmental policies, and the benefits of linking them more closely.
- Section 3 provides a brief description of key developments in environmental policy planning, the development of environmental institutions and the application of policy instruments in China.
- Section 4 evaluates the developments presented in Section 3 and suggests areas for further action.
- Section 5 discusses the rationale for involving the public in environmental management. This section also presents examples of improved public access to information and public participation in environmental decision-making.
- Section 6 summarizes key conclusions and recommendations for further reform.

2. Good governance and environment

Good governance is defined as "the ability to assure effective, efficient and democratic functioning of government institutions through sound, coherent and inclusive processes, for the national and global common good" (OECD, 2000a). Environmental protection is an important public policy concern in OECD and other countries, as a healthy environment is an essential human right and an important element of long-term economic and social development (OECD, 2001c; OECD, 2001d). This part of the report presents the basic relations between good governance and environmental policies and the benefits of linking them more closely in China.

2.1. Key elements of good governance in environmental policies

Over the years, the traditional view of environmental issues as externalities has gradually been replaced by a more proactive view of environmental management that stresses its potential economic and financial benefits and its contribution to establishing better governance and sustainable development practices. As a result, government regulations and institutions in OECD member countries have gone through major changes during the last decade (OECD, 2000b; OECD, 2001b; OECD, 2004). Environmental bodies in OECD member countries have been at the forefront in developing good governance practices, notably by fostering greater openness and participation in decision-making. Many environmental concerns have been amplified by the public, which has demanded governments to protect and improve the environment as a basic human right.

Progress towards environmental improvement, and sustainable development in general, is influenced by the quality of the overall governance system in place (at whatever level: international, regional, national and sub-national). There are several examples illustrating that good governance supports environmental improvement (OECD, 2002b). At the same time, there are other examples showing that lack of good governance hampers countries' efforts to maximize the benefits of environmental policies and minimize the negative impacts of sectoral policies on human health, the environment and natural resources (OECD, 2001e).

The existence of good governance in public policies is a necessary, albeit insufficient, condition to ensure better environmental management. Improving the state of the environment and sustainable development are two among many objectives of democratic government. Although the institutional and procedural prerequisites for democratic governance are also prerequisites for good environmental management, the latter requires specific elements which are critical to achieving the desired objectives (OECD, 1998a). The most important are:

1. Consensus/science-based objectives (differentiated by time) appropriately reflected in policies, laws and regulations.

2. Appropriate institutional framework for policy development and implementation, including a clear allocation of responsibilities and powers to national and sub-national levels of government.

3. Institutions and instruments for policy integration and coherence, embracing the three pillars of "sustainable development": environmental, economic and social.

4. Provision of information, public participation and access to an impartial judiciary in the development and implementation of environmental policies.

Good governance in general requires the rule of law to ensure the respect and protection of basic human rights; checks and balances between the executive, legislative and judiciary branches; the existence of auditing and accountability mechanisms to review government actions, and a degree of autonomy for local governments. Good environmental management contributes to, and benefits from, good overall governance. It is an essential component of the sustainable development of nations.

2.2. Why is good governance needed in China's environmental policy?

Undoubtedly, environmental pollution and resource degradation are severe in China. They negatively impact human health and quality of life, as well as economic and social development. The key problems (Economy, 2004; SEPA, 2002; Stockholm Environmental Institute and UNDP China, 2002; OECD, 2002a; World Bank, 2001) include:

1. Contamination of fresh water resources with urban, industrial and agricultural effluents and wastes results in decreasing access to good quality drinking water and pollution-related illnesses. More than 75% of the waters in rivers flowing through China's urban areas is unsuitable for drinking or fishing. There have been serious outbreaks of waterborne disease, as well as long-term health problems in riverside communities reflected in rising rates of spontaneous abortions, birth defects, and premature deaths. Water pollution in rivers and coastal areas impacts fisheries, aquaculture and leisure activities.

2. Air pollution by particulates as well as other gases from energy production, manufacturing and transport, provoke periods of smoke and haze. By 2002, China had become home to six of the 10 most polluted cities in the world. This adversely affects human health, results in "acid rain" (which now affects about one-third of China's territory, including one-third of its farmland) and contributes to the build-up of greenhouse gases in the atmosphere. Air pollution alone, primarily from coal burning, is responsible for over 300 000 premature deaths per year.

3. Degradation and destruction of forests leads to massive soil erosion and desertification (desert now covers 25% of China's territory).

4. China's best cultivated land is being lost to unsustainable agricultural practices and expanding urban and industrial areas, as well as to the developing network of roads and railways. Household and industrial waste continue to accumulate.

5. Due to the reasons mentioned above, almost all of China's unique and globally significant biodiversity resources are under stress.

A study conducted in 1995 (World Bank, 1997) showed that air and water pollution damage, especially the dangers that fine airborne particulates pose to human health, have been estimated to be at least USD 54 billion a year – or nearly 8% of China's GDP. Furthermore, the analysis of the scale of pollution damage suggests that real GDP is less than the GDP measured if environmental pollution and other social loss are included into the accounting system. The Chinese authorities have launched a pilot project to reflect environmental impacts in the measurement of GDP, but at present, there are no internationally agreed methodologies for doing this. Many researchers (Rogers *et al.*, 1997) also point out that GDP growth in China continues to significantly reduce the opportunities of future generations to enjoy natural resources and the environmental base for meeting their needs.

The environmental problems in China did not happen accidentally. China's population of 1.3 billion, coupled with rapid industrialization and urbanization as well as rapidly growing GDP per capita, create huge pressure on the environment and the demand for resources. China's coal-dominant energy and industrial structures contribute to serious indoor and outdoor air pollution in cities and rural areas. The 30 million people living in poverty increase the pressures on natural resources and environment. At the same time, China is not a country rich in all resources: for example, water resource per capita is only one-fourth of world average level, and that of arable land is only one-seventh of world average level.

The Chinese leadership considers that environmental degradation and unsustainable management of natural resources have become an obstacle to further economic development and the well-being of the population. Addressing environmental problems has become a state priority and there is a clear recognition that more ambitious and concerted policies are needed to stop further environmental degradation.

Developing and applying good governance in environmental policies in China can enhance the impact of these policies and improve the capacity of the administration to pursue effective and efficient regulations and policy instruments. It will also help to mobilize the information and energies of all concerned parties, including citizens and the regulated community.

3. Description of the framework for environmental policy

Addressing environmental problems requires a mix of policy and institutional actions. The key elements of this mix are: *i)* consensus-based strategies and policies backed by robust analysis; *ii)* appropriate institutional framework for policy development and implementation at the national and sub-national level; and *iii)* instruments for policy integration and coherence, which can embrace three pillars of "sustainable development": environmental protection, economic development and social cohesion.

This part presents the development of policy planning in China, the process of building the institutional set-up for environmental management and reform of China's environmental regulatory framework.

3.1. Environmental policy planning

The changes in political and economic development in the late 1970s unlocked the possibilities for closer co-ordination between economic development and environmental protection. Strategically, the Party and the central government already stressed at that time that sustainable development was one of the key elements to guide the development of the country and that environmental protection was one of the most important parts of reform and modernization. Methodologically, they called for two shifts that have significant impacts on environmental governance, that is, from a "planned" economy to a "socialist market" economy and from an "extensive" to an "intensive" pattern of economic growth.

The preparations for the 1972 United Nations Conference on the Human Environment (UNCHE) gave the first impetus for introducing environmental management within the Chinese Government. The first country-wide discussion on environmental protection was launched in 1973 at the National Conference on Human Environment, a national follow-up to the UNCHE. Subsequently, analyses of the environmental consequences of economic development were carried out by a group of experts and officials under the State Council. This work resulted in a 1974 report *Key Points in the Environmental Protection*.

However, this analytical work was not fully translated into practice for nearly two decades. The first PRC environmental protection law was promulgated in 1979, but it was applied for "trial implementation". The "trial" status was only changed in 1989 when a new Environmental Protection Law was introduced, providing a solid legislative base for existing *ad hoc* enforcement programmes (see Box 17.7).

The beginning of the 1990s witnessed a relative increase in the attention devoted to environmental problems. In March 1991, the then-Premier of the State Council Li Peng stated at the National People's Congress (NPC) session that environmental protection was a basic policy of China. The Eighth Five-Year Plan approved by the NPC in 1991 listed environmental protection among the "major tasks and important targets for the following five to 10 years". However, the Plan, which aimed to improve and better co-ordinate environmental planning, control pollution emissions and the generation of industrial waste, and strengthen monitoring and enforcement, was still implemented more on paper rather than in practice.

The 1996 Fourth National Conference on Environmental Protection was the turning point in the reform of environmental policies. The conference, for the first time, defined explicit environmental objectives, duties and plans for the end of the 1990s and the next century. Former President Jiang Zemin pointed out that "environmental protection is to conserve natural resources and improve the productivity". The conference, again for the first time, placed pollution control and ecological conservation as two parallel tasks. The conference also recommended approaches to control "total amount of pollutants" and described in detail China's "Transcentury Green Project", which included over 800 water pollution abatement projects. After the conference, the whole country initiated large-scale campaigns for pollution control and ecological construction in key cities, watersheds, regions and ocean zones. The results of the Fourth National Conference provided important inputs to the provisions of the Ninth Five-Year Plan for the Social and Economic Development of China.

The subsequent Tenth Five-Year Plan for Social and Economic Development, adopted in 2000, contained a specific Five-Year Plan for Environmental Protection. The environmental plan set new goals for the following five years, building on the provisions of the previous plan. Emphasis continued to be placed on further reducing all forms of pollution, including reducing the length of polluted sections in the main rivers, reducing acid deposition across China and more vigorously addressing pollution from agricultural sources. Other goals included slowing down the trend in the destruction of natural habitats and improving environmental quality in major municipalities and regions. Table 17.1 presents selected examples of policy objectives and targets established under the Tenth Five-Year Plan.

Table 17.1. **Examples of environmental targets and indicators in the Tenth Five-Year Economic and Social Development Plan (2001-05)**

Issue	Specific targets and indicators
Environmental protection in river basins	Achieving higher water quality in state-controlled sections of seven major river basins and major lakes. Total elimination of the state-controlled sections in major rivers with the lowest quality of water.
Acid rain and SO_2 control	Reduction of sulphur dioxide and total suspended particulates by 10%. Reduction of sulphur dioxide concentration in urban air within the "acid rain control zone" and the "SO_2 control zone".
Urban environmental protection	Improvement of air quality in 50% of defined medium-sized and large municipalities. Meeting relevant water quality national standards by all centralized potable water sources in urban areas. Achieving a 50% rate of centralized sewage treatment in urban areas. Increase the rate of urban waste treatment to 50%.
Total pollutant discharge control	Achieving progress in "one control – meeting two standards" over the period of five years. Reduction of total amount of air pollutants (SO_2 emissions to the level of 19 million tons and industrial dust discharges to the level of 12.5 million tons). Reduction of the total chemical oxygen demand discharge to the levels of 12.5 million tons. Reduction of the total industrial solid waste to 36 million tons.
Nature protection	Increasing the total number of nature reserves to 1 200 with the area of 11.2 million hectares. Increasing the percentage of land designated as nature reserves from 10 to 13% of the total land area. Achieving the rate of forestry coverage to 18.2% of the total land area.

The Tenth Five-Year Plan also introduced concepts of "green" consumption and "circular" economy,[4] which aimed to help to promote economic development with less pollution and to better integrate environmental considerations into economic development. Coupled with the new development strategy, these concepts play an important role in further development of China's environmental policies.

3.2. Institutional framework

3.2.1. Historical development of state environmental institutions

Even though an institutional framework for environmental management in China was only set up relatively recently, it has already undergone several reforms and adjustments. There are more than 2 500 environmental administrative institutions that exist at the state, provincial, municipal and county levels and more than 100 000 people are involved in management, monitoring, supervision, statistical analysis, scientific research and environmental education. However, the institutional set-up is still far from being effective and efficient. Institutional capacity to design, implement and enforce policies lags behind the requirements of curbing environmental problems associated with China's rapid economic development.

The first version of China's top environmental body was the Environmental Protection Bureau, a unit with a staff of 20 set up in 1974 under the State Council. The office concentrated on general environmental planning and had no authority over environmental management at the sub-national level. In 1982, three years after the promulgation of the trial environmental law, the State Council set up the Ministry of Urban and Rural Construction and Environmental Protection, incorporating the Environmental Protection Bureau within its structure.

Subsequent reorganisations in 1984 and 1988 elevated the status of the environmental bureau to a separate office. Its staff size doubled from 60 to 120 persons and it had dual subordination: to the Ministry of Construction and, at the same time, to the State Council's Environmental Protection Commission, which was an important forum for co-ordinating environmental management among different bodies. Eventually, the Bureau was brought out from under the Ministry of Construction and renamed the National Environmental Protection Agency (NEPA). In making this change, the State Council increased the administration's authority, more than doubled the number of staff (from 120 to 320), and signalled that the State Council attached importance to environmental protection. Like main line ministries, NEPA had direct links to the State Council.

In 1998, China's environmental administration was transformed again, renamed the State Environmental Protection Administration (SEPA). But this time it was upgraded to a ministerial rank, however without a permanent seat in the Council. The restructuring involved consolidating the functions of NEPA and some of the Ministry of Forestry staff. Furthermore, the fact that senior officials from other restructured ministries (Geology and Mineral Resources and the Chemical Industry) had been appointed vice administrators of SEPA gave this institution even greater weight. In the new structure, the administration, with ministerial rank and its head reporting directly to the Vice Premier in charge of environmental protection, is in a better position to influence other government bodies. Notwithstanding these changes, SEPA remains far less powerful than some other key ministries or bodies.

An important role in environmental decision-making was played by the Commission of Environmental Protection of the State Council. It consisted of key persons from 31 ministries and commissions and several representatives of large enterprises and the media. The Commission played an active role in policy-making, co-ordinating environmental efforts of ministries and assisting in resolving controversies in the proposed laws related to the environment. However, the 1998 reorganisation dismantled the State Council's Environmental Protection Commission. This change was regarded as a step which weakened the possibilities for proper co-ordination of environmental measures within the State Council.

3.2.2. Current institutional framework

3.2.2.1. National level

Currently, the following government organisations are involved in environmental protection at the national level:

1. The Environmental and Resources Protection Committee (ERPC) of the NPC is responsible for developing, reviewing and enacting environmental laws. It is also responsible for supervising the implementation of environmental regulations and performance evaluation of the government in the environmental sector. In the 1990s, the ERPC developed into a forum for discussing environmental issues of particular concern to the NPC.

2. A number of sectoral ministries and administrations of the State Council are involved in natural resource and environmental management, playing different but sometimes critical roles in environmental management. Their areas of responsibility are presented in Box 17.1. One of the Vice Premiers is responsible for environmental issues in the Council.

3. Within the government, SEPA is the highest administrative body responsible for environmental protection. Even though it does not have a permanent seat in the Council, the SEPA Administrator participates in State Council meetings when environmental matters are discussed.

4. SEPA is responsible for developing environmental policies and programmes and, to some extent, supervising Environmental Protection Bureaus (EPBs) (see below). SEPA, which has a staff of around 300 people, develops regulations only for projects undertaken by the sectoral bodies at the national level, or activities that are of national significance. In all other cases, EPBs implement industrial pollution control rules and deal with enterprises on a daily basis.

> **Box 17.1. Government bodies involved in environmental management in China**
>
> - **State Environmental Protection Administration** (SEPA) is the highest administrative body responsible for environmental protection. It is responsible for developing environmental policies and programmes and supervising Environmental Protection Bureaus (EPBs). SEPA implements rules for projects undertaken by national-level bodies and activities that are of national significance.
> - **National Development and Reform Commission** (NDRC) develops the overall economic plans for the country, including environmental strategies and plans.
> - **Ministry of Finance** (MOF) must approve foreign loans and domestic financial allocation related to environmental projects/programmes.
> - **Ministry of Construction** is responsible for urban environmental issues, especially environmental infrastructures, such as water supply and wastewater treatment plants and solid waste management.
> - **State Forestry Administration** is responsible for forest conservation, afforestation, biodiversity and wildlife management.
> - **Ministry of Water Resources** controls soil erosion, groundwater quality, and carries watershed management outside urban areas.
> - **China Meteorology Administration** has responsibilities in regional air quality management (it also takes part in the climate change negotiations).
> - **Ministry of Agriculture** (MOA) is responsible for management of agricultural chemicals, aquatic natural reserves, agro-biodiversity and grasslands. It also regulates township and village enterprises.
> - **Ministry of Land and Resources** is responsible for land use planning, mineral and marine resource management, and land rehabilitation. It is also responsible for mapping and cadastral (land ownership) management.
> - **Ministry of Communications** shares responsibility with SEPA on vehicle emissions control, the implementation of which falls on the Public Security Bureaus.
> - **Ministry of Health** is responsible for monitoring the quality of drinking water and the incidences of related diseases.
> - **Ministry of Science and Technology** is the leading body in the development of environmental sciences and technology. It co-ordinates various environmental research programmes in the whole country, including co-operation with international partners.
> - **State Oceanic Administration** is responsible for management of coastal and marine waters, including marine biodiversity conservation.

3.2.2.2. Sub-national level

Several administrative units at the sub-national level play a role in environmental protection in China. In each province, EPBs oversee compliance with national and local level environmental and pollution control regulations and standards. These bureaus are part (including their funding) of the provincial administration (Governor's Office). SEPA has limited direct influence over EPBs although it provides them with guidance on the implementation of policies and regulations. Only recently, SEPA has acquired a say in the selection of the heads of local EPBs.

EPBs also exist at the prefecture/municipal, district/counties administration levels. Each work unit within the administrative system reports to both an upper level department of the same functional area and the government of a geographical area. For example, the prefecture/municipal EPB reports to the provincial EPB and at the same time to the mayor's office. Similarly, at the lower level, the county/district EPB reports to the prefecture/municipal EPB and at the same time to the Office of the County Magistrate (or head of a district). For a number of years, townships and villages have not had environmental units. Only in some cases have individuals been assigned to oversee environmental management.

The EPBs have a number of affiliated units, such as an Environmental Monitoring Centre (responsible for ambient and emission monitoring), an Inspection Unit (responsible for enforcement of regulations and collection of pollution charges), a Research Institute (responsible for technical analysis and research) or an Environmental Investment Unit (managing pollution levy funds). Most of these units are public service units (PSUs, see Chapter 2) and have been supported by state funds to provide services for the government and the public simultaneously. Most recently, however, some of them have undergone changes in their status and management which, in many cases, led to commercialization of some of their services. These institutions, now coupled with universities, may in the future provide consultancy services to the government, the public and enterprises on a competitive basis.

Other institutions at the provincial (and similarly at the lower levels) influencing environmental policies include Environmental Protection Committees of People's Congresses and Environmental Protection Commissions of the People's Governments. The Environmental Protection Committees of People's Congresses approve local environmental regulations, review work carried out by the lower level administrations and keep them informed about environmental problems raised by citizens. The Environmental Protection Commissions of People's Governments, which typically consist of high-level officials (directors and deputy directors), are responsible for co-ordinating EPBs work with other government organs. Members of the Environmental Protection Commissions of People's Governments meet on an *ad hoc* basis to co-ordinate activities related to pollution abatement, settle disputes and respond to accidents.

Other administrative units, such as mayor's offices, planning commissions and economic commissions, as well as industrial, finance and urban construction bureaus are engaged in the environmental policy implementation at the sub-national level (see Box 17.2).

3.3. Regulatory framework

Compared to other developing countries, China has a relatively well-developed regulatory system with more then 2 000 laws issued in the area of environmental protection. However, the design and implementation of policy instruments could be improved.

Over the centuries, China's leaders relied on a highly personal system of moral suasion with few environmental regulations and no codified environmental laws (Economy, 2004). The environmental protection system was highly decentralised and typically based on frequent campaigns and mass mobilisation efforts (see Box 17.7). However, China's regulatory framework for environmental protection has been gradually developed over the past few decades. In 1979, the NPC Standing Committee promulgated a provisional version of China's basic environmental law, the PRC Environmental Protection Law for Trial Implementation. This statute required polluters to comply with pollution and waste-discharge standards, directed enterprises to assess environmental impacts of proposed

> Box 17.2. **Involvement of administrative and sectoral units in environmental protection at sub-national level**
>
> **Mayor's offices** take key decisions on large investment projects involving industrial development and environmental protection. They also settle disputes between the municipal EPBs and enterprises supervised by a municipality's industrial bureaus. In some cities, the mayor heads the Environmental Protection Commission of a People's Government.
>
> **Planning commissions** at the county level and above are responsible for reviewing the environmental protection plans of EPBs and for integrating them into local economic and social development plans. Despite these arrangements, environmental and economic components of development plans are not always consistent. This occurs, in part, because different bodies often fail to communicate with each other during plan preparations.
>
> Many **industrial bureaus** play a significant role in day-to-day industrial pollution abatement. A number of industrial bureaus have environmental protection divisions (EPDs) that assist enterprises associated with their bureaus with technical aspects of pollution control. EPDs also help settle disputes and improve communications between enterprises. EPDs have generally more contacts with their affiliated enterprises and know more about their pollution problems than EPBs. In comparison to EPB staff, the educational background of EPD personnel enables them to be more familiar with technologies employed in factories.
>
> **Finance bureaus** manage city revenues and expenditures and play important roles in the pollution discharge fee system. The bureaus also approve the annual plans of municipal EPBs for use of pollution levy funds.
>
> **Urban construction bureaus** oversee the construction and operations of wastewater treatment plants. Some tensions exist between construction bureaus and EPBs over who should collect fees from enterprises that release waste, violating effluent standards and flowing into municipal treatment plants. There are also tensions over the enforcement of discharge standards for releases from municipal wastewater treatment works, which are built and operated by urban construction bureaus.

projects, and required new projects to satisfy applicable environmental standards. This statute also established national and local environmental administrations with powers to enforce environmental legal requirements. Following a 10-year trial period, the formal Environmental Protection Law of the People's Republic of China came into effect in 1989. This legal act now constitutes the main legal basis for China's environmental protection system. In addition, the recently revised Criminal Law makes provisions for criminal sanctions, in case of egregious harm to the environment and/or natural resources. As the 1990s witnessed reform in economic and sectoral regulations, environmental requirements have also been reformed. They gave greater emphasis to a "preventive approach" and to shifting the responsibility to polluters to pay for environmental damage.

Presently, China possesses an extensive regulatory framework that, in theory, should safeguard the environment. At present, provisions for environmental management are included in the regulations at state, provincial and local levels with more than 30 environmental administrative regulations, more than 70 rules, and about 400 national environmental standards. Examples of specific regulatory instruments applied in China are presented in Box 17.3.

Box 17.3. **Regulatory instruments applied in China's environmental policy**

Emission/discharge and ambient (quality) standards

The 1989 PRC Environmental Protection Law authorized SEPA to establish two types of national standards: ambient (environmental quality) standards and waste discharge/emission standards. Ambient standards are illustrated by restrictions on the maximum allowable concentration of a pollutant in water, air or soil. Discharge/emission standards establish a limit on the maximum permissible concentration of a pollutant in industrial emissions or discharge (*e.g.* mercury in a factory wastewater release). Local governments may create ambient and discharge standards for pollutants not specified in national standards, and they may also establish stricter limit values for pollutants included in national discharge standards. For a long time, China's effluent standards only constrained discharge concentrations and were met by diluting wastewater with uncontaminated water. As a result, pilot schemes have been launched to introduce "mass-based" controls on total provincial discharges. In this connection, another programme, called "two compliance policy", has been launched. This programme aims to promote compliance with discharge standards and ambient standards at the same time (hence "two compliance") to help the move from concentration-based to mass-based or total pollution load control.

Discharge permit system (DPS)

Under the DPS, EPBs issue permits that limit both the quantities and concentrations of pollutants in an enterprise's wastewater and air emissions. DPS rules require enterprises to register with EPBs and apply for a permit. EPBs then allocate allowable pollution loads to enterprise, issue discharge permits and enforce permit conditions. Unlike other systems and programmes, the DPS has not been backed by legislation, but is based on administrative edicts.

Pollution control within deadlines

Under the 1989 PRC Environmental Protection Law, government can require polluting enterprises to reduce their waste releases by specific dates. Clean-up deadlines for enterprises can only be imposed by national or local People's governments, but local governments sometimes give EPBs the authority to set deadlines. Enterprises that do not abate pollution on time risk being fined or shut down.

Environmental impact assessment (EIA) and reporting systems

The EIA requires every project with a potential negative effect on the environment to be reviewed to assess its environmental impacts. Project proposals should contain an analysis of environmental impacts and the corresponding preventive measures, and be submitted to the environmental administrative authorities for screening. After the review of the proposal, the applicant needs to engage a qualified firm to prepare an Environmental Impact Report. It is only after the approval by the national or regional environmental administration that the project can be formally launched.

"Three synchronisations" system

The system of "three synchronisations" (called also "Three Simultaneous Steps") requires that: *i)* the design; *ii)* the construction; and *iii)* the operation of a new industrial enterprise (or an existing factory expanding or changing its operations) must be synchronised with the design, construction and operation of an appropriate pollution treatment facility. Once the construction of the project is completed, inspection and approval by environmental administrations are required (for large projects, or in case of a dispute at the local level, the

Box 17.3. **Regulatory instruments applied
in China's environmental policy** *(cont.)*

approval has to be confirmed by the national level authority). If project operations begin without the approval from the local EPB, the owner of the project can be sanctioned. In many instances though, the sanctions have not been applied and there are many departures from the above-mentioned procedures, especially by many TVEs. Overall, however, this programme has played an important role in stimulating investment in pollution-abatement facilities at industrial enterprises, especially at new factories.

Centralized pollution control

Until the 1980s, China's pollution reduction efforts focused on treatment by individual enterprises. This strategy has not always been effective as the costs of individual treatment plants were higher per unit of waste treated than in cases of larger centralized plants. Recognizing the possible economic advantages of building large treatment plants, the State Council and SEPA issued documents requiring governments at all levels to promote centralized control of waste within their jurisdictions.

To complement the regulatory system, economic instruments have been adopted to curtail environmental pollution, especially from industry. Discharge fees are calculated based on concentrations in effluents. These are applied to industrial emissions across China covering discharges of wastewater, waste gases, solid waste, noise and low-level radioactive waste. Pollution levies are collected by EPBs and earmarked for environmental purposes.

Other economic instruments have been introduced. Since 1989, an ecological damage compensation system has been introduced in some provinces and cities. Experiments with sulphur dioxide taxes and product charges have been undertaken in some provinces and cities. The application of these instruments has been expanded over time.

In addition, financing mechanisms for environmental protection have been set up by the government. These included: funds for enterprise expansion and redevelopment, municipal maintenance funds, earmarked grants from revenues raised by the pollution levy and provision for retention of enterprise-owned profit resulting from waste reuse and access to bank credits.

4. Governance challenges

Previous sections presented historical developments of policy and institutional framework in China. This section evaluates these developments and suggests areas for further action.

4.1. *Environmental policy planning*

A review of environmental policy development between the late 1970s and the beginning of the 21st century shows that environmental policy planning has only become more result-oriented, systematic and consistent over the last 10 years, in the context of developing the Ninth and Tenth Five-Year Plans. The scope of environmental policies has become more specific and policy objectives clearer. The plans specified both the priority geographical areas for actions (such as the Yangtze and Yellow Rivers; Three Rivers: Huaihe, Haihe and Liaohe; Three Lakes: Taihu, Dianchi, Chaohu; Beijing municipality; major municipalities areas) as well as topical issues (such as industrial pollution control, urban environmental quality, protection of the rural environment and nature conservation). The Tenth Five-Year Plan in particular contained important new features such as the development of concrete objectives and numerical targets. It also enlisted environmental indicators which were to assess progress in implementing the established policies against established targets.

Furthermore, the policy-making process has become more open to the views of local governments and the public as more consultative meetings have been conducted. A number of new management approaches have been adopted on the basis of experience from the local level rather than based on the views of "technocrats and experts". Furthermore, the approval procedures of draft plans have become more open and transparent. After being drafted by expert groups, the plans are discussed with different stakeholders. These changes have made central government, along with provincial governments, more interested in performance, rather than just the planning process itself. Although no slogan such as "process-to-performance" was explicitly raised by the central government, environmental management in practice became performance-oriented and focused on "impacts on the ground".

Calls for the elaboration of environmental legislation to strengthen environmental compliance, as well as the assessment of needs for environmental investment and an increase in environmental expenditure, were important new elements included in the most recent plan.

However, environmental policy development is still driven by a top-down approach inherited from the planning era. The assessment of the results from the previously implemented plans has been infrequent and not open to public scrutiny. This can impede the identification of "real" (as opposed to "perceived"[5]) causes of environmental problems and limit the possibilities for finding appropriate solutions and calibrating regulations and instruments to increase their effectiveness. Another problem with designing environmental policies has been that not enough attention has been paid to ensuring coherence between national and sub-national policy objectives and targets. This has led to duplication of efforts or leaving gaps in priority areas.

One possible approach to address these problems could be a wider application of a "planning cycle" that is applied in a number of OECD member countries. The "planning cycle" includes explicit objectives and target-setting, evaluation of progress in achieving them, providing feedback to policy makers and adjusting priorities on the basis of lessons learned. Such evaluation has to include relevant stakeholders and answer questions raised by different interest groups.[6]

Policy planning in China also lacks robust financial analysis of the necessary funding to address environmental problems, and more importantly, the assessment of funding sources and developing strategies for closing funding gaps. There are various methods for assessing funding gaps. A methodology developed by the OECD (presented in Box 17.4, together with the description of its application) can be a particularly useful tool in this regard. The explicit presentation of funding gaps, combined with a robust analysis of possible funding sources could be a powerful instrument for environmental administrations in their discussions with other relevant government bodies over funding for environmental improvement.

Box 17.4. **Water management in Sichuan Province**

China's rapid urbanisation is generating a demand for urban infrastructure that is calling into question existing policy, institutional and financial arrangements. The OECD recently concluded a study to develop a strategy to finance wastewater infrastructure in Sichuan Province, including related changes in the governance of the water sector that would need to be implemented (OECD, 2005a, forthcoming).

Tools for analysis

The analysis of the financing of the wastewater sector in Sichuan Province was supported by the Environmental Financing Strategy methodology, which includes a specialized software application developed at the OECD for transition and developing economies.

The Environmental Financing Strategy is a standardized methodological framework supported by a software FEASIBLE© which facilitates the preparation of realistic, multi-year programmes of action for environmental sectors that require heavy capital investments in public infrastructure. It is also used to evaluate the financial viability and affordability of existing infrastructure development programmes and plans. Its targeted users are public sector officials from the ministries (or sub-national authorities) in charge of environmental and water infrastructure.

The FEASIBLE© model requires specific, technical city-by-city data on the present size and state of infrastructure. It calculates investment, maintenance and operational expenditure that would be required to reach specific targets determined by local policy makers. These expenditure requirements are subsequently compared with forecasted levels and sources of finance. All sources of finance (public, private, domestic, foreign, etc.) and all financial products can be simulated. Through this comparison, the model calculates the financing deficits or surpluses, both annual and accumulated. Not only the magnitude of total cash flow deficits/surpluses is presented, but also the structure of the financing gaps can be extracted, *e.g.* coverage of investment costs by various funding sources, coverage of operation and maintenance costs, etc.

These results help policy makers understand where the main bottlenecks are and where/when/what additional policy interventions are needed to facilitate effective financing of infrastructure development programmes.

Results of analysis

The overall conclusion of the study was that, on present trends, wastewater infrastructure development targets would not be met; these targets are broadly comparable to the water-related Millennium Development Goals which aim to halve the proportion of people without access to safe water and sanitation by 2015.

Current financing arrangements in Sichuan Province rely excessively on public budgets, and would be unsustainable in the future. The report analyses various finance options and suggests that users and taxpayers will probably need to pay more. At the same time, it identifies some regulatory and institutional reforms that would need to accompany efforts to mobilize additional financial resources, including the following:

- The institutional arrangements for the wastewater sector at the national level do not allow resources to be used in the most efficient manner. They are biased in favour of construction of treatment plants, whereas the greatest need for capital expenditure is for sewage networks. They should be re-examined.

> Box 17.4. **Water management in Sichuan Province** (cont.)
>
> - The existing tariff system should be reformed. Water tariffs are kept well below cost-recovery levels, ostensibly to protect the poor. However, this is undermining the financial sustainability of the sector and benefiting richer segments of the population as much as, if not more than, the poor. Tariff reform, together with more targeted subsidies for the poor, would lead to more efficient use of public funds and reduce demand for water resources and related infrastructure.
>
> - The projected financial burdens on taxpayers and users suggest that more will need to be done to spread the increase of user charges over time by greater recourse to debt financing. However, this implies that current legislation prohibiting municipalities from borrowing from commercial banks, issuing bonds, or extending guarantees to municipal utilities would have to be reformed. This is turn would involve broad reform of the municipal finance framework to ensure, among other things, that municipalities did not incur excessive debt.
>
> - Relations between municipalities and water utilities should be redefined. Utilities should concentrate on the core business of service delivery municipalities should be responsible for establishing the policy and regulatory framework within which utilities operate. In many OECD member countries, performance contracts between municipalities and utilities specify the responsibilities that each will assume, including the financial contribution that municipalities will provide for utilities. Reform of municipal finance to enable municipalities to raise debt financing would help avoid the current practice whereby local governments offer implicit, unsanctioned utilities to borrow from commercial banks. It is not clear what the level of this "hidden" municipal debt might be.
>
> - The status of water utilities should be re-assessed. Property rights to infrastructure should be clarified. Utilities should be given more financial and operational autonomy, and be held accountable for it. For wastewater utilities, this would mean granting them authority to collect user charges (they do not have this at present) and to use them to finance their operations. This would also generate more incentives for efficiency. Consideration should also be given to merging water supply and wastewater utilities, or at least providing for joint billing and collection. This would increase efficiency, help to address non-payment and help increase the willingness to pay of consumers for wastewater services.

4.2. Institutional framework

Over the past two decades, China's environmental institutional framework has been broadened and strengthened. It included the creation of a central autonomous authority responsible for developing environmental policy. Elevating SEPA to ministerial level strengthened its position within the government. An extensive framework of environmental administrations at the provincial and other sub-national level has also been created.

The measures taken were influenced by broader institutional changes applied to the whole government system, which included streamlining the central administration, decentralization and further emphasis on effectiveness and efficiency in China's governmental structures. Even though the changes consolidated the position of environmental administrations, several features of the existing framework impede their ability to achieve established environmental objectives.

4.2.1. Lack of co-ordination between environmental and sectoral decision-making

SEPA is mandated to develop and implement environmental policies, but it cannot succeed without collaboration with other government bodies, as many environmental responsibilities are shared. Instead of co-operating, different bodies tend to compete for limited resources and influence. For example, SEPA relations with the State Oceanic Administration are contentious with regard to the monitoring and responsibility over the coastal environmental quality. SEPA relations with the Ministry of Water Resources on watershed management are also tense, as both bodies consider watershed environmental management as their priority. Although the State Council attempted to address the problem by setting up watershed water resources protection bureaus, subordinated to both Ministry of Water Resources and SEPA, the results have not been positive.

There are several reasons for such lack of co-operation. Firstly, the historical status of SEPA and the EPBs adversely affect co-ordination efforts. Even though SEPA and the EPBs now have similar ranks to other ministries and bureaus, they are still considered as lower grade bodies, as in the early 1980s they were parts of the Ministry of Urban and Rural Construction and its municipal bureaus. The uncooperative attitude of urban, industrial or other bureaus to EPBs makes it difficult for those, and SEPA, to resolve differences and co-ordinate policies. Secondly, SEPA is often perceived by enterprises, local governments and sectoral ministries as an environmental "policeman" who impedes economic growth (Stockholm Environmental Institute and UNDP China, 2002). Finally, there are no effective mechanisms to co-ordinate activities and to safeguard the achievement of environmental objectives. Such a situation occurred especially after the abolition of the Environmental Protection Commission of the State Council which played an important role in decision-making and in co-ordinating environmental and sectoral policies. As a result, SEPA often develops a defensive attitude towards co-ordination and narrows the scope of its activities to issues which do not require collaboration with other bodies.

In order to improve the situation, the Chinese authorities may consider various options. One could be to elevate SEPA to full membership of the Cabinet with the same rank as other ministries. This arrangement exists in a number of OECD member countries. Another approach could be the creation of a high-level co-ordination and communication mechanism for integration of decision-making within the whole government, similar to the former Environmental Protection Commission of the State Council. Such a mechanism could ensure that environmental considerations are taken into account in setting sectoral policies; overlaps and contradictions would be reduced, and synergies between the work of different bodies maximized. It is also suggested that the activities of the existing China Council for International Co-operation on Environment and Development could provide important contributions to the work of such a co-ordination mechanism (see Box 17.5).

4.2.2. Conflicts between national and local decision-makers

Environmental administration at the local level is susceptible to interference by local leaders due to the relationships between the vertical and horizontal lines (*tiaokuai guanxi*). Lower level EPBs report to higher level EPBs (and ultimately to SEPA), but the funding and supervisory functions are provided by the provincial or lower level administration. The environmental regulatory and enforcement functions have not been given sufficient autonomy from, and authority over, institutions promoting economic development. The local governments often have different views from SEPA on the balance between development and environment, particularly in cases where the local government may be

Box 17.5. **China Council for International Co-operation on Environment and Development**

The China Council for International Co-operation on Environment and Development (CCICED), which was established in 1992, provides a forum for dialogue between high-level Chinese representatives and their OECD counterparts on issues related to environment and development.

The objectives of CCICED are to:

- provide strategic advice and policy recommendations to the Chinese Government on how to ensure sustainable economic growth, protect and improve China's environment, and safeguard long-term supply and safety of energy and natural resources;
- foster international co-operation between China and the international community on critical issues of environment and development, such as relevant planning, projects, scientific development, technology transfer, training, etc.;
- provide advisory service to the Chinese Government on important decision-making in the field of environment and development, and to assess the economic, social and environmental impacts of such decision-making;
- provide the Chinese Government with international experience in the field of environment and development in the context of globalization, information technology, and scientific and technological innovation, and at the same time to assist China in introducing its accomplishments and experience to other countries;
- help enhance China's capacity in participating in negotiations of international agreements aiming to alleviate global environmental problems; and
- play an advisory and assisting role in promoting public awareness and public participation in environmental protection.

The Council is composed of 40-50 high-level Chinese and international members. The chairmanship is held by the Vice Prime Minister of the State Council of China. The Chinese Council members are ministers, vice ministers, and distinguished scholars working on environment and development issues. These Council members participate in the activities of CCICED in their personal capacities.

CCICED establishes a number of short-term task forces, according to need and on a continual basis, to carry out research on the urgent priority issues related to China's environment and development. Council meetings are held once a year to review research reports and policy recommendations developed by the task forces (currently, 12 task forces exist), and make recommendation to the Chinese Government.

the whole or part-owner of a polluting enterprise or municipal activity. When such enterprises are threatened with sanctions because of non-compliance, a different department of the government – typically the economic or development planning department – may intervene to limit the actions of a local EPB. This tendency is reinforced when entrepreneurs or managers of firms hold positions in the local Party committee, People's Congress or in the local governments (Ma and Ortolano, 2000).

This is not to say that EPB leaders are totally subservient to local leaders. Indeed there are cases reported to SEPA each year involving EPB leaders in conflict with local administrations. However, since the senior managers of EPBs are nominated by, and dependent on sub-national administrations, the policies of local governments generally prevail in cases of conflict.

Another factor that adversely affects environmental management at the local level is the incentive structure for career advancement. The promotion schemes are based on performance in pursuing narrowly defined economic development and employment. As environmental problems are perceived by some as slowing down economic growth, they tend to be ignored. Although this pattern is changing, especially by the recent attempt to develop "green GDP", the incentives for environmental protection remain weak. And finally, leaders in China are usually appointed for short-term contracts. This does not allow them to adequately understand existing problems and does not provide an adequate incentive to develop longer term sustainable development visions and strategies.

Most recently, efforts have been made to address some of the problems mentioned above. The appointments of the heads of sub-national EPBs must now be endorsed by a higher-ranked environmental administration. At the same time, lower-level EPBs were strengthened by receiving an independent administrative status.[7] In addition, central government assigned explicitly the responsibility for environmental protection to the provincial, municipality and country/district governmental administration rather than leaving it only as a duty of the sub-national EPBs. However, mechanisms for holding the government administration accountable for achieving environmental objectives have yet to be developed.

Notwithstanding the abundance of experience accumulated in OECD member countries on integrating economic and environmental policies and decoupling environmental pollution from economic growth, and the application of indicators for assessing the implementation of environmental and sectoral policies,[8] these issues are among the most frequently discussed aspects of environmental policy implementation.

4.2.3. Gap between mandate and capacity at the national and sub-national levels

Environmental administrations in China lack capacity for effective environmental management. The 1990s witnessed an increase in the importance attached to environmental issues by political leaders and the enhancement of the position of the state environmental administration. For example, cities as Dalian, Shanghai and Xiamen routinely invest a significant percentage of their local government revenues in environmental protection and have developed relatively well staffed and well funded EPBs. At the same time, however, a gap was growing between the widening mandates assigned to SEPA and the decline in staff and financial resources. This gap extends to many EPBs at the provincial level. The funding of compliance monitoring activities and control of point-source pollution, in particular, are inadequate in relation to the task assigned.

The tensions between EPBs and Environmental Protection Departments (EPDs) of industrial bureaus mentioned before also contribute to management problems. As EPDs have a greater capacity than EPBs to help enterprises to design ways to meet environmental rules, many company managers are more prepared to co-operate with EPDs than with EPBs.

A World Bank survey of 300 townships in China showed that weaknesses in environmental management capacity are even more pronounced at this level (World Bank, 2001). Only a small portion of township governments have designated employees responsible for environmental management. Their functioning is subordinated to the local township management which usually has close relations with village and township enterprises (TVEs). Even though the TVEs have been largely transformed into private enterprises, they still have a very close relationship with local government in regard to tax and employment, as well as personal links. Thus, environmental management at the local level is weak, although 1 422 environmental protection units were established recently at the township level. This was a step in the right direction which could provide a basis for rectifying the situation.

There is a clear need to strengthen the capacities of environmental administrations in China and to align responsibilities with funding. As a matter of priority, SEPA should review staffing at all levels to assess the gap between their obligations and capacities and identify actions needed to bring them into better alignment to address priority issues. One approach could be for SEPA and EPBs to concentrate their efforts on a smaller number of priority issues, focusing on problems which are potentially solvable. Since pollution in some rural areas is severe and there is a lack of appropriate institutions/staff, the institutional setting at this level is in particular need of review.

In addition, mechanisms for continuous training for SEPA and EPB staff should be established to ensure regular and sustainable skill enhancement and information provision on new regulations and approaches to environmental management. Selected local training institutions should become regional centres of excellence. These environmental training and research institutions should cater not only for the personal capacities of environmental and enforcement officers to deal with environmental issues but also strengthen the capacity of staff to co-ordinate their activities with sectoral bodies.

As government institutions in China are often overloaded with administrative tasks and lack time for thorough research of policy options, they need additional support from experts. The establishment of environmental "think-tanks" could open up the market for consulting services in the environmental field which could play an instrumental role in forging effective and efficient solutions in light of the latest scientific research.

4.2.4. Inadequate and contradictory approach to funding of environmental administrations

The lack of financial resources for environmental administrations is creating perverse incentives with deleterious environmental impacts. Many EPBs have become dependent on the pollution levies they collect, which yield substantial revenues and are used to cover their operating costs. They could retain as much as 20% of the non-compliance pollution fees they collect.[9] For many EPBs, the imposition and retention of these fees are essential for their survival. In many cases, EPBs want to establish unjustifiably strict limits to yield maximum income for the office rather to ensure compliance. This approach is reinforced by the central authorities' calls for self-supporting government entities. Local government cuts in funding of EPBs also encourage the drive to maximise fee-based revenues. In this context, EPBs prefer to keep enterprises polluting and paying their pollution levy rather than making them comply with discharge standards and stop paying.

Furthermore, many EPB affiliates generate substantial revenues by conducting EIAs on proposed development projects. This leads to potential conflicts of interest when EPB staff evaluate impact assessment documents prepared by their colleagues in EPB affiliates.

Therefore, an analysis of the financing of environmental institutions should be carried out with the view to removing perverse incentives linked to the role of EPBs in collecting pollution fees and fines (e.g. by reallocating the responsibility for collecting pollution levies to other institutions, such as tax authorities). The analysis should also consider the longer term view of ensuring adequate funding from the national budget, which is the case in many OECD member countries. A recent OECD review of funding schemes of enforcement bodies provides examples of possible approaches (OECD, 2005b).

4.3. Regulatory framework

The regulatory and enforcement framework developed in China for industrial pollution is quite comprehensive as it includes command and control, economic, and other instruments. The system has been continuously updated and expanded to improve effectiveness and cover priority issues. Experimentation in pilot projects has helped improve the design of new approaches. However, the system suffers from a number of shortcomings. These include:

1. ambiguity and lack of coherence in some legal requirements, including the lack of clearly defined rights and responsibilities of different parties;
2. a non-transparent enforcement system, with considerable and largely unaccountable discretion vested in environmental officials and inspectors; and
3. limited involvement of courts in addressing conflicts and penalising non-compliance.

These problems and possible solutions, are described briefly in the sections below.

4.3.1. Lack of clearly defined law requirements and responsibilities

In principle, China's laws on environmental protection contain general requirements with which the regulated community should comply. However, these provisions are not supported by implementation regulations which further define the responsibilities of various parties and make detailed implementation provisions. So, for example, environmental protection departments cannot enforce the law effectively as the legal basis for their actions is lacking. In some cases, such as in the pollution levy system, fees are established by administrative order rather than by higher level laws approved by the State Council. This leaves these regulations open to challenge by enterprise managers, given the lack of appropriate binding legal status. In addition, related instruments, such as permits and pollution levies, are not always consistent, which makes the system difficult to administer (see Box 17.6).

To address these problems, the Chinese authorities should launch a review of environmental legislation to eliminate important discrepancies and gaps between the laws and executive regulations. The legislative and rule-making processes should be made more transparent to build consensus between regulating entities, the regulated parties and the public. At present, most OECD member countries use regulatory impact analysis (RIA) (OECD, 1997a; OECD, 1997b) also in environmental policies. Such analysis includes both regulatory appraisal and regulatory evaluation.[10] RIA can improve the quality of legislation by reviewing the consistency of the proposed laws with existing regulations, reducing costs and enhancing their effectiveness. China may learn from applying this tool in the OECD region. Allowing more public participation in the regulatory process at all stages, from drafting of environmental legislation to enforcement activities, can help to improve policy effectiveness and to address potential inconsistencies early in the legislative process.

At the same time, policy instruments should be enhanced by designing their optimal mixes to increase their effectiveness and efficiency in addressing particular environmental problems. Such mixes could include emission standards, permit systems and economic instruments applied in a coherent manner, and also differentiate these approaches between various groups of the regulated community (e.g. large and small/medium-size enterprises). Recent OECD experience from developing packages (mixes) of policy instruments in OECD member countries and in Eastern Europe could serve as examples (OECD, 2003a).

Box 17.6. **China's discharge permit system**

During late 1980s, SEPA introduced a discharge permit system that aimed to limit both concentration and mass flows of pollution. This was stimulated by the fact that in some cities, although national effluent standards had been satisfied, the quality of watercourses continued to deteriorate because there were no constraints on the total mass of pollutants discharged into rivers. When the permit programme was introduced, it was inconsistent with the long-standing discharge fee system. Although discharge fees are calculated using concentrations in effluent standards, the permit system is based on both mass flow rates and concentrations of pollutants in discharges. Moreover, the allowable concentration in permits can be different from limits in effluent standards. This leads to confusion as to which of the two concentration limits should be met by enterprises. It has also raised the question as to whether the existing concentration-based fee programme should be replaced by a new fee system based on allowable concentrations and mass flow rates in permits. This lack of consistency between pollution limits in discharge permits and effluent standards frustrated many EPB staff. They felt it would be difficult to implement the permit programme without changing the existing fee system. At the same time they felt powerless to change the fee programme because both effluent standards and the method of calculating fees were specified by law.

In addition, the permit system required EPBs to establish, for each regulated enterprise, limits on concentrations and mass flow rates of pollutants in the wastewater released by enterprises. National rules governing the procedure for writing permits did not require concentration limits to be as stringent as effluent standards. Since the concentration restrictions of many permits were less demanding than those applying to effluent standards, it was common to find enterprises that satisfied permit conditions while violating effluent standards.

4.3.2. *Non-transparent and "pragmatic" enforcement system*

In general, local EPBs are responsible for the routine supervision and management of the polluters within their jurisdiction. Firms are required to meet the national standards of pollution discharges which are subject to environmental regulations. In cases where standards are exceeded, existing firms may be sanctioned for excessive pollution or denied registration when applying for their environmental permit.

EPB enforcement personnel, however, have considerable discretion to determine how they will enforce environmental requirements. In the current institutional context, EPBs must exercise discretion consistent with local government priorities. They have little opportunity for taking enforcement action as they are likely to be opposed by local leaders or powerful bodies. In this context, for example, difficulties have also been experienced in ensuring that recently introduced economic instruments achieve their expected objectives. Although the EPBs issue notices to collect discharge fees, the level of the amounts of fees is generally negotiated rather than calculated using formulas detailed in regulations.

The approach applied in China is considered as "pragmatic" enforcement, in which the choice of enforcement action has more to do with the particular case at hand than the strict compliance with environmental rules. Pragmatism is reflected in EPBs reliance on *guanxi*[11] with regulated enterprises. Many EPB staff believe that the way to bring most enterprises into compliance is by developing mutual understanding, providing technical and financial assistance, and negotiating reasonable compliance deadlines.

Such a "pragmatic" approach has been applied with some success in China, but frequently EPB staff stop short of revoking permits for serious violation of their conditions or choose not to fine enterprises for non-compliance in order to maintain harmonious relations (*guanxi*) with enterprises. Accusing enterprises of violating permit conditions is considered to be risky, as it could lead to a "loss of face" of enterprise managers. Some EPB staff also believe that penalising an enterprise may have the opposite effect of removing the incentive for compliance in the future (Ma and Ortolano, 2000).

To address this problem, appropriate compliance assurance strategies should be developed which enable strict, fair and timely response to non-compliance, while creating incentives to improve compliance and rewards for better environmental behaviour. Experience from applying such strategies exists in several OECD member countries, including examples of "compliance assistance" which use negotiations with enterprises over, for example, compliance schedules. However, the limits of such approaches are clearly specified in the regulations and are open for public scrutiny (USEPA, 1992; OECD, 2003a).

In any case, the discretionary powers of enforcement personnel in China should be limited, and delineated precisely in the regulations. More use could be made of public pressure to achieve compliance with environmental requirements. Implementation of such a policy would also require awareness-raising campaigns and capacity building efforts.

Some enterprises in China are also able to escape the supervision of local EPBs by asking local officials to sign permit documents without the approval of environmental administrations. Moreover, some local governments set up "umbrella" schemes, prohibiting the environmental enforcement authorities to inspect, impose and collect fees and fines from firms which are seriously polluting, but are considered as important to the local economy. There are also cases where county governments revoked EPB decisions to fine an enterprise or did not permit the local EPB to apply for a court order to execute an administrative fine. Such interference renders environmental enforcement ineffective. The ultimate check on this system is when the pollution leads to demonstrable impacts on human health and environment.

Other countervailing forces are specially-arranged environmental campaigns by the central government (see Box 17.7). EPBs view environmental enforcement campaigns as opportunities to enhance their credibility with polluters and demonstrate their accomplishments to higher level officials.

4.3.3. Limited involvement of courts in addressing conflicts and penalizing non-compliance

The laws and regulations provide environmental administrations with some administrative powers, such as the authority to issue warnings and impose an administrative fee in cases of minor non-compliance. However, the authorities do not have adequate instruments to address serious non-compliance. For example, they cannot shut down production lines or whole enterprises, suspend accounts of enterprises, or order people to be detained for serious breach of environmental regulations leading to casualties. This is in contrast with the taxation, commercial and industrial government departments that do possess such powers.

Some of these options would be possible through recourse to the courts. However, EPBs rarely use this path. There are several reasons for this. Firstly, in China parties in dispute prefer to resolve their differences using informal negotiations in which

Box 17.7. **Environmental campaigns by the Chinese Government**

In the 1960s and 1970s, the Chinese Government's main approach to economic and social challenges was through campaigns. Policies that were set at the central level and implemented through large government investment programmes were supported by administrative control measures and propaganda campaigns. This approach dominated the response to environmental issues in the early 1980s and continues to be important today. The measures include: banning certain activities, closing down production lines or whole enterprises, large-scale physical investments and mobilizing communities.

The campaign to clean up the Huai River serves as an example. The call to "harness the Huai River" was introduced by the Chinese Government in the 1970s. The river, which runs through four provinces in China's heavily industrialized eastern coast, remained seriously polluted, despite years of pollution control and reduction. As a response, more than 1 000 plants were shut down as part of the "campaign to control pollution". Furthermore, in 1995 more than 1 500 separate projects were launched in support of government priorities, with an investment totaling over USD 18 billion. These investments were accompanied by efforts to crack down on heavy polluters. Between 1995 and 2000, more than 84 000 heavily polluting plants were shut down, including oil refineries, cement plants, thermal power plants and metallurgical mills. Most of the plants closed were privately owned small businesses scattered across the country and far away from the reaches of state-sponsored infrastructure investments.

These examples reveal how the campaign approach has evolved over the years. In the 1970s, campaigns were often sectoral and relied purely on administrative bans and investments. Increasingly, they have become inter-sectoral, relying also on a regulatory framework and are complemented by social measures. This "campaign" approach has contributed greatly to improving some aspects of the environment. Its main strength has been its power to mobilize broad and deep support from across society to address a key issue, often in support of a "magic number"* or a patriotic slogan. Campaigns are believed to ensure the focus of efforts on issues that matter to people – such as pollution – rather than on technical challenges or means – such as emissions standards. These campaigns helped to some extent to set and to illustrate the priorities of governmental policies.

This approach also has its weaknesses, however. In the past, it has not been clear how priorities were set and environmental campaigns initiated. Usually, the launch of a campaign was associated with publicity, but once an issue became less fashionable, implementation may have faded away. Many of the closed polluting plants re-opened, with the support of local governments. Also, once an issue was identified, insufficient attention was given to determining the most cost-effective methods to achieve the goals set, as the campaigns gave an automatic focus on big spending schemes. Campaigns tend to work against sectoral co-ordination since one body has usually been responsible for each campaign. Finally, the *ad hoc* nature of campaigns makes it difficult for the private sector to adjust.

* Chinese numerology has its roots in Taoist traditions and the ancient and contemporary Chinese consider numbers a mystical part of the universe and use them in slogans.

Source: Stockholm Environmental Institute, UNDP (2002), *China Human Development Report 2002. Making Green Development a Choice.*

compromises are made by opposing sides in order to reach a consensus. Third parties often facilitate conflict resolution by means of mediation and conciliation. Although legal institutions have become increasingly important in China, mediation and conciliation continue to play a strong role, particularly in the context of environmental policy implementation. This approach comes from a Confucian tradition which emphasizes moral values and moral instructions (not fear of legal sanctions) as a basis for guiding behaviour and maintaining social order. At the same time, the legal system has been used as a means to implement state policies rather than a mechanism for articulating and guaranteeing the rights of the citizens.

Secondly, the Chinese legal system is still underdeveloped and trained judges are short in supply. Some legal specialists point out other inadequacies of the court system, such as judicial ignorance of the law, corruption, pressures on judges from local governments and high-level officials, and the inability of courts to enforce their own decisions. Furthermore, even when courts are used, the letter of the law is only one of several factors considered in enforcing environmental rules. Courts decide on the cases by relying on official policy, the views of local governments and a court's individual sense of justice and fairness in contractual dealings. Factors as *guanxi* between EPB staff and enterprise managers, interventions by local officials and an enterprise's profitability may lead to outcomes that are far from those specified in environmental regulations.

Additional reasons why courts are not used more frequently include: most EPBs want to avoid the costs of gathering data needed to support legally convincing evidence; many EPBs lack staff with legal training; vaguely drafted statutes often make it difficult to allocate liability; negotiations are more likely to preserve EPB *guanxi* with enterprises and provide a better basis for future co-operation. Finally, the vagueness of many Chinese environmental regulations does not provide an unambiguous basis for judges to adjudicate on environmental issues.

Even though greater involvement of the court system in enforcing environmental requirements may be time and resource consuming, this path should be encouraged. The courts can assist in reviewing the coherence of legislation; they can help to interpret the ambiguities of regulations and review the clarity and propriety of the delegation of administrative authority. More efforts are also needed to ensure the public's rights and awareness of the possibility of bringing cases of serious environmental pollution (which result from deliberate actions by individuals or enterprises) to court. Penalizing serious civil or criminal offences has proven to be an effective mechanism for creating a deterrence effect in a number of OECD member countries.

5. Access to environmental information and public participation in environmental decision-making

For years, little was known about pressures on the environment or the long-term effects of economic activities in China. The environment was seen as a resource to be used, and potentially dangerous consequences were ignored in the face of important political, economic or social considerations. In some cases the repercussions were known, but dismissed as trivial or to be dealt with later. Even when negative environmental effects became apparent, environmental information and decision-making were often kept secret. Information was difficult to come by and action taken to protect the environment tended to be top-down and based on governmental priorities. People who were affected by the activities were often kept aside and had little to say.

Since the beginning of the 1990s, in light of the visible failure of some of the environmental protection policies, the Chinese authorities have been challenged by a rising new force – the public. The media, academic institutions, non-profit organisations and individuals are demanding better information about the state of the environment and expressing a desire to influence public policies. The government increasingly recognizes the potential of these players and is taking steps to encourage them. The following sections show some of the most prominent examples of public access to information and public participation in environmental decision-making.

5.1. Provision of, and access to environmental information

Article 11 of the Environmental Protection Law of the People's Republic of China (1979, amended in 1989) stipulates that "the competent departments of environmental protection administration under the State Council and governments of provinces, autonomous regions and municipalities directly under the central government shall regularly issue bulletins on environmental situations".[12] Similar provisions appear in China's sectoral laws, such as the Air Pollution Prevention and Control Law, the Water Pollution Prevention and Control Law, the Marine Environment Protection Law and the Environmental Noise Prevention and Control Law. In line with these requirements, at the provincial level, SEPA and EPBs provide information about the state of the environment in a variety of forms, including State of the Environment Reports, bulletins, brochures, and news releases.

The first report on the state of China's environment was published in 1990. Its main objective was to make the public and society familiar with the environmental situation. Since 1991 the SEPA publishes State of the Environment Reports on an annual basis. Since the construction of the "Government Online" project in 1998, the reports have also been posted on the Internet.

The compilation of State of the Environment Reports are also carried out by EPBs at various levels. These reports are supported by data from other ministries such as the Ministry of Agriculture, the State Forestry Administration, the Ministry of Water Resources, the Ministry of Health, the China Meteorology Administration, the State Oceanic Administration, the Ministry of Land and Resources and the National Bureau of Statistics. Their contents include information about environmental pollution, state of the ambient environment and information about environmental protection measures. The reports also contain environmental indicators. Starting from 1998, reports include information about biodiversity and climate change. The structures of the reports are based on a methodological framework "Stress – Status – Response" which follows the "Pressure – State – Response" model adopted by OECD member countries.[13]

Governments of provinces, autonomous regions and municipalities directly under the central government issue their own annual State of the Environment Reports. Some provinces issue weekly and daily reports (see Box 17.8) and publish the State of the Environment Reports on the Internet. At the time of writing, reports at city level were not yet being produced.

In addition to State of the Environment reports at national and provincial level, reports on the environmental situation in key environmental management regions and river basins are produced. For example, in 1997, NEPA issued the *Report on Ecological and Environmental Monitoring in the Three Gorges Region of the Yangtze River*, publicizing the ecological and environmental status of the Three Gorges reservoir area as well as of the upstream area ranging to the estuary of the Yangtze River. The main indicators of this

> Box 17.8. **Weekly and daily environmental reporting**
>
> Weekly and daily reports on ambient air quality are released to the public. Information which is compiled in these reports is based on routine monitoring of several common pollutants stipulated in the national Standard on Ambient Air Quality, and assessment results of the urban air quality. In 1997, the tenth session of the Third Environment Commission of the State Council decided that a weekly report system on urban ambient air quality* should be established in 47 key cities in the country. The city of Nanjing was the first in China to publish weekly air quality reports through newspapers and TV. Currently, *China Environmental News* releases environmental quality reports for 46 key cities every Saturday. *China Environmental News* also publishes the air quality indices of key cities on the Internet.
>
> After more than two years of weekly bulletins of urban air quality in key cities, in 1999, the Chinese authorities decided to issue daily air quality reports in 42 key cities, replacing the original urban air quality weekly reports. There are plans for five more coastal cities to be involved in the scheme. The classification criteria and pollutants were also adjusted in daily air quality reporting. The weekly and daily reports have been presented through the media: radio, TV, newspapers, 168 telephone information stations, information highways and street displays.
>
> The release of urban air quality weekly/daily reports has played a positive role in enhancing the standing of the government and increasing the environmental awareness of citizens.
>
> * Monitoring data included such pollutants as SO_2, NO_x and Total Suspended Particulates.

report included monitoring networks, engineering progress, socio-economic development, natural eco-environment status, eco-environmental experimental stations, polluting source emission status, environmental quality status, and human health in the reservoir area. The compilation of the report was carried out by China's National Environmental Monitoring Centre and some 18 other units, including the National Climate Centre, the Eco-Environmental Monitoring Centre of the State Forestry Administration, the Chinese Yangtze River Three Gorges Engineering Development Group Company and the State Seism Bureau. At present, reports on the water quality of key river basins are also published periodically in the newspapers, including *China Environmental News* and *People's Daily*.

However, some reports on the environmental situation (especially in urban areas) are classified as confidential and are available only to senior staff of environmental protection departments at various levels. The *Environmental Quality Briefs* are provided to leaders of environmental protection departments. The main contents and indicators include information about air quality, acid rain pollution, urban river water quality, water quality of the main river systems, pollution of lakes and reservoirs, offshore marine water quality and radioactive environmental quality.

Information technology has been playing an important role in promoting public awareness of environmental issues. The public can express their opinions on environmental issues, and various organisations and individuals have established more than 2 000 environmentally-related Web sites. However, in China, there are significant restrictions on Internet use, as the state provides the Internet service directly or intervenes in commercial Internet services. Citizens may be fined, questioned, or even imprisoned for messages deemed seditious or expressing dissent from government policies.

Recently, central and local governments have been using a more systematic mechanism for disclosure of environmental information to influence the environmental behaviour of enterprises. An example of the successful application of an environmental performance rating and information disclosure scheme in China is presented in Box 17.9. This scheme is a good example of providing a platform for communication between different stakeholders, including the government, industry and the public.

5.2. Public participation in environmental decision-making

Public participation is one of the key concepts underpinning the principles and practice of good governance. Meaningful participation of relevant stakeholders can increase the effectiveness and efficiency of policies. Public participation can also bring legitimacy, improve credibility and accountability of decision-makers and decision-making processes. Stakeholders can identify conflicts and signal potential problems that managers may have overlooked at an early stage. When all stakeholders have a voice and time is taken to find acceptable solutions, public confidence in the fairness of the decision increases, as well as their involvement in their implementation.

Public involvement in decision-making may make it harder to reach the final decision. However, experiences in OECD member countries indicate that public involvement can ensure the durability of decisions and that policies reflect public values. Public participation can also help offset any undue influence of interest or lobby groups over the regulatory system. Benefits of public participation include:

1. improving the quality of decisions (the public may provide site-specific knowledge or offer suggestions that satisfy a wider range of interests);
2. building trust in institutions;
3. resolving conflict among competing interests (resulting in longer lasting and more satisfying decisions, helping to overcome gridlocks);
4. educating the public and stimulating its active engagement in environmental improvement.

5.2.1. Forms of public participation

Legal provisions in China require the authorities to provide information about the state of the environment but also to allow individuals to participate in decision-making processes. The regulations also describe a number of possibilities through which citizens can participate in decision-making. In many cases, however, these mostly depend on the political circumstances in which decisions are made, on the type of decisions that are being made, and on the time and budget available to receive public input.

A tradition allowing Chinese citizens to make complaints to government authorities has existed for centuries and was continued after the political changes of 1949. Citizens can express dissatisfaction to specially assigned offices at various levels of government. To reduce the risk of retaliation, many people send unsigned letters of complaint.[14] In addition to relying on government offices and visits, citizens can direct their concerns about environmental matters to:

1. EPBs, as many of them have "complaint divisions" to hear public concerns;
2. mayor's offices, as many cities have a vice mayor whose responsibilities include environmental protection, and the staff of this office deal with citizens' complaints; and

Box 17.9. **Environmental information disclosure and performance rating in China**

The State Environmental Protection Administration (SEPA) has become interested in public disclosure as a means to complement traditional regulatory instruments. Since 1989, SEPA and its predecessor NEPA have maintained a list of enterprises with excellent environmental performance. Enterprises are included on the list following the recommendation of provincial Environmental Protection Bureaus, after being vetted by a national Panel of Evaluation and Assessment whose representatives include SEPA, the General Environmental Monitoring Station of China and other ministries. By 1997, this assessment had been conducted six times, and 500 enterprises had been awarded the title of "Nation-wide Advanced Enterprise on Environmental Protection". Over time, numerous enterprises have been removed from the list for failure to maintain standards consistent with the award. However, over 180 enterprises have retained their excellent ratings.

Chinese regulators have recently been influenced by the rapid spread of pollution disclosure systems in other Asian countries in the wake of pilot programmes which were initiated by Indonesia and the Philippines, in collaboration with the World Bank.

Since late 1998, SEPA and the World Bank experts have worked together to establish a "Green-Watch", a public disclosure programme for industrial polluters. Adapted from Indonesia's PROPER, the Green-Watch rates industrial environmental performance from best to worst in five colours – green, blue, yellow, red and black. The ratings are disseminated to the public through the media. Two municipal-level pilot Green-Watch programmes have been implemented. Reactions to these programmes have been positive, and SEPA currently plans to launch pilot programmes in other areas, in preparation for nation-wide implementation of public disclosure. The Green-Watch draws on five principal sources of information: self-monitoring reports, inspection reports, records of public complaints, regulatory actions and penalties, and surveys that record characteristics of the firms that are relevant for rating environmental performance.

The rating system incorporates emission information for 13 regulated air and water pollutants. Pollutant discharges are rated by total quantity and concentration. Solid wastes are rated in three dimensions: production, disposal and recycling.

The rating process involves a detailed account of a firm's behaviour in several dimensions. Environmental management is graded with respect to: timely payment of pollution discharge fees, implementation of the National Pollutant Discharge Reporting and Registering Programme, the Standardized Waste Management Measures, and other administrative regulatory requirements. Internal environmental monitoring, staff training and internal document preparation are taken into account. In addition, the rating system considers the efficiency of resource use, its technological level and the quality of its environmental management system.

The rating scheme is comprehensive, voluntary and offers participants an opportunity to discuss their rating with the authorities before it is disclosed. After being set, the ratings are sent to the programme's steering board for final checking and ratification prior to public disclosure. To ensure accurate press reports, journalists are invited to a detailed presentation of the programme, including an explanation of the rating system and demonstration of the software that is used for ratings development.

Source: Hua Wang, Jun Bi, David Wheeler (2002), *Environmental Performance Rating And Disclosure: China's Greenwatch Program*, Development Research Group, World Bank.

3. local People's Congresses and their Environmental Protection Committees, and citizens frequently bring environmental complaints to their elected representatives.

Many cities have established hotlines for residents to report environmental problems. For example, Dalian City (Liaoning Province) installed a 24-hour telephone hotline to receive citizens' complaints about environmental pollution. The city has a radio talk-show that gives people an opportunity to discuss their environmental problems. Frequently, citizens first complain to the factory causing the problems and turn to government authorities or the media only if the factory is not responsive. In such cases, EPBs receive anonymous telephone calls tipping them off about factories violating environmental rules.

Letters, visits and telephone calls to EPBs represent other ways of registering environmental complaints. However, citizens also have the right to sue companies that pollute and EPBs that fail to comply with environmental requirements. Although citizens do not often use their right to bring suits, the number of citizen-based environmental court actions is rising.

In addition, there are more interactive mechanisms which allow the public to express their opinion about governmental policies and to actively influence them. These mechanisms include regulatory mechanisms, such as EIA procedures, and informal instruments, such as government consultations with citizens through town meetings, hearings or advisory panels. Selected forms of public participation and their current application in China are presented in Box 17.10.

5.2.2. Types of non-governmental actors

Few environmental non-governmental organisations (NGOs) exist in China. Organised civil protest movements against environmental problems have not yet taken place as they did in some OECD member countries when environmental problems reached comparable levels. The mass media, however, has begun to play an increasing role in exposing cases of violation of environmental laws and regulations, providing environmental data and information to the public, and reporting on pollution episodes and accidents. This has helped to mobilize the public to exert pressure on business behaviour and governmental decision-making.

The 1996 State Council Decision Concerning Certain Environmental Issues signalled a turning point by strongly encouraging both the media and citizens to expose illegal actions that caused environmental damage. By the late 1990s, the media and environmental NGOs had become increasingly influential. NGOs worked with the media to cover environmental affairs, to publicize NGOs activities and gain public support. The campaign for the selection of Beijing as a venue for the 2008 Olympic Games contained a highly visible environmental aspect due to public pressure.

Although NGOs are starting to play an important role in environmental protection in China, they do not have the same opportunities or autonomy as NGOs in OECD member countries. All Chinese NGOs must be registered and approved by the government. Indeed, many are established to meet the objectives of government authorities. Some administrations at the sub-national level still limit freedom of speech, or the right to associate, effectively making it impossible to form a voluntary group.

The laws regulating the registration of civic organisations change frequently. China's 1998 Registration Regulations for Social Organisations imposes a number of requirements to establish NGOs. These include the need to have a sponsoring institution,

Box 17.10. **Forms of public participation in environmental decision-making in China**

Environmental impact assessment (EIA). EIA is an officially established process of analyses that detail the anticipated effects of planned projects or activities on local and regional areas. An EIA can explore options and alternatives for mitigating these effects. EIAs have recently become critical planning documents in China, and often provide legal ramifications on whether the project goes forward or needs to be modified to reduce potentially negative impacts. China formally issued the Environmental Impact Assessment Act in 2002 which became effective from September 2003. The Act requires all projects or plans to have undergone an EIA before the government can approve it. Public participation is required as one of the key components of EIA. In April 2004, the "Tieben Steel Company" in Jiangsu Province was closed by the central government because it violated EIA requirements. While the extent of public involvement in EIAs varies among different projects, EIAs can provide an opportunity for the public to comment on proposed projects and suggest alternatives. They can also include explicit procedures for government authorities to review and consider written comments, which are then factored into the authority's decisions.

Public hearings. Public hearings have been one of the most widely used approaches in China's environmental management and urban planning. Hearings have frequently been applied by local governments in project site selection and urban planning. The hearings provide the opportunity for all interested parties to express public feedback on proposed projects, laws, environmental policies or planning. Such hearings, announced via radio, newspapers or other media, are particularly important for stakeholders who may not be able to express their views clearly in writing. They can provide a forum where stakeholders can inform each other about their opinions and ascertain where they stand, as well as give decision-makers a sense of the diversity of public opinions. However, in many cases the hearings are simply informative, which may reduce their effectiveness. Sometimes, more emphasis is put on opinions from experts than those from ordinary citizens. Hearings involving substantive evaluation, where different project proposals are vetted publicly or details of project design are debated, are less frequent.

Advisory committees. This is another often-used channel in China. Usually, experts from academic institutions are asked to participate in such committees. Advisory committees allow participation that is more in-depth and continuous, and thus potentially much more influential. In principle, these committees should allow a diverse set of perspectives to be involved in crafting policies, designing and modifying projects to reduce impacts and assessing the distribution of costs and benefits. However, most of the committees involve a narrow group of carefully selected experts.

Document reviews. Provision for public comments of project documents, policy analyses or other background can be an important mechanism for soliciting meaningful public input to decision-making. Over the past several years, especially after the SARS epidemic, the government has realized the importance of information disclosure. Seeking public comments on documents and reports can also increase the accountability of decision-makers – as well as the perceived legitimacy of decisions – since there is a public record of project details and decisions. However, in practice a number of official documents are not available even to experts and non-governmental organisations. Sometimes documents are not freely shared within the government. Documents are sometimes kept as "private products" by different government departments, and disclosed for a charge.

> Box 17.10. **Forms of public participation in environmental decision-making in China** (cont.)
>
> ***Informational meetings.*** Even though government bureaus and environmental managers hold meetings at local, provincial, or national levels to provide basic information about proposed plans and projects, such events are not frequent. They are used on a project-by-project basis and may occasionally affect the project decision-making process. If arranged on a systematic basis, such meetings can help build public support, identify local concerns and develop collaboration with local groups. With the increase of environmental awareness, the public may oppose projects and plans with unfavourable environmental effects more often. In order to allow more informational meetings during the decision-making process, specific legal requirements need to be adjusted.
>
> ***Forums.*** In China, some forums are organised to provide a channel for special interest groups to participate in environmental issues. More than 10 forums have been held in the past, such as the Forum for Women and the Environment and the Forum for China's Young Environmental Entrepreneurs.

fewer than 50 members and a minimum level of financial resources. The regulation also disallows the existence of two organisations in the same field or sector, and in the same jurisdiction. Those organisations that choose to avoid these restrictions and remain unregistered are unable to enter into contractual relations, such as obtaining telephone lines or leasing office space. Nor can they offer personnel benefits like pensions and medical insurance, or have their own bank account, making it harder to attract staff and funding.

NGOs have limited ability to obtain information. Much important information on the environment is considered confidential and distributed only to high-level government officials. Notwithstanding the limited access to information and other restrictions faced by NGOs, they have undertaken campaigns to stop polluting activities and conducted studies of environmental issues aimed at influencing national leaders. Some NGOs carry out research that explores new approaches to environmental planning and decision-making. Some examples of participants in the consultations on governmental policies are presented in Box 17.11.

5.3. *Suggestions for promoting access to information and public participation*

As discussed above, access to information and public participation has progressed in China over recent years. General information about the state of the environment and public policies is provided by the government; citizens can express their dissatisfaction with the decisions of the authorities and, if necessary, bring their complaints to the administrative or the court system. According to media reports, the increased public attention, which resulted from better access to information about levels of pollution charges and penalties, has reduced the abuse of power and misuse of pollution charges. However, the government, official NGOs as well as the media often confine themselves merely to "lecturing" the public on the need to protect the environment rather than informing the public on problems and solutions.

To remedy this situation, the authorities may need to put more effort into gathering, updating and disseminating environmental information that is relevant to their functions. In particular, they should collect information from private parties or any other groups, that

> **Box 17.11. Key non-governmental actors**
>
> **Research institutions, training centres and other academic organisations.** Even though these institutions are not governmental departments, they usually have very close relationships with the government. They are usually non-profit organisations which provide services for the government and society. Originally, the government provided financial support for these organisations, but in recent years such support has been discontinued. As a result, some of these organisations have become profit-making organisations, while others have retained their original status.
>
> **Associations registered in civil departments.** By 2003, there were more than 100 national societies, associations, foundations and promotion societies in China, such as the China Environmental Protection Foundation, the China Environmental Sciences Society and the China Environmental Industry Association. In addition, there are also societies and associations at the local level.
>
> **"Government-sponsored" NGOs.** While these "semi-public" or "semi-official" environmental groups may not be independent, they can still be effective, given their high-level connections. At the same time, such organisations are not likely to rally any large-scale activity against the state or business sector, and the scope of their work is correspondingly circumscribed.
>
> **Registered companies with the purpose of promoting environmental protection.** Since the law required that all non-profit organisations must associate with a government department, some civil organisations have registered as companies. However, their major activities are still non-profit.
>
> **University student associations.** By 2001, there were 184 environmental associations in 176 universities and colleges. This number did not include the very active associations in Hong Kong, China and Macao. A national association has been established to co-ordinate the activities of different universities. Even though students from primary and secondary schools are not excluded from environmental activities, there are very few associations at this level.
>
> **Groups associated with international NGOs, registered or unregistered.** These groups have their own names and organise activities independently. The most popular are "Friends of the Earth" and "Volunteers of Green Garden".

undertake or wish to undertake activities that could significantly affect the environment. Information disclosure and performance rating schemes, currently in a pilot phase, should be replicated in other parts of the country, as these are potentially powerful vehicles which combine the provision of environmental information to the public and generate public pressure on polluters.

Moreover, in the case of an imminent threat to human health or the environment, all information, which could enable the public to take measures to prevent or mitigate harm arising from the threat, should be disseminated immediately.

Not only should information be available and disseminated, but it should also be provided in a transparent manner and be effectively accessible. The government needs to pursue the dissemination of environmental information in the form of environmental reporting and information which can be presented and disseminated by the media. A national report on the state of the environment should also be published and disseminated at regular intervals. Such measures would ensure that information is updated and is easily accessible to the general public. This would certainly facilitate public enquiries on the quality of the environment and impacts on human health. Moreover, the information should become progressively available in electronic databases and on the Internet.

By enhancing environmental awareness, supporting environmental associations and providing the necessary training, society can become an active implementation agent. The government should remove barriers to the development of environmental non-governmental groups so that they could participate more autonomously in the development and implementation of environmental policy. They should be also allowed to raise their own resources for operations, either through membership fees or services provided to the public. These steps would contribute to the emergence of a civil society.

Studying the mechanisms for public participation in OECD member countries can help to apply proven solutions, approaches and procedures adapted to the Chinese context. The adaptation of the provisions of the Recommendation of the Council on Environmental Information on Access to Information and Participation in Environmental Decision-Making[15] or the provisions of the UNECE[16] Convention on Access to Information, Public Participation in Decision-making and Access to Justice in Environmental Matters (so called Aarhus Convention) can provide useful models in this regard (see Box 17.12).

6. Conclusions and recommendations

6.1. Progress in developing and implementing environmental policies and key challenges

Since the inception of its policy of reform and opening-up in the late 1970s, China has achieved remarkable progress in sustaining high economic growth rates and rising incomes that have eased poverty, reduced infant mortality and lengthened life expectancy. However, China entered this period with already heavy pollution loads. Rapid industrialisation and urbanisation have exacerbated environmental problems. The quality of surface and ground waters, air in urban areas, land and natural resources, including forestry, has been seriously affected. This in turn has adversely affected human health and the productivity of natural resources. Environmental quality in rural areas has been deteriorating as a result of expansion of TVEs and intensive and unsustainable farming practices. The Chinese authorities recognized that previous patterns of economic growth were not environmentally sustainable. As the state of environment continues to deteriorate, the potential for maintaining fast economic growth may be affected.

China's policies and the institutional setting for environmental protection have undergone several transformations over the past few decades, reflecting different stages of government restructuring and an increasing emphasis placed by political leaders and the government on environmental issues. Starting from late 1970s, the protection of the environment has received growing attention. Initial steps to create environmental laws were modest and spread over time. The late 1990s and the beginning of the new century witnessed an important acceleration in the development of a comprehensive regulatory and institutional framework for environmental management. Experience which has accumulated over the years helped to improve the effectiveness of environmental regulations and institutions. The public was also more engaged to promote better compliance with environmental requirements.

Box 17.12. **Examples of international instruments on strengthening the use of environmental information and public participation in decision-making**

OECD Recommendation of the Council on Environmental Information (1998)

OECD member countries consider that openness in information and wide availability of public information on environmental issues is conducive to: *i)* more cost-effective policies; *ii)* greater accountability to all stakeholders concerned; and *iii)* increased public awareness and participation. Similarly, public awareness of environmental conditions and risks is considered essential to the protection of human health and the environment. Therefore, in 1998 the OECD Council adopted the Recommendation on Environmental Information. This document calls on the member countries to:

1. Intensify efforts to improve as far as necessary the quality and relevance for environmental policy of data and information systems on the environment and related economic variables, and in particular:
   - improve monitoring and data collection concerning environmental pressures, conditions and responses, including explanatory information about current environmental changes;
   - encourage all appropriate levels of government to collect environmental data in order to enable them to monitor progress in environmental policies which they implement;
   - promote co-operation on environmental data among different administrations and government levels;
   - develop co-operation in sharing methodologies and improving data comparability and collection systems, drawing on work done in various member countries and in the framework of international organisations;
   - promote periodic assessment by regional or local authorities of environmental situations in their jurisdiction.

2. Further develop and use indicators to measure environmental performance, and in particular:
   - establish indicators of progress concerning implementation of national and sub-national policies on the environment, eco-efficiency and sustainable development;
   - systematically compare achieved results with relevant objectives of environmental policies and, where appropriate, related international commitments;
   - pay particular attention to the availability, reliability and international comparability of indicators concerning international environmental issues.

3. Establish effective mechanisms to better inform the public, decision-makers and the authorities on environmental and sustainable development conditions and issues, and in particular:
   - encourage appropriate levels of government to make publicly available reports on the results of public policies and related actions;
   - use modern effective information communication methods to enable timely, easy and inexpensive access to large volumes of information;
   - promote co-operation on dissemination of environmental information among different administrations and government levels as well as non-governmental organisations concerned.

4. Provide public access on request to non-confidential information on non-compliance as well as on sanctions levied for violation of environmental laws.

5. Support educational efforts towards enabling the public to make use of available environmental information.

Box 17.12. **Examples of international instruments on strengthening the use of environmental information and public participation in decision-making** (cont.)

UNECE Convention on Access to Information, Public Participation in Decision-making and Access to Justice in Environmental Matters (1998)

The UNECE Convention on Access to Information, Public Participation in Decision-making and Access to Justice in Environmental Matters (so called Aarhus Convention) was adopted in 1998 in the Danish city of Aarhus at the Fourth Ministerial Conference in the "Environment for Europe" process. It was described by United Nations' Secretary-General Kofi Annan as "the most ambitious venture in environmental democracy undertaken under the auspices of the United Nations".

The Aarhus Convention links environmental and human rights. It seeks to strengthen the role of members of the public and environmental organisations in protecting and improving the environment for the benefit of future generations. Through its recognition of citizens' environmental rights to information, participation and justice, it aims to promote greater accountability and transparency in environmental matters. Specifically, it aims to:

- allow members of the public greater access to environmental information held by public authorities, thereby increasing the transparency and accountability of government;
- provide an opportunity for people to express their opinions and concerns on environmental matters and ensure that decision-makers take due account of these;
- provide the public with access to review procedures when their rights to information and participation have been breached, and in some cases to challenge more general violations of environmental law.

To date, the Convention has been ratified by 30 European countries. Although the Convention is regional in scope, it is in fact open to accession by countries throughout the world.

These policies, together with significant changes in the structure of the economy, especially in the rural sector, contributed to mitigating environmental pressures in many areas. For example, the gross value of industrial output doubled between 1991 and 1998 while total discharge of major pollutants increased only slightly. Water pollution, especially from small enterprises and TVEs, decreased significantly, emissions of particulates and other pollutants have been curbed, pressures on water quality from the use of pesticides and fertilisers in agriculture have also decreased. In many cases, however, the positive changes resulting from structural changes and environmental policies have been offset by the sheer scale of pollution and natural resource consumption stemming from the fast-growing market economy and continuing population growth.

While there is some evidence that environmental policies have had some effect, there is also scope for improvement. The policies still often have a declarative character and lack realism. The low effectiveness of policies is also influenced by a lack of coherence among environmental regulations, conflicting interests at different levels of the administration, and lack of technical capacity and resources available to environmental institutions to carry out their duties. The incentive framework within which enforcement bodies work at sub-national level (generally favouring development over environment) results in widespread non-compliance with environmental requirements. These problems are further magnified by slow progress in engaging sectoral bodies and the public at large in addressing environmental problems.

6.2. Contradicting responsibilities at different levels

As described above, a general trend of devolution and decentralization has shifted the implementation of environmental policies towards local governments. As a result, sub-national EPBs are now assuming greater responsibility for environmental protection and natural resources management. However, the subsidiarity principle[17] of governance is seldom recognized in designing policy actions and optimising functions that could be allocated to various levels of government. Although the central government authority should be able to intervene at any time to prevent abuses at the local level, it should also clearly delegate and allocate responsibilities for various environmental management matters between different levels of administration to ensure that the specific problems can be tackled using local knowledge and capacities.

Given China's enormous size and complexity, a thorough analysis is required to analyse and resolve contradictions between horizontal and vertical responsibilities at all levels.[18] Options may include: delegating more regulatory authority over all but the smallest industrial enterprises to provinces and municipalities and away from counties, and increasing supervision of lower levels by higher levels through performance audits and public reporting. This could also include increasing the role of SEPA in managing EPBs. All these can help to guarantee a fair, effective and transparent framework of policy-making and enhance the institutional capacity in the implementation. Once analysis is completed, appropriate changes need to be included in the legislation.

6.3. Recommendations for better governance in environmental policies

In view of the above, the institutional and procedural prerequisites for good environmental management are:

- consensus/science-based objectives (differentiated by time) appropriately reflected in policies, laws and regulations;
- appropriate institutional framework for policy development and implementation, including a clear allocation of responsibilities and powers between national and sub-national levels of government;
- institutions and instruments for policy integration and coherence, embracing the three pillars of "sustainable development": environmental, economic and social;
- provision of information, public participation and access to an impartial judiciary in the development and implementation of environmental policies.

In order to further promote better environmental policies based on good governance principles, the Chinese authorities may wish to consider the following issues.

6.3.1. Improving policy planning

The current approach to environmental planning may benefit from a wider application of the "planning cycle" approach used in a number of OECD member countries. It includes setting explicit objectives and targets, evaluating progress in achieving them, providing feedback to policy makers and adjusting priorities on the basis of "results of the ground" and lessons learned. Such an approach requires the participation of relevant stakeholders. Analysis of the costs of achieving environmental goals, combined with a robust analysis of possible funding sources, could be a powerful instrument for environmental administrations in their discussions with other relevant government bodies over resources for environmental improvement.

6.3.2. Strengthening inter-sectoral policy co-ordination

As most issues related to sustainable natural resource use and environmental management cut across lines of administrative responsibilities, effective ways are needed to co-ordinate the work of different bodies, to reduce overlaps and contradictions, maximize synergies and adjust problems. In the current situation of weak co-ordination of environmental and other policies, the Chinese authorities may consider various options. One could be the elevation of SEPA to the full status of ministry and full membership of the Cabinet. This arrangement exists in a number of OECD member countries. Another approach could be the creation of a high-level co-ordination and communication mechanism for integration of decision-making within the whole government similar to the State Council's Environmental Protection Commission. Such a mechanism could ensure that environmental considerations are taken into account in setting sectoral policies, overlaps and contradictions are reduced and synergies between the work of different bodies are maximized. Such a body would need to be established at a suitably high governmental level and provided with sufficient resources to carry out a co-ordinating role. Lessons learned from the CCIED could be helpful in this regard.

6.3.3. Clarifying responsibilities

Taking account of China's size and complexity, a thorough review of the vertical and horizontal distribution of responsibilities in the environmental realm could help identify ways to make the system more vertically and horizontally integrated. Options may include: delegating more regulatory authority over all but the smallest industrial enterprises to provinces and municipalities and away from counties, and increasing the supervision of lower levels by higher levels through performance audits and public reporting. This could include increasing the role of SEPA in managing EPBs. All these can help to guarantee a fair, effective and transparent framework of policy-making and enhance the institutional capacity in implementation. Once analysis is completed, appropriate changes need to be included in the legislation.

6.3.4. Strengthening capacities

There is a need to strengthen capacities of environmental administrations in China and align responsibilities with funding. As a matter of priority, SEPA should review staffing at all levels to assess the gap between their responsibilities and capacities and identify actions needed to bring them into better alignment to address priority issues. This may involve SEPA and EPBs concentrating their efforts on "core" public functions and a smaller number of priority issues and focusing on problems which are potentially solvable. Since pollution in rural areas is severe, and there is a lack of suitable institutions/staff, the institutional setting is in particular need of review.

In addition, mechanisms for continuous training for SEPA and EPB staff should be established to ensure regular and sustainable skill enhancement and information provision on new regulations and approaches to environmental management. Selected local training institutions should become regional centres of excellence. These training and research institutions should cater not only for the personal capacities of environmental and enforcement officers to deal with environmental issues, but also strengthen the capacity of staff to co-ordinate their activities with sectoral bodies. As government institutions in China are overloaded with administrative jobs and lack time for thorough research of policy options, they need additional support from experts. The establishment of environmental "think-tanks", which can be contracted to carry out analysis and research as well as open up the market for consulting services in the environmental field, could play instrumental roles in forging effective and efficient solutions in light of the latest scientific research.

6.3.5. Making regulations coherent, efficient and effective

Environmental laws and regulations could be made more consistent, transparent and non-discriminatory. The Chinese authorities should launch a review of environmental legislation to eliminate important discrepancies and gaps between the principal laws and executive regulations. The legislative and rule-making processes should be made more transparent to build better relations between regulating entities, the regulating parties and the public. RIA applied in a number of OECD member countries can improve the quality of legislation by eliminating contradictions between various regulations, reducing the costs and enhancing effectiveness. Allowing more public participation in the regulatory process at all stages, from drafting environmental legislation to enforcement activities, can help improve policy effectiveness and address potential inconsistencies early in the legislative process.

At the same time, the government has to continue to diversify approaches and environmental tools to provide a better fit between solutions developed and the problems being experienced in different parts of the country. The "one size fits all" approach played a useful role in the past, but is increasingly inadequate to meet current demands. Impacts of policy instruments should be enhanced by designing their optimal mixes with the objective of increasing effectiveness and efficiency of these instruments in addressing priority environmental problems. Such mixes should include emission standards, permitting system and economic instruments applied in a coherent manner to differentiate these approaches between large and small and medium-sized enterprises. Recent OECD experience in developing mixes of policy instruments in OECD member countries and in Eastern Europe could serve as examples.

6.3.6. Strengthening compliance assurance

Appropriate compliance assurance strategies should be developed which enable strict and timely response to non-compliance, while creating fair incentives to improve compliance and reward for better environmental behaviour. Experience from the application of such strategies exists in several OECD member countries. At the same time, however, the discretion of enforcement personnel should be limited and described precisely in regulations. More use could be made of public pressure to achieve compliance with environmental regulations. Implementation of such a policy would require awareness-raising campaigns and capacity building efforts.

6.3.7. Increasing provision of information and promoting participation of the public

Promoting public participation in environmental decision-making should continue to be one of the key objectives of the state and local environmental administration. By enhancing environmental awareness, encouraging environmental associations and providing training, the public can become an active implementation agent.

The government should enhance the dissemination of environmental information in the form of environmental reporting and information, particularly for use by the media. Information disclosure and performance rating schemes are potentially powerful vehicles, combining the provision of environmental information to the public and generating public pressure on polluters. This approach, currently in a pilot phase, should be replicated in other parts of the country, especially in smaller cities, western provinces and rural areas.

A national report on the state of the environment should also be published and disseminated at regular intervals. Such measures could ensure information is updated and is easily accessible to the general public. It would certainly facilitate public enquiries on the quality of the environment and impacts on human health. Moreover, environmental information should become progressively available in electronic databases and on the Internet to facilitate access.

The government should remove barriers to the development of environmental non-government groups so that they could participate more autonomously in the development and implementation of environmental policy. They should also be allowed to raise their own revenues for operations, either through membership fees or services provided to the public.

Studying mechanisms for public participation in OECD member countries can help to apply the best approaches, and procedures in a way that is adapted to the Chinese context. The adaptation of the provision of the OECD Recommendation of the Council on Environmental Information or the provisions of the UNECE Convention on Access to Information, Public Participation in Decision-making and Access to Justice in Environmental Matters (so called Aarhus Convention) can provide useful models in this regard.

Notes

1. This chapter was written by Krzysztof Michalak, Non-member Countries Division, Environment Directorate, OECD. An important contribution to the chapter was provided by Professor Jun Bi from the School of the Environment, Nanjing University, Nanjing, China.
2. Statement made at the Third Plenary Meeting of the Sixteenth National Congress of the CPC.
3. This "scientific development strategy" (also called a "second generation development strategy" or a "new development strategy") was formally promoted at the Third Plenary Meeting of the Sixteenth National Congress of the CPC in October 2003.
4. The core part of "circular" economy is the circular (closed) flow of materials and the use of raw materials and energy through multiple phases. The "3R" principles (reduction, re-use and recycle of materials and energy) are often cited to describe the three possible approaches in practice.
5. Some environmental problems may be less "visible", but may still have a higher impact on the health of the population or lead to a higher economic damage, also in the longer term.
6. The example of the development of the Netherlands' National Environmental Policy Plans (NEPP1 and NEPP2) is particularly comprehensive and could serve as a model for China.
7. As of 2000, all 31 provincial EPBs were given the status of independent bodies and 30 of them were first-tier institutions. All city-level EPBs were independent bodies, and most were first-tier, while about 70% of county EPBs were independent.
8. A number of examples can be found in the *OECD Environmental Performance Reviews*.

9. In addition, they retain some percentages of other payments for late payment or long-term payment. Ma, Xiaoying and Leonard Ortolano (2000).

10. **Regulatory appraisal** is the *ex ante* assessment of proposed new or revised regulation, whereas **regulatory evaluation** refers to the *ex post* assessment of existing regulations. Evaluation may be undertaken either for the environmental regulatory system as a whole or for individual regulatory instruments.

11. The Chinese word *guanxi* is frequently translated as "social connections". *Guanxi*, which has long been an element of Chinese life, is based on a blend of exchanges and mutual affection that "create feelings of responsibility and obligation on the one hand and indebtedness on the other". In general, *guanxi* is maintained by trading favours over long periods. These exchanges are often viewed as creating a resource that can be used to "get things done". Ma and Ortolano (2000).

12. *www.ccchina.gov.cn/english/source/ca/ca2003091813.htm*.

13. See OECD (1998) and further OECD publications on environmental indicators and performance assessment.

14. In many provinces, anonymous notes account for between 25-50% of all citizens' complaint letters.

15. Adopted by the OECD Council at its 922nd session on 3 April 1998, see: *www.oecd.org/findDocument/0,2350,en_2649_34303_1_119672_1_1_1,00.html*.

16. United Nations Economic Commission for Europe, for document see: *www.unece.org/env/pp/welcome.html*.

17. This principle calls for delegating/allocating the responsibility for addressing a specific problem to the lowest possible level where issues can be effectively managed and problems addressed most effectively and efficiently.

18. For an example of discussion about the allocation of responsibilities between various administrative levels see "Encouraging Environmentally Sustainable Growth" in *OECD Economic Reviews: Poland*.

Bibliography

Economy, Elizabeth (2004), *The River Runs Black: The Environmental Challenge to China's Future*, Cornell University Press.

Environmental Protection Law of the People's Republic of China (1979, amended in 1989), available at *www.ccchina.gov.cn/english/source/ca/ca2003091813.htm*.

Jun, Bi (2004), *Environmental Governance in China – Background Report*, unpublished paper.

Ma, Xiaoying and Leonard Ortolano (2000), *Environmental Regulation in China: Institutions, Enforcement and Compliance*, Lanham, Maryland and Oxford, England, Rowman and Littlefield.

OECD (1997a), *Reforming Environmental Regulation in OECD Countries*, OECD, Paris.

OECD (1997b), *Regulatory Impact Analysis. Best Practices in OECD Countries*, OECD, Paris.

OECD (1998a), *Review of the Development and Implementation of the National Environmental Action Programmes in Central and Eastern Europe*, EAP Task Force, OECD, Paris.

OECD (1998b), *Towards Sustainable Development: Environmental Indicators*, OECD, Paris.

OECD (2000a), *Analytical Report on Sustainable Development: Institutions and Decision-Making for Sustainable Development*, OECD, Paris.

OECD (2000b), *Environmental Performance Reviews (1st Cycle: 1993-2000): Conclusions and Recommendations from 32 Countries*, OECD, Paris.

OECD (2001a), *Economic Reviews: Poland*, OECD, Paris.

OECD (2001b), *Environmental Outlook*, OECD, Paris.

OECD (2001c), *Environmental Strategy for 21st Century*, OECD, Paris.

OECD (2001d), *Ministerial Communiqué from the OECD Council Meeting at the Ministerial Level: Towards a Sustainable Future*, 16-17 May 2001.

OECD (2001e), *Review of Environmental Compliance and Enforcement Efforts in Eastern Europe, Caucasus and Central Asia*, EAP Task Force, OECD, Paris.

OECD (2002a), *Environmental Priorities for China's Sustainable Development in China in the World Economy: The Domestic Policy Challenges*, OECD, Paris.

OECD (2002b), *Governance for Sustainable Development: Five OECD Case Studies*, OECD, Paris.

OECD (2003a), *Developing Effective Packages of Environmental Policy Instruments in Eastern Europe, Caucasus and Central Asia*, OECD, Paris.

OECD (2003b), *Guiding Principles for Reform of Environmental Authorities in Transition Economies of Eastern Europe, Caucasus and Central Asia*, EAP Task Force, OECD, Paris.

OECD (2004), *Environmental Strategy: Review of Progress*, OECD, Paris.

OECD (2005a), *Financing Strategy of the Urban Wastewater Sector in Selected Municipalities of the Sichuan Province in China*, OECD, Paris, forthcoming.

OECD (2005b), *Review of Funding of Environmental Enforcement Agencies in selected OECD and Central European Countries*, EAP Task Force, OECD, Paris.

Rogers, Peter, Kazi Jalal, Bidu Lohani, Gene Owens, Chang-Ching Yu, Christian Dufournaud and Jun Bi (1997), *Measuring the Environmental Quality in Asia*, Harvard University Press, Cambridge, MA, USA.

State Environmental Protection Administration (SEPA) (2002), *Report on the State of the Environment in China*, Beijing, China.

Stockholm Environment Institute and UNDP China (2002), *China National Human Development Report 2002 – Making Green Development A Choice*, Oxford University Press.

United Nations Economic Commission for Europe (1998), *Aarhus Convention*, available at www.unece.org/env/pp/welcome.html.

US Environmental Protection Agency (USEPA) (1992), *Principle of Environmental Enforcement*.

World Bank (1997), *Blue Water, Clear Sky*, World Bank.

World Bank (2001), *China: Air, Land, and Water: Environmental Priorities for a New Millennium*, World Bank.

PART IV

Chapter 18

Higher Education Finance and Quality

Table of Contents

Summary 539

Higher Education – Finance and Quality 540

  1. Background 540

  2. China's higher education reform programme 543

      2.1. Appropriate public support for reform 544
      2.2. Equity in access, attainment and achievement 544
      2.3. Support for an increased local participation in policy-making ... 545
      2.4. Inter-sectoral and intra-sectoral co-ordination 545
      2.5. Development of a regional, national, and international emphasis . 545
      2.6. Affordability, flexibility and sustainability 546
      2.7. Encouragement of supplementary resource mobilization 547

  3. The reform process 547

      3.1. Structural reform 547
      3.2. Financial reform 548

  4. How is higher education financed? 549

      4.1. Quality effects of the financial self-responsibility system 550

  5. Existing system-wide quality management instruments and practice 552

Notes 556

Bibliography 556

List of tables

18.1. Enrolment in different HEIs between in China 541
18.2. Employment rates of HEI graduates in 2000 555

Summary

In its quest to become a major player in the global market, China has made impressive strides in many domains, not least in the area of higher education. The Chinese Government recognizes the key role of education in realizing its goals in other domains, and the Ninth Five-Year Plan (1996-2000) and the current Tenth Five-Year Plan (2001-06) have seen enrolment in tertiary institutions more than double from 9.4 million in 2000 to 20 million in 2004. It has also witnessed the rapid rise in the number of non-government (*min ban*) institutions that compete with the older, better-established state ones.

The experience of OECD member countries in addressing the need to increase participation rates in response to economic challenges and rising skill requirements with due regard to maintaining quality, equity of access and adequate financing, are of great interest to China as it enters into the 21st century.

Between 1995 and 2000, the per capita expenditure in higher education and the per capita current cost almost doubled while the government share declined, offset by a tripling of tuition fees.

To nurture a nucleus of "key universities" of high quality, the government inaugurated the "985" and "211" projects. The latter injected more than RMB 40 billion into the system during the Ninth Five-Year Plan and even more was injected through the "985" programme. Coupled to a shift from a very elitist system, the decentralization of most higher education institutions to provinces and municipalities, and the introduction of tuition fees have led to a sea change of the higher education sector. These changes have been the subject of public discussion and have wide political and popular support.

Questions of quality and, despite the massive increase in provision, equity of access remain. Both are closely linked to the urban/rural divide and the very different economic performance of eastern *vs.* western regions. Tuition and student loans are additional barriers to access which the government recognizes need to be addressed over the coming years. Quality has improved with the Ministry of Education now being responsible for regulatory control under the supervision of the State Council. Quality is reinforced through qualification, excellence and random assessment depending on the level of the institution.

Decentralization of the personnel management function has had a profound impact on the performance of individual faculties and of higher education institutions, and bonuses and other supplementary sources represent a major part of the income for teaching and research staff.

The number of graduates seeking employment increased from 1.15 million in 2001 to 2.80 million in 2004. Further learning outcome measures are necessary and statistics on the employment conditions of graduates have begun to be published, reflecting the growing problem of the labour market structure and the imbalance of demand and supply of qualified human resources.

Higher Education – Finance and Quality[1]

1. Background

The Ministry of Education's *2003-2007 Action Plan for Revitalising Education* (hereafter "the Action Plan") states that: "Education represents the basis of fundamental long-term development. In order to fully realize the building of a prosperous society and the great task of revitalising the Chinese nation, it is necessary to persevere in implementing the strategy of developing the country through science and education and strengthening the nation through the cultivation of talent." The Action Plan reinforces and expands on existing reforms to increase coverage and quality of compulsory education, especially in rural areas, on development of top ranking universities and post-secondary teaching quality. It also supports *min ban* (non-governmental) institutions and formulates an outline of Chinese educational development for 2020.

During the Ninth Five-Year Plan (1996-2000), higher education in China went through major structural changes and substantially expanded its intake of full-time students. Structural changes took place at two major levels. First, regulatory control and financing of higher education were modified and, second, comprehensive universities were created through mergers of single disciplinary and professional higher education institutions (HEIs). As part of the modifications, HEIs were given greater autonomy to manage their own resources and operations. The overall goal was to rationalize the education system and to improve its performance so as to meet the social and economic needs of the country.

Coupled with these structural reforms, policy regarding higher education has gone through a major reorientation, shifting away from an elite-based to a mass-based education system by enlarging the total number of enrolments, which reached 19 million students in 2003 compared to 9.4 million in 2000 (see Table 18.1). For 2004, the enrolment rate is 19% or 20 million students. While the structural realignment and the streamlining of the regulatory function have undoubtedly helped improve the effectiveness of the education system, the dramatic increase of student numbers may exert a negative influence on the quality of education and may, in turn, hinder the stated goal of improving China's human capital resource base.

Perhaps no tension is greater in modern China than that between the desire to provide increased access to education at all levels and the equally strong desire to maintain and increase educational quality to "world-class" standards. In resolving this tension, China will face a serious set of policy questions. Among the most pressing issues will be the following:

1. Reduction of rural-urban and province-to-province disparities and income/social class inequalities in the provision of quality education at all levels.

2. Improved retention of female, low-income and minority pupils at least for the compulsory cycle.

Table 18.1. **Enrolment in different HEIs between in China**
Number of students in thousands

	1990	1995	1998	2000	2002	2003
Overall enrolment rate in higher education[1]	3 822.4	5 621.9	6 430	9 390	15 126.2	19 000.2
Post-graduate students	93.0	145.4	198.9	301.2	501.0	651.26
Students enrolled in the degree programmes of regular colleges and universities	2 062.7	2 906.4	3 408.8	5 560.9	9 033.6	11 085.6
Students enrolled in the degree programmes of colleges and universities of continuing education	1 664.4	2 570.1	2 822.2	3 536.4	5 591.6	5 591.6

1. Overall enrolment number includes post-graduate students, students of regular colleges and universities, students of tertiary continuing education institutions, students of military academies, students who registered for the diploma examinations, students of TV universities, students of self-study programmes.

Source: *China Annual Educational Statistics: 1990-1999*, Renmin Education Publisher, 1991-2000. *Educational Statistic Report, 2000*, Development and Planning Division, Ministry of Education, Vol. 1, cited in National Research Institute of Educational Development, *2001 Green Paper on Education in China: Annual Report on Educational Policy in China*. Beijing: Educational Science Publishing House, p. 11. *Educational Statistic Report, 2004*, Development and Planning Division, Ministry of Education, Vol. 1.

3. Greater equalisation of the fiscal capacity to support education among the provinces and local authorities with central authorities emphasizing a policy formulation, quality monitoring and resource equalisation role.
4. Increased utilization of instructional technology, especially where necessary to offset lower levels of teacher preparation or other instructional disadvantages.
5. Improved relevance of skill training in secondary and post-secondary "professional education" and greater freedom of informed choice by higher education students in their selection of specializations and careers.
6. Greater reliance on student tuition, improved loan systems and private education alternatives to finance increased participation at the post-secondary level with the objective of freeing central and provincial/local funds to be used more for development of advanced post-graduate training, improving quality assurance activities and equity concerns.
7. Closer monitoring of employment patterns and creation of effective feedback of this information into both government and private educational decision-making.
8. Continued focus on quality development in higher education's "211" (to develop 100 world-class institutions during the 21st century) and "985" projects (a further expansion of assistance for excellence initiated in May 1998 which involves a broader group of institutions including those in the "211" project) in higher education, but with more emphasis on the second tier of quality institutions than has occurred over the last five years.

None of these policy concerns are unfamiliar to educational professionals of China. What is needed, however, is a more systemic analysis of how these policy options interact with one another. For example, the large growth in private higher education has helped to pacify social demand at the first-degree level but is creating a greater future demand for places in graduate education. Similarly, increased success in retaining students through compulsory education will create greater demands for both professional and traditional higher education. For the foreseeable future, every education policy "solution" will create its own set of special new demands on the education system. China potentially has the human and financial capital to meet these challenges, but immediate and effective response to these policy concerns is essential.

In tandem with the structural reforms and enrolment expansion, financing of higher education has also gone through a dramatic change. At present, tertiary education institutions are classified into different categories of status[2] and accordingly receive financing and other provisions from different sources, namely from national, provincial or local governments. Of the total of about 1 300 HEIs, only just over 100 are now under the direct supervision of the Ministry of Education (MOE). The rest are supervised and funded by provincial or municipal governments, and a comprehensive funding formula has been devised for budgetary purposes. Between 1995 and 2000 the government share (at central, provincial and local level) of higher education revenue in public institutions declined from 70% to 56%. Even though the absolute level of government financing continues to increase, the current levels of per student government expenditure cannot be maintained if the system is to expand as quickly and as responsively to societal and employment demand as higher education planners wish. For example, the gross enrolment rate (enrolment relative to the 18-22 year old cohort) is expected to climb from 11.3% in 2000 to 45.0% in 2020. This increase in total demand is unprecedented in higher education, anywhere in the world.

Between 1995 and 2000, the per capita expenditure in higher education and the per capita current cost almost doubled while the government share has declined relatively. Over this same period, average tuition and fees tripled to help offset this. In 2000, 22.2% of total expenditure and 27.7% of current expenditure per capita were financed by student tuition and other fees (compared to 13.5% and 17% respectively as recently as 1995).

In a detailed financial survey of public degree granting institutions (Hu Ruiwen and Chen Guoliang, 2002) conducted in 1997, the sources of current fund revenue were as follows:

Central government	11.0%
Provincial governments	35.6%
Local governments	3.9%
Tuition	19.0%
Sales and services	22.2%
Other sources	8.3%

The share of public *versus* private sources of funding varies in OECD member countries. Norway, for example, has 96.9% public financing and 3.1% private, whereas the Republic of Korea has 15.9% public and 84.1% private financing. The mean for all OECD member countries is 78.2% public and 21.8% private financing (OECD, 2004).

Since 1997, the share of government contributions has continued to decline and the dependence on institutional sources (including tuition) has grown significantly to offset this. This financing arrangement, based as it is on reducing the share of government responsibility while simultaneously substantially increasing aggregate enrolments and increasing quality, will have a direct and dramatic impact on the teaching capacity and capability of individual HEIs. It might also inadvertently exert a negative impact on the effectiveness of the higher education programmes.

This systemic vulnerability to significant variations in quality within Chinese higher education is made more apparent when one considers the targeted resource allocations made to key universities (see description of the "985" and "211" projects below) and key disciplines for special project funding and other preferential treatment. These effects, combined with the already existing locational advantages and disadvantages of individual

HEIs, pose the greatest challenge to equitable quality enhancement and financing efficiency for the coming years.

The "211" project is the Chinese Government's endeavour aimed at strengthening approximately 100 institutions of higher education and key disciplinary areas as a national priority for the 21st century. It is funded through a co-financing mechanism involving the state, local governments and higher education institutions. In line with the existing administrative system of higher education, funding comes mainly from central departments and local governments which have jurisdiction over the universities concerned. Special funds earmarked by the state serve to initiate, support, guide and readjust the development of the project.

The special funds allocated by the central departments and local governments are used mainly to subsidise the development of the national key disciplinary areas, the public service system of higher education, and the infrastructure improvement in a small number of universities necessary for raising the overall institutional quality. During the first round of "211" (from 1995 to 2000), total funding was RMB 10.9 billion, of which RMB 2.8 billion special funds was earmarked by the state, RMB 3.2 billion paid by central departments having jurisdiction over the universities concerned, RMB 2.5 billion from local government, RMB 2.4 billion raised by the universities themselves and RMB 115 million raised from other sources. Additional funds of RMB 7.5 billion from departments and local government have been allocated for infrastructure improvement at specific universities. For the second round of "211", the goal is to double the total funding. While funding for "985" is not published, it is said to be considerably more than "211".

Other components of ongoing higher education reform consist of investment reform, recruitment and job placement reform, and "inner-institute" management reform, in addition to teaching reform. These individual reforms directly and indirectly affect the quality of the final outcome of higher education. These and related questions of quality and finance formed the framework for the OECD Review[3] which was organised around three major topics: key aspects of the Chinese reform of higher education; quality management in Chinese higher education; and, the financing of higher education in China and the rationale for its support.

2. China's higher education reform programme

The recent reform of higher education within China initiated in the Ninth Five-Year Plan and through the 2003 Law on the Promotion of Private Education has dealt with the need for increases in quality (including relevance of the education provided) and the means for mobilizing adequate financial resources to meet both quality and expansion objectives. It has been characterized by four major actions: i) a shift from a primary emphasis on elite higher education to more concern with increased access; ii) the decentralization of institutional affiliations of HEIs to provincial and municipal authorities and greater attention to institutional autonomy; iii) the allowance for, and even facilitation of, non-governmental *min ban* higher education; and iv) the introduction of a cost-sharing approach through greater reliance on student tuition and other fees to finance higher education costs.

While the government is determined to maintain a number of "world-class" universities, it has recognized the need to meet the aspirations of the rapidly growing population of secondary school graduates who wish to continue their education to the tertiary level. Recognizing the limits on central government financial and human resources, China has decentralized dramatically. From 1990 to 2000 the number of higher education institutions affiliated with central ministries and agencies declined from 354 to 111 and the number affiliated with provincial and municipal authorities increased from 721 to 1 114. By 2003, less than 10% of the institutions of higher education were directly affiliated with a central agency (although, because the central institutions are larger on average, the proportion of higher education students in these institutions is still proportionally greater).

Whereas no private institutions existed in 1990, over 100 were active in 2003. This sector is the fastest growing part of higher education, both in terms of numbers of institutions and total enrolment. A second form of educational privatization has taken place within certain public institutions where selected disciplines within a public university or college may operate as a private or quasi-private unit of the institution. Indeed, tuition and other fees are now charged to many students within the public institutions regardless of whether they are in the "private" or traditional part of the establishment. This cost sharing is both necessary (to finance the desired improvements in quality and access) and equitable (in that students, the major beneficiaries of higher education, are expected to pay some share of the costs of their own education).

2.1. Appropriate public support for reform

Higher education, like all education and training programmes, can affect the lives of the Chinese population profoundly. Because of this, a natural conservatism exists in that change can rarely occur without some fear of loss or uncertainty of the specific results. During this phase of the Chinese higher education reform it was attempted to make clear why changes are required in the higher education system and the manner in which individuals, groups and society will be affected by these changes. In this way, the proposed changes in policy and in programmes for higher education have gained sufficient political and popular support to be implemented and sustained. While much of the work of the reform process is inherently technical in nature and content, ultimately the higher education reform programme is a process that requires broad acceptance from society at large to be effective. The reform appears to have been designed with appropriate attention directed to, and sensitivity shown for, the political, cultural and social considerations involved in the various reforms at both the governmental and institutional levels. However, in the area of cost-sharing, the need for "social marketing" of these policies will become more critical as the share of total costs borne by students and their families increases. Similarly, support for loan programmes for students will require that both students and their families be aware of the benefits and the risks of debt-financed educational opportunities. Finally, the legal framework for the effective operation of private education, both general and tertiary, needs to be more fully elaborated – from such basic concerns as land ownership to difficult matters of standards, quality and intellectual property.

2.2. Equity in access, attainment and achievement

The major access/equity issues traditionally identified for China are the differences between locations (among provinces and urban *versus* rural) and social classes (an issue even in a previous "classless" society). Equity issues may be analyzed in terms of access, retention and graduation as well as for learning achievement and the opportunities for employment. Equity assessments also can be made in terms of access to funding and to specific resources such as qualified instructors, appropriate instructional materials and other learning resources (laboratory facilities and information technology). At present, the higher education management information system is not sufficiently developed to provide data to measure and monitor resource equity. Such a system would assist the authorities to better target state subsidies.

A special equity concern in all societies is gender equity and China has a strong and improving record concerning higher education and tertiary training systems. However, it is necessary to determine whether achievement or programme selection (especially in some more overtly vocational and technical areas) represent a systematic pattern of inequality for women. In addition, the employment opportunities for women may be examined to illustrate the extent to which the gains in gender equity apparent in China's higher education and tertiary training systems are actually translated into fully equitable employment opportunities for female graduates.

2.3. Support for an increased local participation in policy-making

The reforms encouraged by China for the higher education sector area should be co-ordinated with the more general reorientation of the long-term social policy framework in the nation. The central government would issue broad higher education planning guidelines; the provincial, municipal and institutional administrators would then respond with comments, criticisms and alternative suggestions. The central authorities could then develop more detailed proposals and, following further review by sub-national officials, the revised proposals for higher education could be implemented. Central responsibility for key decisions would be retained, but an even greater opportunity would exist for local participation and review. Such an interactive model is already being used to some extent in the higher education reform in China and should be strengthened and expanded to include greater participation by the private sector. Even if only in an advisory capacity, suggestions from private-sector institutions and from employers can only strengthen the overall implementation process for higher education reform.

2.4. Inter-sectoral and intra-sectoral co-ordination

The location of higher education responsibility within different government agencies at the national and sub-national levels continues to have the potential of fragmenting the planning and implementation processes for the sector. All higher education activities, in whatever ministry or agency they are conducted, also should attempt to co-ordinate with the activities of other sub-sectors (an obvious example would be co-operation between the education and labour ministries). Similarly, better co-ordination should be encouraged for higher education institutions with activities outside the public sector (including international institutions operating alone or in concert with domestic institutions). It is recognized in China that higher education development will depend on the larger economy to provide funds for support of education, training, research and development activities and to employ or otherwise utilize the graduates that are produced. This close linkage between education and the economy is important to ensure that the system is in congruence with the needs of Chinese society.

2.5. Development of a regional, national, and international emphasis

The size and complexity of China requires that both a regional and a national orientation be appropriate for many higher education programmes. Institutions in all parts of the nation should attempt to incorporate curricular and other adaptations to meet the specific needs of their regional communities and potential employers while at the same time producing graduates who are nationally and internationally employable. Public and individual interests in China will be best served by making the large majority of higher education programmes more effective regional and national resources for development. Programmes that serve these societal needs will also be serving the needs of individual citizens.

Finally, Chinese specialists in research, administration, evaluation, and curriculum must have the resources and other support necessary to form strong international networks. The nature of higher education development is not limited by national boundaries, but each nation must have the capacity to examine the costs and benefits of each new development and decide whether it is appropriate for their own society or culture. Adaptation, more than simple adoption, of international progress will be the key for Chinese institutes of higher education. Similarly, as the higher education reform programme continues to progress in China, Chinese experts should increasingly be prepared to share their findings and advances with international colleagues through publications, seminars, workshops, and other forms of dissemination.

2.6. Affordability, flexibility and sustainability

China has paid close attention to an obvious, but too frequently ignored, criterion for evaluation of higher education reform activities: the reform programme activities must be affordable within the budget levels assigned to them. Too often, a large gulf exists between a reform programme's goals and its realized effects because the programme was designed for a budget level substantially greater than that finally realized. Affordability must continue to be a criterion for higher education programme design in China or else it will just become an explanation for why a particular reform programme activity has not succeeded. A prior concern for China, of course, has been whether the higher education development programmes are receiving an appropriate priority within the government budget. Of greatest concern, perhaps, are the capital investment demands that will be required over the next 20 years to realize the quality and enrolment objectives of China's higher education reform programme. Estimates of the supplemental capital funds needed vary, but it is certain that these needs will be massive over the next two decades.

Affordability is always a joint function of financial capacity, costs and potential effectiveness (*i.e.* it is easier to justify financing a higher education activity that is effective). Affordability issues within higher education in China are especially of concern because the rapid development of individual academic fields means that expensive investments can be made in technologies or activities that quickly become outdated or irrelevant. Flexibility and sustainability are essential to assure effective use of monies invested in higher education programmes.

The higher education reform programme in China has been designed to encourage flexibility through recurrent analysis and policy adaptation. Planning steps are reconsidered periodically (at least yearly) and adjusted to fit the emerging realities of China's social and economic environment. The flexibility to adapt is the key determinant of system and institutional success in higher education.

Sustainability refers to the ability of the higher education reform programme activities to continue efficient operation after the initial phase of government support is over. This is an especially crucial consideration for government higher education projects that involve short-term financial assistance and for private sector higher education activities that involve government subsidisation that is for a finite period only (including the example of provision of land or other property). In both cases, the critical question is whether the positive effects of the short-term higher education project can be sustained after government assistance comes to an end. If not, then one must question the value of an education intervention that will cease or be dramatically reduced after the project period is concluded. Because of the rapid evolution of knowledge in the higher education technology fields, China must be prepared to monitor and adapt higher education projects (such as "211" or "985") to promote sustainability as well as immediate effectiveness.

2.7. Encouragement of supplementary resource mobilization

All projects in a higher education reform will require financial and human resources. While some of these interventions cannot be self-financing because of their nature, all do have the responsibility of exploring ways in which additional resources might be generated for their support. For example, activities to expand computer availability in universities and colleges should stipulate how the new costs will be shared among the central and provincial governments, local communities, private companies and individuals. Training in computer skills could be financed in part through the utilization of existing facilities made available on a part-time basis by the private sector; and training workshops should prepare local government administrators and private sector personnel to deal with citizens and private sector companies to generate supplementary funds for their education and training activities. Over time, with the steadily rising participation rate in tertiary education, an increasing share of the costs of higher education development and dissemination in China is likely to become the responsibility of the private sector and of individuals. While initially the Chinese Government must play a major role in financing as well as co-ordination, the long-term comparative advantage of the central government is in facilitation, co-ordination, quality control and information management of higher education activities – not just their finance.

3. The reform process

Faced with constant changes in the social, economic and political environments, higher education is being forced to balance the need to adapt to the changing requirements of professional competencies, to maintain academic and scientific rigour in research, to keep pace with scientific developments, and to serve the nation's political and social objectives. One of the central issues related to the development of higher education is: How do China's current reform measures impact the quality of higher educational outcomes in general and the quality of the learning process in particular and how can this relationship be improved?

3.1. Structural reform

The current structural reform of the Chinese higher education system is primarily geared towards rationalizing and strengthening the policy and regulatory functions of China's educational system. Regulatory control of the education sector is now centralized within the MOE with oversight from the State Council. Previously, 24 different line ministries supervised and administered their own colleges and universities, each of which offered specialized professional degree programmes which resulted in relatively high unit (per student or per graduate) costs, low efficiency in resource mobilization and utilization, and stagnation in terms of educational quality. At the national level, this service delivery structure also caused sub-optimal use of scarce educational resources, human and financial, resulting in the establishment of diverse, and often inconsistent, educational and professional qualification standards, and hampered the desired scientific research and technological development within the HEIs. Instead of functioning as a central policy-making organisation, MOE was more akin to a multi-level administrative unit attempting to co-ordinate higher educational activities across departmental and functional boundaries.

The structural streamlining and centralization of the regulatory and management responsibilities in the MOE has improved the opportunity for more effective utilization of educational resources and allows for the establishment of unified qualification standards for learning outcomes and accreditation for granting degrees. It also allows the MOE to become more of a policy-oriented and facilitating organisation and less of a regulatory enforcement mechanism. This seems to have created a much more favourable environment to ensure greater effectiveness of the higher education system in China and the necessary conditions to achieve higher quality in college and university education.

3.2. Financial reform

Previously, the government was responsible for all HEIs and their provision. A new management system has been established wherein the government takes major responsibility in providing educational services at all levels with the active participation of society and individuals. Non-governmental colleges and universities commonly referred to as *min ban* have been created across the country and have become a distinguishable force in providing expanded access to professional and higher education. For instance, some are even accredited for granting bachelor degrees. With WTO membership, China will most likely experience an even greater participation of the international education providers in its domestic educational market. Indeed, the number of foreign universities that operate joint programmes with Chinese universities is constantly rising. This could be a positive trend, as long as the educational products fit with the demands of the Chinese job market and support China's long-term sustainable development **and** as long as consumers (students and employers) are provided adequate information about the true costs and benefits of these courses and programmes.

Greater participation from non-state actors in providing higher education helps complement the limited national education budget which amounts to a relatively low 3.4% of GDP (OECD average is 5.8% of GDP), at a time when most HEIs are in need of substantial new investments in upgrading their teaching facilities, living conditions for students, research capacities and, in quite a few cases, the quality of their instructional faculties. The level of development of HEIs seems to be positively correlated with the economic development of their localities. In other words, significant discrepancies regarding teaching capacities and equipment exist between HEIs belonging to the rich coastal provinces and HEIs belonging to the less-developed inland provinces and regions. Comparisons of "quality" of education in this context are hard to define in terms of instructional "value-added" given that the starting points and social conditions vary dramatically.

Resources from the social sector as well as from the private sector (companies and individuals) have been mobilized to fill part of the gap for some of the less advantaged institutions. Exceptional *min ban* universities have developed impressive infrastructure and learning technology. However, it is not clear how many other *min ban* HEIs are equipped with comparable educational capacities. Similarly, in the state-owned universities, teaching staff of an international standard are said to remain scarce. This is a particularly challenging situation, since *min ban* HEIs tend to use more part-time (often, staff who have full-time positions at a state institution) or retired faculty personnel. Excessive use of such personnel can curtail opportunities for student-instructor interaction outside the classroom and could restrain the development of resident knowledge centres needed for academic excellence and development. In addition, it leaves state institutions with the burden of health care and retirement contributions. Some form of cost-sharing and definition of maximum part-time work outside of the principal working place should be defined.

Although *min ban* universities and schools receive no state subsidies and are not eligible for research funding, they are provided with royalty-free land use and tax exemption, and some enjoy financial self-sufficiency and even generate a surplus of income over costs. More than 10 years after the establishment of the first *min ban* schools, the participation of non-state and non-Chinese actors in the Chinese education market remains limited in scope and still "experimental" relative to total enrolment. Laws concerning the ownership of educational properties are recent or under discussion. The Law on the Promotion of Non-State Schools took effect on 1 September 2003. The intent of this legislation is to clarify the rights and responsibilities of these institutions. Public perception of these non-state HEIs is mixed and therefore provides additional motivation for these HEIs to strive for excellence and recognition. One trend, nevertheless, seems to be clear: the participation of the non-state sector in providing higher education services will continue to increase, probably proportionally as well as in absolute numbers. At present, there are 10 major *min ban* HEIs out of a total of just over 100 private HEIs. This number of prominent *min ban* HEIs will most likely change rapidly with the law governing private sector provision of higher education.

Both the *min ban* universities and colleges and the foreign HEIs supplement and extend the existing higher education capacities in China. Their presence also adds an element of competition that could be positive in raising the quality of education and in increasing higher education access of the student population as long as a stringent qualification system is applied when granting degrees. *Min ban* HEIs have to be sensitive to the needs of students and employers and continuously need to redefine their programme and curricula in order to survive financially. Thus, there is a high likelihood that these *min ban* HEIs would come up with some innovative curricula (products) which combine a multidisciplinary approach targeting specific job profiles. The need remains, however, for *external* monitoring of the quality of the learning process and for on-going feedback regarding competency attainment of graduates and their ability to be integrated into the job market.

4. How is higher education financed?

In 1996, approximately 85% of funding came from the national contribution, but by 2000, the level had dropped to under 70%. It continues to decline whereas tuition fees represent an increasing share. Significant levels of tuition fees and widely available student loans are both relatively new concepts in China. Increased student fees were introduced in 1994 and a broad loan scheme in 1999, concomitant with the current administrative reforms in higher education mentioned above. These two innovative funding mechanisms – tuition and loans – should be allowed to evolve together. Although the tuition for a leading university can be up to EUR 4 000, the average is closer to EUR 1 000 for full-time students. These very significant increases in the levels of tuition fees required to fund the greatly expanded higher education system can only be borne by students and their families if a much more flexible student loans scheme becomes available. A more widely applicable loan scheme is vital from an equity point of view.

At present, public universities and colleges are funded through four broad income streams (each of which has several components): *i)* a *per capita* payment made to the institution by the central government for MOE institutions and provincial government for other HEIs, against an agreed quota of students; *ii)* additional government funds provided (mainly) to the top universities under the "985" and "211" project schemes;[4] *iii)* tuition fees that are fixed by provincial governments on the basis of educational costs and "affordability";[5] and *iv)* additional income that universities and colleges are able to raise through supplementary teaching, research and other activities.

All public institutions receive the per capita grants. The top research-oriented universities receive significant additional sums from the "985" and "211" projects and often generate significant levels of additional income. More instructionally-oriented universities and colleges have to rely almost entirely on tuition (from quota and non-quota students) to supplement their per capita allocations. Private universities are financed from a combination of tuition and entrepreneurial earnings.

A trial student loan scheme was introduced in 1999 and since then about 800 000 students have taken out loans. This is a relatively low proportion of students (about 10 to 15%), and it often benefits those who are from advantaged or middle-class families rather than those from the least advantaged, due to the stringent payback requirements representing more than 20% of annual salary (outlined below), and the fact that the bulk of the money goes directly to the institution with little left for living expenses.

The loan scheme has four principal features. First, students in financial hardship may be loaned sums of up to the cost of their tuition fees and residential charges during their courses of study. Second, the loans are made by the national banks. Third, while they are studying, students are charged only half the interest due on these loans, and the other half is paid by the government. Fourth, on completion of study, the loans become liable for full interest and normally are scheduled to be repaid over the following four years (*i.e.* in seven or eight years in total from initial debt). However, extension of the repayment period to six or even eight years after graduation, may be granted in certain circumstances, such as if the student proceeds to postgraduate study (however, students who receive such extensions must pay the full interest rate during this time of extension). These provisions, while better than no loan programme at all, are much more restrictive than those found in most OECD member countries and less generous and flexible than those found elsewhere in Asia.

Lower average starting salaries and increased graduate unemployment has led to a higher default ratio which in turn has made banks less willing to provide loans. The new Education Action Plan 2005-2007 of the MOE acknowledges this problem and the government's commitment to find solutions.

4.1. *Quality effects of the financial self-responsibility system*

State subsidies no longer cover all the operational costs and HEIs have to generate approximately 50% of the funds needed to cover their recurrent costs and research. On the budgetary side, HEIs are encouraged to establish collaboration with industry. Such collaboration is considered to be mutually beneficial and could help to reinvigorate the HEIs and facilitate innovation. This university-industry collaboration should also provide additional revenue for the HEIs.

The degree of success in this respect varies among different HEIs. Prestigious HEIs with substantial intellectual capital and accumulated technical know-how appear to enjoy great success in obtaining corporate sponsorships and research contracts and in offering continued education programmes and executive development. Does this financial self-responsibility system spur innovation and quality improvement within HEIs? There seems to be no clear-cut answer to this question. In pursuit of financial benefits, HEIs could potentially neglect the basic teaching and research activities for which they were created and focus instead on the more lucrative consulting and training activities. In this case, innovation could still be possible but the institutions' regular students might not be the beneficiaries and could even have their interests placed at risk.

On the other hand, partial financial self-responsibility has generated the needed momentum for management reform within institutions and for product and curricula development. Accompanying the partial financial autonomy, consumers of educational products (students and employers) are increasingly conscious of the differences in product quality offered by the various HEIs. Financial reform in the education sector is gradually achieving its intended objectives to reduce the relative financial burden of education investment on the state and to use financial levers to improve the management of HEIs and their instructional and research performance. Have the recent financial reforms helped to improve the quality of education? Experiences from other countries show that market mechanisms need to be coupled with sound regulations and feedback mechanisms in order to ensure the proper functioning of HEIs and the quality of educational experience and outcome.

The decentralization of the personnel management function and salary systems to the individual HEIs provided the institutional administrations with the needed managerial leverage to strengthen their performance management. This new approach has had a profound impact on the performance of individual faculties and of HEIs. For example, in the appointment of individuals, emphasis is now placed more on professional qualifications and academic achievements than on political credentials. Instead of distributing the performance bonus according to the "rights of the employee", the actual bonus is determined on the basis of performance results and on the level of individual contributions. Increasingly, income from bonuses and other supplementary sources for the high performers has surpassed the actual base salary itself and now constitutes a major part of the total personal income for teaching and research staff. The Action Plan 2005-2007 flags the need for a periodic standardized professional assessment system for teaching staff with certification criteria.

The current income structure of the personnel at public HEIs consists of the following elements: the **basic salary** (which is promulgated jointly by the Ministry of Personnel and the Ministry of Education), and the **university supplement**, the **college supplement** and the **department supplement** (the major part of these last three components of the staff member's personal income are directly tied to the individual HEIs "business" activities outside of the regular teaching programmes). Revenue generation, thus, has become a major driving force in the development of this sector. As a direct result, the motivation of personnel is described as much improved.

A potential pitfall that could deflect the educational reform from its course, however, is the emergence of "profit"-seeking behaviour and short-term opportunistic choices on the part of both individuals and HEIs. Profit-seeking and short-term, opportunistic behaviour can be fundamentally detrimental to more basic scientific innovations and breakthroughs, and could also undermine the quality of teaching and learning. In recent years, Chinese consumers of educational services have been driven by personal career objectives rather than societal objectives and consumers have not always had the information or the incentive to be particularly selective. In the past, the higher education "market" was supply-driven and highly regulated. This led to the production of graduates and research that did not necessarily coincide with society's needs (in type, quantity or quality). However, a demand-driven, unregulated market will not automatically or inevitably encourage efficiency or innovation of education outputs. A teaching staff, busy with various official teaching assignments, involved in special training courses for part-time students, and occasionally employed by more than one institution, will find it hard to invest the time and effort required to improve their teaching materials and teaching methodology. Management is more than motivation – it must consider what institutional goals staff are being motivated to achieve.

5. Existing system-wide quality management instruments and practice

The Academic Degrees Committee (ADC) of the State Council is responsible for defining the standards for the degrees of Bachelor, Master and Doctor and the MOE has established a Disciplinary Guidance Committee whose task is to define the academic standards of Bachelor degrees in all disciplines (curricula and content) for recognition of academic titles and certificates.

At the institution level, a Committee for Accreditation, supported by the Ministry's Educational Development and Planning Division, defines the qualification procedures for assessing the educational capacities for granting permission to establish HEIs. Requirements for accreditation purposes focus on the specific areas of faculty composition, research, quality of teaching and facilities (including key laboratories and library volumes). Both HEIs and research institutes can be accredited to offer academic degrees of postgraduates recognized by the government. The ADC is responsible for examining the qualifications of the HEIs and research institutes to offer academic degrees.

In addition to the initial accreditation, a system of operational monitoring and assessment has also been put in place. HEIs are subject to periodic appraisal and evaluation of their academic programmes and their right to grant degrees. An objective of this systemic quality control process is to raise the level of general education provision requirements and to improve the overall quality of HEIs. The assessment and evaluation is organised at two levels reflecting the difference in administrative responsibilities. The MOE deals with policy matters and the establishment of the rules and regulations, while the provincial education authorities are responsible for operating and implementing these policies.

Mechanisms exist to allow for recurrent assessments of the quality of HEIs. As a consequence, the HEIs' accreditation to grant academic titles is either renewed or cancelled (the latter is rare). Depending on the gravity of the situation, HEIs can be sanctioned through probation or even removal from the recognized programme registrar at MOE. Approval of doctoral and professional programmes is given by the MOE, and the Provincial Education Commissions decide on the establishment of Master-level and undergraduate programmes. This division of labour is part of the educational structural reform and should improve the effectiveness and efficiency of the assessment and evaluation function. Another objective of this decentralization is to ensure the responsiveness of the HEIs to local development needs.

Although standardized assessment procedures and criteria have been in use since the 1980s, the popular perception persists that some HEIs offer superior quality of education while others are perceived as being "diploma mills" which provide sub-standard education. This perception is partially supported by the employment records of graduates from different categories of HEIs. Market perception continues to be reinforced by the admission criteria based mostly on the universal entrance examination scores. Lastly, the distinction of "nationally accredited" *versus* "provincial" or "local" HEIs continues to have direct implications in terms of the perceived and actual quality of teaching staff and in terms of educational capabilities since better endowed schools attract higher quality teachers. A rigorous application of education assessment would help to ensure the minimum conditions and quality of education, no matter what type of higher education institution and wherever located.

The evolution of higher education assessment in China can be separated into two phases. The discipline assessment phase, focusing on specific disciplines, existed from 1985 to 1994. The comprehensive assessment phase lasted from 1995 to 2001 and consisted of the assessment of the educational capacities of HEIs and of the actual teaching process and learning outcomes. During this phase, 20% of the 220 HEIs evaluated were not able to fulfil the required minimum standard.

Starting in 2002, a new procedure, a five-year cycle system, was put in place. Every university is to be evaluated once every five to six years by specifically established independent assessment bodies. This task should be carried out by a non-governmental organisation, the National Evaluation Institute for Degree Granting Education (NEIDGE), which was founded in 1994 to pioneer the development of this procedure. However, given the conservative nature of the education sector, reservations exist concerning the viability of entrusting a third-party institution and the idea of peer review with such a direct policy task of government. To address this concern, the MOE might find it useful to consider such quality certification systems as ISO 10015 (International Quality Standard for Training) or the EFQM (European Foundation for Quality Management).

At present, there are three types of institutional assessment and evaluation for HEIs in China, namely, Qualification Assessment, Excellence Assessment (*xuanyu pinggu*) and Random Assessment. The first qualification assessment is focused on HEIs with relatively weak institutional capacities and less experience with undergraduate education. Its objective is to ensure the minimum standards for operating as an HEI. Excellence Assessment is meant for HEIs with good institutional capacities, high teaching levels and a relatively long history of undergraduate education. It serves as a benchmark. Random Assessment is meant for HEIs falling in between the first two categories and is carried out on an *ad hoc* basis. The purpose of all of these assessments is to determine the quality of teaching and to monitor the existing conditions of HEIs.

The impact of the evaluation process to date is said to have been positive. Actual improvements concerning the administration and quality of education have been observed by the MOE. On the other hand, it has become apparent that greater investment is needed in parts of the higher education infrastructure and especially in post-graduate studies. Findings from these assessments have resulted in increased financial appropriations for the higher education system and significant enlargement of the post-graduate level of higher education. Today, a substantial percentage of graduates from the key universities go on to post-graduate studies and pursue academic and research-oriented career paths at their universities. This should boost the future quality of teaching.

The evolving system of higher educational assessment and evaluation in China has enhanced transparency regarding the actual functioning of the HEIs and created competition among them through publicly available ranking. Institutional administrators and provincial officials alike take pride in receiving recognition for high performance and are motivated to strive for higher rankings. In the foreseeable future, Chinese consumers of educational products might be able to make better-informed choices regarding their higher educational options and be less driven by the allure of traditional (and often out-dated) reputations alone. Even though it is unrealistic to imagine that all 1 300 HEIs would or could reach the same level of excellence, it could ensure that all students have access to a minimally acceptable level of higher education.

Provincial and municipal governments are developing their own assessment and evaluation standards applicable to their respective local HEIs. This move could be very positive and lead to the translation of the general national framework into location-specific solutions. Shaanxi Province, for example, ranked fourth nationwide in regard to its comprehensive educational infrastructure and assets. In 2001, there were six national, 36 provincial and 10 private HEIs with 370 000 regular students and 330 000 self-study students in Shaanxi. Although Shaanxi is one of the leaders in "exporting" higher education services within China, *i.e.* recruiting a large percentage of out-of-province students to study in Shaanxi, only a small percentage of outside graduates actually stay and work in the province. Its initiative in developing its own assessment and evaluation standards could potentially set the example for other provinces and autonomous regions in the Western part of China to do the same, and for making regional HEIs more oriented toward serving local labour market and development needs.

Approaches to self-assessment vary greatly from comprehensive assessment systems to more rudimentary instruments. Most HEIs have installed some form of self-assessment mechanism. Key concerns of the HEIs are related to the quality of teaching. Evaluation methods involve end-of-course evaluation by students, peer reviews and in-class inspection. More external oriented methods also exist, such as obtaining inputs from employers and the alumni. These discussions and feedback are used for curriculum development, to check on quality of teaching and to provide direction for future research. Some HEIs are considering benchmarking themselves against schools from other countries by using data provided by the MOE through informational links provided by the OECD and other international organisations.

So far, all the assessment and evaluation activities appear primarily to focus on knowledge acquisition and related performance. Output measures tend to focus on the number of PhD dissertations, research papers, projects, awards, etc. Little has been said about students' emotional intelligence, creativity and ability to cope with stress, etc. These are all attributes important in today's work environment. The question requiring an answer from HEIs most urgently is: What happens to the soft targets of learning, such as personality development, critical thinking and individual creativity, which require more than classroom learning but mentoring and teacher-student interaction? Additional learning outcome measures need to be considered to deal with these learning dimensions.

It has been mentioned by many HEIs that the employment rate of their graduates is used as an indicator of superior quality of a university. Both the central and provincial governments have started to publish statistics on the employment conditions of graduates from HEIs as performance measures. This development reflects a growing problem of the labour market structure and the imbalance of demand and supply of qualified human resources. The employment situation of the class of 2000 graduates with different levels of educational attainment and from different categories of HEIs is reported in Table 18.2. Generally speaking, graduates from prestigious key universities have few difficulties in finding a job or being assigned a job immediately after graduation. In contrast, graduates from local HEIs in general have much greater difficulty in finding employment quickly.

Table 18.2. **Employment rates of HEI graduates in 2000**

I. Graduate schools			
PhD holders 95.8%		Master degree holders 95.8%	
II. Universities			
Graduates of 4-year HEIs under MOE 90.12%	Graduates of 4-year HEIs under other central ministries 76.2%	Graduates of 4-year HEIs recently transferred to MOE 81.6%	Graduates of 4-year HEIs under local governments c.a. 70%
III. 2- or 3-year higher professional college			
Graduates of 2- or 3-year HEIs under MOE 44.9%	Graduates of 2- or 3-year HEIs under other central ministries 45%	Graduates of 2- or 3-year HEIs newly transferred to MOE 55.7%	Graduates of 2 or 3-year HEIs under local governments c.a. 30%

Source: "China Youth Daily", 12 October, 2000, cited in Zhang, L. (2001), *2001 Green Paper on Education in China*, Beijing: Educational Science Publishing House.

The number of higher education graduates seeking employment increased from 1.15 million in 2001 to 2.80 million in 2004, more than doubling in just three years. Employment is more than an aggregate problem of finding jobs for so many new employees, however. A serious structural problem exists in that the graduates have often prepared in specializations for which there is not sufficient demand. The current extraordinary growth of the Chinese economy will help government deal with this in the short run, but in the long run plans must be made to attack both the aggregate and the structural problem.

It should be understood that it is not only the graduates living in the economically depressed areas who have difficulties in either being assigned or finding a job. About 10% of the university graduates in Shanghai, one of the most prosperous coastal cities, are unemployed in the first 12 months after graduation.

Sub-optimal utilization of higher-educated talents presents both economic and social challenges. In a society where university graduates are still relatively rare in supply, where the economy continues to grow and the need for skilled workforce remains high, why is it that an average of 20% of the university graduates and 50% of the graduates from non-degree colleges cannot find jobs? This may be partially due to migration from the countryside to the cities. Graduates who moved to major cities are in general reluctant to return to their home towns, thus adding to the high unemployment rate and long job search periods of new graduates. Some Chinese specialists believe that the fit between higher education and the competence requirements of the current labour market might be another contributor to this mismatch. Encouraging HEIs to take more interest in the future career opportunities of their students would help to partially mitigate the sizeable unemployment of HEI graduates.

In this context, incorporating the employment rate of HEI graduates as one of the MOE outcome assessment criteria would make an impact on HEI educational objectives and curriculum design. This could help create a better fit between education outputs and labour market demands, in turn fostering a more optimal use of limited education resources through full utilization/employment of graduates. Seen from a management point of view, both educational planning at the local level and at the local HEI level need to be more market- and practice-oriented in order to ensure higher returns on investment.

Notes

1. This paper was written by Ian Whitman, Programme for Co-operation with Non-member Economies, Directorate for Education, OECD.
2. TEIs (tertiary education institutions) consist of universities, 4- and 2-year colleges, 3-year colleges (polytechnics), advanced vocational education institutions (community colleges) and branch schools. Adult TEIs consist of radio/TV universities, workers'/peasants' colleges, institutes of administration, educational colleges (in-service training courses), independent correspondence colleges, evening schools, short-cycle courses.
3. OECD Review of Financing and Quality Assurance Reforms in Higher Education in the People's Republic of China [EDU/EC/NME(2004)1].
4. These are non-recurrent project grants, usually for capital projects such as laboratories, sports facilities or dormitories.
5. These fees are currently set at about 25% of actual cost levels determined by an algorithm developed by the MOE.

Bibliography

Development and Planning Division, Ministry of Education (2004), *Educational Statistic Report 2004*, Vol. 1, Ministry of Education, Beijing.

Hu Ruiwen and Chen Guoliang (2002), *Chinese Higher Education Development: Restructuring the Financial System*, Shanghai Academy of Educational Sciences, Shanghai.

OECD (2001), *Thematic Review of the First Years of Tertiary Education – People's Republic of China Country Note*, OECD, Paris.

OECD (2003), *Review of Financing and Quality Assurance Reforms in Higher Education in the People's Republic of China*, OECD, Paris.

OECD (2004), *Education at a Glance*, OECD, Paris.

People's Republic of China, *China Annual Educational Statistics 1990-1999*, Renmin Education Publisher, 1991-2000.

Zhang, L. (2001), *Educational Statistic Report 2000*, Development and Planning Division, Ministry of Education, Vol. 1 cited in National Research Institute of Educational Development, 2001 *Green Paper on Education in China: Annual Report on Educational Policy in China*, Beijing Educational Science Publishing House, Beijing.

Postface by the Business and Industry Advisory Committee (BIAC) to the OECD*

---

* The Business and Industry Advisory Committee (BIAC) to the OECD is an independent organisation officially recognised by the OECD as being representative of the OECD business community. The BIAC members are the major industrial and employers' organisations in the 30 OECD member countries.

Good Governance: Key for Long-Term Business Engagement

1. Introduction

China continues to attract foreign businesses on a large scale, notwithstanding the fact that weaknesses in governance are still regarded as a major obstacle. With a record USD 53.5 billion in foreign direct investment (FDI) in 2003 and preliminary official estimate of USD 60.6 billion in 2004, it might be tempting to conclude that China has proven itself generally exempt from this trend. However, improving the investment environment is essential to secure long-term investment.

Thus, BIAC businesses consistently call for good governance as a vital prerequisite for making the operating environment for foreign direct investment as well as for domestic investment in China more stable and predictable. China would be well advised to move from an incentive-based system for attracting and retaining investment to one based on principles of good governance and the rule of law.

The chapters of this publication convincingly cover timely suggestions for improving the Chinese governance system.

BIAC can report that although macroeconomic policies, market size and risk environment are important determinants of private sector investment decisions, there is a growing consensus amongst members that the quality of business regulations and the institutions that enforce them are of at least equal importance. A solid regulatory environment has consistently proven decisive to the success of many emerging market economies. China will be no exception.

Indeed, a critical focus for a firm weighing a long-term decision to invest is the reliability and clarity of a host government's administration and the transparency of its decision-making process. Investors will often seek answers to the following questions before committing scarce resources to a venture:

- How efficient and transparent is the host government's decision-making process?
- Is there sufficient coordination between the various ministries and institutions responsible for setting policy and overseeing regulation for relevant sectors of the economy?
- Can decision-makers be readily identified and held accountable? Can they be trusted to make timely and binding decisions after adequately consulting stakeholders, including the business community?
- Are different levels of government (local, provincial, national or regional) supportive of one another or do they tend to work at cross purposes?

While China has made some progress in this regard, our members also report that doing business in China is unlike doing business anywhere else. An inescapable sub-text of this message is that there is still a great deal to be done to improve transparency and reduce the current complexity of administrative procedures at all levels of government. Following some of the recommendations in this OECD Governance Project would be an important step forward.

1.1. Modern governance for investment

For every country, no matter its size, location or level of development, attracting investment is a competitive exercise. Thus, all countries and local communities alike must be prepared to provide business with the right environment, including a transparent and predictable policy framework, if they are to be selected as the site for a new or expanded operations base. Important elements of a sound environment for foreign investors generally include:

- The absence of discriminatory administrative measures such as screening and approval requirements for foreign investments and the absence of ownership, control or performance requirements as a condition of entry. As a first step, ownership restrictions and performance requirements could be disaggregated.

- The content of national laws, such as planning regulations, corporate disclosure requirements or labour relations, must be framed in a manner that is stimulating to private investment, both domestic and foreign.

- Host states should offer constitutional guarantees for the peaceful enjoyment of private property and may want to reinforce these by the conclusion of bilateral investment treaties (BITs) with home governments of investors, requiring international minimum standards of treatment for foreign investors; *BIAC commends the Chinese Government for its recent proposal to enshrine private property rights in its constitution. While commending China for having signed a large number of bilateral investment treaties in the past, we hope that these negotiations will continue in line with recent developments in international investment agreements.*

- While efficient and transparent customs legislation and procedures are prerequisites for entering the market, a high standard intellectual property law and vigorous enforcement enhances the chance to attract high-quality FDI; *China is to be commended for passing strong IPR legislation, but its enforcement remains a pre-eminent problem for foreign investors – and one which is also of increasing concern to domestic investors. Continued weak enforcement will discourage technology transfer and the development of R&D centres in China, jeopardising the quality of future investment.*

- Finally, an established and reliable banking and legal system as well as a predictable regulatory and fiscal environment, including an efficient, accountable and predictable judicial system are essential ingredients for an attractive investment environment. *BIAC strongly supports the Chinese Government's recent efforts to improve the health of the Chinese financial system and considers it crucial to the country's continued development. The uniform application of law to foreign investors by Chinese judges, however, remains a serious concern, especially away from major centres like Beijing and Shanghai.*

2. Transparency for investment

There are many ways of discouraging foreign investors. While obvious market entry restrictions and discrimination against foreign investors are thankfully on the decline, there are few limits to bureaucratic ingenuity. Deliberately non-transparent regulatory systems may well serve as equally efficient hidden barriers to investment. In China, the experience of the foreign business community has been mixed.

Fundamentally, internationally-agreed rules and procedures governing transparency, and the enforcement thereof, enhance a government's commitment to the rule of law and would also contribute favourably to China's overall business climate. For business, knowing what the rules of the game are, how the rules are implemented and how they may be changed creates an enabling environment which enhances the quantity and quality of trade and investment.

Especially for countries like China where investors may still have the perception of a high risk of policy reversals and policy uncertainties, there is a strong argument for establishing transparency not only through national laws and regulations but also by entering into binding international agreements. This enhances international investors' perception that the regulatory structure of an investment regime is stable and predictable.

Many such credibility-enhancing instruments are in place world-wide already (OECD Code for the Liberalisation of Capital Movements, OECD National Treatment Instrument, BITs, Free Trade Areas, WTO provisions) and must be used more widely to lock in transparency requirements in national investment regimes.

From a business point of view, transparency:

- Reduces the risk and uncertainty premium associated with cross-border trade, investment and service transactions.
- Enables firms – foreign and domestic – who risk the capital of their shareholders and the savings of their employees accumulated in pension plans, to make better, less risky decisions as to where and how capital resources will be deployed.
- Promotes stability. When transparent rules are accompanied by transparent procedures for introducing changes in rules, business can plan and invest on a long-term basis. Long-term investment brings greater benefits to a recipient country than short-term investment.
- Reduces opportunities for bribery and corruption, *i.e.* "the hidden tax" that benefits the privileged few at the expense of the population at large.
- Helps to insure that rules and any exemptions do not constitute a hidden barrier to trade, investment, and services.
- Helps to delineate the line between the promotion and application of public policy objectives and where those objectives may become a burden or barrier to trade, investment and services, whether or not intended.
- Fills in the "gaps" on trade, investment and service rules where obligations may be "thin" or limited, *e.g.* in BITs, licensing requirements, physosanitary and sanitary measures.
- Reduces opportunities for governments to place firms in a situation of "conflicting requirements" – being subject to differing rules on the same subject matter by a home country or host country.
- Helps to level the playing field among competing firms – foreign, domestic and state-owned – allowing firms and their workers to compete and be rewarded on the basis of their best offerings.
- Promotes democratic values by providing the greatest opportunity for the views of the populace to be heard and acted upon.

Postface by the Trade Union Advisory Committee (TUAC) to the OECD

Raising Labour Standards in China: The Governance Challenge[1]

1. Introduction

The TUAC welcomes the OECD report on Governance in China. The development of a system that can protect the rights of all workers in China and so ensure social progress at the same time as economic development is one of the central challenges that China faces. Addressing the question of how the Chinese state and the multilateral system can effectively integrate 750 million workers – one-quarter of the world's workforce – into the global economy, requires reflection on the wider governance challenge. Economic globalization means that should China fail in addressing these challenges, the repercussions would be felt around the globe, both economically, socially and politically. We all therefore face a shared responsibility to ensure that China succeeds in meeting these twin challenges of economic development and social reform. We have the national, regional and international institutions and standards to enable this common endeavour to be realised.

2. Labour market trends in China

Access to a decent job with good wages, safe and healthy working conditions, and regular training and up-skilling are among the most fundamental aspirations of all workers. So too is access to affordable social insurance and an adequate retirement income. The wrenching economic and social change as China transforms from an agrarian-based labour force to one based on industrial and service sectors also demands well-funded anti-poverty programmes, active labour market and training programmes, and proactive regional and industrial policies. The right to join a trade union of their own choosing and to bargain collectively are key basic human rights for all workers, including China's. They are also conditions for ensuring that Chinese labour law which is broadly positive is applied in practice.

The progress made by the Chinese authorities in some of these areas needs to be acknowledged. Major poverty reduction advances have been made. In cities and along the Eastern coastal strip affected by foreign investment, economic growth has reduced poverty and raised living standards. However, these gains remain unevenly spread geographically, affect different population groups, and have disproportionate gender outcomes. And, as noted by the government, poverty reduction has slowed dramatically of late, and in some areas reversed. Income inequality persists and is increasing dangerously, threatening both stability and future economic growth. The top 20% of households now account for over 42% of income, while the poorest 20% receive just 6.5%, with an even wider divide in rural areas. Meanwhile, environmental degradation, including water pollution, is posing a central challenge to the sustainability of development.

Although some workers enjoy first world working conditions, the daily reality for the majority and in particular the estimated 100 million plus of migrant workers in the new "private" sector is one of insecurity. Mass rural unemployment and under-employment have resulted in increasing migration and increasing urban unemployment, appalling workplace health and safety standards and the collapse of a social, health and pension system. Women are suffering most in the current situation with a greater likelihood of being laid off and discriminated in recruitment; widening wage gaps, and concentration in low-paid jobs. Those working in Special Economic Zones may be required to present a family planning certificate in order to obtain a residency permit. Official non-governmental organisations, such as the All China Women's Federation, and other such bodies raise these points, but these abuses continue.

Meanwhile, the bulk of the estimated 40% of workers in the private sector face perilous working conditions. Notwithstanding reasonably positive laws and regulations covering workplace health and safety, China ranks as one of the most dangerous countries in the world to work in. It is underscoring the importance of the implementation in the practice of laws, and the development of a legal rights culture, including a fully independent and adequately resourced judiciary, necessary for formal laws to have effect. Official figures recorded 11 402 fatal accidents and 12 554 workers' deaths along with 13 218 instances of occupational diseases in 2001. Miners are particularly vulnerable.

3. Trade union rights

Many of the abuses of working conditions and non-observance of labour laws stem from the lack of pressure of accountable trade unions in the new workplaces. When it comes to workers' rights as human rights (the core labour standards of the International Labour Organization, ILO),[2] China stands in violation of the basic right of freedom of association. Workers' rights of association are also protected by the International Covenant on Civil and Political Rights, which China signed in 1998 and is preparing to ratify. Workers' rights to form and join the trade union of their own choice are also enshrined in the International Covenant on Economic, Social and Cultural Rights, which China ratified in 2001, whilst making the reservation that this could only be implemented in a manner "consistent with the relevant provisions of the Constitution of the People's Republic of China, Trade Union Law and Labour Law".[3]

The authorities face a strategic choice concerning the future role of the official Chinese trade union body, the All-China Federation of Trade Unions (ACFTU). The move to an economic system based on the market, the privatisation of state-owned enterprises, and the dismantling of the old command and control system with all that implies in terms of workers' vulnerability to abuse, requires a counterbalancing trade union movement independent of management and political control to represent those workers. However, the ACFTU struggles to fulfil that role under its current constitution and *modus operandi*. Therefore, as worker unrest accelerates and spreads, driven by structural change and the failure to implement labour laws in the private sector, the ACFTU is often incapable of negotiating with management a peaceful resolution, resulting in public unrest, and a crackdown by the authorities.

The revised Trade Union Law (2001) opened some space for contesting trade union elections, and there has been some experimentation with less control and interference over workplace worker representation.[4] It is particularly worthwhile to note that the government wants to expand the role of collective bargaining in wage-setting. The main driving force for this are the Chinese workers themselves, however pressure from some foreign multinationals concerned about their brand image is said to also be helping. The authorities have recently announced moves in support of ACFTU-led organizing drives (Wal-Mart being a prime example). And in a few instances, they have not interfered when workers have sought independent legal representation, when alleged to have committed offences that in OECD member countries are recognised as fully legitimate and legal. OECD member country trade unions have helped and continue, where possible, to help their Chinese counterparts. Some TUAC and International Confederation of Free Trade Unions affiliates offer training programmes for ACFTU officials in the skills of collective bargaining, and offer other logistical support, as does the ILO. Beyond that, some Global Union Federations (GUFs), which organise on a sectoral basis are doing the same, and in some instances have negotiated Global Framework Agreements with western-based multinational enterprises. One example is that between the International Federation of Building and Wood Workers Union (IFBWW) and Ikea, which includes China-specific programmes.[5]

For its part, the TUAC is seeking with the OECD to promote the OECD Guidelines for Multinational Enterprises which set out OECD governmental expectations on socially responsible behaviour by multinational enterprises. The TUAC User's Guide on the Guidelines has been translated into Chinese. TUAC is seeking to develop a dialogue on how the promotion of internationally accepted standards for corporate responsibility can, among other things, benefit China's development, including labour standards, environmental protection and resource exploitation.

Beyond this, there is a need for a comprehensive and strategic approach led by the Chinese authorities to develop freedom of association, and the exclusion of industrial relations related activities from criminal laws.

Notes

1. The Trade Union Advisory Committee (TUAC) to the OECD is an interface for trade unions with the OECD. It is an international trade union organisation which has consultative status with the OECD and its various committees. This note was based on work by Roy Jones.

2. For various reasons many commentators overlook the fact that key labour rights are in fact human rights explicit within the 1948 UN Declaration on Human Rights, and codified in subsequent Covenants. Moreover, the ILO, a specialized tripartite UN agency, has the authority to negotiate, set, and deal with labour standards. Of major significance was the adoption by the 1998 International Labour Conference of the ILO Declaration on Fundamental Principles and Rights at Work. The Declaration groups together what are known as "basic workers' rights" (the core) relating to: freedom of association and the effective recognition of the right to collective bargaining; the elimination of all forms of forced or compulsory labour; the effective abolition of child labour; and the elimination of discrimination in respect of employment and occupation. These core workers' rights are the subject of ILO Conventions, which carry the full weight of international law.

3. See *www.unhcr.ch*.

4. See *http://ihlo.org/item2/item2-1.htm*.

5. Some trade union national centres and GUFs take a different approach to working with the ACFTU, and even those such as the IFBWW recognise their relationships are not at the expense of the goal of freedom of association and collective bargaining rights. Beyond that, the international labour movement is cautious that relations with the ACFTU should not obscure the fact that at present, it remains a Party-controlled organisation at least at the central level.

Glossary

Acronyms

ABC	Agricultural Bank of China
ACFSMC	All-China Federation of Supply and Marketing Cooperatives
ACFTU	All-China Federation of Trade Unions
ADB	Asian Development Bank
ADBC	Agricultural Development Bank of China
ADC	Academic Degrees Committee
AIC	Administration for Industry and Commerce
AMC	Asset Management Company
AQSIQ	General Administration of Quality Supervision, Inspection and Quarantine
ASBE	Accounting Standards for Business Enterprises
BAS	Basic Accounting Standard
BBS	Bulletin Board System
BIAC	Business and Industry Advisory Committee to the OECD
BIT	Bilateral Investment Treaty
BJPID	Basic Juridical Person Information Database
BOC	Bank of China
BPID	Basic Population Information Database
CBI	Copyright-based industry
CBRC	China Banking Regulatory Commission
CCA	China Consumer Association
CCB	China Construction Bank
CCDI	Central Commission for Discipline Inspection
CCGLC	Code of Corporate Governance for Listed Companies
CCICED	China Council for International Co-operation on Environment and Development
CCID	China Computer Industry Development Research Institute
CCPD	Corruption-related Crime Prevention Department
CCPIT	China Council for the Promotion of International Trade
CCOIC	China Chamber of International Commerce
CICPA	Chinese Institute of Certified Public Accountants
CIETAC	China International Economic and Trade Arbitration Commission
CIRC	China Insurance Regulatory Commission
CMAC	China Maritime Arbitration Commission
CNAO	China National Audit Office
CNNIC	China Internet Network Information Centre
CNPC	China National Petroleum Corporation
COFCO	China National Cereals, Oils and Foodstuffs Corporation

CPA	Certified public accountant
CPC	Communist Party of China
CPPCC	Chinese People's Political Consultative Conference
CSRC	China Securities Regulatory Commission
CTAIS	China Tax Administration Information System
DAAA	Division of Administration of Accounting Affairs (within the Ministry of Finance)
DPS	Discharge Permit System
DRC	Development Research Center of the State Council
EBF	Extra-budgetary funds
ECID	Economic Crimes Investigation Division
EFQM	European Foundation for Quality Management
EIA	Environmental Impact Assessment
EPB	Environmental Protection Bureau
EPD	Environmental Protection Division
ERPC	Environmental and Resources Protection Committee
FDI	Foreign direct investment
FIE	Foreign-invested enterprise
FIFO	First In First Out
GDDS	General Data Dissemination Standard
GDP	Gross domestic product
GERD	Growth expenditure on research and development
GFC	OECD Global Forum on Competition
GFS	Government Finance Statistics
GUF	Global Union Federation
GNP	Gross national product
G2B	Government-to-business
G2C	Government-to-citizen
G2G	Government-to-government
HEI	Higher education institution
HSBC	Hong Kong and Shanghai Banking Corporation
IACC	International Anti-Counterfeiting Coalition
ICBC	Industrial and Commercial Bank of China
ICFTU	International Confederation of Free Trade Unions
ICSID	International Centre for the Settlement of Investment Disputes
ICT	Information and communication technology
IFBWW	International Federation of Building and Wood Workers Union
IFC	International Finance Corporation
IFCAL	International Federation of Commercial Arbitration Institutions
ILO	International Labour Organization
IPO	Initial public offering
IPR	Intellectual property rights
JSB	Joint stock bank
LIFO	Last In First Out
LTS	Local Tax Service
M&A	Merger and acquisition
MEID	Macro Economic Information Database

MII	Ministry of Information Industry
MLR	Ministry of Land and Resources
MOA	Ministry of Agriculture
MOE	Ministry of Education
MOF	Ministry of Finance
MOFCOM	Ministry of Commerce
MOH	Ministry of Health
MOLSS	Ministry of Labour and Social Security
MOST	Ministry of Science and Technology
MPS	Ministry of Public Security
MWR	Ministry of Water Resources
NBS	National Bureau of Statistics
NCAC	National Copyright Administration of China
NDRC	National Development and Reform Commission
NEIDGE	National Evaluation Institute for Degree Granting Education
NEPA	National Environmental Protection Agency
NGO	Non-governmental organisation
NPC	National People's Congress
NPL	Non-performing loans
NPO	Non-profit organisation
NRSGID	Natural Resource, Space and Geography Information Database
NRSMEO	State Council Leading Group for National Rectification and Standardization of Market Economic Order
NTS	National Tax Service
PBC	People's Bank of China
PCT	Patent Co-operation Treaty
PKI	Public Key Infrastructure
PPP	Purchasing power parity
PRC	People's Republic of China
PRO	Public research organisation
PSB	Public Security Bureau
PSU	Public service unit
QBPC	Quality Brand Protection Committee
QFII	Qualified Foreign Institutional Investor
QSIIRC	Qualitative Study of Internet Information Resources in China
R&D	Research and development
RCC	Rural credit co-operative
RIA	Regulatory Impact Analysis
RMB	Renminbi
SAFE	State Administration of Foreign Exchange
SAIC	State Administration of Industry and Commerce
SARS	Severe Acute Respiratory Syndrome
SASAC	State-owned Assets Supervision and Administration Commission of the State Council
SAT	State Administration of Taxation
SCILG	State Council Informatization Leading Group
SCIO	State Council Informatization Office

SCOLA	State Council's Office for Legislation Affairs	
SCOPSR	State Commission Office for Public Sector Reform	
SCORES	State Council Office for Restructuring Economic Systems	
SCSC	State Council Securities Commission	
SEPA	State Environmental Protection Administration	
SERC	State Electricity Regulatory Commission	
SETC	State Economic and Trade Commission	
SEZ	Special Economic Zone	
SGA	State Grain Administration	
SINOPEC	China Petroleum and Chemical Corporation	
SIPO	State Intellectual Property Office	
SOCB	State-owned commercial bank	
SOE	State-owned enterprise	
SPS	Sanitary and phytosanitary	
TBT	Technical barriers to trade	
TDC	Treasury Disbursement Centre	
TSB	Technical Supervisory Bureau	
TRIPS	Trade Related Aspects of Intellectual Property Rights	
TRQ	Tariff Rate Quotas	
TUAC	Trade Union Advisory Committee to the OECD	
TVE	Township and Village Enterprise	
UNCHE	United Nations Conference on the Human Environment	
UNECE	United Nations Economic Commission for Europe	
UNDP	United Nations Development Programme	
VAT	Value-added tax	
VPN	Virtual Private Networks	
WFOE	Wholly-foreign-owned enterprise	
WIPO	World Intellectual Property Organization	
WTO	World Trade Organization	

Terms in Chinese

bangong yewu ziyuan xitong	The Administrative Professional Resources System
bianzhi (system)	civil service personnel establishment
Chuizhi	Direct subordination relationship
dahui jiang, xiaohui jiang, tiantian jiang	reiterate in all meetings, large or small, on a daily basis
Danwei	Work unit
faren gu	Legal person shares
Fashu	Uncle Fa
Ganbu	Cadre
geren gu	Publicly issued and freely tradable shares
Gongwuyuan bangong ting	General Office of the State Council
guanxi	Social connections
guojia gu	State shares
Guojia tongjiju	National Bureau of Statistics
Guowuyuan xinxihua gongzuo lingdao xiaozu	State Council Informatization Leading Group

Guowuyuan zhengdun he guifan shichang jingji zhixu lingdao xiaozu	State Council Leading Group for National Rectification and Standardization of Market Economic Order
gongkai (rules)	Public (rules)
gongzhong jiandu	Public supervision
hexie shehui	Harmonious society
hukou (system)	Household registration (system)
jiabao fukuafeng	Wind of falsification and embellishment
jiguan	Government organ
jinbao	Golden Social Security
jincai	Golden Finance
jindun	Golden Shield
jinguan	Golden Customs
jinhong	Golden Macro
jinka	Golden Card
jinnong	Golden Agriculture
jinqiao	Golden Bridge
jinshen	Golden Audit
jinshui	Golden Water Conservancy
jinshui	Golden Tax
jinzhi	Golden Quality
kexue fazhan guan	Scientific Development Concept
liangtiao tujing xietiao yunzuo	"Two ways, synchronously operating"
luoji geli	Logically separated
min ban	Non-governmental education organisations
neibu (rules)	Internal (rules)
neiwang	Internal network
nongye danwei	Agricultural unit
qiye	Enterprise
qiye danwei	Industrial unit
sange daibiao	Three represents
sige xiandaihua	Four modernizations
shehui tuanti/shetuan	Social organisation
shiye danwei	Public service unit, PSU
shiye bianzhi de jingfei	Work-related costs
tiaokuai guanxi	Relationships between the vertical and horizontal lines
waiwang	External network
wenbao wenti	Clothing and food
weifan caijing jilu	Offence of accounting violations
wuli geli	Physically separated
xiagang	Laid-off workers
xiao jinku	Little gold storage
xiaokang (society)	Well-off (society)
xiaozu	Groups of 30 to 40 households (remnants of production teams of the collective era), often *de facto* collective owners of land

xibu kaifa	Western Development Programme
xingzheng danwei	Administrative unit
xingzheng guizhang	Departmental rules and administrative notices or guidance
xingzheng jingfei	Basic administrative costs
xingzheng lingdao	Administrative leadership
xinxiban	Informatization offices
xinxi gudao	Information islands
xinxihua	Informatization
xinxi zhongxin	Information centres
xitong	Grouping of functionally related bureaucracies
xuanyu pinggu	Excellence assessment
yewu lingdao	Business leadership
yewu zhidao	Business guidance
yibashou gongcheng	Top Leadership Project
yi xinxihua daidong gongyehua	The utilization of informatization to propel industrialization
zaidi	Statistical data compilation based on geographic locality
Zhengguiban	National Office for Rectification and Standardization of Market Economic Order
zhengwu gongkai	Open governance
zhongfa	Issued by the CPC
Zhongguo guoqing yanjiuhui	China State of the Nation Research Society
Zhongguo huaxin xinxi jishu kaifa gongsi	China Huaxin Information Technology Development Company
Zhongyang jigou bianzhi weiyuanhui	State Commission Office for Public Sector Reform, SCOPSR
Zhongguo shichang xinxi diaochaye xiehui	China Market Information Survey Association
Zhongguo tongji zixun youxian gongsi	China Statistical Consulting Company Ltd.
Zhonggong zhongyang bangong ting	General Office of the CPC
zhua da fang xiao	"Grasping the big and releasing the small"

OECD PUBLICATIONS, 2, rue André-Pascal, 75775 PARIS CEDEX 16
PRINTED IN FRANCE
(42 2005 09 1 P) ISBN 92-64-00842-X – No. 53929 2005